ECONOMIC THEORY
AND
OPERATIONS ANALYSIS

Prentice-Hall International Series in Management

ATHOS AND COFFEY	*Behavior in Organizations: A Multidimensional View*
BALLOU	*Business Logistics Management*
BAUMOL	*Economic Theory and Operations Analysis, 4th ed.*
BOLCH AND HUANG	*Multivariate Statistical Methods for Business and Economics*
BOOT	*Mathematical Reasoning in Economics and Management Science*
BROWN	*Smoothing, Forecasting, and Prediction of Discrete Time Series*
CHAMBERS	*Accounting, Evaluation and Economic Behavior*
CHURCHMAN	*Prediction and Optimal Decision: Philosophical Issues of a Science of Values*
CLARKSON	*The Theory of Consumer Demand: A Critical Appraisal*
COHEN AND CYERT	*Theory of the Firm: Resource Allocation in a Market Economy*
CULLMAN AND KNUDSON	*Management Problems in International Environments*
CYERT AND MARCH	*A Behavioral Theory of the Firm*
FABRYCKY AND TORGERSEN	*Operations Economy: Industrial Applications of Operations Research*
FRANK, MASSY, AND WIND	*Market Segmentation*
GREEN AND TULL	*Research for Marketing Decisions, 3rd ed.*
GREENLAW, HERRON, AND RAWDON	*Business Simulation in Industrial and University Education*
HADLEY AND WHITIN	*Analysis of Inventory Systems*
HOLT, MODIGLIANI, MUTH, AND SIMON	*Planning Production, Inventories, and Work Force*
HYMANS	*Probability Theory with Applications to Econometrics and Decision-Making*
IJIRI	*The Foundation of Accounting Measurement: A Mathematical, Economic, and Behavioral Inquiry*

Prentice-Hall, Inc.
Prentice-Hall International, Inc., *United Kingdom and Eire*
Prentice-Hall of Canada, Ltd., *Canada*
Dunod Press, *France*
Maruzen Company, Ltd., *Far East*
Herrero Hermanos, Sucs, *Spain and Latin America*
R. Oldenbourg, Verlag, *Germany*
Ulrico Hoepli Editore, *Italy*

ECONOMIC THEORY

AND

OPERATIONS ANALYSIS

fourth edition

WILLIAM J. BAUMOL

Department of Economics
Princeton and New York Universities

PRENTICE-HALL, INC., Englewood Cliffs, New Jersey 07632

Library of Congress Cataloging in Publication Data

BAUMOL, WILLIAM J.
  Economic theory and operations analysis.

  (Prentice-Hall international series in management)
  Includes bibliographies and index.
    1. Microeconomics.   2. Economics, Mathematical.
3. Operations research.   4. Mathematical analysis.
I. Title
HB135.B38 1977   330'.01'84   76–46591
ISBN 0–13–227132–X

© 1977 by Prentice-Hall, Inc.,
Englewood Cliffs, N.J. 07632

Printed in the United States of America

10 9 8 7

PRENTICE-HALL INTERNATIONAL, INC., London
PRENTICE-HALL OF AUSTRALIA, PTY. LIMITED, Sydney
PRENTICE-HALL OF CANADA, LTD., Toronto
PRENTICE-HALL OF INDIA PRIVATE LIMITED, New Delhi
PRENTICE-HALL OF JAPAN, INC., Tokyo
PRENTICE-HALL OF SOUTHEAST ASIA PTE. LTD., Singapore
WHITEHALL BOOKS LIMITED, Wellington, New Zealand

To Ellen,
who used to like marmalade,
and Daniel,
who used to like jam.

Contents

Prefaces

Preface to the First Edition

The last few years have brought with them a happy increase in rapport between the economic theorist and the managerial economist. This development has involved their simultaneous realization that business practice can be a fertile source of more abstract analytical ideas and that the theorist's rigorous tools can make an important contribution to the analysis of applied problems. That, in essence, is the spirit in which this book was written.

The subject of this book is economic theory, *not* operations research. The volume is intended to offer the reader both a systematic exposition of received microeconomic analysis, and an intuitive grasp of the many recent developments in mathematical economics that have too long remained a mystery in the private possession of the specialists (who, it must be admitted, have always been willing and anxious to share their secrets). The discussions of applications of economic theory to the tools of operations research and to business analysis are primarily illustrative, and though a considerable portion of the body of operations research equipment is described, the result can by no means be considered to constitute a survey of the field. As one reader has suggested, this book is intended to be more helpful to an operations researcher who wishes to learn economics than to an economist who desires a systematic education in operations research.

For their helpful comments and suggestions on all or part of the manuscript I must thank Forman Acton, Wroe Alderson, S. T. Beza, W. W. Cooper, Robert Dorfman, Ralph Gomory, Herman Karreman, Robert Kuenne, Harold Kuhn, Don Patinkin, Gardner Patterson, Maurice Peston, and, above all, Alvaro Lopez and Richard Quandt. The devoted labors of my research assistant, Charles Frisbie, and the extraordinary workmanship of my secretary, Mrs. C. B. Brown, were of immeasurable help. The role of my several years' experience with the management consulting firm of Alderson Associates, Inc., will be apparent in many parts of the book. I must also acknowledge my sincere gratitude to the Ford Foundation, whose grant to the Department of Economics at Princeton helped to finance both the research involved in the more original portions of this volume and the typing of the manuscript.

Finally, I must thank the editors of the several journals involved, as well as my co-authors, Ralph Gomory and Philip Wolfe, who graciously permitted me to reprint portions of the following articles: "On the Role of Marketing Theory," *Journal of Marketing*, Vol. XXI (April, 1957); "Selecting an Appropriate Model for an Operations Research Problem," Vol. VIII (November, 1955), "Solution of Management Problems Through Mathematical Programming," Vol. IX (May, 1956), "Operations Research Applied to Marketing Problems," Vol. X (March, 1957) and "A Guide to Operations Research Methods," Vol. X (April, 1957), all in *Cost and Profit Outlook;* "Community Indifference," *Review of Economic Studies*, Vol. XIV (1946–47): "On the Theory of Oligopoly," *Economica*, Vol. XXV (August, 1958); "Marginalism and the Demand for Cash in Light of Operations Research Experience," *Review of Economics and Statistics*, Vol. XL (August, 1958); (P. Wolfe co-author), "A Warehouse-Location Problem," *Operations Research*, Vol. 6, No. 2 (March–April, 1958); "Economic Theory and the Political Scientist," *World Politics*, Vol. VI (January, 1954); "Activity Analysis in One Lesson." *American Economic Review*, Vol. XLVIII (December, 1958); (R. Gomory co-author), "Integer Programming and Pricing," *Econometrica*, Vol. 28 (1960); and "The Cardinal Utility Which Is Ordinal," *Economic Journal*, Vol. LXVIII (December, 1958).

Preface to the Second Edition

No doubt it is in the nature of things that revised versions of books appear as "second edition—*expanded*." This book is no exception. Though two chapters from the first edition have been expunged, on balance the book has grown at a rate not too dissimilar to the GNP.

There have been only a few minor changes in the text itself, most notably an attempt to improve the explanation of the basic theorem of linear programming. A substantial number of exercises have been added, and brief discussions of the applications of differential calculus to standard economic theory have been inserted at the ends of Chapters 9, 11, 13, and 14. The five new chapters include one on duality, one on linear programming and production, one on statistical problems in demand estimation, and two on capital theory and its applications. The duality chapter and the chapter on demand estimation and its appendix provide elementary materials that are, I believe, particularly difficult to find elsewhere. This is especially true of the latter, which discusses some of the econometric techniques for dealing with simultaneous equation problems and treats such subjects as least squares bias, identification, and simultaneous equation estimates in an intuitive manner.

As usual I find myself deeply indebted to a number of persons for their very substantial help in the preparation of this second edition—to my colleagues Harold Kuhn, Burton Malkiel, Richard Quandt, and Frederic Scherer for their many suggestions, to Robert Bushnell for his revision of the chapter on computers, to Edward Pearsall for proofreading and supervising the preparation of the new diagrams, and to Mrs. C. B. Brown for her superb workmanship in the preparation of the manuscript. To all of these I am most grateful. To those others whose assistance has momentarily slipped my mind, I can only apologize.

Preface to the Third Edition

This edition differs from its predecessor largely in the addition of some fairly extensive materials on the Kuhn-Tucker Theorem, including a discussion of a number of its important applications in economics. Several exercises using these materials are intended to demonstrate how this powerful theorem can be applied to obtain qualitative results in economic analysis. In addition, the discussion of the simplex method has been modified and, I hope, improved, at several points.

Professors A. W. Tucker and H. W. Kuhn were extremely generous in helping me at various stages in the revision. Thus they must get the credit not only for the substance of the new material, but for drawing, most gently, to my attention several weaknesses in the presentation in an earlier draft.

I am also heartily indebted to the many students who over the years have made a sport of catching errors in the book. I do not delude myself, however, that it is even yet nearly free of mistakes. I grow increasingly convinced that the species has evolved to a point where it reproduces itself and multiplies, so that no sooner has one generation of errors been brought under control than it is replaced by a host of successors sprung forth apparently from nowhere.

Finally I want to thank for their help in the final task of preparation of the new edition the several very competent secretaries, who were more patient with me than I deserved, and Mr. Stephen E. Kagann, who conducted so capably the latest hunt for inaccuracies.

Preface to the Fourth Edition

If this book had feelings, no doubt—like GBS on his 90th birthday—it would be somewhat surprised to find itself alive and apparently well in its fourth metamorphosis. I, too, have been surprised and delighted by the increasing frequency with which younger colleagues throughout the profession tell me that they have been subjected at some time to its materials; happily, as far as I could tell, the experience did not elicit their lasting resentment.

When it was first written, the book was intended to guide readers to the frontiers of economic analysis. This new edition represents continued dedication to that goal. Frontiers have a way of moving, and the contents of the volume have had to change accordingly. I have added discussions of a variety of what I believe to be important materials on topics such as the duality analysis of consumption and production (including Shepherd's lemma), the Ramsey-Boiteaux theorem on quasi-optimal pricing under a budget constraint, properties of quasi-concave utility functions and their relationship to ordinal theory, and the reswitching debate in the Cambridge-Cambridge controversy. Many of these have never before appeared in a textbook or have been dealt with only cursorily. Although some of the new materials are, in the nature of the case, somewhat more difficult than the discussions of the standard theory, they have been tested in classes by myself and others and, as far as I can judge from both written and oral comments and from examination results, they have passed the test of comprehensibility.

The new edition contains two essentially new chapters—one on comparative statics (Chapter 13) and the other on duality theory in consumption and production (Chapter 14). In addition, five chapters have been revised extensively—those on the neoclassical theory of consumption and production (Chapters 9 and 11), the chapter on welfare theory (21), and the chapters on distribution (24) and capital theory (26). Finally, the organization of the book has been revised on the basis of economic area covered, rather than on the degree of novelty of the materials.

As always, my debts are great, and words are the only coin I have to offer in repayment.

My greatest debts, for painstaking reading and detailed and invaluable comments, are to Elizabeth Bailey, David Folkerts-Landau, Lester Lave, and Jerome Hass. Their suggestions added to my labors, but that additional effort was thoroughly worthwhile.

In addition, I received very useful comments on all or part of the manuscript from Sebastian Arango, Alan Blinder, Michael Rothschild, Vu Viet, and the members of my first-year graduate class in microeconomics at Princeton in the Fall of 1974.

I was helped in the task of revising the reading lists by Roger Klein, Wassily Leontief, Charles McCallum, Janusz Ordover, Richard Quandt, and Andrew Schotter. To all of them I offer my sincere thanks.

Finally, and most strongly, I must express my appreciation to Sue Anne Batey, my research assistant and secretary at Princeton, for her intelligent assistance, her ingenuity in grasping the intent of my unintelligible intentions, her ability to bring order out of chaos, and, above all, her qualities as a human being.

W.J.B.
Princeton and New York Universities

ECONOMIC THEORY
AND
OPERATIONS ANALYSIS

ANALYTIC TOOLS
OF
OPTIMIZATION

one

Optimization
and an Example
from Inventory Analysis

1

1. Optimization—a Basic Viewpoint

One of the hallmarks of the economic theorist's (and the operations researcher's) approach to the analysis of business behavior and business problems is the concept of optimization. In business practice it is common to see management's decisions made on the basis of some set of fixed numbers which are meant to represent the extent of the opportunities open to the firm. For example, businessmen frequently arrange for market surveys to estimate how much of their products they will be able to sell in the next year or some other period in the future. On the basis of such figures, which management seems to treat as fixed constants (under some such name as "market potential"), it decides how much raw material to put into inventory, how many salesmen to hire, etc.

This sort of reasoning is the antithesis of the approach of the economic theorist and the operations researcher. In their analyses, one starts from the position that there is no one fixed amount of any commodity which buyers are prepared to purchase. Rather, sales will depend on price, advertising expenditure, and a host of other variables whose values may be under the businessman's control. For this reason, the number of salesmen to be hired should not be based on any fixed estimate of future sales, for *the size of the sales force helps, in turn, to determine the sales volume.*

Instead of a fixed sales figure, optimality analysis therefore deals with an array of possibilities, often infinite in number. Which of these possibilities will in fact occur depends on the decisions made by the executives in question. The analyst, then, does not confine his analysis to a single possible decision, treating it as though it were the businessman's only option, because ordinarily he will have a wide set of choices open to him, any one of which may permit him to stay in business or even to prosper. He may, with relative impunity, surely spend somewhat more or somewhat less on advertising, make an upward or downward change in the size of his sales force, in his inventory levels, and often in his prices, though the effects of these alternatives are rarely investigated in the standard market survey. The approach of optimality analysis is to take these alternatives into account and to ask which of these possible sets of decisions will come *closest* to meeting the businessman's objectives, i.e., which decisions will be best or *optimal*.

2. Optimality Analysis in Operations Research

The foregoing does not mean that in applied operations research work the analyst even pretends to be able to find the best of all possible decisions. The data are too inaccurate, the tools of analysis are often too blunt, and the operations researcher's acquaintance with the details of the firm's operations and his general business "know-how" are usually too limited for him to be able to come up with anything more than approximations to the ideal of the true optimum. Nevertheless, an analysis which is specifically designed to look for optimal decisions, crude and approximative though it may be, is very likely to do much better than the workable but relatively arbitrary rules of thumb of obscure origin which play so prominent a part in business practice.

It is easy to provide illustrative examples of these standard business decision rules:

1. *Inventory levels.* The quantity of any product which company X carries in inventory is kept (approximately) equal to the amount which its customers normally buy in sixty days or some other such fixed period.

2. *Pricing.* The price of any of company X's products is set at its cost per unit plus a standard fixed percentage "mark-up."

3. *Advertising budgeting.* A fixed per cent of the firm's revenues (sales) is more or less automatically set aside for advertising.

These crude rules often exhibit serious shortcomings. For example, we will see later in this chapter that the inventory rule of thumb (1) is likely to result in excess inventories of some items and insufficient stocks of others, and in later chapters it will be shown that the pricing rule (2) is unlikely to maximize profits or sales or anything else which the businessman may be expected to consider important.

Most businessmen recognize these rules of thumb for what they are—rough but serviceable management tools. The operations researcher, by systematically seeking to determine the very best of the available possibilities, may at least hope to do better than the old standard rules of thumb.

3. The Role of Optimality in Economic Analysis

The economist's interest in optimization is of another sort entirely. At least in part his position, relative to that of the operations researcher, is somewhat analogous to the physicist's relation to the engineer. A primary aim of the economist is to understand business behavior rather than to make recommendations to businessmen. His understanding of economic processes provides part of the foundation for the analysis of the operations researcher.

The concept of optimality is important to the economist for his analysis, theoretical and applied, of public policy problems; but it also helps him to understand the behavior of businessmen, consumers, and other members of the economy. It is at least possible that sheer business acumen and experience permit management and other economic units to arrive at decisions which come close to being optimal. Moreover, in business, competition may soon eliminate firms whose decision-making is consistently poor. To the extent that these assertions are valid, optimality analysis should serve as a relatively good predictor of economic behavior; that is, it should provide a reasonably good explanation of actual economic decisions and activities. In economic theory it is therefore customary to employ an optimality premise in discussing the behavior of firms, consumers, and other economic units. It is simply assumed that these units' decisions are approximately optimal, and the consequences of this assumption are then usually presented as a rough description of economic behavior in the real world. Thus, in effect, the economist tells us only what a rational individual, who is also a well-trained and efficient calculator of optimal decisions, would do in his economic activities.

Because of this orientation of so much of economic analysis, the theory of optimal decision-making will constitute a central theme of this book.

4. Illustration: A Simple Inventory Problem

The reader may well feel, with some justification, that he has always believed in optimal decisions and that the concept involves relatively little that is new. Two aspects of the approach, however, are likely to be novel. The first is the explicit consideration of the entire relevant range of possibilities. Rather than considering whether the firm can maintain its position with a $2 million advertising budget, we try to examine the effect of each and every possible budget, say between $.5 million and $4 million. A second feature of the optimality calculation which is apt to be novel is the drawing together of these materials into a more systematic and rigorous analysis. These two aspects of optimization are, perhaps, best brought out by illustration. For this purpose let us examine the simplest (and, therefore, the crudest) of the models of inventory analysis. It is to be emphasized that this model is selected only for expository purposes; the reader must keep in mind that for this reason it is necessary to ignore many crucial features of real inventory problems. He should notice, however, how far the analysis carries us on the basis of very little initial information. It pulls implications from the model much as a magician pulls rabbits out of a hat—we know that the rabbits must have been there to begin with, but their presence was by no means obvious, and the skill with which they are produced is often impressive.

Our analysis deals with a retailer who (perhaps on the basis of contracts) confidently expects to sell some fixed amount, call it Q^* units, of one of his commodities over the next year at a predetermined price, with demand spread evenly throughout the year.[1] How much inventory should he keep on hand? He has considerable choice in the matter. For example, if $Q^* =$ 100,000 units he can meet his demand by having the entire amount delivered to his warehouse at the beginning of January, keeping it in stock until it is gradually depleted by shipments to his customers; alternatively, he can have 50,000 units delivered to him right after the first of the year and another equal amount on July 1. Still another alternative is to have four quarterly deliveries of 25,000 units, and so on.

Now the first alternative (receipt of the whole amount at the beginning of the year) involves an inventory which begins with 100,000 units and ends with zero,[2] so that his average inventory is 50,000 units. Similarly, the second (two-delivery) procedure involves inventories which begin with 50,000 units and end with zero, so that in this case the average stock on hand is 25,000 units, etc. Thus, by ordering more and more frequently, the required average inventory level can be made smaller and smaller.

Here, then, is the range of possibilities which our optimality analysis

---

[1] An asterisk is written after the Q to indicate that this letter represents a definite number which is known to the firm. This convention will be used throughout this section to distinguish such numbers from the variables whose values are the unknowns of the analysis.

[2] Of course, in practice it is normally never planned to have inventory run out altogether. For unexpected demands or delays in deliveries could then embarrass the businessman who had no stocks on hand to service the waiting customers. In the analysis which follows the reader can, therefore, if he wishes substitute some minimum inventory quantity M^* for this zero whenever it appears. He will find that no change in the analysis results.

must consider: The basic question is, how far should this process of cutting down on inventory be carried? A smaller inventory, of course, saves money on inventory *carrying costs:* that is, on storage costs, interest cost on the cash used to buy the inventory, etc. But, on the other hand, there is a *reorder cost* involved in placing and delivering an order, and since a smaller inventory involves more frequent orders and deliveries, if management decides on too small an average inventory level these costs may become prohibitive. Determination of the optimal inventory level involves a systematic balancing of the savings in inventory carrying costs against the increased reorder costs which reduced inventory will require.

5. Determination of the Cost Relationship

To find the optimal inventory level (the level which does the job at minimum cost) we must now go through the rather painful process of finding mathematical expressions for these two types of costs:

1. *Carrying cost.* We saw in our example that the average inventory level is one-half the amount received in a shipment. Thus, in general notation, let the quantity delivered to our retailer be D units per shipment (if it is all delivered in January, $D = 100,000$ units in our example). Then, as has been assumed, if demand is spread evenly throughout the year, inventory would fall at a steady rate from the day it is delivered until it is used up. Thus the inventory must fall gradually from D to zero so the average inventory level must be

$$\frac{D + 0}{2} = \frac{D}{2}.$$

Now let k^* (dollars) represent the interest and other carrying cost involved in holding one unit of inventory for one year. Then the total carrying cost will be the annual carrying cost per unit times the (average) number of units in inventory $= k^*D/2$.

2. *Reorder cost.* If 100,000 units are to be sold and 25,000 units are delivered per shipment, then clearly $4 = 100/25$ deliveries will be required over the course of the year. More generally, if Q^* is to be sold over the course of the year and D is delivered each time, the required number of deliveries is Q^*/D.

Suppose, moreover, that the cost per delivery is related to the amount delivered by the expression $a^* + b^*D$ where a^* and b^* are some numbers. Here b^* may be interpreted as the shipping cost per item so that the cost of sending D items is b^*D dollars. Similarly, a^* represents costs such as bookkeeping and long-distance telephoning for orders—in other words, costs whose magnitude is not seriously affected by the amount involved in the shipment.

We can now calculate the total annual reordering cost; it will equal the number of deliveries multiplied by the cost per delivery, i.e.,

$$\frac{(a^* + b^*D)Q^*}{D} = \frac{a^*Q^*}{D} + \frac{b^*Q^*D}{D} = \frac{a^*Q^*}{D} + b^*Q^*.$$

The total cost which our retailer lays out on his inventory is the sum of these two costs: the carrying and the reorder cost. It is therefore equal to

$$C = \frac{k^*D}{2} + \frac{a^*Q^*}{D} + b^*Q^*.$$

This is the relationship which we have been seeking.

6. The Optimality Calculation

Let us pause now to examine what has so far been accomplished. In effect, the only unknown in the preceding equation is the (optimal) value of D, the amount to be delivered per shipment. Once this number is determined the entire problem is solved, because we can automatically know the corresponding average inventory level ($= D/2$) and the number of times per year shipments should be ordered ($= Q^*/D$).

But once we have found our equation, the solution of the problem is reduced to a simple problem of computation, for the equation gives us a direct relationship between costs and the alternative values of our variable, D. For example, suppose the numbers in the equation were $Q^* = 100$ (thousand), $k^* = 8$, $a^* = 60$, and $b^* = 3$. Then the equation becomes

$$C = \frac{8D}{2} + \frac{60 \times 100}{D} + 3 \times 100$$

or

$$C = 4D + \frac{6000}{D} + 300.$$

With such an equation the optimal value of D can be approximated by a number of trial calculations. One can simply take a number of alternative values of D, substitute them in turn into the equation, and compute the corresponding values of C, thus finding, roughly, the value of D which gives the lowest cost. For example, setting $D = 10$ (thousand units) we obtain $C = 40 + 600 + 300 = 940$, and similarly, when $D = 20$, $C = 680$, and so on, as shown in the following table:

D	10	20	30	40	50	60	70	80	...
C	940	680	620	610	620	640	666	695	...

Examination of this table readily suggests the (correct) conclusion that the optimal value of D is approximately 40 (thousand) units per delivery.

Thus, by finding the inventory cost equation we have obtained all the information required for the solution of our problem. An equation of this variety is called an *objective function* because it shows how the firm's objective (cost minimization) is affected by the different values of the variable in question. We shall encounter such objective functions throughout this book.

In effect, then, the inventory problem has now been solved. However, an additional bit of mathematical analysis will enable us to extract a great deal of additional information from this solution. The standard methods of the differential calculus (Chapter 4) can be used to obtain from our cost equation another equation which gives us the optimal value of our variable D. This equation is[3]

$$D = \sqrt{\frac{2a^*Q^*}{k^*}}.$$

This result gives us the optimal average inventory level $D/2$ and the optimal reorder quantity, D, corresponding to any levels of sales volume Q^*, unit carrying cost k^*, and fixed reorder cost a^*. The result is, therefore, not tied to any particular numbers such as $Q^* = 100$, $k^* = 8$, etc., as was our numerical computation. As a result, this equation can be used to see what happens to the optimal value of D when some of these numbers change. It can readily be seen to indicate, as might be expected, that the optimum inventory level $D/2$ should be increased when sales Q^* go up. It also calls for an increase in the size of each delivery D (a reduction in the number of deliveries) when the reorder (delivery) cost a^* increases.

---

[3] *Proof:* The optimal value of D is that which minimizes total inventory cost, C. We therefore differentiate C with respect to D, set the derivative dC/dD equal to zero, and solve for D. We obtain

$$\frac{dC}{dD} = \frac{k^*}{2} - \frac{a^*Q^*}{D^2} = 0 \quad \text{or} \quad \frac{k^*}{2} = \frac{a^*Q^*}{D^2}.$$

Multiplying both sides by $2D^2/k^*$ we obtain

$$D^2 = \frac{2a^*Q^*}{k^*} \quad \text{or} \quad D = \sqrt{\frac{2a^*Q^*}{k^*}}.$$

Similarly, inventory should be reduced if the carrying cost k^* goes up (because k^* appears in the denominator of the fraction).[4]

More surprising, and perhaps more important, is that this formula indicates *inventory should increase only in proportion to the square root of sales.* In other words, if sales of some item double, inventory should not be doubled—it should be increased to much less than 200 per cent of its original amount. As was mentioned earlier in this chapter, many firms fix their inventory at some constant percentage of sales volume (a fixed number of weeks' worth of sales are kept in inventory) so that if one item sells five times as much as another, they will tend to keep five times as large an inventory of the former, which, as our result shows, means that they are keeping too much of the former, too little of the latter, or both. In fact, substantial savings have often been achieved because the last equation and related results have led analysts to recognize that the standard rule of thumb tends to yield excessive inventories of the popular, large-sales-volume items and insufficient inventories of the goods whose sales are relatively modest.[5] Thus we see that even with our highly oversimplified inventory model an optimality analysis can, if used with sufficient caution, produce significant practical results.

REFERENCES

Introductory Books

Magee, J. F., *Production, Planning and Inventory Control,* McGraw-Hill Book Company, New York, 1958.

Whitin, Thompson M., *The Theory of Inventory Management,* 2nd edition, Princeton University Press, Princeton, N.J., 1957.

---

[4] Note that b^* does not appear in the equation for optimal D. This means that no change in the value of b^* should lead to any change in inventory level in this situation. Intuitively, this perhaps slightly surprising result can be explained by noting that if the total amount, Q^*, to be shipped over the year is fixed, then there is nothing that can be done to save on shipping charges which are proportionate to the amount shipped. These charges will add up to b^*Q^* dollars over the year and no change in inventory levels can reduce this number.

[5] This conclusion can be made intuitively plausible in a closely related problem—that of maintaining inventory against unforeseen customer demands. Items whose sale is small are frequently bought by just a few customers so that demand for such a good is likely to be erratic, because it is subject to the sudden caprice of its few buyers. Hence, if the firm is to be reasonably sure it has enough on hand to meet these demands, it must carry relatively large stocks of these low- but erratic-sales-volume goods. On the other hand, the demand for a commodity which has many customers is unlikely to be much affected in an unforeseen manner by the whims of any particular buyer because when some demands are low those of other customers are apt to be high. Hence for such

More Advanced Volumes

Arrow, Kenneth J., Samuel Karlin, and Herbert Scarf, *Studies in the Mathematical Theory of Inventory and Production*, Stanford University Press, Stanford, Calif., 1958.

Morse, Philip M., *Queues, Inventories and Maintenance*, John Wiley & Sons, Inc., New York, 1958.

---

larger-volume goods an inventory which is not nearly as high in proportion to its sales may be expected to provide an adequate reserve against most unforeseen demands. Thus, here again, the optimal size of inventory will normally increase less than proportionately with sales volume.

Some Elementary
Mathematics

2

This chapter provides an explanation of a number of elementary but fundamental mathematical ideas. It discusses the meaning of and notation for a function of one and of many variables, the equation of a straight line and a few other simple relationships, the definition of "slope," the definitions and elementary rules of manipulation of exponents and a matter of notation—the $\sum$ (sigma) representation of a sum. All of these concepts appear frequently in the literature of economics and occur later in the book. The reader who is not sure of himself on these topics would therefore do well to master this material before proceeding; he should not find it difficult. Readers who are familiar with these concepts clearly need not waste their time on this chapter.

1. Functions

The expression $y = f(x)$, which is read "y is a function of x" (and does *not* represent some number x multiplied by another number, f), means that there is some, perhaps unspecified, relationship between the values of

---

* The material in this chapter is far more rudimentary than the contents of the chapters which follow. However, many readers may have forgotten the logic behind such fundamental concepts as linear equations, negative exponents, etc. This material is therefore presented for review to facilitate the reading of some subsequent portions of this book.

the variables y and x. That is, for some values of x, such a relationship specifies corresponding values for y. Such a functional relationship is summarized in the following table:

x	1	5	6	9	10
y	15	-22	0	9	12

This states that when $x = 1$ then $y = f(1) = 15$. Similarly, the value of y which corresponds to $x = 5$, i.e., $f(5)$, is equal to -22, etc. Basically then, $y = f(x)$ is a symbol which represents such a table of values. Sometimes it may represent a specific algebraic relationship such as $y = 15x^2 \log x + 3$ from which we can compute the corresponding table of values, but this will not always be the case.

There are many economic examples of such functional relationships. Thus, some simple models contain a demand function of the form $Q_d = f(P)$ which states that Q_d, the quantity demanded of some commodity, depends on P, the price of the item. If it is desired to introduce a second functional relationship (e.g., a supply function) which is to be distinguished from a functional relationship that was previously introduced, then other symbols such as F, g, ϕ (the Greek letter phi), or f_1 may be used instead of f. Thus, the supply function might be written $Q_s = g(P)$, where Q_s represents the quantity of the commodity which is supplied.

The quantity of the commodity which is demanded may, and in fact does, also depend on the values of variables other than price. For example, it may depend on the level of consumer income, Y, and on the volume of advertising expenditure, A. This is a multivariable demand function which is written symbolically as $Q = f(P, Y, A)$. A somewhat more general notation is $Q = f(x_1, x_2, \cdots, x_{15})$ which states that the value of Q is dependent on the values of 15 different variables. Here x_1 may represent price, x_2 consumer income, etc. Still greater generality can be achieved by representing the number of variables by the symbol n, in which case we write $Q = f(x_1, x_2, \cdots, x_n)$, meaning that the value of Q depends in some way on the values of each of some unspecified number of variables.

2. Slope

The slope of a line is a measure of steepness. For this purpose the following convention is employed: One simply calculates how much the line rises per unit move *to the right*. That is, if moving four units to the right involves a two-unit rise in the graph, we say that its slope is $\frac{2}{4} = 0.5$, i.e., that it rises at an (average) rate of one-half unit as one moves one unit to the right.

This is illustrated in Figure 1. As we move four units to the right below straight line LL' from point A to point B, the curve climbs two units to point C. Specifically, the slope of the curve is given by the increase in the vertical coordinates of points A and C divided by the increase in their horizontal coordinates. That is, it is equal to

$$\frac{y_1 - y_0}{x_1 - x_0} = \frac{4 - 2}{7 - 3} = \frac{2}{4} = 0.5.$$

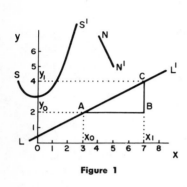

Figure 1

A line such as segment NN' which goes downhill as we move to the right is said to have a *negative slope*. In this case, since its level diminishes two units as we move one unit to the right, it is of slope -2.

The difference between a line which is straight and one which is not is that the slope of a straight line never changes. The line LL' is equally steep in the vicinity of point A and in that of point B. By contrast, at the bottom of curve SS' the line is fairly flat, but it grows steeper as we move up along it either to the right or the left, so that its slope increases in numerical value.

3. Linear and Other Simple Equations

The equation $y = \frac{1}{2}x + 3$ and the more general equation $y = ax + b$ (where a and b are any numbers) are called *linear*. If the reader were to use such an equation to compute a table of values for x and y, and then plotted these figures on a graph, he would find that he had drawn a set of points all of which lie along a straight line; $y = ax + b$ is therefore called a *linear equation*.

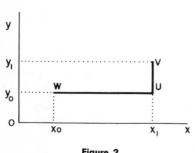

Figure 2

We can prove that this must be so without much difficulty. In the preceding section it was indicated that a straight line may be defined as one whose slope never changes. To prove that $y = ax + b$ is represented by a straight line, we must therefore show that the slope of the graph is a constant (a fixed number such as a or b). Now consider any two points such as W and V (Figure 2) which lie on the graph of this equation, where the remainder of the graph of the equation is not shown in order to avoid prejudging its shape. As we have seen, the slope of this graph is $(y_1 - y_0)/(x_1 - x_0)$. But, since both points lie on the graph of $y = ax + b$, this equation tells us that there is a relationship between y_0 and x_0 and a similar relationship between y_1 and x_1: $y_0 = ax_0 + b$ and $y_1 = ax_1 + b$. Substituting these expressions for y_0 and y_1 into the expression for the slope we obtain

$$\text{slope of } (y = ax + b) = \frac{y_1 - y_0}{x_1 - x_0} = \frac{(ax_1 + b) - (ax_0 + b)}{x_1 - x_0}$$

$$= \frac{ax_1 + \cancel{b} - ax_0 - \cancel{b}}{x_1 - x_0} = \frac{ax_1 - ax_0}{x_1 - x_0}$$

$$= \frac{a(\cancel{x_1 + x_0})}{(\cancel{x_1 + x_0})} = a.$$

Thus we have proved that *the slope of the graph of $y = ax + b$ is always equal to the number a, the coefficient of the term ax.* For example, the graph of $y = 6x + 3$ is of slope 6, which remains unchanged throughout the length of the graph. Hence that graph must be a straight line, as was to be proved.[1]

The constant, b, in our linear equation can also be given a simple interpretation. Consider the point on the graph where $x = 0$, i.e., the point where the graph crosses the y axis. There we have

$$y = f(0) = a \cdot 0 + b = b.$$

In other words, b is the *y intercept*—the value of y (the height of the graph) at the point where it crosses the vertical axis.

It can be shown by similar arguments that the graph of a three-variable relationship such as $y = 3x + 4z - 6$ is the three-dimensional analogue of a straight line—a plane in a three-dimensional diagram whose three axes represent the values of x, y, and z. More generally, by analogy, we use the term *linear equation* for any relationship such as

$$y = a_1x_1 + a_2x_2 + \ldots + a_nx_n + b,$$

where y, x_1, x_2, $\cdots$, x_n are all variables and a_1, a_2, $\cdots$, a_n and b are all constants.

The second-degree nonlinear equation $y = x^2 + 3$ has the graph SS' in Figure 1, as may be verified by plotting some points. Similarly, other

---

[1] It is easily shown that the converse is also true, i.e., that any straight line will match an equation of the form $y = ax + b$. For let a^* be the slope of any such line and let b^* be its y intercept (see below). Then this line must be the graph of $y = a^*x + b^*$.

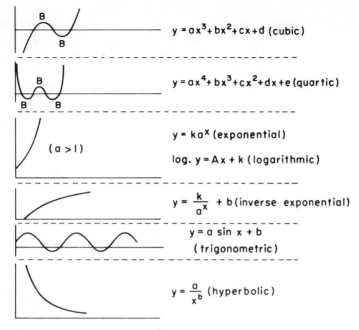

$y = ax^3 + bx^2 + cx + d$ (cubic)

$y = ax^4 + bx^3 + cx^2 + dx + e$ (quartic)

$y = ka^x$ (exponential)

log. $y = Ax + k$ (logarithmic)

$y = \dfrac{k}{a^x} + b$ (inverse exponential)

$y = a \sin x + b$
(trigonometric)

$y = \dfrac{a}{x^b}$ (hyperbolic)

Figure 3[2]

types of equation have characteristic graphic forms, some of which are indicated in Figure 3. Note that the number of "bumps," B, in an nth-degree polynomial equation

$$y = a_1 x^n + a_2 x^{n-1} + \cdots + a_n x + b$$

is (usually) one less than the degree, n, of the equation (though there are exceptional equations for which this is not true). Thus, the third-degree equation

$$y = ax^3 + bx^2 + cx + d$$

has one hill and one valley, the quartic has one peak and two valleys, etc. The next graph, the exponential $y = ka^x$, exhibits an explosive, roughly geometric (cumulatively increasing) growth rate. The inverse type of relationship $y = k/a^x + b$ can level off, with the fractional term gradually approaching zero. The trigonometric functions, $y = a \sin x + b$ and $y = \cos x + b$, form a perfectly symmetrical and repetitious cyclical

[2] For reasons which will become clearer in Sections 4 and 5 below, exponential and logarithmic equations are very closely related and, indeed, one can usually be translated into the other. That is, of course, why they have similar graphs.

pattern. Finally, the relationship $y = a/x^b$, of which the frequently encountered rectangular hyperbola, $y = a/x$ or $xy = a$, is a special case, approaches the axes asymptotically; that is, it comes closer and closer to the axes but never quite reaches them. Of course, many other types of relationship exist and each has its characteristic graph.

PROBLEMS

Show that $3y + 6x + 9 = 0$ is a linear equation. Prove that its slope is -2. Generalize this result to explain why any equation of the form

$$a_1x_1 + a_2x_2 + \cdots + a_nx_n = k$$

is linear. Here the a's and k are any (unspecified) constants (numbers).

4. Exponents: Definitions and Elementary Rules of Manipulation

Negative, fractional, and zero exponents may seem puzzling at first, but these are all extensions of the standard definition

$$x^n = x \cdot x \cdot \ldots \cdot x \ (n \text{ times}),$$

i.e., x multiplied by itself n times. *As a special case of this definition we have* $x^1 = x$.

Now suppose we multiply, say, x^2 by x^3. By this definition,

$$x^2 \cdot x^3 = (x \cdot x) \cdot (x \cdot x \cdot x) = x \cdot x \cdot x \cdot x \cdot x = x^5.$$

Generalizing,[3] we obtain the fundamental

RULE 1. *Multiplication:* $x^a \cdot x^b = x^{a+b}$, that is, the product of two identical terms, each raised to a different power, is equal to that same term, this time raised to the *sum* of the two powers.

In other words, to multiply power terms we add their exponents. An analogous rule applies to division. For example, to divide x^6 by x^2 write

$$\frac{x^6}{x^2} = \frac{x \cdot x \cdot x \cdot x \cdot x \cdot x}{x \cdot x} = x \cdot x \cdot x \cdot x = x^4.$$

Hence we conclude

RULE 2. *Division:* $x^a/x^b = x^{a-b}$.

---

[3] To generalize this and the arguments that follow we need merely substitute letters for the numbers in the illustrative "proofs." For example,

$$x^a \cdot x^b = \underbrace{(x \cdot x \cdot \ldots \cdot x)}_{a \ x\text{'s}} \underbrace{(x \cdot x \cdot \ldots \cdot x)}_{b \ x\text{'s}} = \underbrace{(x \cdot x \cdot \ldots \cdot x)}_{(a+b) \ x\text{'s}} = x^{a+b}.$$

Thus, to divide exponent terms, subtract the exponent of the denominator from that of the numerator.

This rule seems obvious so long as a is greater than b $(a > b)$. But it is also extended verbatim to cases where this does not hold, e.g., to division of x^4 by x^6, which is then written $x^{4-6} = x^{-2}$. Several significant consequences follow. If we divide x^a by x^a, the result is clearly equal to unity. But by Rule 2, $x^a/x^a (= 1) = x^{a-a} = x^0$. Hence,

RULE 3. *Zero exponents:* $x^0 = 1$, for *any* (nonzero) number x.

A consequence of Rule 2 and Rule 3 can be obtained by taking the reciprocal of x^a. This is equal to $1/x^a$, which by Rule 3 is equal to x^0/x^a, or by Rule 2, it is equal to $x^{0-a} = x^{-a}$. This, then, yields the definition of a negative exponent, i.e.,

RULE 4. For any x and a, the expression x^{-a} represents the reciprocal of x^a.

To raise a term, x^a, to a higher power, e.g., to square x^3, we multiply this term by itself to obtain

$$x^3 \cdot x^3 = (x \cdot x \cdot x)(x \cdot x \cdot x) = x^{3 \cdot 2} = x^6.$$

More generally,

RULE 5. *Powers:* x^a raised to the bth power is equal to x^{ab}, so that, to raise such a term to the power b, one multiplies the old exponent by b. Similarly, to undo this operation, e.g., to take the square root of x^6, we get $\sqrt{x^6} = x^3 = x^{6/2}$. More generally,

RULE 6. *Roots:* The bth root of x^a is $x^{a/b}$. In particular, $x^{1/b}$ is the bth root of $x(= x^1)$.

5. Logarithms

The ways of manipulating exponents just described are widely used to simplify computational problems. The facts that multiplication can be reduced to *addition* of exponents and that a number can be raised to a higher power by multiplication provide the basis for logarithmic computation. This section is not intended to teach the reader how to use logarithms in computation; a much longer and more detailed exposition is required for this purpose. Rather, it seeks to illustrate how the results of the previous section can be employed and to review the simple basis of the elementary theory of logarithms, which is often forgotten by many who use the device.

Given any number k, we define the logarithm of k (to the base 10) to be a number which satisfies the following relationship: $k = 10^{\log k}$. That is, log k is a number such that, if one raises 10 to the power log k, then the result is equal to k.

Since these so-called common logarithms are all powers of 10, they can be combined according to the rules for the manipulation of exponents. For example, to multiply two numbers, a and b, observe that (by Rule 1 of the previous section)

$$a \cdot b = 10^{\log a} \cdot 10^{\log b} = 10^{\log a + \log b}.$$

Hence we conclude

RULE 7. *Logarithmic multiplication:* To multiply two numbers, a and b, use a table of logarithms to find the number whose logarithm is equal to $\log a + \log b$.

Similarly, to raise any number k to the power a we note that (by Rule 5)

$$k^a = (10^{\log k})^a = 10^{a \log k}.$$

Therefore

RULE 8. *Logarithmic calculation of powers:* To raise any number k to any power a, find the number whose logarithm is equal to $a \log k$.

To illustrate the economy which these rules permit, the reader may wish to consider what sort of labor would be involved, without the use of logarithms, in calculating, e.g., $100 \, (1.05)^{25}$, the value after twenty-five years of a \$100 security which carries an interest of 5 per cent, compounded annually, and where the interest is allowed to accumulate.

6. $\sum$ Notation

A final item in this collection of miscellaneous mathematical background material is a standard notation for addition, employed at a number of points in this volume. Let x_1, x_2, x_3, and x_4 be symbols used to represent four numbers, say $x_1 = 5$, $x_2 = 0$, $x_3 = -2$, and $x_4 = 12$. The Greek letter $\sum$ (upper-case sigma) is used to indicate summation. The addition of these four numbers is then written as

$$\sum_{i=1}^{4} x_i \,.$$

This means: Add the numbers x_i which are obtained, successively, by letting i be equal to 1, then letting i be equal to 2, all the way up to $i = 4$. This is the significance of the notation above and below the $\sum$. The number (called a *summation index*) which is below the $\sum$ indicates the first term to be included in the sum, and the number above the $\sum$ represents the last term in the sum. Several examples should make this clear:

$$\sum_{i=1}^{4} x_i = x_1 + x_2 + x_3 + x_4 = 5 + 0 - 2 + 12 = 15.$$

Similarly,

$$\sum_{i=1}^{3} x_i = x_1 + x_2 + x_3 = 5 + 0 - 2 = 3$$

and

$$\sum_{i=2}^{4} x_i = x_2 + x_3 + x_4 = 0 - 2 + 12 = 10.$$

A slightly more subtle example is the $\sum$ representation of the power series[4]

$$1 + y + y^2 + y^3 + y^4 + y^5 + y^6 \text{ which is just } \sum_{i=0}^{6} y^i.$$

Where a large number of terms is involved, this notation saves both space and time.

PROBLEMS

1. Write out in $\sum$ notation
   (a) the linear equation

$$y = a_1 x_1 + a_2 x_2 + a_3 x_3 + a_4 x_4$$

   (b) the polynomial equation

$$y = a_0 + a_1 x + a_2 x^2.$$

2. Write out term by term

   (a) $\sum_{i=0}^{3} a_i x^{3-i}$

   (b) $\sum_{i=1}^{3} i^2.$

---

[4] The reader will recall from Rule 3 of Section 4, above, that any number raised to the zeroth power is equal to 1. Specifically, $y^i = 1$ when $i = 0$.

Marginal Analysis

3

1. Marginal Reasoning and the Logic of Decision-Making

There is a common element to all decision problems which is expressible in the apparently trivial question, "Is it worthwhile?" A firm considering an improvement in product quality, a consumer considering the purchase of a bottle of wine, or a government agency considering the organization of another research project must all ask the same question—whether the action in question will *add* sufficiently to the benefits enjoyed by the performer to make it worth the cost. This is the heart of marginal decision-making—the statement that an action merits performance if and only if, as a result, the actor can expect to be *better off than he was before*.

Although this proposition seems obvious enough, the fact that it is frequently violated in practice suggests that it requires some examination. First let us see how a decision which runs counter to this rule is likely to arise. Consider the following example: A manager is empowered to hire an additional salesman. He decides to send this man to St. Louis rather than to Cleveland because last year's orders per salesman were $60,000 in St. Louis and $43,000 in Cleveland. But it is possible that the difference in returns per salesman in the two cities occurred just because the size of the sales force in the former was well adapted to the number of retailers whereas the sales force in the latter was spread too thinly. If so, the new salesman may *add* little, if anything, to the company's orders in the sales-man-saturated St. Louis market, but in Cleveland he might produce a substantial increase in sales. Clearly, if the firm's objective is to maximize its orders, it would in this case be better to send the man to Cleveland.

The figure giving the size of orders per salesman is referred to as the *average* return per salesman, whereas the *increase* in sales which results from the presence of an additional salesman is called the *marginal* return. The manager in the illustration was (inadvertently) acting contrary to the firm's interests by sending a salesman to the city where the *average* return per salesman was higher rather than to the area where his *marginal* return (the amount he could add to company sales) was higher. A basic theorem of this section, then, is that *the best interests of a firm, a consumer, or any other economic unit require that any decision take into account the magnitude of the marginal yield which it promises.*

As will be shown in the next chapter, the marginal analysis is very closely related to the classical mathematical tool of optimality analysis—the differential calculus. A marginal datum may be interpreted, roughly, as a first derivative, and most of the findings of this chapter can readily be translated into calculus terms as is shown occasionally in footnotes.

Marginal analysis, because it can be explained with the aid of arithmetic examples, has a distinct expository advantage. But, on the other hand, in this form it is a relatively blunt calculating instrument to which many of the powerful analytic theorems of the differential calculus described in the next chapter do not apply.

2. Theorems on Resource Allocation

To emphasize further its importance for decision-making, let us now examine two fundamental propositions of the marginal analysis. The first of these is designed to determine the *magnitudes* of the variables which constitute an optimal decision: How much should be spent on newspaper advertising? How far should price be cut? How many pounds of plums should a consumer buy? The paradoxical answer to a question of this sort is

RULE 1. *Optimal activity level:* The scale of an activity should if possible be expanded so long as its *marginal* net yield (taking into account both benefits and costs) is a positive value, and the activity should, therefore, be carried to a point where this *marginal* net yield is zero.[1]

This result is paradoxical because it suggests the question, "Why

---

[1] This is no more than the standard calculus proposition that to maximize any $y = f(x)$ it is necessary that the first derivative, dy/dx (the marginal effect of x on y), be zero. It is, however, very important to realize that this is a necessary but not a sufficient optimality condition, i.e., all optima to which it is relevant must satisfy Rule 1, but not all situations which meet the requirements of the rule will be optima. To separate the sheep from the goats we must satisfy in addition the very important *second-order conditions* described in Section 9 of this chapter. See also Section 2 of Chapter 15 for an illustrative application of this point.

shouldn't we quit while we're still ahead?" Why not stop advertising when the marginal return on a dollar of advertising is, say, $1.75? The answer, here, is that a firm which makes such a decision is voluntarily missing the opportunity to make even more money. An additional dollar spent on advertising will leave the firm 75 cents (= $1.75 − $1.00) ahead, and failure to take advantage of the opportunity therefore leaves the firm 75 cents poorer.

Of course, the firm may not have any more funds to lay out on advertising. In that case the rule cannot be followed. That is the significance of the proviso in Rule 1 that the marginal yield of any activity should be reduced to zero *whenever possible*. As we shall see in later chapters, this remark lies behind the role of mathematical programming.

Another possible objection to Rule 1 is that the firm may have a better use for its money than expansion of the scale of the activity that happens to be under discussion. A dollar spent on improved quality control may perhaps yield $1.97, as against the $1.75 return to an additional advertising dollar; therefore advertising should not be increased until something is done to take advantage of the quality-control profit opportunity. By itself this argument leads only to the conclusion that more should ultimately be spent on both activities. If there is enough money available, and both of these types of expenditure yield diminishing marginal returns, an optimal budget will provide enough funds to expand *both* activities until each of them has a zero marginal yield. But where funds are limited so that this ideal cannot be attained, we have a second fundamental rule of marginal analysis:

RULE 2. *Relative activity levels:* For optimal results activities should, wherever possible, be carried to levels where they all yield the same marginal returns per unit of effort (cost).

For, where this condition does not hold, the decision-maker is missing an opportunity to benefit by reallocating some of his resources from an activity with the smaller marginal return to one with a larger marginal yield. In the previous example, he can benefit by budgeting more money for quality control rather than for advertising. The transfer of one dollar from advertising (marginal yield $1.75) to quality control (marginal yield $1.97) must yield a clear gain of $1.97 − $1.75 = 22 cents, in effect giving him something for nothing! Hence, generally, unless Rule 2 is satisfied, he cannot possibly be getting the maximum yield from his resources; his resource allocation among alternative activities can only be optimal if all his expenditures yield the same marginal return.

3. Totals, Averages, and Marginals: Their Arithmetic Relationships

It is customary to explain the arithmetic of marginal analysis with the aid of a table such as Table 1.

TABLE 1

No. of Units	Total *x*	Average *x*	Marginal *x*
0	0	—	0
1	80	80	80
2	180	90	100
3	270	90	90
4	280	70	10
5	250	50	−30

The last three columns have been labeled "Total," "Average," and "Marginal *x*" to indicate that these are purely arithmetic relationships which are valid whether we are interested in total, average, or marginal revenue, cost, profit, or utility. That is, the reader can substitute any of these words for the letter *x* and end up with a valid table.

One may, perhaps, get a better grasp of the relationship if the numbers are, for the moment, interpreted as the examination grades of a group of five men. The first row indicates that before any of the papers has been marked the total grade is zero. The marginal grade is then, by convention, also considered zero (nothing has yet been added to the total), but there is no meaning to the concept of "average grade" when there are no papers. The first paper, however, gets an 80 (marginal grade = addition to total grade = 80) so that the total of all grades so far is 80, and the average grade is also 80. The second paper gets 100 (marginal grade 100) which brings the total up to 180 and pulls the average up to $(80 + 100)/2 = 90$, and so on.[2] We see, then, that *the marginal figure is defined as the amount which is added to the total by each additional paper.* The average (arithmetic mean), of course, has the usual connotation: the total divided by the number of units.

Three relationships emerge from this illustration, each of which will play some role in the subsequent discussion:

RULE 3. *First units:* The total, average, and marginal figures for the first unit are identical (so long as total *x* for the zeroth unit is zero).

For example, the total, average, and marginal grades of the first paper in Table 1 are all 80. Similarly, if a farmer sells one cow for $50, his marginal revenue (the addition to his income produced by selling one cow) is $50, his revenue per cow sold (average revenue) is $50, and his total revenue is also $50. An exception to this apparently inviolable rule will emerge in Section 6 of this chapter.

---

[2] The fifth man must have done something unusual, since his paper receives a grade of minus 30!

RULE 4. *Relation between total and marginal figures:* The total figure is always the sum of the preceding marginal figures.

For example, the total grade of the first three papers, 270, is the sum of the grades of these papers, 80 + 100 + 90. This rule follows from the definition of the marginal figure as the addition to the preceding total figure (the current total is the sum of the preceding increments to it). Finally, we have the somewhat more complicated

RULE 5. *Relation between average and marginal figures:* For the average to rise, the marginal figure must be above the average figure; for the average to remain unchanged, the average and marginal figures must be equal; for the average to fall, the marginal figure must be below average.[3]

For example, in Table 1, when the average figure rises from 80 to 90, the marginal figure, 100, *lies above* the corresponding average figure, 90. The reason is easily seen—the average of a group of grades can only be raised by adding a paper whose grade is above average.

For similar reasons, the table shows that when the average remains unchanged at 90, the latest grade (the marginal figure) must itself be just average, i.e., 90. And when the average grade then falls to 70 it must have been pulled down by a below-average grade, i.e., 10.

This last rule is often misunderstood to state that, when the average figure falls, the marginal must also *fall;* when the average remains unchanged, the marginal must remain unchanged, etc. Such a conclusion is false. For example, while the average figure remains unchanged at 90 when the third paper is graded, the marginal figure *falls* from 100 to 90.

4. Geometry of Marginal Analysis: Total x Curves

The preceding rules help us to find geometric relationships among the average, marginal, and total concepts. First, let us draw a graph describing the *total* profitability of advertising expenditure (Figure 1) and show how

---

[3] A general proof of this result can also be obtained with the aid of a little differential calculus:

Let Q represent quantity, or number of units (the item in the first column of Table 1) and let A be an average figure. Then the corresponding total figure is AQ (e.g., total revenue equals average revenue multiplied by the number of units sold). The marginal figure, M, is the derivative of the total figure with respect to the independent variable Q, i.e.,

$$(1) \qquad M = \frac{dAQ}{dQ} = A + Q\,\frac{dA}{dQ}.$$

From this equation Rule 5 follows readily. For example, when the average figure is rising, we have $dA/dQ > 0$, and it follows that $M > A$, etc.

the corresponding marginal and average figures can be read off from it. This total profit curve, as its name implies, indicates how total profits will vary with the firm's advertising expenditure. It plots data like those in column 2 of Table 1 against the information in column 1. For example, point A in Figure 1 indicates that $3 million spent on advertising will yield a total of $4 million in profit to the firm. The average profit (profit per advertising dollar) is then $4 million/$3 million = $1.33, approximately. But, in this ratio the $4 million is represented by line segment RA,

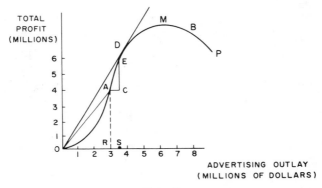

Figure 1

while the $3 million is depicted by OR. Hence, the average profitability of expenditure OR is RA/OR, *which is the slope of* OA, *the straight line from the origin to point* A. In other words, we have

R ULE 6. *Average x and total curves:* Given any point A on a curve representing total *x*, the corresponding average *x* figure at that point is the slope of the straight line, OA, which connects point A with the origin.

This rule permits us to conclude by inspection that between points A and D the average profitability of advertising has risen, for the slope of line OD is clearly greater than that of OA. In fact, the point of maximum *average* profitability is D, the point of tangency between the total profit curve, OP, and the straight line OD, to the origin. The reader may readily check that at points to the right of D, such as M, the average profit will be lower than it is at D because the corresponding line segment through the origin, OM, is less steep than OD.

The *marginal* productivity of advertising at point A is also measured by a slope, but this time by the slope of the total profit curve itself. For marginal profitability is defined as the increment in profit per unit addition to advertising expenditure. But if advertising expenditure goes up from OR to OS, i.e., by amount AC, equals say \$500,000, the curve shows that total profit will rise by amount CE, equals say \$1,800,000. Hence, marginal profitability will equal

$$\frac{1,800,000}{500,000} = \frac{CE}{AC} = \text{the slope of the total profit curve at } A.$$

Thus, the general

RULE 7. *Marginal x and total curves:* Given any point A on a curve representing total x, then marginal x is equal to the slope of the curve at point A.

As an exercise in the use of Rules 6 and 7, we may note that at point A the total profit curve slopes more steeply than does straight line OA. This means that marginal profits at A must exceed average profits so that, by Rule 5, above, average profits must be rising. We have already seen that this is in fact the case since the slope of OD exceeds that of OA. Observe also that at point D, just at the point where average profit stops rising, OD has the same slope as the total profit curve, so that average and marginal profits are equal, again as Rule 5 would lead us to expect.

The graphic interpretation of marginal x as the slope of the total x curve (Rule 7) also casts some light on the fundamental Rule 1 of this chapter, that the optimal level of any activity requires its marginal yield to be zero. Thus, in Figure 1 we note that at advertising expenditure \$3 million, the profit curve has a positive slope (a positive marginal profit yield of advertising). At point B the curve is going downhill (negative marginal profit). Neither of these can be a (profit) optimum advertising expenditure, for at A profits can be increased by advertising more, whereas from B the firm can raise its profits by advertising less. Only at M, where the profit curve is neither rising nor falling, so that the slope of the profit curve is zero, can the advertising expenditure level have reached its optimum value. But that is precisely what Rule 1 asserts for this case—an optimal advertising outlay for a profit-maximizing firm requires that the marginal profit yield of advertising (the slope of the total profit curve) be zero.

5. Marginal and Average x Curves

So much for the "total x curves." We can also draw both "average x" and "marginal x" curves in a similar way (Figure 2). Their general relationship is largely determined by Rule 5 and Rule 3. Rule 3 tells us that the two curves must start out together (point C).[4]

To the right of point C the relative height of the two curves is governed by Rule 5. Thus, it will be observed that output OQ_2 is the point of minimum average costs Q_2M, so that there the average cost curve is horizontal (average neither rising nor falling). At that output marginal and average

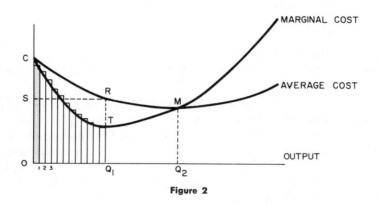

Figure 2

costs are equal (intersection point M). To the right of this point, where average costs are rising, marginal costs lie above them. To the left of Q_2, where the average cost curve has a negative slope, the marginal cost curve lies below the average cost curve.[5]

Just as marginal and average x can be shown on a total x diagram, it is possible to represent total cost in terms of Figure 2. This can be done in two different ways—one in terms of the average cost curve and one in terms of the marginal cost curve.

(a) *Average curve representation of total x.* Since total cost equals average cost (cost per unit) multiplied by the number of units produced, then the total cost of output OQ_1 is $OQ_1 \times Q_1R$, which is the area of the rectangle OQ_1RS. In other words

RULE 8. *Total x and average curves:* The total cost of any output OQ is

---

[4] There is a minor difficulty here. Average cost is not defined for zero units and is only equal to marginal cost when output = 1 unit (compare Table 1). Hence they should meet somewhere to the right of the vertical axis. However, it is usually implicitly assumed, as is done here, that the unit of measurement is very small, so that our first unit lies at a microscopic distance from the origin. The two curves can then be taken to start out from a point practically on the vertical axis.

[5] But it will be noted that in the interval Q_1Q_2 marginal cost is *rising* even though average cost is falling.

the area of the *rectangle* inscribed under the average cost curve which has OQ as its base.

(b) *Marginal curve representation of total x.* Alternatively, we can find another area which represents total profit, this time with the aid of the marginal revenue curve. By Rule 4, total cost is the sum of the preceding marginal costs. But the marginal cost of the first unit is the area of the thin, shaded rectangle next to the vertical axis, since its height is the height of the marginal cost curve at that point. Similarly, the marginal cost of the second unit produced is represented by the next rectangle, etc. Therefore the total cost of producing OQ_1 units equals the sum of the preceding marginal costs equals the sum of the areas of all the thin rectangles equals area OQ_1TC. More generally,

RULE 9. *Total x and the marginal curve:* The total cost of producing OQ

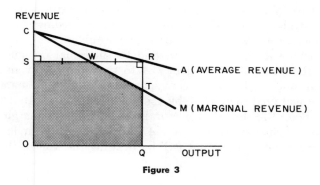

Figure 3

units of any commodity is that portion of the area under the marginal cost curve which lies above line OQ.

We can use these two representations of total x to derive a construction for the marginal curve from any average curve which is given to us. First, we assume that both curves are straight lines (Figure 3). It will now be proved that, given the average revenue curve CA, we obtain the marginal revenue curve by drawing in *any* horizontal line SR which ends on this average revenue curve, finding the midpoint W of SR, and drawing in the straight line CM which (in accord with Rule 3) begins at the same point as the average revenue curve and goes through this midpoint W. To prove the theorem the reader will have to go through the painful process of re-calling a bit of high school geometry.

Step 1: The total revenue from any output OQ is given either by the area of rectangle $OQRS$ inscribed under the average revenue curve or by area $OQTC$ under the marginal revenue curve. Hence, if the two curves are drawn correctly, the two areas must be equal.

Step 2: Since these two areas have shaded area $OQTWS$ in common, it follows that right triangles SWC and WTR must be equal in area.

Step 3: Moreover, angle SWC must be the same as TWR (opposite angles of a vertex are necessarily equal). Therefore triangles SWC and WTR must be similar (two angles in common) as well as being equal in area.

Step 4: These triangles must, as a result, be congruent so that we must have $SW = WR$, as was to be proved. In sum,

Rule 10. *Straight-line marginal and average curves:* Given any straight-line average curve, to find the corresponding marginal curve, draw a straight line which begins where the average curve cuts the vertical axis, and goes through the midpoint of any horizontal line to the average curve.

Where the average curve is not a straight line the construction is a bit more complex. We operate, in effect, by approximating the curve by a number of straight-line segments and using the preceding construction on these segments one at a time. For example, given the curved average revenue curve VA^* (Figure 4), to find the marginal revenue at output OQ, draw the straight-line tangent CA to the average revenue curve at that output, and construct the corresponding straight-line marginal curve (call it the marginal line) CM, by the method just indicated (Rule 10). The point T, on CM directly below R, is then also on the marginal revenue curve to our original average curve VA^*, at that output. Similarly, we find the marginal revenue at output OQ' by drawing the tangent line $C'A'$ to

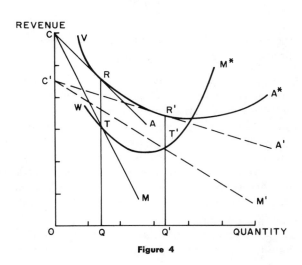

Figure 4

average curve VA^* through point R' (output OQ'). Now treat that straight line as an average revenue curve and find the corresponding marginal line $C'M'$, and the point T' on that line *which corresponds to output OQ'* is the marginal revenue for this output. In this way we can obtain as many marginal points T, T', $\cdots$ as we wish, and the locus of these points WM^* is the marginal revenue curve which we seek. In sum,

RULE 11. *General marginal and average curves:* To find the marginal curve to an average curve which is not straight draw a straight line tangent to the average curve at some output Q, find the corresponding marginal line to this tangent by Rule 10, and thereby find the marginal point on that line at output Q. The marginal curve which we seek is the locus of all such marginal points.[6]

6. Marginal Analysis and Fixed Costs

Fixed costs are defined as costs whose magnitude does not vary with the level of output, at least within some range. For example, the rent of a factory may be the same whether that factory is going full blast or running at half capacity (but once demand exceeds the factory's capacity, rental becomes a variable cost if a second factory is put into operation). Similarly, the cost of an automobile license is the same whether the car is used to travel 5,000 or 30,000 miles in a year. The special features of a fixed cost are (1) that it all comes in one big lump once it is decided to enter on the operation, but (2) after it is incurred a further expansion in output makes no difference in its magnitude.[7]

These features are illustrated by the fixed cost figures in Table 2. This table is completely analogous to Table 1 (which should now be interpreted, for purposes of comparison, as a table of total, average, and marginal *variable* cost).

It will be observed that the total fixed cost figure ($2,000) remains the same throughout, no matter what the number of units, even if no units

---

[6] A short proof can be given with the help of Equation (1) of footnote 3, above. This equation states that

$$(1) \qquad\qquad M = A + Q\,\frac{dA}{dQ}$$

where M is the marginal x, A is average x, and Q is quantity (number of units). Consider, now, the straight-line average curve CA and curved average curve VA^* which are tangent at point R. At that point the outputs OQ are equal on both curves, their average revenues QR also coincide, and because they are tangent, their slopes dA/dQ must also be the same. Hence, by Equation (1), at that output the marginal values QT corresponding to the two curves must be the same—find one and you have the other.

[7] It is also shown in the chapter on integer programming that fixed costs can cause computational difficulties because of these characteristics.

TABLE 2

No. of Units	Total Fixed Cost	Average Fixed Cost	Marginal Fixed Cost
0	2000	—	2000
1	2000	2000	0
2	2000	1000	0
3	2000	666⅔	0
4	2000	500	0
5	2000	400	0

are produced or sold. Thus, once a train runs, it costs the same even if it goes empty, and (in the absence of bankruptcy) a contract to buy a fixed amount of raw material must be honored even if none of it is used.

Skipping to the marginal fixed cost column, we see that it, too, follows a very simple pattern. The very decision to go into an operation saddles management with its fixed costs—even before anything is produced. So, by convention, the zeroth unit is taken to expend the entire $2,000 (the marginal cost of the zeroth unit is $2,000). Thereafter, production of any further units adds nothing to fixed costs (the marginal fixed cost of the first unit, and any unit thereafter, is zero).[8] A curve of marginal fixed costs, therefore, must always have the same shape—it coincides with the axes of the diagram. For, to the right of the origin, marginal fixed cost is always zero so that there the marginal cost curve lies along the horizontal axis, while at the origin the marginal cost is not zero (it rises above the horizontal axis along the vertical axis).

The pattern of the average fixed cost curve is hardly more complicated. As our table shows, and for obvious reasons, the larger the number of units produced, the smaller will be the average fixed cost. The fixed costs are thereby spread over more units. However, the decline in average fixed costs is gradual, and though the average figure becomes smaller and smaller as the number of units increases, it never reaches zero. No matter by how large a number we divide $2,000 (no matter how thin the overhead costs are spread), there will still remain *some* unit cost which is greater than zero.[9]

---

[8] In calculus terms, if T is total cost and Q is the number of units, then marginal cost is dT/dQ which equals zero whenever T is a constant (as it is for a fixed cost).

[9] The average fixed cost curve satisfies a simple mathematical relationship. Let K be total fixed cost and x be the number of units produced. Then average fixed cost, y, is the total fixed cost divided by the number of units, i.e., we have the equation $y = K/x$. This is an equation which is rather familiar in the literature. Its graph, which is called a rectangular hyperbola, is doubtless one of the economists' most popular curves— second only to the straight line. A rectangular hyperbola is depicted in Figure 3a of Chapter 9 and some of its properties are described in Section 4 of that chapter where it enters into the discussion of the theory of consumer demand.

As a final observation on fixed costs, as illustrated by Table 2, notice that, for the first unit, *average* fixed cost is \$2,000, whereas *marginal* fixed cost is, as usual, zero. We see, then, that fixed costs violate Rule 3 of Section 3 of this chapter, which states that for first units marginal x and average x are always equal. That rule holds only so long as the total cost (or total x) of zero units is zero.[10]

So much for the purely fixed costs. In practice, of course, costs are usually neither entirely fixed nor entirely variable. If we refer to such expenses as combined costs, we have, by definition,

total combined cost = total variable cost + total fixed cost.

It is then easy to show from this definition that we have completely analogous relationships for average and marginal costs:

average combined cost = average variable cost + average fixed cost[11]

and finally

marginal combined cost = marginal variable cost + marginal fixed cost.[12]

Moreover, since (except for the zeroth unit) marginal fixed cost is always zero, we have

marginal combined cost = marginal variable cost,

---

[10] For if the zeroth unit has a positive marginal (total) cost, M_0, then the total cost of the first unit produced will be $M_0 + M_1$ where M_1 is the marginal cost of that unit. As a result, the average cost of that one unit will be $(M_0 + M_1)/1 = M_0 + M_1$ which is not equal to M_1, the marginal cost of the first unit.

[11] *Proof:* Writing TCC for total combined cost, etc., we have from our definition $TCC = TVC + TFC$. Dividing both sides of this equation by Q, the number of units, we obtain $TCC/Q = TVC/Q + TFC/Q$. But, again, by definition, $TCC/Q = ACC$, etc., so that we have our result $ACC = AVC + AFC$.

[12] *Proof:* Let TCC (20) represent the total combined cost of the 20th unit produced, etc. Then, from our definition, we have

TCC (20) $= TVC$ (20) $+ TFC$ (20)   and TCC (19) $= TVC$ (19) $+ TFC$ (19).

Subtracting the latter equation from the former, we obtain

TCC (20) $- TCC$ (19) $= TVC$ (20) $- TVC$ (19) $+ TFC$ (20) $- TFC$ (19).

But since, by definition,

MCC (20) $= TCC$ (20) $- TCC$ (19),   etc.,

we have our result, MCC (20) $= MVC$ (20) $+ MFC$ (20). More generally, the same argument also obviously holds for any Qth unit, as well as for the 20th. Alternatively, this follows directly from the rules of the differential calculus, for if $TCC = TVC + TFC$, we have

$$dTCC/dQ = dTVC/dQ + dTFC/dQ.$$

that is (except at a zero output level), fixed costs never affect marginal costs in any way—a result which will be applied at a number of points later in this volume.

7. Average vs. Marginal Figures in Business Practice

In business operations one often encounters rule-of-thumb calculations which serve as substitutes for the operations researcher's optimality computations. When these business calculations are explicit, they are frequently made in terms of *average* rather than marginal quantities, that is, in terms of the elements of the third rather than those of the fourth column of Table 1. We have already seen in Section 1 that decisions based on such average data are not likely to be anywhere near optimal, yet it is tempting to reason on the basis of unit (average) costs or revenues or profits, largely because of the difficulty of marginal data collection. It is almost always harder to obtain marginal figures than to acquire average data, for several reasons:

1. Almost all accounting information is in the form of average or total rather than marginal figures. Tax computations and a number of other uses of accounting data require that this be so and this usage is well ingrained by tradition.

2. By its very nature, marginal information often represents the answers to hypothetical questions—information beyond the range of the firm's actual experience. One must ask, for example, what will be the effect on the firm's profits of an increase in expenditure of type A (the marginal profitability of A), whether or not the firm has ever tried it. But note that this hypothetical question is precisely what *must* be answered in rational decision-making to determine whether or not to increase expenditure A. That is exactly why these difficult-to-obtain marginal figures are essential for good decision-making.

3. Even where some relevant data are available from the past history of a company, it is much easier to collect the statistics required for average than for marginal figures. A single observation, that the total cost of producing 500 units of some output is $15,000, yields the information that its average cost is $15,000/500 = $30. But it takes at least one more observation, say, that the total cost of 510 units is $15,050, to yield the guess that the marginal cost is $5 (since it costs an additional $50 to increase output by 10 units). And, in practice, many more than two observations will usually be required for any sort of reliable guess on marginal magnitudes. As we have seen, marginal x (e.g., cost) is the slope of a total x (cost) curve, and it is surely rash to guess at the slope of any such curve on the basis of only two statistical observations.

Another reason for the popularity of the concept of the average cost or unit profit is that it is so simple and straightforward. Anyone knows that if profits per unit are high, the firm must be making money. But, as we have already seen, this sort of "practical" reasoning can be seriously fallacious. To illustrate the point once more, the decision to produce more of a commodity which brings in a healthy profit per unit (average profit) may be very costly to the firm, as Table 1 readily shows. There the unit profit on the product varies between $50 and $90 and this may appear to be a very healthy rate of return if the average cost of the item is, say, in the vicinity of $30. Nevertheless, the decision to increase the output of this good from 4 to 5 (million) units is tantamount to incurring a loss of $30 (marginal profit = −30)! As is shown there, the increased output can actually reduce the firm's total take by this amount, despite the high level of average profit.

The use of average data in *any* optimization problem can lead to such unsatisfactory results. The logic of the difficulty is not hard to explain. For example, in any allocation problem—say the reassignment of advertising funds—the question is not whether money *already* spent in publicizing product *A* has brought high returns. What must be determined is whether the spending of *additional* money can be justified. It may well be that the public is already saturated with singing commercials, contests, and free samples of product *A*, and although the money already spent on the item brought in very satisfactory returns, more such company expenditures on this product might even repel the public. Rather, the money may be better spent on the promotion of some product *B*, on which previous outlays were so niggardly as to be almost completely ineffective, but where the payoff to *additional* expenditures may be large because they permit some sort of public perception threshold to be reached.

8. Averages as Approximations to Marginal Figures

It is clear, then, that wherever there is a difference between average and marginal data, it is the latter which must be given prior consideration in an optimization problem.[13] Unfortunately, as has been shown, marginal data may be difficult and in some cases, for practical purposes, impossible to come by. It is therefore sometimes necessary to make do with average figures. For this purpose one must understand the relationship between average and marginal figures to recognize the circumstances under which the one can be expected to provide a reasonably good approximation to

---

[13] However, average figures must also always be consulted—marginal data may show the *best* that can be done, but if even this "best" arrangement involves an average loss of $2 per unit, it may be optimal to drop that segment of the business altogether.

the other, and to determine, when this is not the case, what sort of rough adjustments in the average data can be made to bring them closer to the unknown marginal figures.

For this purpose we can again employ Rule 5 of Section 3 [and Equation (1) of footnote 3]. This yields the following correction procedures:

1. Suppose the average figure rises as the number of units increases (e.g., as production, advertising expenditure, warehouse size, or the number of trucks used by the company goes up). Then, since marginal x must be above average x, any average figure must be revised upward to obtain an estimate of the corresponding marginal figure. Moreover, the more rapid the rise in average x, the greater will be the correction required.

2. Similarly, when average x is falling, the marginal figure will lie below the average figure, so that any average should be reduced to obtain the corresponding marginal datum.

3. Only when average x is neither increasing nor decreasing will the two figures coincide so that the average figure will need no readjustment.

In more concrete economic terms, this means that the following types of adjustment must be made to estimate marginal from average data:

(a) In cost figures, if there is reason to believe there are economies of large-scale production (falling average costs), marginal cost will be less than average cost, so that the average cost figure must be adjusted downward to yield a better approximation to the marginal cost figure. On the other hand, if observation suggests the presence of important diminishing returns, the average cost figure must be adjusted upward.

(b) In the case of productivity figures, the reverse holds. Economies of large scale (increasing average product per dollar of outlay) require an upward revision of average product figures to yield a "guestimate" of marginal product, and diminishing returns require that the average figure be reduced.

(c) In the case of revenue data, since demand (average revenue) curves are normally downward sloping, the marginal revenue will be lower than the average revenue. The more inelastic the demand, the greater the difference will be.[14]

A little experience in looking about and asking the proper questions should soon permit the analyst to recognize the presence of such phenomena as economies of large scale and diminishing returns, and on this basis to use the preceding rules to obtain rough marginal data.

---

[14] By the methods shown in the footnotes of Chapter 9, Section 4, it can be shown that the relationship is $mr = ar(1 - 1/E)$, where E is the price elasticity of demand.

These results show that there is something intermediate between the counsel of perfection which regards anything but marginal data as absolutely useless for decision-making and the uncritical calculations which employ average or total figures largely as they are received from the accountants' records. Because economic information is, in any event, notoriously inaccurate, it may be that the crude and approximative marginal figures which are obtained with the aid of the preceding rules will often be as satisfactory as anything that can reasonably be hoped for. Even if this is not quite true, experience seems to suggest that such rough adjustments will in many cases eliminate the bulk of the error which arises from the use of average data as a basis for decision-making. It is even plausible that efforts to obtain better marginal data will sometimes cost more than they can add to the profits of the firm.

9. First- and Second-Order Optimality Conditions

The marginal rules for optimal decision-making which have been discussed so far in this chapter all suffer from a serious omission. Even in the context within which they have been described they represent *necessary* but not *sufficient* conditions for an optimum. That is, any arrangement which is optimal must satisfy these rules, but there are likely to be some alternative *nonoptimal* situations which also satisfy our marginal, or *first-order*, conditions.

This point is discussed in detail in Section 5 of Chapter 4. However, it is of such importance that it must be called to the reader's attention here as well.

The logic of the first-order requirement that an activity should, if possible, be carried to a point where its marginal yield is zero has already been discussed in Section 4. As will be recalled, it was pointed out that the marginal analysis seeks the highest point on the graph representing profit (or whatever other variable one desires to maximize) by hunting for a level point such as M in Figure 1. Only at such a level point (i.e., only at a point where the marginal yield of a small decision change is zero) can we be at the top of a smoothly curved hill of the sort depicted in the diagram. At any point such as E or B where the marginal yield is nonzero, we must be either on the upward- or downward-sloping side of the hill. Hence, unless the marginal yield is zero we cannot be at a maximum, and the maximization method of the marginal analysis, then, consists in the hunt for points (output levels) where marginal yield is zero.

Once having found any such points we can be certain that all points which have been ruled out (i.e., all points corresponding to nonzero marginal yields) are not the maximum which we seek. However, it is perfectly possible that among the points which remain to us—those whose marginal yields are zero—there will be some which are *not* maximal. This possibility is illustrated in Figure 4 of the next chapter. There points A and B as well as all points on the segment CD are of zero slope—they correspond to zero marginal yields. Yet only A is a true maximum. Points on CD lie on a plateau whereas point B is a minimum!

Therefore, to be sure whether we have found a maximum or a minimum when we have located a point whose marginal yield is zero, we must examine it in terms of what are called the *second-order conditions*.[15] These require for a *minimum* that in the vicinity of the point in question the curve be U-shaped so that our level point does, indeed, lie at the bottom of a valley. On the other hand, for a *maximum* the second-order conditions require that in the neighborhood of our point the curve take the shape of an *upside-down* U. A systematic and precise formulation of these second-order conditions is provided in the next chapter.

We conclude, then, that only if *both* the first-order (zero marginal yield) and second-order (curvature) conditions are satisfied can we be certain that we have found the maximal point. The same two types of condition must, of course, be examined in the search for a minimum.

10. Global, Local, and Corner Maxima

If the second-order conditions are satisfied throughout a graph, no further problems of principle will usually arise. But in some cases the second-order conditions will hold only for limited ranges of the figure or they may not even be satisfied at any point in a graph. In that case we may run into several added troubles.

The first of these is the possibility that we may have a multiplicity of maxima—a series of little hills at various locations on the landscape (Figure 5). Here we have four profit hilltops, A, B, C, and D.

True, one of them, C, towers above the others and is the highest point which we undoubtedly wish to find. Such a highest point is called the *global* maximum while the other hilltops are referred to as *local* maxima. But, unfortunately, the first- and second-order conditions are satisfied as perfectly at points A, B, and D as they are at the global maximum C. There is, then, no way in which the standard techniques of marginal analysis can by themselves distinguish between global and local maxima. Other computational difficulties which arise in the presence of the two types of maxima will be discussed in the chapter on nonlinear programming.

---

[15] The reader who has studied some differential calculus will recognize the second-order condition as the usual requirement that the second derivative be negative in the case of a maximum and positive for a minimum. See Section 5 of the next chapter.

There is also a second possible cause for concern which is particularly likely to arise when the second-order conditions are violated. This is the *corner* maximum, although that sort of maximum may occur even if the second-order conditions hold. Figure 6 depicts corner maxima of both types. Suppose we are dealing with a plant whose output capacity is limited to Q_{cap}. Suppose, moreover, that its total profit function is DD' whose shape clearly violates the second-order conditions. Note that the maximal point on such a curve is not likely to occur somewhere in the vicinity of its center. Rather, its highest point will typically occur at one of its ends, point L (zero output) or point M (capacity output). Such a maximum which occurs where a curve cuts one of the axes or at some other end point of its relevant range is called a *corner* maximum (in contrast with the other type of maximum, the *interior* maximum, such as M in Figure 1).

The figure also depicts a corner maximum which occurs with a profit

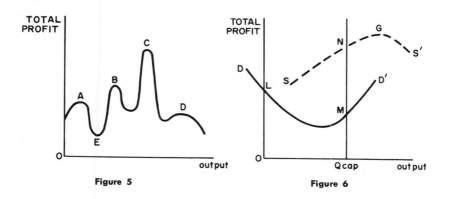

Figure 5   **Figure 6**

function which satisfies the second-order conditions (curve SS'). Here the highest attainable point is not the level point G, but the corner maximum point N which corresponds to the capacity output.

For our present purposes corner maxima are important because they cause the usual rules of the marginal analysis to break down. Notice that at none of the maximum points in Figure 6—L, M, or N—is the pertinent profit curve level. That is, none of those points fulfills the requirement that marginal yield be equal to zero. Since the marginal analysis cannot cope with corner maxima, it was necessary to invent a special analytic procedure, mathematical programming, to deal with these and other closely related phenomena.

It must be observed before we leave this subject that the occurrence of corner maxima is rather common in economic problems. For, by definition, a point lies above one of the axes in a diagram whenever the value of the corresponding variable is zero. Thus, if a firm finds that it can maximize its profits by eliminating some product from its line (reducing that output to zero), it must have attained a corner maximum. The same must also be true of a consumer who decides to purchase only some of the many commodities which are offered for sale to him (for any one of the remaining items i his quantity purchased will be $Q_i = 0$). This must be so because a corner maximum is one where the value of at least one variable has, as it were, been pushed as far as it can go and zero is, of course, as far as an output can be reduced. We may notice also why the marginal condition breaks down in this case. Once an output has been reduced to zero, even if its marginal yield is *negative* so that a further cut would be desirable, there is nothing anyone can do about it. We have reached our optimal position even though marginal yield is *not* zero.

In many areas of economic analysis it has proved convenient to proceed on the assumption that the relevant maxima were of the interior rather than the corner variety. However, the importance of maxima of the latter sort must not be forgotten. Their significance and the methods by which they are analyzed will become clearer in the chapters on mathematical programming and activity analysis.

11. The Second-Order Conditions and Stability

One characteristic of the second-order conditions remains to be cleared up. In some earlier writings, solutions which satisfy both the first- and second-order conditions were referred to as *stable* equilibria, while solutions which satisfy the first-order but *not* the second-order conditions were called *unstable* equilibria. It is easy to see why this terminology was employed. If someone departs from a solution point of the first variety, e.g., from quantity Q_A in Figure 4 of Chapter 4, he is motivated to try to return to the equilibrium point Q_A. On the other hand, if something pushes someone away from Q_B where the second-order condition is violated, he will have no desire whatsoever to return to that quantity.

However, more recently it has been pointed out that this terminology is misleading. Q_B is nowadays *not* called an unstable equilibrium quantity. Rather, it is now clear that Q_B is no equilibrium at all. Not only is there no motivation to return to Q_B after leaving it; there is really no reason for anyone to wish to go there in the first place. *An "equilibrium" may be defined as a set of variable values which, once attained, do not automatically set change-producing forces into motion.* But even though the first-order maximum conditions are satisfied at Q_B no one will want to stay at that quantity—it is a minimum and the value of output will automatically be changed from Q_B by any rational decision-maker.

On the other hand, Q_A is an equilibrium point. Once the maximizing decision-maker gets there he will do nothing to move away. But this is no reason to consider it stable. *Stability* of an equilibrium means that *if for some reason there is a displacement from the equilibrium point the system will eventually return at least reasonably close to that point*. Why, then, may we doubt that Q_A will be stable? The answer is that, though the decision-maker may *want* to make things move toward Q_A, there is many a slip . . . . Suppose, for example, that Q_A is an inventory level and that the company reduces its production if inventory happens to be above Q_A and increases its output if inventory is below that level. Then it is possible (and it does happen in practice) that companies' production-control rules lead to over-compensation. If inventory starts out above Q_A, production may be curtailed so sharply that inventory level falls well below its target. This, in turn, may cause an extreme increase in production and a rebuilding of surplus inventory, and so on, *ad infinitum*. Here we see, then, that though the objective of management is perfectly clear—it seeks to attain the equilibrium (profit-maximizing) inventory level Q_A—the dynamics of its adjustment process prevent it from attaining that level. The equilibrium just is not stable. But we are able to test for stability only by examining explicitly the dynamics of the adjustment process, and the second-order conditions, at least by themselves, do not enable us to settle the issue.

REFERENCE

Robinson, Joan, *The Economics of Imperfect Competition*, Macmillan & Co., Ltd., London, 1933, Chapter 2.

Maximization, Minimization, and Elementary Differential Calculus

4

1. Differential Calculus and Marginal Analysis

Before we get down to the differential calculus and its relationship to marginal analysis, it is necessary to translate the marginal concept into algebraic notation. Suppose, for example, that an additional $5 in advertising expenditure were to increase a firm's sales by $100. We then evaluate the marginal sales contribution of advertising as $100/5 = 20$. In algebraic notation, if S represents sales volume and A symbolizes the amount of advertising, it is customary to represent an addition to (change in) S and A by ΔS and ΔA respectively,[1] so that the marginal sales contribution of advertising may be written as $\Delta S/\Delta A$.

It will be noted that this expression does not specify whether the change in advertising expenditure is large or small—in the numerical example we took $\Delta A = \$5$. But this ambiguity leads to a further difficulty because it means that the value of the marginal yield figure itself may not be determined. For example, suppose we encounter a rather extreme diminishing-returns case in which the first thousand dollars adds $40,000 to the sales of a small retailer, but a second thousand in advertising adds very little more, and a third thousand poured into a saturated market repels customers

---

[1] Δ is the (upper-case) Greek letter delta.

and actually reduces sales by \$10,000. If we take $\Delta A = \$1,000$, then the marginal yield,

$$\frac{\Delta S}{\Delta A} = \frac{40,000}{1,000} = 40.$$

But if $\Delta A = \$2,000$, we have

$$\frac{\Delta S}{\Delta A} = \frac{40,000 + 0}{2,000} = 20$$

and finally, if $\Delta A = \$3,000$, we obtain

$$\frac{\Delta S}{\Delta A} = \frac{40,000 + 0 - 10,000}{3,000} = 10.$$

In other words, the value of the marginal yield of advertising varies with the magnitude of ΔA, the magnitude of the increment in advertising expenditure whose effect we decide to consider, and it is easy to see that a similar problem arises even in less extreme examples.

The heart of the difficulty is that if ΔA is a large number, the marginal measure becomes a rather crude over-all representation of the effects of a change in expenditure, and it therefore becomes a relatively blunt decision-making tool. For example, if a marginal computation is made using $\Delta A = \$3,000$ in the preceding illustration, we have already noted that we obtain

$$\frac{\Delta S}{\Delta A} = \frac{40,000 + 0 - 10,000}{3,000} = 10.$$

In other words, this calculation indicates that a dollar in advertising adds \$10 to this retailer's sales and may suggest to him that it pays hand over fist to spend even more on promotion. But a more detailed calculation shows that he should actually have stopped after his first \$1,000 promotional outlay.

We see, then, that the larger the magnitude of the investigated change in a decision variable whose effect we calculate, i.e., the larger the value of the denominator in the marginal value fraction, the cruder becomes the marginal measure. It becomes a rough average measure of the effects of advertising or whatever we happen to be examining, and, as in the preceding example, it may conceal more than it reveals.

This naturally suggests that we ought to stick to very small changes. But, at least in principle, so long as we pick any fixed value for the increment in the decision variable, i.e., if we take $\Delta A = \$2$, we are faced with the problem that a calculation employing an even finer unit of change might give us even more detailed and perhaps different information.

The basic approach of the differential calculus is designed to cope with precisely this problem. It proceeds by operating, conceptually, with smaller and smaller units and *taking as the value of the marginal fraction the limit of the value of these fractions as the magnitude of the denominator decreases indefinitely.* For example, suppose we obtain the data in the following table:

ΔA	8	4	2	1	0.5	0.25	etc.
ΔS	30.4	13.6	6.4	3.1	1.525	0.75625	$\cdots$
$\Delta S/\Delta A$	3.8	3.4	3.2	3.1	3.05	3.025	$\cdots$

As we consider smaller and smaller changes in advertising expenditure, their contribution to sales also grows correspondingly insignificant,[2] e.g., as advertising expenditure drops from 8 to 2, its contribution to sales falls from 30.4 to 6.4. But the ratio of these magnitudes, $\Delta S/\Delta A$, may nevertheless vary relatively little because both numerator and denominator are going in the same direction. In our rather obviously cooked-up example the ratio $\Delta S/\Delta A$ shows a remarkably simple pattern, and it is easy to see where it is heading. Keep up the process of cutting down on ΔA long enough and the difference between the corresponding value of $\Delta S/\Delta A$ and the number 3 will not be worth mentioning—it can be made to approximate 3 to whatever degree of accuracy we desire. In standard mathematical terminology we say that *as ΔA approaches zero the fraction $\Delta S/\Delta A$ approaches the limit* 3. This limit number 3 is represented by the symbol dS/dA or, sometimes, by S' and is called the *first derivative of sales with respect to advertising expenditure.*

More generally, then, the first derivative dy/dx of any variable, y, with respect to another variable, x, may be described as the limit value of the marginal change in y per unit change in x when the change in x is made to be smaller and smaller, i.e., when the change approaches zero. This combination of concepts—the notion of a limit number which is approached by an infinite sequence of numbers and the definition of the derivative—is the foundation of differential calculus.

---

[2] Of course it must be recognized that this illustration is economic nonsense. Increases in most types of advertising cannot be bought in units as small as $8—one cannot even talk to an advertising man for that price. It should also be noted that a minimum level of expenditure is likely to be required before the advertising has any impact on sales, but the table does not assume that we start off with zero advertising. We may be asking whether the firm should *increase or decrease* its current million-dollar budget so that even if ΔA is only $6 the total A is increased to $1,000,006.

2. Rules of Differentiation

Let us see now how these definitions can be employed. Suppose that we have, by statistical or other means, obtained an algebraic relationship between sales and advertising expenditure. To illustrate the logic of the procedure, we consider three (rather implausible) cases:

(a) $S = 50,000$ (S a constant unaffected by A).

(b) $S = 3A$ (relationship of proportionality).

(c) $S = 3A^2$ (second-degree relationship).

The first two cases are trivial and we can easily guess at the derivatives that will be involved. In the first case sales are fixed and independent of the level of advertising so that we may conclude, correctly, that $dS/dA = 0$, i..e, that the marginal sales yield of advertising is zero. This is a special case of the general

RULE 1. *Constants:* The derivative of any constant with respect to any variable is always zero.

The second (linear) case is only slightly more complex. It is obvious that the expression in question tells us that every unit increase in A increases sales by \$3, for sales then increase from $3A$ to $3(A + 1) = 3A + 3$. Therefore, $dS/dA = 3$. We thus have

RULE 2. *First-degree terms:* In any first-degree relationship $y = bx$, where b is any number, we have

$$\frac{dy}{dx} = b.$$

It is only in the third-case relationship $S = 3A^2$ that the calculation becomes slightly more complicated and that it seems worth going through a systematic derivation of the value of dy/dx. The following rather simple algebraic argument is typical of the procedures used in arriving at the various differentiation formulae which are listed below. If the reader understands it thoroughly, he will have some comprehension of the elements of the logical structure of the differential calculus.

Our object is to evaluate dS/dA in the case $S = 3A^2$. For this purpose we begin by determining the marginal fraction $\Delta S/\Delta A$, then finding what happens to it as ΔA approaches zero, just as described in the previous section. We start off by adding any increment ΔA to the A in our equation $S = 3A^2$ to see what effect this has on S. This changes the value of S, so that, by the definition of ΔS, the procedure replaces S by $S + \Delta S$. We therefore obtain

Step 1:

$$S + \Delta S = 3(A + \Delta A)^2 = 3[A^2 + 2A\ \Delta A + (\Delta A)^2] \quad \text{(by squaring and multiplying out)}$$

$$= 3A^2 + 6A\ \Delta A + 3(\Delta A)^2.$$

But we are looking for ΔS, not for $S + \Delta S$. We therefore subtract the expression $S = 3A^2$ from the preceding $S + \Delta S$ equation. This gives us

Step 2:

$$\Delta S = S + \Delta S - S = 3A^2 + 6A\ \Delta A + 3(\Delta A)^2 - 3A^2 = 6A\ \Delta A + 3(\Delta A)^2.$$

That is,

$$\Delta S = 6A\ \Delta A + 3(\Delta A)^2.$$

We now find the marginal sales contribution of advertising, $\Delta S/\Delta A$, by dividing both sides of the equation for ΔS by ΔA to obtain

Step 3:

$$\frac{\Delta S}{\Delta A} = \frac{6A\ \Delta A}{\Delta A} + \frac{3(\Delta A)^2}{\Delta A} = 6A + 3\ \Delta A.$$

But the derivative, dS/dA, is the limit of $\Delta S/\Delta A$ as ΔA approaches zero (written $\Delta A \rightarrow 0$), i.e., (in conventional notation) we calculate

Step 4:

$$\frac{dS}{dA} = \lim_{\Delta A \rightarrow 0} \frac{\Delta S}{\Delta A} = \lim_{\Delta A \rightarrow 0} (6A + 3\Delta A) = 6A,$$

that is, the term $3\Delta A$, which clearly approaches zero when ΔA approaches zero, simply drops out in the limit. Hence we have our result for $S = 3A^2$, that in this case $dS/dA = 6A$.

More generally (the derivation follows the preceding one step by step)[3] we have

---

[3] There is one complication. Raising $(x + \Delta x)$ to the bth power is ordinarily more complicated than squaring it. If b is an integer (a whole number) we employ the binomial theorem of high school algebra to multiply out $(x + \Delta x)^b$. The proof then proceeds exactly as above.

Note that Rules 1 and 2 are both special cases of Rule 3 in which $b = 0$ and $b = 1$, respectively.

RULE 3. *Power terms:* For any constants a and b, if $y = ax^b$, then

$$\frac{dy}{dx} = bax^{b-1}.$$

Example: The derivative of $4x^{10}$ is $4 \cdot 10x^9 = 40x^9$.

Several other frequently used rules of the differential calculus are now given and their use illustrated:

RULE 4. *Sums:* The derivative of a sum of several terms is the sum of the derivatives of these terms, i.e., if $y = y_1 + y_2$, then

$$\frac{dy}{dx} = \frac{dy_1}{dx} + \frac{dy_2}{dx}.$$

Example: Given $y = 500 - 2x + 5x^4$. We know by Rules 1–3 that the derivative of 500 is zero, that of $-2x$ is -2, and that of $5x^4$ is $4 \times 5x^3 = 20x^3$. Hence, in this case,

$$\frac{dy}{dx} = 0 - 2 + 20x^3 = -2 + 20x^3.$$

RULE 5. *Miscellaneous formulas:*

(a)	if $y = a \sin bx$,	$dy/dx = ab \cos bx$
(b)	if $y = a \cos bx$,	$dy/dx = -ab \sin bx$
$(c)^4$	if $y = ae^{bx}$,	$dy/dx = bae^{bx}$.

Thus, in particular, ae^x is an expression (indeed the only expression) which is equal to its own derivative, i.e.,

(d)	if $y = ae^x$,	$dy/dx = ae^x(= y)$
$(e)^5$	if $y = a \log_e bx$,	$dy/dx = a/x$.

---

[4] Here e ($= 2.718$ approximately) is the number that represents the principal which would accrue after one year if one dollar were compounded at *every* instant over the year at a 100 per cent (annual) rate of interest. This number occupies an extremely important position in the differential calculus, particularly in the theory of growth.

[5] $\text{Log}_e x$ (the logarithm of x to the base e) is defined by the relationship $x = e^{\log_e x}$. In other words, $\log_e x$ is a number L, such that when e is raised to the power L the result is equal to x. This number has most of the convenient properties of the common logarithm (i.e., the logarithm to the base 10; $x = 10^{\log_{10} x}$). For example, by the definition that $e^a \cdot e^b = e^{a+b}$, for the product of any two numbers x and z,

$$x \cdot z = e^{\log_e x} \cdot e^{\log_e z} = e^{\log_e x + \log_e z}.$$

Thus two numbers can be multiplied by adding up their logarithms (to the base e) and then finding the number whose logarithm is equal to this sum.

One reason logarithms to the base e are employed in much scientific work is that they have such a simple differentiation rule.

RULE 6. *Products:* The derivative of the product of two expressions is the product of the (undifferentiated) second expression multiplied by the derivative of the first plus the first multiplied by the derivative of the second; that is, if $y = y_1 y_2$, then

$$\frac{dy}{dx} = y_2 \frac{dy_1}{dx} + y_1 \frac{dy_2}{dx}.$$

Example: Given $y = 6x^4 \sin\left(\frac{1}{3}x\right)$ find dy/dx. We know by Rule 3 that the derivative of $6x^4$ is $24x^3$, and by Rule 5a that the derivative of $\sin\left(\frac{1}{3}x\right)$ is $\frac{1}{3}\cos\frac{1}{3}x$. Hence by Rule 6,

$$\frac{dy}{dx} = 24x^3 \sin\left(\frac{1}{3}x\right) + 6x^4\left[\frac{1}{3}\cos\left(\frac{1}{3}x\right)\right]$$

$$= 24x^3 \sin\left(\frac{1}{3}x\right) + 2x^4 \cos\left(\frac{1}{3}x\right).$$

RULE 7. *Division:* If y is the ratio of two expressions, its derivative is the denominator multiplied by the derivative of the numerator *minus* the numerator multiplied by the derivative of the denominator all divided by the square of the denominator[6]; i.e., if $y = y_1/y_2$ then

$$\frac{dy}{dx} = \frac{y_2(dy_1/dx) - y_1(dy_2/dx)}{y_2^2}.$$

Example: If $y = \log_e x/e^{3x}$ then, since the derivative of $\log_e x$ is $1/x$ and that of e^{3x} is $3e^{3x}$, we have

$$\frac{dy}{dx} = \frac{e^{3x}(1/x) - 3(\log_e x)e^{3x}}{(e^{3x})^2}$$

where, by definition, $(e^{3x})^2 = e^{6x}$.

RULE 8. *The chain rule:* If y is a function of some variable z whose value is, in turn, a function of another variable, x, then the derivative of y with respect to x equals the derivative of y with respect to z multiplied by the derivative of z with respect to x, i.e.,

$$dy/dx = dy/dz \cdot dz/dx.$$

To illustrate Rule 8, consider the four illustrative functions (1) $y = e^z$, where $z = 5x^3$; (2) $y = \sin z$, where $z = e^x$; (3) $y = \cos z$, where $z = \sin x$; and (4) $y = 5z^2$, where $z = \log_e x$. Their derivatives are

(1') $e^z 15x^2 = 15x^2 e^{5x^3}$

(2') $(\cos z)e^x = e^x \cos e^x$,

(3') $-\sin z \cos x = -\sin(\sin x)\cos x$, and

(4') $10z/x = 10\log_e x/x$.

---

[6] Rule 7 can be derived directly from Rules 6, 3, and 8.

The chain rule also permits us to take relatively complicated functions and break them into two simpler components each of which can be differentiated separately. For example, consider the relationship (1'') $y = e^{(5x^3)}$.

By arbitrarily setting $z = 5x^3$ in (1'') it is immediately transformed into our first problem (1) to which the chain rule applies immediately. Similarly, we transform (2'') $y = \sin(e^z)$, (3'') $y = \cos(\sin x)$, and (4'') $y = 5(\log_e x)^2$ into (2), (3), and (4) by setting, respectively, $z = e^x$ in (2''), $z = \sin x$ in (3''), and $z = \log_e x$ in (4'').

Thus, in general terms given the function of a function $y = g[f(x)]$ we may rewrite it as $y = g(z)$, where $z = f(x)$. Rule 8 enables us to divide up and conquer such a problem. To find dy/dx we obtain the more easily found derivatives dy/dz and dz/dx and then get our answer just by multiplying them together.

Example: Given $y = \log_e(3x^2)$, to find dy/dx we write

$$y = \log_e z \qquad z = 3x^2$$
$$dy/dz = 1/z \qquad dz/dx = 6x$$

and therefore, substituting into the equation of Rule 8, we have (since $z = 3x^2$)

$$\frac{dy}{dx} = \frac{dy}{dz} \cdot \frac{dz}{dx} = \frac{1}{z}(6x) = \frac{6x}{3x^2} = \frac{2}{x}.$$

PROBLEMS

Differentiate the following:

1. $y = 11x^7 - 16x^2 + 3$
2. $y = -4x^{12} + 17^2 + 2\cos 4x$
3. $y = 7x^{-6}\ (= 7/x^6)$
4. $y = e^{3x}\sin x$
5. $y = e^{3x}/\sin x$
6. $y = e^{3x}/\log x$
7. $y = 3\sin 5x^4$
8. $y = 8e^{2x^{-2}}$

3. Geometric Interpretation: The First-Order Maximum Condition

It is useful at this point to translate the derivative into graphic terms. Consider the relationship between the quantity Q of a commodity marketed by some firm and the total profit R which accrues to it. Such a graph is depicted as curve PP' in Figure 1.

First, it will be recalled that the slope of a line is defined as the increase in its height per unit move *to the right*. For example, as we move to the

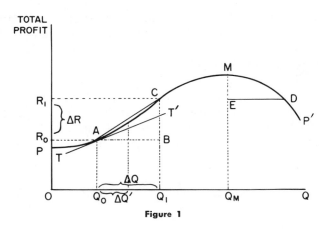

Figure 1

right from point Q_0 to Q_1, the curve rises from R_0 to R_1. Hence its (average) slope over this stretch is $(R_1 - R_0)/(Q_1 - Q_0)$ or BC/AB. Similarly, we note that as we move to the right from point E to point D, the graph goes downhill, so that the slope EM/ED is negative (there is a *negative* increase in the height of the curve).

Now the marginal profitability of an increase in output ΔQ is defined as ΔR over ΔQ. But it will be observed that ΔQ, the increment in Q, is $Q_1 - Q_0$ and, similarly, that ΔR is $R_1 - R_0$. Hence the slope of the curve and the marginal profitability are the same number. More generally, let y be some variable whose value depends on x. Then the slope of the curve of this relationship represents the marginal effect on y of a change in x.

It will be noted that the slope of the curve changes as we move along the diagram. That is why the value of $\Delta R/\Delta Q$ is ambiguous and why we turn to the concept of the derivative. By letting the interval which represents ΔQ grow smaller and smaller, it more and more closely approximates a single point. That is, if from ΔQ we shift our attention to smaller interval $\Delta Q'$, and so on, we ultimately approach a state where nothing is left but point Q_0. We then interpret the derivative of the function at point Q_0 as the slope of the graph at that point.

However, this slope itself cannot be defined in the same way as the slope of a finite interval, because at a point there is neither a change in Q nor any change in R. That is, at A there is neither a ΔQ nor a ΔR, or if we wish, they are both equal to zero.

This is where the limit process is invoked. The slope at A is *defined* as the limit of the slope of AC as ΔQ approaches zero. Geometrically, this limit turns out to be the slope of the tangent TT' at point A. We see this by noting that our original marginal figure $\Delta R/\Delta Q$ is the slope of straight-line chord AC. Our second approximation is the slope of a shorter chord beginning at A, etc. It is clear intuitively that this sequence of slopes approaches the slope of the tangent TT'.

In sum, the derivative of any relationship between y and x with respect to x at some value x^* of x is represented by the slope of the tangent (at point $x = x^*$) to the curve which represents the relationship.

We can use this interpretation to discuss the problem of optimization. Suppose management desires to maximize the firm's total profits. The total profit graph in Figure 1 is shaped like a hill, and the output OQ_m which maximizes profits is the point directly below the peak of the hill M.

This gives us a derivative criterion for locating point M. At points to the left of Q_m the slope of the curve (the derivative) is positive. Such points cannot be optimal because a movement to the right from any one of them will increase profits. Similarly, any point to the right of Q_m cannot be optimal because there we are going downhill (negative derivative) so that a retreat (a reduction in the size of output Q) will increase profits. Only when the derivative is zero, so that we are neither at the upgrade nor downgrade side of a profit hill, is it possible for us to be at an optimal point. Note that this condition is satisfied at point M, the top of the profit curve, which is level because it is the border line between the uphill and the downhill segments of the curve.

This result corresponds to our first-order maximum condition of marginal analysis rule 1 (Section 2 of Chapter 3) that any activity should, if possible, be carried to a point where its marginal net benefit (its first derivative) is zero.

Example: Find the output Q which maximizes profit R when given the relationship $R = 300 + 1,200Q - Q^2$.

Differentiating, we have

$$\frac{dR}{dQ} = 1,200 - 2Q.$$

Hence the only point at which this derivative is zero is where

$$1,200 - 2Q = 0,$$

i.e., where $2Q = 1,200$ or $Q = 600$.

4. Nondifferentiability and Limited Variable Range Problems

The results of the preceding section may be summed up as the following first-order rule: To find the value of x which maximizes the value of y, given some relationship $y = f(x)$ between these variables, find the derivative, dy/dx, set it equal to zero, and solve for x. This procedure is, indeed, widely applicable but it has important limitations which must be understood clearly. We shall now examine several cases in which the rule is meaningless, inapplicable, or completely incorrect. Each of these cases is of fundamental importance and not just a minor exception to be acknowledged summarily and then forgotten.

Case 1. Discontinuities and Kinks

In Figures 2a and 2b we represent relationships between y and x which exhibit two important types of irregularity. At point B there is a sharp corner or *kink* in the graph. Above point x_a there is an even more serious type of irregularity—the graph has a complete break, or *discontinuity, AA'*. The difficulty is that at such points the slope, that is, the derivative, is not even defined. There is no tangent to the curves at the points directly above x_a or x_b. It is to be noted that points A and B both represent maxima of the functions, i.e., at x_a or at x_b, y becomes as large as possible. But at

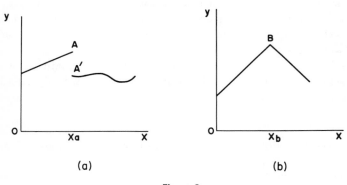

(a)   (b)

Figure 2

neither point is dy/dx equal to zero because we cannot even impute the usual meaning to the concept at such a point. Hence we conclude:

In the presence of kinks or discontinuities the derivative is not defined, so it may not be possible to employ the maximization criterion $dy/dx = 0$.

Case 2. Limitations on the Values of the Variables

In Figures 3a and 3b are represented two cases in which the levels of output Q are restricted. The unlikely situation in Figure 3a might be referred to as the crop restriction subsidy case. Here the firm is in the peculiar position that the less it produces and sells, the higher the profit it makes. Clearly, however, the smallest output Q which the firm can produce is zero, so that this is the point of maximum profits. Actually, analogous situations are frequently encountered in the multiproduct firms which are typical of our economy. If the production of one of the outputs of the firm incurs a loss, the most profitable (least costly) output of that product will be zero, though the total profit of the firm as a whole (R) may be a positive

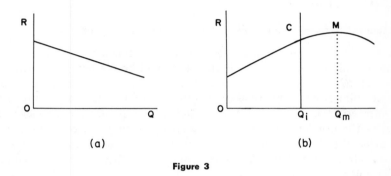

(a)   (b)

Figure 3

number because its other products bring in enough money to keep the company in the black.

In this situation we note that at the point of maximum profits the slope of the graph is negative ($dR/dQ < 0$) so that a further decrease in output, if it were possible, would appear to be called for. But, since such a reduction is not possible, we must be satisfied with a level of production at which the calculus maximization criterion fails: dR/dQ, i.e., the marginal profit yield of Q is not equal to zero.

A similar difficulty occurs in somewhat more striking form in the situation shown in Figure 3b. Here we assume that the firm has a limited output capacity and that it can therefore produce no more than quantity OQ_i. In this diagram there is a level maximum point M, at which the derivative maximum condition $dR/dQ = 0$ is satisfied. However, this maximum is economically irrelevant because the firm cannot attain it even though it might well like to do so. The maximum profit feasible point is, in fact, C, where $dR/dQ > 0$, so that the derivative maximization rule is violated.

The two cases so far considered in which this rule breaks down can be handled effectively only by means of a totally new approach for the determination of optimal values of the variables. In the simple examples shown in Figures 2 and 3 the optimal values of x and Q are, of course, obvious on inspection. Particularly in Figure 3b the answer seems easy—to maximize its profits the firm should produce as much as it can. But when the number of variables involved is considerable, as it usually is in practice—for example, when the firm is dividing up its limited productive capacity among many hundreds of products—the answer is far from obvious.

To deal with such optimization problems (frequently encountered in economics) where the marginal maximization condition fails, a new body of analysis, called *mathematical programming*, has been developed. This analysis, which has turned out to be of very great significance for economics and business decision-making, is discussed in considerable detail in the next four chapters.

5. Second-Order Conditions of Maximization and Minimization

A totally different but less serious sort of difficulty for the calculus maximum rule is illustrated in Figure 4. It will be observed that the condition $dR/dQ = 0$ is satisfied not only at the maximum point A. It also holds at point B where profit is at its minimum (!) and at any point in the level stretch CD. Except in the mathematical programming cases discussed in the previous section, we may conclude that wherever profits are maximized $dR/dQ = 0$, but the converse is *not* true: We may be at an output such as OQ_B, where $dR/dQ = 0$, and yet profit will not be maximized at that point.

The source of the difficulty is easily seen. The marginal maximization condition dR/dQ assures us only that we are at a level stretch on the profit hill—we are neither going uphill nor downhill. But being on a piece of level ground is obviously no guarantee that we are on top of a hill.

To take care of this difficulty we need some more information. We require another condition (called a *second-order condition*) which assures us that we have just stopped going uphill, and that if we go any further we will begin to descend. If this is true, and if we are at a level point, we must clearly be at the top of a hill. This elementary and apparently trivial argument lies behind a considerable body of relatively deep analysis.

Unlike the problems of the preceding section, our present difficulties can normally be taken care of with the help of the differential calculus. The second-order condition which has just been described is essentially a requirement about the behavior of the slope of the curve. The (first-order) condition $dR/dQ = 0$ states that the slope must be zero at a profit-maximizing point. The second-order condition states that the slope must previously have been positive, i.e., that there $dR/dQ > 0$ (we must have been

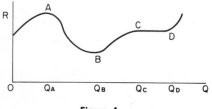

Figure 4

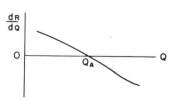

Figure 5

going uphill as we moved toward point A from the left) and that thereafter the slope must become negative (further movement to the right, i.e., further increases in production after output level OQ_A, must reduce total profit). In sum, the second-order condition requires that dR/dQ fall as output increases. These two requirements are summarized graphically in Figure 5. Here, rather than representing *total* profit on the vertical axis, as we did before, we have instead measured the *marginal* profitability of output, dR/dQ, along that axis. The first-order condition, then, requires that the graph cut the horizontal axis $(dR/dQ = 0)$ at the profit-maximizing output OQ_A. *The second-order condition requires that the slope of the marginal curve at that point be negative,* so that dR/dQ will be positive to the left of Q_A and negative to its right.

This second requirement is a condition which refers to the behavior of the curve in Figure 5. It states that the slope of the dR/dQ curve must be negative. But dR/dQ is, in turn, itself a slope—the slope of the profit graph. Hence our second-order condition is a statement about the slope of a slope. It involves what is called *a second derivative.*

The process used to find a second derivative (written d^2y/dx^2 or y'') is a simple repetition of that used to find the first derivative. We just differentiate (to find a slope) and then differentiate again (to find the slope of the slope curve). For example, given $y = 4x^3$, we know that $dy/dx = 12x^2$ and (by repeated differentiation) $d^2y/dx^2 = 24x$.

In sum, the second-order rule states: To find the maximum value of any relationship between two variables, y and x, compute dy/dx and determine the values of x for which this has the value zero. If for any of these values of x we also find that d^2y/dx^2 is negative (dy/dx falling, as in Figure 5), then this is a true maximum point.

Minimization, too, can occur in an optimality calculation. For example, instead of maximizing profit we may wish to find the output level which minimizes total cost. The preceding rule is easily modified to deal with this sort of problem. The reader should convince himself that the only required change in the second-order condition is that in minimization the second derivative must be positive.[7]

Example: Find the maximizing value of x for

$$y = 100 + 12x - x^3.$$

Here $dy/dx = 12 - 3x^2$, so that if $dy/dx = 0$ we must have

$$12 - 3x^2 = 0, \quad \text{i.e., } 3x^2 = 12, \quad x^2 = 4, \quad x = \pm 2.$$

---

[7] Actually, slightly weaker conditions will do in both cases. If the second derivative is zero but the fourth derivative d^4y/dx^4 is negative, the point in question is still a maximum; if this derivative is positive, it is a minimum. A similar result holds for the case where the fourth derivative is also zero but the sixth is not, and so on.

To find which of these two numbers (if either) yields a maximum value of y, we find that $d^2y/dx^2 = -6x$, which is negative for $x = +2$ and positive for $x = -2$. Hence $x = +2$ yields a maximum value of y:

$$100 + (12)(2) - (2)^3 = 116$$

and $x = -2$ yields a minimum value of y:

$$100 + (12)(-2) - (-2)^3 = 84.$$

One more important warning is still required. There is a pitfall in the definition of the words "maximum" and "minimum" as used in ordinary discussions involving the differential calculus. A maximum is used to denote the top of a hill in the graph of the function. But the graph may contain several hills (each is then called a *local maximum*) and the calculus procedure as described offers us no guarantee that we have found the

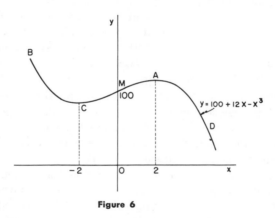

Figure 6

highest hill (called a *global maximum*). Moreover, the graph may contain higher points which are not hilltops. This was in fact the case in the last example whose graph is shown in Figure 6. It is to be noted that our (local) maximum point A is below points such as B and our (local) minimum point C is above points such as D. In this case no global maximum or minimum points exist because y keeps going downhill indefinitely as we move to the right beyond A and it rises indefinitely to the left of C. Hence it is pointless to look for a global maximum or minimum here. But even in a problem in which there are a number of local maxima, one of which is a global optimum, the differential calculus methods just described will not do the trick. However, mathematical programming has made some progress in dealing with this problem.

PROBLEMS

1. Find the second derivatives of
   (a) $y = 3x^5 + 15x$
   (b) $2 \log 4x$.

2. (a) Does $y = 50 + 90x - 5x^2$ have a maximum or a minimum? What is the value of x at that point?
   (b) How about $y = 15x^2$?

6. Maximization in Many-Variable Relationships: Partial Differentiation

Usually more than two variables will be involved in an economic relationship. For example, total profit R will depend not only on the level of output Q. It will also depend on the firm's advertising expenditure A, on the price P charged for some competing product, and so on. If these four variables, R, Q, A, and P, were the only ones involved, we would write

$$R = f(Q, A, P),$$

which is read, "R is a function of Q, A, and P." This means only that the level of total profit depends in some specified manner on the levels of the firm's output, its advertising expenditure, and the price of the competing product.

Given such a multivariable relationship, we may again ask about the effect of a change in Q, A, and P on total profits. In doing so we investigate the marginal profit effects of a change of one or more of these variables. In particular, we may wish to see what happens when we vary the value of one of the variables and the values of the others do not change from given amounts. As is to be expected, there is a form of the derivative which corresponds to such an "other things being equal" marginal concept. It is called the *partial derivative*. For example, if we wish to examine the effect (at a point) of a change in advertising expenditure on total profit for any specified and unchanging levels of Q and P, we compute the partial derivative of total profit with respect to advertising expenditure, which is written $\partial R/\partial A$.

The procedures for partial differentiation are a simple and intuitively comprehensible extension of the ordinary differentiation process. We just treat as constants all variables other than the two which are directly involved. This is the natural interpretation of the idea that the values of all other variables are held constant. An example will make this clear. Given

$$y = 5x^4 + 55x^3 \log z + 3xz - 12z^2 + 4$$

to find $\partial y / \partial x$ we treat z as a constant so that the relationship may be rewritten as

$$y = 5x^4 + (55 \log z)x^3 + (3z)x - (12z^2 - 4).$$

None of the terms in parentheses contains either a y or an x, so that each such term is treated as a constant number, i.e., for purposes of partial differentiation our relationship is treated like the equation

$$y = ax^4 + bx^3 + cx + d$$

where a, b, c, and d are constants. Thus we have

$$\frac{\partial y}{\partial x} = 4ax^3 + 3bx^2 + c = 20x^3 + 3(55 \log z)x^2 + 3z.$$

The term $d = -(12z^2 - 4)$ drops out in partial differentiation with respect to x because the derivative of a constant is always zero.

Employing the partial differentiation concept, we can now extend our discussion of the calculus minimization and maximization criteria. We shall discuss only the first-order conditions because the second-order conditions are rather complex in this case and we defer their discussion to Chapter 13.[8]

Figure 7 is a geometric representation of a three-variable case. Here the graph of the profit relationship is a three-dimensional hill. Any point on the "floor" of the diagram represents a pair of values of Q and A. For example, point K represents a situation in which the firm decides on output level OQ_k and on advertising expenditure OA_k. Moreover, the profits to be earned by this output-advertising expenditure combination are represented by the length of the vertical line KK' from point K to the point K' on the profit surface directly above it.

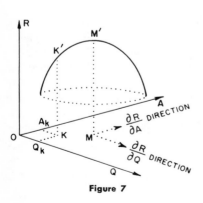

Figure 7

[8] These conditions have in fact played an important role in comparative statics analysis. The conditions are discussed and used in the Mathematical Appendix to

Here the profit-maximizing output-advertising expenditure combination is obviously M, and it will be noted that at its highest point, M', the profit surface is again level. This means that the slope of any cross section is zero at that point (for otherwise we would be going uphill or downhill and hence we would not be at a maximum). In particular, this means that as we move directly toward the right (increase Q and hold A constant) we must find the profit surface level, i.e., we must have $\partial R/\partial Q = 0$. Similarly, a small move directly toward the rear of the diagram (increasing A and holding Q constant) must also encounter a level profit surface so that $\partial R/\partial A = 0$.

More generally, in the $n + 1$ variable case, $y = f(x_1, \cdots, x_n)$, if we are to be at a maximum point, we must have the n relationships

$$\partial y/\partial x_1 = 0, \qquad \partial y/\partial x_2 = 0, \qquad \cdots, \qquad \partial y/\partial x_n = 0$$

so that no small change in value in any of the variables x_1, x_2, $\cdots$, x_n will increase y. These are the first-order maximum or minimum conditions in the many-variable case.

The way this helps us to find the maximizing or minimizing values of the variables x_1, x_2, $\cdots$, x_n is now straightforward, at least in principle. The conditions $\partial y/\partial x_1 = 0$, etc., are n equations in the n unknowns; and if they can be solved simultaneously for the values of the x's, they will yield the maximum or minimum values (if the appropriate second-order conditions are satisfied).

Example: Assuming that the second-order conditions are satisfied, find the profit-maximizing values of Q and A. Given the relationship

$$R = 400 - 3Q^2 - 4Q + 2QA - 5A^2 + 48A$$

we take $\partial R/\partial Q$ and $\partial R/\partial A$ and set them equal to zero to obtain

$$\frac{\partial R}{\partial Q} = -6Q - 4 + 2A = 0, \qquad \text{i.e., } -6Q + 2A = 4$$

$$\frac{\partial R}{\partial A} = 2Q - 10A + 48 = 0, \qquad \text{i.e., } 2Q - 10A = -48.$$

To eliminate the terms containing the A's, multiply the first equation by 5 to obtain

$$-30Q + 10A = 20$$

J. R. Hicks' *Value and Capital*, 2nd Edition, Oxford University Press, New York, 1946, and in Chapter IV and Appendix A of Paul A. Samuelson's *Foundations of Economic Analysis*, Harvard University Press, Cambridge, Mass., 1948. For a good introductory exposition see James M. Henderson and Richard E. Quandt, *Microeconomic Theory*, McGraw-Hill Book Company, New York, 2nd ed., 1971, especially Chapters 2 and 3.

and add this to the second equation to yield

$$-28Q = -28 \quad \text{or} \quad Q = 1.$$

Substitution of this value into the first equation gives

$$-6 \times 1 + 2A = 4 \quad \text{or} \quad 2A = 10, \quad \text{so that } A = 5.$$

Hence $Q = 1$ and $A = 5$ are the output and advertising expenditure levels which maximize total profit.

PROBLEMS

Which values of the variables satisfy the first-order maximum or minimum conditions in the following relationships?

1. $R = 737 - 5Q^2 + 22A + QA - 4A^2 + 17Q.$
2. $y = 83.4 + x^2 + 26x - 6xz - 36z + 2z^2.$

7. Total Differentation

Total differentiation is a natural extension of the idea of partial differentiation. If we have an n-variable function, $y = f(x_1, x_2, \cdots, x_n)$, then the partial derivative $\partial y / \partial x_1$ is the effect of a small change in x_1 on y *all other things being held equal*, i.e., it is the effect on y of a change in x_1, (hypothetically) holding $x_2, \cdots, x_n$ constant, whether or not in reality these values are affected by x_1. Thus, we may ask about the effect of a rise in the price charged by a firm, x_1, on the demand for its own products, y, on the assumption that competing firms were not to change their prices in response. But in fact competitive price responses do sometimes occur, so that if we want to determine the final net outcome of the chain of events set off by a change in x_1, we cannot stop with the corresponding partial derivative. We must instead use an expression, the *total derivative*, that takes into account not only the direct influence of the change in x_1 on y but also its indirect influence via its effects on the other variables, $x_2, \cdots, x_n$.

The formula for the *total differential of y* is

$$dy = \frac{\partial y}{\partial x_1} dx_1 + \frac{\partial y}{\partial x_2} dx_2 + \cdots + \frac{\partial y}{\partial x_n} dx_n,$$

or dividing through by dx_1, we obtain the formula for the *total derivative* of y with respect to x_1 (recalling that $dx_1/dx_1 = 1$),

$$\frac{dy}{dx_1} = \frac{\partial y}{\partial x_1} + \frac{\partial y}{\partial x_2}\frac{dx_2}{dx_1} + \cdots + \frac{\partial y}{\partial x_n}\frac{dx_n}{dx_1}.$$

This fundamental result will be used repeatedly in the book. An intuitive interpretation of these formulae is not difficult. The second of these equations, for example, states that the effect of x_1 on y is composed of two parts: Its direct effect, $\partial y/\partial x_1$, plus the sum of its indirect effects via all other variables x_i, each such indirect effect being given by $(\partial y/x_i)(dx_i/dx_1)$, the product of the effect of x_1 on x_i and of x_i on y. This equation almost strikes one as too simple to be true. In effect it states that to find the total effect of x_1 on y one takes its direct effect and each of its indirect effects via other variables in turn and simply adds them up.

It is quite easy to indicate the derivation of these formulae. Dealing, for simplicity of notation, with the two-variable case $y = f(x_1, x_2)$, we obtain the formula for the total differential as follows:

By definition

$$\Delta y = f(x_1 + \Delta x_1, x_2 + \Delta x_2) - f(x_1, x_2)$$

or simultaneously subtracting and adding $f(x_1, x_2 + \Delta x_2)$,

$$\Delta y = [f(x_1 + \Delta x_1, x_2 + \Delta x_2) - f(x_1, x_2 + \Delta x_2)]$$
$$+ [f(x_1, x_2 + \Delta x_2) - f(x_1, x_2)]$$

$$= \frac{f(x_1 + \Delta x_1, x_2 + \Delta x_2) - f(x_1, x_2 + \Delta x_2)}{\Delta x_1} \Delta x_1$$

$$+ \frac{f(x_1, x_2 + \Delta x_2) - f(x_1, x_2)}{\Delta x_2} \Delta x_2.$$

But, by definition, the limit of the second fraction, as Δx_2 approaches zero, is $\partial f/\partial x_2$, and the analogous interpretation holds for the first fraction. Consequently, taking limits as Δx_1 and Δx_2 simultaneously approach zero, Δy approaches dy, etc., and our last equation approaches

$$dy = (\partial f/\partial x_1) \, dx_1 + (\partial f/\partial x_2) \, dx_2,$$

which is our desired result.

PROBLEM

1. Find the total differentials of the following:

(a) $y = 2x_1^2 x_2^3$

(b) $y = 2x_1^2 + 4x_2^3$

(c) $y = f(x_1, x_2) + x_2^2$.

8. Constrained Maxima: Lagrange Multipliers

We have already come across a number of cases in which the range of variation of the variables was restricted. Maximization or minimization in such cases becomes a problem of finding the largest or smallest values which can be achieved within the permitted ranges of the variables. A problem of this sort is said to be one of *constrained* maximization, and the relationships which restrict the range of variation of the variables are called *constraints* or *side conditions*. Problems involving constraints occur frequently in economics, as we shall see in the next chapter.

The relationship between a constrained and an unconstrained maximization problem can be illustrated with the aid of a geographic analogy. If we seek the location of the highest point on earth, we will end up with the latitude and longitude of the peak of Mount Everest. But if this altitude maximization problem is constrained by the condition that we must remain within the continental limits of the United States, two changes will occur: (1) we will end up with different latitude and longitude numbers, and (2) the height of the maximum point will be decreased. Of course, if the constraint had instead only required us to stay within the Asiatic continent, rather than the United States, our original (unconstrained) answer would have remained valid. Hence we conclude that a constraint usually will, but need not always, change the values of the "independent variables"; it usually will (but need not) decrease the value of the item being maximized, and, at best, it will leave that value unaffected.

Let us now consider a specific maximization problem. A firm has 100 (thousand) dollars to spend on labor and raw materials in the next year. Let L be the quantity of labor it hires and let its (annual) price per unit be 2 (thousand dollars). Moreover, let the quantity of raw material bought be M, and let it have a price of 1 (thousand dollars) per unit. Then the firm is operating under the budget constraint that its total expenditure on these two items be 100, i.e., that

$$2L + M = 100.$$

For subsequent reference it is important to note that this constraint is an *equation*. Suppose, moreover, for purposes of illustrative simplicity that the firm's output Q is related to L and M via the following improbable production function:

$$Q = 5LM.$$

To get as much output as possible out of its budget the firm must find the values of L and M which maximize Q but which satisfy the budget constraint. Again, in this section we deal only with first-order conditions.

One fairly straightforward way of solving this constrained maximum problem is to use the constraint to eliminate one of the variables. Thus

$2L + M = 100$ gives $M = 100 - 2L$, and substituting this expression for M in the production function $Q = 5LM$ gives

$$Q = 5L(100 - 2L) = 500L - 10L^2.$$

We are then left with an ordinary unconstrained maximization problem involving only the two variables Q and L. This is solved, as before, by setting the first derivative equal to zero to determine the value of L, i.e., by solving

$$500 - 20L = 0,$$

which gives $L = 25$. Now, substituting this into the budget constraint equation, we find that $M = 100 - 2L = 50$. This, then, is the solution. It will pay the firm to obtain twenty-five units of labor and fifty units of raw material.

Before discussing a second and far more powerful method of solving such constrained maximum or minimum problems, let us examine the problem geometrically. In Figure 8a the straight line BB' is the graph of the budget constraint $100 = 2L + M$. This graph shows how the budget constraint restricts the range of values of the variables L and M. It does not just set fixed upper or lower limits on their values. Rather, it states that only certain combinations of these values are admissible, i.e., those which satisfy the budget equation so that (like combination L_a and M_a) they are represented by points on this line. In economic terms, only combinations of labor and raw material quantities whose total value is equal to 100 are to be considered. All other points such as C or D represent input combinations which do not meet the firm's budget requirements.

Now, suppose we place Figure 8a flat on the floor and erect over it a graphic representation of the production function $Q = 5LM$. This is done in Figure 8b in which surface $OUVW$ represents the production function,

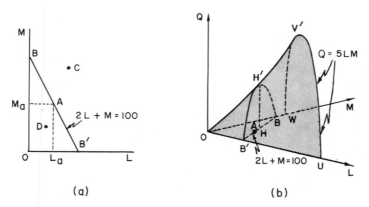

(a)   (b)

Figure 8

i.e., for each combination of inputs L and M it shows how much will be produced.

In the constrained maximization problem we are not interested in the entire production surface. We consider only that part of the surface which corresponds to admissible input combinations whose locus is line BB' on the floor of the diagram. The locus of the corresponding outputs is the arc $BH'B'$ above line BB'. The optimum point which we seek is clearly point H, which lies below the highest point on this arc, i.e., it yields the highest *attainable* production level, HH'.

The method of solution which already has been described involves our using the budget constraint to eliminate one of the variables. This is tantamount to our taking a cross section of the diagram which contains both line BB' and arc $BH'B'$. In this way one of the dimensions is eliminated from the diagram and we are left with an ordinary maximization problem in two dimensions (variables).

Unfortunately, the method does not always work. The constraint does not always take the simple form of our budget equation, so that it is not always possible to eliminate one of the variables directly. For example, if (in some nightmare) we encountered the constraint

$$\frac{L^M \log LM}{\sqrt{1 - L^2/M^5}} = 4,$$

we would find it difficult to solve for M in terms of L as we did before. Such cases must be dealt with by the method of *Lagrange multipliers*, which is, in any event, of far greater theoretical interest. Rigorous justification of this procedure is beyond the scope of this book but it will be described and explained intuitively.

It will be recalled that in the unconstrained maximization problems we proceeded by differentiating partially with respect to each variable in turn and setting each of these partial derivatives equal to zero. This gave us as many equations as variables and normally these could be solved for the optimum values of the variables. This method usually breaks down when there are constraint equations in the problem; for, in addition to the "partial derivative equal to zero" conditions, the constraint equations must also be satisfied. This means that the problem contains more equations than unknowns and is therefore, in normal circumstances, over-determined.[9] To get out of this difficulty we introduce some artificial unknowns, as many as there are constraints, to increase the number of unknowns to equality with the number of partial derivative equations and

---

[9] It is not true that equality of the number of equations and unknowns either guarantees or is necessary for solvability of a system of simultaneous equations. However, there is some presumption that this will be so. See below, Chapter 23, Section 1.

constraint equations. These artificial unknowns are called *Lagrange multipliers*.

Let us rework our example to show how the method works, meanwhile offering some justification for the procedure. First we take our constraint $2L + M = 100$ and bring all the terms over to one side of the equation to obtain

$$2L + M - 100 = 0.$$

Next, we multiply the resulting expression on the left by an unknown constant λ[10], and add the result to the production function $Q = 5LM$ to obtain the so-called Lagrangian expression

$$Q_\lambda = 5LM + \lambda(2L + M - 100).$$

The basic point is, roughly, that if the constraint is always satisfied the expression in parentheses will be equal to zero so that the Lagrangian expression Q_λ will behave exactly in the same way as does the production function. Whatever values of L and M maximize the one will automatically maximize the other. But the Lagrangian expression contains *three* symbols whose values are unknown, namely λ, L, and M. We may then solve the problem by differentiating partially with respect to each of the three unknowns, set the three results equal to zero, and solve these three equations for the three unknown values. This yields

$$\frac{\partial Q_\lambda}{\partial L} = 5M + 2\lambda = 0$$

$$\frac{\partial Q_\lambda}{\partial M} = 5L + \lambda = 0$$

$$\frac{\partial Q_\lambda}{\partial \lambda} = 2L + M - 100 = 0 \quad \text{(which is the budget constraint equation).}$$

Now the reader will note that when we set the partial derivative with respect to λ equal to zero we *automatically guarantee that our constraint will be satisfied*. This was *arranged for* when we multiplied λ by the constraint expression in the Lagrangian function Q_λ. But, as we have seen, since the constraint is satisfied ($2L + M - 100 = 0$), we must have $Q_\lambda = Q$ and the solution to the Lagrangian problem then necessarily solves the original problem as well. That, roughly, is the rationale of the Lagrangian method.

Our three equations can be solved by multiplying the second equation through by 2 and subtracting from it the first equation to obtain $10L = 5M$ or $M = 2L$. Substituting this into the last equation we obtain $4L = 100$ or $L = 25$, and another simple substitution yields $M = 50$, $\lambda = -125$,

---

[10] λ is the Greek letter lambda, which is usually used for this purpose.

the same result as before, except that, in addition, we have now obtained a value for λ.

It can be shown that this value of λ itself has a significant economic interpretation. In this case, $-\lambda$ is the marginal productivity of money—it indicates how much would be added to output if the input budget were increased from 100 to 101. We can check this roughly by noting that this dollar could be used to buy another unit of M, which would increase output from

$$Q = 5LM = 5 \cdot 25M = 125M \qquad \text{to} \qquad Q + \Delta Q = 125(M + 1)$$
$$= 125M + 125$$

so that

$$\Delta Q(= \Delta Q/1 = \Delta Q/\Delta M) = 125 = -\lambda.$$

More will be said about the interpretation of Lagrange multipliers in a later chapter.

Finally, we note that if the problem has more than one constraint equation, to obtain the Lagrangian expression we multiply each of the constraints by a *different* unknown Lagrange multiplier and add them all to the original expression whose value is to be maximized.

Example: Maximize

$$y = 10xzw - 3w^2$$

subject to $x + z + w = 12$ and $x - w = 2$.

We rewrite the constraints as $x + z + w - 12 = 0$ and $x - w - 2 = 0$, and multiplying these, respectively, by λ_1 and λ_2 we can write the Lagrangian expression

$$y_\lambda = 10xzw - 3w^2 + \lambda_1(x + z + w - 12) + \lambda_2(x - w - 2).$$

The maximum (or minimum) value is then found from the equations

$$\frac{\partial y_\lambda}{\partial x} = 10zw + \lambda_1 + \lambda_2 = 0$$

$$\frac{\partial y_\lambda}{\partial z} = 10xw + \lambda_1 = 0$$

$$\frac{\partial y_\lambda}{\partial w} = 10xz - 6w + \lambda_1 - \lambda_2 = 0$$

$$\frac{\partial y_\lambda}{\partial \lambda_1} = x + z + w - 12 = 0$$

and
$$\frac{\partial y_\lambda}{\partial \lambda_2} = x - w - 2 = 0,$$

where the last two lines are the constraint equations.

PROBLEMS

1. By both methods find the values which satisfy the first-order conditions for maximization of

(a) $y = 10xw - 2w^2$ subject to $x + w = 12$
(b) $R = 737 - 8Q^2 + 14A + QA - 4A^2 + 20Q$ subject to

$$2Q + A = 2.$$

2. Write out the Lagrangian expression for the problem: maximize

$$y = \log x^3 w$$

subject to

$$\cos x \cos w = 0.3 \quad \text{and} \quad \frac{x}{w^5} + e^w = 10.$$

9. Some Economic Applications of the Differential Calculus

In economics the differential calculus has had many fruitful applications. In fact, as we have already noted, economists have invented a special terminology for this technique, referring to it as *marginal analysis*. This application arises naturally in an investigation of the decision-making of business firms, consumers, and other economic units. For, in pursuing their goals, these units may be taken to *maximize* some measure of achievement, whether it be profits, national income, or some other such variable. It is convenient at this point to list some of the functional relationships which recur most frequently in the work of the economist:

(1) a production function, $Q = f(z)$, which records how the required quantity of labor or some raw material, z, varies with the production level Q of some commodity, e.g., Q may represent the number of shoes produced per week by a shoe factory;

(2) a cost function $C = g(Q)$, which records the total expense C associated with production level Q;

(3) a demand function $P = F(Q)$, which shows how high a price P can be charged per unit if it is desired to sell Q units of a commodity. In other words, it shows how much of the commodity consumers will demand at different levels of the price;

(4) a revenue function $P \cdot Q = QF(Q)$, which shows the total income of the firm when it sells Q units of a commodity at the price P per unit;

(5) a utility function $U(Q)$, which measures the pleasure that the individual derives from the possession of some quantity Q of some commodity.

Economists have then adopted the following terminology:

$$\text{marginal utility is the name given to } \frac{dU}{dQ}$$

$$\text{marginal product refers to } \frac{dQ}{dz}$$

$$\text{marginal cost refers to } \frac{dC}{dQ}$$

$$\text{marginal revenue refers to } \frac{d(PQ)}{dQ}.$$

Suppose now that a businessman desires to earn as much total profit, R, as he can. This means that he desires to make as large as possible the difference between his total receipts (revenue) PQ and his total costs C. In other words, he seeks to maximize

$$R = PQ - C.$$

We can now see what level of production Q is most profitable. In ordinary circumstances, R will be maximized when its derivative vanishes, i.e., when

$$\frac{dR}{dQ} = \frac{d(PQ)}{dQ} - \frac{dC}{dQ} = 0$$

or

$$\frac{d(PQ)}{dQ} = \frac{dC}{dQ}.$$

In other words, maximum profits require that *marginal cost be equal to marginal revenue*. This is a fundamental result in the economic theory of the firm, which will be discussed again later.

Example 1: *Optimal production level.* Suppose the relevant portion of the demand function is

$$P = 100 - 0.01Q,$$

where Q is the weekly production. This equation states that as more of the commodity is put on the market its price must fall. If price is measured in cents, it means that price must fall by 1 cent for every 100 additional units of the commodity which appear on the market each week. Suppose also that the cost function is given by

$$C = 50Q + 30,000.$$

It is easy to verify that

$$\text{total revenue} = PQ \quad = 100Q - 0.01Q^2$$

$$\text{marginal revenue} = \frac{d(PQ)}{dQ} = 100 - 0.02Q$$

$$\text{marginal cost} = \frac{dC}{dQ} \quad = 50$$

so that maximum profit involves

$$\text{marginal cost} = \text{marginal revenue}, \quad \text{i.e., } 50 = 100 - 0.02Q.$$

This means that the most profitable level of production will be

$$Q = \frac{50}{0.02} = 2{,}500 \text{ units per week.}$$

At that level of production, price will be

$$P = 100 - 0.01Q = 100 - 25 = 75 \text{ cents}$$

and total profit per week will be

$$R = PQ - C = 75 \times 2{,}500 - (30{,}000 + 50 \times 2{,}500) \text{ cents} = \$325.$$

Example 2: *The incidence of a sales tax.* Suppose, in the preceding example, the government decides to levy a tax of 10 cents per unit of product sold. What will happen to price, quantity sold, and total profit?

Total cost now becomes

$$C = 50Q + 10Q + 30{,}000 = 60Q + 30{,}000.$$

Maximum profit again requires marginal cost to equal marginal revenue, which now involves

$$60 = 100 - 0.02Q.$$

This yields

$$Q = 2{,}000 \text{ units per week}$$

$$P = 80 \text{ cents}$$

$$R = \$100$$

We thus have the results

	Before Tax	After Tax
Tax/unit	0	10
Weekly output	2,500	2,000
Price (cents)	75	80
Weekly profit ($)	325	100

Particularly noteworthy is the result that it does not pay the businessman to pass on the full 10 cents tax rise to the consumer—rather it is most profitable in this case to raise his price by only 5 cents!

Example 3: *Fixed costs.* Let the firm's total cost be given by $C = k + c(Q)$. That portion of the firm's costs, k, which do not change when its output Q changes is called its *fixed cost.* The firm's marginal cost is obtained, by differentiation, to be

$$\frac{dC}{dQ} = \frac{dc(Q)}{dQ}.$$

It will be observed that the constant term, k, has dropped out in the course of this differentiation. As a result, marginal costs are the same no matter what the value of k, i.e., no matter what changes occur in the firm's fixed costs (cf. Section 6 of the previous chapter).

This leads us to a rather surprising result. Since a change in fixed costs does not affect the firm's marginal cost (nor clearly, its marginal revenue), the price-output combination at which marginal cost equals marginal revenue will be unaffected by any such change. In other words *if the firm maximizes its profits, a change in fixed cost will affect neither its output level nor the price of its product!*[11]

PROBLEMS

1. Give verbal definitions of marginal utility, marginal cost, marginal revenue, and marginal product.

2. A commodity is sold at a *fixed* price P per unit. A consumer, in buying Q units of the commodity, tries to maximize the difference between the utility $U = f(Q)$, derived from his consumption of the commodity and the total amount PQ which he has to pay. Show that to maximize $U - PQ = f(Q) - PQ$ he should buy so much of the commodity that its marginal utility is equal to its price.

3. Elasticity of demand is a measure of the responsiveness of quantity demanded to price changes, which is given by

$$\frac{\% \text{ change in quantity demanded}}{\% \text{ change in price}} = \frac{100\, dQ/Q}{100\, dP/P} = \frac{P}{Q}\frac{dQ}{dP}.$$

If the demand function $Q = F(P)$ is such that when price is cut purchases increase by an amount just sufficient to keep total revenue unchanged, the demand equation is $PQ = K$ (a constant). Show that in this case elasticity of demand $= -1$.

4. Let $c = g(Q)$ be the cost per unit of producing a commodity, C the total cost of producing that commodity, and Q the number of units produced. Then, by definition, $C = cQ$. Prove that if Q is at such a level that costs per unit are at a minimum (is this an efficient level of production?), we will also have marginal cost equal to c.

---

[11] The rationale of the rule that the profit maximizer's prices should not be changed when fixed costs change is discussed in Chapter 15, below.

5. Suppose *total* cost $C = 120Q - Q^2 + 0.02Q^3$ and $P = 114 - 0.25Q$.

(a) What level of Q yields minimum costs *per unit c*?

(b) Does this level of output yield maximum profit?

(c) At how many levels of output is marginal cost equal to marginal revenue?

(d) Are these all profit-maximizing outputs? (Evaluate the second derivative of the total profit.)

6. Consider the demand and cost functions

$$P = a - bQ$$
$$C = w + vQ,$$

where a, b, w, and v are positive constants. Suppose the government imposes on the producer a tax of t dollars per unit of output and that as a result it pays to raise price from P dollars to P^* dollars. Show that $P^* - P = \frac{1}{2}t$, i.e., that it pays the manufacturer to shift only one-half of the tax onto the consumer if he is to maximize his profits.

7. Find the sign of the second derivatives of the profit functions in the preceding problem. Why are they relevant?

REFERENCES

Allen, R. G. D., *Mathematical Analysis for Economists*, Macmillan & Co., Ltd., London, 1938, Chapters VI–XIV.

Chiang, Alpha C., *Fundamental Methods of Mathematical Economics*, McGraw-Hill Book Company, New York, 1967.

Crum, W. L., and J. A. Schumpeter, *Rudimentary Mathematics for Economists and Statisticians*, McGraw-Hill Book Company, New York, 1946.

Intrilligator, M. D., *Mathematical Optimization and Economic Theory*, Prentice-Hall, Inc., Englewood Cliffs, N.J., 1971, Chapter 3.

Thomas, G. B., Jr., *Calculus and Analytic Geometry*, Addison-Wesley Publishing Co., Inc., Reading, Mass., 4th ed., 1968.

Williamson, R. E., R. H. Crowell, and H. F. Trotter, *Calculus of Vector Functions*, Prentice-Hall, Inc., Englewood Cliffs, N.J., 3rd ed., 1972.

Linear Programming

5

Programming, both linear and nonlinear, is entirely a mathematical technique. Its economic content is therefore nil. This is no mere classificatory quibble. It means that programming per se can never tell us anything about the operation of any part of the economy. Like the calculus or any other branch of mathematics, it can only help us to find the implications of the economic information which we already have or are willing to assume. To the extent, then, that economists were responsible for the development of programming,[1] they may be said to have been productive in areas outside their own fields, as they have been in the past when they formulated the largely technological law of diminishing returns, or when, by inventing the marginal analysis, they stumbled, a few centuries too late, on what is essentially a crude version of the differential calculus.

1. Some Standard Programming Problems

Programming is concerned with the determination of the optimal solutions to problems. As a result, it is well suited to the analysis of rational

---

[1] Several economists have made important contributions. Notable among these are T. C. Koopmans, R. Dorfman, and W. W. Cooper. But if any one person is to be named as the father of programming, we must undoubtedly award the honor to mathematician George Dantzig, inventor of the first successful (and still one of the most efficient) general computational techniques, the simplex method. Important contributions have been made by mathematicians such as the Russian L. V. Kantorovich, who first formulated the problem, H. W. Kuhn, A. W. Tucker, A. Charnes, and others.

behavior. It has, therefore, like the marginal analysis, been somewhat less successful in describing what is than in indicating what (given some pre-assigned goals) ought to be. Some of the most fertile applications of programming have involved welfare economics and advice to businessmen, both of which aim to tell the relevant persons how they can most efficiently go about working toward their objectives. Let us indicate briefly a few of the business problems to which programming is most frequently applied.

(1) *Optimal product lines and production processes.* When operating at a high output level a firm is likely to run into a variety of capacity limitations. Its factory size, the amount of time available on different machines, its warehouse space, and its skilled personnel—any or all may constitute bottlenecks, some of which are prohibitively expensive or even impossible to eliminate in the short run.

A crucial characteristic of such a situation is that the production of a relatively unprofitable item or the use of a production process which makes liberal use of the scarce facilities may take up valuable capacity that can better be used in more economical processes and in the manufacture of more lucrative commodities.

There is no simple solution, such as complete specialization in the one "most efficient process" for producing the one item which makes "most profitable" use of scarce facilities since, except by pure accident, there may be no process or no product which is economical in its use of all of the firm's limited facilities at once. One item may make good use of machine capacity and may therefore yield the highest profit per scarce machine-hour, whereas another may make more effective use of limited warehouse space. Production of only the former would find warehouses completely loaded before machine time was fully employed, while the latter product, since it is not bulky, might leave warehouses half empty even if the firm's machines were to turn out nothing else.

(2) *Transportation routing.* In the selection of transportation routes, especially where a firm has many plants and its processes involve trans-shipment of items in various stages of production, substantial savings can be expected from careful planning of commodity movements. If the firm employs its own trucks or other transport facilities, the problem is to route them in a way that incurs as little cost as possible. Where the firm employs others to do its transporting, the computations may be further complicated by peculiarities in the transportation rate structure, for then the firm's objective is not to minimize ton-miles but to minimize payments to the carrier, and the two do not always correspond.

(3) *Meeting product specifications.* Many contracts include a number of minimum specifications which must be met by the product, and sometimes the manufacturer will set up such standards for himself. Usually there is a variety of ways in which these specifications can be met. For example, an

animal feed may require X units of protein per bag, Y of carbohydrates, Z of vitamin B, etc. Each of the grains combined in the animal feed contains some of the nutrients, and it is therefore possible to make a bag of feed meet these specifications in many different ways. A very inexpensive ingredient may contain much starch and very little else, so to meet the standards it may be necessary to add some more expensive ingredients. But which ingredients should be added and in what proportion? Or will it prove cheaper to begin with somewhat more costly ingredients which supply a better balance of all the nutrients?

The least-cost combination of meeting specifications is basically a programming problem. This technique has, for example, been employed in just this fashion, i.e., in mixing animal feeds, as well as other areas such as in the blending of gasolines. Programming techniques have been employed in many other business problems. They can help determine optimal inventory levels and have been used to solve production problems such as in the cutting of paper and cloth in a way which minimizes raw material waste and in the job assignment of specialized personnel.

2. Characteristics of Programming

What is the common element in all of these situations which makes them amenable to programming analysis? It is clear that all of them require a search for "best" values of the variables. But there is something more involved which makes the usual tools of the calculus or marginal analysis inapplicable. In many problems of optimization there is a complication in that the outcome, to be acceptable, must meet certain conditions. For example, the problem of fencing in 20 square feet at minimum cost involves the determination of that shape of plot which will save on fencing most effectively. But any saving which is achieved by fencing only 19 or 21 square feet will be unacceptable. This, then, is essentially a problem of finding the best way of meeting a very precise specification which the mathematician calls "a side condition." So long as the specifications are so precise (the area must be 20 square feet, no more or less, or the starch content of a 100-pound bag of feed must be exactly so many calories, etc.), the optimization problem can usually still be dealt with by calculus (marginal) techniques, as was shown in Section 8 of the previous chapter.[2]

However, it is characteristic of many business problems that specifications are not precise but provide only minimum requirements that must be met. Or the specification, rather than stating the precise extent to

---

[2] Even here there is an important exception. The mathematical form of the precise specification (side condition) is an equation. If the graph of the equation is discontinuous or kinked, calculus methods cannot be depended on to work. The reason is that these techniques find an optimum by computing the slope of the relevant graphs to investigate whether it is possible to go "uphill" (toward higher profits). Where the graph of a function is discontinuous or kinked, its slope is, for obvious reasons, not even defined.

which a facility will be used, may indicate only the maximum capacity which is available. Any output which overshoots the quality standards or does not fully utilize some part of capacity is not necessarily ruled out. Here the side conditions are inequalities rather than equations. That is, they do not state that X must equal 500 but only that X must be no less than 500.[3]

This sort of side condition characterizes each of the business problems which has been described. In the optimum-product-line and production-process problem there are maximum capacities to be dealt with. In meeting specifications at minimum cost, each specification is such an inequality. In the transportation-routing and plant-location problems, the presence of such restrictions on the businessman's decisions is less obvious, but they are nevertheless there and play a fundamental role in the computation. There can be limitations on the size and cargo-carrying capacity of the trucks, trains, or ships to be routed. But the more relevant capacity limitation is a peculiar one which states that in no case is it possible to ship negative amounts from one place to another! This rather silly-sounding restriction is important partly because things like this are never obvious to an electronic computer and, unless it is specifically forbidden to do so, the computer will assign negative shipments from some supply sources to some destinations. For the machine will reason that if it is profitable to reduce some shipments to zero, it may be still more profitable to reduce these shipments even further!

For the economic theorist, such nonnegativity requirements are important for a far more fundamental reason. Like an electronic computer, marginal analysis is, by itself, incapable of taking account of them. To return to the more familiar optimal-output problem, for the competitive firm we note that the rule of the marginal analysis is that the output of any item should be at a level at which marginal cost is equal to price. But for an unprofitable item marginal cost may only be equal to price at an impossible negative output level. That is, in a case of increasing costs, even at zero output cost need not have fallen back to the level of price.

---

[3] The reason marginal techniques break down in the presence of inequality side conditions is easily illustrated with the aid of a simple graph (Figure 3b of Chapter 4). Marginal analysis finds, e.g., the point of maximum profits by locating the point at which marginal profit (the slope of the total profit curve) equals zero (output OQ_m in the figure). That is the meaning of the standard marginal-cost-equals-marginal-revenue condition. But suppose output is limited by the inequality that production cannot exceed OQ_i. Then our problem is to find out whether the point of maximum attainable profit is OQ_i or some point to its left (which is no easy problem in the N-dimensional N-variable case). But for this the first-order conditions of the marginal analysis cannot be employed, for at the optimum point in the diagram, OQ_i, the marginal criterion, marginal profit equals the slope of the total profit curve equals zero, is obviously invalid. See Chapter 4, Section 4, for a more complete discussion of the cases in which the calculus maximization criteria are not directly applicable.

Of course, no moderately sane economist making a graphic analysis will ever recommend a negative output. But where a large number of inter-dependent decisions have to be made, the calculations may all have to be done with the help of mathematical reasoning. And a mathematical analysis, based on marginal equalities such as marginal cost equals price, must in such a case yield nonsense results unless we impose on the calculation the explicit requirement that the variables be given no negative values. We will come to this point again later.

Programming, then, is the mathematical method for the analysis and computation of optimal decisions which do not violate the limitations imposed by inequality side conditions. In almost all cases the method of computation is a so-called iterative procedure. Just as the term *"ragout"* disguises the fact that it is only stew, though presumably an elegant one, this fancy term is used to dignify a systematic trial-and-error procedure. The answer to a programming problem will ordinarily not be arrived at directly. Instead the solution is found by groping toward it. But the trial-and-error procedure is not pure guesswork. It is systematic in that it usually involves at least the first two of the following features:

1. There is a mechanical rule which determines, after each step, exactly what the next step is to be on the basis of the results of the trial just completed. One purpose of this feature of the method of solution is that it makes electronic computation possible. Most of these mechanical brains unfortunately possess no judgment of their own so they must be told what to do in every contingency. This is like teaching a human the rules of algebra before giving him an algebraic problem to solve. In any event, a mechanical rule stating what must be done at each succeeding trial in the trial-and-error procedure is useful because in a problem complicated by a great number of variables and interrelationships, human judgment can go badly wrong and can result in an inefficient, even totally ineffective, search for the answer.

2. A second characteristic feature of the systematic trial-and-error procedure is a proof that the method has been constructed in a way which guarantees that each trial will yield values which are closer than the preceding one to the correct answer. This very important feature assures the calculator that he is always getting closer to his result and is not wasting his time by going off in a wrong direction. We shall see later, in our discussion of the simplex method, how this sort of guarantee can be built into a computation procedure. Of course, such a guarantee can only be provided where there is a mechanical rule which specifies step by step what will be done. Otherwise, successive steps are unpredictable, and it is then not possible to say in advance whether they will be closer to or farther from the correct answer.

3. For a large class of problems there are available trial-and-error

procedure rules which are guaranteed to yield precisely the correct result after a finite number of steps. In other cases where this is not possible, one can hope to calculate a maximum error, and to be able to say, for example, that the result of the most recent trial is at most one-tenth of 1 per cent from the correct answer.

Where the problem is one involving *linear* programming, there are several computational methods many of which yield a precise answer after a finite number of steps. The simplex method, the method of fictitious play, and the complete-description method are all linear programming computational techniques. In the next section we will see what is involved in the linearity of a programming problem.

3. Algebra and Geometry

First, let us set out the equations of a typical linear programming problem.

Consider a profit-maximizing firm which can produce any of the four products w, x, y, and z whose outputs are W, X, Y, and Z and whose profits per unit of output are, respectively, 5, 3, 2, and 7. Then the total profits of the firm are given by $5W + 3X + 2Y + 7Z$. (Here, e.g., W and X may represent outputs of the same product manufactured by different "processes," i.e., with the use of different input proportions.) Suppose, moreover, the firm has available only 50,000 square feet of warehouse space and 32,000 machine-hours. If the manufacture of one unit of w requires 0.5 hours of machine time, that of x requires 2 hours of machine time, etc., we have an inequality relationship (which is called a "constraint" or "side condition") such as

$$0.5W + 2X + 1.9Y + 3.1Z \leq 32,000,$$

which states that no more of these outputs can be manufactured than the available machine time permits. Assume also that there is a similar warehouse-space constraint which is written out below. We can see now that the programming problem can be written:

(1) $\begin{cases} \text{maximize profits: } 5W + 3X + 2Y + 7Z \\ \text{subject to the constraints} \\ 0.5W + 2X + 1.9Y + 3.1Z \leq 32,000 \text{ (available machine time)} \\ 10W + 1.2X + 7Y + 4Z \leq 50,000 \text{ (warehouse capacity)} \\ \text{and the nonnegativity requirements} \\ W \geq 0, \quad X \geq 0, \quad Y \geq 0, \quad Z \geq 0. \end{cases}$

This is the standard form for a programming problem. It consists of three parts: (1) the function (e.g., profits or costs) whose value is to be maximized or minimized, which is called *the objective function*, (2) the ordinary *structural* (capacity) constraints, and (3) the nonnegativity conditions on the variables, e.g., $W \geq 0$.

This problem is called "linear" because the expression to be maximized and the inequalities involve only the variable multiplied by constants and added together (as in an equation for a straight line such as $y = 5x + 3$). There are no X^2's, 5 sin Y's, log Z's, or more complex expressions. We may note that this linear model employs an assumption of competitively or otherwise fixed input and output prices and constant returns to scale in production.[4] These premises enter in two ways. First, from the information that profit per unit of w is 5, we can only compute the profit from producing 10 units of w at $5W = 50$ because the assumption of constant returns to scale and constant input and output prices implies that costs, revenues, and profits will all rise precisely in proportion with the level of output. (We observe again that w is *defined* in such a way that it must always be produced with the same input proportions—in this analysis a change in the amount of scarce machine time used per unit of output is described as a shift from the manufacture of, say, w to that of x.) The linearity of the inequalities also rests on the assumption of constant returns to scale—the amount of warehouse space occupied by product y is assumed strictly proportionate to Y, the level of output of that item.[5]

Let us now look at some programming geometry. First, we must see how an inequality is represented graphically. Consider the inequality $2X + Y \leq 5$. (This may be interpreted, e.g., as a warehouse capacity limitation.) In Figure 1 any point such as P on the line LL' which represents the equation $2X + Y = 5$ (and represents full use of capacity) clearly satisfies the inequality. But, in addition, any point such as Q, R, or S which lies below and to the left of LL' also satisfies the inequality because it involves values of X and Y smaller than those which completely use up the capacity. We note, then, that while a two-variable equation is represented by a line, a two-variable inequality is represented by a region. Indeed, a linear two-variable inequality is represented by drawing a straight line which divides the plane into two regions called "half-spaces," one of which contains all points satisfying the inequality.

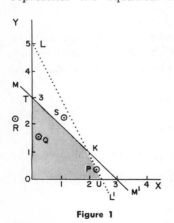

Figure 1

---

[4] For a definition and discussion of the "constant returns" case see Chapter 11.

[5] Where the facts of the situation do not warrant these assumptions even as an approximation, we may be forced to employ techniques of nonlinear programming. Usually these are, at best, more complicated, as indicated in Chapter 7.

Let us see what happens if, in addition, the variables must satisfy a second inequality, say $Y + X \leq 3$ represented by the half-space to the left of line MM'. All of the points which satisfy both inequalities must lie below both lines MM' and LL', so that we are left with the region bounded by the broken line MKL'.[6] Further inequalities may bound the region from all sides—e.g., the addition of the inequalities $X \geq 0$, $Y \geq 0$ leaves us with the shaded region in the diagram. This area is called the *feasible region* because every point such as Q which lies within it or on its boundary represents a combination of values of the variables (the output levels of X and Y) which does not violate the constraints, i.e., any such output combination is within the firm's capacity. For this reason, every point such as Q or P, in the feasible region, represents what is called a *feasible solution* to the programming problem.

We can now represent the entire programming problem diagrammatically by adding to Figure 1 a third dimension which we use to represent profits (Figure 2a). A surface $ORR'R''$ shows the profit that can be earned by any combination of our two outputs x and y. The XOY plane which constitutes the floor of the diagram is the same as the graph of Figure 1 or Figure 2b. Thus point K, for example, is a combination of outputs X and Y. If this combination, say, is capable of yielding \$100 in profits, we erect above point K the vertical line KK' whose length is 100 units. The profit surface $ORR'R''$ is the locus of all points such as K' whose height indicates the profits which are yielded by the output combination represented by the point K directly below.

In the *linear* programming case this profit surface $ORR'R''$ is always a plane through the origin (equation: profit $= aX + bY$, where a and b are constants).

Alternatively (Figure 2b) this situation can be depicted in a two-dimensional diagram where the profits are shown by iso-profit curves. Any two points on such a curve represent combinations of outputs X and Y which yield the same profits—e.g., profits at output combination R are the same as at output combination K. In a *linear* program these iso-profit curves are always straight lines, and they are parallel. For, a typical profit equation in a two-variable linear program is

$$\text{profit} = 3X + 2Y.$$

The curve representing a \$50,000 profit level therefore has the equation

$$50{,}000 = 3X + 2Y, \quad \text{i.e.,} \quad Y = -\tfrac{3}{2}X + 25{,}000$$

---

[6] Note that while two linear equations in two variables will normally leave us with only one possible point (the intersection of the two straight lines), two or more linear inequalities will often still leave us an unlimited number of points to choose from. Thus, there is nothing necessarily wrong with, say, a system of 5 inequalities in 3 unknowns even though we usually prefer to have no more equations than unknowns.

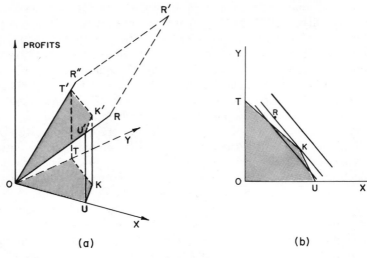

(a)   (b)

Figure 2

so that the profit indifference curve is a straight line whose slope is $-\frac{3}{2}$. Similarly, the line representing a \$70,000 profit level will be higher than and of the same slope as the \$50,000 line. The indifference curves of a linear program will therefore be a series of parallel straight lines. Further, moving to higher and higher curves will always increase profits.[7]

The objective of a programming calculation is to pick the *optimal* (in our examples, the most profitable) among the feasible output combinations. In geometric terms, this is represented by the point in the feasible region which happens to lie beneath the highest point on the profit surface $ORR'R''$, i.e., the feasible point which lies on the most valuable profit indifference curve.

It follows from the result that a move to a higher indifference curve always increases profits, that the optimal point of a *linear* program will always lie on the boundary of the feasible region.[8] The logic is simple. Any commodity whose production is profitable will continue to be lucrative as its output expands because there will be neither diminishing returns to scale nor unfavorable effects on input and output prices. It will, therefore, always pay to expand production until some capacity limit is reached, i.e.,

---

[7] There is an exception to this result when the outputs in question bring in losses rather than profits. In such a case profits may decrease when we move to higher indifference curves. However, this exception does not affect the rest of the argument.

[8] It will be shown in Chapter 7 that where a programming problem is nonlinear, most of the preceding theorems need not hold. The profit surface need not be a plane, the iso-profit curves need not be parallel straight lines, and an optimal point need not occur on the boundary of the feasible region.

until the boundary of the feasible region is attained. In fact, in a linear program, since the profit indifference curves are straight lines, there will always be at least one optimal solution (an optimal point) which occurs at one of the corners O, T, K, or U of the feasible region. For the optimal point will always either be a corner "tangency" point, such as K in Figure 2b, or, if the straight-line indifference curves are parallel to one of the segments of the feasible region's boundary, say to TK, then the entire segment *including corners T and K* will be optimal.

This important result, called the *basic theorem of linear programming*, will presently be restated and reinterpreted. However, its computational significance should at once be apparent. In seeking the optimal solution in Figure 2b we can ignore almost all of the infinite set of points in the shaded feasible region and examine only the profitability of our four corner points O, U, K, and T.

Though the economy of calculation introduced by this result is really remarkable, the reader should not be misled by our simple two-variable, two-constraint example into thinking that the basic theorem transforms programming into a trivial problem. As we shall see presently, in any real programming problem the number of corners of the feasible region is likely to be astronomical, and only a really powerful computational technique can hope to arrive at an optimal selection among them.

4. Slack Variables, Feasible Solutions, and Basic Solutions

For later use both the programming problem and the basic theorem of linear programming need to be restated somewhat. First, let us employ our numerical example to illustrate the required reformulation of the linear programming problem. For this purpose we make use of two additional symbols, T and C, to represent unused machine time and warehouse capacity, so that the statement $C = 10,000$ means that 10,000 square feet of warehouse space remains unused. T and C are called *slack variables* (in contrast, variables such as W, X, and Y will be called *structural* or *ordinary variables*). With the aid of these symbols our problem (1) can be written in a manner to which we shall refer as the *equality form* of the program:

$$(2) \quad \begin{cases} \text{maximize } 5W + 3X + 2Y + 7Z \\[4pt] \text{given the constraints} \\[4pt] \quad 0.5W + 2X + 1.9Y + 3.1Z + T = 32,000 \\[4pt] \quad 10W + 1.2X + 7Y + 4Z + C = 50,000 \\[4pt] \text{and the nonnegativity requirements} \\[4pt] W \geq 0, \quad X \geq 0, \quad Y \geq 0, \quad Z \geq 0, \quad T \geq 0, \quad C \geq 0. \end{cases}$$

Thus by adding two new *nonnegative* slack variables, we have been able to change all of the inequalities into equations except, of course, for the nonnegativity requirements. To interpret T and C in a manner comparable with the other variables, we may consider these slack variables to represent costless processes whose function is to "use up" otherwise unemployed machine time and warehouse capacity. In solving a programming problem we are interested also in the optimal values of these slack variables, for they indicate which of the firm's facilities will constitute bottlenecks (facilities whose slack variables have value zero) and to what extent there should be idle capacity in the remaining facilities.

We now give two other useful definitions.

Feasible solution: Any values of our variables (W, X, Y, Z, T, and C) which satisfy *both* the constraints and the nonnegativity conditions are said to constitute a feasible solution.

Basic solution: Any set of values of our variables in which the number of nonzero-valued variables (either ordinary or slack) is equal to the number of constraints is called a basic solution.

The latter, apparently arbitrary definition, is highly important and is best grasped with the aid of an illustration. Consider the following three alternative possible solutions to our problem:

1st possible solution:

$$W = 0, \qquad X = 16{,}000, \quad Y = 0, \quad Z = 0, \quad T = 0, \qquad C = 30{,}800$$

2nd possible solution:

$$W = 2{,}000, \quad X = 0, \qquad Y = 0, \quad Z = 0, \quad T = 31{,}000, \quad C = 30{,}000$$

3rd possible solution:

$$W = 0, \qquad X = 0, \qquad Y = 0, \quad Z = 0, \quad T = 7{,}000, \qquad C = 16{,}000.$$

Since our problem contains two ordinary (structural) constraints, our first possible solution is a basic solution *because it involves exactly two nonzero-valued variables,* $X = 16{,}000$ and $C = 30{,}800$. For a similar reason the second solution is nonbasic—it contains three nonzero-valued variables, one more than the number of constraints. The reader should verify that the third solution is a basic solution. He should also note that our first solution is feasible (since each variable is assigned a nonnegative value and since, substituting the proposed values $W = 0$, $X = 16{,}000$, etc., into the constraint equations in (2), we see that both equations are satisfied). Similarly, he should check that solution 2 is feasible while solution 3 is not.

Let us now interpret diagrammatically our three new concepts: slack variable, feasible solution, and basic solution. For this purpose consider

Figure 3, which represents the following single-constraint two-variable problem:

$$\text{maximize} \quad P_x X + P_y Y$$

$$\text{subject to} \quad a_x X + a_y Y + T = K$$

$$X \geq 0, \qquad Y \geq 0, \qquad T \geq 0,$$

where X and Y are our ordinary (structural) variables, T is a slack variable, and P_x, P_y, a_x, a_y, and K are constants. Our constraint can also be written without a slack variable as $a_x X + a_y Y \leq K$ and it will be recalled that line CC' is the graph of the equation $a_x X + a_y Y = K$. That is, at any point on CC' our constraint resource is used completely to capacity so that our slack T must be equal to zero. However, at points below CC' some of our resource K must be left over (i.e., $a_x X + a_y Y < K$) so that we must have $T > 0$. Moreover, the further we go below CC' the more unused K we will have, i.e., the greater must be the value of T. This, then, is how our slack variable appears in the graph. It is zero at any point on the constraint line and takes a positive value at any point in the feasible region which does not lie on the constraint line. Now we can see that any point in Figure 3 represents values of our three variables X, Y, and T, so any such point may be said to represent a "candidate" solution. It then follows at once that any point in the feasible region represents a feasible

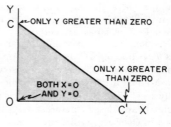

Figure 3

solution: It specifies values for our ordinary variables X and Y and our slack variable T; the point also satisfies our constraint (it does not lie above CC') and it satisfies our nonnegativity requirements (the point does not lie below or to the left of the axes).

It is also possible to show that any and all *basic* feasible solutions are represented by corners of the feasible region, i.e., points 0, C, C' are the three basic feasible solutions of our problem. For at point C we have $Y > 0$ and $X = 0$, and in addition, since this point lies on CC', the slack variable T equals zero. Hence, with one constraint and one nonzero-valued variable the solution represented by C is basic. Similarly, the solution at C' is $X > 0$, $Y = 0$, $T = 0$, which is also basic. Finally, since the origin lies below CC', it leaves unused capacity, so $T > 0$, i.e., at point 0 we have the basic feasible solution $X = 0$, $Y = 0$, $T > 0$. Moreover, no other feasible point represents a basic solution. For example, at any point in the interior of the diagram we have $X > 0$, $Y > 0$, $T > 0$, which, in our one-constraint case, is certainly not a basic solution.[9]

5. The Basic Theorem and the Simplex Method

We may now bring together the two major conclusions of the preceding sections: (1) that an optimal solution can always be found among the corner points 'and (2) that a corner point represents a basic solution. From these we deduce the following version of the *basic theorem of linear programming:*

In any linear programming problem an optimal solution can be found by considering only the basic solutions. That is, there will always exist an optimal solution in which the number of nonzero-valued variables (both ordinary and slack) is *exactly* equal to the number of constraints in the problem.[10]

----

[9] The logic of the argument that corners represent basic feasible solutions may be seen more easily with the aid of an n-constraint two ordinary variable problem. Assuming each of the constraints initially took the form of an inequality, each such constraint will now contain one slack variable so that there will be n slacks in the problem, making $n + 2$ variables altogether.

Now, along each constraint line the corresponding slack variable will equal zero (just as $T = 0$ along CC' in Figure 3), while along the X axis $Y = 0$ and along the Y axis we have $X = 0$. Hence, at a point on *any* line bordering the feasible region some one variable is equal to zero. Since at a corner in our two-dimensional diagram two such lines normally meet (e.g., CC' and the X axis meet at point C') at a corner, we will have *two* zero-valued variables. Therefore, because there are $n + 2$ variables altogether, at a corner exactly n of them will ordinarily be nonzero. In sum, since at a corner n variables take nonzero values in an n-constraint problem, the corner point must represent a basic solution.

This argument also shows why noncorner points in the feasible region represent nonbasic solutions. The same argument can also be extended to a case involving a multiplicity of ordinary variables, though this requires a diagram of as many dimensions as ordinary variables (with one axis for each variable).

The entire discussion abstracts from the special problem of *degeneracy*, which is discussed briefly in the next footnote. Degeneracy occurs if, fortuitously, more than two of the lines bounding a feasible region happen to meet at the same corner point. The reader will recognize that then more than two variables will have zero values at such a corner point and the preceding argument has to be modified for such cases.

[10] Some other types of solution sometimes occur. We have seen that if our iso-profit lines are parallel to a constraint line then there are some optimal noncorner points (involving a number of nonzero-valued variables which exceeds the number of constraints). However, in such circumstances these nonbasic optimal points are no better than the adjacent corner (basic) points, which are also optimal.

An exception to the basic theorem as stated is the case of *degeneracy* defined in the preceding footnote, in which more than two constraint lines happen to pass through a corner point (or more than n-constraint hyperplanes coincide at a point in the n ordinary

This is really a very surprising result. It states that for a firm which has, say, twelve inputs of fixed capacity and is producing 500 products, a linear programming calculation will indicate that the company can maximize its profits by cutting its product line (the number of nonzero-valued ordinary variables) down to no more than twelve items! This result should properly be viewed with suspicion and it must be recognized that its validity depends completely on the validity of the linearity assumption, as will be shown in our discussion of nonlinear programming. In practice, a businessman must be very sure to confirm the linearity of his problem before accepting such radical advice.

We can grasp the rationale of the basic theorem by recognizing that if there are constant returns to scale and there is only one constraint, say only machine time is limited, it will pay to expand up to capacity the production of only one item—that good which yields the highest profit per machine-hour. This is so because there are no diminishing returns to the production of this item, so that if it is the most profitable of products in its use of machine time at any output level it will continue to be the most profitable as its output increases. But if warehouse space, too, is limited, it will usually also be profitable to introduce a second item, one which yields a high return per unit of warehouse space, and so on. In sum, it will normally pay to introduce additional outputs only as the number of constraints (scarce inputs) is increased.

The basic theorem also enables us to grasp the enormous magnitude of the task of calculation which linear programming performs and thus to recognize its truly remarkable achievement. Let us deal with what, in practice, is a *very* small problem—that of a firm which is considering ninety possible goods from among which it will select its product line. Suppose that it has ten scarce resources so that it may be expected to produce ten items or less. The number of basic solutions in the problem is the number of combinations of ten nonzero-valued variables which can be selected from among the 100 variables (ninety ordinary variables and ten slacks) in the program. The standard calculation of the arithmetic of permutations and combinations tells us that the number of such combinations is in excess of 17,000,000,000,000! Thus, if a hard-working management were to devote no more than one second to the examination of each of these possible product-line combinations and were to devote 12 hours per day and 365 days per year to the task, elementary arithmetic indicates that the job would require

---

variable case). Here the solution may involve less than m nonzero-valued variables in an m-constraint problem.

In practice most degeneracy problems can be dealt with easily by the introduction of a tiny artificial shift into one of the constraint lines so that it no longer passes exactly through the intersection of the others. In the remainder of the book it will be assumed that our problems are not degenerate.

more than one million years to complete! What happens when such decisions are made by traditional methods is that only a very small subset of the possible combinations is actually considered and, as a result, the likelihood that some of the best possibilities will be overlooked is very great indeed. Linear programming has to its credit a very noteworthy achievement in permitting solutions to such problems to be found (with the aid of computers) in a matter of minutes or even seconds.

The simplex method[11] is the computational technique most frequently used to deal with problems such as that just described and with other problems which are vastly larger—some of them involving many thousands of variables and constraints. It is therefore rather pleasant to discover that a method powerful enough to deal with such difficult problems is fairly simple in principle. Before going on to study the details of the simplex method, it is useful to look briefly at the process as a whole. It will be recognized that at the heart of the method is the basic theorem's assurance that an optimal solution can always be found among the corners of the feasible region and that all other points in the diagram can be ignored in the calculation. In outline, the method proceeds as follows:

1. Find any basic solution—i.e., any corner of the feasible region (this is not as easy as it sounds—if the origin is a corner of the feasible region as in our diagrams, it can save a lot of trouble to start here). Suppose then we start at O (Figure 1).

2. Compute the profits at point O and at the adjacent corners T and U.[12]

3. If one or both of the latter yield higher profits than does O, move to the corner which offers more profit (per unit of output), say to U.

4. Now repeat steps 2 and 3 substituting point U for point O. Thus compute profits at K and see if they are higher than those at U; if so, move to K; otherwise stay at U. In this way, by successive elimination, we must eventually find the optimal point.[13] This sounds much easier than it is in practice. Most of the work arises in just locating the (adjacent) corners of the feasible region.

---

[11] The name was not chosen to imply that the procedure is simple. Roughly, a simplex may be described as the N-dimensional analogue of a triangle. The outline of the computations, below, indicates that the method consists in successive investigation of adjacent corners of a figure which can be broken up into a series of simplexes.

[12] This is not quite accurate. In practice, we only compute the change in profits resulting from a small move in the direction of T or U. A theorem states that in a linear problem if such a small move is profitable, so is the move all the way to T or U (because in a *linear* program there are no diminishing returns).

[13] We do not have to try every point because it can be shown that if no move to an *adjacent* corner increases profits we are at an optimum. If both O and K are less profitable than U, it is unnecessary to try T.

6. The Initial Basic Solution, Feasibility and Optimality Criteria

For reasons which will soon be given it is convenient to make one slight and final modification in the formulation of problem (2) by bringing all of the terms involving ordinary variables over to the right-hand side of the equations:

(3)

$$\begin{cases} \text{maximize} \quad \text{profits} = 0 + 5W + 3X + 2Y + 7Z \\ \text{subject to} \\ T = 32{,}000 - 0.5W - 2X - 1.9Y - 3.1Z \\ C = 50{,}000 - 10W - 1.2X - 7Y - 4Z \end{cases}$$

or, in more general notation,

(3a) $$\max Z = a_{00} + a_{01}X_1 + \cdots + a_{0n}X_n$$

subject to

(3b) $$t_1 = a_{10} + a_{11}X_1 + \cdots + a_{1n}X_n$$
$$\cdot \cdot \cdot \cdot \cdot \cdot \cdot \cdot \cdot \cdot \cdot \cdot \cdot \cdot \cdot$$
$$t_m = a_{m0} + a_{m1}X_1 + \cdots + a_{mn}X_n$$

(3c) $$\text{all} \quad t_i \geq 0 \quad \text{and all} \quad X_j \geq 0,$$

where the X_j are ordinary variables, the t_i are slack variables, and the a_{ij} are constants. (The notation X_j is used to represent any one of the numbers, $X_1, X_2, \cdots, X_n$ and similarly t_i and a_{ij} represent any one of the t variables and any of the a's, respectively.)

This form (3) has substantial advantages, because, as will now be shown, it permits us to accomplish three important things. Just by inspection we can (a) write out a basic solution, (b) check whether this solution is feasible, and (c) check whether it is optimal.

(a) *The basic solution.* The first step in the simplex method is to find some (any) basic feasible solution. In many cases, a basic feasible solution is easily obtained by setting all ordinary variables equal to zero and setting each slack variable equal to the corresponding capacity figure. For then we have

RULE 1. *A basic solution:* A basic solution of (3) is

(4) $T = 32{,}000, \qquad C = 50{,}000, \qquad \text{and} \qquad W = X = Y = Z = 0$

or, in the more general case [Equations (3a) to (3c)],

(4a) $t_1 = a_{10}, t_2 = a_{20}, \cdots, t_m = a_{m0}$ and $X_1 = X_2 = \cdots = X_n = 0.$

Since there are exactly as many nonzero variables as there are constraints (two or m), (4) and (4a) are clearly basic solutions.

This is the solution in which all facilities are left idle and the only nonzero activities are disposal activities. It is the basic solution represented by the origin in the previous diagrams. It will ordinarily be far from an optimal solution since, if it were optimal, the best alternative open to the businessman would be for him to close up his firm altogether. Nevertheless, this basic solution is so easily found that it is usually a good idea to employ it as a starting point for the calculation.

(b) *Feasibility check.* If and only if all of the constant terms $a_{10}, a_{20}, \cdots,$ a_{m0} in (3b) are nonnegative the basic solution (4a) is feasible, i.e., it satisfies all of the requirements (3b) and (3c). Equations (3b) are clearly satisfied by (4a), as we can see by substitution, and since the variables take on the non-negative values $a_{10}, a_{20}, \cdots, a_{m0}$ and zero, the nonnegativity requirements (3c) are also clearly satisfied. Hence, we can tell at once by just looking at (3b) whether (4a) is feasible since

RULE 2. *Feasibility:* The basic solution (4) is feasible if and only if all of the constant terms $a_{10}, a_{20}, \cdots, a_{m0},$ in (3b) are nonnegative.

Before describing the equally simple optimality test, it is necessary to outline the rest of the computational procedure. It will be observed that all of the variables which take nonzero values in our basic solution (4a) appear on the left-hand side of (3b) whereas all of the zero-valued variables appear on the right-hand side of (3a) and (3b). It is this convenient arrangement which permits us to say that the solution (4) is feasible if the constant terms in (3b) are nonnegative. Therefore, whenever we try out a new basic solution in our computational procedure we will rewrite the equations in the corresponding form—the variables which at that stage are possibly nonzero on the left, and all other variables on the right. We will thus proceed as follows:

We will keep moving from basic solution to basic solution (from corner to corner in our diagrams). This means we will want one variable X_j which was previously zero to become nonzero, and one variable t_i which was formerly nonzero in solution (4) to become zero. In this way we keep the right number of positive elements in the solution for the solution to continue basic [as many positive elements as constraints (3b)].

In making these substitutions and rewriting the system in form (3) each time (with nonzero variables on the left), naturally the coefficient (a_{ij}) figures will be replaced by new values, and these new values must be computed for each step. Each time, moreover, we must stop to see whether we have arrived at the optimum which we are seeking. We then have the following convenient test for optimality:

(c) *Optimality check.* Suppose we reach a stage where all of the revalued coefficients a'_{oj} of the variables in the objective function (3a) are negative (or zero). It can be seen by inspection that the corresponding solution (4) for this stage of the operation is not only basic and feasible, but it must be optimal. For if the objective function at that stage is, say, $Z = 23 - 7X'_1 - 12X'_2$, where X'_1 and X'_2 are the variables which appear on the right in (3) at that stage of the computations, then since X_1 and X_2 must take nonnegative values, the largest possible value of Z (i.e., 23) will be obtained by setting $X_1 = X_2 = 0$. In other words, any other basic solution, in which either X_1 or X_2 must be positive, cannot possibly yield a higher profit, Z. Thus

RULE 3. *Optimality:* A basic solution such as (4a) is optimal if and only if none of the coefficients of the objective function (3a) corresponding to that basic solution is positive.

This condition, that the coefficients of the X_i be nonpositive, has, incidentally, a simple economic interpretation. The coefficient of X_i in the objective function is the contribution to total profit of an additional unit of X_i (the marginal profit of X_i). If the coefficients of the X_i are all negative or zero, all of the X_i will yield negative or zero marginal profits. Hence it will not pay to introduce any of these activities into the firm's operations—the optimal solution will require all of these $X_i = 0$.

Let us now examine the details of the computation with the aid of a two-variable numerical example:

$$\text{maximize}\quad 2.5X_1 + 2X_2$$

subject to

$$X_1 + 2X_2 \le 8{,}000$$

$$3X_1 + 2X_2 \le 9{,}000$$

$$X_1 \ge 0, \qquad X_2 \ge 0.$$

To put this problem into our standard form (3) we must insert two slack variables, S_a and S_b, and bring all terms involving the ordinary variables X_1 and X_2 over to the right. This gives us

(3′)
$$\text{maximize}\quad Z = 0 + 2.5X_1 + 2X_2$$

subject to

$$S_a = 8{,}000 - X_1 - 2X_2$$

$$S_b = 9{,}000 - 3X_1 - 2X_2$$

$$S_a \ge 0, \qquad S_b \ge 0, \qquad X_1 \ge 0, \qquad X_2 \ge 0.$$

We write out the table or *matrix* of coefficients corresponding to system (3′) at this stage of the computation. This is just a table which provides a convenient summary of the numerical data in our system (3′).

		1	X_1	X_2
	$Z =$	0	(2.5)	(2)
(5)	$S_a =$	8,000	-1	-2
	$S_b =$	9,000	(-3^*)	(-2)

Our first basic solution is clearly

$$(4') \qquad S_a = 8{,}000, \qquad S_b = 9{,}000, \qquad X_1 = X_2 = 0$$

so that in matrix (5) the zero-valued variables X_1 and X_2 appear at the top and positive-valued variables appear along the left side. The equals signs after the variables indicate that the matrix represents a system of equations each with terms involving the variables X_1, and X_2 and a constant term (i.e., a term in which the coefficient is multiplied by unity, rather than by a variable).

7. The Next Basic Solution: The Pivoting Process

Next, we wish to arrive at a new basic solution and the corresponding matrix for this following step. To do this, we must give a positive value to one of the variables which was zero in the previous solution (4′) and a zero value to one of the formerly nonzero variables. That is, in the next matrix we will want to move one of the top variables, say X_1, over to the left side, and move one of the left-hand (formerly nonzero) variables, say S_b, over to the top. In such a case where we are interchanging the roles of X_1 and S_b we say we are pivoting on the corresponding element, -3, in the S_b (horizontal) row and X_1 (vertical) column in the matrix, and we mark that element with an asterisk.

How we choose which element to interchange will be examined presently. First we must discuss the effect of the interchange. Consider first the equation in which element S_b appears,

$$S_b = 9{,}000 - 3^*X_1 - 2X_2,$$

where the asterisk is retained on the -3 to remind us that it is the pivot.

We require that this and the other constraints (3′) continue to hold since the firm's capacity limitations continue unchanged. But we now want these constraints rewritten with a new arrangement of the variables, i.e., with S_b on their right in place of variable X_1. We want the preceding equation to be replaced by an equivalent equation with X_1 on the left and S_b on the right. This new equation is obtained by dividing through by the coefficient of X_1, i.e., by the pivot element -3^*, and transposing, to obtain

$$(6) \quad X_1 = \frac{-9{,}000}{-3^*} + \frac{1}{-3^*} \, S_b + \frac{2}{-3^*} \, X_2 = 3{,}000 - \frac{1}{3} \, S_b - \frac{2}{3} \, X_2.$$

This is our new third equation and its coefficients are, therefore, the elements of the last row of the next matrix (7).

(7)   (incomplete)

	1	S_b	X_2
$Z =$			
$S_a =$			
$X_1 =$	3,000	$-\frac{1}{3}$	$-\frac{2}{3}$

Similarly, to obtain the remaining terms in the matrix, we must replace the former zero-valued variable, X_1, by the new zero variable S_b in the other two equations of (3'). For this purpose we substitute the expression (6) for X_1 into the objective function and the other constraint in the original system (3'). We obtain

$$Z = 0 + 2.5 \left(\frac{-9{,}000}{-3^*} + \frac{1}{-3^*} \, S_b + \frac{2}{-3^*} \, X_2 \right) + 2X_2$$

$$S_a = 8{,}000 - \left(\frac{-9{,}000}{-3^*} + \frac{1}{-3^*} \, S_b + \frac{2}{-3^*} \, X_2 \right) - 2X_2.$$

By collecting terms we obtain the new coefficients of our variables S_b and X_2 in these equations and the new constant terms. These are the remaining elements of the new matrix (7). Thus, we have

$$Z = \left(0 - \frac{(2.5)\,(9{,}000)}{-3^*} \right) + \frac{2.5}{-3^*} \, S_b + \left(2 - \frac{(2.5)\,(-2)}{-3^*} \right) X_2$$

(8)

$$S_a = \left(8{,}000 - \frac{(-1)\,(9{,}000)}{-3^*} \right) + \frac{-1}{-3^*} \, S_b + \left(-2 - \frac{(-1)\,(-2)}{-3^*} \right) X_2,$$

that is,

(9)
$$Z = 7{,}500 - \tfrac{5}{6}S_b + \tfrac{1}{3}X_2$$
$$S_a = 5{,}000 + \tfrac{1}{3}S_b - \tfrac{4}{3}X_2.$$

These are the coefficients of the first and second rows of matrix (7):

		1	S_b	X_2
	$Z =$	7,500	$-\tfrac{5}{6}$	$\tfrac{1}{3}$
(7)	$S_a =$	5,000	$\tfrac{1}{3}$	$-\tfrac{4}{3}*$
	$X_1 =$	3,000	$-\tfrac{1}{3}$	$-\tfrac{2}{3}$

Equations (6) and (9) or, alternatively, matrix (7) give us our next trial basic solution. By an extension of Rule 1 we have for this solution $S_b = X_2 = 0$, so that $S_a = 5{,}000$ and $X_1 = 3{,}000$. By Rule 2 this is a feasible solution. Note also that we now have profit, $Z = 7{,}500$, which is a considerable improvement over the previous zero profit level of matrix (5).

We are now ready to choose another pivot and repeat this procedure as many times as necessary until an optimal basic solution (as indicated by Rule 3) is found. That is all there is to the simplex method. Once we have found out how to choose the pivot element (Section 9), we shall then have gone over the entire procedure.

8. Special Pivoting Rules[14]

However, before going on it is convenient to describe a method which avoids a good deal of the work involved in the preceding equation-manipulating procedures. The four rules which follow reduce the entire pivoting process to some very elementary arithmetic. Unfortunately, a statement of the rules does not make light or interesting reading. However, experi-

---

[14] This section makes rather tedious reading. However, it does show a way in which the simplex computation can be considerably simplified. The reader may prefer to skip this and all except the first and last paragraphs of Section 10 (in which the method is reviewed) or he may prefer to return to this material later.

ence indicates that once the reader has employed them on a problem he will find them exceedingly easy to use and to remember.

The coefficients of Equation (6) of the previous section illustrate the following two rules for finding the elements in the new simplex matrix which replace the elements in which the pivot previously appeared [the last row in matrix (5)][15]:

RULE 4. *Pivot element:* The element which replaces the old pivot $(-3*)$ is simply the number 1 divided by the old pivot element $(1/-3*)$, i.e., it is the reciprocal of the old pivot element.

RULE 5. *Other pivot row elements:* Any other element in this row of the matrix is obtained by changing the sign of the corresponding old element and dividing by the old pivot element. For example, the lower left-hand element, 9,000 in matrix (5), is replaced by $-9,000/-3* = 3,000$. Similarly, Equations (8) illustrate the following rules for the replacement of the remaining elements of the matrix:

RULE 6. *Other pivot column elements:* Any other element in the (vertical) column which contained the old pivot is replaced by the corresponding old element divided by the old pivot. Thus, the number 2.5 in the second (pivot) column of (5) is replaced by $2.5/-3* = -5/6$ in the new matrix (7).

RULE 7. *All other elements:* The last rule for the transformation of the remaining elements of (5) is also the most complicated of the four, but a little practice can make it fairly easy to follow: To replace, e.g., the element 2 in the upper right-hand corner of (5), consider its position relative to that of the pivot element. Now find the corner elements, one in the pivot row and one in the pivot column [the circled elements 2.5 and -2 in matrix (5)], which together with the pivot element and the element to be replaced (the other circled elements) form the four corners of a rec-

---

[15] A general proof is the following: Let the original equation of (3b) which contains the pivot element a_{vw}^* be

$$t_v = a_{v0} + a_{v1}X_1 + \cdots + a_{vw}^*X_w + \cdots + a_{vn}X_n.$$

Then, to solve for X_w (the new nonzero variable) in terms of t_v (the variable whose value will be zero in the next basic solution) we divide through by the pivot, a_{vw}^*, and transpose terms to obtain

$$(6a) \qquad X_w = -\frac{a_{v0}}{a_{vw}^*} - \frac{a_{v1}}{a_{vw}^*}X_1 - \cdots + \frac{1}{a_{vw}^*}t_v - \cdots - \frac{a_{vn}}{a_{vw}^*}X_n$$

so that Rules 4 and 5 hold generally.

tangle. Then follow the formula[16]

(10)   new element = corresponding old element

$$- \frac{\text{product of the two (other) corner elements}}{\text{old pivot element}}$$

e.g.,
$$\frac{1}{3} = 2 - \frac{(2.5)\,(-2)}{-3*}$$

so that $\frac{1}{3}$ is the upper right-hand element in the next matrix (7).[17]

9. Choosing the Pivot

We need only one more result and our description of the simplex method is complete. We need only decide which element to choose as the pivot element. Here we have two rules:

RULE 8. *Choice of pivot column:* The pivot element is (as a matter of good computational strategy) chosen to come from that column, w, which has the largest positive top element.

---

[16] The reader may find the following alternative formulation easier to remember because of its symmetry. Form the cross product of circled elements in (5), which is given by

cross product = old element times pivot element minus the product
of the other two corner elements.

Then we have the following formula, which the reader may readily show to be equivalent to (10):

$$\text{new element} = \frac{\text{cross product}}{\text{old pivot element}}.$$

[17] In the general case Rules 6 and 7 are obtained by substituting the last equation (6a) in footnote 15 for X_w in the general (nonpivot-row) equation of (3a) or (3b):

$$t_i = a_{i0} + a_{i1}X_1 + \cdots + a_{iw}X_w + \cdots + a_{in}X_n.$$

This substitution yields

$$t_i = a_{i0} + a_{i1}X_1 + \cdots$$

$$+ a_{iw}\left(-\frac{a_{v0}}{a_{vw}^*} - \frac{a_{v1}}{a_{vw}^*}X_1 - \cdots + \frac{1}{a_{vw}^*}t_v - \cdots - \frac{a_{vn}}{a_{vw}^*}X_n \right) + \cdots + a_{in}X_n$$

or, collecting terms,

$$t_i = \left(a_{i0} - \frac{a_{iw}a_{v0}}{a_{vw}^*} \right) + \left(a_{i1} - \frac{a_{iw}a_{v1}}{a_{vw}^*} \right)X_1 + \cdots + \frac{a_{iw}}{a_{vw}^*}t_v + \cdots + \left(a_{in} - \frac{a_{iw}a_{vn}}{a_{vw}^*} \right)X_n$$

in which the bracketed expressions give us formula (10) (Rule 7) and the unbracketed coefficient gives us Rule 6, above.

Thus in matrix (5) the pivot column, w, must be the second column because its top element, 2.5, is positive and larger than that of any other column. To see why we choose the pivot column by this rule, note that by picking this second column for our pivot column we have decided to make the corresponding variable X_1 [or X_w, in the general matrix (11) in footnote 18] nonzero in the next basic (corner) solution. But the positive number 2.5 is the coefficient of X_1 in the objective function. We are, therefore, introducing a variable (an output), X_1, whose marginal profit, 2.5, is positive and greater than the marginal profit of any other formerly zero variable (e.g., the profit derivable from the introduction of a unit of X_2 is only 2). This is precisely what we want to do in order to increase profit rapidly at the next step.[18]

But which of the numbers in this column, w (the second column), should be chosen as the pivot element? Here we have another rule:

RULE 9. *Choice of pivot element:* Take each *negative* element in the chosen column and use it to divide the corresponding element in the first column. The element for which the resulting quotient is smallest in absolute value (i.e., smallest, ignoring sign) must be chosen as pivot.

For example, in matrix (5) the pivot is to be chosen from the second column whose only negative elements are -1 and -3. Dividing the cor-

---

[18] We choose our pivot column in this way because at each step of the computation we desire to increase the value of the objective function (total profit) which is the element in the upper left-hand corner of the matrix (a_{00}). We therefore want to choose our pivot in a way which will, by formula (10), increase the value of this element a_{00}. In the general matrix (11) we note that if a_{vw}^* is chosen as pivot the two circled corner

$$
\begin{array}{ccccccc}
 & & 1 & \cdots & X_w & \cdots & X_n \\
Z = & & \left(a_{00}\right) & \cdots & \left(a_{0w}\right) & \cdots & a_{0n} \\
 & & \cdots & \cdots & \cdots & \cdots & \cdots \\
(11) \quad t_v = & & \left(a_{v0}\right) & \cdots & \left(a_{vw}^*\right) & \cdots & a_{vn} \\
 & & \cdots & \cdots & \cdots & \cdots & \cdots \\
t_m = & & a_{m0} & \cdots & a_{mw} & \cdots & a_{mn}
\end{array}
$$

elements which complete the a_{00}-pivot rectangle include one element, a_{v0}, from the first column and one, a_{0w}, from the first row. The former, a_{v0}, must be nonnegative because we began with a feasible solution. Hence, if we pick a_{0w} *positive and our pivot negative* (by rule 9), the fraction $-a_{v0}a_{0w}/a_{vw}^*$ must be positive. Hence by formula (10) since this is the change in a_{00}, it follows that a_{00} will be increased.

responding first-column elements by these numbers, we have the quotients $8,000/-1 = -8,000$ and $9,000/-3 = -3,000$. The latter of these is clearly the smaller in absolute value and hence the corresponding element -3 of the column in question *must* be chosen as pivot.

The reason we must choose this element can be explained intuitively.[19] When we introduce the new output X_1 into the solution, some of the firm's limited productive capacity must be diverted from its current outputs and used for the production of X_1. Thus, the quantities of other outputs will be reduced. We can increase the quantity of the profitable output X_1 only so long as sufficient capacity remains to be taken away from other outputs. We therefore must stop increasing the output of X_1 when the production of some other commodity, call it W, is cut down to zero, for any further increase in X_1 would require a negative output of W, which is impossible. W will, then, be the output which is cut to zero in the next basic solution, i.e., the pivot element will be in the row of the old matrix (5) which corresponds to output W.

To find which will be commodity W we must find which output is first reduced to zero by an expansion of the production of X_1. Let us therefore see what happens to each of the previously nonzero "outputs," S_a and S_b, when we increase X_1 in matrix (5). By the first constraint equation in (3'), a unit increase in X_1 decreases the output of S_a by 1 unit [the second element in the pivot column of matrix (5)—i.e., the element in the S_a row and X_1 column of that matrix]. Since there are 8,000 units of S_a to begin with in the previous solution (4') [the element in the S_a row and first column of matrix (5)], it will take $8,000/1 = 8,000$ units of X_1 to reduce S_a to zero.

Now, compare the effect of the increase in X_1 on S_b. By the second

---

[19] A rigorous proof which is relatively simple but not very intuitive is the following: We require all the elements a'_{i0} in the first column of the next matrix to be nonnegative so that the next basic solution will also be feasible. But by (10) that new element will be

$$a'_{i0} = a_{i0} - \frac{a_{iw}a_{v0}}{a^*_{vw}}.$$

If this is to be nonnegative for every such element i, we must have (for negative a_{iw} and a^*_{vw})

$$a_{i0} - \frac{-a_{iw}a_{v0}}{-a^*_{vw}} \geq 0, \quad \text{i.e.,} \quad \frac{a_{i0}}{-a_{iw}} \geq \frac{a_{v0}}{-a^*_{vw}}$$

so that the pivot element a^*_{vw} must yield such a fraction which is no larger than that corresponding to any other element a_{iw} in the same column w.

The reader should show that if some a_{iw} is not negative we must always have $a'_{i0} \geq a_{i0} \geq 0$ so that such elements can never be reduced to zero (a_{iw} cannot be the pivot), nor can they produce a nonfeasible solution ($a'_{i0} < 0$). That is why this proof deals only with negative a_{iw}, and why the pivot element must always be negative.

equation in $(3')$ a unit increase in X_1 decreases S_b by 3 units [the element, 3, in the S_b row and X_1 column of matrix (5)], and since there are 9,000 units of S_b to begin with (the element in the S_b row and first column), S_b production will be eliminated altogether with a $9,000/3 = 3,000$-unit output of X_1. Hence S_b will be reduced to zero before we can reach the 8,000-unit output of X_1 needed to eliminate output S_a. It is therefore impossible to expand the output of X_1 beyond 3,000 units, and S_b will be the output which is reduced to zero in the next basic solution; that is, the element, -3, in the S_b row and X_1 column must be the pivot in matrix (5) because the ratio $9,000/3$, the output of X_1 which reduces S_b to zero, is smaller than $8,000/1$, the corresponding figure for output S_a. This is our Rule 9 for the choice of pivot element.

10. Illustration: Another Pivot Step

This completes the discussion of the simplex-method computation. However, the reader may have found it confusing on first reading, and a careful description of the computation of the next matrix may help to pull the preceding material together into a clear pattern. We notice that in the previous matrix (7) there is only one column (the last) whose top element is positive. The pivot must therefore be chosen from this column (Rule 8). Both remaining elements in this column are negative, and to choose the pivot we must find the quotients obtained by dividing the corresponding first-column elements by these. The quotients are

$$\frac{5,000}{-\frac{4}{3}} = -3750 \quad \text{and} \quad \frac{3,000}{-\frac{2}{3}} = -4,500.$$

Since the former is the smaller quotient in absolute value, $-\frac{4}{3}$, the element in the S_a row and X_2 column, becomes the pivot element (Rule 9). That means the roles of variables X_2 and S_a are to be interchanged in the next matrix, where S_a will be reduced to zero and X_2 will become positive. The new matrix is then produced as follows:

1. Interchange X_2 and S_a in the column and row headings so that the third column is now labeled S_a and the second row is called X_2.[20]

2. The pivot element $-\frac{4}{3}$ in (7) is replaced by its reciprocal $-\frac{3}{4}$, and the rest of the elements of the pivot row are replaced by the corresponding old elements in (7), each multiplied by -1 and divided by the pivot $(-\frac{4}{3})$,

---

[20] The reader who omitted the special computational techniques of Section 8 is reminded that the remainder of this section [except for matrix (12) and the last paragraph of the section] is just a review of these methods so this material should be skipped by him.

as shown in matrix (12a) (Rules 4 and 5):

$$(12a) \quad
\begin{array}{c}
Z = \\[4pt]
X_2 = \\[4pt]
X_1 =
\end{array}
\quad
\begin{array}{c}
1 \qquad\quad S_b \qquad\quad S_a \\[4pt]
\boxed{\begin{array}{ccc}
 & & \\
-\dfrac{5{,}000}{-\frac{4}{3}} & \dfrac{-\frac{1}{3}}{-\frac{4}{3}} & -\frac{3}{4} \\
 & &
\end{array}}
\end{array}
\quad = X_2 =
\begin{array}{c}
1 \qquad\quad S_b \qquad\quad S_a \\[4pt]
\boxed{\begin{array}{ccc}
 & & \\
3750 & \frac{1}{4} & -\frac{3}{4} \\
 & &
\end{array}}
\end{array}
$$

3. The remaining elements of the pivot column in (7) are replaced by the corresponding old elements each divided by the pivot $(-\frac{4}{3})$ as shown in matrix (12b) (Rule 6):

$$(12b) \quad
\begin{array}{c}
Z = \\[4pt]
X_2 = \\[4pt]
X_1 =
\end{array}
\quad
\begin{array}{c}
1 \qquad\quad S_b \qquad\quad S_a \\[4pt]
\boxed{\begin{array}{ccc}
 & & -\frac{1}{4} \\[6pt]
 & & \\[6pt]
 & & \frac{1}{2}
\end{array}}
\end{array}
$$

4. Finally, the remaining elements in matrix (7) are replaced by use of formula (10) of Rule 7 as shown in matrix (12c):

$$(12c) \quad
\begin{array}{c}
Z = \\[20pt]
X_2 = \\[20pt]
X_1 =
\end{array}
\quad
\begin{array}{c}
1 \qquad\qquad\qquad\qquad S_b \qquad\qquad\qquad\qquad S_a \\[4pt]
\boxed{\begin{array}{ccc}
7{,}500 - \dfrac{(5{,}000)\,(\frac{1}{3})}{-\frac{4}{3}} & -\dfrac{5}{6} - \dfrac{(\frac{1}{3})\,(\frac{1}{3})}{-\frac{4}{3}} & \\[20pt]
 & & \\[6pt]
3{,}000 - \dfrac{(5{,}000)\,(-\frac{2}{3})}{-\frac{4}{3}} & -\dfrac{1}{3} - \dfrac{(\frac{1}{3})\,(-\frac{2}{3})}{-\frac{4}{3}} &
\end{array}}
\end{array}
$$

$$
\begin{array}{c}
Z = \\[4pt]
= X_2 = \\[4pt]
X_1 =
\end{array}
\quad
\begin{array}{c}
1 \qquad\quad S_b \qquad\quad S_a \\[4pt]
\boxed{\begin{array}{ccc}
8{,}750 & -\frac{3}{4} & \\[6pt]
 & & \\[6pt]
500 & -\frac{1}{2} &
\end{array}}
\end{array}
$$

If we now combine the information in (12a), (12b), and (12c), we obtain our new matrix (12):

		1	S_b	S_a
	$Z =$	8,750	$-\frac{3}{4}$	$-\frac{1}{4}$
(12)	$X_2 =$	3,750	$\frac{1}{4}$	$-\frac{3}{4}$
	$X_1 =$	500	$-\frac{1}{2}$	$\frac{1}{2}$

It will be noted that all (except the first) of the elements in the top row are negative. These negative numbers are the marginal profitabilities of the items S_b and S_a, whose outputs are now zero. Hence, by Rule 3, *the corresponding basic solution is optimal* (any nonzero value of S_b and S_a must decrease profit, Z). By (4) this solution is $X_2 = 3,750$, $X_1 = 500$, $S_b = S_a = 0$, and it yields $Z = 8,750$ in profit.

PROBLEMS

1. Maximize $R = 3x + 7y + 6z$ subject to

$$2x + 2y + 2z \leq 8$$
$$x + y \qquad \leq 3$$

$x \geq 0, y \geq 0, z \geq 0.$

2. Maximize $R = 4x + 3y$ subject to

$$x + 3.5y \leq 9$$
$$2x + y \leq 8$$
$$x + y \leq 6$$

$x \geq 0, y \geq 0.$

3. Maximize $R = 4x + 6y$ subject to

$$\tfrac{1}{2}x + y \leq 4$$
$$2x + y \leq 8$$
$$4x - 2y \leq 2$$

$x \geq 0, y \geq 0.$

4. Maximize $R = 4x + y$ subject to

$$x + 2y \leq 5$$
$$3x + 2y \leq 4$$

$x \geq 0, y \geq 0.$

11. Cases Where the Origin is not a Feasible Solution

We started our discussion of the simplex computation by assuming that a feasible basic solution can be found by setting all variables except the slack variables equal to zero. In this way we obtained our first basic solution (4) from which all subsequent trial solutions were derived. Unfortunately, many programming problems are inconsistent with such a solution. Some of the constraints may lack slack variables because they were equations to begin with. Even if this difficulty does not arise, a basic solution in which all variables, except the slack elements, are given the value zero may not be feasible.

For example, consider a program with an inequality of a sort that arises typically out of a minimum-requirements specification. A simplified illustration is an advertising budgeting problem that aims to minimize the cost of getting 160 million exposures among noncollege audiences (the number of times one of the company's advertisements is seen or read by some such person—two persons seeing the same ad or one person seeing two different ads each counts as two "exposures"). Because of the nature of the product, the company wants at least 60 million exposures to involve persons with family incomes over \$8,000 per year, and at least 80 million exposures to involve persons between 18 and 40 years of age. The issue is to decide how to divide the company's budget between magazine and television advertising. Survey information indicates the size and composition of the audiences of the two media. The following table provides all the relevant information:

	Magazine	Television
Cost per ad (thousands of dollars)	40	200
Noncollege audience per ad (millions)	4	40
Audience (per ad) with income over \$8,000 (millions)	3	10
Audience (per ad) ages 18–40 (millions)	8	10

This states, for example, that each magazine advertisement reaches 4 million noncollege graduates, 3 million persons with an income over \$8,000 per year, etc. Now let m and t represent the number of magazine and television advertisements under consideration by the firm, and let α be its total advertising cost. The cost minimization problem, then, is given by the following program:

Minimize $\alpha = 40m + 200t$

subject to

(13)
$$4m + 40t \geq 160 \quad \text{(noncollege requirement)}$$
$$3m + 10t \geq 60 \quad \text{(income requirement)}$$
$$8m + 10t \geq 80 \quad \text{(age requirement)}$$
$$m \geq 0 \qquad t \geq 0.$$

Using slack variables the constraints may be rewritten as

(13a)
$$4m + 40t - l_1 = 160$$
$$3m + 10t - l_2 = 60$$
$$8m + 10t - l_3 = 80$$
$$m \geq 0, \qquad t \geq 0, \qquad l_1 \geq 0, \qquad l_2 \geq 0, \qquad l_3 \geq 0.$$

Here, the nonnegative slack variables, l_1, l_2, and l_3, must be *subtracted* from the left-hand sides of their respective constraints because (unlike the machine time-warehouse capacity constraint problem described earlier in the chapter) the activity levels now to be decided upon must produce a result (e.g., reach an audience) *greater* than or equal to some predetermined level (160 million), not less than or equal to some capacity figure, as before, Hence, if the advertising campaign were to produce an acceptable 164 million noncollege exposures, we must subtract $l_1 = 4$ million from this number to make it equal to the 160 million requirements figure.

Suppose, now, that we try to proceed as we did previously and attempt to obtain an initial feasible basic solution by setting both of our structural variables, m and t, equal to zero. By (13) this yields the absurd result $0 \geq 160$, $0 \geq 60$, $0 \geq 80$, or, alternatively, by (13a), $-160 = l_1 \geq 0$, $-60 = l_2 \geq 0$, and $-80 = l_3 \geq 0$, none of which, obviously, can be true. Hence the approach we used before to begin our simplex calculation, taking the origin as our initial basic solution, just does not work. The reason, in economic terms, is very simple. Where our constraints represent maximal capacities as in the output problem earlier in this chapter, a solution in which all outputs are zero is certainly *feasible* (if not very profitable). Zero outputs will obviously not overstrain the capacity of the firm's facilities. But now, where the constraints represent minimum results that are required for acceptability, zero activity levels will not do the trick. The firm cannot possibly obtain 160 million audience exposures with zero advertising of both varieties. It follows that the easy method we have used previously to find our initial basic solutions, that is, setting all our structural variables equal to zero, does not always work.

We will see in the next chapter that there is an easy alternative procedure that works in most problems that arise naturally out of economic issues.

Duality theory will permit us to substitute for a problem such as (13) another problem, called the dual, for which the origin *is* a feasible basic solution. In the course of finding the solution to this dual problem we will see that we also obtain, automatically, the solution to the initial ("primal") problem (13).[21]

For the moment we will have to content ourselves with a graphic solution of problem (13) which should be illuminating. In Figure 4a we have represented the three constraints in (13). For example, the reader should verify that the line EE'_1 labeled "exposures" represents the equation $4m + 40t = 160$; i.e., it gives all combinations of m and t that just barely satisfy the first constraint, which requires a total of 160 million audience exposures. Similarly II' and AA' correspond, respectively, to the income and age requirement constraints.

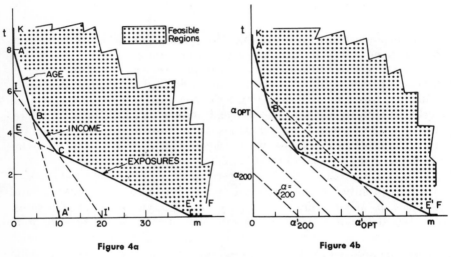

Figure 4a   Figure 4b

Now, since our constraints are all "greater-than-or-equal-to" requirements, feasibility means that each and every one of the minimum requirements represented by the constraint lines must *at least* be met. That is, any point, if it is to represent a feasible combination of m and t, must lie *on or above each and every one* of the constraint lines. The feasible region therefore is the shaded region representing all points that do not lie below any of the constraint lines. This is the shaded region on, or above and to the right of, the polyhedral boundary $KABCE'F$.

---

[21] An appendix to the following chapter will also describe an alternative and somewhat more time-consuming calculation that works generally, even in the unusual cases where the dual method does not.

Our objective now is to minimize total costs—to get onto the lowest of the iso-cost lines that can be reached from the feasible region (Figure 4b). To find these lines we utilize the total advertising cost function, $\alpha = 40m + 200t$. Any iso-cost line is obtained by setting α equal to some constant. For example, taking $\alpha = 200$ we obtain the equation $200 = 40m + 200t$ which is represented by the straight-line segment labeled $\alpha = 200$. All the other iso-cost lines are parallel to this one, since a change in the value of α does not affect the coefficients of m and t in the cost equation and, hence, does not change the slope of the iso-cost line.

The lowest of these iso-cost lines that can be reached from the feasible region is obviously the one labeled α_{opt}, and it touches the feasible region at corner point C. Thus, C represents the optimal solution and we read from the graph that it corresponds, at least approximately, to the values $m = 10$, $t = 3$.

That completes our graphic solution. However, several additional observations may be illuminating. Once we have found the approximate solution to a linear program graphically, it is generally easy to go on to determine the solution values precisely. As usual in linear programming, a solution will occur at some corner of the diagram. In the two structural variable cases that can be handled diagrammatically, two constraint lines will always meet at such a corner. Thus, once we know which corner and, hence, which constraint lines go through the solution point, we can find the coordinates of the solution point by solving the two corresponding constraint equations simultaneously. In the case in Figure 4 the optimal point C is the intersection of the exposures and the income constraint lines. Consequently, we can find the values of m and t by solving simultaneously the two corresponding constraint equations

$$4m + 40t = 160$$
$$3m + 10t = 60.$$

The reader can verify directly from these equations that the optimal solution is in fact given *exactly* by $m = 10$, $t = 3$, the values we had read off from Figure 4.

There is one other observation that we can usefully draw from the graph. We note in Figure 4 that the origin lies outside the feasible region. This is in clear contrast with the cases represented in Figures 1, 2, and 3, where the origin is a corner of the shaded feasible region. That gives us another way of seeing why, in our earlier calculations, we could start off by taking the origin as our initial basic-feasible solution, but why we can no longer do so in the problem (13) which we are now discussing.

REFERENCES

Beale, E. M. L., *Mathematical Programming in Practice*, Pitman, New York, 1968.

Charnes, A., and W. W. Cooper, *Management Models and Industrial Applications of Linear Programming*, Volumes I and II, John Wiley & Sons, New York, 1961.

Dantzig, George B., *Linear Programming and Extensions*, Princeton University Press, Princeton, N.J., 1963.

Dorfman, Robert, Paul A. Samuelson, and Robert M. Solow, *Linear Programming and Economic Analysis*, McGraw-Hill Book Company, New York, 1958.

Gale, D., *The Theory of Linear Economic Models*, McGraw-Hill Book Company, New York, 1960.

Gass, S. I., *Linear Programming: Methods and Applications*, 3rd ed., McGraw-Hill Book Company, New York, 1969.

Zionts, S., *Linear and Integer Programming*, Prentice-Hall, Inc., Englewood Cliffs, N.J., 1974.

Duality

6

1. The Dual Problem

With every linear programming maximization problem it has proved useful to associate a closely related minimization problem and vice versa. Such pairs of problems are called *dual linear programming problems*.[1] The analysis of dual programming problems has attracted a great deal of attention among both economists and mathematicians, for a number of reasons:

1. Duality yields a number of powerful theorems which add substantially to our understanding of linear programming.

2. Duality analysis has been very helpful in the solution of programming problems. Indeed, as we shall see, it is frequently easier to find the solution of a programming problem by first solving its associated dual problem.

3. The dual problem turns out to have an extremely illuminating economic interpretation which, incidentally, shows that old-fashioned marginal analysis is always implicitly involved in the search for an optimal solution of a linear programming problem.

Before we turn to the economic interpretation of the dual, it will be desirable to describe the meaning of duality in a purely abstract manner without any reference to meaning or interpretation. At the end of this

---

[1] The basic ideas of duality theory were first suggested by John von Neumann. The theory was first rigorously developed by David Gale, Harold Kuhn, and A. W. Tucker.

section, given any linear programming problem, the reader should be able to write out its dual. In this chapter we change our notation from that which was used before this point. The reason will be explained presently.

Consider the general linear programming problem which we will call the *primal* problem:

$$\text{maximize} \quad \Pi = P_1Q_1 + P_2Q_2 + \cdots + P_nQ_n$$

$$\text{subject to} \quad a_{11}Q_1 + a_{12}Q_2 + \cdots + a_{1n}Q_n \leq C_1$$

(1)

$$a_{m1}Q_1 + a_{m2}Q_2 + \cdots + a_{mn}Q_n \leq C_m$$

$$Q_1 \geq 0, \cdots, Q_n \geq 0.$$

Suppose a mischievous gremlin were let loose on this linear programming problem and decided that he would turn everything he possibly could on its head. There are a number of obvious things he would think of. For the word "maximize" he would substitute "minimize." For the symbol $\geq$ he would substitute $\leq$. Furthermore, a nice way to add to the resulting confusion might be to put the capacity figures $C_1, C_2, \cdots, C_m$ where the unit profit figures, $P_1, P_2, \cdots, P_n$, used to be and vice versa. For good measure he might reverse the order in which the constants appear in the inequalities, or better yet, he might rewrite them so that instead of reading across we would now read down. That is, where a_{12} was formerly the second constant in the first inequality, he would now make it the first constant in the second inequality. In other words, by reading across in the first inequality we would formerly have found the constants, a_{11}, a_{12}, a_{13}, etc. Now we would find those same constants not by reading across from left to right, but by reading down from the first inequality to the second to the third, etc. Finally, to cap the confusion, our gremlin would probably decide to get rid of our original variables $Q_1, Q_2, \cdots, Q_n$ altogether and substitute for them an entirely new set of variables $V_1, V_2, \cdots, V_m$. Having done all this he would end up with the linear programming problem which may be written as follows:

$$\text{minimize} \quad \alpha = C_1V_1 + C_2V_2 + \cdots + C_mV_m$$

$$\text{subject to} \quad a_{11}V_1 + a_{21}V_2 + \cdots + a_{m1}V_m \geq P_1$$

$$a_{1n}V_1 + a_{2n}V_2 + \cdots + a_{mn}V_m \geq P_n$$

$$V_1 \geq 0, \quad V_2 \geq 0, \cdots, V_m \geq 0.$$

This new program produced by the gremlin is precisely what we call the dual. Before going further, let us recapitulate the characteristics of the two problems which give them their remarkable symmetry:

  1. If the primal problem involves maximization, the dual involves minimization, *and vice versa.*
  2. If the primal involves $\geq$ signs, the dual involves $\leq$ signs, and vice versa.
  3. The profit constants P_j in the primal problem replace the capacity constants C_i, and vice versa.
  4. In the constraint inequalities the coefficients which were found by going from left to right are positioned in the dual from top to bottom, and vice versa.
  5. A new set of variables appears in the dual.
  6. Neglecting the number of nonnegativity conditions, if there are n variables and m inequalities in the primal problem, in the dual there will be m variables and n inequalities.

Finally, it should be noted that if we were to let our gremlin loose again and have him do his work on the dual problem, he would end right back with the problem with which he started. That is, if he were to take the dual problem and subject it to all the abuses which he had heaped on our original linear program, he would find that in the end he would have undone all his mischief. The dual of the dual problem is the original linear programming problem itself. It follows that, given such a pair of problems, it is entirely arbitrary which of them is referred to as the primal and which as the dual. Each one of them is the dual of the other.

These rules for the construction of the dual are illustrated in the following pair of numerical linear programming problems. The reader should verify that these problems do indeed constitute one another's dual. In order to emphasize that minimization problems also have a dual we have selected as our illustrative primal program the minimization problem (13) of Chapter 5.

	Primal Problem	*Dual Problem*
	minimize	maximize
	$\alpha = 40m + 200t$	$R = 160V_1 + 60V_2 + 80V_3$
	subject to	subject to
(2)	$4m + 40t \geq 160$	$4V_1 + 3V_2 + 8V_3 \leq 40$
	$3m + 10t \geq 60$	$40V_1 + 10V_2 + 10V_3 \leq 200$
	$8m + 10t \geq 80$	
	$m \geq 0, t \geq 0$	$V_1 \geq 0, V_2 \geq 0, V_3 \geq 0.$

It will be observed, in our illustration, that the primal problem involves three variables and two structural constraints, whereas the dual problem involves two variables and three constraints. It should also be pointed out that one feature is not tampered with in going from a linear programming problem to its dual—the inequalities of the nonnegativity condition retain their directions. That is, both in the primal and in the dual problem each variable is required to be greater than or equal to zero.

Before proceeding further it is convenient to rewrite our general primal and dual programs, this time including the slack variables so that the structural constraints become equations. We obtain

<table>
<tr><td align="center">Primal Problem</td><td align="center">Dual Problem</td></tr>
<tr><td>maximize</td><td>minimize</td></tr>
</table>

$$\Pi = P_1 Q_1 + \cdots + P_n Q_n \qquad\qquad \alpha = C_1 V_1 + \cdots + C_m V_m$$

subject to   subject to

$$a_{11} Q_1 + \cdots + a_{1n} Q_n + U_1 = C_1 \qquad a_{11} V_1 + \cdots + a_{m1} V_m - L_1 = P_1$$

(3)   . . . .

$$a_{m1} Q_1 + \cdots + a_{mn} Q_n + U_m = C_m \qquad a_{1n} V_1 + \cdots + a_{mn} V_m - L_n = P_n$$

$$Q_1 \geq 0, \cdots, Q_n \geq 0, \qquad\qquad V_1 \geq 0, \cdots, V_m \geq 0,$$

$$U_1 \geq 0, \cdots, U_m \geq 0 \qquad\qquad L_1 \geq 0, \cdots, L_n \geq 0.$$

Here the U_i and L_j represent, respectively, the primal and dual slack variables. It should be noted that in our dual program, since the constraints are "greater than or equal to" inequalities, the slack variables L_j are *subtracted* from the left-hand side of the equations. To give a simple example, in translating the inequality $3Q_1 \geq 7$ into an equation we must rewrite it as $3Q_1 - L = 7$, where, as usual, $L \geq 0$.

PROBLEMS

1. Write out the dual of the following problem:

maximize $\Pi = 6Q_1 + 2Q_2$

subject to

$$4Q_1 + Q_2 \leq 5$$
$$3Q_1 + 2Q_2 \leq 7$$
$$Q_1 + Q_2 \leq 3$$
$$Q_1 \geq 0, \qquad Q_2 \geq 0.$$

2. Show that the dual of your answer is the original programming problem.

3. Write out the dual to the program in Problem 1 in slack variable form.

2. Economic Interpretation of the Dual Problem

It is convenient to begin our interpretation of the dual problem in a manner which seems extremely artificial. But the reader will see the artificiality of the interpretation disappear rapidly as the analysis proceeds, and the very real significance of the duality theorems will make this abundantly clear.

Let our primal program be a standard production problem, that is, the problem of determining the profit-maximizing output levels for the firm's various products, subject to a number of scarce input (capacity) constraint limitations. The costs of the company's fixed inputs C_1, C_2, $\cdots$, C_m may not enter directly into its accounting profit calculations, particularly if the warehouses, factories, and other facilities which these symbols represent have been completely amortized. Nevertheless, it must be recognized that without these inputs the firm could not have earned its profits. Suppose, then, that the businessman in question decides to determine what portion of the profit on each of his products he "owes" to each of the inputs. In the economist's jargon, he will undertake to *impute* all of the company's profits to its scarce resources. For this purpose, he will seek to calculate an artificial accounting price or value V for each of his inputs and to choose a magnitude for each V such that the sum of these computed values of the scarce inputs going into any of his products, say shoes, is high enough to account for his profits on shoe production. That is, values of the V's should be chosen so that, if possible, the net profit from shoe production (and the net profit from each other company output) would be zero if each scarce input C_i were to cost V_i dollars per unit.[2]

It must be emphasized that the zero profit condition in this problem is not directly related to the zero profit requirement for long-run equilibrium under perfect competition. In our imputation analysis zero profit is an accounting requirement. If accounting values V are proposed which do not impute profits completely to the scarce inputs, these accounting values must be raised until the unimputed residue has been eliminated.

We shall now show that the variables V_1, V_2, and V_3 in the dual program of the numerical problem in the exercises of the preceding section can be interpreted as the required accounting values of the firm's three scarce resources. Let us assume that our three scarce resources are, respectively, warehouse space, machine time, and inspection time, so that our original linear programming problem tells us that the firm has available to it 5 (million) cubic feet of warehouse space, 7 (hundred) hours of machine

---

[2] We will see that some commodities which the firm considers producing may end up yielding negative accounting profits. That is, their gross profits are less than the value imputed to the scarce resources needed to produce them. As the reader may surmise, these are the items which will be excluded from the firm's *optimal* product line.

time, and 3 (hundred) hours of inspection time. V_1 may then be described as the accounting value to the firm of a unit of warehouse space, V_2 as the accounting value of a unit of machine time, and V_3 as the accounting value of inspection time. Suppose we tentatively accept this interpretation.

Let us now look at the first inequality in the dual problem and show that it is no more than an explicit statement of our no-accounting-profit requirement for the first item in the firm's product line, Q_1. It will be remembered that the coefficient 4 of the variable V_1 in that inequality had a very definite meaning in our primal problem. There it represented the number of units of warehouse space used to produce one unit of output 1. Similarly, the second coefficient 3 in our dual inequality, that is, the coefficient of V_2, in our primal problem represented the amount of machine time needed to produce a unit of output 1. Finally, the coefficient of the V_3 in our dual inequality represented the number of units of inspection time needed to produce a unit of output 1. In sum, the three coefficients, the 4, and 3, and the unity represent the quantities of the three different inputs which go into a unit of commodity 1. Now, if each unit of warehouse space is worth V_1 dollars, then four units of warehouse space would be worth four times V_1 dollars and, similarly, if each unit of machine time is worth V_2 dollars, the three machine-time units would be worth $3V_2$ dollars, and, finally, the one unit of inspection time would be worth one times V_3 dollars if each unit is worth V_3. We see, then, that the expression on the left-hand side of our inequality, $4V_1 + 3V_2 + 1V_3$, has a straightforward economic interpretation, given the meaning which has tentatively been assigned to our variables. That sum is the total value of the inputs which is necessary to produce one unit of output of commodity 1.

Only one more step is needed to complete our interpretation of this inequality. We must now recall what is signified by the number 6 on the right-hand side of that relationship. Going back to our primal problem once more, we see that the 6 is the unit profit one obtains by producing our first commodity. Each unit of commodity 1 which is manufactured yields \$6 to the firm. Our first inequality can now be read to state the following: The value of the inputs going into the production of a unit of commodity 1 must be greater than or equal to the profit which the firm makes by producing a unit of commodity 1. Our first inequality, then, states that we must assign to each of the inputs a value sufficiently great to impute to them all the profits of output number 1. Just as the first inequality of the dual program serves to impute the profits of commodity 1, so the second inequality imputes all the profit of each unit of output 2 to the company's scarce inputs. It states that the values of the three inputs which are used to make a unit of commodity 2 must account fully for the \$2 of profit which are yielded by a unit of commodity 2.

We will see presently why it is convenient to write these constraints as inequalities rather than equations, that is, why we do not directly require that values of the inputs be exactly equal to the profits. However, one simple reason can be indicated now. The need for inequalities in the constraints follows directly from the fact that the number of variables and the number of structural constraints in a programming problem need not be the same. In our dual problem we have three variables and two inequalities. We could just as easily have had, say, six variables and fifteen inequalities. If we had attempted to write those fifteen constraints as equations rather than inequalities, we would have had a system involving fifteen equations in six unknowns, and obviously this is likely to run us into difficulties, for usually it is impossible to satisfy a system of equations containing more equations than unknowns. Since, therefore, in such a situation we may be forced to relinquish equality in part of the system, we have chosen between the two apparently less desirable alternatives, overimputation and underimputation, and decided to favor the former. That is, we have said, "If it is absolutely necessary to assign a value to the inputs employed which is either greater than or less than profit, let us assign a total value which is greater than the profit."

But once we have stated the inequalities in this way, it may appear that there is no problem at all in solving our linear program. We need just assign values as capriciously high as we wish to each of the inputs and we can be sure that they will more than account for all of the profits. What prevents this sort of arbitrary solution is that our dual problem requires us to *minimize* $\alpha = 5V_1 + 7V_2 + 3V_3$. The value of the dual objective function, α, also has an economic interpretation which follows directly from our preceding discussion. It will be recalled that the company has five units of warehouse space in its possession so that the total value of the warehouse space available to the firm will be $5V_1$ and, similarly, the total value of the machine time available to the firm will be $7V_2$ because there are seven units of machine time at the firm's command, and so on. Hence $\alpha = 5V_1 + 7V_2 + 3V_3$ represents the total value of all of the inputs which the firm has under its control. To summarize, then, *the dual problem requires us to find the very smallest valuation of the company's stock of inputs which completely accounts for all of the profits of each of the outputs.*

We may conclude this preliminary discussion of the interpretation of the dual problem by ascribing an economic meaning to the dual slack variables $L_1, \cdots, L_n$. From our dual problem in (3) we see that, for example, L_1 is given by

$$L_1 = (a_{11}V_1 + a_{21}V_2 + \cdots + a_{m1}V_m) - P_1.$$

But P_1 is the profit per unit of output 1, while, as we have just seen, the expression in parentheses is the accounting value of the resources used in producing a unit of output 1 (since a_{11} is the amount of input 1 used in a unit of output 1 so that $a_{11}V_1$ is the value of the amount of input 1 used in the production of output 1, etc.). We can, therefore, rewrite the last equation as

$$L_1 = \text{(value of resources going into a unit of output 1)}$$

$$- \text{(the unit profit of output 1)}.$$

Thus, we may consider L_1 to represent a sort of *relative loss* figure for product 1, for if L_1 is positive it tells us that the resources used in producing output 1 are worth more than the profits yielded by that commodity. We shall presently return to these dual slack figures and see precisely what is meant by the "loss" which they represent.

Let us now review the interpretation we have given the variables in our pair of programming problems. Our primal and dual problems involve the following four types of variable:

Q_j the (*quantity of*) *output* of product j (the primal ordinary variables)
U_i the *unused capacity* of input i (the primal slack variables)
V_i the *value* (accounting price) of input i (the dual ordinary variables)
L_j the accounting *loss* per unit of output j (the dual slack variables).

Primal variable Q_j and dual variable L_j, then, both refer to *outputs*, while dual variable V_i and primal variable U_i both refer to *inputs*. This information is summarized schematically in the following table:

	Primal Variable (physical quantities)	*Dual Variable* (in money units)
Refers to outputs	Q_j	L_j
Refers to inputs	U_i	V_i

The interpretation of these four types of variable must be understood clearly before the reader can hope to master the economic implications of the dual. It should also be noted that the primal variables Q_j and U_i refer, respectively, to physical output and input quantities and so must be measured in units such as tons, square feet, kilowatt hours, etc. On the other hand, both dual variables V_i and L_j refer to pecuniary magnitudes and can be measured in a monetary unit such as the dollar.

So far the reader may well have the feeling that our interpretation of the dual program is rather strained. We have forced an odd sort of economic meaning onto our dual but there appears to be little reason for an economist or anyone else to be interested. However, the mathematicians have proved a number of theorems about the dual problem which dramatically breathe life and power into the entire construct.

3. Some Duality Theorems

In this section several of the most pertinent theorems of duality theory will be described rather briefly. They and their derivations are discussed in somewhat greater detail in Appendix A to this chapter.

As a preliminary matter, we may mention the following rather useful theorem. Suppose we have found any *feasible* solution to the primal problem and this solution yields as the value of the objective function (the total profit figure) the number Π^*. Suppose, moreover, that we have found some feasible solution to the dual problem which yields the number α^* for the value of the dual objective function. Then Π^* will never exceed α^*, i.e., we will have $\Pi^* \leq \alpha^*$. This theorem tells us, in effect, that the company's total profit Π will never exceed α, the accounting value assigned to the company's scarce inputs. Actually, that result is hardly surprising since, as we saw in the last section, in constructing the dual problem we had done it in a way which may well overimpute company profits but will certainly leave no part of company profits unimputed to the scarce inputs. Somewhat less obvious is

Duality Theorem I: The maximum value of Π will be exactly equal to the minimum value of α, and *any* pair of *feasible* solutions for which $\alpha = \Pi$ must be optimal.

This theorem states that despite our apparent willingness to over-impute profits if necessary, everything comes out well in the end! When *optimal* solutions have been found for the primal and dual problems we will have assigned a total value α to the company's scarce resources which is exactly equal to total profit Π! As an example, it will be recalled that in the illustrative problem of Sections 6–10 in Chapter 5, *maximum* profit was equal to 8,750, as was shown in matrix (12). Theorem I then tells us that the *minimum* value of the objective function of the dual problem will also be $\alpha = 8,750$. Furthermore, it tells us that if we find any primal and dual solutions for which $\alpha = \Pi = 8,750$, we need look no further. We will then have found our optimal solutions.

Another basic duality result is described by the next proposition:

Duality Theorem II: In a pair of optimal solutions, the firm will produce only commodities whose accounting loss figures L are zero. In addition, in such optimal solutions only inputs which are used to capacity will receive a nonzero accounting valuation V. Moreover, any pair of feasible solutions to the primal and dual problems which satisfy this requirement must be optimal!

Symbolically, this theorem may be written:

$$in\ an\ optimal\ solution\ Q_j L_j = 0\ for\ each\ commodity\ j,$$
$$and\ U_i V_i = 0\ for\ each\ input\ i.$$

This set of equations is referred to as the *complementary slackness* conditions.

To see the connection between the symbolic and the verbal statements of Theorem II, note that, e.g., the equation $Q_1 L_1 = 0$ requires either that $Q_1 = 0$ or that $L_1 = 0$ (or both). This means that if $Q_1 > 0$ (if output of commodity 1 is positive), then we must have $L_1 = 0$ (its accounting loss must be zero). Similarly, if $L_1 > 0$ (commodity 1 involves an accounting loss), then we must have $Q_1 = 0$. The interpretation of the other equations in Theorem II is similar and is left to the reader.

Theorem II, then, is reassuring. It tells us that the dual values make some economic sense—inputs which are in excess supply to the firm are given a zero accounting value V and commodities which are associated with a nonzero accounting loss are those which, optimally, should not be produced.

Looked at the other way, the theorem tells us that from the optimal solution of the dual problem we can immediately make a number of predictions about the solution to the primal; we can be sure, in advance, which outputs will not be produced and which inputs will be used to capacity. For example, as will be shown later in this chapter, the solution to the dual of the illustrative linear programming problem (3') of Sections 6–10 in Chapter 5 is $L_1 = 0$, $L_2 = 0$, $V_a = \frac{1}{4}$, $V_b = \frac{3}{4}$. With the aid of Theorem II these figures tell us to expect both outputs 1 and 2 to be produced and that both inputs will be used to capacity. Indeed, this turns out to be the case, for it will be recalled that the solution to the primal problem is given by matrix (12) of Chapter 5 and is $Q_1 = 500$, $Q_2 = 3,750$, $U_a = 0$, $U_b = 0$.

We may also observe, specifically, that all the equations of Theorem II are satisfied by the pair of solutions just given, for we have

$$Q_1 L_1 = (500)(0) = 0, \quad Q_2 L_2 = (3,750)(0) = 0, \quad U_a V_a = (0)(1/4) = 0,$$

and

$$U_b V_b = (0)(3/4) = 0.$$

Perhaps the more surprising part of the theorem is its converse portion—the assertion that *any* pair of feasible solutions for which all $Q_j L_j = 0$ and all $U_i V_i = 0$ must be optimal. It is rather plausible that an optimal evaluation of the L's and V's should have us produce no item which involves a "loss" L and should impute no value to an input which goes partially unused, but intuitively it is not easy to see why no more than this is required to guarantee optimality in a pair of solutions. Nevertheless, this converse proposition is valid and its proof, which is not very difficult (once Theorem I has been derived) is given in Appendix A of this chapter.

Further duality theorems tell us more about the meaning of the dual variables V_i and L_j and should convince the reader of their real economic significance.

First, let us examine the input valuation variables V_i. As an example, suppose input i is machine time. Then, as we have said, V_i is simply the dollar value which is assigned to an hour of time of this piece of equipment. Now it is natural for the economist to feel that the value which should be assigned to time on such an item is its marginal revenue product (its marginal contribution to the profits of the firm). And this is usually what V_i turns out to be. As is indicated in Appendix A, normally V_i *is equal to the marginal profit contribution of input i!* That is, V_i tells us (approximately) what would be added to the firm's profits if somehow the company could increase its available machine time by one hour (per day). More precisely, (wherever the profit function Π has a derivative) we have

$$V_i = \partial\Pi/\partial C_i,$$

where C_i is the total capacity of input i (the total amount of machine time available to the firm). In other words, if we were to make two *independent* programming calculations, one calculation with the aid of the primal problem alone to determine the value of $\partial\Pi/\partial C_i$ and another calculation with the aid of the dual to find the optimal value of V_i, comparison of the two figures after both computations were completed would show them to be precisely equal![3]

Let us turn now to our other pecuniary variable L_j, the dual slack

---

[3] To determine the marginal profitability of input i, we may proceed as follows. Suppose the available amount of input i is, say, $C_i = 9$; solve the primal problem for the optimal value of Π using this C_i figure. Now substitute for $C_i = 9$ the value $C_i + \Delta C_i = 9 + \Delta C_i$ (where some very small number may be used for the ΔC_i). Then solve the primal problem again, only with this increase in the capacity of input i, to yield the increased profit figure $\Pi + \Delta\Pi$. It is now a straightforward matter to find $\Delta\Pi/\Delta C_i$. As an example, the reader may verify that, if in our illustrative programming problem (3') in Chapter 5, the first capacity figure C_a is increased from 8,000 to 8,001, the optimal solution matrix which was previously given by (12) in Chapter 5 now becomes

	1	U_b	U_a
$\Pi =$	$8{,}750\frac{1}{4}$	$-\frac{3}{4}$	$-\frac{1}{4}$
$Q_2 =$	$3{,}750\frac{3}{4}$	$\frac{1}{4}$	$-\frac{3}{4}$
$Q_1 =$	$499\frac{1}{2}$	$-\frac{1}{2}$	$\frac{1}{2}$

Thus C_a has increased by $\Delta C_a = 8{,}001 - 8{,}000 = 1$, while Π has risen by $\Delta\Pi = 8{,}750\frac{1}{4} - 8{,}750 = \frac{1}{4}$. Hence, we have $\Delta\Pi/\Delta C_a = \frac{1}{4}$. Comparison with the dual value as given later in this chapter shows that $V_a = \frac{1}{4} = \Delta\Pi/\Delta C_a$, as our theorem asserts. However, it should be pointed out that this is not always sure to happen, for our theorem tells us that $V_i = \partial\Pi/\partial C_i$, and not that $V_i = \Delta\Pi/\Delta C_i$, i.e., the theorem only holds in the limit, as ΔC_i approaches zero, and then only if there is no discontinuity in the profit function which would prevent differentiation.

variable. This is the accounting loss per unit of output j. That is, we have from our dual constraints

$$L_j = V_1 a_{1j} + V_2 a_{2j} + \cdots + V_m a_{mj} - P_j,$$

where P_j is the actual profit per unit of output j and the remaining terms represent the accounting costs of the scarce inputs used up in producing a unit of item j. By construction, these accounting costs are designed to impute profits completely to the firm's scarce resources, so, at best, for any output j the unit profit P_j will just cover the accounting cost $\sum V_i a_{ij}$. The accounting loss L_j associated with such items will be zero. On all other items we will have $L_j > 0$, i.e., there will be a net accounting loss.

What is the meaning of such an accounting loss? It only implies that the inputs used in producing the item in question would be more valuable elsewhere. That is, the profit on this item does not cover the marginal contribution to profitability which could be obtained by using the same inputs in the production of some other goods. Thus, the accounting losses are only losses relative to the most profitable alternatives. To illustrate the point, suppose it took the same scarce resources to produce a handbag and a pair of shoes and that their unit profitability were, respectively, $P_h = \$5$ and $P_s = \$7$. If these were the only outputs being considered by the firm, we would then have $L_h = \$2$ and $L_s = 0$. That is, *even though the firm nets $5 on every handbag it produces*, it still loses $2 compared to the amount it could be making by transferring these resources to shoe production. The accounting loss on shoe output L_s is zero because shoe manufacturing is the company's most profitable alternative, i.e., it loses no opportunity for further gain by keeping bottleneck inputs tied up in shoe production. Thus L_h and L_s turn out to be what the economist has always called the *opportunity costs* of these items.

It is noteworthy, then, how these time-honored concepts of economic theory, the marginal product and the opportunity cost, have sneaked back into the analysis. No one has put them into the analysis of the primal production problem which proceeds largely in terms of the relevant physical and technological considerations. Yet always hiding behind this primal problem is the dual, which informs us that if we want to determine the optimal magnitudes of our outputs and the optimal allocation of our bottleneck inputs, we should value the inputs in terms of their marginal (profit) yields and produce only the items for which the opportunity costs, so evaluated, are zero. This indicates, in fact, that no matter how technocratic the bias of the planner and how abhorrent to him are the unplanned workings of the free market, every optimal planning decision which he makes must have implicit in it the rationale of the pricing mechanism and the allocation of resources produced by the profit system. It is noteworthy that these results have led to the open and well-publicized reintroduction of marginal analysis into Soviet economics by Russian mathematicians working on the application of linear programming to economic planning.

4. Duality and Decentralized Decision-making

There is another related aspect of the matter which has attracted considerable attention. The dual accounting prices V_i can serve as a device for steering decentralized decision-making along an optimal course. Consider, for example, a firm with a large number of plants each of which makes some use of over-all company resources. If plant A uses more of the company's central warehouse space, less will be available to plant B and vice versa. Top management can, of course, allocate its bottleneck resources among the various plants by making a master plan and deciding, plant by plant, input by input, how much should go where. This is the method of direct centralized planning and decision-making.

However, duality theory points to an alternative approach. Suppose management is in a position to calculate the values of the dual accounting prices V_i by an ordinary programming computation. (The enormous practical problems likely to be involved in obtaining the required statistics and the difficulties caused by nonlinearities must, however, not be forgotten by the reader to whom the procedure sounds delightfully simple.) Top management is now in a position to say to all plant directors, "You can have as much of every input as you want. However, for every unit of input which you employ, the company will debit you with the dual value of the item" (presumably some more palatable term would be used). It is to be noted that our second duality theorem tells us that items which should be produced in an optimal solution (i.e., for which the optimal $Q_j > 0$) will ordinarily be those which will yield no accounting loss $(L_j = 0)$. That is, only these items will yield unit profits sufficient to cover the dual value charge on the inputs used to produce them. Thus, if they are effective profit-makers, plant managers can be left to decide by themselves which items should be included in the product line, for commodities which are not optimal from the point of view of the company will cause the plant to incur a loss.[4] The perfect plant manager will just break even

---

[4] There still remains the problem of determining *how much* of each profitable item to produce. Under linear programming assumptions which rule out diminishing returns to scale, all items which are profitable should be produced in amounts as large as resources will permit. Unfortunately this still leaves a substantial calculation problem because increased production of one commodity will mean that fewer resources will remain available for use in the production of other items. Thus, the dual pricing approach only takes care of part of the job of providing efficient decentralized decision-making arrangements. There are, however, somewhat related linear programming methods also involving dual prices, which, at least in principle, can handle the entire matter.

because the dual accounting prices are calculated so as to eat up all profits, but they will cause no loss only if all his product-line decisions are optimal. Thus dual pricing can, at least in principle, serve as a substitute for centralized control and it can open the way to efficient decentralized decision-making. In fact, such an approach is now being employed in some industrial applications and, as will be indicated in Chapter 21, it has even been suggested as an appropriate device for the government to use in a socialistic economy, where, it has been implied, the method can help to attain the goals of socialism at a relatively low cost in central control and loss of individual initiative.

5. Solution of the Primal and Dual Programs

It will be shown in this section that our method for solving the primal linear programming problem immediately yields the solution to the dual problem without further calculation. To see how it does so we first write out a pair of small problems in our standard form as follows:

<table>
<tr><td align="center">Primal</td><td align="center">Dual</td></tr>
</table>

$$\text{Max } \Pi = 0 + P_1 Q_1 + P_2 Q_2 + P_3 Q_3 \qquad \text{Min } \alpha = 0 + C_1 V_1 + C_2 V_2$$

subject to   subject to

$$U_1 = C_1 - a_{11} Q_1 - a_{12} Q_2 - a_{13} Q_3 \qquad L_1 = -P_1 + a_{11} V_1 + a_{21} V_2$$

$$U_2 = C_2 - a_{21} Q_1 - a_{22} Q_2 - a_{23} Q_3 \qquad L_2 = -P_2 + a_{12} V_1 + a_{22} V_2$$

all Q's, U's nonnegative $$L_3 = -P_3 + a_{13} V_1 + a_{23} V_2$$

all V's, L's nonnegative

Notice the differences in sign in the right-hand sides of the constraint equations of the primal and dual problems. This difference occurs because in our original constraint equations (3) the primal slack variables U_i appear with a plus sign while the dual slack variables L_j appear with a minus. Now we may write the two problems in matrix form to obtain

<table>
<tr><td align="center" colspan="5">Primal Matrix</td><td colspan="4" align="center">Dual Matrix</td></tr>
<tr><td></td><td align="center">1</td><td align="center">Q_1</td><td align="center">Q_2</td><td align="center">Q_3</td><td align="center">1</td><td align="center">V_1</td><td align="center">V_2</td></tr>
<tr><td align="right">$\Pi =$</td><td align="center">0</td><td align="center">P_1</td><td align="center">P_2</td><td align="center">P_3</td><td align="right">$\alpha =$</td><td align="center">0</td><td align="center">C_1</td><td align="center">C_2</td></tr>
<tr><td align="right">(4) $U_1 =$</td><td align="center">C_1</td><td align="center">$-a_{11}$</td><td align="center">$-a_{12}$</td><td align="center">$-a_{13}$</td><td align="right">$L_1 =$</td><td align="center">$-P_1$</td><td align="center">a_{11}</td><td align="center">a_{21}</td></tr>
<tr><td align="right">$U_2 =$</td><td align="center">C_2</td><td align="center">$-a_{21}$</td><td align="center">$-a_{22}$</td><td align="center">$-a_{23}$</td><td align="right">$L_2 =$</td><td align="center">$-P_2$</td><td align="center">a_{12}</td><td align="center">a_{22}</td></tr>
<tr><td></td><td></td><td></td><td></td><td></td><td align="right">$L_3 =$</td><td align="center">$-P_3$</td><td align="center">a_{13}</td><td align="center">a_{23}</td></tr>
</table>

These matrices exhibit fully the remarkable symmetry of the primal and dual problems. Neglecting differences in signs, the dual matrix is merely the primal matrix flipped over so that the lower left-hand and upper right-hand corners have exchanged places. In addition, there is a change in the sign of every element except those in the first column of the primal (first row of the dual) matrix.

These observations suggest a measure which can achieve considerable economy of notation. All essential information can be preserved in the following *combined* matrix:

$$
\begin{array}{c}
\begin{array}{cccc}
1 & Q_1 & Q_2 & Q_3
\end{array} \\
\begin{array}{rl}
\Pi = & \boxed{\begin{array}{cccc}
0 & P_1 & P_2 & P_3 \\
C_1 & -a_{11} & -a_{12} & -a_{13} \\
C_2 & -a_{21} & -a_{22} & -a_{23}
\end{array}}
\end{array}
\end{array}
$$

(5)

with row labels $\Pi =$, $U_1 =$, $U_2 =$ and right labels 1, V_1, V_2, and bottom label $\alpha = -L_1 = -L_2 = -L_3 =$

Several essential characteristics of this combined matrix should be observed.

1. The combined matrix (5) is simply the primal matrix in (4) with the dual variables entered along the right and lower sides to indicate their position in the dual matrix in (4). For example, since L_1 appears beside the second *row* in the dual matrix in (4), it is written next to the second *column* in (5). From (5) we can at once reconstruct our dual matrix by just interchanging the rows with the columns and reversing the signs of all elements except those in the first column of (5).

2. Each *primal* structural variable is paired with the corresponding *dual slack* variable, and each *primal slack* variable is paired with the corresponding *dual* structural variable. For example, the third column corresponds to variables Q_2 and L_2, while the second row corresponds to the two variables U_1 and V_1. We see that the primal and dual variables are always paired in exactly the same manner as they are in duality Theorem II.

3. As usual, the primal variables appearing at the top of the matrix (5) take the value zero, in the current basic solution (i.e., $Q_1 = Q_2 = Q_3 = 0$), while the primal variables at the left obtain their values from the first column of (5) (i.e., $\Pi = 0$, $U_1 = C_1$, $U_2 = C_2$). In the original dual matrix in (4) the same rule holds, but because (5) is a flipped over representation of (4), things appear a bit inverted when we get to the values of the dual variables in (5). Here *the zero-valued dual variables are those at the right* ($V_1 = V_2 = 0$) and *the values of the dual variables at the bottom are given*

by the elements of the first row with their signs reversed (i.e., $\alpha = 0$, $L_1 = -P_1$, $L_2 = -P_2$, $L_3 = -P_3$). For this reason, as a reminder, minus signs have been inserted before the dual variables which appear beneath the matrix.

These three characteristics of the combined matrix continue applicable throughout the simplex calculation. Now consider some pivot operation, say the one in matrix (5) of Chapter 5, which involves an interchange of the primal variables we now call Q_1 and U_b. Suppose in the dual problem we were to pivot in a way which interchanges the corresponding dual variables L_1 and V_b. It is easy to prove by applying the pivoting rules of Section 8 of Chapter 5 to the dual matrix that *the new primal matrix and the new dual matrix again combine into a single matrix exactly analogous with* (5)! That remarkable result enables us to go through the simplex procedure step by step simply by carrying out the calculation for the primal problem alone. As an example, we reproduce as combined matrices the three primal simplex matrices (5), (7), and (12) of Chapter 5 for our illustrative problem (3′) in that chapter:

1st Matrix

	1	Q_1	Q_2	
II =	0	2.5	2	1
U_a =	8,000	-1	-2	V_a
U_b =	9,000	-3*	-2	V_b

$\alpha = \quad -L_1 = \quad -L_2 =$

2nd Matrix

	1	U_b	Q_2	
II =	7,500	$-\frac{5}{6}$	$\frac{1}{3}$	1
U_a =	5,000	$\frac{1}{3}$	$-\frac{4}{3}$*	V_a
Q_1 =	3,000	$-\frac{1}{3}$	$-\frac{2}{3}$	L_1

$\alpha = \quad -V_b = \quad -L_2 =$

(6)

3rd Matrix

	1	U_b	U_a	
II =	8,750	$-\frac{3}{4}$	$-\frac{1}{4}$	1
Q_2 =	3,750	$\frac{1}{4}$	$-\frac{3}{4}$	L_2
Q_1 =	500	$-\frac{1}{2}$	$\frac{1}{2}$	L_1

$\alpha = \quad -V_b = \quad -V_a =$

Each of these matrices satisfies all three characteristics of combined simplex matrices which have just been described. In particular, the first matrix yields the basic dual solution $V_a = V_b = 0$, $\alpha = 0$, $L_1 = -2.5$, $L_2 = -2$ (since $-L_1 = 2.5$ and $-L_2 = 2$, so that the values of L_1 and L_2 are obtained by *changing the signs* of the elements in the first row). Similarly, the third matrix (which provided the optimal solution to the primal problem) yields the dual basic solution $L_2 = L_1 = 0$, $\alpha = 8{,}750$, $V_b = \frac{3}{4}$, $V_a = \frac{1}{4}$.

Indeed, this last basic solution is also the *optimal* solution to the dual problem. The optimal solution can always be found in this way, from the first row of the optimal combined matrix. For, as will be shown next, this dual solution simultaneously satisfies two criteria:

> *The dual feasibility criterion*, which requires all entries in the first row of the combined matrix (except for the element in the left-hand corner) to be negative; and *the dual optimality criterion*, which requires all elements in the first column of the combined matrix (except for the upper left-hand element) to be positive.

First let us examine the logic behind the optimality criterion. We do so in several steps:

1. It will be recalled that in a maximization problem the optimality criterion requires every element in the first row of the matrix (except for the profit figure) to be negative because then only products with negative marginal profits will have been assigned zero output levels. Correspondingly, in a *minimization* problem (view it as a problem of cost minimization), the optimal values of the coefficients of the dual objective function will all be *positive* because any process which has a negative coefficient (so that it *reduces* total cost) should be employed by the firm [it should *not* be represented by one of the dual variables at the top of our original dual matrix (4)].[5]

2. Because the combined matrix may be viewed as the dual matrix "lying on its side," the first *row* of the combined matrix yields the basic solutions of the dual, as we have seen, and *the first column of the combined matrix gives the coefficients of the dual objective function.* The reader should verify that the initial dual objective function in (6) is $\alpha = 0 + 8{,}000V_a + 9{,}000V_b$ corresponding to the entries 0, 8,000, and 9,000 in the first column of the first of our three combined matrices.

3. We conclude that *the optimality criterion for our dual problem requires all elements in the first column of the matrix to be positive.* This is because the first column of the combined matrix corresponds to the first row of the dual matrix, and these are the elements which do not change sign in the transition from the dual to the combined matrix [compare the dual matrix in (4) with combined matrix (5)].

---

[5] For example, if our problem is to *minimize* $\alpha = 90 + 3V_1 - 6V_2$, we clearly do not want $V_2 = 0$.

The reader may well feel at this point that something has gone seriously wrong. True, the last of our three matrices (6) satisfies the dual optimality criterion, because the entries in the first column (excluding the α figure) are the positive numbers 3,750 and 500. But the other two matrices in (6) also satisfy the criterion—surely they cannot all be optimal! The difficulty is that the dual solutions corresponding to these first two matrices, while they do meet the optimality criterion, must be rejected because they are not even feasible. We saw, for example, that the solution proposed in the first matrix involves $L_1 = -2.5$ and $L_2 = -2$. But these figures clearly violate the nonnegativity requirements $L_1 \geq 0$, $L_2 \geq 0$. Indeed, we can generalize these observations and conclude that any combined matrix which corresponds to a *nonoptimal* solution to the *primal* problem must yield a *nonfeasible* solution to the dual problem. For if the primal solution is not optimal, at least one of the elements in the top row of the matrix must be positive, and hence (after the required change in sign) the value of the corresponding dual variable must be negative. This observation also yields our *dual feasibility criterion*, which requires that *all entries in the first row of the combined matrix be negative.*

In sum, when and only when we have found an optimal matrix for the primal problem, the corresponding combined matrix will yield an optimal dual solution. For in such a matrix the elements of the first column must be positive (to assure that the primal solution is feasible) and the elements of the first row must be negative (to assure optimality of the primal solution). It follows that the dual solution must be feasible (because the elements of the first row are all negative) and optimal (because the first column elements are positive).

Specifically, the solution given by the last matrix in (6) is, therefore, the optimal solution to our dual problem, and it has been read off directly from the optimal primal matrix without any further calculation!

For the same reasons it is possible to solve the primal problem by first dealing with the dual problem, that is, by solving the dual problem, thereby obtaining the solution to the primal problem as a costless bonus. This is called the *dual simplex method* and was developed by E. C. Lemke. Which of these two methods it pays to use is a matter of convenience or computational efficiency since the dual and primal problems are usually not equally easy to solve.

The option of solving a problem either directly or through its dual has an important application in cases such as the primal problem (2) for which $Q_1 = Q_2 = \cdots = Q_n = 0$ is not a feasible solution so that we cannot use this as our initial basic solution. Frequently in such cases the dual problem is not characterized by similar difficulties. For suppose in the primal problem we have only "greater than or equal to" constraints, such as $0.6M + 2T + 0.7R \geq 23$ in (2). This requirement is clearly not satisfied by $M =$

$T = R = 0$. But in such a case the dual problems will have only "less than or equal to" constraints such as $9V_1 + 2V_2 \leq 400$, which are satisfied by $V_1 = V_2 = 0$. Hence, in such circumstances, it is possible to solve the primal problem by working only with the dual problem and starting off with the basic solution corresponding to the origin of the dual problem's feasible region, where all the ordinary variables $V_1, V_2, \cdots, V_m$ are equal to zero. In such a situation, we can avoid the additional work required by the use of the feasibility program which was invented to deal with problems in which the origin is not a feasible solution. [6]

PROBLEMS

1. What is the dual basic solution given by the second matrix in (6)?

2. Is this solution feasible? Explain.

3. Given simplex matrix

	1	U_2	Q_1	U_1	
$\Pi =$	300	-2	-4	-1	1
$Q_2 =$	9				L_2
$U_3 =$	7				V_3

$$\alpha = -V_2 = -L_1 = -V_1 =$$

(a) What is the corresponding solution to the primal problem?

(b) What is the corresponding solution to the dual problem?

(c) Show that both solutions are feasible.

(d) Show that both solutions are optimal.

(e) Show that duality Theorem I is satisfied.

(f) Show that duality Theorem II is satisfied.

---

[6] See Appendix B to this chapter. However, the approach just described may not work if the primal contains both "less than or equal to" and "greater than or equal to" constraints, for then the same is likely to be true of the dual program.

We can tell by direct inspection of the simplex matrix when it is possible to proceed by way of the dual in the manner just described. Feasibility for the primal problem requires all elements in the first column to be positive. Feasibility for the dual problem requires all elements in the first *row* of the combined matrix to be *negative*. If the first of these conditions is met, we can proceed by solving the primal problem directly. If only the second condition is satisfied, it is strategic to proceed via the dual. If it happens simultaneously that both conditions are satisfied, the reader should verify that we have found a matrix whose solutions are feasible *and optimal* for both primal and dual, and there is then nothing further to compute.

4. Why can the following *not* be a pair of optimal solutions?

$$Q_1 = 17, \quad Q_2 = 0, \quad U_1 = 2, \quad U_2 = 4, \quad U_3 = 0, \quad L_1 = 0,$$

$$L_2 = 5, \quad V_1 = 8, \quad V_2 = 0, \quad V_3 = 6.$$

5. Solve the advertising problem (13) of Chapter 5, confirming the graphic solution $M = 10, t = 3$.

6. Another Look at the Simplex Method

Our dual theoretic approach to the solution of linear programming problems can also offer us new insights into the nature of the simplex method. In Chapter 5 we described this method as a sequence of steps in which we go from basic solution to basic solution, always seeking at each step to improve matters—to increase profits in a profit maximization problem, or to decrease costs in a cost minimization problem.

We can now obtain readily an alternative and rather illuminating way of looking at the simplex procedure. We have seen from our duality theorems that an optimal solution to a pair of dual programs is given by any pair of *feasible* primal and dual solutions that satisfies the so-called "complementary slackness" conditions

(7)
$$Q_1 L_1 = 0, \quad Q_2 L_2 = 0, \quad \cdots, \quad Q_n L_n = 0$$

$$U_1 V_1 = 0, \quad U_2 V_2 = 0, \quad \cdots, \quad U_m V_m = 0.$$

Thus, for every pair of values Q_j and L_j at least one of the two variables must be zero and for every pair U_i and V_i at least one of these variables must be zero. The strategy of the simplex method is to examine various combinations of values of the Q_j, L_j, U_i and V_i, all of which satisfy this complementary slackness property, and to find among them a set of values that satisfies the feasibility requirement of the primal and the dual problems. It does so by starting from a set of values of the variables that satisfy the complementary slackness requirements, (7). If these are not feasible it then takes, say, some zero-valued Q, call it Q_k, and next time around permits $Q_k \neq 0$ but instead sets $L_k = 0$. Simultaneously it does the same for some pair of variables U_w and V_w. Such an interchange is precisely what constitutes a pivot step.

All of this is readily illustrated by the following schematic simplex diagram:

Zero-valued variables

	1	Q_1	Q_2	$\cdots$	Q_n		
$\pi =$	0	P_1	P_2	$\cdots$	P_n	1	
$U_1 =$	C_1	$-a_{11}$	$-a_{12}$	$\cdots$	$-a_{1n}$	V_1	
$U_2 =$	C_2	$-a_{21}$	$-a_{22}$	$\cdots$	$-a_{2n}$	V_2	Zero-valued variables
$\cdots$						$\cdot\cdot$	
$U_m =$	C_m	$-a_{m1}$	$-a_{m2}$	$\cdots$	$-a_{mn}$	V_m	
	$\alpha =$	$-L_1 =$	$-L_2 =$		$-L_n =$		

Notice that each of the primal variables on top of the matrix and each of the dual variables on its right are assigned the value zero, while the corresponding variables on the left and the bottom of the matrix are, in general, nonzero. Obviously, such a set of values satisfies the complementary slackness requirements (7). However, as we have seen in the preceding section, these values will not generally be primal and dual feasible, i.e., we will not generally meet all the requirements

(8)
$$U_1 = C_1 \geq 0, \cdots, U_m = C_m \geq 0$$
$$-L_1 = P_1 \leq 0, \cdots, -L_n = P_n \leq 0,$$

for if this last set of feasibility conditions were all satisfied we would already have arrived at an optimal solution since our current basic solution satisfies (7).

If the feasibility criteria (8) are not met, we then undertake a pivot step. Say, for the sake of illustration, that the pivot element is a_{m2}.

In the case the next simplex matrix takes the form

$$1 \qquad Q_1 \qquad U_m \qquad \cdots \qquad Q_n$$

$\pi =$	$\cdots$	1
$U_1 =$	$\cdots$	V_1
$U_2 =$	$\cdots$	V_2
$\cdots$	$\cdots$	$\cdots$
$Q_2 =$	$\cdots$	L_2

$$\alpha = \qquad -L_1 = \qquad -V_m = \qquad \cdots \qquad -L_n =$$

where the entries inside the matrix are not indicated. What has happened in this pivot step is that instead of

$$Q_2 = 0, \; L_2 \lessgtr 0 \qquad V_m = 0, \; U_m \lessgtr 0, \text{ as before,}$$

we now have

$$L_2 = 0, \; Q_2 \lessgtr 0, \qquad U_m = 0, \; V_m \lessgtr 0.$$

In this way we have interchanged the assignment of zeros, as between two primal variables, Q_2 and U_m, and as between two dual variables, L_2 and V_m, in such a way as to guarantee that the complementary slackness conditions will remain satisfied. In the process, the values of all of the nonzero-valued variables will have changed and perhaps they will now all be feasible and, hence, optimal. If not, one goes on to still another pivot step, and so on.

The strategy of the simplex method, then, may be summarized as follows: One goes from basic solution to basic solution for the primal and the dual simultaneously. The pivoting rules are designed to guarantee that in this process one never will double back on one's steps—no basic solution will ever be encountered twice in the calculation process. The pivot steps are conducted in a way that also guarantees that the complementary slackness requirements (7) are always satisfied. Since there is only a finite number of basic solutions (corners of the feasible region), eventually this process must arrive at a solution that is feasible if any such solution exists (cf. Appendix A, Theorem 6). At that point the simplex method will have brought the calculation to the optimal solution that is desired.

APPENDIX A: ON THE DERIVATION OF THE DUALITY THEOREMS

This appendix undertakes to indicate some of the approaches which have been employed in proofs of the duality theorems. In general, the mathematical arguments are intended merely to be suggestive rather than rigorous.

Before getting to the theorems themselves we establish a key preliminary result due to A. W. Tucker, from which most of our duality theorems can readily be derived. Given any feasible solutions of the primal and dual problems, this proposition describes a general relationship between the values of the primal and dual objective functions Π and α in terms of the other variables of the two problems:

$$(1) \qquad \alpha - \Pi = \sum_i U_i V_i + \sum_j Q_j L_j.$$

In words, this equation states that for *any* pair of feasible solutions, the value of the dual, α, exceeds the value of the primal by the sum of the values of the primal slacks U_i, each multiplied by the corresponding dual ordinary variable V_i plus the sum of the primal ordinary variables Q_j, each multiplied by the corresponding slack variable.

To derive this equation we must examine the constraints of the primal and dual problems which establish the requirements of feasibility. In slack variable form these constraints may be written

	Primal	*Dual*

$$
\begin{array}{cc}
\sum_j a_{1j}Q_j + U_1 = C_1 & \sum_i V_i a_{i1} - L_1 = P_1 \\
\cdot \quad \cdot \quad \cdot \quad \cdot & \cdot \quad \cdot \quad \cdot \quad \cdot \\
\sum_j a_{mj}Q_j + U_m = C_m & \sum_i V_i a_{in} - L_n = P_n.
\end{array}
$$

(2)

Multiplying the first primal equation through by V_1, the second by V_2, etc., and then multiplying the first dual equation by Q_1, etc., we obtain

$$
\begin{array}{cc}
\sum_j V_1 a_{1j}Q_j + U_1 V_1 = C_1 V_1 & \sum_i V_i a_{i1}Q_1 - L_1 Q_1 = P_1 Q_1 \\
\cdot \quad \cdot \quad \cdot \quad \cdot \quad \cdot & \cdot \quad \cdot \quad \cdot \quad \cdot \quad \cdot \\
\sum_j V_m a_{mj}Q_j + U_m V_m = C_m V_m & \sum_i V_i a_{in}Q_n - L_n Q_n = P_n Q_n.
\end{array}
$$

(3)

Now adding together the primal constraints in (3) and remembering the dual objective function,

$$(4) \qquad \alpha = \sum_i C_i V_i,$$

we obtain

(5)
$$\sum_i \sum_j V_i a_{ij} Q_j + \sum_i U_i V_i = \sum_i C_i V_i = \alpha.$$

Similarly, by adding together the dual constraints in (3) and using the primal objective function,

(6)
$$\Pi = \sum_j P_j Q_j,$$

we have

(7)
$$\sum_i \sum_j V_i a_{ij} Q_j - \sum_j L_j Q_j = \sum_j P_j Q_j = \Pi.$$

Since the first terms in (5) and (7) are identical, we obtain the required relationship $\Pi + \sum L_j Q_j = \alpha - \sum U_i V_i$, which is clearly equivalent to the Tucker equation (1).

From (1), we observe at once

Theorem 1: For any feasible solution to the primal problem and any (not necessarily related) solution of the dual we have for the values of the objective functions $\alpha \geq \Pi$. This follows from (1) because feasibility requires

(8) $L_j \geq 0, \quad Q_j \geq 0, \quad U_i \geq 0, \quad \text{and} \quad V_i \geq 0 \quad \text{for all } i \text{ and } j.$

A simple extension of the argument gives us

Theorem 2: If, for some particular pair of feasible solutions, we have $\alpha^* = \Pi^*$, those feasible solutions of the primal and dual problems must also be optimal. Incidentally, we shall see presently that the converse of Theorem 2 is also valid—for any pair of optimal solutions we must have $\alpha = \Pi$.

To derive Theorem 2, observe that if any other feasible solution of the primal problem yields a value of the objective function Π^{**}, we must have, by Theorem 1, $\Pi^{**} \leq \alpha^*$, so that, by hypothesis, any such $\Pi^{**} \leq \Pi^*$, i.e., Π^* must be the maximal value of Π. The proof that α^* is the minimal value of α is precisely analogous and the reader should go through it as an exercise.

Viewed intuitively, Theorem 1 has, in effect, established any α as a ceiling on possible values of Π, and the logic of Theorem 2 is that a Π which reaches such a ceiling (any $\Pi^* = \alpha^*$) must be maximal. A similar argument applies to α^* with any Π acting as a floor to the possible values of α.

It is Theorem 2 rather than its converse (which is more difficult to prove) that is most useful in application. For Theorem 2 tells us that if by means of the simplex method we find *any* pair of *feasible* solutions for which $\pi = \alpha$, we can be sure we have arrived at a pair of *optimal* solutions.

Next, from (1), we deduce

Theorem 3: Any pair of feasible solutions will yield $\Pi = \alpha$ if and only if, for *each i* and *each j* $U_iV_i = 0$ and $L_jQ_j = 0$.

Proof: By (8) if any $L_jQ_j \neq 0$ that product must be positive and, similarly, if any $U_iV_i \neq 0$, we must have $U_iV_i > 0$. In either such case

$$\sum L_jQ_j + \sum U_iV_i$$

must be positive because it is a sum of nonnegative terms not all of which are zero. Thus, if and only if such a situation occurs we must have $\alpha > \Pi$. Q.E.D.

Theorem 4: If a pair of solutions is optimal, they must satisfy $\alpha = \Pi$.

This is the converse of Theorem 2 and states that in *every* pair of optimal solutions the values of the primal and dual objective functions must coincide.

For a rigorous proof we refer the reader to any more-advanced book on programming. However, a brief intuitive discussion may be illuminating. Consider any pair of feasible solutions to a primal and dual program for which $\alpha \neq \pi$. Can these be optimal? We will suggest now why they cannot. A glance at the key Tucker equation (1) indicates that if $\alpha \neq \pi$ we must have, since all the variable values are nonnegative, either

$$U_iV_i > 0 \text{ for some input, } i, \text{ or}$$

$$Q_jL_j > \text{ for some output } j, \text{ (or both).}$$

The first of these inequalities implies that we are not using all of the available quantity of input i ($U_i > 0$) even though its marginal yield is positive ($V_i > 0$). Such a solution clearly cannot yield maximum profits. Similarly, if $Q_jL_j > 0$, we must be producing an output, j, which incurs an opportunity loss ($L_j > 0$), also clearly violating a fundamental requirement of optimality. Hence, any solution for which $\alpha \neq \pi$ is seen necessarily to fail the optimality requirements that we long ago learned from marginal analysis. Thus, only if $\alpha = \pi$ can the solution be optimal, just as Theorem 4 asserts.

We come now to the very important theorem that confirms the legitimacy of our interpretation of the dual variable V_i as the marginal yield of input i. Specifically, we have

Theorem 5: If the derivative $\partial\pi^0/\partial C_i$ exists, we must have

$$V_i^0 = \frac{\partial\pi^0}{\partial C_i}.$$

Unfortunately, a rigorous proof of this result is rather difficult. A graphic argument can be utilized to indicate the validity of the result and to suggest

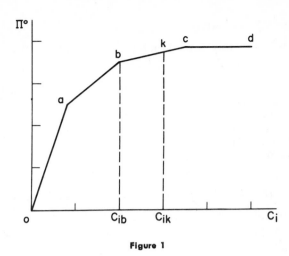

Figure 1

the character of the extension of Proposition 5 to the important class of cases where $\partial \pi^0 / \partial C_i$ does not exist, but even that is too lengthy to be appropriate here.[7]

Theorem 6: If there is a feasible solution to the primal problem and a feasible solution to the dual problem, then both problems also possess an optimal solution.

Outline of Proof: There are only two ways in which a programming problem can fail to have an optimal solution: (a) if it involves a contradiction so that it possesses no solution, or (b) if the value of the objective function

---

[7] For these materials see M. L. Balinski and W. J. Baumol, "The Dual in Nonlinear Programming and its Economic Interpretation," *Review of Economic Studies*, Vol. XXXV, July 1968.

In intuitive terms, in trying to find $\partial \pi^0 / \partial C_i$ we are investigating what happens to potential profits as we increase the capacity, C_i, of the firm's ith input, i.e., as we "ease" the firm's ith constraint, $a_{i1}Q_1 + \cdots + a_{in}Q_n \leq C_i$. Obviously, an increase in the available capacity of input i will generally increase the profits the firm can earn. Specifically, it is not difficult to show that in a linear programming problem the relationship between π^0 and C_i will have the piecewise linear shape shown by curve *oabcd* in Figure 1, where the graph $\pi^0 = f(C_i)$ increases monotonically with C_i but gradually levels off (diminishing returns to input i alone). Now, if the actual value of C_i in a numerical programming problem happens to be represented by a point like C_{ik} that does not lie below a "kink" in the graph, then the derivative, $\partial \pi^0 / \partial C_i$, clearly exists and we can show that in this case the value of the dual variable, V_i, will be equal to that derivative, i.e., to the slope of the segment *bc*. On the other hand, suppose that in a numerical problem the value of C_i is like that shown by C_{ib}, i.e., it lies below a kink, b, in the profit curve. Here the slope of the profit curve is no longer defined. However, even for this case we can show that V_i will lie somewhere between the slope of segment *ab* and the slope of segment *bc*, i.e., between the value of $\partial \pi^0 / \partial C_i$ just to the left of point b, and its value just to the right of b.

is unbounded so that there is nothing to prevent it from "becoming infinite." [Examples of problems which have no solution: case a; Max $\Pi = 6x + 3y$

subject to

$$x \geq 5 \quad \text{and} \quad x - 2 \leq 2.$$

Since x cannot be both greater than 5 and less than 4, this problem has no solution.

Example of case b; Max $\Pi = 6x + 3y$

subject to

$$x \geq 5.$$

Here x can be increased without limit and so, therefore, can Π. There is, then, no finite maximum value of Π.] But if both the primal and dual problems possess feasible solutions, neither of them can involve a contradiction (condition a, above). Moreover, let Π^* and α^* be the values of Π and α corresponding to these solutions. Then by Theorem 1, above, for any solutions $\Pi \leq \alpha^*$ and $\Pi^* \leq \alpha$. Thus it is impossible for Π to increase without limit or for α to decrease without limit, i.e., both Π and α are bounded (condition b). Thus both our conditions for the existence of an optimal solution are satisfied and so both the primal and dual problems must have an optimal solution.

We come now to the Lagrange multiplier theorem.

Theorem 7: The value of $\Pi = \sum P_j Q_j$ will be maximized subject to the inequality constraints $\sum a_{ij} Q_j \leq C_i$ if and only if the unconstrained Lagrangian expression

$$(9) \qquad \Pi_\lambda = \sum_j P_j Q_j - \sum_i \lambda_i \left(\sum_j a_{ij} Q_j - C_i \right)$$

also attains its maximum, and where the ith Lagrange multiplier, $\lambda_i = V_i^0$, is the optimal value of the ith dual variable, so that the Lagrangian expression (9) becomes

$$(10) \qquad \Pi_\lambda = \sum_j P_j Q_j - \sum_i \sum_j V_i^0 a_{ij} Q_j + \sum_i C_i V_i^0.$$

Moreover, the corresponding Lagrangian function for the dual problem is identical with (10) except that in the α_λ expression it is not the V_i but the Q_j which are assigned their optimal values, Q_i^0.

This theorem tells us, among other surprising things, that the Lagrangian method of the differential calculus can also be applied to linear programming problems despite the fact that the constraints are inequalities

and that they have not been changed into equations by the insertion of
slack variables!

The correspondence between the Lagrangian expression for the primal
and dual problems can readily be verified by the reader by forming the α
equation just as we derived that for Π_λ in (10). Let us ignore for the moment the requirement that any variables take optimal values in (10).
This gives us a generalized Lagrangian expression which we denote by
$L(Q, V)$, i.e.,

$$(11) \qquad L(Q, V) = \sum P_j Q_j - \sum \sum V_i a_{ij} Q_j + \sum C_i V_i$$
$$= \Pi - \sum \sum V_i a_{ij} Q_j + \alpha.$$

Clearly, by (10), $L(Q, V^0) = \Pi_\lambda$, and, similarly, $L(Q^0, V) = \alpha_\lambda$. Now we
shall prove that any value of Q which maximizes Π subject to our primal
constraints must also maximize $\Pi_\lambda = L(Q, V^0)$.

By (5) and (7), we have for any α and any Π

$$\alpha \geq \sum \sum V_i a_{ij} Q_j \geq \Pi,$$

and even for the optimal V_i

$$(12) \qquad \sum \sum V_i^0 a_{ij} Q_j \geq \Pi.$$

But by Theorems 2 and 4, for optimal solutions

$$(13) \qquad \alpha^0 = \sum \sum V_i^0 a_{ij} Q_j^0 = \Pi^0.$$

Thus, by (12) and (13), $\Pi - \sum \sum V_i^0 a_{ij} Q_j \leq \Pi^0 - \sum \sum V_i^0 a_{ij} Q_j^0$.
Hence comparing

$$L(Q, V^0) = \Pi - \sum \sum V_i^0 a_{ij} Q_j + \alpha^0$$

with

$$L(Q^0, V^0) = \Pi^0 - \sum \sum V_i^0 a_{ij} Q_j^0 + \alpha^0$$

we see at once that
$$L(Q^0, V^0) \geq L(Q, V^0).$$

Thus, it follows that the values Q_i^0 which maximize Π must also maximize
the value of the Lagrangian expression $L(Q, V^0) = \Pi_\lambda$, which is what we
were to prove.

The corresponding result for the dual problem is left as an exercise for
the reader. The converse of the theorem [i.e., any values of Q which
maximize $L(Q, V^0)$ must also maximize Π subject to our constraints] is a
little more difficult to prove and the derivation will therefore not be given
here.

This theorem will be referred to again in the discussion of the Kuhn-
Tucker theorem in the next chapter. However, a geometric interpretation

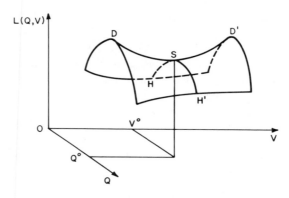

Figure 2

may first be indicated briefly. Our theorem states that the optimal Q_j will *maximize* $\Pi_\lambda = L(Q, V^0)$. Similarly, the dual formulation of the theorem states that the optimal V_i will minimize $\alpha_\lambda = L(Q^0, V)$. Hence, for $V_i = V_i^0$ we will have $L(Q, V)$ maximal for optimal values of the Q's and for $Q_j = Q_j^0$ it is minimal for optimal values of the V's. Our situation is as that shown in Figure 2 for the trivial case where there is one primal variable, Q, and only one dual variable, V. S is the point on the $L(Q, V)$ surface corresponding to the optimal value Q^0 of the primal variable and the optimal value V^0 of the dual variable. Moreover, S is the lowest point in the valley DSD' which is obtained by varying the value of V. Finally, S is the highest point on the hill HSH' to which $L(Q, V)$ can be brought by varying the value of Q. It should be obvious from the shape of the surface why S is called a *saddle point*.

APPENDIX B: THE INITIAL BASIC SOLUTION AND THE "FEASIBILITY PROGRAM"

We have seen that in many cases in which the origin is not a feasible solution for a program, rather than solving the original problem, one can instead solve its dual. This is possible wherever the origin is a feasible solution for the dual. However, there can arise cases in which neither for the primal problem nor the dual program is the origin a feasible point. First we will see how such a case can arise. Then a method by which one can solve such a problem will be described.

If we look again at the primal and dual matrices (4), we see that the origin is a feasible solution for the primal if and only if all the $C_i \geq 0$. For, then, if we set all $Q_j = 0$ we obtain the feasible solution $U_1 = C_1 \geq 0$, $U_2 = C_2 \geq 0$, etc. Similarly, from the dual matrix in (4) we see that its origin is a feasible solution for the dual if and only if all $P_j \leq 0$, for then at the origin, where all the dual structural variables, U_i, are equal to zero, we have the feasible solution $L_1 = -P_1 \geq 0$, $L_2 = -P_2 \geq 0$, etc.

Hence, we can solve either the primal or the dual problem in the normal manner unless there is at least one $C_i \leq 0$ *and* at least one $P_j \geq 0$, as the reader can verify by writing out such a problem in algebraic form. There will be no such difficulty if the maximization problem of the pair of dual programs contains only the normal sort of capacity constraints in which the use of resources must be less than or equal to their capacity. Similarly, it does not arise in the usual sort of minimization problem in which all the constraints are minimum acceptability conditions such as "the advertising program must reach *at least* 80 million people aged 18–40."

Where, however, constraints of both varieties enter a single problem, difficulties may arise. For example, suppose the firm's objective is to maximize its profits $\pi = 9Q_1 + 2Q_2$ from the quantities, Q_1 and Q_2, of its two outputs, subject to a warehouse capacity constraint:

$$3Q_1 + Q_2 \leq 6$$

and a contractual constraint specifying a minimum total output of the two items that must be delivered:

$$Q_1 + Q_2 \geq 3.$$

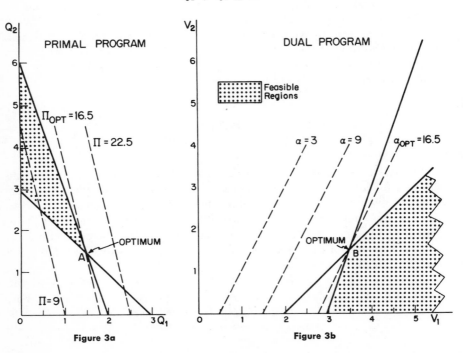

Figure 3a   **Figure 3b**

Figure 3a shows the (shaded) feasible region for this program and Figure 3b shows the feasible region for its dual. It is obvious that the origin is not feasible for either program.

Next, if we put the slack variable $U_1 \geq 0$, $U_2 \geq 0$ into the two constraints we obtain readily

(1)
$$U_1 = 6 - 3Q_1 - Q_2$$

$$U_2 = -3 + Q_1 + Q_2,$$

so that the simplex matrix for our program becomes

(2)

	1	Q_1	Q_2
$\pi =$	0	9	2
$U_1 =$	6	−3	−1
$U_2 =$	−3	1	1

Since this contains the negative number −3 in the first column, we see again that the origin is not a feasible solution for the primal problem. Similarly, since it contains the positive numbers 9 and 2 in the first row, the origin is not a feasible solution for the dual. Neither problem, then, can be solved by the usual procedure that starts from the origin as its initial feasible solution.

If a problem taking this inconvenient form does possess at least one feasible solution,[8] there is an ingenious procedure invented by Michel Balinski which enables us to deal with the programming calculation in a fairly straightforward manner.[9] What the procedure does is to take a nonfeasible simplex matrix such as (2) and by a sequence of pivot steps transform it into a matrix giving one of the feasible basic solutions of the problem. Once this is done one can proceed to find the optimal solution of the problem by applying the normal simplex procedure to the feasible matrix found through the Balinski procedure.

---

[8] It is conceivable that it might not have any feasible solutions. This will occur if the constraints impose inconsistent requirements. For example, a program obviously will have no nonnegative solution if it contains the constraint

$$Q_1 + 3Q_2 \leq -2$$

or if it has the pair of constraints $Q_1 \leq 5$, $Q_1 \geq 12$. Of course, where the set of constraints is large and involves many variables, inconsistencies are far harder to detect than they are in trivial and transparent cases such as the preceding.

[9] The discussion that follows is fairly specialized and the reader may prefer to omit it.

The nature of the method is best explained by example:

Step 1: Rewrite the matrix moving all rows with negative first entries (i.e., the infeasible portions of the solution) to the top of the new matrix. Thus, since in matrix (2) only the last row has a negative entry, we move that last row to the top of the matrix to obtain the new matrix

(3)

	1	Q_1	Q_2
$U_2 =$	-3	1	1
$\pi =$	0	9	2
$U_1 =$	6	-3	-1^*

This changeover is carried out just for convenience and obviously involves no substantive change in any of the relationships of the program.

The objective now is to rewrite the problem, if possible, in a way that gets rid of all the negative entries in the first column, since it is these negative entries that are the source of the nonfeasibility in our initial solution.

Step 2: We now treat the first row in the new matrix as a psuedo-objective function and begin moving toward the maximum value of this function by the usual pivoting steps of the simplex process. This again produces no substantive change in the programming problem itself because, it will be recalled from Chapter 5, a pivot step only rewrites the equations and inequalities of the program expressing one subset of variables in terms of the others. Just as the equation $y = 3x + 6$ is equivalent to $x = y/3 - 2$, a linear program after a pivot step remains the same in substance and changes only in form.

The purpose in moving toward a maximum of the value of the first entry in the matrix (which started out negative) is to see whether there is *any* pivoting transformation of the program which replaces that negative entry by some positive number. In terms of matrix (3), we want to pivot in a way that will replace the $-3 = U_2$ in the upper left-hand corner of matrix (3) by some positive number, and the obvious way to go about it is to move toward the maximal value[10] of U_2. We do this, as usual, by picking a pivot element from a column with a positive top entry, say the

---

[10] If it were, unfortunately, to turn out that the *maximal* value of U_2 were only, say, -0.6, then obviously no positive replacement for the negative first entry would be possible, and in such a case it would follow by definition that the problem in question possessed no feasible basic solution (no basic solution with all entries in the first column positive).

last column in matrix (3). However, the choice of pivot row in the Balinski process has two additional provisos: (a) Never take a pivot element from a row corresponding to the objective function of the original problem [row 2 of matrix (3)],[11] and (b) never take a pivot element from a row with a negative first entry [there happen to be none other than row 1 in illustrative matrix (3)].[12]

We now pivot in the usual way, on the pivot element -1, obtaining as our new simplex matrix (as the reader can verify)

	1	Q_1	U_1
$U_2 =$	3	-2	-1
$\pi =$	12	3	-2
$Q_2 =$	6	-3	-1

(4)

Because of the simplicity of the illustrative problem, this one pivoting step has yielded us a feasible solution because there are no longer any negative entries in the first column. If any had remained, we would simply have repeated our procedure, bringing another row with a negative entry to the top of the matrix (step 1) and moving toward a maximum of this new pseudo-objective function (step 2).[13]

---

[11] We avoid this since such a pivot element would move π, the objective variable, over to the top of the matrix, i.e., to the right-hand side of the equations or inequalities of the program, and it is never appropriate to do that since we always want to express π in terms of the other variables, not the other variables in terms of π.

[12] We never take an entry from a nonfeasible row because the pivot row is chosen so as to make certain that the pivot step does not transform any initially positive first entry into one which becomes negative after the next pivot step (see footnote 19 of Chapter 5). That is, the pivot row is selected in a way which prevents the introduction of a nonfeasible variable value into the solution by a badly chosen pivot step. But to prevent this we need only consider those variables whose values were nonnegative before the pivot step in question, i.e., those rows whose first entries were nonnegative to begin with.

[13] It may seem at first blush as though this further pivoting step might reintroduce negative entries into the first column in places where they had previously been eliminated. That is, suppose in (4) the last entry had indicated $Q_2 = -6$. Might not the process of getting rid of that minus sign reintroduce a negative value for U_2 which we have just gotten rid of? It is not difficult to show that such a mishap can never occur if the pivoting process is carried out correctly, for it is proved in footnote 19 of Chapter 5 that if the pivot element is chosen by the rules of Section 9 no pivot step will ever replace a positive entry in the first column by a negative one.

In our case, since (4) is now a feasible solution we now move on to

Step 3: Move the row corresponding to the true objective function [the second row in (4)] back to the top of the matrix, obtaining

$$
\begin{array}{c c c c}
 & 1 & Q_1 & U_1 \\
\pi = & 12 & 3 & -2 \\
(5) \qquad U_2 = & 3 & -2 & -1 \\
Q_2 = & 6 & -3 & -1
\end{array}
$$

Step 4: Now, if the solution is not optimal, proceed with the usual simplex calculation starting from the feasible simplex matrix that the Balinski procedure has provided. In our example, (5) is obviously not an optimal solution since the second entry in the top row is still positive. We therefore select a pivot element from that column and continue on with the simplex calculation until the optimum is found.

The procedure is really quite straightforward and appears to be rather efficient computationally. To summarize, what the Balinski procedure does is to move us from a basic solution which is not feasible (the origin) to some other basic solution that is feasible so that we can apply the usual simplex procedure to its matrix. It does this by taking the variables with initially nonfeasible values (those whose values are initially negative) and substituting for the initial programming problem an equivalent problem whose (pseudo-) objective is to maximize (in turn) the values of those variables whose initial values are negative. It does this by moving the corresponding rows to the top of the matrix and proceeding by the usual pivoting steps to increase the values of the offending variables until all negative values have been eliminated.

PROBLEM

Verify from (2) and from the dual of (2) that points A and B in Figures 3a and 3b are in fact the respective optimal solutions of the primal and the dual.

REFERENCES

Charnes, A., and W. W. Cooper, *Management Models and Industrial Applications of Linear Programming,* Volumes I and II, John Wiley & Sons, Inc., New York, 1961.

Dantzig, George B., *Linear Programming and Extensions*, Princeton University Press, Princeton, N.J., 1963.

Intrilligator, M. D., *Mathematical Optimization and Economic Theory*, Prentice-Hall, Inc., Englewood Cliffs, N.J., 1971, Chapter 5.

Nonlinear Programming *

7

In economic terms nonlinear programming may be described as the analysis of constrained maximization problems in which diminishing or increasing returns to scale are present. For example, by doubling *all* its inputs a firm may find that it can increase its profits by only 47 per cent. This may occur because, for some reason, its physical outputs cannot keep pace, or because it becomes increasingly difficult to sell additional outputs so that selling costs yield diminishing returns and/or the prices of its products fall.

1. Algebraic Notation and Example

In a nonlinear program the algebraic expressions which occur in either the objective function (e.g., the profit or cost relationship) or in the constraints or both will involve nonlinear terms such as X^3 or 5^x or $\cos X$. Thus, rather than representing the profit relationship by a simple linear expression such as $5X + 3Y + 7Z$, we use the more general functional notation total profit $= f(X, Y, Z)$, which states simply that profit is dependent in some way on the quantities of the three outputs, X, Y, and

---

* Some of the material in this chapter may be considered conceptually difficult. However, it is recommended that readers of the two preceding chapters read at least Sections 1 through 6, for only by contrast with nonlinear programming can the limitations and peculiarities of the *linear* programming case be fully understood.

Z. Similar notation is used for the constraints, so that the general nonlinear programming problem may be written in the usual three parts:

1. *Objective function*

$$\text{maximize (or minimize) } f(X, Y, Z, \cdots)$$

subject to

2. *Constraints*

$$g_1 (X, Y, Z, \cdots) \leq c_1$$
$$g_2(X, Y, Z, \cdots) \leq c_2$$
$$\cdot \quad \cdot \quad \cdot \quad \cdot \quad \cdot \quad \cdot \quad \cdot \quad \cdot \quad \cdot$$
$$g_m(X, Y, Z, \cdots) \leq c_m$$

and

3. *The nonnegativity requirements*

$$X \geq 0, \qquad Y \geq 0, \qquad Z \geq 0, \cdots.$$

To show how such a nonlinear programming problem can arise in an economic problem, consider the case where the unit profits P_x and P_y of X and Y are fixed, say $P_x = 5$ and $P_y = 3$. Suppose, however, that because of customer resistance to increased purchasing (a negatively sloping demand curve) the unit profits of Z, P_z, fall continuously as more of this commodity is offered for sale, in accord with the simple *linear* relationship

$$P_z = 200 - 0.005Z,$$

which states that every time another thousand units of Z are offered for sale, its price falls 5 cents. Substituting this expression for P_z into the objective function, that function becomes

$$\text{total profit} = P_xX + P_yY + P_zZ = 5X + 3Y + (200 - 0.005Z)Z$$
$$= 5X + 3Y + 200Z - 0.005Z^2.$$

Note that this contains a Z^2, so it is no longer a linear relationship despite the fact that the demand expression which was substituted for P_z is linear.

2. Geometric Representation: Nonlinear Constraints

It is convenient to consider the effects of nonlinearities on the graph of a programming problem in two separate stages: (1) the effects of non-linearities in the constraints, and (2) the effects of nonlinearities in the objective function.

Let us first examine the constraints. Suppose the problem involves, for example, the inequality

$$X^2 + Y^2 \leq 1.$$

As in the linear programming case, this divides combinations of X and Y into two classes: Feasible (those which meet the conditions specified by the inequality) and infeasible (those combinations of X and Y which violate the inequality). The border line between the region of feasible points and

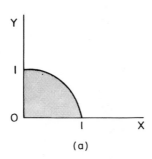

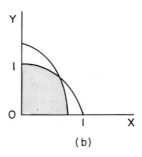

(a)   (b)

Figure 1

those which represent outputs that do not satisfy the inequality is again given by the requirement that *equality* hold in the constraint:

$$X^2 + Y^2 = 1, \quad \text{i.e.,} \quad Y = \sqrt{1 - X^2}.$$

Any point on the graph of this equation represents a combination of X and Y which just manages to squeeze in "under the wire"—it just barely satisfies the inequality. By trying various values of X and computing the corresponding values of Y, or by more sophisticated means, it can be seen that the graph of this relationship is that shown in Figure 1a. Furthermore, if we require X and Y to be nonnegative, the feasible output combinations are represented by the shaded region in this diagram. A second nonlinear inequality might reduce the feasible region to that depicted in Figure 1b.

We see, then, that nonlinear inequalities trace out a feasible region just as do linear inequalities. However, when they are nonlinear the borders of the feasible region will consist, at least partly, of curved lines.

3. Geometry of Nonlinear Objective Functions

For reasons analogous to those just described, the graph of a nonlinear objective function is not a plane as in the linear case. Instead profit functions may be hills or valleys or of totally irregular shape.

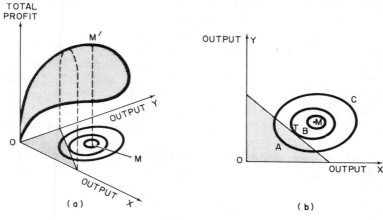

Figure 2

Several such profit relationships and the corresponding iso-profit curves (profit indifference curves) are illustrated in Figures 2, 3, and 4. Figure 2a represents the "best-behaved" type of profit function. For reasons which are discussed later in this chapter, such a function makes life easier for the programmer than does the presence of other types of nonlinear profit functions.

This can be described as a diminishing-returns case—the curvature of the surface (its upside-down U-shaped cross sections) indicates that increases in output yield diminishing marginal returns (see Section 4 of Chapter 11. Indeed, increases in output beyond the profit-maximizing

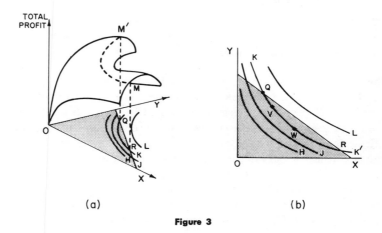

Figure 3

point M must yield diminishing *total* returns, i.e., such an increase in output must obviously reduce total profits.

The iso-profit curves of nonlinear profit functions are not usually parallel straight lines. In this hill-shaped profit function case they are closed curves which lie inside one another. It is also to be noted that, unlike the linear case, the direction of profitable movement can change. For example, in Figure 2b a movement upward and to the right (an increase in both out-puts) will sometimes increase profits and sometimes reduce them. Thus the move from A to B adds to total profits, but a move from T to C reduces them.

An extreme case of this phenomenon is depicted in Figure 3. Here the iso-profit curves have the traditional shape of indifference curves, but there is one difference. Profits increase as we move up from H to J to K.

But curve K corresponds to the maximum profit ridge MM' in Figure 3a, so that if we move further away from the origin, say from an output combination on K to one on L, profits actually fall.

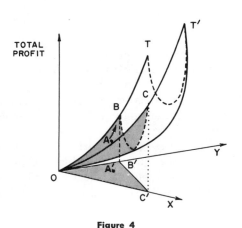

Finally, Figure 4 depicts an important case, that of increasing returns to specialization, where higher values of, say, X bring in ever-increasing marginal yields (the upward curvature of OCT'). After a preliminary discussion of some geometric concepts we shall return to examine some of the problems which such a situation involves.

Figure 4

4. Convex and Nonconvex Regions

The shaded region in Figure 5a is of a variety which is called *convex*. That is to say, it has no dents or holes as does the nonconvex region in Figure 5b. More precisely, a region is defined to be convex if the straight line connecting any two of its points lies entirely inside the region. Thus, if we draw the line connecting any two points, such as M and R in Figure 5a, that line will never leave the shaded area. But if in 5b we try to connect points A and B or B and C in this way, our lines will have to traverse some of the unshaded part of the diagram.

The distinction between convexity and nonconvexity of the feasible region is important for programming. Nonconvexity can make it more difficult for us to find the optimal point, and it can also make it more difficult for us to recognize the point to be optimal when we get there.

1. *Testing for optimality.* Suppose, for the moment, that the objective (profit) function is linear so that the iso-profit curves are parallel straight lines. Then, in a feasible region which is convex, if we find a point such as M from which any *small* move decreases profit, we can be sure that this point is a global optimum, i.e., no move of *any* magnitude will bring in profits higher than those at M. M is a point of "tangency" between iso-profit curve PP' and the boundary of the feasible region.

Because of the convexity of the region, its boundary curves further and further away from iso-profit line PP'. Thus if a small move away from

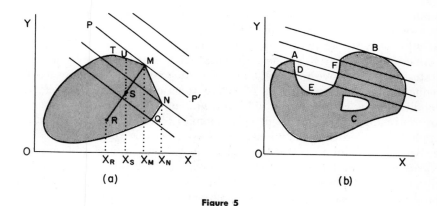

(a)   (b)

Figure 5

M, say to N, reduces profits, we can be sure that any further move in that direction, say to Q, will reduce profits still more.

However, this result does not hold for the nonconvex feasible region in Figure 5b. There, a move from point of tangency A over to D does indeed reduce profits. But if we are patient and nevertheless follow along the boundary of the feasible region, it may begin to curl back upward again (point E) and eventually we may even reach a point B which is also a point of price line-feasible region tangency and which yields profits far higher than those at tangency point A. A point like A which yields higher profit than any other feasible point in its vicinity is called a *local optimum*, whereas the point B which really yields maximum profits is a *global optimum*.

2. *Finding the optimum.* A related problem produced by nonconvexity is that it is more difficult under these circumstances to design an iterative

procedure to find the global optimum. In the convex case (Figure 5a) any move which increases profits (e.g., the move from Q to N) is certain to get us closer to the optimal point, M, because there is only one profit hilltop and any uphill move must bring us nearer to it. But in the case of the nonconvex region a move which increases profits (e.g., the move from E to D in Figure 5b) can move us toward the wrong hilltop, A, and away from the true optimum, B. Hence in such a case an iterative procedure which is designed always to increase profits may very well fail to lead us to the global optimum.

What is the significance of these results? It is, in effect, that near-sighted mathematicians cannot be trusted to solve programming problems in which the feasible region is nonconvex. Any procedure that tells us to test for maximum profits by checking whether a few steps in any direction reduce profits can be considered to involve such a myopic approach. An example of such a procedure is the simple requirement of the differential calculus that the second derivative of the function whose value is to be maximized be negative at the maximum point. For this condition merely states that any move to a point *very near* the maximum point results in a reduction in the value of the objective function, so it is a satisfactory condition only where nearsightedness is no handicap. In other words there are optimality tests and resulting economies of calculation which are in-applicable to problems involving nonconvex feasible regions.

It is important to note that in a *linear* program the feasible region is *always* convex.[1] That is why, in the simplex method, to see whether some corner C of the feasible region is optimal it is only necessary to test the profitability of a move to one of the corners adjacent to C. For if a move to any such corner reduces profits (or increases costs) then any further moves must certainly be disadvantageous. In other words, the simplex method can be classified as a nearsighted calculation method.

---

[1] To demonstrate this it is only necessary to show that if S (Figure 5a) is any point on the line connecting two feasible points such as M and R in the feasible region of a linear program, then S is also feasible (it lies in the shaded region). But S represents an output combination which can be obtained by a suitable scaling down of the activities at M and R. For example, if S is the midpoint of line MR, it represents the sum of half the outputs at M and half the outputs at R (X_S is the midpoint of X_R and X_M, etc.). Now consider any scarce facility k, whose total capacity is K. Since M is feasible, its production must require no more than K units of this facility, and the same must hold for output combination R. But because a linear program involves constant returns to scale, it follows that half of the outputs at M or at R require no more than $\frac{1}{2}K$ units of facility k in their production. Hence S will require in its manufacture no more than $\frac{1}{2}K + \frac{1}{2}K = K$ units of k, i.e., no more of this scarce resource than is available. A similar argument holds for every scarce resource needed to produce S, and it therefore follows that output S must be feasible.

5. Concave and Convex (Objective) Functions

A classification somewhat analogous to that just described for geo-metric regions also holds for the graphs of functions. A function whose graph is like that in Figure 4 is called *convex* while that in Figure 2a is called *concave*. More precisely, a function is called *strictly concave* if, when we draw a straight line connecting any two points A and B on its graph (Figure 6a), the whole of the arc AB, excluding the end points, lies above the straight line AB. The function is called *concave* (but not strictly concave) if its graph contains some linear stretches so that a straight line such as $A'B'$ (Figure 6b) may coincide with arc $A'B'$.

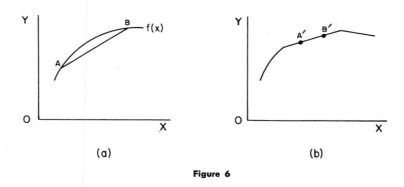

(a)   (b)

Figure 6

Convex and *strictly convex* functions are defined analogously, only here the connecting arc always lies *below* or coincides with the line connecting two points on the graph. It should be noted that a linear function, whose graph is a straight line, a plane, or a hyperplane (n-dimensional analogue of a plane), is always *both* concave and convex.

Objective functions of the "wrong" shape can lead to the same problem as nonconvex feasible regions—they can produce local optima which are not global optima so they can invalidate myopic computational procedures and procedures for testing for optimality. But in this case, which shape is wrong depends on the nature of the problem. As we shall see now, a well-behaved objective function in a maximization problem is apt to be badly behaved in a minimization problem, and vice versa.

A moment's thought indicates why this is so. In a maximization prob-lem, if the function is hill-shaped (concave) all uphill roads lead to the top. In Figure 2a we can confidently proceed by moving upward in *any* direction because all uphill paths end up at the peak. Hence any trial-and-error (iterative) procedure that keeps trying successive output levels which are more profitable than those in the previous attempts will (if it does not move up too slowly) eventually get us to the maximum profit output combination. Moreover, if we are at a point M from which any small move takes us downhill, we know that this point must be the true optimum. The myopic computational techniques and optimality tests both work.

But if in a maximization problem the graph of the objective function contains a valley (it is convex), going in an uphill direction is not guaranteed to get us to the top. If we start uphill from point A in Figure 4, we may land up in point B instead of point C, the global optimum in the shaded feasible region.

In a minimization problem it is easy to see that the situation is reversed—a valley is desirable and a hill is troublesome from the point of view of computation.

> We may sum up by stating that nearsighted computational techniques can be used in a maximization problem if the feasible region is convex and the objective function is concave. In a minimization problem such methods can be employed if the objective function and the feasible region are both convex.

There is another way in which the economist can look at this matter. A graph of a concave function such as Figure 2, if it is a profit function, represents a situation involving diminishing returns, as already noted. But if the figure were to represent a cost function, it should be clear that it would be one involving increasing returns (decreasing marginal costs as output expands). Similarly, convex Figure 4 represents either an increasing-returns profit function or a diminishing-returns cost function. Thus a well-behaved objective function in either the maximization case (concave) or the minimization case (convex) involves diminishing returns. We can, then, restate our main theorem as:

> Myopic computational and optimality testing techniques can be used when the problem involves a convex feasible region and diminishing returns.

The role of diminishing returns in this proposition is easily visualized intuitively—if any departure from a local optimum always involves diminishing returns, then going further and further only makes things worse, so that our local optimum must be a global optimum as well. Indeed, this reasoning can be carried further to indicate that diminishing returns will tend to produce convexity in the feasible region. The stretch EF in the nonconvex feasible region in Figure 5b clearly involves increasing returns to output (increasing marginal profits as output increases). If diminishing returns held throughout, the boundary of the feasible region would curve further and further away from the iso-profit line through local optimum point A so that no other optimum point such as B would be possible.[2] Therefore, *only if we have diminishing returns throughout the feasible region are myopic computational techniques generally legitimate.* This is the final, most compact form of our theorem.

6. Nonlinearities and the Basic Theorem of Linear Programming

It will be recalled from the preceding chapter that there is a central theorem of linear programming which states that the number of variables (including slack variables) whose values are positive in an optimal solution will ordinarily be equal to the number of constraints in the problem. In other words there will always be a *basic* optimal solution to any solvable linear programming problem. In geometric terms, there will then always be an optimal solution which occurs at a corner of the feasible region. This is one of the great computational economies which *linear* programming makes possible. An optimal solution can always be found by examining only the corners of the feasible region, and ignoring the infinite set of points which make up the remainder of the feasible region.

In nonlinear programming this result does not hold. This is easily shown by counterexample. In Figure 2b the optimum point is the point of tangency T between the boundary of the feasible region and the highest attainable iso-profit curve. It will be noted that at point T both X and Y have positive values even though there is only one constraint.

In Figure 3b an even more extreme case is depicted. Here optimal

---

[2] More specifically, it is easy to show that, if the variables represent the magnitudes of several outputs, then convexity of the feasible region is tantamount to diminishing marginal rate of transformation of one output for another (see *Value and Capital*, 2nd edition, Oxford University Press, Inc., New York, 1946, pp. 80–87), for the outer (northeast) boundary of the feasible region (arc TN in Figure 5a) is the production possibility locus (the transformation curve or efficiency frontier), which represents all the maximal output combinations producible with the available quantities of scarce resources (see Chapter 11, Section 7, below). Convexity requires that as we move to the right along this arc its slope diminishes (becomes increasingly negative) or, for some stretches, remains unchanged. But the diminishing slope of TN means that we get diminishing returns in shifting resources out of the production of Y and into the production of X. Thus, an increase in the output of X from X_s to X_m results in only a small decrease in Y (from the ordinate of U to that of M), but a further equal increase in X from X_m to X_n requires a much larger fall in Y. This argument can be extended to the case where there are more variables, or variables other than outputs, to show a general connection between diminishing returns and convexity of the feasible region.

Note that, in this respect, diminishing returns is compatible with a *linear* programming problem, because the feasible region of such a problem is always convex. Cf. footnote 1, above.

points, such as V and W, occur in the interior of the feasible region.[3] It is to be noted, then, that even though there is only one constraint both X and Y are positive. But, in addition, since the facility represented by that constraint is not used to capacity (we are not on the constraint line), the slack variable corresponding to that constraint will also have a nonzero value. Here, then, we have only one constraint and yet every one of the three variables' values is positive!

It is clear, then, that the so-called basic theorem of linear programming need not hold in the presence of nonlinearities. However, the connection between the number of variables whose optimal values are nonzero and the number of constraints does not just descend into chaos. A very important relationship exists between the difference in these two numbers and the structure of the problem. In general we may state that with diminishing returns (a concave maximization or a convex minimization problem) the number of positive variable values will tend to be greater than the number of constraints. In the increasing-returns case the number of positive optimal variable values will generally fall short of the number of constraints. It follows that if we try to approximate a nonlinear problem with a linear programming calculation, then if there are diminishing returns we should suspect that the answer will contain too few positive values, while if it involves increasing returns it will contain too many.

The reason for this result is not difficult to see. First we may note how this follows from the geometry. We consider only the maximization problem, but the argument for the minimization case is perfectly analogous. In Figure 2, the diminishing-returns case, the highest feasible point, that is, the optimal point, will tend to occur toward the center of the diagram where variables take nonzero values. On the other hand, in the increasing-returns case (Figure 4) where the graph curls upward toward the edges of the diagram, maximal points like B and C will occur over the axes where variables take on zero values (X is zero at point B and Y is zero at point C).

But there is an easier way to visualize the relationship between diminishing or increasing returns and the number of nonzero variable values in an optimal solution. When a linear program indicates that a firm with 2,000 products and 17 constraints should cut its line down to 17 or fewer items, it is reasoned implicitly that the combination of products which yields the greatest profits with a small expansion in their outputs will also

---

[3] It is true that this figure also contains two optimal points Q and R which lie on the boundary (but *not on corners*) of the feasible region. But it is easy to see that a slight modification of the drawing could eliminate these by bending down the three-dimensional surface in Figure 3a as it approaches the axes. A simpler example of an optimum point which occurs only in the interior of the feasible region would result if the highest point M in Figure 2 fell inside the feasible region.

continue to be most profitable as their production increases indefinitely. It will then pay to enlarge the output of these most profitable goods as far as possible—until they take over all of the firm's scarce facilities and leave no excess capacity sufficient for the production of other items. But if there are diminishing returns to the production of these goods, then though they start off being the most profitable, after their output expands to some intermediate level the profitability of a further increment in their outputs will fall below that of some other goods and it will then pay to devote some of the company's resources to the output of these other goods, and so on.

That is precisely why our instincts are outraged by the linear programming recommendation that a 2,000-product firm cut its product line down to 17 items, devoting all of its facilities to the production of these goods. We surmise that the firm has spread its production over so many different items because the market calls for them—because it will be difficult or impossible to market as much of the 17 items as the firm has the capacity to produce. There are diminishing returns because of increasing marketing costs. Often careful analysis will indicate that the 2,000-item line is indeed excessive, but that the optimal set of products includes considerably more than the 17 items which will yield most profits to a small output expansion.

For similar reasons, increasing returns tend to call for considerably greater concentration in a few products than does linear programming. If an item which is most profitable becomes even more profitable as its output expands, it will pay to drop other goods from the line to achieve the full benefits of specialization.

Here again, an economic example may help to clarify the situation. In a study of the optimal number and geographic location of a company's warehouses it was found that a linear programming computation might very well suggest that the firm operate a separate warehouse for every customer! For, in the linear case, if a change in warehouse location would reduce the transportation cost of shipping from factory to warehouse to some single customer, it would (if these were the only costs involved) pay to operate such a warehouse. What this computation ignores is the economies in inventory, administration, and bookkeeping, etc., which result from the operation of a small number of larger warehouses. In other words the increasing returns to size of warehouse operation are ignored in the linear programming calculation, which then recommends the operation of too many warehouse installations (too many nonzero variables).

In sum, when a linear programming calculation is employed to deal with a problem which really involves diminishing returns, the linear approximation will recommend too few activities, whereas if the actual problem involves economies of large scale (increasing returns) the linear approximation will call for too many activities. This rule should be helpful in making rough improvements in the results of linear approximations. Even more important, *it warns us of the dangers of a linear calculation where there are nonlinearities present.*

7. Methods of Nonlinear Computation

This section makes no attempt to teach the reader step-by-step procedures for nonlinear computation. The literature contains many special tricks which vary from one type of problem to another, and the field is in a state of rapid change and development. We shall discuss only two general approaches indicating the logic of the procedures which have been employed. It will be noted that the methods which are about to be described are both of the myopic variety. They can only be relied upon to find a global optimum in a diminishing-returns problem. In a case of increasing returns these methods cannot be relied upon to produce more than local optima. There exist principles for the determination of global optima in the increasing-returns case, but they have as yet not been tested to any significant extent.

Dr. Wolfe has described the simplex procedure of linear programming as a "walking" method.[4] That is, the computer steps from one corner to another adjacent corner (always in the right direction), until he finds an optimum. By contrast he has described the techniques of nonlinear programming as hopping and creeping methods. Let us deal first with the former.

The hopping approach applies only where the constraints are linear, even though the objective function is nonlinear. In fact most nonlinear programs which have so far been utilized in practice have been of this variety. In such a case the boundary of the feasible region is composed of a set of joined straight-line segments and is always convex. Indeed, it is identical with the feasible region of linear programming.

In this situation it is nevertheless possible for a unique optimal point to occur away from a corner, as witness the case of point T in Figure 2b, which is an example of this sort of program. The hopping feature of the computational procedure is necessary to get us away from the corner-to-corner movement of the simplex method. In effect, starting off at any point we walk to the next more profitable corner and then hop back to any still more lucrative intermediate point.

To be more specific, let us describe one of the more frequently used hopping procedures in somewhat greater detail. Consider the situation in Figure 7. Suppose at some stage of our computation we have just passed

---

[4] See Philip Wolfe, "Computational Techniques for Non-Linear Programs," Princeton University Conference, March 1957.

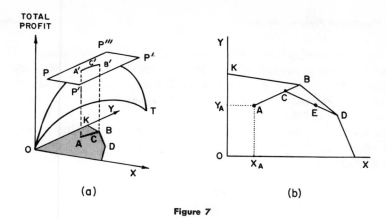

Figure 7

corner K and happen to find ourselves at a point A. We then proceed in the following stages:

Step 1: Fit a plane, $PP'P''P'''$, tangent to the nonlinear profit surface above point A.[5]

Step 2: Use one "round" of the simplex method on the resulting approximative linear programming problem to find a corner, say B, which is more profitable than the previous corner K.

Step 3: Use the differential calculus or some substitute procedure to find the most profitable point, say C, on the straight line connecting A and B, i.e., find the point C on line AB above which the nonlinear profit function is highest. (This is always a "one-dimensional problem," i.e., the graph of alternatives is a straight line, and the computation is therefore not difficult.)

Step 4: Go back to step 1, but start this time from point C and corner B (thus going, e.g., successively to corner D and then back to E, etc.).

These "hopping" methods are slower than the walking methods. Moreover, unlike the walking methods, they do not actually find the solution to a programming problem, but they do approximate it to any desired degree of accuracy, which is enough for all practical applications.

We come now to the "creeping" or, more correctly, the *gradient* methods for solving nonlinear programming problems. Geometrically, they involve our sliding around the feasible region, always in continuous motion (no jumps) and always in a direction which goes uphill (downhill) on the profit (cost) function. These methods can be used even when both the objective function and the constraints contain nonlinearities. Such meth-

---

[5] This is done by taking the profit function to be total profit $= aX + bY$ and setting $a = \partial f/\partial X$ and $b = \partial f/\partial Y$, where $f(X, Y)$ is the true nonlinear profit function and the partial derivatives are evaluated at point A', i.e., at $X = X_A$ and $Y = Y_A$.

ods were first proposed for problems relating to programming by George Brown and von Neumann. Samuelson later showed that they bear some analogy with the way in which a market mechanism can approach its equilibrium. The basic idea of the gradient methods is very simple. Suppose it is desired to find the outputs which maximize profit, $R = f(X_1, \cdots, X_n)$, where the X_i are the outputs of the firm's different products. A gradient method sets up the differential equation (in which t represents computing time elapsed)

$$\frac{dX_i}{dt} = \frac{\partial R}{\partial X_i}.$$

This states that we increase the quantity X_i of commodity $i (dX_i/dt > 0)$ in the trial solution, so long and only so long as this increase in X_i results in a rise in the firm's profits. Moreover, we make this time rate of increase in output, X_i, proportionate (equal for an appropriate time unit) to its marginal profitability $(\partial R/\partial X_i)$. In other words, we increase (decrease) all quantities whose rise leads to higher (lower) profits and, in effect, give a priority ordering to the changes in the different quantities in proportion to their profit contribution. Moreover, we impose the condition that any quantity which falls to zero be stopped at that point

$$[\partial X_k/\partial t = 0 \quad \text{if} \quad X_k = 0 \quad \text{and} \quad \partial R/\partial X_k < 0$$

(i.e., if X_k has just been falling)] so that we do not get into the economic nonsense of negative outputs. This is the essence of the gradient methods. If the problem is one involving diminishing returns throughout, the solution to the gradient-method differential equations will converge, over time, to the true maximum, i.e., the quantities, X_i, will all approach their profit-maximizing values. Gradient methods can also be employed in linear programming computations. There is reason to believe that they are slower than the simplex method when an accurate solution is required, but there is not yet enough computational experience for a firm statement on this matter.

Still another, indeed, so far one of the most successful methods of dealing with nonlinear programming problems involves the use of "piecewise linear" approximations. Clearly, a circle can be approximated to any desired degree of accuracy by an inscribed polygon. Similarly, other well-behaved curves can be approximated by connected straight-line segments. In this way the objective function and constraints of a nonlinear program can be approximated linearly, and the resulting approximation can be handled by variants of the simplex method of linear programming.

REFERENCES

Arrow, K. J., Leonid Hurwicz, and H. Uzawa, *Studies in Linear and Non-Linear Programming*, Stanford University Press, Stanford, Calif., 1958.

Luenberger, D. G., *Introduction to Linear and Nonlinear Programming*, Addison-Wesley, Reading, Mass., 1973.

Mangasarian, O. L., *Nonlinear Programming*, McGraw-Hill Book Company, New York, 1969.

Whittle, P., *Optimization Under Constraints: Theory and Applications of Nonlinear Programming*, Wiley-Interscience, New York, 1971.

Zangwill, W. I., *Nonlinear Programming: A Unified Approach*, Prentice-Hall, Inc., Englewood Cliffs, N.J., 1969.

Kuhn-Tucker Methods*

8

1. Kuhn-Tucker Analysis[1]

We come now to a class of theorems of nonlinear programming that have been the focal point of the mathematician's interest in the subject. These theorems are deeper than the material on programming covered in the preceding three chapters. The basic theorems were contributed by H. W. Kuhn and A. W. Tucker.

It will be recalled from Chapter 4 that a maximum or minimum problem involving only equality constraints, and which is amenable to treatment by standard calculus techniques, can be approached by the classical method of Lagrange multipliers. This method utilizes an "artificial" Lagrangian problem that is related to the original problem in one important respect: Their solutions are the same. In bare outline, construction of this artificial substitute problem involves the following steps:

1. Take each of the constraints and bring all of the terms over to one side of the equation—e.g., rewrite $X + Y = 5$ as $X + Y - 5 = 0$.

2. Multiply each of the constraints by a variable whose value is unspecified, this variable being the Lagrange multiplier. For example, the preceding constraint becomes $\lambda(X + Y - 5) = 0$.

---

* This chapter is somewhat more advanced than the preceding discussions of programming analysis.

[1] The following discussion generalizes some of the materials in Appendix A of Chapter 6.

3. Add together all of the constraints (each multiplied by its own Lagrange multiplier) and then add this sum to the objective function. This sum is called the *Lagrangian expression*; e.g., if the problem is to maximize $X^2 + 3XY + Z$ subject to $X + Y = 5$ and $XZ = 10$, the Lagrangian expression is

$$X^2 + 3XY + Z + \lambda_1(X + Y - 5) + \lambda_2(XZ - 10),$$

where λ_1 and λ_2 are two different Lagrange multipliers.

We now can state the central theorem of Lagrange multiplier theory, which asserts that, in a wide class of problems, any values of X, Y, and Z which maximize the value of the objective function subject to the stated constraints will also maximize the (unconstrained) Lagrangian expression and vice versa. In other words, we are given a choice—we can either solve the original constrained maximization problem or we can instead solve the *totally different* problem of maximizing the value of the Lagrangian expression, a problem that involves no constraints. Either procedure automatically solves both problems. Naturally, we then choose the alternative that is easier, and often the easier procedure will be the Lagrangian method. We will see presently that besides its usefulness as a computational device, the Lagrangian approach offers us a great deal of additional analytical power.

Professors Kuhn and Tucker have extended this approach to mathematical programming. We will find it convenient first simply to describe their results and the corresponding methods without attempting to justify any of the assertions made in the process. It will facilitate the discussion to leave explanations to a later section. In sum, the Kuhn-Tucker analysis tells us that:

1. For a wide class of programming problems (including all linear problems and all diminishing-returns nonlinear problems) a Lagrangian expression can be formed in exactly the way described above for the calculus case, and this Lagrangian expression will have the same useful property:

Whatever values of the variables maximize (minimize) the value of the original objective function subject to its equality or inequality constraints will maximize (minimize) the value of the Lagrangian expression (subject only to the nonnegativity conditions for the variables).

This first proposition is, in essence, the main Kuhn-Tucker theorem.

2. The Lagrangian expression has another interesting property, which will be explained further in item 4, below. Suppose, to be concrete, that we are dealing with a maximization problem. Then we have the following rather curious result: If we treat the Lagrange multipliers as variables, then the original problem will have been solved when and only when we have found the values of the original problem's variables which maximize the

value of the Lagrangian expression *and the values of the λ's which minimize that value.* In more technical terminology we call this solution a saddle point. [See Appendix A to Chapter 6 and Section 5 of Chapter 18, which explain this terminology. The graph of the Lagrangian function has a saddle-like shape and the optimal point is the top of a hill when looked at from one direction, and the trough of a valley when looked at from another (Figure 2 of Chapter 6).]

3. In particular, for reasons that will be suggested toward the end of the chapter, in a linear programming problem these Lagrange multipliers turn out to be the optimal values (the "prices") of the dual problem.[2] Moreover, *given any primal problem and its dual, the Lagrangian expressions for the two problems are identical!*

(This theorem is a direct consequence of the duality theorems of Chapter 6. It has already been discussed in Appendix A to that chapter and will be derived explicitly at the end of Section 2.) For this reason we will henceforward use the symbols for our dual structural variables, $V_1, V_2, \cdots, V_m$, to denote the Lagrange multipliers which we have heretofore referred to as $\lambda_1, \lambda_2, \cdots, \lambda_m$.

4. In fact, this duality relationship leads directly to the maximization-minimization (saddle-point) property described in 2, above. For suppose our primal problem is a maximization problem in which the object is to maximize profit (Π). Then the dual problem must be a minimization problem whose objective is to minimize accounting cost (α). Let $L(Q_1, \cdots, Q_n, V_1, \cdots, V_m)$ represent the common Lagrangian expression for the two problems, and let us designate it in briefer notation as $L(Q, V)$. Let Q^0 represent the optimal set of Q's for the primal problem and let V^0 represent the optimal set of V's for the dual. The Lagrangian approach then rests on the following assertions: (a) the value of the primal variables $Q_1, \cdots, Q_n$, which maximize Π, must also be those which maximize $L(Q, V^0)$ i.e., the Lagrangian expression for the primal problem in which we have set $\lambda_i = V_i^0$.

Similarly, the values of the dual variables $V_1, \cdots, V_m$ which minimize α must also minimize $L(Q^0, V)$. Hence we have the minimax (saddle-point) result:

If we find a combination of Q's and V's which constitutes a solution to the primal and the dual problems, respectively, then for these values the Lagrangian expression $L(Q, V)$ will have the lowest value which any V's can give it and the highest value which any Q's can give it.

---

[2] The reader may well wonder whether one can construct a dual problem corresponding to a given nonlinear primal problem and whether analogous properties hold for the nonlinear dual. The answer is that duals can be constructed for wide classes of nonlinear problems, and that analogous results do apply. While the nonlinear dual objective func-

Before proceeding to discuss the main mode of utilization of the Kuhn-Tucker theorem we may describe very briefly several other applications of the theorem:

1. It provides a helpful interpretation (as dual prices) of Lagrange multipliers in the linear and portions of the nonlinear programming theory, which sheds some light on Lagrange multiplier theory in general.

2. It is, in many cases, helpful in computation, giving us alternative means for solving a given programming problem. In particular, it has been helpful in the gradient methods of solution.

3. Perhaps most important from the point of view of the mathematician, the Kuhn-Tucker theorem serves as a so-called existence theorem in mathematical programming. That is, there are some programming problems which are unsolvable (they have no solution) because they involve inconsistencies or because there is no effective upper bound to the value of the objective function (so that the sky is the limit—there is no finite *maximum* value). Before we try to solve a problem it is desirable to know whether a solution even *exists*—because if it does not exist there is no point in wasting time looking for it. An existence theorem is a criterion which can tell us whether a solution to a given problem exists, even if it does not show us how to go about finding that solution. The Kuhn-Tucker theorem provides such an existence criterion, for it states that, for the class of programming problems for which it is valid, a problem has a solution if and only if the corresponding Lagrangian conditions can be satisfied.

2. The Form of the Lagrangian Expression

In the Kuhn-Tucker analysis it is particularly easy to become confused about the signs of the terms used in constructing the Lagrangian expression. The difficulty arises out of the presence of inequality constraints in which, unlike the case of an equation, there is an asymmetry between the transfer of terms from the right- to the left-hand side of the relationship and the transfer in the opposite direction. Since much confusion can result from an error in signs in the formulation of the Lagrangian, before going further let

---

tion is somewhat more complicated than the dual's objective function in the linear case, the dual constraints are the obvious nonlinear generalization of the linear dual constraints. In economic terms, the nonlinear dual constraint requires that the *marginal* profit yield of output j be no greater than the accounting value of all the *marginal* input requirements of output j.

For further references on duality in nonlinear programming see Philip Wolfe, "A Duality Theorem for Nonlinear Programming," *Quarterly of Applied Mathematics*, Vol. 19, 1961, and M. L. Balinski and W. J. Baumol, "The Dual in Nonlinear Programing and Its Economic Interpretation," *Review of Economic Studies*, Vol. XXXV, July 1968.

us go through the rather uninteresting step of describing a standardized procedure that is designed to reduce the likelihood of this sort of mistake. The procedure is described in the following two rules, which, for the moment, are offered with no attempt at explanation, but which will be justified in footnote 4.

RULE 1. Write each constraint so that all nonzero terms appear on one side of the inequality or the equals sign and only a zero appears on the other side of the expression. *In a maximization problem all inequality constraints should be rewritten in the form $S \geq 0$, where S is the sum of all nonzero terms, while in a minimization problem the inequality should be reversed, i.e., the relationship should be written in the form $S \leq 0$.*

Example: Suppose a maximization problem contains the constraint $Q_1^2 + 2Q_2 \geq 4$. This should be rewritten in standard form (by Rule 1) as $-4 + Q_1^2 + 2Q_2 \geq 0$.

RULE 2. To form the Lagrangian, multiply each of the resulting expressions, S_i, by its own Lagrange multiplier, V_i, and *add* the resulting product to the original objective function. After all these additions have been completed one has obtained the requisite Lagrangian whose maximum (or, rather, whose saddle point) remains to be found.

To summarize, if our problem involves maximization of $\Pi = f(Q_1, \cdots, Q_n)$ subject to the constraints $g_1(Q_1, \cdots, Q_n) \leq c_1; \cdots;$ $g_m(Q_1, \cdots, Q_n) \leq c_m$, then the Lagrangian function is $L(Q, V) = f(Q_1, \cdots, Q_n) + V_1[c_1 - g_1(Q_1, \cdots, Q_n)] + \cdots + V_m[c_m - g_m(Q_1, \cdots, Q_n)]$. The Kuhn-Tucker theorem then asserts that if we find the Q's for which $L(Q, V)$ is a maximum and the V's for which this function is a minimum, *subject only to the nonnegativity conditions $Q_j \geq 0$, $V_i \geq 0$,* we will have found the solutions to the original primal and dual problems.

Example: Consider the program

$$\text{maximize} \qquad \Pi = Q_1^3 + Q_1 Q_2$$
$$\text{subject to,} \qquad Q_1 - 10 \leq -Q_2^5$$
$$Q_1^2 + 2Q_2 \geq 4$$
$$Q_1 \geq 0, Q_2 \geq 0.$$

After rewriting our constraints as indicated in Rule 1 we have as our Lagrangian expression

$$L(Q, V) = Q_1^3 + Q_1 Q_2 + V_1(10 - Q_1 - Q_2^5) + V_2(-4 + Q_1^2 + 2Q_2),$$

which is constrained only by the nonnegativity conditions $Q_1 \geq 0$, $Q_2 \geq 0$, $V_1 \geq 0$, $V_2 \geq 0$. The reader will note that because we are dealing with a maximization problem each constraint has been rewritten as a "greater than or equal to" relationship.

We can now apply the rules for the formation of the Lagrangian expression to demonstrate our earlier assertion about the relationship between the Lagrangians for a pair of dual linear programs. Specifically, we will show that $L(Q, V^0)$, the Lagrangian for a primal problem, is, term by term, identical in form with the Lagrangian for its dual, $L(Q^0, V)$, accepting for the moment the unproved assertion that the values of the Lagrange multipliers for the primal are the V_i^0, the optimal values of the dual structural variables, and that the values of the Lagrange multipliers for the dual are the Q_j^0, the optimal values of the primal structural variables.

Proof: In general notation we have as our primal problem

$$\text{Max} \qquad\qquad \Pi = \sum_{j=1}^{n} P_j Q_j$$

subject to

$$\sum_{j=1}^{n} a_{ij} Q_j \leq c_i \qquad (i = 1, \cdots, m).$$

By Rules 1 and 2, this corresponds to the Lagrangian problem

$$\text{Max} \qquad L(Q, V^0) = \sum_{j=1}^{n} P_j Q_j + \sum_{i=1}^{m} V_i^0 (c_i - \sum_{j=1}^{n} a_{ij} Q_j).$$

Similarly, the dual program can be written

$$\text{Min} \qquad\qquad \alpha = \sum_{i=1}^{m} c_i V_i$$

subject to

$$\sum_{i=1}^{m} a_{ij} V_i \geq P_j \qquad (j = 1, \cdots, n).$$

whose Lagrangian problem is

$$\text{Min} \qquad L(Q^0, V) = \sum_{i=1}^{m} V_i c_i + \sum_{j=1}^{n} Q_j^0 (P_j - \sum_{i=1}^{m} a_{ij} V_i).$$

A glance at both of the preceding Lagrangian expressions indicates that each is a special case of the general Lagrangian form

$$L(Q, V) = \sum P_j Q_j + \sum V_i c_i - \sum\sum V_i a_{ij} Q_j.$$

The primal Lagrangian problem, then, is to maximize $L(Q, V)$ with V_1, $\cdots$, V_m set, respectively, equal to $V_1^0, \cdots, V_m^0$ and the dual problem is to minimize the same function with the values for the $Q_1, \cdots, Q_n$ set equal to $Q_1^0, \cdots, Q_n^0$. Thus the solution is what is called a *saddle point* for the general function $L(Q, V)$, with that function maximized with respect to the values of the Q_j's and minimized with respect to the values of the V_i's.

3. The Kuhn-Tucker Conditions.

The observation that a constrained maximization problem can be translated into an unconstrained Lagrangian expression is highly illuminating in itself. But we have seen in the discussion of the subject in the context of the differential calculus that many of the uses of this transformation depend on the next step, the employment of the first-order conditions for the maximization of the Lagrangian expression $L(Q_1, \cdots, Q_n, V_1, \cdots, V_m)$. That is, in the analysis and solution of a constrained maximum problem in the calculus we make use of the requirement that all of the partial derivatives of this expression must be equal to zero., i.e., that

(1) $$\partial L(Q, V)/\partial Q_j = 0 \qquad (j = 1, 2, \cdots, n)$$

and

(2) $$\partial L(Q, V)/\partial V_i = 0 \qquad (i = 1, 2, \cdots, m).$$

It will be recalled that one normally proceeds to solve simultaneously these $n + m$ equations for the optimal values of our $n + m$ variables $Q_1, \cdots, Q_n, V_1, \cdots, V_m$.

It is natural to ask whether a similar strategy can be extended to programming problems—to cases involving inequality constraints. The Kuhn-Tucker analysis assures us that, if the relevant functions are differentiable, such an extension is indeed possible and shows just how it can be done.

First, however, we must be careful to recall that conditions of the sort we will be discussing are by themselves necessary but not sufficient for a set of variable values to constitute a maximum of the Lagrangian and hence of the original constrained maximum problem. That is, if our first-order conditions are violated, the candidate solution certainly cannot constitute a maximum. But even if the first-order conditions are satisfied, it is still possible that the proposed solution will not do. We can be sure that the variable values under consideration will do the trick only if, in addition to the first-order conditions, they satisfy the requirements of the second-order conditions.

Though it is possible to weaken the second-order requirements somewhat, for our purposes we may take the following to constitute the second-order conditions (here it does not matter whether we are dealing with a programming problem or one to which the calculus can be applied).

Second-Order Conditions:

a. The set of constraints must define a feasible region which is everywhere convex.

b. For a local maximum the original objective function must be concave in the neighborhood of the maximum point, while for a local minimum it must be convex. If these concavity-convexity conditions hold throughout, the extreme point will be a global maximum (or minimum).

The logic of these second-order requirements has already been discussed earlier in this chapter.

We may now turn to the crucial first-order requirements, called the Kuhn-Tucker conditions. It will be seen that they are indeed an extension of the corresponding requirements of the differential calculus in which the first derivatives are set equal to zero. The following are the Kuhn-Tucker conditions for a maximization problem—the direction of the inequalities simply requiring reversal for a problem of minimization:

Kuhn-Tucker Maximum Conditions:

(3) $$\partial L(Q, V)/\partial Q_j \leq 0 \qquad (j = 1, 2, \cdots, n)$$

(4) $$Q_j[\partial L(Q, V)/\partial Q_j] = 0 \qquad (j = 1, 2, \cdots, n)$$

(5) $$\partial L(Q, V)/\partial V_i \geq 0 \qquad (i = 1, 2, \cdots, m)$$

(6) $$V_i[\partial L(Q, V)/\partial V_i] = 0 \qquad (i = 1, 2, \cdots, m)$$

$$Q_j \geq 0, \ V_i \geq 0.$$

The reader will note that the two sets of conditions of the differential calculus case (1) and (2) have been replaced by four sets of conditions, two of them involving inequalities. Moreover, it is the inequality Kuhn-Tucker conditions (3) and (5) that correspond, respectively, to the differential calculus requirements (1) and (2), while the two remaining condition sets seem basically new. In the next section we will examine the logic of these requirements. But first we must make certain that the reader understands their construction.

For this purpose we return to the illustrative Lagrangian function of the preceding section:

$$L(Q, V) = Q_1^3 + Q_1 Q_2 + V_1(10 - Q_1 - Q_2^5) + V_2(-4 + Q_1^2 + 2Q_2).$$

The reader may verify directly by differentiating partially that the corresponding Kuhn-Tucker conditions are

(3a) $$\begin{cases} \partial L/\partial Q_1 = 3Q_1^2 + Q_2 - V_1 + 2V_2 Q_1 \leq 0 \\ \partial L/\partial Q_2 = Q_1 - 5V_1 Q_2^4 + 2V_2 \leq 0 \end{cases}$$

(4a) $$\begin{cases} Q_1 \partial L/\partial Q_1 = Q_1(3Q_1^2 + Q_2 - V_1 + 2V_2 Q_1) = 0 \\ Q_2 \partial L/\partial Q_2 = Q_2(Q_1 - 5V_1 Q_2^4 + 2V_2) = 0 \end{cases}$$

(5a) $$\begin{cases} \partial L/\partial V_1 = 10 - Q_1 - Q_2^5 \geq 0 \\ \partial L/\partial V_2 = -4 + Q_1^2 + 2Q_2 \geq 0 \end{cases}$$

(6a) $$\begin{cases} V_1(\partial L/\partial V_1) = V_1(10 - Q_1 - Q_2^5) = 0 \\ V_2(\partial L/\partial V_2) = V_2(-4 + Q_1^2 + 2Q_2) = 0 \end{cases}$$

$$Q_1 \geq 0, \ Q_2 \geq 0, \ V_1 \geq 0, \ V_2 \geq 0$$

It will be observed that these have been grouped and numbered to correspond, respectively, to the general Kuhn-Tucker conditions (3), (4), (5), and (6).

4. Rationale of the Kuhn-Tucker Conditions

As we will see now, the Kuhn-Tucker conditions are the natural generalization of the calculus requirements (1) and (2) to take account of the possibility that the maximum or minimum in question can occur at a boundary point (a corner solution) rather than at an interior point (see Chapter 3, Section 10). The calculus requirements are generally appropriate only if the extremum (i.e., the maximum or minimum) occurs at a point at which all of the variables (including slacks) take nonzero values—at a point not on any of the boundaries of the feasible region. The Kuhn-Tucker conditions, as we shall see now, apply to either case. The role of the novel requirements (4) and (6) is, in effect, to determine whether the interior or corner maximum rules apply. Naturally, *this issue arises only because the variables are constrained to take nonnegative values*, since otherwise $Q_i = 0$ would no longer be a boundary point.

An intuitive view of the matter is simple enough. Consider the maximization of $y = f(x_1, x_2, \cdots, x_n)$ subject to all $x_i \geq 0$. Suppose, first, that we are at a point at which the value of x_1 can either be increased or decreased (an interior point, as far as this variable is concerned). Then (point A in Figure 1) by the usual logic of the marginal analysis we must have $\partial y/\partial x_1 = 0$, for otherwise either a rise or a fall in the value of x_1 could increase the value of y, and so y could not be at its maximum.

On the other hand, suppose we are testing for the possibility of a corner maximum at which $x_1 = 0$. Here, of the three possibilities $\partial y/\partial x_1 = 0$, $\partial y/\partial x_1 < 0$, and $\partial y/\partial x_1 > 0$, we can only rule out the last. That is, if $\partial y/\partial x_1 > 0$, then one can increase the value of y by raising x_1 above the corner value $x_1 = 0$ so that $x_1 = 0$ cannot possibly be the coordinate of a maximum point. However, if $\partial y/\partial x_1 = 0$, the point with $x_1 = 0$ (point B

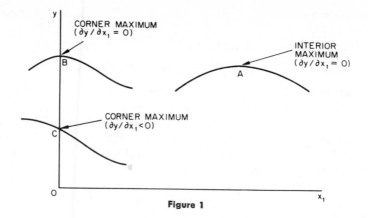

Figure 1

in Figure 1) may be a maximum for the usual reasons, while if $\partial y/\partial x_1 < 0$ it may be a maximum point simply because it is impossible to reduce the value of x_1 any further (point C in Figure 1). We conclude

RULE 3. Given a differentiable function $y = f(x_1, \cdots, x_n)$
(a) For an interior maximum it is necessary that $\partial y/\partial x_i = 0$ ($i = 1, 2, \cdots, n$).
(b) For a corner maximum it is necessary that $\partial y/\partial x_i \leq 0$.
(c) For a corner minimum it is necessary that $\partial y/\partial x_i \geq 0$.

The reader should check for himself that part (c) of Rule 3 follows directly by the same reasoning that explains the use of the reversed inequality for the maximization case.

We observe next that (4) and (6), the two completely novel requirements among the Kuhn-Tucker conditions, serve essentially to determine which of the two regimes applies: whether the corner or the interior maximum conditions are pertinent. Consider first the condition

(4) $$Q_j[\partial L(Q, V)/\partial Q_j] = 0.$$

This can be translated into the equivalent requirement

(4′) either $Q_j = 0$ or $\partial L/\partial Q_j = 0$ (or both).

The implication should be clear. If the value of Q_j under consideration is nonzero (interior maximum case) then (4) requires $\partial L/\partial Q_j = 0$, the condition which we have seen to be necessary in this case. However, if we are at a corner where $Q_j = 0$, then (4) or, more obviously, (4′) tells us that $\partial L/\partial Q_j$ may or may not be equal to zero. However, now we see by Kuhn-Tucker condition (3) that we then must have $\partial L/\partial Q_j \leq 0$, which, by Rule 3, is the requirement for a corner maximum.

Similarly, (6) can be translated into

(6')   either $V_i = 0$ or $\partial L / \partial V_i = 0$ (or both).[3]

This tells us, analogously with the interpretation of (4') that for $V_i \neq 0$ (an interior point), we must have $\partial L / \partial V_i = 0$, while for $V_i = 0$ (a corner), comparison with (5) tells us that $\partial L / \partial V_i \geq 0$. Here the inequality is reversed from that in (3) because, it will be recalled, we seek a saddle point of $L(Q, V)$, i.e., we are looking for values of Q and V at which $L(Q, V)$ is at a *maximum* with respect to the Q and is at a *minimum* with respect to the V. Thus, by Rules 3b and 3c we require $\partial L / \partial Q_j \leq 0$ and $\partial L / \partial V_i \geq 0$ just as is specified by Kuhn-Tucker conditions (3) and (5).

To summarize, the Kuhn-Tucker conditions are a natural generalization of the calculus requirements for an extremum. While the latter apply only to interior maxima, the former adapt themselves automatically to corner or to interior maxima as the circumstances require. The Kuhn-Tucker approach, then, permits us to treat a programming problem in two steps. First, by employing a Lagrangian expression for the original constrained maximization problem, we substitute a saddle-point problem involving no constraints other than the nonnegativity requirements. Second, by use of the Kuhn-Tucker conditions we are able to choose among both interior and corner points and thereby to arrive at the true extremum, provided that the second-order conditions are satisfied.

PROBLEMS

Write the Lagrangian expressions and the Kuhn-Tucker conditions for the following problems.

1. Maximize $\Pi = 7Q_1^2 - 2Q_1Q_2 + Q_2^3$

   subject to $Q_1 + Q_2 \leq 400$
   $$Q_1Q_2 \geq 200.$$

2. *Minimize* the value of Π in the preceding problem subject to the same constraints.

3. Minimize $\Pi = 6Q_1Q_2^2$

   subject to $2Q_1^2 + Q_2 \geq 50$
   $$Q_1 \leq 10.$$

5. Interpretation of the Kuhn-Tucker Conditions

Some additional observations will shed further light on the economics of the Kuhn-Tucker conditions and on the nature of their workings. It will be

---

[3] The reader may recognize a resemblance between the explanation offered for (4) and (6) and the duality theorems $U_iV_i = 0$ and $L_jQ_j = 0$ which were described in Section 3 of Chapter 6. The similarity is no coincidence as will be shown in the next section.

recalled that (by bringing all terms over to one side) the typical constraint in our problem may be written as

$$(7) \qquad\qquad 0 \leq c_i - g_i(Q_1, \cdots, Q_n).$$

The Lagrangian function is obtained by multiplying the right-hand side of this expression by its Lagrange multiplier, V_i, and adding it (and all other such constraint expressions) to the original objective function $\Pi = f(Q_1, \cdots, Q_n)$. The explicit form of the Lagrangian function is, therefore,

$$(8) \qquad L(Q, V) = f(Q_1, \cdots, Q_n) + \sum_i V_i[c_i - g_i(Q_1, \cdots, Q_n)].$$

We can now see at once the meaning of the Kuhn-Tucker condition (5), $\partial L / \partial V_i \geq 0$, for by direct differentiation of (8) this becomes

$$(9) \qquad\qquad \partial L / \partial V_i = c_i - g_i(Q_1, \cdots, Q_n) \geq 0,$$

which is identical with our original constraint (7).

In other words, Kuhn-Tucker *condition* (5) *is simply the ith constraint equation itself*, in somewhat disguised form. That is how the Kuhn-Tucker conditions guarantee that in solving the Lagrangian problem the constraints of the original problem are satisfied, even though no explicit constraints appear in the Lagrangian formulation of a problem. This remark suggests how the Lagrangian approach permits one to substitute for a constrained maximum problem one involving no constraints. The Lagrangian expression is simply constructed in such a way that in the process of maximizing the latter, as a consequence of the requirement $\partial L / \partial V_i \geq 0$ for all i, the original constraints are automatically satisfied.[4]

---

[4] We can now finally explain the conventions about the construction of the Lagrangian which are embodied in Rules 1 and 2 of Section 2, above. The point in these rules is to construct a Lagrangian expression having the properties we desire. Specifically, we want $L(Q, V)$ to have a form that guarantees that the Kuhn-Tucker condition $\partial L / \partial V_i \geq 0$ is equivalent to the ith primal constraint, and that the Kuhn-Tucker condition $\partial L / \partial Q_j \leq 0$ is the same as the jth dual constraint (as discussed later in this section).

To see how this is accomplished, recall that by Rule 1 one rewrites the ith primal constraint as $S_i \geq 0$, where S_i is the sum of all nonzero terms in the constraint. This sum, S_i, is then multiplied by $+V_i$ (Rule 2) to yield the term $V_i S_i$. Thus, the Kuhn-Tucker requirement (5) $\partial L / \partial V_i \geq 0$ gives us, by direct differentiation, $S_i \geq 0$, our original constraint, as we desired. Now suppose that instead of following Rule 1, we had brought all the terms in the original constraint over to the other side of the inequality to yield $-S_i \leq 0$. Multiplying $-S_i$ by V_i, we obtain the Lagrangian term $-V_i S_i$, so that Kuhn-Tucker condition (5) now becomes $-S_i \geq 0$, which is clearly *not* the original constraint. Thus, if we bring the terms of the constraint over to the "wrong" side in violation of Rule 1, the method will not work because the original constraints will not, generally, be satisfied.

There is an alternative interpretation of (5) which is also important and which immediately offers us an economic translation of Kuhn-Tucker condition 6. For this purpose recall that the ith primal slack variable, U_i (unused capacity), is defined by a rewriting of the primal constraint as

$$g_i(Q_1, \cdots, Q_m) + U_i = c_i \qquad \text{or} \qquad U_i = c_i - g_i(Q_1, \cdots, Q_m).$$

Comparison with (9) shows at once that our Kuhn-Tucker condition (5) can now be rewritten simply as

$$\partial L/\partial V_i = U_i \geq 0.$$

In other words, the derivative of the Lagrangian with respect to V_i, the ith Lagrange multiplier, is just U_i, the ith slack variable, and so Kuhn-Tucker condition (5) amounts simply to the requirement that the values of the slack variables be nonnegative!

Moreover, making the substitution $\partial L/\partial V_i = U_i$ into Kuhn-Tucker condition (6) we obtain

$$V_i \, \partial L/\partial V_i = V_i \, U_i = 0.$$

This is nothing more or less than the familiar duality theorem which states that either U_i, the unused capacity of resource i, equals zero, or that V_i, the marginal valuation of that resource, is zero (or both). There is thus a very good explanation for the structural resemblance between the implications of the duality requirement $U_i V_i = 0$ and those which we obtained from requirement (6) in the preceding section.

We may now quickly offer analogous interpretations of Kuhn-Tucker conditions (4) and (5). In the dual of our programming problem let T_j represent the dual slack variable in the jth dual constraint. It will be recalled from Chapter 6 that this can be interpreted as the opportunity loss incurred by the production of a unit of output j.[5]

Then, by direct analogy with the preceding discussion of Kuhn-Tucker conditions (5) and (6), it can be shown that

(a) The jth Kuhn-Tucker condition (3) is equivalent to the jth constraint of the dual problem.

(b) Condition (3) may be rewritten as

$$-\partial L/\partial Q_j = T_j \geq 0 \qquad (j = 1, \cdots, n),$$

i.e., it is the nonnegativity requirement for the dual slack variable and the partial derivative of L with respect to Q_j is simply minus one, times the slack variable T_j.

---

[5] We no longer use L_j to denote the value of the dual slack variable, to avoid confusion with $L(Q, V)$, which is employed in this chapter to represent the Lagrangian function.

(c) Condition (4) may be rewritten as

$$T_j Q_j = 0 \qquad (j = 1, \cdots, n),$$

which is the standard proposition of duality theory stating that output j should not be produced ($Q_j = 0$) unless it incurs no opportunity loss ($T_j = 0$), i.e., it states that $Q_j = 0$ or $T_j = 0$ (or both).

6. Why It Works

We are now in a position to offer a heuristic explanation of the Kuhn-Tucker theorem. That is, we can now grasp why a set of values of the Q's and V's that solve the Lagrangian problem must also be solutions for the primal and dual problems, respectively. In particular, we can see why the optimal values of the V's, the dual structural variables, can serve as the values of the corresponding Lagrange multipliers, i.e., why we have $V_i^0 = \lambda_i$ where V_i^0 is the optimal value of V_i.

Note that we are *not* asserting that the original programming problem and the Lagrangian problem are equivalent. Neither problem is simply a rearranged version of the other. The analysis states only that these two problems happen to yield the same answer. That is, *we will have proved that we have found the correct Lagrangian if we can show that its solution is also a solution to the original primal and dual programming problems.* In sum, to prove that the Lagrangian expression is correct we need only show that "it works"—that it yields the desired solution to the original problem.

For this purpose we show now how the Kuhn-Tucker conditions for the Lagrangian assure that any solution for the Lagrangian problem must automatically accord with the constraints and the objective function of the original problem.

A. *The original constraints:* We have just seen that the Kuhn-Tucker conditions (3) and (5) (together with the nonnegativity requirements $Q_j \geq 0$, $V_i \geq 0$) are equivalent to the constraints of the original primal and dual programs. Hence, since the solution of the Lagrangian problem must satisfy Kuhn-Tucker conditions (3) and (5), they must satisfy the original primal and dual constraints as well.

B. *The objective function:* The objective function of the Lagrangian problem is

$$L(Q, V) = \Pi + \sum V_i[c_i - g_i(Q_1, \cdots, Q_n)].$$

But Kuhn-Tucker condition (6) asserts that for any i

$$V_i \partial L / \partial V_i = V_i[c_i - g_i(Q_1, \cdots, Q_n)] = 0.$$

Hence, in any solution that satisfies the Kuhn-Tucker conditions, all of the last terms in the preceding expression for $L(Q, V)$ must drop out and the objective function of the Lagrangian problem becomes simply

$$(10) \qquad\qquad L(Q^0, V^0) = \Pi,$$

which is the value of the objective function of the original (primal) problem.

In exactly the same manner we can show that these values of Q and V must yield

$$(11) \qquad\qquad L(Q^0, V^0) = \alpha$$

so that the Lagrangian then takes the value of the dual objective function. Thus, to summarize, we have shown in intuitive terms that a solution that satisfies the Kuhn-Tucker conditions for the Lagrangian (and the non-negativity conditions for the variables) must satisfy the constraints for the original problems and must equate the value of the Lagrangian to that of the objective function of the primal (the dual). With the original objective functions coinciding with the Lagrangian expression and all the original constraints satisfied, it need no longer be surprising that the Q and V which satisfy the Lagrangian problem as constructed are also the solutions to the original primal problem and its dual.

As a matter of fact a simple argument now shows rigorously that a solution of the Lagrangian problem must satisfy the original primal and dual, for we have just shown that for $Q = Q^0$ and $V = V^0$ satisfying the Kuhn-Tucker conditions for the Lagrangian, these values must satisfy the primal and dual constraints and so must be feasible. We have, in addition, by (10) and (11),

$$\alpha = L(Q^0, V^0) = \Pi.$$

But, it will be recalled, the duality theorems of Chapter 6 tell us that this is a necessary and sufficient condition for optimality of the solution. For any pair of feasible solutions to the primal and dual that yield $\alpha = \pi$ *must* also be optimal solutions to those problems. Hence, Q^0 and V^0 must be the optimal solutions for the original primal and dual problems.

We have thus shown that the Lagrangian function as described by Rules 1 and 2 is constructed correctly—it "works" in the sense that its solution is also the solution to the original primal and dual problems. Incidentally, this also provides the rationale for our use of the dual variable values V_i^0 as the Lagrange multipliers for the primal problem and the use of the Q_j^0 as the Lagrange multipliers for the dual. For the Lagrangian function that we have just shown to "work" uses the V_i^0 and the Q_j^0 in just that way. Thus this procedure is correct because it yields the correct solution to the original problems, which is all we require of it.

7. Theoretical Applications of the Kuhn-Tucker Conditions

The Kuhn-Tucker conditions can be helpful in the solution of specific numerical problems. But economists have used them primarily to deal with more general qualitative problems. That is, the conditions can be used to derive *general* conclusions about the nature of the solutions, even where programming problems involve rather general functions *the values of whose parameters are not specified*. Thus, while the simplex method can handle only a numerical objective function such as $\pi = 3Q_1 + 5Q_2$, the Kuhn-Tucker analysis can work with more general objective functions such as $\pi = a_1Q_1 + a_2Q_2$, or even $\pi = f(Q_1, Q_2)$. As a result, the Kuhn-Tucker conditions may perhaps constitute the most powerful single weapon provided to economic theory by mathematical programming. There is no known general expression for the solution of a general programming problem. Unlike a differential calculus problem, in a programming computation we can only find the solution of a specific program all of whose parameters are known, determining this solution through a process of successive numerical approximations. It is therefore a manifestation of the very great power of the Kuhn-Tucker analysis that it does permit us to arrive at general qualitative conclusions about the behavior of the solutions to nonnumerical problems. A few examples will show precisely how this is accomplished.

Example 1: *Inelastic demands.* Evidence, which is perhaps superficial, suggests that some of the commodities or services produced by multiproduct "natural" monopolies face markets whose demands are quite inelastic, at least throughout what the businessman considers the relevant range of prices. It is well known that the presence of such items causes problems for the standard theory of profit maximization. This is so because such a commodity always yields a negative marginal revenue.[6] Therefore the firm can increase its profits by raising its price, thus reducing its sales volume. For this increases its total revenue, and, since the company now sells less, it simultaneously reduces its total cost. Let us examine the equilibrium of the firm in such circumstances. In the following discussion we suppose for simplicity that only two items are sold by the firm. Marginal costs are assumed to be positive throughout.

Let Q_1 and Q_2 be the quantities sold of the two items,

$P_1(Q_1)$, $P_2(Q_2)$ be their prices,
$MR_1 = \partial P_1 Q_1 / \partial Q_1$, $MR_2 = \partial P_2 Q_2 / \partial Q_2$ be their marginal revenues,
$C(Q_1, Q_2)$ be the total cost function, and
MC_1, MC_2 be the commodities' respective marginal costs.

---

[6] *Proof:* Elasticity of demand is defined as $E = -\dfrac{P}{Q}\dfrac{dQ}{dP}$ and for marginal revenue we have the expression

$$MR = \frac{dPQ}{dQ} = P + Q\frac{dP}{dQ} = P\left(1 + \frac{Q}{P}\frac{dP}{dQ}\right) = P\left(1 - \frac{1}{E}\right).$$

Thus, if demand is elastic $(E > 1)$, then $MR > 0$, and if demand is inelastic, $MR < 0$.

We derive

Proposition 1: The profit-maximizing firm, one of whose products has an inelastic demand, will always end up at a corner maximum at which Q_1, the quantity of that item sold, is (virtually) zero or is as small as regulatory stipulations permit.

Proof: Our firm's problem is to maximize profits,

$$\Pi = P_1Q_1 + P_2Q_2 - C(Q_1, Q_2),$$

subject to the minimum output requirements,

$$0 < m_1 \leq Q_1, \qquad 0 < m_2 \leq Q_2.$$

Our Lagrangian becomes

$$L(Q, V) = P_1Q_1 + P_2Q_2 - C(Q_1, Q_2) + V_1(Q_1 - m_1) + V_2(Q_2 - m_2).$$

Since there are two structural variables and two Lagrange multipliers, this problem yields eight Kuhn-Tucker conditions. However, only four of them explicitly involve Q_1, the variable in which we are interested. Thus, the Kuhn-Tucker conditions that are relevant for our purposes are

(a) $\partial L/\partial Q_1 = MR_1 - MC_1 + V_1 \leq 0$

(b) $Q_1 \partial L/\partial Q_1 = Q_1(MR_1 - MC_1 + V_1) = 0$

(c) $\partial L/\partial V_1 = Q_1 - m_1 \geq 0$

(d) $V_1 \partial L/\partial V_1 = V_1(Q_1 - m_1) = 0.$

By condition (c) for $m_1 > 0$ we must have $Q_1 > 0$. Therefore, by (b) we must have $MR_1 - MC_1 + V_1 = 0$. We know (footnote 6) that a commodity whose demand is inelastic has a negative marginal revenue, i.e., that $MR_1 < 0$. Thus, since $V_1 = MC_1 - MR_1$, this means $V_1 > 0$. Therefore, by (d) it follows that $Q_1 = m_1$, that is, Q_1 will set at its minimum permissible level, as was to be shown.

Notice the basic procedural trick that recurs again and again in this sort of application. We usually focus initially on one of the Kuhn-Tucker *equations*, (4) or (6), rather than the inequalities, (3) or (5). Thus, taking a Kuhn-Tucker condition such as $Q_i \partial L/\partial Q_i = 0$, we try to verify one of the two alternatives such a condition permits. If we happen to know $\partial L/\partial Q_i > 0$, then we deduce $Q_1 = 0$. Alternatively, if we know $Q_1 > 0$, we have instead of the inequality, $\partial L/\partial Q_i \geq 0$ as specified by condition (3), the equation $\partial L/\partial Q_i = 0$. This equation can be used to help us to solve for the value of Q_i and the other variables. The same device, it will be noted, is also used in deriving the economically more important results that follow.

Example 2: *Peak load pricing.* Suppose that the demands of a perfectly competitive firm vary by hour of day so that in some hours its capacity is fully utilized (peak periods) while at other times demand is slow so some capacity remains underutilized (off-peak periods). Then we have:

Proposition 2: The profit-maximizing outputs will be such that prices at off-peak periods will merely cover marginal operating costs (raw materials, labor, etc.) while in peak periods the prices will exceed marginal operating costs. The sum of the excesses of these prices over marginal operating costs for all peak periods will just add up to marginal capital cost, i.e., they will sum to the marginal cost of increasing capacity.

Notation: Let

$$Q_1, Q_2, \cdots, Q_{24}$$

represent quantity demanded during each of the 24 hours of the day

$P_1, P_2, \cdots, P_{24}$ be the corresponding prices,

y be the hourly output capacity,

$C(Q_1, \cdots, Q_{24})$ be the daily total operating cost, and

$g(y)$ be the daily cost of capital (capacity).

We assume that all $Q_i > 0$, i.e., that some output is sold during each hour of the day. Total profit per day will obviously be

$$\sum_{i=1}^{24} P_i Q_i - C(Q_1, \cdots, Q_{24}) - g(y),$$

which the firm maximizes subject to the twenty-four capacity constraints:

$$Q_1 \leq y$$
$$\cdots \cdots$$
$$Q_{24} \leq y.$$

Our Lagrangian function becomes

$$\Pi_\lambda = \Sigma\, P_i Q_i - C(Q_1, \cdots, Q_{24}) - g(y) + \Sigma\, \lambda_i(y - Q_i).$$

Since competition is assumed to be perfect, prices are not affected by the firm's outputs, i.e., $\partial P_i/\partial Q_i = 0$. Our Kuhn-Tucker conditions are then

(a) $$\frac{\partial \Pi_\lambda}{\partial Q_j} = P_j - \frac{\partial C}{\partial Q_j} - \lambda_j \leq 0 \qquad (j = 1, \cdots, 24)$$

(b) $$Q_j \frac{\partial \Pi_\lambda}{\partial Q_j} = 0 \qquad (j = 1, \cdots, 24)$$

(c) $$\frac{\partial \Pi_\lambda}{\partial y} = -\frac{\partial g}{\partial y} + \Sigma \lambda_i \leq 0$$

(d) $$y\frac{\partial \Pi_\lambda}{\partial y} = 0$$

(e) $$\frac{\partial \Pi_\lambda}{\partial \lambda_j} = y - Q_j \geq 0 \qquad (j = 1, \cdots, 24)$$

(f) $$\lambda_j \frac{\partial \Pi_\lambda}{\partial \lambda_j} = \lambda_j(y - Q_j) = 0 \qquad (j = 1, \cdots, 24).$$

Since we have assumed all $Q_j > 0$, it follows from (e) that $y > 0$ (that is, if capacity, y, were zero, nothing could be produced).

Now that we know that all Q_j and y are positive, by (b) and (d) we have $\partial \Pi_\lambda/\partial Q_j = 0$ and $\partial \Pi_\lambda/\partial y = 0$, that is, (a) and (c) become the equations

(a') $$\frac{\partial \Pi_\lambda}{\partial Q_j} = P_j - \frac{\partial C}{\partial Q_j} - \lambda_j = 0$$

(c') $$\frac{\partial \Pi_\lambda}{\partial y} = -\frac{\partial g}{\partial y} + \Sigma \lambda_i = 0.$$

Furthermore, since in any off-peak period, t, there is, by definition, excess capacity, we must have $y > Q_t$, that is, by (f), for such a period we must have

$$\lambda_t = 0.$$

Hence by (a') the first part of our theorem follows at once: For any off-peak period, t,

$$P_t - \frac{\partial C}{\partial Q_t} = 0;$$

that is, for any off-peak period, price will optimally be equal to marginal operating cost, $\partial C/\partial Q_t$.

For any peak period, s, we may, however, have $\lambda_s > 0$ in which case, by (a'), price will exceed its marginal operating cost by a supplementary amount equal to λ_s, i.e.,

$$P_s = \partial C/\partial Q_s + \lambda_s.$$

Moreover, by (c') the sum of these supplements for all peak periods together will be exactly equal to the marginal capacity cost, $\partial g/\partial y$, that is,

$$\Sigma \lambda_i = \frac{\partial g}{\partial y}.$$

This completes the derivation of Proposition 2.

There is a public policy analogue of this theorem.[7] It states that in off-peak periods, since there is excess capacity, demand should be encouraged by charging a price as low as possible without incurring a loss on the marginal unit sold, i.e., by charging a price that covers only the marginal operating cost, $\partial C/\partial Q_t$. However, since peak period demand presses on capacity, any increase in this demand must require additional capital, and it must therefore cover its marginal capital cost, $\partial g/\partial y$. These, then, are the basic principles of optimal peak-hour and off-peak pricing, i.e., the principles relevant for the setting of daytime and evening electricity rates, telephone rates, etc. It suggests, for example, that there may be something irrational about the common practice on trains, toll bridges, etc., under which discount tickets are available to commuters who travel, typically, at the peak hours. For the commuter ticket tends to encourage utilization of these facilities at the most crowded period, an influence whose desirability may well be questionable.

PROBLEMS

1. Suppose that instead of seeking to maximize profits the firm desires to maximize its physical sales volume $Q_1 + Q_2$ subject to the rate of return (relative profit) constraint $\Pi \geq (Q_1 + Q_2)S$, i.e., $P_1 Q_1 + P_2 Q_2 - C(Q_1, Q_2) \geq (Q_1 + Q_2)S$, where S is a constant representing the minimum acceptable *rate* of profit, $\Pi/(Q_1 + Q_2)$. If $MR_1 < 0$, $MR_2 > 0$, and both marginal costs are equal ($MC_1 = MC_2$), prove that a maximum requires $\Pi = (Q_1 + Q_2)S$ and $Q_1 = 0$.

2. What are the implications of our marginal revenue assumptions for the elasticities of demand of the two products? Explain in economic terms, therefore, why no solution with $Q_1 > 0$ can be expected to be optimal.

3. Suppose the firm produces a single product whose output is Q and that its sales are affected by its advertising expenditure, A. If the firm is trying to maximize its total revenue, $R(Q, A)$, subject to a profit constraint $\Pi = R(Q, A) - C(Q) - A \geq m$, where the marginal revenue of advertising and the marginal cost of output are both positive ($\partial R/\partial A > 0$, $\partial C/\partial Q > 0$), prove, assuming $Q > 0$ in the solution, that we must have $\Pi = m$, $\partial R/\partial Q > 0$ and $\partial \Pi/\partial Q < 0$.

4. What is the economic interpretation of the results obtained in the solution to Problem 3? (Hint: What do they imply about the relative magnitudes of the profit-maximizing output, the unconstrained revenue-maximizing output, and the constrained revenue-maximizing output?)

---

[7] The theorem was derived with the aid of Kuhn-Tucker analysis in S. C. Littlechild, "Peak-Load Pricing of Telephone Calls," *The Bell Journal of Economics and Management Science,* Autumn 1970, pp. 191–210. The result was previously formulated by Steiner, Williamson, and others; see P. O. Steiner, "Peak Loads and Efficient Pricing," *Quarterly Journal of Economics,* March 1964, pp. 54, 64–76; and O. E. Williamson, "Peak-Load Pricing and Optimal Capacity Under Indivisibility Constraints," *American Economic Review,* September 1966, pp. 56, 810–27. Reprinted as "Peak-Load Pricing," in R. Turvey, ed., *Public Enterprise,* Penguin Books, Inc., Baltimore, 1968, pp. 64–85.

5. (Proposition due to Averch and Johnson[8]) Suppose that a profit-maximizing firm has a single output and two inputs, capital and labor, whose respective quantities are Q, x_1, and x_2 so that its profit function is $\Pi = PQ - c_1 x_1 - c_2 x_2$, where $c_1 > 0$ and $c_2 > 0$ are the respective unit costs of capital and labor. If the firm's profit is limited to some fixed proportion of its capital so that $\Pi \leq Kx_1$. $K > 0$, and $x_1 > 0$, $x_2 > 0$, prove that $\dfrac{\partial PQ}{\partial x_1} \Big/ \dfrac{\partial PQ}{\partial x_2}$ cannot equal c_1/c_2 as would be the case in the absence of the constraint, i.e., the regulatory constraint will distort the relative proportions of capital and labor used by the firm. Assume $0 < \lambda < 1$, where λ is the Lagrange multiplier. (This can be proved, on the assumption $K > 0$ and the premise that the constraint effectively reduces the firm's total profits.)

6. Discuss the significance of the Averch-Johnson result (Problem 5) for regulatory policy relating to public utilities.

REFERENCES

Averch, Harvey, and Leland L. Johnson, "Behavior of the Firm Under Regulatory Constraint," *American Economic Review*, Vol. 52, December 1962.

Bailey, Elizabeth E., *Economic Theory of Regulatory Constraint*, D. C. Heath & Company, Lexington, Mass., 1973.

Dorfman, R. A., P. A. Samuelson, and R. M. Solow, *Linear Programming and Economic Analysis*, McGraw-Hill Book Company, New York, 1958, Chapter 8.

Intrilligator, M. D., *Mathematical Optimization and Economic Theory*, Prentice-Hall, Inc., Englewood Cliffs, N.J., 1971, Chapter 4.

Kuhn, H. W., and A. W. Tucker, "Nonlinear Programming," in J. Neyman (ed.), *Proceedings of the Second Berkeley Symposium on Mathematical Statistics and Probability*, University of California Press, Berkeley and Los Angeles, 1951.

Roberts, Blaine, and David L. Schultze, *Modern Mathematics and Economic Analysis*, Norton, New York, 1973.

---

[8] See Harvey Averch and L. L. Johnson, "Behavior of the Firm under Regulatory Constraint," *American Economic Review*, Vol. LII, December 1962.

DEMAND
AND PRODUCTION
THEORY

two

Demand Curves, Utility Surfaces, and Indifference Maps

9

1. Demand Curves

The demand curve is among those devices of economic theory which have found frequent employment in applied economics. In its traditional form, it sums up the response of consumer demand to alternative prices of a product—it can tell management what may be expected to happen to the demand for one of its outputs if the price of that item is changed.

This information is summarized in a graph (the demand curve itself) which shows how much will be demanded at every possible (hypothetical) price over the relevant range (Figure 1). For example, point D_0 on the demand curve DD' indicates that at price OP_0 the consumer, or group of consumers, for whom the curve is drawn will wish to purchase OX_0 units of the product.

Several features of the demand curve should be noted:

1. It is customary to represent the price level on the vertical axis and the quantity demanded on the horizontal axis.[1]

_____

[1] This arbitrary convention would seem to be an inappropriate arrangement because in the present discussion we treat quantity demanded as the dependent variable and price as the independent variable. The origin of this practice is that this curve together with a supply curve has traditionally been used in the analysis of price determination in a competitive industry as described in Chapter 16, Section 3. However, even here the price cannot be considered a dependent variable since, in the supply-demand analysis, price and quantity are determined simultaneously.

2. The graph may refer to the demand of an individual consumer, or it may describe the aggregated demands of a group of consumers constituting a market. The market demand curve is obtained from the demand curves of the individuals composing it by adding up, for each price in turn, the quantities all the individual consumers demand at that price. That is, one adds the individual demand curves *horizontally* to obtain the market demand curves.

3. The demand curve assumes that there is no change in the values of other pertinent variables. Specifically, prices of other goods and consumer incomes are among the other things that are assumed to remain equal.

4. The graph depicts the situation at a single point in time, say 4:33 p.m. on June 12. Hence, all but one of the prices and quantities must be hypothetical—the curve must generally answer the "iffy" question: "If price were OP, how much would this (these) consumer(s) buy?"

5. The curve is generally assumed to have a negative slope. In economic terms, this is the plausible assertion that, other things being equal, more of the commodity would be demanded (OX_1 rather than OX_0) if the price were lower (OP_1 instead of OP_0). However, two exceptions should be mentioned: Cases of snob appeal and cases where consumers judge quality by price. Commodities like expensive jewelry may be purchased precisely because their price is high, and a fall in their price might reduce their snob

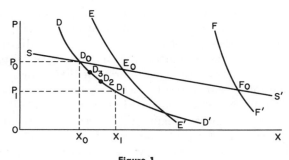

Figure 1

appeal and therefore, perhaps, their sale (although enough poorer consumers might then be induced to buy the items to make up for the loss of affluent customers). Similarly, when consumers have no ability to judge the quality of a good directly and use price as an indicator of quality, as they probably often do, a reduction in its price may cut into the demand for a good. The negative slope of the usual demand curve will be discussed again later in this chapter, along with another exceptional case that has been discussed widely in the theoretical literature.

It is important to recognize the *isotemporal* character of the demand curve—the fact that every one of its points represents one of the hypothetical possibilities available *for some given moment*. This property is a common feature of *all* the relationships used in static analysis, i.e., of virtually all the relationships in this book. This characteristic is troublesome both for empirical application and for comprehensibility of economic analysis by laymen. Yet, this attribute of our static relationships is not imposed as a mere caprice or as a means to introduce analytical complexity or elegance.

Rather, we use relationships that are isotemporal because most of our analysis concerns itself one way or another with *optimal choice*. Behavioral analysis in economic theory usually proceeds on the assumption that the decision-maker always arrives at decisions that are optimal in terms of his objectives; welfare analysis seeks to determine what decisions are optimal from the point of view of the public interest; etc. But we saw in Chapter 1 that, by definition, optimization analysis consists of the explicit or implicit comparison of the financial consequences of the choices available to the decision-maker. The need for isotemporal relationships follows at once. Suppose a seller is considering the selection of a price for 4:33 p.m. on June 12 and the price possibilities under consideration are $12.99, $14.99, and $16.99. Obviously, the relevant consideration for the decision-maker is how much he will sell if he selects the first of these possibilities, how much he will sell instead if he selects the intermediate-price candidate, etc. But that is precisely the information that an isotemporal demand curve gives—it tells us how much would be sold *if some one or another of the possible prices is the one that is selected for the moment to which the decision pertains*. In sum, since optimization requires explicit comparison of the possibilities available at the time to which the decision applies, the relevant relationships (curves) *must* describe (and contrast) just those hypothetical possibilities for that time period.

2. Shifting Demand Curves: Demand Functions

Since the demand curve is defined to pertain only to a particular time, its shape and position are likely to change with the passage of time. At one moment DD' is the relevant demand curve, but at another instant the curve has the shape EE'. Such a change is described as a *shift* in the demand curve. This is contrasted with a *movement along* a demand curve, say from point D_0 to D_1.

A shift in a demand curve is normally accounted for by a change in the value of some of the variables which affect demand. For example, a rise in consumer income can lead to an upward shift in the demand curve from DD' to EE'. This means that at *any given price*, such as OP_1, the consumer(s) will demand more than before the shift. It should be noted, however, that if price happens to rise sufficiently at the same time, say to OP_0, consumers may end up buying less despite an outward shift in the demand curve. In such a case, the shift in demand is accompanied by an offsetting movement *along* the curve.

Besides income, many other variables can affect the position of the curve. A change in the amount of advertising, a change in price or quality, or the advertising approach of a competing product—even a change in the weather—can shift a demand curve. Some of the relevant variables may even be intangible and unquantifiable—for example, a change in consumer tastes can cause a shift in a demand curve—although we may prefer to go behind this phenomenon and seek the variables which account for the taste change.

To summarize, demand is a function of many variables such as price, advertising, and decisions relating to competing and complementary products. The relationship which describes this entire many-variable interconnection is called the *demand function*. By contrast, the demand curve deals only with two of these variables, price and quantity demanded, and ignores the others, or, rather, assumes that their values are held constant. Indeed, the distinction between a movement along and a shift in a demand curve may be described in terms of the variables involved. Any change in quantity demanded which results only from a variation in price is a movement along the curve, whereas change in the value of any other variable in the demand *function* is likely to shift the demand *curve*.

Several concluding observations about the distinction between shifts in and movements along the demand curve are relevant:

1. Phrases such as "a rise in demand" are ambiguous and should be avoided, since it is not clear whether they refer to a shift in or a movement along the curve.

2. The distinction is often important for applied economics. For example, the statement that a reduction in demand is deflationary is valid only if it refers to a downward shift in the demand curve, since a leftward movement (a decrease in quantity demanded) along a negatively sloping demand curve must, by definition, be concurrent with a rise in price. One can find cases where this has been misunderstood by legislators who thereupon have made nonsensical statements on inflation policy. Similarly, the sort of increase in demand which is most eagerly hoped for in a business firm will involve a shift in the demand curves for its products. In fact, it will normally result from autonomous changes in the values of the variables which are entirely outside the management's control. There is usually

some cost to the firm when the quantity of its products demanded increases as a result of a change in the firm's advertising expenditure, or in the incidental services which it provides to its customers, or in some other of its demand curve-raising activities. But an upward shift in demand which occurs because of a rise in national income or favorable weather comes to the company free.

3. The possibility that demand curves can frequently shift implies that a statistical investigation of the shape of such a curve requires the aid of relatively powerful methods. There is a serious difficulty in the obvious approach, which involves our taking price quantity data for a number of months and plotting them on a graph. For example, if in October OX_0 units were sold at (average) price OP_0 (point D_0 in Figure 1) whereas November and December sales were represented by points E_0 and F_0, respectively, this method would have us draw in the statistical "demand curve" SS', which, as we can see, really resembles *none* of the true demand curves (the DD' curve for October, the EE' curve for November, and the FF' December curve). The difficulty is that the true demand curve has shifted over this period. The naïve statistical method which has just been described does not even indicate this fact and it certainly offers us no means of correcting for it.

More sophisticated methods have been designed to deal with this so-called *identification* problem, and, more generally, with the econometrics of simultaneous equation estimation. However, it is desirable to defer discussion of these techniques until later.[2]

3. Elasticity: A Measure of Responsiveness

The most obvious piece of information we desire of a demand function (or from economic relationships of other varieties) is an indication of the effect on the "dependent" variable of a change in the value of one of the other variables. In the case of the demand curve, this involves measurement of the response in quantity demanded which can be expected to result from a given change in the price of the commodity.

The obvious measure of responsiveness is, of course, what we may call the marginal demand contribution of a price change, $\Delta x/\Delta p$, or the corresponding derivative, dx/dp, the change (fall) in quantity demanded caused by a unit change (rise) in price. It will be observed, incidentally, that this measure is the reciprocal of the slope of the demand curve $\Delta p/\Delta x$ (or dp/dx), so that the flatter the demand curve, the greater will be the value of this measure of responsiveness to price change. This peculiarity results from the oddity in the conventional drawing of the demand curve

---

[2]See the next chapter and its appendix.

which has already been noted—the fact that the value of the apparently dependent variable, quantity, is measured along the horizontal axis, and that of the independent variable, price, along the vertical axis. We might well get a better intuitive grasp of the degree of price responsiveness of a demand curve if the diagram were turned on its side.

In any event, the obvious measures of responsiveness, $\Delta x/\Delta p$ and dx/dp, are subject to a drawback which has led theorists to employ instead another measure—elasticity. The difficulty with, say, $\Delta x/\Delta p$ is that it deals with the absolute changes in quantity and price, which makes it difficult to compare the responsiveness of different commodities. Commodities are measured in different units—labor in hours, land in acres, and whiskey in fifths or quarts. There is no simple way of comparing a 20,000-quart increase in the quantity of Scotch demanded with a 3,000-acre rise in that of land. In economics it is difficult, because of the very nature of the animal, to impose uniform units on all the relevant magnitudes as is done in physics.

But the problem extends beyond the dissimilarity of units, because, even in the measurement of price change, the magnitudes are not readily comparable. Consider a 1-cent fall in the price of a package of bubble gum and an equal fall in the price of an automatic dishwasher. We might not be surprised to find bubble gum sales booming when habitués discover the bargain in this brand of the confection, but it is difficult to believe that a one-penny reduction in dishwasher prices would even be noticed. Though the measure $\Delta x/\Delta p$ would therefore almost certainly yield a much higher number in the case of chewing gum than in that of major household appliances (a much greater change in quantity demanded per penny price reduction), we would surely hesitate to conclude from this that the demand of the former was significantly more price-sensitive.

Theorists have concluded, from such considerations, that an appropriate measure of responsiveness of demand to price changes should employ percentage rather than absolute change figures. A 1 *per cent* (rather than a one-penny) fall in price then becomes the standard of comparison, so that the change in dishwasher price in our illustration is discounted as an insignificant price fall in comparison with that of the bubble gum.

Employing these percentage terms we have the definition

price elasticity of demand for item X

$$= -\ \frac{\text{percentage change in quantity of } X \text{ demanded}}{\text{percentage change in the price of } X}.$$

The only peculiarity in the definition which remains to be explained is the presence of the minus sign before the fraction. This is inserted to make the elasticity number nonnegative. When the demand curve is negatively inclined, a rise in price (Δp positive) will lead to a fall in quantity (Δx

negative) so that in our elasticity fraction the numerator and denominator will be of opposite sign. Therefore the fraction will be a negative number, and a minus sign is needed to make the number positive. The insertion of this sign in the elasticity formula is, then, just a matter of linguistic convenience.

For our purposes it is necessary to define the elasticity measure somewhat more specifically. The percentage change in any quantity, x, is defined as 100 times the change in x, i.e., as $100\Delta x$, divided by x. For example, if quantity rises from 10 to 15, we have $\Delta x = 15 - 10 = 5$ and the percentage rise in x is $100\Delta x/x = 500/10 = 50$ per cent. Similarly, the percentage change in p is given by the expression $100\Delta p/p$. Therefore we have, by our definition of elasticity,

$$\text{price elasticity of demand} = -\frac{100\Delta x/x}{100\Delta p/p} = -\frac{\Delta x/x}{\Delta p/p}$$

(since we can divide both numerator and denominator by 100).

Moreover, since division by a fraction, $\Delta p/p$, is the same as multiplication by its reciprocal, $p/\Delta p$, we obtain the expression

(1) $$\text{price elasticity of demand} = -\frac{\Delta x}{x} \cdot \frac{p}{\Delta p} = -\frac{\Delta x}{\Delta p} \cdot \frac{p}{x}.$$

This expression, which will be used throughout the remainder of the elasticity discussion, helps now to describe two different elasticity concepts: *point elasticity* and *arc elasticity*. Arc elasticity is a measure of the *average* responsiveness to price change exhibited by a demand curve over some finite stretch of the curve such as $D_0 D_1$ in Figure 1. One complication is inherent in the concept. In the elasticity formula (1), when price changes from P_0 to P_1 it is clear that $\Delta x = X_1 - X_0$, the change in quantity bought (Figure 1), and that $\Delta p = P_1 - P_0$. But what are the values of x and p? Since a range of values of x occurs along arc $D_0 D_1$, no unique value of this variable is called for by the definition. It is customary for this purpose to use the average of the two end values of x, that is, to set $x = (X_1 + X_0)/2$, and to do the same for the percentage change in price. Hence the arc elasticity of demand is defined by the expression

$$-\frac{\Delta x}{\Delta p} \cdot \frac{p}{x} = -\frac{X_1 - X_0}{P_1 - P_0} \cdot \frac{(P_1 + P_0)/2}{(X_1 + X_0)/2}$$

so that, multiplying both numerator and denominator by 2, we have

(2) $$\text{arc (price) elasticity of demand} = -\frac{X_1 - X_0}{P_1 - P_0} \frac{P_1 + P_0}{X_1 + X_0}.$$

Point elasticity of demand is the corresponding concept for each particular point on the demand curve. But, at any such point there is no change in price ($\Delta p = 0$) or in quantity. We therefore define point elasticity in much the same way as the derivative concept in Chapter 4. That is, we take point elasticity to be the limit of the arc elasticity figure as the arc $D_0 D_1$ is made smaller and smaller, first being cut down to $D_0 D_2$, then to $D_0 D_3$, etc. We thereby arrive at the definition

(3) $$\text{point price elasticity of demand} = -\frac{dx}{dp} \cdot \frac{p}{x},$$

where the derivative dx/dp has been substituted for $\Delta x/\Delta p$ in the elasticity definition (1).

Before leaving the question of definitions, it is well to point out that the elasticity concept can be (and has been) adapted to measure responsiveness in variables other than quantity and price. For example, we may measure the responsiveness of the supply, s, of some commodity to a change in interest rate, i, as

$$\text{interest elasticity of supply} = -\frac{\text{percentage change in supply}}{\text{percentage change in interest rate}}$$

$$= -\frac{ds}{di} \cdot \frac{i}{s}.$$

Similarly, when the price, p_j, of one commodity, j affects the quantity demanded, x_k, of another commodity k it is customary to define

$$\text{cross elasticity of demand} = \frac{dx_k}{dp_j} \cdot \frac{p_j}{x_k}.$$

The reader should try defining such concepts as the income elasticity of imports and the interest elasticity of investment.

4. Properties of the Elasticity Measure

The basic elasticity formula (1) permits us to see a relationship between an elasticity measure and the corresponding marginal measure of responsiveness, $\Delta x/\Delta p$, with which the elasticity discussion began. Elasticity is simply the marginal measure multiplied by the fraction $-p/x$.

This observation, in turn, helps us to see one of the peculiarities of the elasticity measure. Consider a straight-line demand curve like that in Figure 2. It is tempting to guess that the elasticity of such a demand

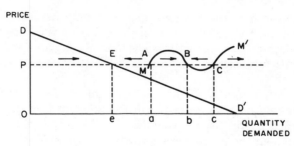

Figure 2

curve is the same throughout the length of the curve. Such constancy does hold for the marginal measure of price responsiveness, $\Delta x/\Delta p$, since it is the reciprocal of the slope of the demand curve which does not change along a straight line. There are two cases in which the elasticity measure also behaves in this way: If a demand curve is vertical (a fixed quantity demanded no matter what the price, so that $\Delta x/\Delta p = 0$), its elasticity is zero throughout, and at the other extreme, a horizontal demand curve has "infinite elasticity." But in any other straight-line case, such as DD' in Figure 2, *elasticity* is not constant. Indeed, it varies continuously from zero at point D' on the horizontal axis to any number as high as we like when we get close to the vertical axis (so that elasticity is said to approach infinity as we move toward point D)!

The reason for the variability in the elasticity of a straight line is readily seen from our last elasticity formula. We have just noted that the first fraction in this expression, $\Delta x/\Delta p$, retains the same value throughout the graph. But that is not true of the second fraction, p/x. At point D', we have $x = OD'$ and $p = 0$ so that $p/x = 0$, and hence the price elasticity of demand is zero also. As we move toward the left along the demand curve, the numerator of p/x increases while the denominator, x, approaches zero. Hence the value of the fraction grows larger and larger without limit and the same is consequently true of the price elasticity of demand.[3] We conclude that, except in the zero elastic vertical case and the infinite elastic horizontal case, elasticity of demand is certainly not constant along a straight-line demand curve. This complication is a price which we pay for using percentage figures instead of absolute figures in the elasticity measure.

---

[3] Note that I have avoided speaking of the elasticity being infinite at point D, where $x = 0$. Here the elasticity is not even defined because an attempt to evaluate the fraction p/x at that point forces us to commit the sin of dividing by zero. The reader who has forgotten why division by zero is immoral may recall that division is the reverse operation of multiplication. Hence, in seeking the quotient $c = a/b$ we look for a number, c, which when multiplied by b gives us the number a, i.e., for which $cb = a$. But if a is not zero, say $a = 5$, and b is zero, there is no such number because there is no c such that $c \times 0 = 5$.

However, even here there is an important compensation. Though the connection may at first not be obvious, the following theorem will lead us to a type of curve whose elasticity *is* constant throughout and which will offer us some useful insights.

Elasticity Proposition 1: Given any segment of the demand curve, a change in price within that segment will have no effect on the product px (price multiplied by quantity demanded) if and only if the elasticity of demand throughout the range is exactly equal to unity. More specifically, a change in price from p_0 to p_1 will yield $p_0 x_0 = p_1 x_1$ if and only if the elasticity of the arc $D_0 D_1$ is unity, and each and every intermediate price change will also leave px unaffected if and only if point elasticity is unity at *every* point along this arc.[4]

The product px represents the amount which the consumer would spend and which the seller would therefore receive if quantity x were bought at price p. This theorem therefore states that if the price elasticity of his demand is unity, a fall in price will induce the consumer to increase his purchases by exactly the amount needed to keep his total outlay the same as it was initially. This is certainly plausible intuitively, for we may view a price reduction as having an expenditure-increasing effect (more demanded) and an expenditure-reducing effect (a lower price paid for each unit purchased). When the elasticity of demand is unity, the percentage fall in price is, by definition, exactly equal to the percentage rise in quantity demanded, and it is therefore believable that these two effects will then exactly offset one another, as the theorem asserts.

The theorem describes, implicitly, the type of demand curve along which elasticity of demand is constant. Specifically, it tells us that the elasticity will take the constant value unity along any curve characterized by the equation $px = K$ (any constant). Such a curve is called a *rectangular hyperbola* and has the shape of one of the curves depicted in Figure 3 (where different curves correspond to different values of K). That a

---

[4] The following argument demonstrates both Propositions 1 and 2 in terms of point elasticity. The arc elasticity proofs are just matters of tedious algebraic manipulation.

Proof (of Propositions 1 and 2): We want to determine the relationship between the elasticity, E, and the effect of a change in price, p, on total expenditure, $px = p \cdot f(p)$, where $x = f(p)$ is the equation of the demand curve. Then the effect of a change of a price on total expenditure is (by the formula for the derivative of a product)

$$\frac{d[pf(p)]}{dp} = p\frac{df}{dp} + f\frac{dp}{dp} = p\frac{dx}{dp} + x\frac{dp}{dp} = p\frac{dx}{dp} + x = x\frac{p\,dx}{x\,dp} + x = -xE + x$$

$$= x(1 - E).$$

Hence, a change in price will leave xp constant, $d[p \cdot f(p)]/dp = 0$, if and only if $E = 1$. Similarly, $d[p \cdot f(p)] > 0$ if and only if $E < 1$ (demand inelastic), etc.

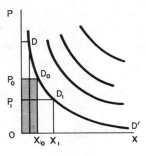

Figure 3

curve $px = K$ is of such a shape can be seen by noting that if our demand curve is DD', then, e.g., at price OP_0, consumer expenditure $OX_0 \times OP_0$ is represented by the area of the shaded rectangle $OX_0D_0P_0$ ($=$ height OP_0 multiplied by width OX_0). Similarly, at price OP_1 expenditure is depicted by area $OX_1D_1P_1$. Since expenditure is constant along a demand curve of unit elasticity, it follows that all such rectangles must be equal in area. Hence the unit elastic demand curve must approach the axes of the diagram asymptotically, for as such a rectangle gets taller it must become narrower in order for its area to remain equal to that of its fellow expenditure rectangles. Moreover, such a demand curve must not touch either axis for at a point of intersection with an axis either p or x is zero so that px must equal zero rather than K. It can be shown, incidentally, that demand curves of constant elasticity 2 or $\frac{3}{4}$ or any other number are asymmetrical relative to the axes but roughly similar in shape to rectangular hyperbolas.

We may use a geometric argument to extend our first elasticity theorem as follows:

Elasticity Proposition 2: If a demand curve has elasticity less than unity (it is *inelastic*), a *rise* in price will *increase* consumer expenditure, px, and *vice versa*. If the curve has an elasticity greater than unity (it is *elastic*), a *fall* in price will increase consumer expenditure and *vice versa*.

A proof has already been provided in a footnote. The two elasticity theorems just given lie behind much of the use of the elasticity concept in applied economics. They are met, for example, in the analysis of problems of taxation, international trade, and pricing by private business. As a simple illustration, note that it will not ordinarily pay a firm to reduce the price of a product whose demand is inelastic, because this price reduction will tend to increase the number of units sold and hence the firm's total raw material, labor, and other costs, but, by Proposition 2, *it will also decrease the firm's revenue px*—clearly a losing proposition! As a second illustration, consider a country suffering from a "gold shortage." In such a case, popular writers often recommend that the country devalue its currency, thus making its products cheaper and hence leading foreigners to import more. There are a number of complications to be considered, but the one which is relevant for our purposes is the possibility that the elasticity of the foreigners' demand for that country's exports may be less than unity. Thus the country may find, after devaluing, that though it is shipping more abroad, it is actually earning less gold than before!

PROBLEMS

1. Given the definition of arc elasticity of demand as shown in Equation (2), prove that if total expenditure is constant along an arc, so that $P_1X_1 = P_2X_2$, then the arc elasticity must be unity.
2. If a firm's price elasticity of demand is greater than 1, can you say from this alone whether a fall in its price is profitable? Why?

5. Utility Analysis of Demand

Economic theory has long sought to go behind the obvious and observable demand phenomena which are summed up in the demand function in an attempt to explain these observations in terms of the structure of consumer desires. It seemed immediately apparent that there is some connection between demand and the *utility* of the commodity, i.e., the subjective benefit which the consumer obtains from its possession. But to classical economists this connection appeared to be limited largely to the fact that items totally without utility would not be demanded at all. To show that there is little or no connection with price, they called attention to the fact that water, which is essential to life and therefore to be considered of very great utility, commands only a very low and often no more than a zero price, whereas diamonds, whose utility was said to be less than that of water, are notoriously expensive.

This "diamond-water" paradox was explained by an analysis which was the focal point of the economic literature at the turn of the century. It was argued that the price of a commodity was determined not by its *total* but by its *marginal* utility. For this discussion it is convenient to evaluate the marginal utility of a commodity, X, in money terms (the amount of money the consumer is just willing to give up for another unit). The connection between price and marginal utility is that if to some rational consumer the marginal utility of some item, X, when he holds A units of X is more than its price, he can increase his welfare by purchasing some more units of X. This is so because, by definition, in these circumstances he receives more value than he gives up in such an exchange. Similarly, if the marginal utility of an Lth unit of the commodity is less than its price, the consumer can benefit by buying less than L units. He should, therefore, always buy such an amount of X that its marginal utility is equal to its price.[5]

The marginal utility theorists carried their analysis considerably further. For one thing, they argued, largely on introspective grounds, the more we possess of a commodity, the less we value an additional unit—the famous "law" of *diminishing marginal utility*. Partly, it was stated, this is so because we give priority to more highly valued uses—if we have only one piece of cake, we feed it to our child; if we have two, we divide it between husband and wife and a third we give to our mothers-in-law.

The marginal utility analysis of pricing and the diminishing marginal utility proposition can quickly dispose of the diamond-water paradox. The relative scarcity of diamonds results in their having a high *marginal* utility and, therefore, a high price, while the relative abundance of water means that its *marginal* utility and, consequently, its price will be low despite its high *total* utility.

This law of diminishing marginal utility was also used as an explanation of the negative slope which is alleged to characterize most simple demand curves. The argument is that if the marginal utility of a commodity falls when the consumer purchases more of the item, he can only be induced to buy more of a good by a fall in its price.

Another important function of the law of diminishing marginal utility arises out of the need for *second-order* equilibrium conditions. It will be recalled (Section 5 of Chapter 4) that a marginal equation such as "price equals marginal utility" is not enough to guarantee that the consumer is getting the maximum possible utility for his money. There may be several purchase levels at which the equation holds. For example, referring back to Figure 2, we see that if the marginal utility curve has the peculiar shape of curve MM' and price is OP, then there are three purchase levels Oa, Ob, and Oc at which marginal utility equals price. However, these are not all optimal purchase levels. In fact, two of these, Oa and Oc, are extremely *dis*advantageous to the consumer! If, for example, the consumer increases his purchase quantity from Oa (direction of an arrow), he enters a region where marginal utility exceeds price, and it will pay him to increase the amount he buys even more. Only when he gets to the true equilibrium point B (where marginal utility is diminishing—the curve of MM' has a negative slope) does it pay him to stop increasing his purchases. Similarly,

---

[5] More formally, if x is the amount of X purchased, and if $u(x)$ is the total utility of the purchase (measured in dollars), the consumer presumably seeks to maximize the difference between this total utility and his expenditure, px, i.e., he seeks to maximize $u(x) - px$. Differentiating with respect to x and setting the result equal to zero, we obtain $du/dx - p = 0$, i.e., $p = du/dx$, the marginal utility of x units of good X.

from quantity Oc it pays the consumer either to increase or decrease his purchases—not to stay at Oc (direction of the arrows). In sum, even if price equals marginal utility but marginal utility is *increasing* (points A and C), the consumer is at a point of *minimum*, not maximum, net gain. The "price equals marginal utility" condition only assures us that the consumer is on neither the uphill nor the downhill side of a total utility hill, but this means that he may be either at the top of the hill or the bottom of the valley (see Figure 4 of Chapter 4). Only if marginal utility is diminishing (as at point B) do we know that he must be at a point of *maximum* net gain. [6] From B it pays him to move neither to the right nor to the left (see arrows at point b). Finally, if the law of diminishing marginal utility is valid, the entire marginal utility curve will have a negative slope (curve DD' in Figure 2). There will then be only one point, E, where marginal utility is equal to price, and it will always pay the consumer to move toward the corresponding purchase level, Oe (arrows). The law of diminishing marginal utility thus guarantees that there will be only one possible equilibrium level, Oe, and that it will possess an element of stability—consumers will always be motivated to move toward that point.

At the beginning of this section we employed a monetary measure of marginal utility to make our comparison between the price of a commodity and its marginal utility. The marginal utility of X in money terms was defined as the maximum amount of money which a consumer is willing to pay for an additional unit of X. But the marginal utility theorists were generally dissatisfied with such a measure, for when money becomes scarcer, they maintained, its subjective marginal value will increase, like that of any commodity. Hence, an attempt to measure the marginal utility of X by asking the person how much *money* an additional unit is worth to him is like calculating length with a rubber ruler which stretches as we measure. Marginal utility must, according to this view, be measured in its own, subjective, units—we may call them utils. Some noted economists believed that subjective introspective experiments can be conducted successfully and that marginal utility, measured in utils rather than some directly observable unit (like money), can be known to diminish. That is, by thinking about our own feelings about additions to our holdings of, say, packages of spaghetti, we can come to be sure that additional packages are

---

[6] This is of course the second-order condition—the requirement that if we are maximizing, the second derivative of the maximand must be negative. In the current case (see the preceding footnote) the maximand is $u(x) - px$ whose first derivative with respect to x is $mu_x - p$, where we write mu_x for marginal utility of x. The second derivative, then, is dmu_x/dx, which is required to be negative by the second-order conditions. That is, marginal utility must be declining, as the text asserts.

worth less and less to us in these absolute units (which corresponds to no objective experience that any of us has ever had). This view can be referred to as the *neoclassical cardinal utility* position.[7]

6. Indifference Maps: Ordinal and Cardinal Utility

Many theorists, who classify themselves as *ordinalists*, believe that measurement of subjective utility on an absolute scale is neither possible nor necessary. They question the validity of the introspective data of neoclassical cardinal utility and maintain that all consumer behavior can be described in terms of preferences, or rankings, in which the consumer need only state which of two collections of goods he prefers, without reporting on the magnitude of any numerical index of the strength of this preference.

The geometric device employed to represent this sort of ordinal preference information is the indifference map (Figure 4a). In this diagram

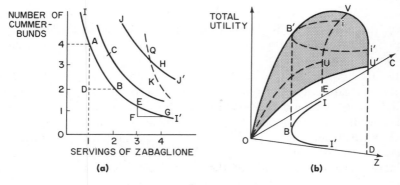

Figure 4

quantities of different commodities are measured along the axes, so that, for example, point A on indifference curve II' represents a collection of commodities consisting of one serving of zabaglione and four cummerbunds. It represents no more than this, and this datum, by itself, contains no information about the consumer in question. In particular, *it does not mean*

---

[7] That view is briefly discussed again in Chapter 17, where it is contrasted with von Neumann-Morgenstern cardinal utility, an entirely different sort of construct despite the similarity in nomenclature. Neoclassical cardinalism is also mentioned in the next section, where it is contrasted with the ordinalist position.

that he is indifferent between the four cummerbunds and the serving of Italian dessert. We note also that every possible combination of these two items can be represented by a point in this diagram.

We may now define an indifference curve as the locus of points each of which represents a collection of commodities such that the consumer is indifferent among any of these combinations. For example, the presence of point B on curve II' means that the consumer is indifferent between *collections* A and B, that is, between the combination of four cummerbunds and one serving of zabaglione (point A) and the combination which consists of two units of each of these items (point B). The indifference map consists of the infinite set of indifference curves such as II' and JJ' (there is, by assumption, one through every point in the diagram) of which only a few can be shown in any actual drawing.

If, for reasons which will be discussed presently, we go along with the assumption that the consumer prefers combinations represented by points on higher indifference curves (e.g., he prefers collection C to A), the indifference map provides us with a complete and simple report on the consumer's ordering of all possible combinations of the two items, for if two combinations are represented by points on the same indifference curve, the consumer is indifferent between them, and in any other case he prefers that collection which is represented by a point on a higher indifference curve.

Let us digress briefly to see how the indifference map is related to the neoclassical cardinal utility representation of the consumer's tastes, leaving until Sections 14–19 a discussion of utility functions in an ordinal analysis. The three-dimensional Figure 4b shows the same consumer's utility surface, which is constructed as follows: Lay Figure 4a on a horizontal surface to constitute the floor of the diagram. Any point, such as B, on this floor again represents a collection of these two items. Now suppose we have somehow found out the number of utils which this collection, B, can yield to the consumer. We erect over point B a flagpole BB', whose length is equal to the number of utils. Similarly, such a flagpole is erected above every point on the floor of the diagram representing the utility of every possible combination of the two items. For example, DU' is the utility of the collection of OD servings of zabaglione (and zero cummerbunds), whereas EU is the utility of OE cummerbunds. If we now stretch a canvas over the top of the collection of flagpoles, this canvas is the consumer's *cardinal* utility surface, $OUVU'$ (shaded surface).

Since all combinations of consumer goods represented by points on an indifference curve II' have equal utility, the flagpoles above such a curve must all be of equal height, i.e., the portion of the utility surface which lies directly above an indifference curve (such as IBI') must all be of a single height (curve $iB'i'$). In other words, the consumer's indifference curves are the contour lines (iso-utility lines) of his utility surface. They are the loci of commodity combinations of equal utility, just as the contour lines on an ordinary geographic map are loci of combinations of latitude and longitude of equal height above sea level.[8]

However, to an ordinalist there is one important respect in which this geographic analogy does not hold. A contour line on an ordinary map is labeled by a number which indicates the height of its points above sea level. But an indifference curve bears no number to indicate the corresponding height of the utility surface—no cardinal utility number is attached to the curve. Hence indifference curves do not contain cardinal utility information—they only record preferences—the order in which the consumer ranks the various commodity combinations. From utility information we can deduce preferences; the consumer prefers the item whose utility is highest—but the converse is not true: The statement that the consumer prefers A to B gives us no numerical utility magnitudes.

7. Properties of Indifference Curves

The slope of an indifference curve has a significant economic interpretation. For example, in Figure 4a we see that the arc AB has the slope AD/DB. But in moving from point A to B the consumer loses AD (2) cummerbunds and gains DB (1) serving of zabaglione. Since A and B are indifferent, it must mean that the DB unit gain in his zabaglione holdings just compensates him for his AD unit cummerbund loss. Thus the absolute (i.e., positive) value of the slope, $AD/DB = \frac{2}{1} = 2$, indicates that it takes one serving of zabaglione to supply heart balm to the consumer for the loss of two cummerbunds. This absolute value of the slope, called the consumer's *marginal rate of substitution of zabaglione for cummerbunds*, therefore represents the number of units of the latter whose loss can be made up by a unit gain in the former. It is the consumer's psychological rate of exchange between the two commodities.

We can also show that this slope (which in the rest of this chapter is taken to mean its *absolute value*) is equal to the fraction (marginal utility of zabaglione/marginal utility of cummerbunds),[9] that is, the marginal

---

[8] If we describe the utility surface by means of a function $u = f(x_1, \cdots, x_n)$, where x_i is the quantity of good i consumed, then the equation of an indifference curve is $f(x_1, \cdots, x_n) = k$ (constant) with different indifference curves corresponding to different values of k.

[9] *Proof:* If arc AB is sufficiently small, the utility loss involved in giving up AD units of cummerbunds is the marginal utility of such a unit (mu_c) multiplied by AD, the number of units involved, i.e., the loss in giving up $AD = (AD) \times (mu_c)$. Similarly, the utility gain involved in acquiring DB units of z is $(DB) \times (mu_z)$, where mu_z represents the marginal utility of zabaglione. Since the gain and the loss just offset one

rate of substitution of Z for C equals

$$\text{slope of } II' \left(= \frac{\Delta c}{\Delta z} \right) = \frac{\text{marginal utility of } Z}{\text{marginal utility of } C}$$

where z and c represent, respectively, the quantities of zabaglione and cummerbunds.

Two features of this result bear some discussion:

1. In the equation

$$\frac{\Delta c}{\Delta z} = \frac{\text{marginal utility of } Z}{\text{marginal utility of } C}$$

it is noteworthy that c appears in the *numerator* of the left-hand fraction but in the *denominator* of the fraction on the right-hand side of the equation and that the reverse holds for z. This inverse relationship between Δc and the marginal utility of c is easily explained. $\Delta c = AD$ units of C is the amount of C which the consumer is willing to give up for $\Delta z = DB$ units of Z. But the more valuable C is to him (the greater the marginal utility of C), obviously the less the consumer will be willing to give up in exchange for Δz; i.e., the smaller will be Δc; hence the inverse relationship.

2. A second thing to be noted is that marginal *utility* seems to have sneaked back into the analysis despite the ordinal nature of the indifference map. However, its return is not as serious as it may appear from the point of view of the ordinalist. Only the *ratio* of two marginal utilities ever

---

another (points A and B are indifferent), we have $AD \times mu_c = DB \times mu_z$. Dividing both sides of the equation by $mu_c \times DB$ we obtain the required result:

$$mu_z/mu_c = AD/DB = \text{the slope of } II'.$$

Alternatively, one can obtain the equation of the text from the expression for the utility function, $u = f(c, z)$, and the formula for total differentiation (Chapter 4, Section 7). Since along an indifference curve total utility must be constant, we must have $du = 0$ or

$$du = \frac{\partial u}{\partial c} \, dc + \frac{\partial u}{\partial z} \, dz = 0.$$

Bringing the first term over to the right and dividing through by $dz \, \partial u/\partial c$ we obtain at once

$$\frac{dc}{dz} = - \frac{\partial u/\partial z}{\partial u/\partial c},$$

which is the relationship in the text.

occurs in indifference analysis. In such a ratio we measure the marginal utility of one commodity not in terms of utils but in terms of the other commodity. We ask how much of C an additional unit of Z is worth (the marginal rate of substitution of Z for C). Thus we are, in effect, back to measuring marginal utility in terms of money, or some other commodity, and that is perfectly satisfactory to the ordinalist.

In indifference curve analysis it is customary (at least implicitly) to make these assumptions about the psychology of the consumer:

Assumption 1 (nonsatiety): The consumer is not oversupplied with either commodity, i.e., he prefers to have more of C and/or Z.

Assumption 2 (transitivity): If A, B, and D are any three commodity combinations and if A is indifferent with B and B is indifferent with D, then the consumer is also indifferent between A and D. This condition simply requires that the consumer's tastes possess a conceptually simple type of consistency.

Assumption 3 (diminishing marginal rate of substitution): Consider two collections represented by points along the same indifference curve (e.g., A and E in Figure 4a). Then if at one of these points, E, the consumer has a relatively small supply of one commodity, C, and a relatively large supply of the other, then at E the marginal utility of the relatively scarcer C will be large in comparison to that of Z, i.e., the consumer will there be willing to give up only a relatively small amount of C in exchange for an additional unit of Z. Thus, in Figure 4a, at point A the consumer is willing to give up AD units of C for an additional unit of Z. But at point E, where C is scarcer, he is only willing to pay the smaller number EF units of C for the same increment in his holdings of Z.

These assumptions permit us to deduce four properties of indifference curves which normally characterize their drawings:

PROPERTY A (*by Assumption 1*). An indifference curve which lies above and to the right of another represents preferred combinations of commodities.

Proof: Consider the indifference curves II' and JJ' in Figure 4a, and combination B on II' and Q on JJ'. Since point Q is above and to the right of point B, it involves more of both commodites C and Z. Hence, by Assumption 1, the consumer must prefer Q to B, and therefore he must prefer every point on JJ' (all of which are indifferent with Q) to any point on II'.

PROPERTY B. Indifference curves have a negative slope (by Assumption 1).

Proof: Start, e.g., at point A in Figure 4a and move from it to the right so that the consumer holds more of commodity Z as a result. By Assumption 1 the consumer must prefer this new point (he cannot be indifferent between it and A) unless at the same time it involves his having less of the other commodity, C. In other words, if he is to be indifferent between the new point and A, it must lie below A as well as to its right, as does point B.

PROPERTY C. Indifference curves can never meet or intersect, so that only one indifference curve will pass through any one point in the map (by Assumptions 1 and 2).

Proof: Suppose on the contrary that two indifference curves, JJ' and the dashed curve, were to intersect at point Q. Pick point K on the dashed indifference curve and point H on JJ' where H lies above and to the right of K. By Property A (Assumption 1) H must be preferred to K. But H is indifferent with Q, and Q is, in turn, indifferent with K. Hence, by Assumption 2, H must be indifferent with K. Since H cannot be both indifferent with and preferred to K, the intersection of the two curves which led to this self-contradictory result cannot possibly occur.

PROPERTY D. The absolute slope of an indifference curve diminishes toward the right (the curve is flatter at point E than it is at point A) so that the curve is said to be *convex to the origin* (by contrast with SS' in Figure 7, which is said to be concave to the origin). This theorem is a direct consequence of Assumption 3, which states that the marginal rate of substitution of Z for C [which, it will be remembered, is represented by the slope of the curve (neglecting minus signs)] is smaller at E than at A (Figure 4a).

8. Violation of the Premises about Indifference Curves. Satiation and Lexicographical Orderings

While the shapes that have just been described are frequently assumed to hold and are extremely convenient analytically for reasons that will be indicated presently, they are necessarily valid *only* on the psychological assumptions listed at the beginning of the section, i.e., nonsatiety, transitivity, and diminishing marginal rate of substitution. Any or all of these conditions can be violated in reality and there is nothing necessarily pathological about such violations, as will now be shown.

Assume that our consumer ultimately does become sated with zabaglione—after the refrigerator and the freezer are filled with it the householder regards further quantities of the dessert with apprehension and perhaps with hostility. Suppose Z^* is the maximal desired quantity of Z (and similarly, let C^* be the satiation quantity of cummerbunds). What happens to the shape of the indifference curves beyond these quantities?

In Figure 5a we see that rectangle OZ^*SC^* is the region of nonsatiation:

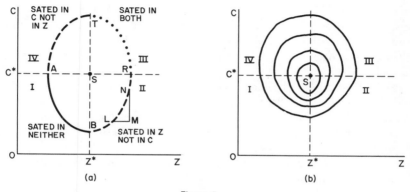

Figure 5

Any point in that region (which has been labeled region I) represents a combination of the two goods which leaves the consumer wanting more of either or both. In that region we see a normally shaped indifference curve—the solid locus AB. However, at any point in region II to the right of Z^* but below C^* (e.g., point L), the consumer still wants more of C but now he desires *less* of Z. Hence if he gets still more Z (the move from L to M) and yet remains indifferent, he must be compensated for the (repugnant) rise in quantity of Z by a desired *rise* in C. Thus the indifference curve in this region must have a *positive* slope. The reader should verify that the same argument holds for region IV in which there is too much C but more Z is still desired. However, in region III, where the consumer has more than he wants of either item, the indifference curve will again acquire its negative slope since there, to compensate him for an *addition* in his unwanted holding of Z, he must be *relieved* of some of his unwanted C. That is, to leave him indifferent a rise in his Z holdings must be accompanied by a fall in his C, and vice versa.

Figure 5b suggests more clearly what is going on by showing a set of several indifference curves. It reveals them to be closed contours, one inside the other, converging to the saturation point, S (sometimes called the "bliss point"), at which the consumer possesses exactly the maximal amounts he wants of each of the two commodities. The indifference curves can be taken as the contour lines of a smooth utility hill with a single maximum point, S, with the surrounding indifference curves representing decreasingly desirable possibilities as they move further from the bliss point.

Thus we see

1. The conventional indifference curves really are only segments of the complete indifference curves—those portions lying in region I, the region of nonsatiation (scarcity). This is, of course, the relevant region for most economic analysis since budgetary limitations do keep consumers from complete satiation in *every* commodity (even the wealthiest of absolute rulers has not been able to afford all the military equipment he wanted for his armies).

2. In other regions the negative slope of the indifference curve need not hold. Moreover, the curve need not be convex to the origin (region III).[10]

3. At points B and T in Figure 5a (zabaglione satiation) the indifference curve is horizontal (a small change in Z neither adds to nor subtracts from his welfare, and so no change in quantity of C is needed to compensate him for such a change). Similarly, at points R and A (cummerbund satiation) the indifference curves are vertical.

It is also possible to think of plausible cases in which the nonintersection property of indifference curves will be violated (intransitivities). This will occur, for example, where the consumer cannot distinguish small differences (1.0003 and 1.0004 ounces of Z look the same to him and seem to assuage his hunger equally). In that case neighboring indifference curves will be equally preferable though one is a tiny bit higher than the other. In this case one says that indifference curves are "thick," that is, they encompass a narrow area rather than a locus (curve) of zero thickness.

Finally, we note that underlying the entire discussion is a premise rarely questioned in elementary texts—the assumption that such curves *exist*. But even that is not necessarily true. It is easy to describe an interesting preference relationship for which no such curves exist. The standard

---

[10] Intuitively, as the quantities of Z rise and C fall as we move from point T toward R in Figure 5a, further additions to the holdings of Z become increasingly unbearable, while further decreases in the excess holdings of C become less urgent. Hence, to get the consumer to accept further increases in his Z he must be compensated by ever-larger declines in his C (increasing marginal rate of substitution).

Actually, this sort of shape of indifference curve can occur also in region I, where it characterizes the behavior of an addict or a collector (the more of either commodity he has, the more urgently he wants even more of it). If addiction to zabaglione were to characterize its consumption, as we move toward point Z^* additional units of this item will become very valuable and additional C comparatively worthless, i.e., the consumer will be willing to trade a small addition in Z for a great loss in C.

counterexample, which is of interest in itself, is called a *lexicographical ordering*, i.e., it uses a ranking criterion analogous to that used in ordering words in a dictionary. Suppose a government of a very poor country with a mild climate considers two objectives: More food (x_1) and more clothing (x_2). Since starvation and malnutrition are serious problems and neither cold nor modesty (!) are considered pressing issues, the government prefers *any* increase in food output *no matter what happens to clothing production*. Then no increase in clothing output can make up for a unit decline in food output. However, the government does favor more clothing output for its decorative and amusement value, provided no food need be given up to get it. Thus, if we start out with 8 units of food and 8 of clothing (point A in Figure 6), the government will prefer any point involving more food than

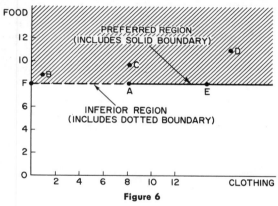

Figure 6

A regardless of the associated quantity of clothing (e.g., points $B, C,$ or D). It will also prefer any point on AE to the right of A (more clothing with no less food). However, it will consider inferior to A any point below A or on the line segment FA to the left of A. Thus, every point in the diagram other than A is either preferable to A or less desirable than A. *There can be no second point that is indifferent to A*, so that no indifference *curve* through A (or through any other point in the diagram) is possible, just as our discussion was intended to show.

PROBLEMS

1. Show the pertinent indifference curve and equilibrium point for a wealthy ruler who has all the zabaglione he can possibly want but wishes he could afford more military equipment.
2. Explain why point F in Figure 6 is considered inferior to A but B, which is very close to F, is superior to A.
3. Explain the analogy between the lexicographical ordering as described in the text and the ordering of words in a dictionary.

9. Price Lines: Consumer Income and Prices

By itself, an indifference map cannot possibly predict consumer behavior because it leaves out two vital types of information—the income of the consumer and the prices of the commodities. The indifference curves do not ask the consumer which combination he believes will give him the most for his money. It is merely a hypothetical ranking of various commodity combinations—perhaps castles in Spain against yachts in Portugal —taking no account of what the consumer can afford.

Price and income information is supplied in an indifference diagram by another curve which is called the *price line* or, sometimes, the *budget line*. Since the axes of the diagram present only quantities of commodities rather than amounts of money, dollar prices and incomes cannot be shown directly. Instead, the price line does the next best thing and indicates what amounts of the commodities a given amount of money can buy.

For example (Figure 7), suppose $50 spent exclusively on commodity Z

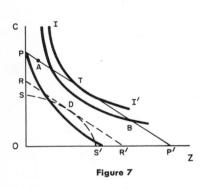

Figure 7

will, at its current price, buy OP' units of that commodity, whereas the same amount spent entirely on C will purchase exactly OP units of that item. Suppose, moreover, that every point such as A on line PP' represents a combination of the two commodities which sells for $50 (e.g., $10 worth of Z plus $40 of C). Then line PP' is a *price* or *budget* line. Such a line is defined as the locus of all combinations of commodities which cost some fixed amount of money (e.g., our illustrative $50).

If the prices of both commodities are fixed, that is, they do not vary with the amounts of the goods which are purchased, the price line will possess the following properties:

1. It will be a straight line.
2. It will have a negative slope.
3. Its slope will be equal to the *negative inverse* of the ratio of the prices of the two commodities, i.e., we will have $\Delta c/\Delta z = -p_z/p_c$, where p_z and p_c are the unit prices of Z and C, respectively.
4. Suppose two price lines involve the same commodity prices but represent the expenditure of different amounts of money (say $50 for PP' and $30 for RR'). Then the two lines will be parallel.

The equation of the price line is, in the fixed price case, given by a simple expression. If the consumer buys z units of commodity Z, his total expenditure on this item will be $p_z z$ (the price per unit, p_z, multiplied by the number of units purchased). Similarly, expenditure on the other commodity is given by $p_c c$ so that total expenditure is given by

$$(4) \qquad\qquad p_z z + p_c c = m,$$

where m is the amount of money spent (our illustrative \$50 for line PP') and is therefore constant along a price line. This, then, is the equation of a price line.[11]

The four properties can readily be generalized to take account of price variability. There are two possibilities: Either that buying in quantity will make the commodities scarce relative to the quantities demanded and so raise their prices to the purchaser (as wages go up when the demand for labor increases), or, on the other hand, that he will be offered discounts if he buys in larger quantities (special today: one elephant, \$200, or two for \$325). The former possibility, which can be interpreted as a case of diminishing returns to an increased number of dollars spent by a large purchaser on a given commodity, will yield a curved price line which, like SS', is concave to the origin (Figure 7). The reason is that as one moves toward the axes from an interior point such as D, a greater proportion of this large consumer's fixed amount of money, m, is spent on one of the commodities; thus near S almost all of it is spent on commodity C. This raises the price of C against the consumer so that his m dollars will buy only OS—which is less than the OR units he could obtain for m dollars if the price of C were fixed at the level it is at point D.

For a completely analogous reason, quantity discounts (increasing returns to increased expenditure on any one item) will result in a budget line which, like II', is convex to the origin.

There remains one point to discuss about price lines. What do they tell us about the consumer's income and the prices of the various products? First, to deal with the information on consumer income which is conveyed by a price line, it is convenient to define the multicommodity analogue of a price line [Equation (4)]—the algebraic budget relationship for all of

---

[11] The four properties of the price line are readily derived from this equation. Dividing both sides by p_c and rearranging terms the equation becomes

$$c = -\frac{p_z}{p_c} z + \frac{m}{p_c}.$$

If we now change our notation, writing y for c, x for z, a for $-p_z/p_c$, and b for m/p_c, this becomes the standard *linear* equation of Chapter 2, $y = ax + b$, with (*negative*) *slope* $a = -p_z/p_c$. The four price-line properties follow directly from this result, as the reader should verify.

Note also that m/p_c = the total amount of C the consumer could purchase if he were to spend all of his income on that item.

the (say, 1,257) different commodities which the consumer buys or considers buying:

$$p_1 x_1 + p_2 x_2 + \cdots + p_{1257} x_{1257} = m,$$

where, e.g., x_2 is the quantity of commodity number 2 purchased and p_2 is its unit price. In such a multicommodity budget equation it is convenient to consider savings to be one of the 1,257 goods which he buys or can buy for his money. On this interpretation, the consumer has no choice but to spend all his money (either on savings or on some other commodity) and the only relevant price line is the one which uses up all of the funds which he has available to him. This price line, then, specifies the consumer's *real income* (or wealth). It tells us just what combinations of commodities he can afford to buy, given prices and his money income.

So much for the income information supplied by a price line. Let us now see what the price line tells us about prices.

Property 3 states that the slope of such a line tells us the *ratio* of the prices of the commodities. If the slope is -2, we know that the price of Z must be twice the price of a unit of C (note again the inverse relationship, $-p_z/p_c = \Delta c/\Delta z$).

To summarize, the price line specifies the real purchasing power which is available to the consumer and the ratio of the prices of the two commodities. But since monetary quantities are not shown anywhere on the diagram, it is impossible for the price line by itself to specify either the level of the consumer's liquid assets or the money price of any commodity.[12]

10. Equilibrium of the Consumer

The consumer who wants to get the most for his money will want to land on as high an indifference curve as his purchasing power permits—the highest indifference curve which can be reached from his budget line. This optimal purchase combination is given by the point of tangency, T, between the price line and indifference curve II' (Figure 7), for it is clear, by inspection of the diagram, that any other point on the price line, such as B, will be intersected by an indifference curve which lies below II'. In this way, the indifference map together with the price line permit us to predict the demand pattern of the "rational" consumer—the consumer who spends his money efficiently in the pursuit of his needs and interests. We say that T is a *point of equilibrium* because once the consumer arrives at

---

[12] However, if we know any one of these values, the others follow at once. For example, if the price of C is known to be \$10 and the price line shows Z to be twice as expensive as C, then the price of Z must obviously be \$20. Similarly, since his money buys OP units of C at \$10 per unit, his expendable money must be OP times \$10.

the decision to purchase the combination of commodities represented by that point, he has no motivation to revise his purchase plans.

The tangency condition of equilibrium immediately yields another equilibrium condition. At their point of tangency the slope of the price line and that of the indifference curve must, by definition, be equal. But we know that the (absolute value of the) slope of the budget line is equal to the (inverse) ratio of the two prices, whereas the slope of the indifference curve is equal to the (inverse) ratio of the two marginal utilities or to the marginal rate of substitution of Z for C. Therefore, in equilibrium we must have

$$\frac{p_z}{p_c} = \frac{mu_z}{mu_c} = \text{marginal rate of substitution of } Z \text{ for } C.$$

This is the marginal condition of equilibrium of the consumer. It resembles the neoclassical equilibrium condition that price must equal the marginal utility of a commodity, but states, instead, that the *ratio* of the marginal utilities of two commodities must equal the *ratio* of their prices.

The logic of this condition is easily demonstrated. Suppose the condition is violated so that, e.g., the first of these fractions is greater than the second. Then, multiplying both sides by the presumably positive number mu_c/p_z, we obtain the inequality $mu_c/p_c > mu_z/p_z$. But if item C costs, e.g., $p_c = \$5$ per unit, we can for \$1 obtain $1/5 = 1/p_c$ units of this item, and $(1/5)mu_c = (1/p_c)mu_c$ therefore represents the utility which can be obtained spending an additional dollar on C. The last inequality therefore states that the consumer can acquire more utility out of an additional dollar spent on C than from another dollar spent on Z. If this is so, he cannot possibly be getting the most for his money—he can get more by reallocating his funds, spending less on Z and more on C. This is illustrated in Figure 7, where we note that at point B the absolute value of the slope of the indifference curve is less than that of the price line (the indifference curve is flatter) so that we have $mu_z/mu_c < p_z/p_c$ and so, as before, $mu_z/p_z < mu_c/p_c$. It therefore pays the consumer to plan to buy less of Z and more of C, i.e., for him to move upward and to the left along the price line from B toward the point of tangency T. We see then that B violates our equilibrium condition and *that it does so in a way which motivates the consumer to move toward the equilibrium point T.* Thus with curves of the usual shape (as in the diagram), the equilibrium point possesses an element of stability. From any other point on the price line the consumer is motivated to move in the direction of the point of tangency.

Indeed, the shape we have assumed for the indifference curves plays an important role in our tangency solution. If any one of the four properties of indifference curves (listed in Section 7, above) were violated, consumer equilibrium would not occur at a point of tangency. Thus, if Property A were violated so that the consumer wished, say, to be on the lowest attainable indifference curve, his optimal point would be P rather than T, i.e., he would end up spending his money exclusively on one commodity. If Property B were violated so that the slope of the indifference curves was not negative, there could be no point of tangency with the negatively sloping price line. If Property C (nonintersectability of indifference curves) were violated, a number of points of tangency might occur (Figure 8a), and if the indifference curves were concave to the origin, in violation of

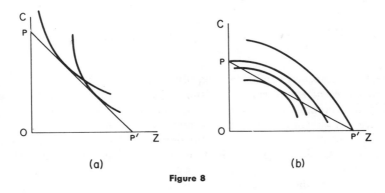

(a)   (b)

Figure 8

Property D, the point of tangency would yield the lowest attainable indifference curve, whereas the highest indifference curve would lie at one of the end points of the price line (P' in Figure 8b), so the rational consumer would again end up spending all of his money on just one commodity! Note that at the point of tangency in Figure 8b the consumer is at the point of *minimum* utility on his price line.[13]

PROBLEM

Show that if indifference curves are positively sloped the optimal point is likely to occur at a corner (an end point of the price line). Interpret this case in terms of Figure 5.

11. Responses to Price and Income Changes

If the income of the consumer increases, his budget line will retain its slope (relative prices remain unchanged) but that line will then shift

---

[13] What has gone wrong here is that while at the tangency point the first-order conditions for a maximum are satisfied (MRS equal to the ratio of prices), the second-order conditions are those required for a minimum rather than a maximum (i.e., it is as though, in a one-variable function, the second derivative were positive).

upward (he can get more goods for his increased money supply). In other words, income changes cause parallel shifts in the budget line, and a set of parallel budget lines (Figure 9a) shows how the consumer's possible purchases will vary with changes in his income. On each such line we can find the equilibrium point of tangency (points T_1, T_2, etc.). The curve OW, which is the locus of all such points, shows how the consumer's purchases of the two commodities will vary when his income changes. Such a curve is called an *income-consumption* curve or, sometimes, an Engel curve (named after an early student of the effects of income changes on consumer expenditure patterns).

Normally, consumers may be expected to increase their purchases of commodities as their incomes rise. But sometimes, if an item is of low quality, demand for it will drop as the consumer's financial position improves and more desirable commodities are substituted for it. Such an item is called an *inferior good*. Plausible examples of inferior goods are recapped automobile tires, poorly made clothing, poor cuts of meat, etc., any of which the consumer may be buying only because he can afford no better. In Figure 9a commodity Z is taken to be an inferior good. This is shown by the relative positions of points T_3 and T_4 (the negatively sloping segment of OW). The latter point lies to the left of the former (it represents a lower quantity of Z) despite the fact that it (T_4) is on a higher budget line and therefore involves a higher income for the consumer.

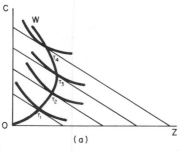 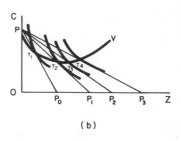

(a)   (b)

Figure 9

Next, we can investigate the effects on the consumer's purchases of changes in the price of one of the commodities. Suppose the price of Z falls, other things remaining equal. This means that the buyer can get more of this commodity for his money (e.g., OP_1 instead of OP_0 in Figure 9b), though he can only obtain the same amount of C as before (quantity of OP). We see, then, that a fall in the price of the item on the horizontal axis leads the price line to flatten out by swinging to the right. Figure 9b represents a number of such price lines and the corresponding equilibrium tangency points. Curve PV, the locus of these points of tangency, shows how changes in the price of Z affect the purchases of *both* commodities. PV is called a *price-consumption curve* or sometimes, particularly in international trade theory, an *offer curve*.

It will be noted that the *income-consumption* curve, OW, begins at the origin (point O) because with zero income the consumer can buy none of either commodity. By contrast, the *price*-consumption curve, PV, characteristically begins at point P, the pivot point of the swinging price line in Figure 9b. The reason is that, as the price line approaches the vertical axis (the price of Z increases further and further), the consumer finds that he gets less and less of Z for his money. Eventually, when its price goes high enough, the consumer will be forced out of buying Z altogether and he will therefore spend all his money on the remaining commodity, C, i.e., he will buy OP units of C and no Z (point P).

The offer curve construction can readily be translated into an ordinary demand curve for the consumer[14] if one of the commodities represented in the diagram is M, the money held by the consumer (Figure 10a). By this device money values are inserted into the indifference map. As before, let PV be the offer curve so that if the consumer buys zero units of the commodity he will have $30 for himself (point P). Now consider point A on

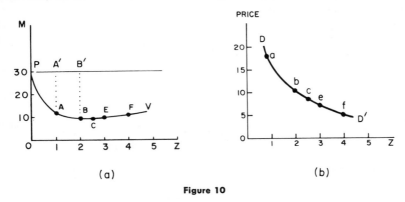

(a)   (b)

Figure 10

the offer curve which represents the consumer possessing $z = 1$ unit of commodity Z and $m = \$12$. Since in moving from P to A he acquired 1 unit of the good but gave up $18 = 30 - 12$ dollars, the price per unit at A must be $18. Thus, point A states that the consumer will buy 1 unit of the commodity if its price is $18. This information is recorded by point a in Figure 10b. Similarly, point B on his offer curve involves the buyer's spending $20 = 30 - 10$ dollars on *two* units of the good so the price *per unit* must be $\$20/2 = \$10$. Hence (point b in Figure 10b) the offer curve

---

[14] It should be noted, however, that even if the consumer has preference patterns for which an indifference map exists (cf. Section 8) it need not follow that a corresponding demand function exists unless the (ordinal) utility function is differentiable.

tells us that he is prepared to buy two units if the price is $10. Points c, e, and f in Figure 10b are derived similarly. These are clearly points on the consumer's demand curve since they indicate how many units he is prepared to buy at different prices. DD', the locus of all such points, is the demand curve for this consumer.

It is noteworthy that the *offer* curve gives us information about the elasticity of the *demand* curve. For example, inspection of PV tells us that to the left of point c the demand curve DD' must be elastic. To see why this is so, note that the unit price at point B ($10) is lower than that at A ($18) but that total consumer expenditure on the commodity at B ($BB' = $20) is greater than that at A ($AA' = $18). Thus a fall in price has produced a rise in total expenditure (the price-consumption curve has a negative slope). By elasticity Proposition 2 in Section 4 of this chapter, expenditure will rise when price falls only if the demand curve is elastic. The reader should have no difficulty showing that DD' is unit elastic at horizontal point c and inelastic to the right of point c.

12. Income and Substitution Effects: The Slutsky Theorem

It is customary to analyze somewhat further the effect on purchases of a change in the price of one of the commodities. The effect, for example, of a fall in the price of Z is classified into categories: the income and the substitution effect. Its lower price makes Z a better buy relative to C than it was before, and, as will be shown presently, that consequence by itself would always induce the consumer to increase his purchase of Z (the Slutsky theorem). This price-ratio portion of the effect of a price change on purchases is called the *substitution* effect. Purchases of Z will be substituted for those of C because Z is *relatively* more price-attractive than it was initially.

But the fall in price of Z also affects the purchases of both commodities in another way—it increases the purchasing power of the consumer's income. This will, in turn, always increase the purchases of *both* commodities provided that neither of them is an inferior good, the demand for which is reduced by an increase in real income. The income effect, then, is the effect *on the consumer's purchases* of the rise in real income which results from a fall in the price of commodity Z. Note that the income effect refers to the resulting change in his purchases and *not* to the change in his real income.

To summarize, a fall in the price of any commodity, X, will affect the consumer's demand for X. This effect may be subdivided into two parts: the substitution effect, which always increases the demand for X, and the income effect, which will increase the demand for X unless X is an inferior good. Thus, ignoring this exceptional possibility, *the demand curve for X must have a negative slope*, i.e., a fall in the price of X must increase the demand for that commodity. Even if X is an inferior good its demand curve will still have a negative slope unless the income effect is stronger than the substitution effect, for, as will soon be shown, the substitution effect of a lower price of X is always a rise in the demand for X. In addition, in practice, the income effect for most consumers' goods is likely to be small because a buyer's outlay on any one commodity constitutes a relatively small proportion of his budget, so a fall in the price of that item alone will not increase his real income significantly.[15]

Two different graphic depictions of the income and substitution effects have been employed in the literature. In Figure 11a and 11b let PP' and PP'' be two price lines involving different prices of commodity Z, and let A and B represent the (tangency) equilibrium points on the two price lines. The total effect of the price change on the amount of Z purchased is, therefore, ab. Our object is to divide ab into two parts—the income effect and the substitution effect. For this purpose the change in position of the price line is divided artificially into two parts: a parallel shift (a change in real income with no change in relative prices) and a pivot or twisting (change in slope) of the price line (a change in relative prices with no change in real income). To accomplish this division we employ an imaginary price line RR' in Figure 11a (or SS' in Figure 11b) which is parallel to one of the price lines (they have the same relative prices) and is, in some sense, at the same real income level as the other. Here is where the ambiguity in interpretation occurs (the source of difference between the two diagrams).

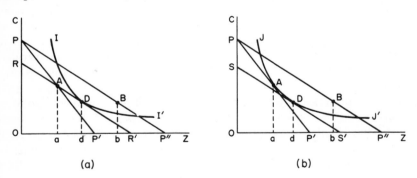

(a)   (b)

Figure 11

---

[15] But, at least as a remote possibility, we see that a very inferior good for which the income effect is very high provides another possible case of a positively sloping demand curve. The other two cases which were mentioned in Section 1 of this chapter (snob appeal and quality judged by price) do not show up in the usual indifference map analysis because each of these involves the consumer's preference structure being changed by the price change. He values platinum collar stays or a brand of frozen chop suey more highly when its price rises. In other words, the consumer's indifference curves shift when there is a swing in the price line—a possibility which has not been considered in the text.

When do two price lines, which are not identical, represent the same real income? One highly persuasive solution is to say that this occurs when they both yield the same satisfaction to the consumer, i.e., they are both tangent to the same indifference curve, as are PP' and SS' in Figure 11b (they are tangent, at points A and D, respectively, to indifference curve JJ'). There is another solution, which is perhaps less satisfying intuitively but which is very useful and which we will need presently. This is to say that RR' (Figure 11a) yields the same income as PP' if RR' passes through point A so that it just gives the consumer enough money to buy combination A, the combination he would buy if PP' were in fact the prevailing price line. In this case, the point of equilibrium, D, on the imaginary price line RR' lies on an indifference curve II', which is not tangent to PP'. Indeed, since line RR' in Figure 11a is higher than SS' in 11b, the indifference curve II' to which RR' is tangent must lie above indifference curve JJ' in 11b, which is tangent to both SS' and the original price line, PP'.

The income and substitution effects can now be read off from the diagrams. The substitution effect is ad, the change in purchase of Z which results from the twisting of the imaginary price line, whereas the income effect is db, the effect of the parallel shift in the price line.

In this two-commodity analysis. Figure 11b can be used to show that when the price of z falls (the price line flattens out), the substitution effect must lead to a rise in the demand for Z, for SS' and PP' are both tangent to the same indifference curve. But since SS' is the flatter price line, its point of tangency, D, must occur to the right of A, the point of tangency of PP' (because the slope of an indifference curve gets smaller toward the right). Hence, with the lower relative price of Z (RR' or SS') the demand for $Z(d)$ will be greater than the demand for Z when the price line is PP'. Unfortunately this argument is not valid when there are more than two commodities so that the consumer's preferences cannot be summed up in a two-dimensional indifference map. Presently, more general proofs of this result, the *Slutsky theorem*, will be presented (Chapter 13, Section 8).

13. The Role of the Income Effect

The reader may well wonder what the fuss is all about—why the mere classification of the effects of a price change into two portions—the substitution and the income effect—should have elicited so much attention in the literature. The essence of the matter is that Eugen Slutsky and, after him, J. R. Hicks and R. D. G. Allen discovered independently that such a price effect has two portions one of which, the substitution effect, is predictable in sign and in many of its other characteristics. For example, we have just seen that the substitution effect of a rise in the price of X on the quantity of X purchased will always be negative (the Slutsky theorem).

But these authors noted that there is another portion of the overall effect (the income-effect portion) whose behavior is unpredictable in general—and it must therefore be stripped away so that the systematic and predictable behavior of the substitution effect can be revealed. This discovery can be likened to a filter which eliminates the static from the transmission of sound so that the underlying message can be made out.

This, then, is the unexalted role of the income effect—it is discussed primarily in order to permit us to remove it. One should not be misled by the subclassification of possible values for the income effect—the statement that for "normal" goods it has one sign and for "inferior" goods it has another. This is only a little more than the use of nomenclature to put a better appearance on our ignorance. What this last subclassification asserts, in essence, is that the income effect can go either way and that we can think of realistic examples of both cases. Hence, we can make firm predictions about demand reactions to price changes only if this undependable portion of the price effect has been removed.

Much of more sophisticated consumer theory proceeds accordingly, discussing matters in terms of "net" concepts—after removal of the income effects—rather than the corresponding gross concepts which correspond more closely to the observable data but whose behavior patterns vary in a manner that defies generalization.

14. Complements and Substitutes

The distinction between substitute and complementary commodities is easily grasped intuitively. Vodka and gin are substitute commodities—they serve the same general purposes, and if we have more of one, we will tend to want less of the other. On the other hand, bread and butter or gin and vermouth are complements—for many consumers they are better together and hence an increase in the availability of one tends to stimulate the demand for the other. But how does one measure these relationships? One straightforward approach makes use of the cross elasticity of demand—the effect of a change in the price of X_1 on the demand for X_2. If goods are substitutes, we expect the cross elasticity to be positive, and we expect the reverse if they are complements, for if X_1 and X_2 are substitutes, a rise in p_1 will decrease x_1 (the quantity of X_1 demanded), and as a result the consumer will seek more of the substitute. Consequently, the rise in p_1 will lead to an increase in x_2, and so the cross elasticity, $(dx_2/dp_1)p_1/x_2$, will be positive. The reverse will be true of complements, for the rise in p_1 will decrease x_1 and hence decrease x_2.

Or will it? The answer is that it always will[16] *unless* the ambiguous

---

[16] For proof of this statement see Chapter 14, Section 9, Proposition 10.

income effect messes matters up once again. For example, suppose the consumer is a relatively impecunious martini drinker. Then a rise in the price of gin may lead him to increase his purchases of cheap vermouth, which he will use instead of the imported variety. It is clearly the income effect which stimulates his consumption of the inferior good, cheap vermouth, as the rise in price of gin reduces the consumer's real income. Thus, though the goods are complements, their cross elasticity will in this case be positive. Similarly, a rise in the price of hamburger may lead a poor family to decrease its demand for steaks even though they are substitutes.

There is worse to come: Because of the asymmetry of the income effect the cross elasticity of demand for good 1 with respect to the price of good 2 may be positive and yet the elasticity of demand for good 2 with respect to the price of good 1 may be negative, for one good may play a small part in the consumer's budget and so a rise in its price will have a negligible income effect while the reverse may be true of the other good.

To make it easier to describe these cases economists use the following classifications:

1. Good 1 is a *gross substitute* for 2 if its cross elasticity of demand with respect to p_2 is positive,

2. It is a *gross complement* if that cross elasticity is negative,

3. It is a *net substitute* if the cross elasticity is positive *after the income effect is removed,*

4. It is a *net complement* if the cross elasticity is negative after removal of the income effect.

15. Compensated Demand Curves

The elimination of the income effect has also been carried out for demand curves, and so much of recent analysis has been carried out in terms of a *compensated demand curve,* i.e., the demand curve after adjustment to remove income effects. This curve describes the result of the conceptual experiment described in the following steps:

a. Start from some initial price-quantity combination.

b. Consider some alternative price, e.g., a price higher than the initial one.

c. Adjust the consumer's income so as to leave him with the real purchasing power he possessed initially; e.g., if price is increased, he must be compensated by an increase in income sufficient to permit him to purchase the initial quantity combination, should he choose to do so.

d. Now examine the effect of the price change on his purchases after the compensation for income effect (step c.).

Graphically the process looks as shown in Figure 12. Here DD' is the ordinary (uncompensated) demand curve. Suppose the initial price-quantity combination is p_a, x_a and we consider the consumer's behavior at the alternative price, p_b. Without compensation his purchases would be reduced to x_b. But to compensate him for the erosion of his purchasing power stemming from the price rise, the consumer is provided a (conceptual) infusion of income. If X is not an inferior good, this means his purchases will not fall quite as much as if he had received no compensation, i.e., instead of going from x_a to x_b they will decrease only to x_c. This means that AC is a *compensated demand curve* through point A. Thus, the compensated demand curve for a rise in price will generally lie to right of the ordinary demand curve (except at the initial point), provided the commodity in question is not an inferior good.

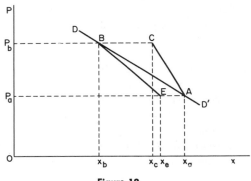

Figure 12

We note at once that there is not just one single compensated demand curve—indeed, there will be a different one for every initial price-quantity combination, i.e., for each initial point (like A) on the ordinary demand curve DD'. Moreover, there are also compensated demand curves for price *decreases*, and these (like curve BE) will usually lie to the left of the ordinary demand curve. For if price falls, in the absence of compensation the consumer's real income will rise. Thus, after enough income has been taken away to offset this gain, if the good is not inferior he will buy less than he would have otherwise. For example, with the lower price, p_a, substituted for p_b the uncompensated quantity demanded will rise to x_a, but with the (negative) compensation to offset the rise in real income accompanying the price fall, quantity demanded will rise only to x_e.

16. Ordinal Utility Functions: Monotonic Transformations

Even in an ordinalist analysis it is often convenient to conduct the calculations in terms of utility functions rather than an indifference map.

By approaching the consumer's decision as a matter of utility maximization subject to a budget constraint one is enabled to use all of the mathematical apparatus of constrained maximization, the powerful Lagrangian techniques, their extension in Kuhn-Tucker methods, etc.

But what utility function can an ordinalist use, since he does not believe that absolute psychic utility can be measured? The answer is that for any given indifference map there is ordinarily[17] an infinity of utility functions any one of which will do just as well as any other. Given two indifference curves A and B with the latter preferable to the former, we can say arbitrarily that any output combination on the former offers 7 utils and the latter 11 utils or instead we can say that A provides 3 utils and B provides 59 utils. As long as points on the preferred indifference curve are assigned the higher utility numbers they provide all the information on preferences that the ordinalist needs for his calculations. We know that above any indifference curve the utility surface is level and that the surface gets higher as we move to higher indifference curves, but no more. The actual height of the utility surface above any indifference curve is left completely unspecified, so that any of an infinite number of utility surfaces is usually consistent with any given indifference map—that is, all of the surfaces in the set will give us the same indifference map. Thus, to an ordinalist the surface in Figure 4b represents only one of the infinite number of utility surfaces consistent with the given indifference map.

The switch from one such acceptable utility function to another is said to involve a *monotonic transformation*. A *transformation* may be described as the replacement of one set of numbers by another. A transformation is monotonic if a higher number in the first set is always replaced by a higher number in the second set. Table 1 illustrates the relationship.

TABLE 1

Goods Collection	a_1	a_2	a_3	a_4	a_5
First set of utility numbers	3	7	9	11	15
Second set of utility numbers	1	2.6	55	59	60
Third set of utility numbers	3	7	10	8	15

We see that the replacement of the first set of numbers by the second is, indeed, a monotonic transformation since whenever the numbers in the first row increase, the numbers in the second also increase. On the other

---

[17] There are some cases that may be considered pathological in which a peculiar indifference map precludes the existence of *any* utility surface consistent with it. This is the so-called integrability problem—an indifference map which permits no utility function is called *nonintegrable*.

hand, the replacement of the first set of numbers by the third is not monotonic, for the 9-util entry in row 1 is replaced by (transformed into) a 10-util entry in row 3, while the 11-util entry is transformed into an 8-util figure. Thus, the figures in row 1 assert that goods combination a_4 is preferable to a_3, whereas the utility figures in row 3 indicate that the preferences are reversed.

If we use $u = f(x_1, \cdots, x_n)$ to describe any one of the infinity of utility functions for a given indifference map, then any monotonic transformation of this function, i.e., any other acceptable utility function, is written

$$u^* = g(u), \qquad dg/du > 0,$$

where g is *any* function of u whose value increases whenever u increases. But that is just what is meant by monotonicity, and it is also precisely what is meant by the $dg/du > 0$. It is important to note that *any monotonic transformation of a utility surface will leave the indifference curves unchanged.*[18]

We will see next that the class of utility functions acceptable to an ordinalist is characterized by a property called *quasi-concavity*, which is extremely useful analytically. But in order to define the concept we must first deal with a preliminary matter.

17. Interior Points on a Line Segment[19]

Consider any two points A and B with coordinates (y_a, x_a) and (y_b, x_b), respectively (Figure 13). Now connect A and B by a line segment. The remainder of the chapter will make heavy use of the formula for the coordinates of any given point on this line segment which is given by the rule that the coordinates of any interior point on the line segment AB

---

[18] It is easy to prove that the indifference curves will be unaffected by the choice between u and u^* as a utility function. The shape of the indifference curve through any point in the indifference map for commodities 1 and 2 is given by the slope of that curve which we know is given by $-mu_1/mu_2 = -(\partial u/\partial x_1)/(\partial u/\partial x_2)$. The issue is what happens to that ratio when the utility function u is replaced by its monotone transform $u^* = g(u)$. But by the chain rule of differentiation (Chapter 4, Section 2, Rule 8) we know that $\partial u^*/\partial x_i = (dg/du) \, \partial u/\partial x_i$. Therefore, with the utility function u^* we deduce that the slope of the indifference curve becomes

$$-\frac{du^*/dx_1}{du^*/dx_2} = -\frac{(dg/du) \, \partial u/\partial x_1}{(dg/du) \, \partial u/\partial x_2} = -\frac{\partial u/\partial x_1}{\partial u/\partial x_2}.$$

Therefore, both utility functions necessarily yield the same number for the slope of the indifference curve through any point in the indifference map.

[19] The remainder of this chapter is made up of relatively advanced material.

will be a weighted sum of the corresponding coordinates of A and B, with a fixed weight, k, applied to *each and every* coordinate of A, and the weight $1 - k$ assigned to *each and every* coordinate of B, and where k is some number between zero and unity. More specifically, we have (in the two-dimensional case) the rather tedious but important

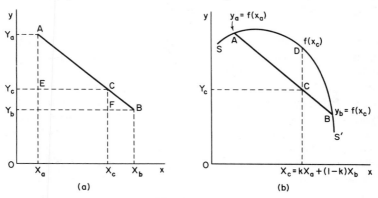

Figure 13

Proposition 3: Let point C with coordinates (y_c, x_c) be any point on line segment AB. Write x_c as a weighted average of x_a and x_b, so that $x_c = kx_a + (1 - k)x_b$, where $0 < k < 1$. (x_c is then called a *convex combination* of x_a and x_b.) Then, the y coordinates of points C, A, and B will satisfy the corresponding equation with the same value of k, i.e., we will have[20] $y_c = ky_a + (1 - k)y_b$. Moreover, $k/(1 - k)$ equals the ratio $(x_b - x_c)/(x_c - x_a)$.

It should be noted that the same result holds in n-dimensional space: Let A and B be two points with respective coordinates $(x_{1a}, \cdots, x_{na})$ and

---

[20] *Proof:* The triangles AEC and CFB are similar. Hence

(i) $\qquad (x_b - x_c)/(x_c - x_a) = FB/EC = FC/EA = (y_b - y_c)/(y_c - y_a)$.

But substituting for x_c the expression $kx_a + (1 - k)x_b$, as given in the text, the first of the preceding fractions becomes

$$(x_b - x_c)/(x_c - x_a) = [(x_b - kx_a - (1 - k)x_b]/[kx_a + (1 - k)x_b - x_a]$$

$$= \frac{k(x_b - x_a)}{(1 - k)(x_b - x_a)} = k/(1 - k).$$

Hence by (i) we must also have

$$(y_b - y_c)/(y_c - y_a) = k/(1 - k) \text{ or } (y_b - y_c) - (ky_b - ky_c) = ky_c - ky_a,$$

which gives us our result: $y_c = ky_a + (1 - k)y_b$.

$(x_{1b}, \cdots, x_{nb})$ and if C is any point in the interior of the line segment connecting A and B, then there exists a number k such that $0 < k < 1$ and such that if x_{ic} is the ith coordinate of C, then $x_{ic} = kx_{ia} + (1 - k)x_{ib}$ for each and every i.

18. Concave and Strictly Concave Functions

Section 5 of Chapter 7 offered intuitive definitions of *concave* and *convex functions*.[21] Using the customary frame of reference—the shape of the surface as viewed from the floor of the diagram—we can envision a concave function as one having the general shape of an inverted bowl, while a convex function is shaped like an upright bowl. When a function is concave, if we take any two points on the surface of the bowl and connect them by a line segment, it is clear intuitively that every interior point on that connecting line segment will lie beneath the surface of the bowl. This characteristic is used by mathematicians to define a concave function.

Specifically, the theorem on the formula for interior points of a connecting line segment (Proposition 3 of the preceding section) is used to define concavity. The general notion is illustrated in Figure 13b in which SS' is the graph of a concave function $y = f(x)$. A and B are any two points on the surface and C is any point on the connecting line segment, and since the curve is concave, C lies below point D on SS' directly above x_c, the x coordinate of C. Now we have

(i) the y coordinate of point D, $y_d = f(x_c) = f[kx_a + (1 - k)x_b]$
by the formula for x_c from the preceding section;
(ii) by Proposition 3 the y coordinate of point $C = y_c = ky_a + (1 - k)y_b = kf(x_a) + (1 - k)f(x_b)$.

Therefore, we have

Definition: The function $y = f(x)$ is *strictly concave* if for any two values of x, call them x_a and x_b, every point $C = (y_c, x_c)$ on the line connecting (y_a, x_a) and (y_b, x_b) lies *below* the corresponding point $D = (y_d, x_c)$ on the graph of the function, i.e., [by (i) and (ii)] if

$$y_c = kf(x_a) + (1 - k)f(x_b) < f[kx_a + (1 - k)x_b] = y_d.$$

Definition: The function $y = f(x)$ is *concave* if for any two values of x, call them x_a and x_b, every point $C = (y_c, x_c)$ on the line connecting points

---

[21] The reader may well want to review the discussion and the distinction between the concept of a convex set (region) and that of a convex function.

$A = (y_a, x_a)$ and $B = (y_b, x_b)$ lies *on or below* the corresponding point $D = (y_d, x_c)$ on the graph of the function, that is, if the $<$ in the previous definition is replaced by $\leq$.

These concepts are readily extended to the $(n + 1)$-variable case $y = f(x_1, \cdots, x_n)$, where we merely write $y_a = f(x_{1a}, \cdots, x_{na})$, etc., and leave all other elements of the definitions of concavity and strict concavity completely unchanged.

Now strict concavity is the natural extension of the second-order maximum condition requiring a negative second derivative of the function being maximized. In effect, strict concavity requires that if the function is differentiable, its second derivatives be negative along *any* cross section, i.e., in any direction in the $(n + 1)$-dimensional (!) graph representing the function. Looked at another way, obviously in seeking to maximize we want the relevant function to be shaped like a hill or an inverted cup, and that is just what we mean by (strict) concavity.

Thus, if we are to analyze consumer behavior in terms of utility maximization, it would be convenient for the utility function to be concave, with the second-order conditions for maximization thereby satisfied. Unfortunately, ordinal utility analysis cannot accept such an assumption. For, as we have seen, given any indifference map, there is an infinity of utility functions corresponding to it, any one of which is as acceptable as any other. Furthermore, as we will confirm next, among those that are acceptable there will be some utility functions that are concave and some that are not. This is shown clearly by Figures 14a and 14b, both of which have the same indifference curves for combinations of x_1 and x_2, yet the first of which has a utility surface that is concave and the latter of which

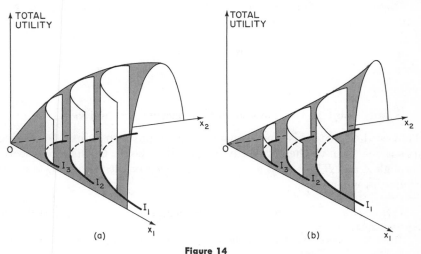

(a)   (b)

Figure 14

does not. The one utility surface is clearly a monotonic transformation of the other, and hence neither is more valid than the other as a representation of the indifference map. Thus, we simply cannot take an ordinalist point of view and yet require a utility function to be concave. Concavity of the utility function essentially has no implications about preferences in an ordinalist world because it is irrelevant for the shapes of the indifference curves. It is therefore just undefinable in any operational or observable terms. Some substitute concept has to be found by the ordinalist to serve the purposes of the second-order conditions. This substitute is a weaker condition, quasi-concavity, to which we now turn.

19. Quasi-Concave Utility Functions

Intuitively, a function is taken to be strictly quasi-concave if it follows one of two behavior patterns: (a) It is *monotonic* throughout; that is, in any direction in which its graph slopes uphill it does so "forever," i.e., for all values of its variables, and in any direction in which it slopes downhill, it also never reverses direction; (b) alternatively, if the function is not monotonic, it will have one single maximum with no other bumps or dents. Where the *second* alternative holds we see that the quasi-concave function does, indeed, resemble a concave relationship, as is illustrated in Figure 14a. But where the first alternative applies, as we will see (Figure 14b) that the shape of a quasi-concave surface may depart significantly from that of one that is concave. The formal definition of quasi-concavity bears some resemblance to that of concavity:

Definition: A function $y = f(x_1, \cdots, x_n)$ is *quasi-concave*, if given any two sets of values[22] of the x's $\mathbf{x}_a = (x_{1a}, \cdots, x_{na})$ and $\mathbf{x}_b = (x_{1b}, \cdots, x_{nb})$, where, say,

$$f(\mathbf{x}_a) \leq f(\mathbf{x}_b),$$

then

$$f(\mathbf{x}_c) \geq f(\mathbf{x}_a)$$

for $\mathbf{x}_c$ any point on the line segment connecting[23] $\mathbf{x}_a$ and $\mathbf{x}_b$.

That is, the function is quasi-concave if given any two points A and B, on its surface, then the height of any intermediate point, C, on a cross section through A and B is at least as great as the lower of the two points A and B. Similarly, we have

---

[22] Note that here we introduce the vector notation $\mathbf{x} = (x_1, \cdots, x_n)$ so that $f(\mathbf{x})$ represents $f(x_1, \cdots, x_n)$.

[23] [so that there exists a k value $0 < k < 1$ such that for any $i = 1, \cdots, n$, $x_{ic} = kx_{ia} + (1 - k)x_{ib}$]

Definition: A function $f(\mathbf{x})$ is *strictly quasi-concave* if for any two values $\mathbf{x}_a$ and $\mathbf{x}_b$ and any point $\mathbf{x}_c$ on the line segment connecting them, $f(\mathbf{x}_c)$ is greater than at least one of $f(\mathbf{x}_a)$ and $f(\mathbf{x}_b)$, i.e., if either

$$f(\mathbf{x}_c) > f(\mathbf{x}_a) \quad \text{or} \quad f(\mathbf{x}_c) > f(\mathbf{x}_b).$$

It is easy to prove

Proposition 4: Every function which satisfies the definition of concavity automatically satisfies that of quasi-concavity, and, similarly, every strictly concave function is automatically strictly quasi-concave.

Though we omit a formal proof, the reason for this result is not difficult to see. By definition, interpreting $\mathbf{x}_a$, $\mathbf{x}_b$, and $\mathbf{x}_c$ as before, a concave function is one for which $f(\mathbf{x}_c)$ is at least as great as a weighted average of $f(\mathbf{x}_a)$ and $f(\mathbf{x}_b)$, i.e., for which $f(\mathbf{x}_c) \geq kf(\mathbf{x}_a) + (1 - k)f(\mathbf{x}_b)$. But then $f(\mathbf{x}_c)$ must obviously be at least as great as the smaller of the two items in the average, which is what quasi-concavity requires.

But while every concave function is therefore automatically quasi-concave, the converse is not true.

Proposition 5: A function which is quasi-concave need not be concave.

That is just what we mean by saying that quasi-concavity is a weaker condition than concavity. There are many functions that are quasi-concave but not concave. An example is all that is needed to prove the proposition. The function $y = x^2$ is clearly not concave for its graph "goes" upward toward the right at an increasing rate somewhat like the surface in Figure 14b, and so the line segment connecting any two points on its graph lies above its graph, not below it as concavity requires. However, $y = x^2$ *is* quasi-concave, for take any two values of x, $x_a < x_b$. For any x_c between them we may write $x_c = x_a + \delta$, $\delta > 0$. Then $y(x_c) = (x_a + \delta)^2 > x_a^2 = y(x_a)$, as is required for strict quasi-concavity.

Thus we have shown that $y = x^2$ is a function that is (strictly) quasi-concave but not concave (or strictly concave).

Next we show

Proposition 6: A quasi-concave function cannot have two (local) maxima.

Proof by contradiction: Suppose the contrary, that $y = f(\mathbf{x})$ is quasi-concave and yet possesses two (separated) local maxima $\mathbf{x}_a$ and $\mathbf{x}_b$. By definition every local maximum point is surrounded by points of lower altitude; therefore there must be a point $\mathbf{x}_c$ on the line segment joining $\mathbf{x}_a$ and $\mathbf{x}_b$ such that $f(\mathbf{x}_c) < f(\mathbf{x}_a)$ and $f(\mathbf{x}_c) < f(\mathbf{x}_b)$. But this contradicts the premise that $f(\mathbf{x})$ is quasi-concave.

This means that if a quasi-concave function has more than one maximum point they must be contiguous with the top of the graph, forming a level plateau.[24] This completes our characterization of the quasi-concave functions themselves. They may have a maximum point, but for a function that is strictly quasi-concave, never more than one, and if they have none, they will be monotonic. They need not be concave and include utility surfaces like that in Figures 14b as well as that in Figure 14a.

Next, we prove a proposition which shows that the quasi-concavity of utility functions is compatible with an ordinalist analysis, which, it will be recalled, treats two utility functions to be interchangeable if one is a monotonic transform of the other.

Proposition 7: Any function $y^* = g(y) = g[f(x)]$ obtained by a monotonic transformation from a quasi-concave (strictly quasi-concave) function $y = f(\mathbf{x})$ must itself also be quasi-concave (strictly quasi-concave).

Proof: By definition of quasi-concavity with $\mathbf{x}_c$, $\mathbf{x}_a$, and $\mathbf{x}_b$ defined as before, $y_c = f(\mathbf{x}_c) \geq y_a = f(\mathbf{x}_a)$. Then by the monotonicity of the transformation $y_c^* = g(y_c) \geq g(y_a) = y_a^*$, which proves the quasi-concavity of y^*, for it shows that y_c^* must also equal or exceed the smaller of y_a^* and y_b^*.

Thus, quasi-concavity is not a characteristic which evaporates as one utility function is replaced by another obtained from the former by a monotone transformation.

Finally, we come to another proposition that reveals the reason for adoption of the premise of strict quasi-concavity for utility functions, for though this premise is weaker than that of strict concavity, it is nevertheless sufficient, if used along with the premise of nonsatiety, to guarantee that indifference curves are convex to the origin. And once that property of indifference curves is satisfied all of the usual analysis of consumer behavior proceeds without difficulty.[25] Thus we conclude our discussion with

---

[24] But if the function is *strictly* quasi-concave, even two such points with equal values of $f(\mathbf{x})$ are impossible. Indeed, we have the following more general proposition: A function that is *strictly* quasi-concave cannot have two *global* maxima $\mathbf{x}_a$ and $\mathbf{x}_b$.

Proof: If both points are global maxima, we must have $f(\mathbf{x}_a) = f(\mathbf{x}_b)$. Hence, if $\mathbf{x}_c$ is any point on the line segment joining $\mathbf{x}_a$ and $\mathbf{x}_b$, we must have by strict quasi-concavity $f(\mathbf{x}_c) > f(\mathbf{x}_a) = f(\mathbf{x}_b)$. But this obviously contradicts the assertion that at points $\mathbf{x}_a$ and $\mathbf{x}_b$ the function $f(\mathbf{x})$ attains a global maximum.

[25] We also need for this purpose the negative slope of the indifference curves and the property that curves farther from the origin are always preferred, but these, as we have seen, follow from the nonsatiety assumption.

Proposition 8: If the consumer is not sated in any commodity (he prefers more of any good or any combination of goods, holding all other quantities constant) and his utility function is *strictly* quasi-concave, then any of his indifference curves (surfaces) will be convex to the origin.

Geometric demonstration: Given a strictly quasi-concave utility function (surface $OSTU$ in Figure 15a), select any two points A and B of equal

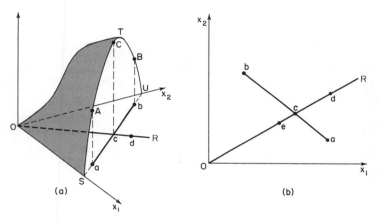

Figure 15

height (utility) on its surface so that their projections a and b on the floor of the diagram (the x_1, x_2 plane) lie on the same indifference curve. Now connect a and b by a line segment and draw any ray (line segment), OR through the origin. To find another point on the (unknown) indifference curve which connects indifferent points a and b we ask where the ray, OR, can intersect that curve. First, we know that the unknown intersection point cannot be point c where OR crosses ab for by the definition of strict quasi-concavity the utility of point c must be greater than the utility of at least one of points a and b and hence c cannot be indifferent to points a and b. Moreover, that point of indifference on OR cannot be a point like d above and to the right of ab since d offers more of both goods x_1 and x_2 than does point c, so that by nonsatiety d must be preferred to c, which is in turn preferred to a and b. So, if there is any point on OR which is indifferent to a and b, it must be a point such as e, which lies below and to the left of ab, but that is exactly what we mean by convexity to the origin of the indifference curve through points a, e, and b.

20. Elementary Mathematics of Demand Analysis

As we have noted, much of standard demand analysis is based on the formulation which takes the consumer to maximize a utility function

$$u = f(x_1, \cdots, x_n)$$

subject to a budget constraint

$$p_1 x_1 + p_2 x_2 + \cdots + p_n x_n = m,$$

where x_i is the quantity of commodity i purchased by the consumer, p_i is its price, and m is the total amount of money available to him. Using a Lagrangian approach to the problem (cf. Chapter 4, Section 8) we obtain the expression

$$u_\lambda = f(x_1, \cdots, x_n) + \lambda(m - p_1 x_1 - p_2 x_2 - \cdots - p_n x_n),$$

which we maximize by setting each of its partial derivatives equal to zero:

$$\frac{\partial u_\lambda}{\partial x_1} = \frac{\partial f}{\partial x_1} - \lambda p_1 = 0$$

$$\vdots$$

$$\frac{\partial u_\lambda}{\partial x_n} = \frac{\partial f}{\partial x_n} - \lambda p_n = 0$$

$$\frac{\partial u_\lambda}{\partial \lambda} = m - p_1 x_1 - \cdots - p_n x_n = 0.$$

Here, by definition, $\partial f/\partial x_i$ is the marginal utility of i. Dividing the preceding equation corresponding to commodity i by the equation which refers to commodity j, we have

(5)
$$\frac{\partial f}{\partial x_i} \bigg/ \frac{\partial f}{\partial x_j} = \frac{p_i}{p_j}.$$

This is the equilibrium condition which was derived in a less formal manner earlier in the chapter. It states that in equilibrium the ratio of the prices of the two commodities must be equal to the ratio of their marginal utilities, i.e., to their marginal rate of substitution.

Let us see finally how the utility function can be used to derive a specific demand relationship.

Example: Suppose a consumer has \$90 available to be divided between commodities A and B, and suppose the unit price of B is fixed at 20 cents. What will be his demand equation for A if his utility function is $u = \log x_a + 2 \log x_b$?

Answer: We are given $p_b = 0.2$ and $m = 90$. By direct differentiation of the utility function we obtain $du/dx_a = 1/x_a$ and $du/dx_b = 2/x_b$. Substituting these into equilibrium condition (5) we have

$$\frac{1}{x_a} \bigg/ \frac{2}{x_b} = \frac{p_a}{0.2}$$

or

$$x_b = 10 p_a x_a.$$

Substitution of this value of x_b, $p_b = 0.2$ and $m = 90$ into the budget $m = p_a x_a + p_b x_b$ yields

$$90 = p_a x_a + 0.2(10 p_a x_a) = p_a x_a + 2 p_a x_a$$

or

$$p_a x_a = 30.$$

This is our desired demand equation, which, incidentally, happens to be a rectangular hyperbola.

To summarize, given a utility function, income, and the prices of all other commodities, we obtain the demand for the remaining commodity by direct substitution into the equilibrium condition (5) and the budget constraint.

PROBLEMS

Find the demand function for commodity A, given
1. $p_b = \$3$, $m = \$20$, $u = 4x_a x_b$.
2. $p_b = \$12$, $m = \$246$, $u = e^7 x_a x_b$.
3. $p_b = \$8$, $m = \$100$, $u = 2x_a - 3x_a^2 + x_b - 4x_b^2 + 782$.

REFERENCES

American Economic Association, George J. Stigler and Kenneth E. Boulding (eds.), *Readings in Price Theory*, Richard D. Irwin, Inc., Homewood, Ill., 1952, Articles 1–4.

Henderson, James M., and Richard E. Quandt, *Microeconomic Theory*, 3rd edition, McGraw-Hill Book Company, New York, 1971, Chapter 2, Sections 1–7.

Hicks, J. R., *Value and Capital*, 2nd edition, Oxford University Press, New York, 1946, Part I and Mathematical Appendix to these chapters. (Rather difficult reading.)

————, *A Revision of Demand Theory*, Oxford University Press, New York, 1956.

Malinvaud, Edmond, *Lectures on Microeconomic Theory*, North-Holland Publishing Company, Amsterdam, 1972, Chapter 2 (rather difficult).

Marshall, Alfred, *Principles of Economics*, 8th edition, Macmillan & Co., Ltd., London, 1922, Book III and pp. 838–840.

Morgenstern, Oskar, "Demand Theory Reconsidered," *Quarterly Journal of Economics*, Vol. XLII, February 1948.

Samuelson, Paul A., *Foundations of Economic Analysis*, Harvard University Press, Cambridge, Mass., 1947, Chapters V and VI. (Highly mathematical.)

Walsh, V. C., *Introduction to Contemporary Microeconomics*, McGraw-Hill Book Company, New York, 1970, Chapters 1 and 3 (axiomatic treatment of utility theory).

On Empirical Determination

of

Demand Relationships

1. Why Demand Functions?

Demand functions, as they are defined in economic analysis, are rather queer creatures, somewhat abstract, containing generous elements of the hypothetical and, in general, marked by an aura of unreality. The peculiarity of the concept is well illustrated by the fact that only one point on a demand curve can ever be observed directly with any degree of confidence, because by the time we can obtain the data with which to plot a second point, the entire curve may well have shifted without our knowing it. A more fundamental but related source of our discomfort with the idea is the fact that the demand relationship is defined as the answer to the set of hypothetical questions which begin, "What would consumers do if price (or advertising outlay, or some other type of marketing effort) were different than it is in fact?" We are, then, dealing with information about potential consumer behavior in situations which consumers may never have experienced. And, since we have very little confidence in the constancy of consumer tastes and desires, all of these data are taken to refer to possible events at just one moment of time—e.g., consumer reactions to alternative possible prices if any of them were to occur tomorrow at 2:47 P.M.

In view of all this, there should be little wonder that people with an orientation toward applied economics occasionally become somewhat impatient with the economic theorist's demand function. Yet no matter how ingenious the circumlocutions which may have been employed, they have been unable to find an acceptable substitute for the concept. For the demand function must ultimately play a critical role in any probing marketing decision process, and there is really no way to get away from it.

For example, to decide on the number of salesmen which will best serve the interests of the firm, it is first necessary to know what difference in consumer purchases would result from alternative sales force sizes. But this is precisely the sort of odd and hypothetical information which goes to make up the demand relationship. It is for exactly the same reason that many large and reputable firms in diverse fields of industry are conducting ambitious research programs whose aim is the determination of their advertising-demand curves, that is, the relationship between their advertising outlays and their sales. So far, these efforts have met with varying degrees of success, and it must be admitted that many of them have not come up with very meaningful results. For the empirical determination of demand relationships is no simple matter and there are many booby traps for the amateur investigator and the unwary. It is no trick at all, on looking over a small sample of the published demand studies, to come up with horrible examples of just about every available type of misstep.

This chapter is designed primarily to point out some of the pitfalls which threaten the investigator of demand relationships. Its aim is to warn the reader to proceed with extreme caution in any such enterprise. No cut-and-dried solutions are offered to the problems which are discussed. This is true for two reasons: first, because many of the methods for dealing with these difficulties are highly technical matters of specialized econometric analysis and so are completely outside the scope of this volume. Second, and more important, solutions are not listed mechanically because there simply are no panaceas; the problems must be dealt with case by case as they arise, and the effectiveness with which they can be handled is still highly dependent on the skill, experience, and judgment of the specialist investigator.

If after reading the chapter the reader is left somewhat worried and uncomfortable, it will have accomplished its purpose. However, it should be emphasized that the problems which are raised, serious and difficult though they be, are not totally intractable and beyond the power of our statistical techniques.

2. Interview Approaches to Demand Determination

Before turning to statistical methods for the finding of demand functions, it is appropriate to say a few words about a more direct method for dealing with the problem—the consumer interview approach. In its most blatant and naïve form, consumers are simply collared by the interviewer and asked how much they would be willing to purchase of a given product at a number of alternative product price levels.

It should be obvious enough that this is a dangerous and unreliable procedure. People just have not thought out in advance what they would do in these hypothetical situations, and their snap judgments thrown up at the request of the interviewer cannot inspire a great deal of confidence. Even if they attempt to offer honest answers, even if they had thought about their decisions in advance, consumers might well find that when confronted with the harsh realities of the concrete situation, they behave in a manner which belies their own expectations. When we get to the effects of advertising on demand, the problems of such a direct interview approach become even more apparent. What is the consumer to be asked—how much more of the company's product he would buy if it were to institute a 10 per cent increase in its spot announcements to its television budget?

Much more subtle and effective approaches to consumer interviewing are indeed possible. Indirect, but far more revealing, questions can be asked. Consumers may, for example, be asked about the difference in price between two competing products, and if it turns out that they simply do not know the facts of the matter, one may be led to infer that a lower product price may have a relatively limited influence on consumer behavior, just because few consumers are likely to be aware of its existence. A clever interview-designer may in this way build up a strategy of indirect questions which gradually isolates the required facts.

Alternatively, consumers may be placed in simulated market situations, so-called consumer clinics, in which changes in their behavior can be observed as the circumstances of the experiment are varied. An obvious approach to this matter is to get groups of housewives together, give them small amounts of money with which they are offered the opportunity to purchase one of, say, several brands of dishwasher soap which are put on display at the clinic, and observe what happens as the posted prices on the displays are varied from group to group. Here again, much more subtle variants in experimental design are clearly possible.

But even the best of these procedures has its limitations for our purpose, which is the determination of the precise form of a demand relationship. Artificial consumer clinic experiments inevitably introduce some degree of distortion because subjects cannot be kept from realizing that they are in an experimental situation. In any event, such clinics are rather expensive and so the samples involved are usually extremely small—too small for confidence in any inferences which are drawn about the magnitudes of the parameters of the demand relationships for the body of consumers as a whole. And large sample interviews which approach the determination of consumer demand patterns by subtle and indirect questions are often highly revealing, but they rarely can supply the quantitative information required for the estimation of a demand equation.

3. Direct Market Experiments

A second alternative approach which is sometimes considered as a means for finding demand relationship information is the direct market experiment. A company engages in a deliberate program of price or advertising level variation. Suppose it increases its newspaper advertising outlay in one city by 5 per cent, in another city it increases this outlay by 10 per cent, and in still a third metropolis a 10 per cent reduction is undertaken. In some ways such a direct experimental approach must always be the most revealing. It gives real answers to our formerly hypothetical questions and does so without subjecting the consumer to the artificial atmosphere of the interview situation or the consumer clinic.

However, direct experimentation has its serious limitations as well.

1. It can be very expensive or extremely risky for the firm. Customers lost by an experimental price increase may never be regained from competitive products which they might otherwise never have tried, and a 10 per cent increase in advertising outlay for any protracted period may be no trivial matter.

2. Market experiments are almost never *controlled* experiments, so that the observations which they yield are likely to be colored by all sorts of fortuitous occurrences—coincidental changes in consumer incomes or in competitive advertising programs, peculiarities of the weather during the period of the experiment, etc.

3. Because of the high cost of the experiments and because it is often simply physically impossible to try out a large number of variations, the number of observations is likely to be unsatisfactorily small. If, for example, it is desired to determine the effects of varied advertising outlay in a national periodical, the company cannot increase the size of its ads which are seen by Nashville readers and simultaneously reduce those which are seen in Lexington, Kentucky. This difficulty has been eased to some extent by the fact that a number of national magazines now put out several regional editions, but by and large the problem remains: Market experiments usually supply information only about a very limited number of alternatives.

4. For similar reasons, market experiments are often of only relatively brief duration. Companies cannot afford to permit them to run long enough to display much more than impact effects. And yet the distinction between impact effects and long-run effects of a change is often extremely significant, as was so clearly demonstrated by the sharp but very temporary drop in cigarette sales when the first announcement was made about the association between smoking and the incidence of cancer. How often has a rise in the

price of a product caused a major reduction in purchases for a few weeks, with customers then gradually but steadily drifting back?

Market experiments do have a role to play in demand relationship determination. They can be important as a check on the results of a statistical study. Or they can provide some critical information about a few points on the demand curve in which past experience is entirely lacking. In some special circumstances experimentation is particularly convenient and has been used in the past, apparently with a considerable degree of success. For example, some mail-order houses have employed systematic programs in which a few special experimental pages were bound inconspicuously into the catalogues distributed to customers within restricted geographic regions, thus permitting observation of the effects of price, product, or even catalogue display variations. However, it should also be clear that market experiments cannot by themselves be relied upon universally to provide the demand information needed by management. Economics is just not a subject which lends itself readily to experimentation, largely because there are always too many elements beyond the control of the investigator and because economic experimentation is often inherently too expensive, risky, and difficult.

4. Standard Statistical Approaches

The third, and generally most attractive, approach to demand function determination attempts to squeeze its information out of sources such as the accumulated records of the past (a time-series analysis), or a comparative evaluation of the performance of different sectors of the market (a cross-sectional analysis). The available statistics on sales, prices, advertising outlays of the most relevant varieties, and other marketing data are gathered together and then analyzed with the aid of the standard statistical techniques.

The basic procedure is simple enough; in fact, as we shall see presently, it is often far too simple, particularly in the case of advertising-sales relationships where, for reasons we will see presently, near-perfect correlations, *which are in fact spurious*, are very common. Suppose, for example, that the following data on company sales and advertising outlays have been accumulated:

TABLE 1

Year	1950	1951	1952	1953	1954	1955	1956	1957
Sales .... (millions of dollars)	67	73	54	62	70	75	79	83
Advertising.................. (millions of dollars)	12	15	13	14	18	17	19	15

Once the figures have been plotted, the pattern formed by the dots can be used in an obvious manner to fit a straight line (see Figure 1) or a curve to them. This line is then taken as the desired advertising-demand curve. Its slope can be used as a measure of advertising effectiveness, that is, it measures the marginal sales productivity of an advertising dollar, Δ sales/Δ advertising outlay. This line can be determined impressionistically simply by drawing in a line that appears to fit the dots fairly well, or any one of a variety of more systematic methods can be used.

The most widely employed and best known of these techniques is the method of least squares,[1] in which the object is to find that line which

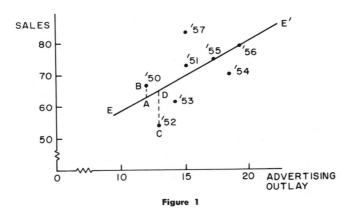

Figure 1

makes the sum of the (squared) vertical deviations between our dots and the fitted line as small as possible, where the deviations are defined as the vertical distances such as AB or CD in Figure 1. The idea is inherently attractive. We wish to minimize deviations because a line which involves very substantial deviations from the dots representing our data surely does not represent the information in a very satisfactory way. But if, in our addition process, a large negative deviation such as AB (that is, a case where the line underestimates the vertical coordinate of our dot) happens to be largely cancelled out by a positive deviation, CD, the sum of the deviations can turn out to be small. This is surely not what we want in looking for a line which does not deviate much from the dots. One can avoid ending up with a line which fits the facts rather badly but in which

---

[1] The next few paragraphs are a very elementary review of the method of least squares and they should be omitted by the reader who has any acquaintance with the subject.

the positive and negative deviations add up to a rather small number, by squaring all the deviation figures before adding them together. Since the square of a negative real number as well as that of a positive real number is always positive, large, squared negative deviations cannot offset large, squared positive deviations, and the sum of squared deviations will never add up to a small number unless our line happens to fit the dots closely.[2]

There exist still more sophisticated techniques for fitting our advertising-demand curve from the data. Although it is often too complex and

---

[2] Other devices (such as the absolute value of the fourth power of the deviation) might accomplish the objective discussed. The reason one chooses to minimize the sum of the *squares* is that under very simple assumptions such estimates have several extremely desirable technical properties, among them, that these estimated parameter values are "best" in the sense that they minimize variance of the estimate and are unbiased in the sense discussed in the appendix to this chapter.

To find the straight-line equation which satisfies our least squares requirement we employ the symbol y_t to represent sales in year t and x_t to represent advertising outlay in that year and let the equation of the line to be fitted be written $y_{ct} = a + bx_t$, where the subscript c in y_{ct} is there to remind us that in our equation the y is a figure calculated from the formula rather than observation. Now we proceed as follows:

Step 1: Define a deviation from our line as

$$y_t - y_{ct} = y_t - (a + bx_t) = y_t - a - bx_t.$$

Step 2: Define a squared deviation as

$$(y_t - y_{ct})^2 = y_t^2 + a^2 + b^2x_t^2 - 2ay_t - 2bx_ty_t + 2abx_t.$$

Step 3: Add the squared deviations

$$\sum (y_t - y_{ct})^2 = \sum y_t^2 + na^2 + b^2 \sum x_t^2 - 2a \sum y_t - 2b \sum x_ty_t + 2ab \sum x_t,$$

where, since a is a constant, $\sum_{t=1}^{n} a^2 = a^2 + a^2 + a^2 \cdots (n \text{ equal terms}) = na^2.$

Step 4: Find the values of a and b (the parameters of our equation) which minimize the sum of the squared deviations. We do this with the aid of the usual calculus procedure, by taking partial derivatives with respect to a and b and setting them equal to zero, thus:

$$\frac{\partial \sum (y_t - y_{ct})^2}{\partial a} = 2an - 2 \sum y_t + 2b \sum x_t = 0$$

and

$$\frac{\partial \sum (y_t - y_{ct})^2}{\partial b} = 2b \sum x_t^2 - 2 \sum x_ty_t + 2a \sum x_t = 0.$$

These last two equations contain, in addition to a and b, only known statistical figures x_t and y_t. The equations can therefore be solved simultaneously to obtain the desired parameter values, a and b, i.e., they determine for us the least squares line $y_{ct} = a + bx_t$. These two equations are usually referred to as the *normal equations* of the least squares method in this most elementary (two-variable straight-line) case. The procedure employed in fitting many variable equations or curvilinear equations is a simple and obvious extension of that which has just been described.

expensive to employ in practice, professional statisticians usually consider the method of maximum likelihood as their ideal. This method requires some information about the probability distribution of the random elements which influence sales. From this probability distribution the statistician determines a likelihood function

$$L = f(x_t, y_t, a, b),$$

where x_t and y_t represent, respectively, advertising expenditures and sales in year t, and a and b are the constants in our advertising-demand equation $y_t = a + bx_t$. This likelihood function is defined as an answer to the following type of question: "Given any specific values of the parameters in our equation, say $a = 5$ and $b = 63$, how likely is it that the demand situation would have generated the statistics $x_{1950} = 12$, $y_{1950} = 67$, etc.?" (Note that these values of sales and advertising are in fact our observed statistical figures taken from Table 1.) Considering all possible values of a and b, we can then employ the differential calculus to find the a and b combination which maximizes the value of the likelihood, L. We will then have found the a and b which provide, in this sense, the best possible explanation of the observed facts, i.e., we will have found that equation $y_t = a + bx_t$ whose parameters a and b are most likely to be the correct values of the true but unknown parameters, given the facts which were actually observed by the data-collector.

It is of interest to note that in some special cases the least squares method turns out to be identical with maximum likelihood. That is, in these fortunate circumstances the least squares calculation becomes equivalent to the maximum likelihood procedure. We shall presently discuss one of the things which may go wrong if the least squares method is employed in situations where it does not yield the same results as the maximum likelihood calculation.

Having described now in highly general and impressionistic terms the methods which are most commonly employed by the statistician to determine relationships, let us now see some of the problems to which they give rise.

5. Omission of Important Variables

Clearly, sales are affected by other variables in addition to the company's advertising expenditure. Prices, competitive advertising, consumer income variations, and other variables also play an important role in any demand relationship. If, therefore, we try to extract from our statistics a simple equation relating sales to advertising outlay alone, and in the process we ignore all other variables, our results are likely to be very badly distorted. We may ascribe to the company's advertising outlays sales trends which are really the result of the behavior of other economic changes. The behavior of other variables can thus conceal and even offset the effects of advertising. To show how serious the results can be, consider the illustrative demand equation

$$(1) \qquad\qquad S = 50 + 4A + 0.02Y,$$

where S represents sales, A advertising expenditure, and Y consumer income. The values given in Table 2 can easily be seen to satisfy the equation precisely, and any standard estimation procedure based on such information can be expected to yield the correct equation.

TABLE 2

Date	1956	1957	1958
Y	3,000	4,000	3,500
A	2	3	2.5
S	118	142	130

But the standard calculation shows that a *two*-variable, straight, least squares line which gives us a (perfect!) correlation between S and A alone (ignoring Y) and which is based on these same values will yield the equation

$$(2) \qquad\qquad S = 24A + 70.$$

This equation asserts that each added dollar of advertising expenditure brings in $24 in sales, instead of the true $4 return shown by Equation (1). In addition, because of the perfect correlation there is, in this case, no residual unexplained variation in S which is left to be accounted for by a subsequent correlation between S and Y, i.e., *this incorrect procedure appears to show that consumer income has absolutely no influence on demand*! The advertising coefficient has been inflated by usurping to itself the influence of Y on sales.

Incidentally, if, instead of proceeding as we just did, we had started off by finding a least squares equation relating sales to consumer income alone, we would have obtained from the same statistics the equation

$$S = 0.024Y + 46,$$

which this time overvalues the influence of income on sales and ascribes absolutely no effectiveness to advertising.[3]

It is clear, then, that more than two variables must usually be taken into account in the statistical estimation of a demand relationship. And, in fact, this is ordinarily done, the estimation usually employing what is called a least squares *multiple regression* technique. However, it should be

---

[3] The correlation between Y and A creates another difficulty in this example. The resulting problems are discussed in the next section.

remembered that even if we include five variables in our analysis but omit a sixth rather important variable, precisely the same difficulties will be encountered. That is, the omission of any important variable, however defined, from the statistical procedure can lead to serious distortions in its results.

This might appear to constitute an argument for the inclusion in the analysis of every variable which comes to the statistician's mind as a factor of possible importance, just as a matter of insurance. Unfortunately, however, we are not at liberty to go on adding variables willy-nilly. The more variables whose influence we want to take into account, the more data we require as a basis for the estimation. If we only have statistical information pertaining to three points in time, it is ridiculous to try to disentangle the influence of fifteen variables. In fact, the statistician requires many pieces of information for every variable he includes in his analysis, if he is to estimate his relationship with a clear conscience.

However, large masses of marketing data are not easily come by. Records are often woefully incomplete; additional data can sometimes be acquired only at considerable expense, and in any event, statistics which go too far back in time are apt to be obsolete and irrelevant for the company's current circumstances. We must, therefore, very frequently be contented with skimpy figures which force us to be extremely niggardly in the number of variables which we take into account, despite the very great dangers involved.

6. Inclusion of Mutually Correlated Variables

Another difficulty which, to some extent, can help to make life easier as far as the problem of the preceding section is concerned arises when a number of the relevant variables are themselves closely interrelated. For example, one encounters advertising effectiveness studies in which income and years of education per inhabitant are both included as variables. Now education is itself very closely related to income level both because higher-income families can afford to provide more education and larger inheritances to their children and because a more educated person is often in a position to earn a higher income.

It may nevertheless be true that education and income do have different consequences for advertising effectiveness. For example, an increase in income without any change in educational level could increase the person's willingness to purchase more in response to an ad, whereas more education not backed up by larger purchasing power might have the reverse effect. But, in general, there is no statistical method whereby these two consequences can be separated, because, for the bulk of the population, whenever one of these variables increases in value, so does the other. Hence, the statistics which can merely exhibit directions of variation might show that, other things remaining equal, whenever sales increased, income also increased, and so (as a consequence?) did education.

In such circumstances if we include both the income and the educational level variables in the statistical demand-fitting procedure, the chances are that the mechanics of the procedure will provide a perfectly arbitrary ascription of the sales changes to our two causal variables. And sometimes the results may turn out completely nonsensical because the standard computational procedure has no way to apply common sense in imputing the total sales change to the separate influences of education and income changes.

Therefore, if in a demand relationship there occur several variables which are themselves highly correlated, it is usually wise to omit all but one of any such set of variables in a statistical study. If this is not done, another powerful source of nonsense results is introduced.

7. Simultaneous Relationship Problems

The difficulties which have so far been discussed, while they can be extremely important and are often overlooked in practice (with rather sad consequences) may, by and large, be considered rather routine and, in retrospect, fairly obvious matters.

We come now to a far more subtle and perhaps a far more serious problem which was only brought to our attention in 1927 by E. J. Working and which has only received serious and systematic attention quite recently, largely as a result of the work of the Cowles Foundation. The problem in question, in a sense, follows from the difficulty which was discussed in the previous section. If there is a close correlation between two variables, it is likely to mean that they are not independent of one another and that there is at least one other relevant equation in the system which expresses the relationship between them. For example, in our illustrative case there might be an equation indicating how income level is ordinarily increased by a person's education. We then end up having to deal with not just a single demand equation, but with a system of several equations in which a number of the variables interact mutually and are determined simultaneously.

Economics is characterized by such simultaneous relationships. The standard example is the price determination process in which a supply equation is involved as well as our demand relationship. Similarly, simultaneous relationships constitute the core of national income analysis. National income depends on the demand for consumer's goods which helps determine the level of profitable production. But the consumption demand equation, in turn, involves national income (as a measure of the public's purchasing power) as a variable. To mention another simultaneous relationship example, the coal mining industry is a customer for steel whose volume of demand depends on coal sales, but the demand for coal itself depends heavily on the amount of coal to be used in producing steel. It is possible to expand the list of simultaneous relationships in economics indefinitely.

The empirical data which are generated by such a set of equations are the information source on which the statistician must base his estimates of the relationships. But since these data are the result of a number of such relationships, the difficult problem arises of separating out the relationships from the observed statistics.

Unless steps are taken to make sure that the influences of the several simultaneous relationships on the data can be and have been separated, there is not the slightest justification for the use of any estimation procedure, such as that depicted in Figure 1, to compute a statistical relationship. Yet it will readily be recognized how frequently this completely fallacious procedure is employed in practice in the form of simple or multiple correlations computed without any attempt to cope with the simultaneous relationship problem. Let us see now how serious are the distortions which can be expected to result.

8. The Identification Problem

In rather general terms our basic problem can conveniently be divided into two parts:

1. In some circumstances the simultaneous relationships (equations) will be so similar in character that it will be impossible to unscramble them (or at least some of them) from the statistics. Such relationships are said to be *unidentifiable*. Presently it will be shown how such an unhappy situation can arise, and it will be indicated that it is unfortunately not unheard of in marketing problems. Clearly, in such a case, we are wasting our time in a statistical investigation of the equation in question. There do exist some mathematical tests which show whether or not an equation is *identified* (i.e., whether or not it is in principle possible to separate it from the other relationships in the system). These tests should always be applied before embarking on the type of statistical investigation under discussion. It must be emphasized that if an equation happens not to be identified, it is impossible even to approximate the true equation from statistical data alone. Market experiments or other substitute approaches must be employed to obtain this information.

2. Even if an equation turns out to be identified, precautions must be taken to ensure that a statistically estimated equation is not distorted by

the presence of the simultaneous relationships. We will see in the next section that an ordinary least squares procedure is likely to lead to precisely this sort of distortion.

In this section we deal with the first of these, the identification problem —the circumstances under which it is, at least in principle, possible to unscramble our simultaneous relationships statistically.

To illustrate, let us consider what is involved in finding statistically an advertising-demand curve such as the one which Figure 1 attempted to construct in a rather primitive fashion. Now while sales are doubtless affected by advertising, as the advertising-demand function assumes, this function is often accompanied by a second relationship in which what we might call the direction of causation is reversed. It is well known that a firm's advertising budget is frequently affected by its sales volume. In fact, many businesses operate on a rule of thumb which allocates to advertising expenditure a fixed proportion of their total revenues. For such a business, then, we will have two advertising expenditure demand relationships: (1) the demand function which shows how quantity demanded, Q, is affected by a firm's advertising budget, $A : Q = f(A)$, and (2) the budgeting equation which shows how the firm's advertising decisions are affected by the demand for its product: $A = g(Q)$.

Both of these relationships may actually be of interest to the businessman. The first, as already stated, is directly relevant to his own optimal expenditure decision. The second, if obtained from industry records, will give him vital information about the behavior patterns of his competitors.

The firm's actual sales and its actual advertising expenditure will, of course, depend on both its advertising budgeting practices (the budgeting equation) and on the demand-advertising relationships. In Figure 2 the graphs of two such hypothetical relationships are depicted.

In Figure 2a we show the two curves which the statistician is seeking. We make ourselves, as it were, momentarily omniscient and thus have no difficulty envisioning the true relationships. However, the information available to the statistician is much more restricted as we shall now see. In our situation the actual advertising expenditure, A, and the volume of sales, Q, are determined, as for any simultaneous equation, by the point of intersection, P, of the two curves.

We now can describe two cases of nonidentification:

Case 1. Neither Curve Identified.

If the two curves were to retain their shape from year to year, that is, *if neither of them ever shifted*, all the intersection points P would coincide or at least lie very close together (Figure 2b). There would only be a single observed point, as in the figure, or the tightly clustered points would form

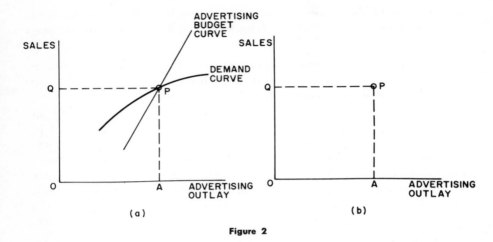

Figure 2

no discernible pattern, and so the shape of neither curve could even approximately be found from the data. We see then, though it may be a bit surprising, that curves which never shift are from this point of view the worst of all possibilities.

Case 2. One of the Curves Not Identified (but the other curve identifiable).

This is a case frequently encountered in practice when the demand curve of one firm is investigated. The data form a neat and simple pattern, but what they describe is the firm's inflexible advertising budgeting practices rather than the nature of the demand for its product. In such circumstances what happens is that the budget curve never shifts but the demand curve does. There will then be a number of different intersection points,

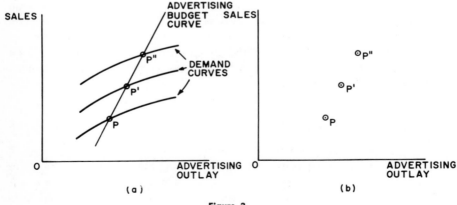

Figure 3

such as P, P', and P'', but they will always describe only the shape of the advertising budget line (Figure 3). *The reader can well imagine how often statistical attempts to find the advertising-demand curve have produced neat linear relationships (and spectacularly high correlation coefficients), though what the triumphant investigator has located (without his knowing it) is a totally different curve from the one he was seeking.* The situation which we have just examined is really ideal from the point of view of the statistician, *provided the relationship which is not shifting happens to be the one he is seeking.* But the question remains: How is he to know when one relationship is standing still, and even if he somehow knows this, how does he determine which one it is? We will see that in the answers to these questions lies the key to the solution of the identification problem.

It will be shown presently that only where both curves shift over time or from firm to firm or from geographical territory to territory can they ordinarily both be identified. However, in this case the difficult task of

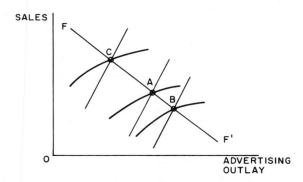

Figure 4

unscrambling the two relationships becomes particularly acute. Figure 4 illustrates how three points, A, B, and C, in a diagram similar to Figure 1 might have been generated by three different (shifted) pairs of our curves. It is noteworthy that the negatively sloping (!) "advertising curve" FF' estimated statistically from these points bears not the slightest resemblance to any of the true curves. Nor, since it is merely a recording of points of intersection, is there any reason why it should. *The shape of* FF' *is not even any sort of "compromise" between those of the budget and advertising-demand curves!* We conclude that where simultaneous relationships are present the standard curve-fitting techniques described in Section 4 and Figure 1 may well break down completely. *Their results are likely to bear absolutely no resemblance to the equations which are being sought!* Such a naïve approach may therefore well be worse than no investigation because misleading information is usually worse than no information at all.

Let us now see how one can, in principle, test whether the relationship we are seeking is identified (potentially discoverable by statistical means).

First we note that, as the model has so far been described, there is no way of accounting for any shifts in either relationship, which, as we have observed, are crucial for our problem. The reason is that only two variables, A and Q, have been considered in the relationships $Q = f(A)$ (the demand relationship) and $A = g(Q)$ (the advertising budget equation).

There must, in fact, be some other influences (other variables) which disturb the relationships between Q and A and produce the shifts in their graphs. These additional variables must be taken explicitly into account. As we know, the demand relationship is likely to involve many variables in addition to A. For example, consumer's disposable income is a variable which affects the volume of sales resulting from a given level of advertising expenditure, though, very likely, it does not enter the firm's budget calculation explicitly but only indirectly via the effects of income on the sales of the company's product. Similarly, the firm's budget policy may be affected by its past dividend payments, which determine how much it can currently spare for advertising expenditure, but this dividend policy will have little or no effect on the demand curve for its products. Suppose, for the sake of simplicity, that the four variables Q, A, Y (the disposable income), and D (the total dividend payments in the preceding year) are the only ones that are relevant to the problem. Our two relationships then become

(3)   the advertising demand function $Q = f(A, Y)$

and

(4)   the advertising budget equation $A = g(Q, D)$.

Here changes in the value of Y are what produce the shifts in the graph of the demand equation which have been discussed. Similarly, changes in D produce shifts in the advertising budget curve.

Now that we have examined how shifts in the two curves are produced we can return to the question of identification. Let us see, intuitively, how the presence of the shift variables in Equations (3) and (4) makes it possible, in principle, to separate the relationships from the statistics (i.e., how the shift variables identify the equations). It will be shown now that Y and D permit the statistician, at least conceptually, to divide up the statistical information in such a way that he is left with situations like that depicted in Figure 3. Such a situation gives him the information that permits him to infer which of the relationships is shifting and which is standing still. That is, he can determine when one graph is not moving while the other shifts around, so that the resulting dots trace out the graph of the equation which is not shifting, the equation he is trying to estimate. The reader should first be warned, however, that the procedure which is

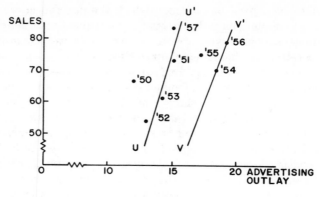

Figure 5

about to be described is not usually a practical estimation (curve-finding) procedure and that other, more sophisticated measures are normally employed for the purpose.

In Figure 5 we replot the data of Figure 1. Let us, in addition, determine for each point the dividend payment, D, for that particular year. Suppose this information is as shown in Table 3 (the corresponding sales and advertising figures are in Table 1).

TABLE 3

Advertising demand point	1950	1951	1952	1953	1954	1955	1956	1957
Total dividend D (\$ millions)	360	297	295	307	428	381	420	300

We note that the dividend values for the points representing 1951, 1952, 1953, and 1957 are fairly close together. Hence, if we are convinced that Y is the only variable which makes for sizable shifts in the advertising budget curve, it is reasonable to assume that all four points lie on (or close to) the same curve; that is, among these points there has occurred little or no shift in the curve. We may, therefore, use these four points (ignoring the others) to locate a budget curve UU' (for income level approximately 300 billion) as shown. Similarly, we can use points for years 1954 and 1956 alone to find the shape of the advertising budget curve VV' which pertains to income level approximately 420 billion, etc. In other words, the additional information on the value of D for each point has permitted us, in principle, to ignore all points which contain information irrelevant to a given advertising budget curve.

We see, then, that if variable D is present in the one equation but not in the other it permits us, in principle, to discover statistical points over which the budget line has shifted but through which the demand curve remains unchanged, thus enabling us to trace out the corresponding *demand curve*.

In an analogous way we were able to trace out a *budget line* in Figure 3, for there the position of the demand curve changed as Y varied, while the budget line remained stationary. But while this enabled us to find the budget line in Figure 3, there the demand curve was unidentifiable because the budget curve never shifted. There is no shift variable such as D in the budget relationship postulated at that point which moves the budget line about and yet permits the demand curve to stay still. This gives us the following result: *One of a pair of simultaneous relationships will be identified if it lacks a variable which is present in the other relationship.* A change in the value of that variable will not affect the position of the curve corresponding to the relationship we are seeking, but it will shift the other curve.

The relevance of the shift variables Y and D for identification can also be seen in another way. Assume that on the basis of *a priori* judgment we have already constructed our model consisting of Equations (3) and (4) in which we postulate in advance that the variable Y is present only in the first of these equations and the variable D appears only in the second. Suppose now that we use any simultaneous equation estimation procedure to find some statistical relationships among the variables Q, A, Y, and D. The system is identified if it is possible, in principle, to obtain one such statistical relationship which is known to be an approximation to Equation (3) (the demand function) and another statistical function which approximates (4) (the budget function), and if it is possible to find out whether any given statistical curve derived in the process represents (3), (4), or neither. Suppose, then, we have obtained some such statistical function from our data on Q, A, Y, or D. How might we be able to tell whether it represents a demand function, a budget function, or a hodgepodge combination of the two? There are three possibilities:

1. Suppose, after our calculations are completed, we discover that the statistical relationship turns out to take the form $Q = F(A, Y, D)$ in which all four variables are present (*all* of their coefficients are significantly different from zero). In that case we know that the statistics have given us a mongrel function resembling neither of the relationships we are seeking, for the equations of our model tell us that neither of the *true* relationships contains *both* variables Y and D.

2. Suppose now that the statistical relationship turns out to have an equation of the form $F(A, Y) = Q$; i.e., D plays no role in the equation. Then we can be fairly sure that no budget function component has sneaked into our statistical equation, for, if the budget equation had somehow gotten mixed into our calculation, the variable D would have shown up in our calculated equation, since it is present in the budget curve (4). The presence of the variable D would have shown at once that the budgeting relationship had intruded into our computation. But since, in the case we

are discussing, we obtain an equation $Q = F(A, Y)$ *from which D is absent,* we conclude that our statistical equation must be an estimate of the demand relationship (3) alone.

3. Similarly, if the form of the statistical equation is $F(A, D) = Q$, it must represent the budget relationship (4) alone.

Thus the two variables Y and D, each of which appears in one and only one of the two *a priori* relationships in our model, have permitted us to identify both equations. For example, the presence of the variable D, which occurs only in the budget equation, acts as a warning signal which notifies us at once when the budget equation has somehow got itself mixed in with our demand information.

9. Least Squares Bias in Simultaneous Systems

Even if it transpires that a set of simultaneous relationships is identified so that it is appropriate to investigate them statistically, the analyst's troubles are not yet over. For the statistical methods which yield satisfactory results in determining the nature of a single relationship are apt to yield seriously biased results in the presence of simultaneous equations.

To show one way in which this may come about notice first that any economic relationships are constantly subject at least to small shifts as the result of minor random occurrences. A sudden change in the weather or a newspaper strike affects department store sales, rumors of a price rise may lead housewives to stock up on a product, and so on. Consequently, a demand curve can never be expected to stand still for very long. Rather, it is likely to shift back and forth so that its position will (at least) vary within a (more or less) narrow band.

Figure 6a illustrates the band within which our illustrative advertising-demand curve usually varies as the result of random disturbances. Suppose first that this is a single relationship situation so that the advertising-demand curve is the only relevant curve. Observed statistics are then likely to fall throughout this band as shown by the points in Figure 6a. The dots form a pattern very similar in shape to the demand curve itself. A least squares line fitted to these data will then tend to follow the same pattern and it will be a rather good representation of the true demand curve which the statistician is seeking.

Now let us contrast this with what happens when there is a second relationship present—our advertising budget line. The range of variation of these two curves is shown in Figure 6b, where both curves may be expected to shift about simultaneously. This means that the intersection points of the two curves are likely to move about within the diamond-shaped region $ABCD$. The dots within that region, then, represent the information which the statistician observes.

This time it will be noted that the pattern of dots does not resemble

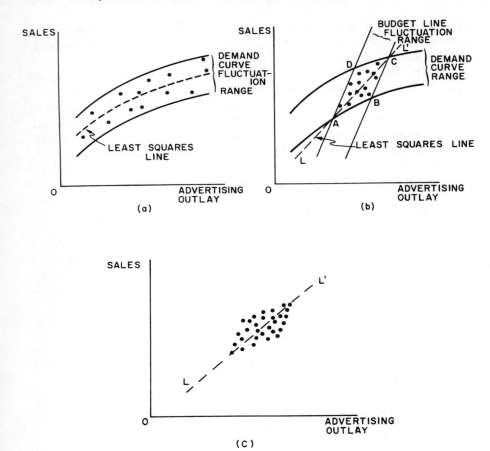

Figure 6

either curve closely. Moreover, a least squares line, LL', fitted to these dots will generally pass approximately through a diagonal of the diamond moving upward and to the right from corner A to corner C. It should be clear to the reader that a diagonal line of this sort should appear to yield a good fit to such a diamond-shaped collection of dots (see Figure 6c). But from our state of omniscience in Figure 6b we can easily see that this least squares line is really a very poor approximation to the advertising demand curve.

All sorts of alternative methods have been devised for simultaneous equation estimation to avoid these difficulties of the standard least squares approach. Aside from the full maximum-likelihood method, which is generally too expensive and cumbersome to be employed in practice, several alternatives have been designed and employed extensively. Noteworthy are the limited information method, the instrumental variables method, and the multiple-stage least squares method (which employs several repeated applications of the least squares technique, designed to correct for its deficiencies). All of these are intended to serve as approximations to the maximum likelihood method.

There is no point in trying to describe these methods here. It is enough for our purpose that the reader has been made aware of the statistical problems caused by the presence of simultaneous relationships and of the fact that methods exist for dealing with these difficulties.

10. Concluding Comments

We have seen, then, how difficult it is to find actual demand relationships in practice. These problems are, to a large extent, a consequence of the very peculiarity of the demand function concept itself—the fact that it represents the answers to a set of purely hypothetical questions and that the information is taken to pertain simultaneously to the same moment of time. Unfortunately, this odd demand relationship turns out to be indispensable to sophisticated decision-making within the firm. We simply have to learn to live with it, and to face up to the difficulties involved in its empirical determination. An essential part of this process is knowledge of the pitfalls which await the unwary investigators who set out to beard the demand function in its lair.

APPENDIX: NOTES ON IDENTIFICATION AND SIMULTANEOUS EQUATION ESTIMATION

The statistical problems created by the presence of simultaneous relationships are not confined only to demand analysis or even to economics. Simultaneous equation problems are nearly universal and occur in research arising out of disciplines as diverse as sociology and medicine. Since interdependence is so common a phenomenon the reader should have no difficulty in thinking up all sorts of illustrative statistical problems in which simultaneous relationships play a critical role. It is therefore worth going into the methods for dealing with such problems in somewhat greater detail. This appendix attempts to explain these on an entirely nonrigorous intuitive basis.

1. Some Identification Theorems

Consider a model consisting of the following pair of simultaneous supply-demand equations for some farm product, in which Q represents quantity sold, P stands for price, Y is an index of consumer income, R is a measure of rainfall, S is the amount of subsidy provided to suppliers, and U_1 and U_2 are two *random shock variables*:

$$Q = A_{10} + A_{11}P + A_{12}Y \qquad\qquad + U_1 \text{ (demand equation)}$$

(1a) $Q = A_{20} + A_{21}P$

$$\qquad\qquad + A_{23}R + A_{24}S + U_2 \text{ (supply equation)}.$$

A "shock variable" may be roughly defined as a random variable which is used to take account of "shocks" or "disturbances" affecting the equations. Those disturbances result from changes in other variables which affect the system but have been ignored, for example, because each taken by itself is insignificant or because they cannot be observed (e.g., psychological variables). A model in which explicit cognizance is taken of such disturbances by the insertion of one or more random shock variables (usually one in each equation, thus accounting for random "shifts" in its graph) is called a *shock model*. In our model, the first equation tells us that the amount of the product demanded will depend on its price and on the level of consumer income, while, according to the second equation, the supply is determined by the price, rainfall, and the extent of the Federal farm subsidy. However, both of these relationships are disturbed by random elements (changes in tastes, in the number of plant-eating insects, etc.). Here the A_{ij} are the constant parameters whose magnitudes are to be estimated statistically.

An equation or a set of equations can be identified only if we possess enough *a priori* information about it, i.e., if each of the equations is known in advance to be sufficiently distinctive from the others. The most important type of such *a priori* restriction consists of information about which variables do, in fact, enter the equation in question. This sort of information can be written in the form

(2) $A_{ij} = 0$ for various specified i and j.

The economic interpretation of this sort of information (or assumption) is obvious: It is believed that the variable X_j does not play any economic role in the ith equation. For example, the dividend payments of a firm may not affect the demands for its products.

More specifically, compare our system of supply-demand equations (1a) with the following more general pair:

$$Q = A_{10} + A_{11}P + A_{12}Y + A_{13}R + A_{14}S + U_1$$

(1)

$$Q = A_{20} + A_{21}P + A_{22}Y + A_{23}R + A_{24}S + U_2.$$

It should be clear that our first equations, (1a), involve the *a priori* restrictions

(2a) $$A_{13} = 0, \qquad A_{14} = 0, \qquad A_{22} = 0.$$

The use for identification purposes of other types of *a priori* restrictions, such as the requirement that just one of the equations involve curvature, has been investigated by econometricians. But restrictions of type (2) have been used most frequently in practical economic problems. These are far easier to handle computationally than the corresponding conditions for restrictions of other types, and for many other types of *a priori* restriction the theory is still in a rather rudimentary form. The theorems which are given below (with no attempt to indicate their proofs) will therefore be confined to the necessary and sufficient conditions for identification with the aid of assumptions of type (2).

Proposition 1: A necessary condition for the identification of the ith equation in a system which is composed of m linear equations with the aid of restrictions of type (2) is that at least $m - 1$ of the parameters occurring in equation i be zero, i.e., that we have for that equation at least $m - 1$ conditions

$$A_{ij} = 0.$$

In our system (1a) we have two equations, so that $m = 2$. To see whether the first equation in that system meets the requirements of the proposition which has just been stated, we note by comparison with the more general system (1) that in the first equation $A_{13} = 0$ and $A_{14} = 0$. Thus we have more than the minimum of $m - 1 = 1$ coefficients required to be zero in order to achieve identification. We say, therefore, that our first equation is *overidentified*. The second equation, however, has only one coefficient missing, i.e., it has only $A_{22} = 0$, so there is no redundant *a priori* information here, and we say that the second equation is *just identified*.

Proposition 2: A *necessary* condition for the identification of the kth equation in a simultaneous system of linear equations under restrictions of type (2) is that for every other equation i there exists one variable X_j which appears in equation i but not in equation k, i.e., for which

$$A_{kj} = 0, \qquad A_{ij} \neq 0.$$

Thus if any two equations in a simultaneous system of linear equations contain exactly the same variables, they cannot be identified. But if each contains one variable which is absent from the other, they may be identified.

Proposition 2 becomes important in a system involving more than two equations. For example, in a set of three ($m = 3$) equations, two of them may each have two coefficients equal to zero, hence satisfying the requirement of Proposition 1, but if both equations lack exactly the same coefficients, Proposition 2 tells us that they will not be identified. This is illustrated in the following system where the first two equations pass the identification test of Proposition 1 but fail the Proposition 2 test:

$$Q = A_{10} + A_{11}X_1 \qquad\qquad\qquad + U_1$$

$$Q = A_{20} + A_{21}X_1 \qquad\qquad\qquad + U_2$$

$$Q = A_{30} \qquad\qquad + A_{32}X_2 + A_{33}X_3 + U_3$$

Proposition 3[4]: A *necessary and sufficient* condition for the identification of the ith equation in the general system

$$A_{11}X_1 + A_{12}X_2 + \cdots + A_{1n}X_n = U_1$$

(3) $\qquad \cdot \quad \cdot \quad \cdot \quad \cdot \quad \cdot \quad \cdot \quad \cdot$

$$A_{m1}X_1 + A_{m2}X_2 + \cdots + A_{mn}X_n = U_m$$

under restrictions of type (2) is the following. Suppose we number our variables so that just the first q variables in the system are absent from equation i, i.e., so that (2) becomes

$$A_{ij} = 0, \qquad j = 1, 2, \cdots, q.$$

Then the matrix, known as the rank criterion matrix,

$$A^* = \begin{bmatrix} A_{11} & A_{12} & \cdots & A_{1q} \\ A_{21} & A_{22} & \cdots & A_{2q} \\ \cdot & \cdot & \cdot & \cdot \\ A_{i-1,1} & A_{i-1,2} & \cdots & A_{i-1,q} \\ A_{i+1,1} & A_{i+1,2} & \cdots & A_{i+1,q} \\ \cdot & \cdot & \cdot & \cdot \\ A_{m1} & A_{m2} & \cdots & A_{mq} \end{bmatrix}$$

must be exactly of rank $m - 1$; i.e., it must contain at least one set of $m - 1$ columns and rows which form a nonzero determinant (of order $m - 1$).[5] Since the matrix has only $m - 1$ rows (*because it excludes the coefficients of the equation, i*, whose identification is being investigated), it obviously cannot be of greater rank than $m - 1$. It can contain no higher order determinant.

---

[4] This proposition involves considerations which are relatively difficult, and readers who are not conversant with elementary properties of matrices and determinants will wish to avoid reading the following paragraphs.

[5] For proof see T. C. Koopmans and W. C. Hood, "The Estimation of Simultaneous Linear Economic Relationships," pp. 135–42, in Hood and Koopmans (eds.), *Studies in Econometric Method*, Cowles Commission Monograph No. 10, John Wiley & Sons, Inc., New York, 1953.

With the aid of Proposition 3 a strong presumption about the identifiability of equation i in system (3) under restrictions of type (2) can be established by inspection. To do this merely take the A_{ij}, which are equal to zero according to (2), i.e., those variables known *a priori* to be absent in the various equations of the system, and substitute zeros for these A_{ij} wherever they appear in the matrix A^*. If A^* is then identically of rank less than $m - 1$, then equation i is not identified. For example, in a four-equation system (where $m - 1 = 3$), suppose we have the A^* matrix

$$(4) \qquad A^* = \begin{bmatrix} 0 & 0 & 0 & 0 \\ A_{21} & A_{22} & A_{23} & A_{24} \\ A_{31} & A_{32} & A_{33} & A_{34} \end{bmatrix} ;$$

then since this contains no nonzero three-by-three determinant, the equation being tested is not identified. On the other hand, if our four-equation system had, in testing for identification of one of its equations, yielded the A^* matrix

$$(5) \qquad A^* = \begin{bmatrix} A_{11} & 0 & 0 & 0 \\ 0 & A_{22} & 0 & 0 \\ 0 & 0 & A_{33} & A_{34} \end{bmatrix} ,$$

we can be confident that the equation being tested will be identified, because A^* involves at least one nonzero third-order determinant [unless subsequent statistical calculation shows that some of the A's in (5) are equal to zero].

Propositions 1 and 2 can readily be shown to be corollaries of Proposition 3.

Example 1: In the system

$$A_{15}X_5 = U_1$$
$$A_{21}X_1 + A_{22}X_2 + A_{23}X_3 + A_{24}X_4 + A_{25}X_5 = U_2$$
$$A_{31}X_1 + A_{32}X_2 + A_{33}X_3 + A_{34}X_4 \qquad\qquad = U_3$$
$$A_{45}X_5 = U_4$$

none of the equations is identified. The second and third equations violate the requirements of Proposition 1 because they each contain less than $m - 1 = 3$ zero coefficients. The reader should verify that the fourth equation yields the A^* matrix given by (4) and hence violates the condition given in Proposition 3 as does Equation (1). Alternatively, the first and fourth together violate Proposition 2 because neither contains a variable which is absent from the other.

Example 2: In the system

$$A_{11}X_1 \qquad\qquad\qquad\qquad = U_1$$
$$A_{22}X_2 \qquad\qquad\qquad = U_2$$
$$A_{33}X_3 + A_{34}X_4 \qquad = U_3$$
$$A_{45}X_5 = U_4$$

all the equations except the third are overidentified. For example, the reader should check that the A^* matrix for the fourth equation is given by (5) and hence this equation is presumably identified. It is, in fact, overidentified since this system has four equations ($m = 4$), but four ($>3 = m - 1$) of the variables do not appear. The third equation is just identified since it has exactly $m - 1 = 3$ variables missing, and since its A^* matrix is

$$\begin{bmatrix} A_{11} & 0 & 0 \\ 0 & A_{22} & 0 \\ 0 & 0 & A_{45} \end{bmatrix},$$

whose determinant is nonzero.

2. Criteria for Evaluating Simultaneous Equation Estimation Methods

As we have seen, an estimation technique is essentially nothing more than a method for deciding on the numerical value of some parameter on the basis of observed statistical information. A considerable variety of alternative estimation techniques exists, and this is particularly true in the case of simultaneous equation problems. In deciding which of the competing estimation methods to use in coping with a particular problem, some obvious practical considerations are relevant. One must ask for each of them whether computer programs are immediately and conveniently available, which of them has been tested by previous use, and how sparing each technique is in its use of expensive computer time.

In addition to this information it is also obviously necessary to know something about the relative virtues of each of these methods from the point of view of statistical theory. Here three basic criteria—bias, consistency, and efficiency—have been employed. These are technical terms, whose meaning is not directly related to the everyday usage of the words, as we shall see.

a. Unbiased estimates. An estimating technique is said to produce unbiased results in some particular circumstances if, were we to go through the estimation process an indefinite number of times, the average (arithmetic mean) of the estimates obtained from the various samples of size m would equal the true value of the parameter to be estimated. That is, consider an attempt by means of a sampling study to find $_tA$, the true value of some parameter A, e.g., the average height of 1,000 men. Suppose we used a sample with twenty-six statistical observations and a given estimating method and obtained an estimate $\hat{A}_1$. In the height estimation case, $\hat{A}_1$ might be the average height of some twenty-six men selected at random from the thousand. Similarly, assume that a second (independent) twenty-six-observation sample were to yield a second estimated value, $\hat{A}_2$, etc. Then the estimating technique would be said to yield unbiased results in these circumstances if the expected value (the arithmetic mean of the $\hat{A}$'s), $E(\hat{A}) = (\hat{A}_1 + \hat{A}_2 + \cdots + \hat{A}_n)/n$, were equal to the true value, $_tA$.

It is noteworthy that deductive methods can be employed to prejudge whether a method will yield biased results. Indeed, it is sometimes possible to predict the magnitude of the bias [the difference between the true value, $_tA$, and the average estimate, $E(\hat{A})$].

b. Consistent estimates. An estimation technique is said to yield consistent results in some particular type of circumstance if, as the size of the sample on which the estimate is based increases, the estimate approaches the true value of the parameter whose value is to be estimated. Thus, suppose this time that $\hat{A}_1$ is the estimate obtained from a twenty-one-observation sample, $\hat{A}_2$ is obtained from a twenty-two-observation sample, etc. Then the estimating procedure is consistent if the successive estimates $\hat{A}_1, \hat{A}_2, \cdots, \hat{A}_m$ come closer and closer to the true value of the parameter, $_tA$, as the sample size, $m + 20$, approaches infinity.

It is to be noted that the term "consistency" denotes a property which is strictly relevant only in cases involving large quantities of data. Thus it is conceivable that some procedures which can be shown to be consistent, and therefore perform well in large-sample problems, may behave very poorly when utilizing the limited data which so frequently are all the economist has available.[6]

A final concept used in evaluating an estimation procedure is

c. Efficiency. An estimating method is said to be efficient if in seeking the true value of a parameter, $_tA$, the estimates $\hat{A}_1, \hat{A}_2, \cdots$ which the method yields on application to different samples differ from one another by a smaller amount than the estimates produced by any other method.

---

[6] Though there is at least a superficial resemblance, the situation is not the same for the bias property. If we know that an estimate is unbiased, we are assured that "on the average" *even small sample estimates* tend to be good approximations.

That is, suppose we take several estimates of A and calculate their variance (or their standard deviation). If it can be shown that this estimation procedure yields variance figures no larger than any other possible estimation technique, it is said to be efficient. Basically, the statement that an estimation procedure is efficient asserts that its estimates of a parameter are dependable and do not vary very much from sample to sample.

Using these concepts we can now go on to discuss some of the standard estimation methods.

3. Maximum Likelihood Method: General Description

The problem of estimation may for present purposes be considered that of finding a set of parameters A_{ij} for the system of equations (3) where the parameters found must satisfy the *a priori* restrictions (2) and where the estimated values of the parameters must in some sense be those which "best" fit the facts (the statistics on which the estimates are based). Let us now use an illustrative problem to try to get a rough idea of what is involved in the maximum likelihood method of estimation, which is the method very frequently considered most desirable by statisticians.

Suppose someone were to select any integer A, then roll two dice, and add to the unrevealed number A the sum of the numbers, U, which came up on the faces of the dice. He then tells us that the total of the two numbers, $A + U$, is 16. Our job is to try to guess his selected number, A. In effect, we have the equation

$$(6) \qquad\qquad 16 = A + U,$$

where U is a random shock variable (the sum of the numbers which came up on the faces of the dice). The problem is to estimate the value of A.

Let us see now how one would go about making this estimate by means of the maximum likelihood method. The possible numbers or sums on the dice range from $U = 2$ ("snake eyes") to $U = 12$ ("boxcars"). But not all of these values have equal probabilities of occurring. The second row of Table 4 shows us, for example, that in repeated tossing of our dice[7] a value $U = 9$ may be expected to turn up twice as frequently as $U = 3$.

We observe, then, that the most likely (frequent) value of U is 7. If that were, indeed, the value of U, then A would have to be $A = 16 - U = 16 - 7 = 9$. In other words, 9 is the value of A which is most likely to

---

[7] To see how these numbers are computed, consider, for example, the entry $U = 4$. This may occur in exactly *three* different ways: The first die may turn up a 1 and the second a 3, or the first die may show a 3 and the second a 1, or both dice may come out 2—hence the entry 3 in the second row under $U = 4$. Similarly, a value of $U = 2$ can only occur in *one* single way, and therefore the first entry in the second row is 1. The rest of the second row of the table is constructed similarly.

occur, given that $A + U = 16$. Hence, our maximum likelihood estimate of A is $\hat{A} = 9$.

To summarize, the maximum likelihood method proceeds as follows. To estimate the value of some parameter (our A) it takes some observation, X (our reported total of 16 for $A + U$), or observations and asks what value of the unknown parameter makes it most likely that the observed statistic would have been generated by the equation or equations in question.

Let us now generalize somewhat, replacing our trivial single-observation case by one involving several (k) statistical observations, the case which usually occurs in practice. It is now convenient to rewrite Equation (6) as

(7) $$X_t - A = U_t,$$

where X_t is the observed value of X at time t, etc. For example, if a successive repetition of our dice-tossing experiment had brought up the numbers 18, 12, etc., after the initial total of 16, we would have $X_1 = 16$, $X_2 =$

TABLE 4

U	2	3	4	5	6	7	8	9	10	11	12
Relative frequency	1	2	3	4	5	6	5	4	3	2	1
A (= 16 − U)	14	13	12	11	10	9	8	7	6	5	4

18, $X_3 = 12$, etc. Suppose, moreover, that the U_t has a joint frequency function, $F(U_0, U_1, \cdots, U_k)$, known *a priori*. This function, of course, corresponds to the entries in the second row in Table 4, which could then have been described as $F(U)$. Substitution into this function from (7) gives us a frequency function involving only the observed statistical values, X_t and the unknown parameter A, $F(X_0 - A, X_1 - A, \cdots, X_k - A)$, which we may rewrite simply as $G(X_0, X_1, \cdots, X_k, A)$. If the values of $X_1, X_2, \cdots$ are given by observation, the only variable in $G(X_0, X_1, \cdots, X_k, A)$ is A. The maximum likelihood estimate of A is then given by the value of A for which this function attains its maximum, i.e., for which the derivative of G, with respect to A,

$$\frac{dG(X_0, X_1, \cdots, X_k, A)}{dA},$$

is equal to zero.

We may, in an obvious manner, extend the discussion to the case of a more general system like (3). There the random variables, U_i, may be considered functions of the parameters A_{ij} and the values of the variables X_{jt} which are to be observed. We must again assume that we know something about the likelihood function for the random variables. Let us use (3) to express the U_i in terms of the A_{ij} and the observed values of the variables X_{jt} and then substitute these expressions for U_i in the likelihood function, $\psi(U_1, \cdots, U_m)$. We thereby obtain the rewritten likelihood function

$$(8) \qquad L = \phi(X_{11}, \cdots, X_{nk}, A_{11}, \cdots, A_{mn}),$$

which is a function of the observed statistics X_{jt} and the unknown parameters A_{ij}.

Given the statistics we may then estimate the values of the parameters as those values of the A_{ji} for which the likelihood function attains its maximum *subject to the constraints imposed by the* a priori *information given by (2)*. This is the essence of the idea behind the maximum likelihood of estimation.

PROBLEM

Calculate the maximum likelihood estimate of A in our dice-throwing experiment if the dice are thrown twice and the reported sums of A and U are 16 on the first throw and 14 on the second. (This problem will be fairly difficult for the reader who knows no elementary probability theory.)

4. Advantages and Disadvantages of the Full-Information Maximum-Likelihood Method

The *full-information,* maximum likelihood method takes into account *all* of the *a priori* restrictions (2) for every equation of the system. As has just been stated, the equations (2) are treated as constraints. The full-information method then proceeds by finding the values of the A_{ij} which maximize L in (8) subject to *all* of the constraints (2). It normally employs the classical differential calculus methods for maximization of the value of a function subject to equality constraints which were discussed toward the end of Chapter 4.

Aside from its great intuitive attractiveness, the method has several advantages from the point of view of statistical theory. In important classes of cases these estimates are consistent and efficient. They are sometimes (but not always) also unbiased.

However, the method also has two important disadvantages. The first, which is a disadvantage to the economic but not necessarily to the statistical theorist, is that we must assume that we have some advance knowledge about the probability distribution of the random shocks, U_i, when in fact it seems difficult to visualize economically relevant cases where we will even have any grounds on which to base a good guess about the nature of this function. In the literature it is customary to assume at least that the distribution of such disturbances will be normal, but it is not easy to find the basis on which this premise is accepted.

The second disadvantage of the full-information maximum likelihood method lies in the complexity of the calculations which it requires except where the probability distribution of the disturbances is normal and the equations happen to be just identified, in which case the maximum likelihood estimates coincide with a form of simple least squares estimate of the parameters of the system (3).[8] Generally, however, the process of computation is apt to be exceedingly slow and expensive, and it is very rarely used in practice. As computers with higher speeds and larger memory capacities have become available, this disadvantage has, however, become somewhat less serious.

5. Structural Equations and Reduced-Form Equations: Definitions

A *structural equation* may be defined, roughly, as one which explicitly results from the (economic) theory, as opposed to an equation which is obtained by mathematical manipulation of structural equations. Thus, our demand-and-supply equations (1a) are structural equations.

The reduced form of equation system (1) may be described as follows: Only the first two variables in the system, Q and P (quantity sold and price), are *jointly determined*, i.e., their values are determined simultaneously by the system of two equations. The other variables, Y (national income), R (rainfall), and S (subsidy level), are not determined by our supply-demand model. They are called *exogenous* because their values are given from outside the equation system. In general, there will be the same number of jointly determined variables as there are equations in the system because these equations must suffice to determine the values of the dependent (jointly determined) variables.

Let us now solve our Equations (1) to obtain expressions for the values of Q and P in terms of the exogenous variables only. Thus we get equations of the form

$$Q = D_{10} + D_{11}Y + D_{12}R + D_{13}S + U_1'$$

(9)

$$P = D_{20} + D_{21}Y + D_{22}R + D_{23}S + U_2',$$

where the D_{ij} are constants and the U_i''s are random variables. This is

---

[8] See Koopmans and Hood, *op. cit.*, pp. 140-55. Also see below, Section 6.

called the *reduced form* of the system of structural equations (1). More specifically, in the case of Equations (1a) we can obtain our second (P) reduced-form equation (9) as follows. Eliminate Q by setting the two equations (1a) equal to one another, thus:

$$A_{10} + A_{11}P + A_{12}Y + U_1 = A_{20} + A_{21}P + A_{23}R + A_{24}S + U_2$$

so that

$$P(A_{11} - A_{21}) = A_{20} - A_{10} - A_{12}Y + A_{23}R + A_{24}S + U_2 - U_1$$

or

$$P = \frac{A_{20} - A_{10}}{A_{11} - A_{21}} - \frac{A_{12}}{A_{11} - A_{21}}Y + \frac{A_{23}}{A_{11} - A_{21}}R$$

$$+ \frac{A_{24}}{A_{11} - A_{21}}S + \frac{U_2 - U_1}{A_{11} - A_{21}}.$$

This is clearly one of our reduced-form equations (9). The other reduced-form equation (for Q) can be obtained similarly by eliminating the P's between our two equations (1a).

It will be noted that each equation now contains only one of the interdependent (jointly determined) variables P and Q. None of the variables on the right-hand side of the equations is jointly determined. The equations of the reduced form are generally not structural. Thus, the equations of the general system (3) would be of reduced form only if (3) happened accidentally to meet the reduced-form requirements to begin with, i.e., if the A parameters which are held equal to zero by the *a priori* restrictions (2) were such that each of the equations in (3) contained only one jointly determined variable.

6. The Reduced-Form Method

As indicated earlier in this chapter, the use of the ordinary least squares method to estimate directly the parameters of a structural equation yields estimates which are biased. Indeed, they will also be inconsistent, so that in terms of the criteria of statistical theory this procedure has little to recommend it. However, it can be shown that it is normally legitimate to use the ordinary least squares method, not in determining parameters A_{ij} for our structural equations, but in estimating the parameters D_{ij} of the reduced-form equations. Because all but one jointly dependent variable has been eliminated from each reduced-form equation, no equation contains two mutually interdependent variables, and, as has been indicated in the body of this chapter, it is this mutual interdependence which produces least squares bias. In effect, the reduced form is not a system of M

simultaneous equations but, rather, it is a set of M *independent* equations, all of which happen to hold. Hence, since simultaneous relationships are essentially not involved in the reduced form, it is legitimate to estimate the parameters of the equations by means of ordinary least squares procedures.

Having found the D coefficients of the reduced form by least squares, it is then necessary to retrace our steps and use these D values to estimate the A parameters of our structural equations (1) or (1a). Specifically, if the system is *just* identified, i.e., there are just exactly enough *a priori* restrictions (2) to ensure identification of each equation in (3), and no more, then we can proceed as follows: (*a*) estimate the D_{ij} of the reduced form by old-fashioned least squares; (*b*) now substitute the resulting reduced-form equations into our structural equations (3) and find the values of the A_{ij} essentially by straightforward algebraic manipulation. In this just-identified case it turns out that the estimates of the structural parameters thus obtained by application of least squares to the reduced form *will necessarily be the same as the full-information maximum likelihood estimates*!

Unhappily, we are rarely so fortunate. The number of constraints [*a priori* restrictions (2)] in the system are frequently more abundant than the minimum necessary for identification, and then no simple and inexpensive shortcut to the full-information maximum likelihood estimates is known. The difficulty is that only if an equation is just identified is it possible to solve in a straightforward manner for the A coefficients of our structural equations in terms of the D coefficients of the reduced-form equations.

Illustration. Suppose in our reduced-form equations (9) the estimated values of the parameters are $\hat{D}_{10} = 5$, $\hat{D}_{11} = 2$, $\hat{D}_{12} = 3$, $\hat{D}_{13} = 1$, $\hat{D}_{20} = 2$, $\hat{D}_{21} = -4$, $\hat{D}_{22} = 0.5$, and $\hat{D}_{23} = 4$, so that our reduced-form estimated equations become

$$Q = 5 + 2Y + 3R + S$$

(10)

$$P = 2 - 4Y + 0.5R + 4S,$$

where the random elements U_1' and U_2' may for the present be taken to have been dropped for simplicity. It will be recalled that our second structural equation in (1a) is just identified because it has one less zero coefficient ($A_{22} = 0$) than the number of equations in the system ($m = 2$).

In general terms this equation together with its *a priori* restriction (2) can be written

(11) $Q = A_{20} + A_{21}P + A_{22}Y + A_{23}R + A_{24}S$

(12) $A_{22} = 0.$

We can substitute for Q and P from our reduced-form equations (10) into (11). This gives us

$$
\begin{aligned}
5 + 2Y + 3R + S &= A_{20} + 2A_{21} - 4A_{21}Y + 0.5A_{21}R + 4A_{21}S \\
&\quad + A_{22}Y + A_{23}R + A_{24}S \\
&= (A_{20} + 2A_{21}) + (-4A_{21} + A_{22})Y \\
&\quad + (0.5A_{21} + A_{23})R + (4A_{21} + A_{24})S.
\end{aligned}
$$

(13)

This equality is supposed to hold no matter what the statistical values of our variables. Hence the constant terms on both sides of Equation (13) must be equal. Similarly, the coefficients of the Y terms on both sides of the equations must be equal, and so on. Writing these conditions out explicitly we end up with the four equations[9]

$$
\begin{aligned}
5 &= A_{20} + 2A_{21} \\
2 &= -4A_{21} + A_{22} \\
3 &= 0.5A_{21} + A_{23} \\
1 &= 4A_{21} + A_{24}.
\end{aligned}
$$

(14)

These equations have the five unknowns A_{20}, A_{21}, A_{22}, A_{23}, and A_{24}. It is only the addition of the *a priori* restriction (12) which gives us the fifth equation required to solve for the values of the A parameters. And, in fact, substituting this zero value of A_{22} into the second equation we readily obtain

$$
\begin{aligned}
\hat{A}_{21} &= -0.5 \\
\hat{A}_{20} &= 6 \\
\hat{A}_{23} &= 3.25 \\
\hat{A}_{24} &= 3,
\end{aligned}
$$

as the reduced-form estimates of the parameters of our second structural equation (1a).

---

[9] More rigorously, we obtain the first of these equations by setting $Y = R = S = 0$ in (13). Similarly, we obtain the second equation by subtracting (14) from (13) and setting $Y = 1$, $R = S = 0$, etc. This procedure is legitimate, since the equation (13) is supposed to be valid for *any* values of Y, R, and S.

It will be noted that we could find these $\hat{A}$ values only because there was exactly one *a priori* restriction (12). If the equation had been over-identified and there had been more than one such restriction, we would have had more equations to determine the values of the A's than there were unknowns, and so we would not have been able to use the reduced-form method to estimate the $\hat{A}$'s.[10]

PROBLEM

Using the reduced-form equations (10) show that the reduced-form method does not permit us to estimate the coefficients of the first of the equations (1a). Why?

7. The Limited-Information Approach

Another approach to simultaneous equation estimation, the limited-information method, is very powerful in that it allows us to estimate the coefficients of a single structural equation without requiring us to undertake any estimation for the remaining structural equations. This fact distinguishes it from the full-information maximum likelihood method which presents us with estimates for *all* coefficients in the system.

The name of the limited-information method refers to the fact that we do not employ the *a priori* restrictions ($A_{ij} = 0$) which pertain to equations other than the one being estimated. Neglect of those other *a priori* restrictions has the distinct advantage that we need not specify the exact form of the other equations in the system. (Often there may be no practical purpose served by specifying these other equations precisely.) We do, however, need some minimal information about these equations. The method does require us to specify all of the exogenous variables that enter the equations in which we are not directly interested.

In sum, the limited-information method reduces the work of model construction. It also eases considerably the difficulties of computation and thus reduces the costs of calculation. However, these gains are unfortunately partially offset by some loss of efficiency: Limited-information

---

[10] More generally, suppose an m equation system contains m jointly determined variables and k exogenous variables. In trying to find the A parameters of one of the structural equations from the D parameters of the reduced equations, we will obtain an equation corresponding to (13) containing $k + 1$ terms on each side—one constant term and one term corresponding to each of the k exogenous variables. Thus we will end up with $k + 1$ equations like (14) to determine the $m + k$ coefficients, A_{ij}, of the $m + k$ variables, but if, and only if, the equation is exactly identified, it will involve $m - 1$ *a priori* restrictions (2), i.e., exactly $m - 1$ conditions $A_{ij} = 0$. Thus we will have $k + 1$ equations like (14) and $m - 1$ equations (2), making $m + k$ equations altogether, the same as the number of unknown estimates A_{ij}. If the structural equation is, however, overidentified, we will end up with more than $m - 1$ equations (2) and we will normally have too many equations to solve for the $m + k$ parameters A_{ij}.

estimates will have greater variability from sample to sample than do full-information maximum likelihood estimates.

8. The Method of Instrumental Variables

Two other methods of simultaneous-equation estimation merit special emphasis. One of these is the method of instrumental variables and the other is Theil's method of two-stage least squares. It will be seen that both of these seek to take advantage of the simplicity of the least squares computations while making some attempt to reduce its deficiencies in a simultaneous-equation problem.

As was indicated earlier, if X and Y are "jointly dependent" variables in a simultaneous system, the least squares estimates of their coefficients will be neither unbiased nor consistent. The basic reason for this is that not only does Y change every time X does, but because of their interdependence, the change in Y, in turn, has a feedback effect on X. Thus, consider the simultaneous system[11]

$$Y = bX + U$$

(15)

$$Y = cX + dZ + V.$$

If we base our estimate of the value of b, in the first equation, on the observed relative movements of Y and X, we are likely to attribute to b more than just the effect of X on Y.

The method of instrumental variables attacks this problem as follows. Instead of estimating b directly in terms of the changes in X and Y, it tries to "net out" the relationship by using the exogenous variable Z as an instrument for this purpose. In effect,[12] rather than estimating b by means of the observed values of $\Delta Y/\Delta X$, it first computes $\Delta Y/\Delta Z$, then calculates $\Delta X/\Delta Z$, and takes as its estimate for b the ratio of these two,

$$\frac{\Delta Y/\Delta Z}{\Delta X/\Delta Z},$$

which, when the ΔZ's cancel out, should give us

$$\frac{\Delta Y}{\Delta X}.$$

Since Z is not a jointly determined variable, neither Y nor X influences the

---

[11] Are both equations in this system identified?

[12] Since the equations in (15) are linear, their coefficients may be interpreted as slopes or first (partial) derivatives. Specifically, if we ignore the U in the first equation, it is clear that $\Delta Y/\Delta X = b$.

value of Z, and so neither $\Delta Y/\Delta Z$ nor $\Delta X/\Delta Z$ is distorted by simultaneous equation feedback effect.[13]

This method can be shown to give at least consistent estimates. Its great disadvantage is that where a number of exogenous variables appear in the system, the choice of Z, the instrumental variable, is arbitrary, but that choice will affect the final results of the calculation. It may be men-

---

[13] More specifically, it will be recalled from our discussion of the least squares method in footnote 2 of Chapter 10 that the least squares estimates of a and b in $Y = a + bX$ are given by the two normal equations. Since in the first equation of our system (15), whose parameters we wish to estimate, the constant term is missing (i.e., we have assumed $a = 0$), the first of the normal equations drops out and the least squares estimate of b is given by the second normal equation with the a term eliminated: $\sum YX = \dot{b} \sum X^2$, i.e., by

$$\dot{b} = \frac{\sum YX}{\sum X^2} .$$

In the instrumental-variables method this estimate is replaced by

$$\dot{b}* = \frac{\sum YZ}{\sum XZ} = \frac{\sum YZ}{\sum Z^2} \bigg/ \frac{\sum XZ}{\sum Z^2} .$$

But it will be noted that the numerator and denominator may themselves each be interpreted as the least squares estimates

$$\hat{\alpha} = \frac{\sum YZ}{\sum Z^2} \quad \text{and} \quad \hat{\beta} = \frac{\sum XZ}{\sum Z^2}$$

of the coefficients α and β in a pair of equations

$$Y = \alpha Z \quad\quad X = \beta Z$$

Now returning to our original simultaneous-equation system (15) in which we want to estimate the value of b, assume for the moment that there are no random influences so that $U = V = 0$. The reader should verify by first eliminating X from Equations (15) and then eliminating Y between these equations that the reduced-form equations of the system are

$$Y = \frac{bd}{b - c} Z \quad \text{and} \quad X = \frac{d}{b - c} Z.$$

These reduced-form equations are two equations of the form $Y = \alpha Z$ and $X = \beta Z$. Moreover, since

$$\alpha/\beta = \left(\frac{bd}{b - c}\right) \bigg/ \left(\frac{d}{b - c}\right) = b$$

our instrumental-variables estimate

$$\dot{b}* = \hat{\alpha}/\hat{\beta}$$

may indeed be considered to constitute an estimate of b.

tioned, finally, that in an equation with more parameters to be estimated, we would need as many instrumental variables as there are parameters.

9. The Method of Two-Stage Least Squares

Theil's method of two-stage least squares can also be applied to a single equation at a time. It starts from a second interpretation of the reason for the inappropriateness of using least squares to estimate b in our first equation in (15). This explanation bases itself on the fact that in a simultaneous equation model X and Y are both functions of the same error or shock variables U and V. That is to say, X and Y are both random variables dependent on U and V, and this fact produces an extraneous relationship between X and Y which makes least squares produce inconsistent estimates. To see this more specifically, we note that the reduced-form equations corresponding to the structural equations (15) must be of the form

$$X = A_1 + A_2 Z + w$$

(16)

$$Y = B_1 + B_2 Z + W,$$

where w and W are random variables which are themselves dependent on U and V. If we actually knew the magnitude of w for each date for which we have a statistical figure for X, our difficulties would be at an end, because we could then rewrite our equation $Y = a + bX + U$ as

$$(17) \quad Y = a + b(X - w) + U + bw = a + b(X - w) + R,$$

where R is the random variable $U + bw$. Now the variable on the right of (17) is no longer the random variable X. Instead it has been replaced by the nonrandom variable $X - w$, i.e., by the values of X with their random components, w, removed. Hence in correlating Y with $X - w$ to obtain $\hat{b}$, we would be dealing with only one variable which contains a random component. It would therefore be perfectly legitimate to use the ordinary least squares method to determine a value for b in (17) because the two variables would no longer be interconnected by common random shocks which can produce spurious correlations between them.

Unfortunately, we have no way of determining the magnitudes of w for each different date for which we have X statistics. At best we can *estimate* w by means of the residuals $\hat{w}$ obtained from a least squares regression calculated for the first reduced-form equation (16). That is, from this equation we obtain for every date t an estimated value[14] of X, $\hat{X}_t = \hat{A}_1 + \hat{A}_2 Z_t$. Subtracting this estimated $\hat{X}$ from the actual value of X for that day as given by our statistics, we obtain our estimate of w for that date[15] as $\hat{w}_t = X_t - \hat{X}_t = (A + A_2 Z_t + w_t) - (\hat{A}_1 + \hat{A}_2 Z_t)$. Theil then proposes that w be replaced by $\hat{w}$ in (17) and that a second regression (hence the name two-stage least squares) be calculated for (17). Thus, by comparing the ordinary statistical values of the Y's, with the revised values $X - \hat{w}$ for the X's (which have been doctored to remove the random influence, w), we obtain a least squares equation for (17) giving us a revised estimate $\hat{b}$. This is the two-stage least squares estimate of $\hat{b}$.

---

[14] Note that the estimation equation for X contains no random term. In effect, we are dealing with the least squares estimating line for the dots in Figure 7. The dots represent the actual statistics, and the height of the line gives us our estimated $\hat{X}$ values.

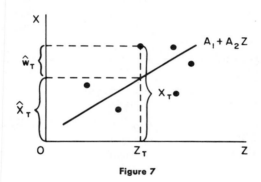

Figure 7

The deviations of the actual dots above and below the line are taken to be due to the random influences which are measured by w. Thus, the random element does not have any influence on the *estimated* X as given by the line. Rather, it is given by the deviations between the actual and the predicted X's.

[15] More specifically, suppose we have the following statistical values for X and Z:

Date	X (actual)	Z	$\hat{X}$ (calculated)	$\hat{w} = X - \hat{X}$
1950	50	20	47	3
1951	53	25	57	-4
1952	41	18	43	-2

and that our reduced-form equation has been estimated as $\hat{X}_t = 7 + 2Z_t$. We easily calculate that since in 1950 Z was 20, then the calculated $\hat{X}_{'50}$ must be $7 + 2(20) = 47$. Similarly, we obtain the estimated (column 4) value $\hat{X}_{'51} = 7 + 2(25) = 57$ and $\hat{X}_{'52} = 43$. We note that none of these estimated $\hat{X}$'s is exactly equal to the actual X values as given in the second column of the table. The last column of the table shows the calculation of the estimated $\hat{w}$ for each year by subtraction of the calculated $\hat{X}$'s from the actual statistical X values.

Although the replacement of w by $\hat{w}$ is theoretically undesirable, it turns out that $X - \hat{w}$ is "sufficiently" nonrandom that the resulting estimates of b are consistent. These estimates are not too difficult to calculate and Theil's method is generally considered to be a significant addition to the list of available methods of estimating the coefficients of structural equations in a simultaneous system.

REFERENCES

Beals, Ralph E., *Statistics for Economists*, Rand-McNally, Chicago, 1972.

Christ, Carl L., *Econometric Models and Methods*, John Wiley & Sons, Inc., New York, 1966.

Goldberger, A. S., *Econometric Theory*, John Wiley & Sons, Inc., New York, 1964.

Hood, William C., and Tjalling C. Koopmans (eds.), *Studies in Econometric Method*, Cowles Commission Monograph 14, John Wiley & Sons, Inc., New York, 1953, especially Chapters III (by T. C. Koopmans), VI (by T. C. Koopmans and W. C. Hood), and IX (by Jean Bronfenbrenner).

Johnston, J., *Econometric Methods*, McGraw-Hill Book Company, New York, 2nd ed., 1974.

Klein, Lawrence R., *A Textbook of Econometrics*, Harper & Row, Publishers, Inc., New York, 2nd ed., 1974, especially Chapters III and IV.

Wonnacott, R. J., and T. H. Wonnacott, *Econometrics*, John Wiley & Sons, Inc., New York, 1970.

Working, E. J., "What Do Statistical 'Demand Curves' Show?" *Quarterly Journal of Economics*, Vol. XLI, 1927.

Zellner, Arnold, *An Introduction to Bayesian Inference in Econometrics*, John Wiley & Sons, Inc., New York, 1971.

Production and Cost

11

1. Production, Inputs, and Outputs

The standard economic discussions of production classify the firm's decision variables into only two categories, *inputs* and *outputs*. An input is simply anything which the firm buys for use in its production or other processes. An output is any commodity which the firm produces or processes for sale.

The term "processing," as it is used here, may denote an act of transportation or storage and does not necessarily imply a manufacturing activity. To an economist, all of these may be equally productive acts. For example, transportation increases the usefulness of the product by bringing it to the location where the consumer needs it—without transportation the item may be just as useless to him as it would be if it were still just a collection of raw materials. Similarly, storage gets the item to the consumer *when* he needs it, just as transportation gets it to him *where* he needs it. The terms "production" and "processing," then, are used in this more general sense, which does not necessarily involve the literal, physical transformation of raw materials.

Management's production decision problems may be considered to fall into four types:

1. How much, in total, shall be spent on the purchase of inputs?
2. How shall this amount be divided among the various types of input?

3. How much of each type of input will be allocated to each type of output?

4. How much of each final product (output) shall the firm produce?

The answers to the questions are the subjects of this and succeeding chapters.

2. The Production Function

Decisions on inputs and outputs cannot, of course, be taken independently. There are technological relationships summarized in the *production function*

$$y = g(r_1, r_2, \cdots, r_m),$$

which states that y is the *maximum* amount of commodity Y which the firm can produce if it uses exactly r_1 units of input 1, r_2 units of input 2, etc.

Knowledge of such a functional relationship presupposes that a set of optimality calculations has already been carried out, explicitly or implicitly, by the firm's engineers or production managers. They must be taken to have examined the many alternative ways in which inputs can be combined to produce any given output and to have selected the most efficient way of using inputs for each potential output of the firm. Thus their calculation is taken to indicate the *maximum* output obtainable from any given combination of inputs. In the following chapter the nature of this implicit optimality calculation will be described in some detail.[1]

Confining our discussion to two inputs to permit the use of two- and three-dimensional graphs, we can represent the production function in a set of diagrams very closely analogous to consumer indifference maps and the utility function in Chapter 9. However, for reasons which will become clear presently (Section 6), it is customary and convenient to represent

---

[1] That chapter discusses the production-decision process using the standard analysis of mathematical programming. It shows that this analysis encompasses *both* the decisions discussed in the next few pages and the optimization computation implicit in the estimation of the production function. That is, it considers not only how much of each output ought to be produced but also at what level each available technological process should be employed. This is handled by a simple device. Suppose there are two processes for producing shoes. Instead of using one variable, y, to represent shoe output, we employ two variables, y_1 and y_2, to represent the quantities produced by the first and second processes, respectively. Then the optimal values of y_1 and y_2 can both be calculated by the standard programming techniques and these values obviously determine, implicitly, the optimal combination of use of shoe manufacturing processes 1 and 2 for that level of output.

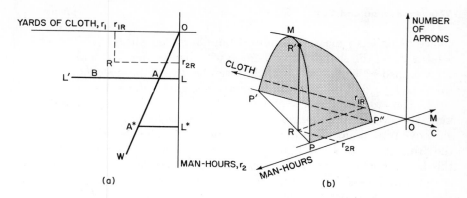

Figure 1

inputs as *negative* amounts, i.e., the use of 75 tons of coal is interpreted as a 75-ton *deduction* from the coal resources utilized by society. Consequently, input axes go either downward or to the left of the origin.

In Figure 1a any point R represents a combination of two inputs—quantity Or_{1R} of cloth and quantity Or_{2R} of labor. Suppose with such a combination of inputs the largest possible output of aprons is RR' (Figure 1). Then point R' is one point on the production surface. The locus of all such points is a bandshell-like surface, a portion of which is shown in Figure 1b as $PP'MP''$.

3. Relative Input Levels and Production

We note that, as it is drawn, the production surface does not extend up to the labor and cloth axes. The reason for this is that at a point such as r_{2R}, which lies on one of the axes, we have a positive quantity of only one input. At point r_{2R} we have Or_{2R} labor and no cloth. We know that with such a combination of inputs it is not possible to produce any aprons, i.e., output at point r_{2R} must be zero. Hence the production surface at that point must be of zero height. That is what also gives the production function the roughly upside-down U-shaped cross section PMP'. This shape indicates that output cannot be produced with only cloth alone or only labor alone and that positive outputs can only be produced by combinations of the two (intermediate points in the diagram). Note that by more careful cutting and workmanship it is possible to save on cloth by increased use of labor so that aprons can indeed be produced with varying proportions of cloth and labor, as the diagram shows.

There are several respects in which the diagram may be misleading:

1. The cross section PMP' need not be symmetrical, for the two inputs need not make similar contributions to output, particularly since the

269

choice of units to measure inputs—man-hours and yards—is completely arbitrary and the shape of the diagram will change when the unit of measure is varied—a square meter of cloth can be used to produce more aprons than can a yard of cloth because a meter is slightly longer than a yard.

2. The cross section PMP' need not be smooth—it may have dents, kinks, or even sharp breaks. For example, consider what happens when we move from point R' in the direction of P'. This involves a reduction in the firm's use of labor and an increased use of cloth. At some point along this line the labor/cloth ratio may become so low that it is necessary to switch to labor-saving equipment, and this switch may produce a sharp rise in output—a break (a sudden rise) in the production surface.

3. Point M, the highest point on the cross section PMP', will *not* normally represent an optimal arrangement. True, it represents a technologically productive combination of inputs, but whether it will pay to employ that input combination depends on relative prices, which we have not yet brought into the picture. That is, whether it will pay to use 10 minutes or 15 minutes of labor per yard of cloth will depend in part on the level of wages, no matter what the physical productivity of labor.

4. Properties of Production Functions: Diminishing Returns

A standard economic assumption affecting the shape of the production function is the "law" of diminishing returns, which is interpreted here to mean (eventually) diminishing marginal productivity. This highly plausible empirical allegation (which seems to be fairly well supported by experience) states that

> As more and more of some input, i, is employed, *all other input quantities being held constant*, eventually a point will be reached where additional quantities of input i will yield diminishing marginal contributions to total product.

The plausibility argument is that, eventually, other inputs will grow short relative to input i, and so additional units of i will be at a growing disadvantage in adding to production. As we hire more and more labor but do not supply the increased labor force with additional workroom equipment or raw material, further additions to the labor force may well be expected to grow less helpful.

The effect of this assumption on the shape of the production surface is readily shown. Consider line LL' in Figure 1a. Point B on this line involves more cloth than does point A. But, *because LL' is parallel to the horizontal cloth axis*, both A and B involve the same quantities of labor input. A line parallel to either axis, then, represents the conditions necessary to test for the presence of diminishing returns—by moving along such a line we can increase the use of one input *while holding the quantity of the other input constant*.

To see now whether the production surface exhibits diminishing returns we must investigate what happens to the production level as we make such a move (from *A* toward *B* on *LL′*). For this purpose we examine the cross section, *LSTB*, of the production surface taken above line *LL′* (Figure 2a). This curve, which is reproduced by itself in Figure 2b, is a total product curve for cloth given the fixed quantity of labor, *OL*. We note that as it is drawn it flattens out as we move toward the left (its slope diminishes with increasing quantities of cloth input). But we know (Chapter 3, Section 4) that the marginal product of cloth is represented by the slope of the total product curve. It follows that as we move to the left

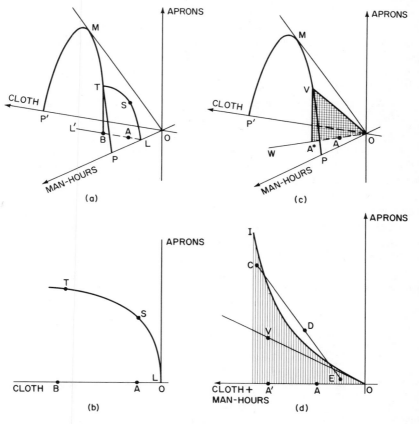

Figure 2

along LL', the marginal product of cloth (the slope of LST) is declining, as the diminishing-marginal-returns assumption requires. To summarize, if (and only if) the production function involves diminishing marginal returns, any cross section taken parallel to *either* input axis will have the gradually flattening shape shown in Figure 2b, and not a constant slope (as does OV in Figure 2d) or an increasing slope (OI in Figure 2d).

5. Properties of Production Functions: Returns to Scale

So far we have examined what happens when any one input is increased by itself. This leads naturally to our next question, what happens when all inputs are increased together, that is, when the production process is expanded exactly *to scale*? For this purpose, let us return again to the floor of our production diagram (Figure 1a). Suppose we begin with some input combination, A, and ask how a doubling of both of the input quantities at A will be represented. We then have the following result:

Draw the straight line OW, which goes through both the origin and point A. Pick point A^* on this line OW so that length $OA^* =$ twice (k times) length OA. Then point A^* represents an exact doubling (multiplication by k) of all of the inputs at point A.[2]

Moreover, it is simple to extend this result to obtain the converse proposition that *any* proportionate increase (decrease) in all of a firm's inputs must be represented by a movement along some straight line, OW, from the origin on the floor of the three-dimensional production diagram (Figure 2c). Note that this straight line need not bisect the angle formed by the axes. For example, in Figure 1a curve OW is relatively close to the labor axis because it represents what looks like a large (constant) labor-to-cloth ratio.

This, then, is how we ask our question: To find out what happens to production when all inputs increase in the same proportion (an increase to scale) we take a cross section OA^*V of our production diagram (Figure 2c) cutting along the straight line on the floor from the origin and examine the shape of this cross section. There are three possibilities:

> 1. *Diminishing returns to scale:* The curve representing the top of the cross section has the shape of $P''M$ in Figure 1b, in which the slope decreases toward the left.

---

[2] *Proof:* Triangles LOA and L^*OA^* are similar because they are both right triangles and they have angle LOA in common. Therefore their sides are proportional, i.e., we have $L^*A^*/LA = OL^*/OL = OA^*/OA = k$. But OL and OL^* are the labor input at points A and A^*, respectively, and LA and L^*A^* are the respective cloth inputs at A and A^*. The result then follows at once.

2. *Increasing returns to scale:* The top of the cross section has an increasing slope, as does OI in Figure 2d.

3. *Constant returns to scale:* The cross section line is straight (OV in Figures 2c and 2d).[3]

This last possibility, which is called the case of a *linearly homogeneous production function*,[4] has received a great deal of attention in the literature. It turns out that such a relationship has extremely convenient mathematical properties, which make it very useful for purposes of analysis. Whenever we are fortunate enough to encounter a production function which (at least approximately) exhibits constant returns to scale, i.e., linear homogeneity, we can at once bring to bear a number of special theorems, several of which will be described presently.

There is also some empirical evidence that the production function for the economy as a whole is not too far from being linearly homogeneous.[5]

Finally, it is almost tempting to argue that production functions will *necessarily* exhibit constant returns to scale. The view is that if, in some sense, all inputs are, say, tripled, what is there to prevent all outputs from being tripled? After all, if we build three identical factories with identical work forces, equipment, and raw materials, will we not obtain three times the output of a single factory? In this view, given constant prices, there are only two reasons why costs (input use) should not vary in exact proportion with output:

1. *Limited input quantities:* If we increase outputs, but there are some factors whose use cannot expand in proportion because their supplies are limited, costs per unit will be driven up because there will be diminishing returns to those inputs whose use is increased.

An alternative proof which also proves the converse, notes that the equation of a straight line through the origin is $y = ax$ (see Chapter 2, Section 3). But input quantities y and x vary proportionately if and only if $y/x = a$ (a constant), which is precisely the same as the equation of the straight line through the origin.

[3] Note that the "spine" of the diagram, OM, which is one such cross section, is also a straight line in this case.

[4] This is the mathematical terminology for the case of constant returns to scale. See Sections 9 and 10 below. Incidentally, the reader would do well to convince himself that a production function can satisfy the "law of diminishing returns" and yet, simultaneously, exhibit constant returns to scale. It should be noted that both of these phenomena occur in linear programming problems.

[5] See Paul H. Douglas, "Are There Laws of Production?" *American Economic Reveiw*, Vol. XXXVIII, March 1948; and Robert M. Solow, "Technical Change and the Aggregate Production Function," *Review of Economics and Statistics*, Vol. XXXIX, August 1957. Cf., however, K. J. Arrow, H. B. Chenery, B. S. Minhas, and R. M. Solow, "Capital-Labor Substitution and Economic Efficiency," *Review of Economics and Statistics*, Vol. 43, August 1961, pp. 225–248.

2. *Indivisibilities:* Some inputs just do not come in small units. We cannot install half a blast furnace or half a locomotive (a small locomotive is not the same as a fraction of a large locomotive). As a result, only if operations are carried on on a sufficiently large scale will it pay to employ such indivisible items. This, it is said, is the only source of economies of large-scale production. In other words, from this point of view all production functions are linear and homogeneous, only, unfortunately, it is not always possible to increase or diminish all input uses in exactly the same proportion.

This position has been criticized on several grounds. First of all, it has been maintained that one cannot generally duplicate all of the elements in a given situation even in principle. A pair of factories in close proximity simply is not the same as a duplication of one factory in isolation. The existence of another nearby factory affects labor morale, air pollution, the cost of labor-force training, etc.

More important, suppose one larger factory is more efficient than two small factories of similar total capacity. Then there is no motivation for a businessman to expand by *duplicating* his original facilities, even if this option is open to him. In other words, if he can obtain increasing returns to scale, he can be expected to take advantage of such opportunities when he expands his output.

There are standard examples of the manner in which such economies can arise. For example, it was shown in Chapter 1 that the optimal inventory level is likely to increase less than in proportion with the scale of a firm's output. In other words, when the firm doubles its sales, it may be foolish to double its inventory expenditures. Here is an increasing-returns case—an economy of large-scale production. Another standard example is the warehouse construction case. Suppose the work in building a cubical warehouse is proportionate to the number of bricks used in its construction and that, within limits, the number of bricks depends strictly on the wall area of the building. It is a matter of elementary geometry that the wall and floor areas will increase as the *square* of the perimeter of the warehouse but the volume of the building (the storage area) will increase as the *cube* of the perimeter. In other words, double the land, bricks, and the brick-laying labor and one more than doubles warehouse capacity. Here is another case of economies of large-scale production.

One must conclude that whether or not the production function of a particular plant is linearly homogeneous or even approximately so is a matter for empirical investigation and cannot be settled by *a priori* considerations. [6]

---

[6] Some of the standard references on this discussion are Nicholas Kaldor, "The Equilibrium of the Firm," *Economic Journal*, Vol. XLIV, March 1934; Paul A. Samuel-

6. Notation for Production Functions and Production Sets: Multiproduct Firms

Elementary discussions usually deal only with single-product enterprises whose output level is y and which uses quantities $r_1, \cdots, r_m$ of m different inputs. Then, as we have seen, the production function may be written as

$$y = g(r_1, \cdots, r_m).$$

For reasons which will become clear in the next few paragraphs, it is convenient to rewrite this function as

$$y - g(r_1, \cdots, r_m) = 0,$$

which, in turn, can be rewritten as

$$f(y, r_1, \cdots, r_m) = 0.$$

If we consider the possibility of waste or inefficiency in the productive process [to deal with the entire *set* of feasible production possibilities and not just the (efficient) production function], the preceding relationships are transformed into the following inequalities:

$$y \leq g(r_1, \cdots, r_m) \quad \text{or} \quad y - g(r_1, \cdots, r_m) \equiv f(y, r_1, \cdots, r_m) \leq 0.$$

The reason we have gone to the trouble of bringing the y inside the functional relationship is that with this notation it is extremely easy to proceed to the corresponding relationships for a firm that produces a multiplicity of outputs. To adapt it to a multiproduct enterprise, with output quantities $y_1, \cdots, y_n$, the preceding form can simply be rewritten

$$f(y_1, \cdots, y_n, r_1, \cdots, r_m) \leq 0,$$

meaning that any one output can be increased either by increasing input use holding other output levels constant, *or*, instead, by reducing other outputs without any change in input use (or by some combination of the two).

son, *Foundations of Economic Analysis*, Harvard University Press, Cambridge, Mass., 1947, pp. 81–87; Edward H. Chamberlin, "Proportionality, Divisibility, and Economies of Scale," *Quarterly Journal of Economics*, Vol. LXII, February 1948; "Comments" by A. N. McLeod and F. H. Hahn and "Reply" by Chamberlin, same journal, Vol. LXIII, February 1949; "Random Variations, Risk and Returns to Scale," Thompson M. Whitin and Maurice H. Peston, same journal, Vol. LXVIII, November 1954; and Harvey Leibenstein, "The Proportionality Controversy and the Theory of Production," same journal, Vol. LXIX, November 1955.

One last modification in notation simplifies this relationship and simultaneously permits us to generalize it somewhat further. Consider some commodity such as electricity which is an input for some firms and an output of some others. A firm may be both a producer and a user of electricity, and its optimality calculation will determine whether or not it pays it to produce more than it consumes, i.e., whether it is a supplier of electricity to others or whether it produces only enough to meet some of its own demand (as in the case of firms that keep standby generators for emergencies). If its output is positive, it is a seller, and electricity is then one of the firm's outputs. If its net output is negative, electricity becomes one of its inputs. We then may let z_i represent *either* the output or the input of item i, with the convention that the item serves as an output if $z_i > 0$ and as an input if $z_i < 0$. This is the primary reason for the convention that *input quantities are represented by negative numbers*. Then, for brevity, writing $w = m + n$, the feasible production set becomes

$$f(z_1, \cdots, z_w) \leq 0.$$

Sometimes it is not convenient to describe the production possibilities in terms of a well-defined function such as $f(z_1, \cdots, z_w) \leq 0$. In that case we simply deal with the set of possible input and output combinations. That is, we use the

Definition: The *production set*, T, is the set of all points $(z_1, \cdots, z_w)$ in w-dimensional space representing all combinations of inputs and outputs that are possible given the available resources and the state of technological knowledge.

7. Iso-Product Curves and Production Frontiers

Consider the production set in two outputs and two inputs given by

$$f(y_1, y_2, r_1, r_2) \leq 0.$$

If we hold both input quantities constant at some levels, call them r_1^*, r_2^*, we can determine all the possible output combinations capable of being produced by that pair of inputs. The resulting locus is called a *production possibility locus*, or a *production frontier*. Figure 3 shows two such curves. The curve SS' shows the output possibilities when the available input combination is r_1^*, r_2^*, while ZZ' is the possibility locus for some other (larger) input combination. Point U on SS' is an *efficient* output combination for input combination r_1^*, r_2^*. Point T is feasible but inefficient since it is

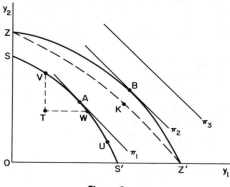

Figure 3

possible with the given inputs to produce any output combination in region TVW, where, in comparison with point T, any such point represents an increase in at least one of the two outputs with no reduction in the other.

The production frontiers have been drawn concave to the origin, indicating that there are diminishing returns to specialization in any one output. Thus, on production frontier ZZ', point Z indicates how large an output, y_2, can be produced if *all* the inputs used along ZZ' were devoted to commodity 2, and, similarly, point Z' represents the maximal output y_1 if all available inputs were devoted to commodity 1. If returns were constant, the feasible input combinations would be represented by the line segment ZKZ' connecting Z and Z'. But since the production frontier in the diagram is ZBZ', which lies outside line ZKZ' everywhere except at its end points, it follows that this firm is more efficient in producing a *combination* of outputs (as at point B) than in specializing in either output by itself (point Z or Z').

A diagram with output quantities (such as y_1 and y_2) on its axes is called *output space*. We can also examine the production set in terms of the input combinations corresponding to any given set of output quantities. The diagram for this analysis represents input quantities on its axes and is referred to as *input space*. For this purpose, while it is not essential, the argument will perhaps be followed more easily if we return to the single-output case: the production function $f(y, r_1, r_2) \leq 0$.

An *iso-product locus* or a production indifference curve is defined as a locus of input combinations all of which are capable of producing the same output level. It is a contour line on the floor of the three-dimensional diagram representing the "latitudes and longitudes" of points of equal height on the production surface. Thus, in Figure 4a, all points on the curve marked "10" represent input combinations capable of producing the same number of aprons (say 10,000 aprons), as indicated by the 10 next to that indifference curve . These production indifference curves normally possess properties which are the same as (or analogous with) those usually assumed for consumer indifference curves (see Section 7 of Chapter 9):

    1. They have a negative slope;
    2. If one indifference curve, X, lies farther from the origin than another indifference curve, Y, then X normally corresponds to a higher output level than Y;
    3. No two indifference curves intersect;
    4. The curves are convex to the origin.

The rationale of each of these properties is so closely analogous with that involved in the theory of the consumer that its investigation is left entirely as an exercise for the interested reader. It also follows by an argument analogous to that for consumer indifference curves that

    5. The slope of an iso-product locus for inputs r_1 and r_2 equals $-mp_1/mp_2$, where mp_1 is the marginal product of input 1, etc.

Only one new feature arises in production indifference curve analysis. A *consumer* indifference curve can be defined as a line of constant utility. But since the entire idea of utility measurement (in this sense) is under suspicion, no attempt was made to put numbers next to each consumer indifference curve to specify the utility level which it represents. In this single-product case the iso-product curve presents no analogous problem for the finicky. The output level of a single commodity is a definable concept and we need feel no compunction about labelling the curves 5, 10, 15, etc., as is done in Figure 4a to indicate the production level to which each curve corresponds.

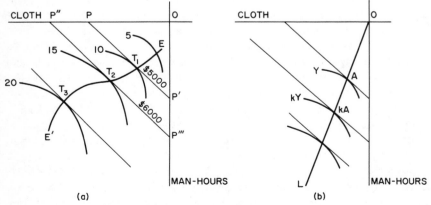

(a)   (b)

Figure 4

8. Price Line and Expansion Path

As previously indicated, the production indifference map (or the production surface) represents only technological information. Such data alone ordinarily do not permit us to determine the firm's optimal decisions, for we lack price information which can tell us what each input gives us *for our money*. This information is supplied to us by the price line (e.g., PP' in Figure 4a). The price line in production analysis is exactly the same as the price or budget line in consumer theory as discussed in Section 9 of Chapter 9—it is not even a matter of analogy. The price line is again a line of constant expenditure—it represents all combinations of labor and cloth which can be bought for a fixed amount of money. Thus, for example, PP' in Figure 4a represents all possible combinations of these two inputs which together cost exactly $5,000.

It will clearly be in the interests of the profit-maximizing (or the revenue-maximizing) firm to obtain as high a level of production for its money as possible. If management is going to spend $5,000, the firm will obtain one of the input combinations represented by the points on line PP'. Management will want to end up on the lowest iso-product curve (the highest output) consistent with this expenditure. This optimal point will be the point of tangency, T_1, between PP' and indifference curve 10. For any other point on PP' must lie on a less lucrative indifference curve. Point T_1, then, represents the optimal input combination for the firm if it should decide to spend $5,000.

But suppose the firm considers also what will happen if it spends some other amount of money, say $6,000. This will involve a parallel shift in the price line, say to $P''P'''$. The optimal input combination (the maximum output for the firm's $6,000 outlay) is given by the point of tangency, T_2. Thus, if we draw in curve EE', the locus of all such points of tangency, we obtain what is called the company's *expansion path*. For the given relative prices of the two inputs (the slope of the price line), the expansion path tells us how the firm's optimal input combination will vary when the size of the company's input budget changes.

The condition that optimal input combinations occur at points of tangency between a price line and a production indifference curve is a geometric representation of the following basic optimality rule (which we will encounter again in this book):

Proposition 1: An optimal combination of any two inputs, I and J, requires that the ratio of their marginal products be equal to the ratio of their prices. Symbolically, we must thus have

$$mp_i/mp_j = p_i/p_j.$$

We have already noted that, by analogy with the argument for consumer indifference curves, the slope of any of the production indifference curves of Figure 4a equals the marginal product of labor over the marginal product of cloth (mp_L/mp_c). Moreover, since the slope of the price line equals the ratio of the two prices (Section 9, Chapter 9), the preceding rule follows at once. Since two tangent curves have the same slope, at a point like T_1 in Figure 4a we must have $mp_L/mp_c = p_L/p_c$.

The rationale of the rule is also readily explained. Rewrite the equation as $mp_L/p_L = mp_c/p_c$. Now, if one added man-hour of labor produces three aprons $(mp_L = 3)$ and costs \$2 $(p_L = 2)$, the ratio $mp_L/p_L = \frac{3}{2} = 1\frac{1}{2}$ tells us that every additional dollar spent on labor yields $1\frac{1}{2}$ aprons. In other words mp_L/p_L is the measure of what the firm gets by putting an additional dollar into labor. Similarly, mp_c/p_c is the corresponding measure of the yield of a dollar spent on cloth. If the two happen to be unequal, say if $mp_c/p_c = 2$, this means that a reallocation of the company budget must be profitable—one dollar taken out of labor outlay and transferred to cloth purchasing will yield a net increase in output of one-half apron. Obviously, then, if mp_c/p_c exceeds mp_L/p_L, the firm must not be buying enough cloth to keep the men appropriately busy—the firm's cloth-labor combination cannot be optimal. Only if the two ratios are equal can the firm be allocating its input expenditures optimally.

The optimal choice of input proportions as just described has its analogue in the choice of relative outputs, which can be examined with the aid of our earlier output-space diagram, Figure 3.

If the prices of y_1 and y_2 are fixed at p_1 and p_2, respectively, the total revenue corresponding to any point y_1, y_2 in the diagram is given by $R = p_1 y_1 + p_2 y_2$. This relationship is represented by a family of parallel straight lines with slope $-p_1/p_2$,

$$ y_2 = -\frac{p_1}{p_2}\, y_1 + \frac{R}{p_2}, $$

the lines such as π_1, π_2, or π_3 in the diagram. Since any possibility locus involves a fixed combination of inputs and hence a fixed expenditure (cost) level for the firm, profit maximization requires the firm to select the highest iso-revenue line on any production frontier. For example, on frontier SS' the highest attainable iso-revenue line is π_1, which is tangent to SS' at point A.

9. Homogeneous and Homothetic Production Functions

This section deals with a very important class of production functions for which the expansion path takes a particularly simple and significant form. This class of production functions, the *homogeneous* functions, is a generalization of the case of constant returns to scale. They are most easily discussed in terms of the single-output case and the most conventional notation for the production functions: $y = g(r_1, \cdots, r_n)$.

We have the

Definition: The function $y = g(r_1, \cdots, r_n)$ is *homogeneous of degree s* in the variables $r_1, \cdots, r_n$ if, when the value of each such variable is multiplied by the same number, k, the value of the function is multiplied by the sth power of k, i.e., if

$$g(kr_1, \cdots, kr_n) = k^s y.$$

In particular, where $s = 1$ we have the case of the *linearly homogeneous function* (*constant returns to scale*), since a proportionate increase in all input values (kr_i) then obviously produces an equiproportionate increase in output, ky.

We note at once that where a production function is homogeneous of degree $s > 1$, increasing returns to scale are present throughout, while if $s < 1$, the function exhibits diminishing returns to scale throughout.

A moment's thought indicates why this is so. For example, if $s = 2$, then an equiproportionate increase in all input quantities by the factor $k > 1$ must increase output by the factor $k^2 > k$. A special case of particular interest is that of a function homogeneous of degree zero ($s = 0$). Here any proportionate increase in $r_1, \cdots, r_n$ produces absolutely no change in y, that is, it "changes" y to $k^0 y = y$. As will be seen in a later chapter, this case is of importance in monetary analysis (rather than production theory) where it is often asserted that a proportionate change in all prices and asset values only represents an inflation in nominal prices but no real change in the price of any commodity and therefore has no effect on the real quantity of any good that is demanded or supplied.

The following three functions, which will be shown to be linearly homogeneous, indicate that such functions need *not* be linear:

$$y_1 = 3r_1 + 2r_2 \qquad y_2 = r_1^7/r_2^6 \qquad y_3 = ar_1^b r_2^{(1-b)}, \qquad (0 < b < 1).$$

In each of these three cases, if we multiply r_1 and r_2 by the same constant, k, the corresponding y will also be multiplied by k. This is obvious in the first (linear) example. In the second example we note that we have, upon multiplication of r_1 and r_2 by k,

$$(kr_1)^7/(kr_2)^6 = k^7 r_1^7/k^6 r_1^6 = kr_1^7/r_2^6 = ky.$$

This example should enable the reader to write out immediately homogeneous functions of any desired degree. For example, a homogeneous function of third degree is, by the same argument, $y = r_1^7/r_2^4$. The third of our examples of a linearly homogeneous function is the widely used Cobb-Douglas function to which we will return presently. The reader should verify its linear homogeneity by substituting kr_1 and kr_2 for r_1 and r_2, respectively.

We have just seen that linearly homogeneous functions are not all linear. The converse is also true: Not all linear functions are linearly homogeneous. For example, in the function $y = 3r_1 + 2r_2 + 6$ if we double r_1 and r_2 we will clearly not double y. Indeed, we see that *any linear function which contains a constant term is not homogeneous*.

Before closing our definitional discussion we present one last concept which represents a generalization of the concept of homogeneity:

A *homothetic function* is any strictly monotonically increasing function of any homogeneous function. That is, if $y = g(r_1, \cdots, r_n)$ is a homogeneous function, then

$$z = F(y) = F[g(r_1, \cdots, r_n)] \text{ is homothetic if } dF/dy > 0.$$

Intuitively, a homothetic production function is related to a homogeneous one much as an ordinal utility function is related to a (neoclassical) cardinal utility function. It will be recalled that given any set of indifference curves we can construct an ordinal utility function consistent with it by assigning an arbitrary "utility" number to each indifference number *provided that this number increases as we move to preferred indifference curves*. That is, we can transform any such ordinal utility numbers into another legitimate set of utility numbers provided that preferred consumption bundles are always assigned higher numbers (that is, provided such a transformation is *monotonic*). In the same way, a homothetic function can be obtained from a homogeneous function by replacing the set of numbers y with a set of numbers z such that if for two values of y we have $y^* > y^{**}$, then $z^* = F(y^*) > F(y^{**}) = z^{**}$. That is, the higher of the two values of y will always be associated with a higher value[7] of z.

10. Some Properties of Homogeneous (Homothetic) Functions

Homogeneous functions play an important role in various areas of economic analysis. We have already seen in Chapter 5 the crucial role of

---

[7] An example of a homothetic function is $z = 3r_1 + 2r_2 + 6$, which is clearly not homogeneous (multiplying r_1 and r_2 by k does not multiply z by a constant power of k). However, it is a monotone transform of the linearly homogeneous function $y = 3r_1 + 2r_2$,

linear homogeneity in the linear programming model of production, and this role will be emphasized further in the next chapter. A similar place is occupied by the concept in input-output theory. It is important in the theory of distribution, as we will see. Homogeneity of degree zero has a significant place in monetary analysis, and so on.

The widespread utilization of this sort of relationship is attributable to its mathematical properties. In this section several of those properties will be described and derived, though their importance will in some cases only be hinted at and left for more detailed discussion at appropriate points in the book.

We have

Proposition 2: Euler's theorem. If a production function $y = g(r_1, \cdots, r_n)$ is homogeneous of degree s, then

$$\frac{\partial g}{\partial r_1} r_1 + \cdots + \frac{\partial g}{\partial r_n} r_n = sy,$$

That is, the partial derivatives of the function, each multiplied by the corresponding variable, add up to s times the value of the function.[8]

Euler's theorem has been used to argue that if the production function is linearly homogeneous (so that $s = 1$) and if each input is paid a price equal to its marginal product [i.e., the unit price, p_i, of resource i is $p\partial g/\partial r_i$ and its total payment is $p_i r_i = p(\partial g/\partial r_i) r_i$], then the sum of the payments to all inputs together will exactly equal the value of total output, py.

---

which can be expressed as $z = y + 6$. An illustrative nonhomothetic function is $y = 3r_1^2 + 2r_2^3$. The reader can verify by the methods of Section 16 that its expansion path will satisfy $r_1/r_2^2 = p_1/p_2 = $ constant, which violates the linearity property of the expansion path of a homothetic function (Proposition 7).

[8] *Proof:* By definition, since the function is homogeneous of degree s,

$$k^s y = g(kr_1, \cdots, kr_n).$$

Taking the total derivative of both sides with respect to k we have by the formula for total differentiation

$$sk^{s-1}y = \frac{\partial g}{\partial kr_1}\frac{dkr_1}{dk} + \cdots + \frac{\partial g}{\partial kr_n}\frac{dkr_n}{dk} = \frac{\partial g}{\partial kr_1}r_1 + \cdots + \frac{\partial g}{\partial kr_n}r_n.$$

This result must hold for *any* value of k. In particular, it must be valid for $k = 1$. But for that value of k the preceding equation becomes

$$sy = \frac{\partial g}{\partial r_1}r_1 + \cdots + \frac{\partial g}{\partial r_n}r_n,$$

which is Euler's theorem.

Next we have

Proposition 3: If a production function is homogeneous of any degree s, the marginal product of each and every one of its inputs will be homogeneous of one lower degree, $s - 1$. That is, if $y = f(r_1, \cdots, r_n)$ is homogeneous of degree s, then any of its partial derivatives, $\partial g/\partial r_i$, will itself be a function of $r_1, \cdots, r_n$ that is homogeneous of degree $s - 1$.[9]

Proposition 4: A homogeneous function of $n + 1$ variables $y, r_1, \cdots, r_n$ can be rewritten as a function of the n variables $y/r_n^s, r_1/r_n, \cdots, r_{n-1}/r_n$.

Proof: In the definition of a homogeneous function, take $k = 1/r_n$ and multiply every variable by this value of k. That immediately yields our desired result:

$$y/r_n^s = g(r_1/r_n, \cdots, r_{n-1}/r_n, 1).$$

Thus, the linearly homogeneous production function $y = f(K, L)$ of the quantities of capital, K, and labor, L, is often written with the output-labor ratio a function of the capital-labor ratio, i.e., $y/L = f(K/L, 1) = F(K/L)$.

Proposition 5: Given two functions of the same variables the first of which is homogeneous of degree s and the second homogeneous of degree t, then a third function obtained by dividing the first function by the second will be homogeneous of degree $s - t$.

Corollary: In particular, if $s = t$, the function obtained by this division process will be homogeneous of degree zero, i.e., multiplication of each variable by k will leave the value of the new function totally unaffected.

The proof of Proposition 5 and its corollary is trivial, for if we write $F^1(r_1, \cdots, r_n)$ for the first of these functions, $F^2(\cdot)$ for the second, and $F^3(\cdot)$ for the ratio of the first to the second, we obtain

---

[9] *Proof:* We are given $k^s y = g(kr_1, \cdots, kr_n)$ or $k^s g(r_1, \cdots, r_n) = g(kr_1, \cdots, kr_n)$. Thus, differentiating with respect to r_1 we obtain

$$k^s \frac{\partial g(r_1, \cdots, r_n)}{\partial r_1} = \frac{\partial g(kr_1, \cdots, kr_n)}{\partial kr_1} \frac{dkr_1}{dr_1} = \frac{\partial g(kr_1, \cdots, kr_n)}{\partial kr_1} k.$$

Thus dividing through by k we obtain our result:

$$k^{s-1} \frac{\partial g(r_1, \cdots, r_n)}{\partial r_1} = \frac{\partial g(kr_1, \cdots, kr_n)}{\partial kr_1}.$$

That is, if we replace every variable r_i in $\partial g/\partial r_1$ by kr_i, then that derivative is multiplied by k^{s-1}. Thus, $\partial g/\partial r_1$ is homogeneous of degree $s - 1$. Obviously, the same result holds for the derivative with respect to any other input, r_i.

$$F^3(kr_1, \cdots, kr_n) = \frac{F^1(kr_1, \cdots, kr_n)}{F^2(kr_1, \cdots, kr_n)} = \frac{k^s F^1(r_1, \cdots, r_n)}{k^t F^2(r_1, \cdots, r_n)}$$

$$= k^{s-t} F^3(r_1, \cdots, r_n).$$

We can now prove

Proposition 6: If the production function is homogeneous of any degree s, then along any ray (a straight line through the origin) the slopes of all the iso-product curves will be identical.

Proof: As has already been noted, for reasons completely analogous to the case of consumer indifference curves, the absolute slope of an iso-product curve between two inputs, 1 and 2, is the ratio of their marginal products, $(\partial g/\partial r_1)/(\partial g/\partial r_2)$. But by Proposition 2, since $g(r_1, r_2)$ is homogeneous of degree s, $\partial g/\partial r_1$ and $\partial g/\partial r_2$ will both be homogeneous of *the same* degree $(s - 1)$. Hence, by the corollary to Proposition 5 their ratio, mr_1/mr_2, will be homogeneous of degree zero. But, along a ray, as we increase the quantity of one input, we increase the other proportionately, i.e., if we increase r_1 to kr_1, we simultaneously increase r_2 to kr_2. Thus, any such move along a ray must leave unchanged the slope of the iso-product locus, $(\partial g/\partial r_1)/(\partial g/\partial r_2)$, since the equation of that slope is homogeneous of degree zero.[10]

Finally, we come to the important

Proposition 7: For any homogeneous (or homothetic) production function in two-input variables, any expansion path will be a ray.

Suppose (Figure 4b) point A on OL is a point of tangency between a price line and indifference curve Y. Then any other point, kA, on line OL must also be such a point of tangency, because all price lines are parallel (if input prices do not change) and the slope of indifference curve kY at kA is the same as that of curve Y at point A, as was just shown. Thus, if any point on line OL lies on the expansion path, so will any other point on this line.

---

[10] It is easy to show that the same result holds for a homothetic production function $y = F[g(r_1, r_2)]$. For in this case, by the chain rule of differentiation, the ratio of the marginal products of r_1 and r_2 is

$$\frac{mp_1}{mp_2} = \frac{dF}{dg}\frac{\partial g}{\partial r_1} \Big/ \frac{dF}{dg}\frac{\partial g}{\partial r_2} = \frac{\partial g}{\partial r_1} \Big/ \frac{\partial g}{\partial r_2}.$$

Since the function $g(r_1, r_2)$ must, by definition, be homogeneous, it follows once more by Propositions 2 and 5 that mp_1/mp_2 is homogeneous of degree zero.

Hence, the expansion path of a linear homogeneous production function will always be a straight line. But, as was shown in Section 5, above, all points on such a line involve the same input proportions. We conclude that with constant returns to scale and fixed input prices there will be just one optimal input proportion (say, 8 yards of cloth per man-hour) which does not change no matter what the level of the firm's output.

This result is quite convenient. For the businessman it means that he need only compute one such figure, and as long as input prices do not change he has no further input-proportion decision problems. The theorem can also be useful for economic analysis, as we shall see in our input-output discussion.

PROBLEM

Prove that if the production function $y = g(r_1, r_2)$ is linearly homogeneous and the *average* product of x_1 is increasing, then the *marginal* product of x_2 must be negative.

11. Cobb-Douglas Production Functions

The Cobb-Douglas function is a type of linearly homogeneous production function which has proved particularly useful for empirical work. The general formula for this function is

$$y = ar_1^b r_2^{(1-b)} \qquad \text{where } 0 < b < 1.$$

The property of this function that makes it particularly attractive is

Proposition 8: The Cobb-Douglas production function is linear if rewritten in terms of the logarithms of its variables.

We have by the usual rules for logarithms of powers and products

$$\ln y = \ln a + b \ln r_1 + (1 - b) \ln r_2.$$

That is, if we write $y^* = \ln y$, $a^* = \ln a$, etc., we have the linear function

$$y^* = a^* + br_1^* + (1 - b)r_2^*.$$

This means that if one has a Cobb-Douglas function one can take advantage of the many simplifications in the process of statistical estimation that are possible in the case of a linear relationship.

One may then ask why do we not simply use a linear production function. The answer is that such a purely linear relationship commits us to premises about reality which we do not want to accept. For example, with a linear production function $y = ur_1 + vr_2 + w$, the marginal product of any input, say input 1, is $\partial y/\partial r_1 = u$, which is a constant. That means that (a) the marginal product of input 1 cannot possibly diminish with the quantity r_1 (it must violate the "law" of diminishing returns) and (b) the marginal product of r_1 must be totally unaffected by the available quantity of other inputs. That is, labor must have the same marginal product whether it has available to it a large quantity of equipment, or a small quantity, or none. Obviously, neither of these implications of the linearity assumption for the production function is really palatable.

However, with a Cobb-Douglas function we have

Proposition 9: The marginal product of an input in a Cobb-Douglas production function decreases when the quantity of that input rises (diminishing marginal returns) and increases when the available quantities of the other inputs rise.[11]

12. Elasticity of Substitution: Response to Relative Input Prices

So far we have taken input prices to be fixed. This is, for example, a crucial premise in the calculation of the expansion path. When this assumption is dropped, it is helpful to have a measure of the responsiveness of the optimal proportions among the firm's inputs to changes in their relative prices. The measure used for this purpose is the *elasticity of substitution*. If a moderate rise in wages relative to the cost of capital leads to a substantial replacement of labor by machinery, we say the elasticity of substitution is large. On the other hand, if in that case there is little change in the capital-labor ratio, the elasticity of substitution is small. Specifically, we have the

Definition: The elasticity of substitution for inputs 1 and 2 is the ratio of the percentage change in their relative quantity, r_1/r_2, to the associated change in their relative price, p_1/p_2. That is, it is given by

$$\sigma = \frac{100d(r_1/r_2)}{r_1/r_2} \bigg/ \frac{100d(p_1/p_2)}{p_1/p_2} = \frac{d(r_1/r_2)}{d(p_1/p_2)} \cdot \frac{p_1/p_2}{r_1/r_2} \; .$$

---

[11] *Proof:* The first and second partial derivatives of the Cobb-Douglas function with respect to r_1 are (by direct differentiation)

$$mp_1 = \partial y/\partial r_1 = bar_1^{b-1}r_2^{1-b} \qquad \text{(which increases with } r_2)$$

and

$$\frac{\partial mp_1}{\partial r_1} = \partial^2 y/\partial r_1^2 = (b-1)bar_1^{b-2}r_2^{1-b} < 0, \qquad \text{since } b < 1.$$

It is easy to see that the elasticity of substitution of two inputs in a production function varies inversely with the curvature of their iso-product curves—the greater their curvature, the smaller the elasticity of substitution. In Figures 5a and 5b we see two pairs of price lines, one pair steep and one flat. One represents a comparatively low price ratio p_1/p_2 for the two inputs and the other a relatively high price ratio.

In Figure 5a, where they are both tangent to a mildly curved iso-product curve, their tangency points T and T' are far apart. That is, the given change in relative prices corresponds to a substantial change in input proportion, r_2/r_1. Thus, in that case, elasticity of substitution is high. The reverse is clearly true in Figure 5b.

The reason for the association between low curvature and high elasticity of substitution is not difficult to see. With a given change in the slope of the price line (a given change in p_1/p_2) the flatter the iso-product curve, the farther along it one must move to find the new point of tangency, i.e., the farther one must move to find the point on the iso-product curve with a slope equal to that of the new price line.

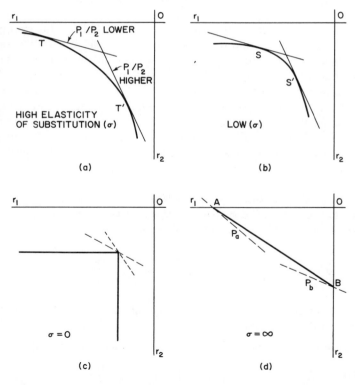

Figure 5

Figure 5c with its right-angled iso-product locus represents the extreme case in which elasticity of substitution is zero. A change in the slope of the (broken) price lines produces absolutely no change in input proportions. On the other hand, Figure 5d represents the opposite extreme—infinite elasticity of substitution. A small change in relative prices from the price line p_a to p_b causes a drastic switch from exclusive use of input 1 (point A) to exclusive use of input 2.

There is, of course, a full range of intermediate cases in which elasticity of substitution is constant throughout but is neither zero nor infinite. For example, a simple but tedious calculation can be invoked to show that the Cobb-Douglas production function yields a unit elasticity of substitution throughout. This and other production functions with constant elasticity of substitution (CES) have proved extremely useful for econometric estimation of production relationships.[1][2]

13. Derivation of Cost Curves[13]

From the firm's expansion path it is fairly easy to find the firm's *total* and *average cost curves*. The total cost curve is, as we know, defined as a curve which shows how total company outlays vary with its level of production, and the average (per unit) cost curve is defined analogously.

It will be recalled that price line PP' in Figure 4a was taken to represent an outlay of $5,000. Thus, point of tangency T_1 on this price line tells us that the maximum output obtainable for that outlay is 10,000 aprons. This information is represented by point C_1 in Figure 6. Similarly, point C_2 in Figure 6 tells us that it will cost $6,000 to produce 15,000 aprons, which is the information given by point T_2 in Figure 4a, and so on. The curve OC in Figure 6, which is the locus of all points like C_1 and C_2, is the company's total cost curve.

It is also possible to find the firm's average cost curve directly with the aid of Figure 4a. For example, point T_1 tells us that the unit cost of producing 10,000 aprons is $5,000/10,000 = 50 cents. We can find the same information for every other point on the expansion path, EE', and by recording these data on another graph (not shown) we obtain the firm's average cost curve.

Alternatively, we can use the methods of Chapter 3 to obtain the firm's average and marginal costs from its total cost curve in Figure 6.

---

[12] The classic discussion of this subject is the article by Arrow, Chenery, Minhas, and Solow, *op. cit.*

[13] For a more systematic discussion of the deeper relationships between cost curves and production functions, see Chapter 14, Sections 11–15. An illustration of the mathematical derivation of a cost function from a production function is provided in Section 16 of this chapter.

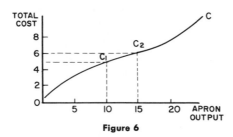

Figure 6

14. Long Run and Short Run: Definitions

Before we go any further, it is necessary to define a bit of economists' jargon: the terms *long run* and *short run*. These do *not* refer to any fixed units of calendar time—we cannot say in advance and without reference to a specific problem that a two-month period lies in the short run and that a five-year period extends into the long run.

Rather, these concepts are defined flexibly in terms of the period over which the company's commitments extend. The very long run is a period so long that all of the firm's present contracts will have run out, its present plant and equipment will have been worn out or rendered obsolete and will therefore need replacement, etc. In other words, the long run is a period of sufficient duration for the company to become completely free in its decisions from its present policies, possessions, and commitments. For example, if the company finds that the demand for its product has increased substantially, it may be ten years before it can afford to redesign its plant and equipment completely in accord with the requirements of this development. Obviously, even that ten-year figure is flexible. The larger the shift in demand, the sooner a reconstruction of the plant will be profitable, so that the length of time that can appropriately be considered to constitute the long run is itself an economic variable.

The other extreme case, the very short run, is that where the firm has a minimum of free choice. In the very short run a firm will not even be able to increase its output in response to increased consumer demand. To do this it must acquire more raw materials, perhaps it must arrange for some of its labor force to work overtime, and it may also have to hire more labor. Even after all of this is arranged, it will take time for the increased production flow to begin rolling off the assembly line. In the very short run, then, the firm can only satisfy increased demands out of inventory.

In between these extreme cases, the very short and the very long run, there are all sorts of intermediate time periods in which the firm can make partial adjustments to any changes in the situation. But in any such in-between period it will find its options circumscribed to some extent by previous commitments.

15. Long-Run and Short-Run Average Costs

These concepts enable us to examine somewhat further the nature of the data which lie behind the firm's cost relationships.

Imagine a firm which is considering renting one of four factories where the owners of these factories all insist on, say, two-year leases. Call these four factories, arranged in increasing order of size, S, T, V, and W. If our firm decides to lease factory S, its average cost curve for the next two years will (other things remaining unchanged) then be given, say, by curve SS' in Figure 7a. The other U-shaped curves in Figure 7a can be interpreted similarly. We see that if, for example, the firm expects to produce and sell output OV_m it will pay its management to rent factory V, the third largest of the available factories. For although factories T and W are also both capable of producing that output, it can be done in plant V at lower unit cost than in either of the other facilities.

Suppose that the firm decides to lease plant T. TT' in Figure 7 will then be its average cost curve for the two-year lease period—its short-run average cost curve. Once it has committed itself to T, if the firm ends up producing output OV_m, it will for the next two years have no choice but to incur average cost V_mK. In other words, the U-shaped curves in the diagram are the alternative *short-run cost curves* available to the firm.

The corresponding long-run cost curve is also apparent from the diagram. For before the firm has made its commitment it will be free to choose the plant size most appropriate for its anticipated output—it will be able to lease that plant which produces its output at the lowest possible cost. Thus with output OS_m it will want to use plant T and produce at unit cost S_mL; with output OV_m it will want to use plant V so that its unit costs will be V_mJ; etc. In sum, the firm's long-run average cost curve will be the heavy scalloped curve $SALBJCW'$. This curve consists of the lowest segments of all of the short-run average cost curves.

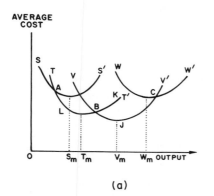

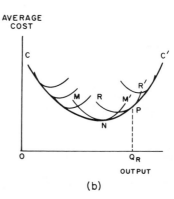

(a)   (b)

Figure 7

Sometimes the firm has an unlimited number of alternatives in picking its plant capacity. This would be the case if it were having an architect draw up plans for a new factory (rather than looking for an existing property to rent). In such a situation there would be an infinity of possible short-run cost curves, some of which are represented in Figure 7b. Here it is to be noted that the scallops can be smoothed out of the long-run cost curve, CNC'. The smooth long-run curve consists, as before, of the "bottom" of the set of the short-run curves. For obvious reasons it is called the *envelope* of the short-run curves.

One interesting theorem follows from these drawings: It will not always pay to use a plant at an output level where it operates at minimum unit costs! For example, in Figure 7a it will pay to rent plant S if it is expected that very low outputs will be called for. But suppose the firm anticipates turning out output OS_m at which plant S is at its "most efficient" (its point of minimum unit costs). At this output, plant T is even more efficient so that it will pay to use T rather than S to produce OS_m. In other words, if it pays to rent plant S, it will only be for the production of outputs well below the technical "capacity" of that plant! A somewhat similar conclusion holds for plant W, as an examination of the cost situation at output OW_m will readily show.

Indeed, in the smooth long-run average-cost-curve case in Figure 7b there will be almost no plant which should be used at its point of minimum cost. For example, consider plant R, whose short-run cost curve touches the long-run curve only at point P (output OQ_R). This, then, is the only output at which it pays to use plant R. But at P curve RR' is tangent to the long-run average cost curve, which happens to have a positive slope at that point. Therefore, at P, curve RR' must also have a positive slope, i.e., P cannot possibly be the minimum point of short-run average curve RR'.

The only exception is plant M, whose short-run cost curve MM' touches the long-run curve at its minimum point N, for there both these curves will be level and so they will both be at their minimum points.

16. Some Elementary Mathematics of Production Theory[14]

Proposition 1 of Section 8 on the optimal combinations of inputs for the firm is easily derived with the aid of the Lagrange multiplier methods of Chapter 4, Section 8. Let the firm's production function be represented by

$$y = g(r_1, r_2, \cdots, r_n),$$

---

[14] We will return to the use of these methods in Chapter 14 in the discussion of duality theory in production.

where r_1 is the quantity of input 1 (say labor) used by the firm, r_2 is the quantity of input 2 (say leather), etc. Given any output level, y^*, the firm will try to produce y^* as cheaply as it can. This means that it is trying to minimize its expenditure, m, on the inputs used to produce y^*, where this expenditure is given by

$$m = p_1 r_1 + p_2 r_2 + \cdots + p_n r_n.$$

Here p_1 is the price of input 1, etc. The firm is trying to minimize m subject to the constraint on its operations given by the production function. To obtain the Lagrangian expression for this constrained minimization problem, we rewrite the constraint into the standard form

$$y^* - g(r_1, r_2, \cdots, r_n) = 0$$

and multiply it by the artificial variable, λ. Adding this to the expression for m, which we are trying to minimize, we have our Lagrangian expression

$$m_\lambda = p_1 r_1 + p_2 r_2 + \cdots + p_n r_n + \lambda[y^* - g(r_1, r_2, \cdots, r_n)].$$

It is minimized by setting each of its partial derivatives equal to zero, in turn, to obtain

$$\frac{\partial m_\lambda}{\partial r_1} = p_1 - \lambda \frac{\partial g}{\partial r_1} = 0$$

$$\cdots \cdots \cdots \cdots \cdots$$

$$\frac{\partial m_\lambda}{\partial r_n} = p_n - \lambda \frac{\partial g}{\partial r_n} = 0$$

$$\frac{\partial m_\lambda}{\partial \lambda} = y^* - g(r_1, r_2, \cdots, r_n) = 0.$$

This is a system of $n + 1$ simultaneous equations which can presumably be solved for the optimal values of our n input variables, $r_1, r_2, \cdots, r_n$, as well as the value of the Lagrangian variable, λ.

In particular, to derive Proposition 1 we rewrite the first two of these partial derivative equations as

$$p_1 = -\lambda \frac{\partial g}{\partial r_1} \quad \text{and} \quad p_2 = -\lambda \frac{\partial g}{\partial r_2},$$

and dividing one equation by the other, we obtain, cancelling out the $-\lambda$'s,

$$\frac{p_1}{p_2} = \frac{\partial g/\partial r_1}{\partial g/\partial r_2},$$

which, noting that $\partial g/\partial r_1$ is the marginal product of r_1, etc., gives us our result in Section 8. The reader should also convince himself that the first n of the partial derivative equations $\partial m_\lambda/\partial r_i = 0$ determines the firm's expansion path.

Example 1: Expansion Path

Find the firm's expansion path expressed in terms of its total expenditure (in dollars) on its inputs, labor, L, and capital, K, given the production function

$$y = 2 \log L + 4 \log K$$

and input prices P_L and P_K.

The object is to maximize output y, subject to the expenditure constraint

$$P_L L + P_K K = M.$$

This yields the Lagrangian expression

$$y_\lambda = 2 \log L + 4 \log K + \lambda(M - P_L L - P_K K).$$

Taking partial derivatives we obtain among our first-order conditions

$$\frac{\partial y_\lambda}{\partial L} = \frac{2}{L} - \lambda P_L = 0, \qquad \text{i.e.,} \quad \frac{2}{L} = \lambda P_L$$

$$\frac{\partial y_\lambda}{\partial K} = \frac{4}{K} - \lambda P_K = 0, \qquad \text{i.e.,} \quad \frac{4}{K} = \lambda P_K.$$

Dividing the first equation through by the second we obtain

$$K/2L = P_L/P_K.$$

Thus, with P_L and P_K given, the right-hand side is a constant, call it a, and the equation becomes $K = 2aL$, which is a straight-line expansion path through the origin.

Example 2: Supply Function

Using the production function and input prices of the preceding problem, determine the supply function of the product whose price is taken to be an unspecified constant, P, and where $P_L = 4$, $P_K = 12$.

The object of the firm is to maximize its profits

$$\Pi = Py - 4L - 12K$$

subject to the constraint imposed by the company's production function as given in Example 1. This yields the Lagrangian expression

$$\Pi_\lambda = Py - 4L - 12K + \lambda(y - 2 \log L - 4 \log K),$$

whose partial derivatives at its maximum are

$$\frac{\partial \Pi_\lambda}{\partial y} = P + \lambda = 0$$

$$\frac{\partial \Pi_\lambda}{\partial L} = -4 - \frac{2\lambda}{L} = 0$$

$$\frac{\partial \Pi_\lambda}{\partial K} = -12 - \frac{4\lambda}{K} = 0$$

$$\frac{\partial \Pi_\lambda}{\partial \lambda} = y - 2 \log L - 4 \log K = 0.$$

These equations clearly have the solution

$$\lambda = -P, \qquad L = \frac{P}{2}, \qquad K = \frac{P}{3}, \qquad y = 2 \log \frac{P}{2} + 4 \log \frac{P}{3},$$

which constitute our supply function as well as derived demand functions for the two inputs.

Example 3: Cost Function

Find the expression giving total cost as a function of output y when the production function is $y = L^2 + K^2$.

We proceed by solving for K and L as functions of y and substituting the result into $M = P_L L + P_K K$. To find the optimal K and L our Lagrangian this time is

$$y_\lambda = L^2 + K^2 + \lambda(M - P_L L - P_K K),$$

which gives us among the first-order conditions

$$2L = \lambda P_L \qquad 2K = \lambda P_K$$

or

$$L/K = P_L/P_K.$$

That is,

$$L = (P_L/P_K)K.$$

Substituting this into the production function we have

$$y = (P_L/P_K)^2 K^2 + K^2 = [(P_L/P_K)^2 + 1]K^2.$$

Writing $a = (P_L/P_K)^2 + 1$ we have

$$K = \sqrt{y/a}$$

and

$$L = (P_L/P_K)\sqrt{y/a}.$$

Thus, the cost function is

$$C = P_L L + P_K K$$
$$= (P_L^2/P_K)\sqrt{y/a} + P_K\sqrt{y/a}.$$

PROBLEMS

Find (a) the expansion path and (b) supply and derived demand function relationships for the following production functions and input prices:

1. $y = 8L^{\frac{1}{2}} + 20K^{\frac{1}{2}}$, $P_L = 1$, $P_K = 5$.
2. $y = -4K^2 + 2KL - 2L^2 + 10K + 3L$, $P_L = 1$, $P_K = 2$.
3. Prove that the following functions are linearly homogeneous:
   (a) $y = 5x_1 + 23.5x_2$
   (b) $y = 7x_1^5/x_2^4 + 3x_2^2/x_1$
   (c) $y = 6x_1^{1/4}x_2^{3/4}$.
4. Show that $y = 3x_1 + 4x_2 + 6$ is not linearly homogeneous.

REFERENCES

American Economic Association, *Readings in Price Theory*, in George J. Stigler and Kenneth E. Boulding (eds.), Richard D. Irwin, Inc., Homewood, Ill., 1952, Articles 5–13 (especially Article 10, "Cost Curves and Supply Curves," by Jacob Viner, also reprinted in R. V. Clemence, *Readings in Economic Analysis*, Addison-Wesley Publishing Co., Inc., Cambridge, Mass., 1950, and in Jacob Viner, *The Long View and the Short*, The Free Press of Glencoe, New York, 1958.

Carlson, Sune, *A Study on the Pure Theory of Production*, P. S. King, London, 1939.

Cassels, John M., "On the Law of Variable Proportions," *Explorations in Economics*, McGraw-Hill Book Company, New York, 1936, reprinted in American Economic Association, *Readings in the Theory of Income Distribution*, The Blakiston Company, New York, 1946.

Henderson, James M., and Richard E. Quandt, *Microeconomic Theory*, 2nd edition, McGraw-Hill Book Company, New York, 1971, Chapter 3.

Hirshleifer, Jack, "The Firm's Cost Function: A Successful Reconstruction?" *Journal of Business*, Vol. 35, July 1962.

Malinvaud, Edmond, *Lectures on Microeconomic Theory*, North-Holland Publishing Company, Amsterdam, 1972, Chapter 3 (rather difficult).

Turvey, Ralph, "Marginal Cost," *Economic Journal*, vol. 79, June 1969.

Linear Programming

and

the Theory of Production

Having summarized the standard neoclassical production analysis of economic theory we shall now reexamine the entire subject, this time making use of our linear programming equipment. It will be recalled that much of our description of linear programming theory in Chapter 5 employed as its main illustration the product-line determination problem in which the object is to find the optimal combination of commodities to be produced by the firm, the quantity of each such item which should be turned out, and the processes by which these goods should be produced. It is this problem which forms the basis of the linear programming analysis of production. The model will therefore constitute the central focus of this chapter.

1. Why a Programming Reexamination of Production Theory?

It was stated in our previous discussion that a linear programming formulation of the production problem involves the implicit assumption that the production function is linear and homogeneous. Having gone into the meaning and implications of this sort of production relationship, it will be profitable to look once more at the linear programming theory of production.

There are other, more fundamental reasons why it is desirable to look at the production decision problem from the programming point of view.

1. In at least one sense, the programming analysis digs deeper than does the neoclassical theory. As has already been stated, the neoclassical theory assumes that the optimal technical production processes have somehow already been determined before the economic theorist gets to work on the problem. This premise is an integral part of the very concept of the production function, for, by definition, that function tells us what is the *largest* possible output which can be obtained for every input combination. That is, it assumes that optimal processes are employed to make those inputs go as far as possible. As we shall see in this chapter, the choice of an optimal combination of production processes, i.e., of an optimal technological arrangement, is no trivial task. It is, however, one which can be handled by the methods of mathematical programming.

2. A second reason it is desirable to reexamine production decision-making from a programming standpoint is that the orientation of the programmer and that of the businessman have a great deal in common. In industry one never hears of concepts such as the production function or the marginal product, even though it is true that these ideas must lie somewhere behind much of management's thinking. Programming theory, though it is, of course, rather abstract and still quite removed from everyday managerial parlance, brings us much closer to the language and the viewpoint of the business world.

However, it will turn out that the two types of approach are really not so different after all and that the analyst whose training is primarily in standard economic theory will find in the programming model a great deal that is familiar to him.

It should be remarked, before proceeding, that in our previous discussion of the linear programming analysis of production we focused our attention on the choice of *product line*—i.e., which items should be turned out and in what quantities. In the present chapter, partly for variety, we concentrate on the choice of *process* for manufacturing these items. But the analysis is really perfectly general and covers both problems. If we interpret the basic variable Q_i as the quantity of commodity i to be produced, we have a product-line analysis. If we interpret Q_j as the quantity of our (single) commodity to be produced with the aid of process number j, our analysis will tell us how much of each process to employ in our technological arrangements. Finally, with a slight change of notation we can use as our basic variables the double-subscripted symbols Q_{ij} to represent the quantity of product i to be produced with the aid of process j. In that case, the same analysis determines both the optimal set of outputs and the optimal production process combination at one swoop.

2. An Alternative Linear Programming Diagram

In our geometric representation of linear programming we have so far employed exclusively one type of diagram. From our present point of view it can be characterized by the fact that its axes were used to measure *output* quantities rather than *input* quantities. More generally, we might say that it concentrated on ends rather than means. In those diagrams any point represents a combination of outputs (or processes) which is a potential solution to the problem. Inputs only made their appearance in the form of the constraint lines, which show us the extent to which the limited availability of the inputs restricts the magnitude of the outputs.

Partly for easier comparison with the diagrams of standard production theory, it is now appropriate to translate the linear programming problem into a different diagram, one in which input quantities are measured along the axes and outputs are indicated with the aid of production indifference curves. In these new diagrams, then, the input requirements become the focus of the representation.[1]

3. Illustrative Example

Since the axes in our diagram will represent input quantities, to avail ourselves of the simplicity of a two-dimensional diagram we will have to take as our illustrative example a two-constraint (two-scarce-input) linear program. We will employ the following case as our illustrative example throughout most of this chapter:

A leather-processing company is engaged, among other operations, in the dyeing of white suede leather. It is limited in its output by the capacity of its dyeing vats and the amount of skilled labor it has available for supervision of its production process. The firm is considering four dyeing processes, or, rather, four variants of its basic procedure. Process 1 involves inspection for defects of a sample from each batch before it is put into the dyeing vats. Process 2 involves inspection of every individual hide. Process 3 also calls for examination of a sample as in process 1, but a considerably smaller proportion of the hides is inspected. Finally, process 4

---

[1] The reader will readily see why the diagrams which are about to be employed are sometimes described by saying that they are represented in *requirements space*, while our previous linear programming diagrams are said to employ *solution space*. It should also be clear that a requirements space representation is possible for any other linear programming problem, such as the diet problem, the transportation problem, etc., and need not be associated exclusively with production analysis as it is in this chapter. The "solution and requirements space" terminology was invented by Charnes and Cooper.

avoids the difficult preinspection process altogether. All hides are dyed and then quickly examined to see if the dye has "taken" satisfactorily.[2]

Let Q_1 be the quantity of dyed leather to be turned out by means of process 1, Q_2 be the amount produced by the second process, 2, etc. Then suppose we have enough data to specify our programming problem as follows:

$$\text{maximize profits} = 0.9Q_1 + 0.75Q_2 + 1.0Q_3 + 1.1Q_4$$

subject to the constraints

$$2Q_1 + 1.5Q_2 + 3.5Q_3 + 7Q_4 \leq 4{,}000$$

$$0.4Q_1 + 0.45Q_2 + 0.35Q_3 + 0.3Q_4 \leq 600$$

and the nonnegativity requirements

$$Q_1 \geq 0, \qquad Q_2 \geq 0, \qquad Q_3 \geq 0, \qquad Q_4 \geq 0.$$

Here 4,000 (gallon-hours per week) is the available vat capacity and 600 (man-hours per week) is the amount of skilled labor the company can use for the production of this dye. Our two limited inputs are thus vat capacity and labor. The first coefficient, 0.9 (dollars) in our profit function, represents the return per square foot of leather treated by means of process number 1, and a similar interpretation holds for the other coefficients in the objective (profit) function. The first number, 2, in our upper constraint indicates the number of gallon-hours of vat capacity which will be taken up by a hide treated by process 1, etc.

4. The Feasible Region

We can now proceed to our new diagrammatic representation. The depiction of the feasible region is completely trivial. It is shown in Figure 1, where, by convention, inputs are shown as negative quantities below and to the left of the origin. Here there is constructed a rectangle $OABC$ bounded by segments OA and OC of the two axes, the vertical line AB below the point which represents 600 labor hours and the horizontal line CB to the left of the point which represents 4,000 gallons of vat capacity. Since a maximum of 600 hours of labor time and 4,000 gallon-hours of vat space are available, only this shaded rectangular region represents feasible input combinations. Thus, for example, point S outside the shaded region represents the use of 4,000 gallons of vat space and 800 labor-hours. Since that much labor time

---

[2] Clearly, it makes no real difference to the analysis that these processes are all described as variants of the same procedure. Process 4, for example, might equally well be a totally different procedure which involves the use of fancier labor-saving equipment, with no change in the discussion of the remainder of the chapter.

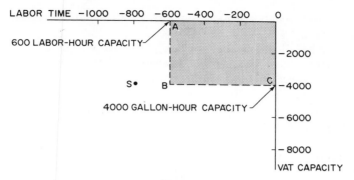

Figure 1

of the required skill is not available to the company, point S is simply not feasible.

5. Representation of a Process

Next we turn to the geometric representation of a production process. But first we must take care of a matter of definition. For our purposes, a production process is *required* to involve fixed input proportions. For example, in our illustrative model, process number 1 involves the use of 2 gallon-hours of vat capacity and 0.4 hours of labor time per square foot of output. This means that 10 square feet of leather will require 20 gallon-hours and 4 labor-hours, 100 square feet involve the use of 200 vat gallon-hours and 40 labor-hours, etc. In other words, no matter how large the output produced with the aid of process 1, it will employ $2/0.4 = 5$ units of vat time per unit of labor time. This constant ratio of input quantities is, in fact, a property which we use to help define a production process. Thus, given some two processes, A and B, if procedure A involves 6 hours of vat time per unit of labor time, while procedure B involves 4 hours of

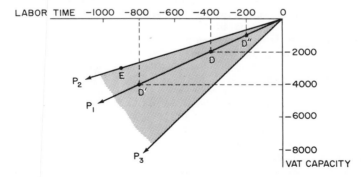

Figure 2

vat time per unit of labor time, A and B are by definition taken to be different processes.[3]

With the aid of this definition we can now readily represent a process diagrammatically. Since our diagram is constructed to show only inputs, a process must be represented in terms of its input requirements. But any production process requires inputs in fixed proportions, as we just stated. And, as was shown in Section 5 of the previous chapter, *the locus of all points involving unchanging input proportions is always a straight line through the origin.* In Figure 2 the line OP_1 represents process 1. Specifically, we see that point D on this line represents the use of 400 hours of labor time and 2,000 vat gallon-hours, so that this point involves the correct input proportions for process 1: two hours of vat capacity for 0.4 hours of labor, and the same is true of any other point on line OP_1. Moreover, a moment of thought indicates that point D must correspond to the production of 1,000 square feet of leather per week (since process 1 requires 0.4 labor hours and 2 vat hours to make 1 foot). Similarly, point D' represents the production of 2,000 square feet of leather. Thus, because it includes all points representing the use of 5 gallon-hours of vat time for every labor hour,[4] every possible output employing process 1 is specified by some point on line OP_1. And, conversely, every point on OP_1 represents an output which can be produced by means of process 1 if sufficient quantities of resources are available. Incidentally, it should be indicated at this point that a "line" such as OP_1, which starts at some definite point, O, but then goes off into space (not stopping at point P_1), is properly called a *ray* not a *line.* This terminology is used in most of the programming literature and it will also be employed here.

---

[3] The converse is, however, not part of our definition. That is, even if some procedure, C, also involves six hours of vat time per hour of labor time, A and C need not be taken to be the same process. An obvious reason is the possibility that A may be vastly more efficient and profitable than is C. For example, procedure A may involve the use of six hours of vat time and one hour of labor time per square foot of leather, while B may require twelve hours of vat time and two hours of labor time for the same purpose. Both methods involve the same vat-labor time ratios, but B is clearly twice as costly as A in the use of these resources. In any event, it would do violence to common sense to exclude by definition the possibility that two different processes are by coincidence equally labor intensive, i.e., that they happen to use the same labor-equipment ratios.

The real peculiarity of our standard linear programming definition of a process is the following: suppose that when some procedure, D, is used to produce more than a certain output, economies of large-scale production become possible and permit savings in the use of vat time. That is, suppose below outputs of 10,000 units the vat-labor time ratio is 6, whereas for higher outputs the ratio falls to 4. In that case, our definition forces us to say that this procedure really consists of two different processes.

[4] Indeed, the equation of the line is $V = 5L$ or $V/L = 5$, where V and L, respectively, represent the quantities of vat and labor time used. Hence the slope of a process ray such as OP_1 represents the input ratios of the process.

In the same way as we found ray OP_1 we now see that ray OP_2 represents process 2. This can be checked by observing that any point on this ray involves the correct input proportions for process 2: For example, point E on this ray represents the use of 3,000 hours of vat time and 900 hours of labor, thus satisfying the 1.5 hours of vat time to 0.45 hours of labor time requirement of process 2.

We end this section by noting that the collection of rays representing such processes constitute a (nonfinite) cone-shaped figure, P_2OP_3 (shaded region). As will be shown in the next section, interior points in the cone represent the concurrent use of several of these processes. In other words, our cone represents the total set of possible production arrangements involving processes 1, 2, and 3.

PROBLEMS

1. What output is represented in Figure 2 by
   (a) Point D''?
   (b) Point E?
2. Show that ray OP_3 represents process 3.
3. Draw in the ray OP_4, which represents process 4.

6. Production Indifference Curves: Construction

Moving one step closer to the diagrams of classical production theory, we can now proceed to construct the production indifference curves of our linear programming model, and in a later section we will use these to derive the profit indifference curves (iso-profit curves) needed for decision-making in the profit-maximizing firm. For the moment let us concentrate our attention on just processes 1 and 3. In Figure 3 we see that point D_1

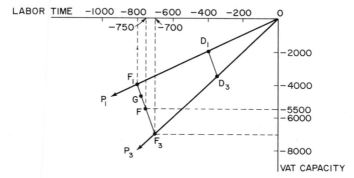

Figure 3

represents 1,000 units of output of process 1, while D_3 represents the same output of process 3. Thus the production indifference curve which involves the production of 1,000 square feet of leather must go through both these points. Similarly, points F_1 and F_3 must both lie on the 2,000-square-foot production indifference curve, etc.

But what about the portion of the 2,000-output indifference curve which lies between points F_1 and F_3? It can be shown (see next footnote for proof) that this section of the indifference curve must be the straight line segment which connects points F_1 and F_3.

The meaning of this statement is really not so clear as it may at first appear. We know that point F_1 represents the inputs required for some level of operation of process 1 and F_3 refers in a similar manner to process 3. But how can we define an intermediate point such as the midpoint, F, of line F_1F_3? There is no process ray going through point F and so we cannot explain it as a level of operation of any such process.

Instead, we must take such interior points as F and G to represent the *input requirements* for the simultaneous use of both processes 1 and 3 in some combination. That is, F represents an output of 2,000 square feet of leather, part of which is produced by means of process 1 and part of which is produced by process 3.

More specifically, it will be shown next that F, the midpoint of the line F_1F_3, represents the *inputs* needed for 2,000 units of output, produced half by one process and half by the other. Similarly, point G, which is $\frac{3}{4}$ of the way along F_1F_3 toward point F_1, represents the use of process 1 and process 3 in the ratio 3/4 to 1/4, i.e., it involves 1,500 square feet produced by process 1 and 500 square feet made by process 3. The reader can readily extend this interpretation to other points on F_1F_3, always remembering that the nearer the point to one of the process lines, the greater the use of that process which it involves.

This interpretation clearly calls for some justification. Let us look more closely at midpoint F. It can be seen to require 750 hours of labor time and 5,500 gallon-hours of vat time. Now it has been stated that F represents a 1,000-unit process 1 output (point D_1) plus a 1,000-unit process 3 output (point D_3). Let us examine the input requirements of these two separate outputs. These figures, which can be read off the diagram or calculated from our constraints are summarized in the following table:

Inputs Employed	Labor	Vat Capacity
Point D_1	400	2,000
Point D_3	350	3,500
Total	750	5,500

It will be noted that the total input requirements of D_1 and D_3 together turn out to be exactly equal to the coordinates of point F! That is, *point F represents precisely the total input quantities which would be required to operate both processes simultaneously at the 1,000-square-foot output level.* And, in the same way, it can be shown that point G represents the inputs needed to produce 1,500 units of output by means of process 1 and 500 units of process 3 output. Since a similar proposition can be proved[5] for every point on line segment F_1F_3, this justifies our interpretation of the line segment, and in particular, shows that F_1F_3 is a segment of our indifference curve.

---

[5] Our theorem states that if A and B represent equal outputs produced by different processes, then any point, C, or line segment, AB, represents the inputs needed to make the same quantity of the commodity by means of a combination of the two processes. The converse, that any such combination is represented by a point on AB, will also be shown to be valid.

Proof: In Figure 4 let OA represent an R-unit operation of process a and OB represent an R-unit operation of process b. Let C be any point on line AB. Construct line DC

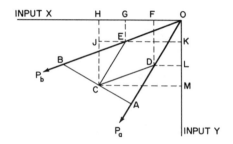

Figure 4

parallel to OB and line EC parallel to OA. Then $OE/OB = AC/AB =$ some number, k. Thus point E represents the fraction, k, of the output at B, i.e., the output level at E is kR, and it is produced by process b.

Similarly, $OD/OA = CB/AB = (AB - AC)/AB = 1 - k$. Thus, point D represents an output of magnitude $(1 - k)R$, produced by process a. Therefore, together, points D and E represent an output of $kR + (1 - k)R = R$ units of production.

Moreover, the two processes thus combined use $OG + OF$ of input x. But $OECD$ is a parallelogram, so that right triangle OFD is congruent with triangle EJC (since $OD = EC$ and angle $DOF =$ angle CEJ). Thus $OF = EJ = GH$. Hence the quantity of x used is

$$OG + OF = OG + GH = OH.$$

Similarly, points E and D together involve the employment of OM units of y. Thus, point C represents these total input quantities, OH of x and OM of y, as was to be shown.

Proof of converse: The converse will be demonstrated by means of an algebraic argument to illustrate an alternative approach. Let X_a and Y_a be the quantities of x and y used at point A, and let X_b and Y_b be the corresponding amounts for point B. Finally, let the equation of line AB be $Y = \alpha X + \beta$. Then since points A and B both lie on this line, we have

(1) $Y_a = \alpha X_a + \beta$ and $Y_b = \alpha X_b + \beta.$

Now consider any combination of the two processes in which process a produces kR units and process b produces $(1 - k)R$ units so that, together, they manufacture R units, as required. Then process a uses kX_a units of x and kY_a units of y, and process

Having established the basic point that line segment F_1F_3 is part of the production indifference curve connecting points F_1 and F_3, we can now construct the rest of the indifference curve as well as other indifference curves without any difficulty. In Figure 5 we now have included the rays which represent three of our processes 1, 2, and 3. Point F_2 on ray OP_2 represents the output of 2,000 square feet of leather by means of process 2.

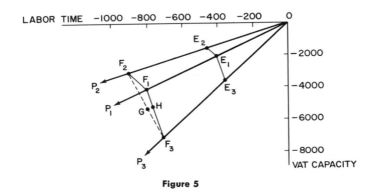

Figure 5

Therefore line F_1F_2 is also part of the 2,000-unit production indifference curve. In a similar way it can be shown that broken line $E_2E_1E_3$ is (a portion of) the 1,000-square-foot output production indifference curve. Other indifference curves in this map can be constructed similarly.

7. Some Properties of the Indifference Curves

One may well ask why we do not draw the straight line F_2F_3 (broken line) representing the 2,000-unit output combinations of processes 2 and 3 and consider points on this line to constitute a relevant portion of the production indifference curve (or area). The answer is that any point on

---

b uses $(1 - k)X_b$ units of x and $(1 - k)Y_b$ units of y. Thus together they employ $kX_a +$ $(1 - k)X_b$ units of x and $kY_a + (1 - k)Y_b$ units of input y. To see whether this input combination is represented by a point on line AB we must test whether these values of X and Y satisfy our equation $Y = \alpha X + \beta$. Substituting our value of X into the equation we obtain

$$Y = \alpha[kX_a + (1 - k)X_b] + \beta = k(\alpha X_a + \beta) + (1 - k)(\alpha X_b + \beta)$$

which by Equation (1), above, equals $kA_a + (1 - k)Y_b$, so that we have

$$kY_a + (1 - k)Y_b = \alpha[kX_a + (1 - k)X_b] + \beta$$

and so our values of X and Y [i.e., $X = kX_a + (1 - k)X_b$ and $Y = kY_a + (1 - k)Y_b$] do indeed satisfy the equation for line AB. Thus, the point representing any such input combination does lie on line AB, as was to be shown. (The reader should satisfy himself that it must lie on the portion of the line $Y = \alpha X + \beta$ which lies between points A and B.)

F_2F_3 (which does indeed represent a 2,000-unit output combination of processes 2 and 3) is necessarily a wasteful arrangement, and it will never occur in an optimal solution. For consider any point, G, on F_2F_3. Corresponding to any such point there will be points on $F_2F_1F_3$, such as point H, which lie above and to the right of G. This means that point H uses less of *both* inputs than does G. But H and G both yield the same outputs. Therefore G clearly represents an inefficient use of resources, is irrelevant for an optimal solution, and can therefore be ignored as far as the 2,000-unit production indifference curve $F_2F_1F_3$ is concerned.

We may now observe the characteristic shape of the production indifference curves of linear programming. They consist of kinked line segments. Their slope is always negative (or at least nonpositive). Their relevant portions are convex to the origin, i.e., they necessarily involve a diminishing (or at least a nonincreasing) marginal rate of substitution.[6]

Thus the production indifference curves of linear programming have the same basic shape as do the corresponding curves of neoclassical production theory except for the fact that the latter are usually taken to be smooth throughout, i.e., they are assumed to contain no kinks or corners. This premise is usually employed in the neoclassical theory to make it

---

[6] For the definition of the terms see the preceding three chapters. To justify our assertion, we need merely note what would occur in an increasing marginal rate of substitution case as depicted by curve $W_2W_1W_3$ in Figure 6. In that case, for reasons which have just

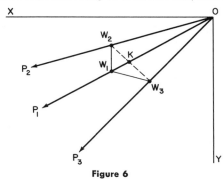

Figure 6

been given, the straight-line segment W_2KW_3, representing a combination of processes P_2 and P_3, is more efficient than any point on $W_2W_1W_3$. Thus, that line would be irrelevant in an optimal solution and W_2KW_3, not $W_2W_1W_3$, would be the pertinent production indifference curve.

The nonpositive slope follows from a similar argument. If (as in the case of SS' in Figure 10b) there were a positively sloping segment whose highest point is S', then every other point on SS' would involve larger quantities of both inputs for the same output. Therefore, the entire segment (except endpoint S') could be ignored on grounds of inefficiency. Strictly speaking, since the firm is taken to maximize profits rather than output, the preceding arguments are not really applicable to the *production* indifference curves that are under discussion here. However, they do hold directly for the profit indifference curves described in Section 6.

easier to apply the differential calculus, which breaks down at a kink (corner) point, such as F_1 in Figure 5, since the slope of the curve at that point is not defined.

Linear programming is, then, compatible with the type of diminishing-returns phenomenon represented by a diminishing marginal rate of substitution of one input for another (see the discussion of this term in the preceding three chapters). That is, if labor can be used to save vat time (e.g., by culling out defective pieces of leather which would otherwise waste vat space), increased use of labor for this purpose (with output remaining unchanged) may yield diminishing returns, i.e., diminishing marginal saving of vat time.

Presently we will see that the ordinary "law" of diminishing returns is also compatible with linear programming, i.e., the marginal yield to increased use of one input may decline, provided the employment of all other inputs remains unchanged. However, linearity does rule out diminishing returns *to scale*. That is, as already stated, it implies that the production function is linearly homogeneous. The diagram behaves accordingly. Recall that such a production function is characterized by indifference curves which are parallel in the sense that they all have the same slope along any straight line from the origin (cf. Section 10 of the previous chapter). But that is precisely what occurs here. In Figure 5 it is readily verified that the slopes of F_1F_3 and of E_1E_3 are equal. For we have (cancelling out all minus signs of the negative input values)

$$\text{slope of } F_1F_3 = \frac{7,000 - 4,000}{700 - 800} = -30$$

and

$$\text{slope of } E_1E_3 = \frac{3,500 - 2,000}{350 - 400} = -30.$$

Similarly, F_2F_1 and E_2E_1 have the same slopes. This illustrates the fact that the production indifference curves have the parallelism property of a linearly homogeneous production function.[7] The reader should observe that

---

[7] This property follows from the constancy of the coefficients in the constraints, which imply that if we double our output, sticking to the use of process 1 or any other specific process or fixed combination of processes, it will require a doubled use of our scarce inputs. That remark by itself shows why the production function in such a case is linearly homogeneous.

The parallelism phenomenon follows from the fact that F_1 involves twice the inputs employed at E_1 (where, say, X_1 and Y_1 of labor and vat time are used) and F_3 involves twice the inputs (X_3 and Y_3) which are used at E_3. Thus the slope of E_1E_3 is $(Y_3 - Y_1)/(X_3 - X_1)$, while the slope of F_1F_3 is $(2Y_3 - 2Y_1)/(2X_3 - 2X_1)$, which (cancelling out the 2's) is clearly equal to the slope of E_1E_3.

More generally, we can show that the corresponding indifference curve line segment which involves k thousand units of output also has the same slope as E_1E_3. For this purpose we employ exactly the same method of proof as was just used for F_1F_3 except that the symbol k is now substituted for the number 2 throughout the argument.

this property incidentally guarantees that the linear programming indifference curves will never intersect.

PROBLEMS

1. Show that point G, which is the midpoint between F and F_1 in Figure 3, involves the inputs required to produce 1,500 units of output by means of process 1 and 500 units of output by means of process 3.

2. Complete the two indifference curves in Figure 5 by taking into account process 4 and the corresponding points E_4 and F_4.

3. Show that it will never be efficient for our firm to use a combination of processes 2 and 4 to produce 2,000 units of output. (Hint: Draw in straight-line segment F_2F_4 in the diagram which constitutes the answer to Problem 2 and compare it with indifference curve $F_2F_1F_3F_4$.)

4. Show from the parallelism feature of the indifference curve that your preceding answer is valid for any output level, i.e., that it is never efficient to use processes 2 and 4 together (so long as processes 1 and 3 constitute available alternatives).

5. Show numerically that F_1F_2 is parallel to E_1E_2 in Figure 5.

8. Profit Indifference Curves

The *production* indifference curves in Figure 5 can readily be translated into *profit* indifference curves.

It will be recalled that the four processes are not equally profitable. In fact, from our objective function,

$$\text{profit} = 0.9Q_1 + 0.75Q_2 + 1.0Q_3 + 1.1Q_4,$$

we note that the unit profits of outputs 1, 2, 3, and 4 are, respectively, 90 cents, 75 cents, \$1, and \$1.10.

In Figure 7 we reproduce production indifference curve $E_2E_1E_3$ from

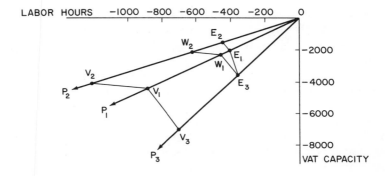

Figure 7

Figure 5. Each of points E_1, E_2, and E_3 represents an output of 1,000 square feet of leather. Let us see what points represent outputs which yield $1,000 in profit.

Since process 3 yields $1 in profit for every square foot of output, point E_3 represents both 1,000 units of product and 1,000 units of profit, i.e., at that point the $1,000 profit and 1,000-unit production indifference curves coincide.

But point E_1 involves considerably less than $1,000 in profit. Specifically, since every unit of process 1 output pays 90 cents, point E_1 represents only $900 in earnings. Thus, to earn $1,000 by means of process 1 we have to manufacture 11.1 per cent more, i.e., 1,111 units must be produced (since $1,111 \times 0.90 = 1,000$ approx.). Hence the point W_1 on ray OP_1 which lies on the $1,000 *profit* indifference curve, is $\frac{1}{9}$ farther from the origin than is E_1. Finally, to find the point of coincidence between this profit indifference curve and ray OP_2, we note that each unit of process 2 output yields only 75 cents, so that it requires $1,333.33\frac{1}{3}$ units of process 2 output to yield $1,000 in profit. This is represented by point W_2, where length OW_2 is exactly $1.33\frac{1}{3}$ times as great as length OE_2. [Once again, this is so, because of the linearity of our program which implies that it takes $\frac{1}{3}$ more of both inputs to produce $1,333.33\frac{1}{3}$ units of output via process 2 (600 hours of labor and 2,000 vat gallons) than is required to produce 1,000 units of output by means of this process (450 hours of labor and 1,500 vat gallons—see the coefficients of Q_2 in our constraints).]

For the same reasons as in the production indifference curves, we can again connect points $W_2W_1E_3$ by straight-line segments and the resulting graph will constitute the relevant portion of the $1,000 profit indifference curve. Other profit indifference curves can readily be obtained in the same way.

As in the case of the iso-product curves, the profit indifference curve will have the parallelism feature characteristic of a linear homogeneous production function. A linear program yields constant profit returns to scale, e.g., a tripling of all the operations of our firm will triple its profits. In other words, we can also obtain additional profit indifference curves in Figure 7 directly by just drawing any other "curve" $V_2V_1V_3$ whose segments are equal in slope to the corresponding segments of indifference curve $W_2W_1E_3$.

Observe, finally, that the less profitable a process happens to be, the further out will we shift a point on that ray to transfer it from a given production indifference curve to a specific profit indifference curve. Thus, the move from E_2 to W_2 is (proportionately) greater than the move from E_1 to W_1 in Figure 7 because process 1 yields 90 cents profit per unit while process 2 offers only 75 cents per unit. Suppose, for a moment, that process 1 were very unprofitable. Then curve $W_2W_1E_3$ might even have become concave to the origin as is curve $W_2W_1W_3$ in Figure 6. In that case, the straight-line segment W_2KW_3 would be closer to the origin than $W_2W_1W_3$, which means that process 1 is then a totally inefficient profit earner—it is simply not worth considering in comparison with a combination of processes 2 and 3, which can yield the same profits with the use of much smaller quantities of input. In exactly the same way, it may happen that a profit indifference curve acquires a positively sloping segment (see Figure 10b, lines WW' or SS'). This segment can then be ignored because the process at the upper end of the segment (process P in Figure 10b) must be relatively unprofitable—it takes larger quantities of both inputs to produce the same profits than does the other process, P'.

9. Graphic Solution of the Programming Problem

We have now obtained a graphic description of both the profit possibilities (Figure 7) and the feasible region as delineated by the availability of

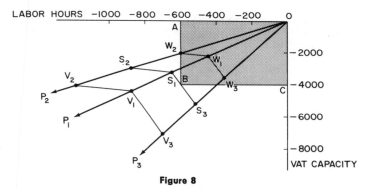

Figure 8

labor and vat inputs (Figure 1). It is now a simple matter to combine the two diagrams by superimposing them one upon the other, and then to find the optimal solution of the programming problem. The two diagrams are combined in this way in Figure 8.

It will be recalled that only points within the shaded rectangle involve input quantities no greater than the amounts available to the company. The object of our calculation is to determine how to earn the largest amount of profit which can be extracted from the available resources. Thus we want to get to the lowest possible profit indifference curve which has any point in common with the feasible region.

Since between any two process rays (the OP's) the segments of the indifference curves have the same slopes, we can, given one of these curves, construct as many other indifference curves as we like. In particular, we can construct the curve $S_2S_1S_3$, which just goes through the lower left-hand corner point, B, of the feasible rectangle. This is the linear programming analogue of the optimal tangency point of classical production theory. Point B, then, represents our optimal solution.

By examining point B we determine the following:

1. Since B lies on line segment S_1S_3, it involves the use of a combination of processes 1 and 3. This illustrates the basic theorem of linear programming—that the solution will usually contain as many nonzero elements as there are constraints in the problem. Where, as in our original linear program, two constraints are involved, there will usually be no more than two production processes employed in an optimal arrangement.[8]

2. Our optimal output involves the use of exactly 600 hours of labor and 4,000 vat gallon-hours—that is, in this case it involves full use of both limited resources of the firm.

---

[8] If there had been three constraints (three inputs), our diagram would have been three-dimensional with three axes to represent the magnitudes of the three inputs (Figure 9). The lightly shaded quasi-cubical region (the rectangular prism) is the feasible region. The production process loci, OP, OP', and OP'', are rays in three-dimensional space, and together they form a cone with flat sides, $OPP'P''$. Corresponding to line segments such as W_1W_3, S_1S_3, and V_1V_3 in Figure 8, we now have the heavily shaded triangles $WW'W''$, $SS'S''$, and $VV'V''$ in Figure 9. These triangles now represent

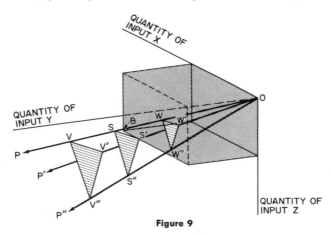

Figure 9

combinations of the *three* processes P, P', and P''. Thus, in this three-constraint case the optimal point, B, involves the use of three processes at once. Here, unlike the two-dimensional case, it may pay to use three processes at once, because, for example, line segment SS'' does not lie between the origin and either segment SS' or $S'S''$. Hence SS'' is not in this sense more efficient than the other segments, and, similarly, neither of the other segments is more efficient than S''. Hence none of these can be ruled out in advance, and so any point of these segments, as well as any combination specified by an interior point of triangle $SS'S''$, represents a legitimate portion of the production indifference surface.

3. Since $S_2 S_1 S_3$ is a little nearer to $W_2 W_1 W_3$ (the \$1,000 curve) than it is to $V_2 V_1 V_3$ (the \$2,000 curve), it yields somewhat less than \$1,500 in profit. More specifically, we note that point S_1 on this same indifference curve involves the exclusive use of process 1 and employs about 3,200 units of vat time (and about 640 labor hours). It must produce an output of approximately 1,600 square feet (since process 1 employs 2 units of vat capacity per square foot of leather, then 3,200 vat gallons will suffice to produce 1,600 square feet). At 90 cents per foot this means a profit of about \$1,440. In fact, a standard simplex calculation of the optimal solution of our programming problem shows that the total profit will be \$1,471.43.

4. Since point B lies approximately $\frac{2}{5}$ of the way toward point S_1 on line $S_1 S_3$, the optimal solution involves approximately $3/5(\$1,440) = \$864$ of profit on process 1 production and $2/5(\$1,440) = \$576$ of process 3 profits.[9] The precise profit figures yielded by a simplex calculation are \$900 on process 1 output and \$571.43 on process 3 output.

PROBLEM

Suppose process 3 were forbidden by law and the company had only processes 1, 2, and 4 to choose among. Find the optimal solution by graphic methods. Check your answer by means of the simplex computation.

10. Alternative Types of Solutions

Figure 10 illustrates several other varieties of solution, some of them "pathological," which sometimes occur in linear programming problems.

Figure 10a represents a rather common situation. Here point B, the lower left-hand corner of the feasible region, lies outside the heavily shaded cone of production possibilities, POP''. In that case, the optimal point is S and not B. The firm's resources will then not be used fully. Specifically, there will be an unused amount of X whose magnitude is indicated by length SB. Moreover, in this situation just one process, P, will be employed exclusively. Thus one process variable, Q, and one slack variable (the unused output of X) will not be equal to zero, again giving us two nonzero variables in this two-constraint case, as the basic theorem of linear programming requires.

A somewhat similar situation is depicted in Figure 10b where, even though point B lies inside the production possibility cone, process P is

---

[9] Since the unit profits on processes 1 and 2 are 90 cents and \$1.00, respectively, this implies physical outputs of $864/0.9 = 960$ units through process 1 and $576/1.0 = 576$ units via process 3. The simplex calculation yields the output values 1,000 and $571\frac{3}{7}$ units for processes 1 and 3, respectively.

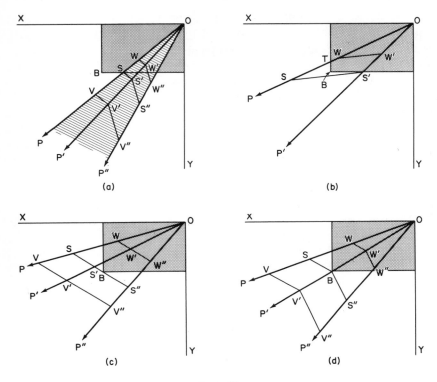

(a)   (b)

(c)   (d)

Figure 10

highly unprofitable, as is indicated by the positive slope of the profit indifference curves SS' and WW'. That is, point S yields the same profit return as does point S', but since S is below and to the left of S', it requires more of both inputs than does S' to obtain these same profits. Hence it will pay to use only process P', the more profitable process, and to use it to the full extent permitted by the company's resources. Thus the optimal point, the point on the lowest indifference curve in the shaded feasible region, is S'. Like S in Figure 10a, our optimal point S' is a basic solution involving one nonzero level of process operation and one nonzero slack variable (unused X).

Figures 10c and 10d represent rather more freakish cases. In Figure 10c two segments such as VV' and $V'V''$ of the indifference curves happen to form one straight-line segment. Since SS' and $S'S''$ together coincide with SS'', there is no disadvantage to using a combination of all three processes, i.e., an optimal solution can be found in which we have simultaneously $Q > 0$, $Q' > 0$, and $Q'' > 0$. However, there is really nothing to be gained by the simultaneous use of all three processes since any three-process solution corresponds to an equivalent two-process solution. For example, point B falls both on SS'' and on $S'S''$, so we can do as well by employing just processes P' and P'' as we would by using all three methods.

Figure 10d is another odd case in which one of the process rays, OP', happens to go through point B, the lower left-hand corner of the feasible region. Here it pays to use only the one process, P'. The basic theorem of linear programming is violated in this case since we have $Q = 0$, $Q' > 0$, $Q'' = 0$, and, since X and Y are both used to capacity, so that both slack variables also take the value zero. Thus, despite the fact that there are two constraints in our problem, its solution involves only one nonzero-valued variable.

Figure 10d represents the phenomenon which is called *degeneracy*. Intuitively it means that one process happens by accident to employ resources in the right proportion to use up the available resources completely (or, in the general case, that this is done by a number of processes smaller than the number of different input resources). Computational experience indicates that such cases are encountered more frequently than might be expected in advance. Degeneracy causes some computational difficulties but they are not usually very serious.

PROBLEM

Show that points O, S', B, and T are the basic solution points in Figure 10b, i.e., they are the points which involve exactly as many nonzero-valued variables as there are constraints in the problem (two). (Cf. Chapter 5 for the definition of the term "basic solution.")

11. Marginal, Total, and Average Input Products

As a final extension of our conventionalization of the linear programming analysis, let us examine the marginal revenue[10] productivity of our two inputs. Simply for the sake of variety let us turn at this point to another programming problem:

$$\text{Max} \quad 4Q_1 + 4Q_2$$

subject to

$$2Q_1 + Q_2 \le x$$

$$2Q_1 + 3Q_2 \le y$$

$$Q_1 \ge 0, \qquad Q_2 \ge 0,$$

where x and y represent the available quantities of the two inputs.

---

[10] The use of *profit* indifference curves in our calculation is the reason it gives us marginal *revenue* products. We obtain a measure of the marginal revenue of input x rather than its marginal profit yield because the cost of obtaining additional units of x is not taken into account in the calculation.

Our profit indifference map is shown in Figure 11a. The horizontal segments such as CD have been added to the indifference curves simply to show that beyond a quantity required by either of the two processes (see, for example, point C), a further addition to the firm's stock of input x *by itself* (leaving the available quantity of y unchanged) will add nothing to output, i.e., it will leave us on the same indifference curve. The reason for the vertical segments (e.g., BA) is perfectly analogous.

Next to each indifference curve a number has also been inserted to indicate the profit level it represents. Thus the 8 at the end of the lower indifference curve indicates that any point on this curve represents an arrangement which will yield a profit of 8 (thousand dollars?).

Let us now investigate the marginal revenue productivity of input x. For this purpose we must keep the quantity of input y fixed and see what happens to total product as additional units of x are made available to the company. Fixing the quantity of y arbitrarily at $y = 4$, and adding successive units to the firm's stock of input x, we obtain, in turn, points E, F, G, etc.

Now at point E we are on the 4 (thousand dollar) profit indifference curve, $ABCD$. Thus, with one unit of x we obtain a total profit of \$4,000. This is recorded as point e on the total revenue product curve in Figure 11b. Similarly, point F in Figure 11a indicates that two units of x permit the acquisition of six units of profit, and this gives us point f in Figure 11b. In this way the entire total revenue product curve can be determined. Note that this curve rises steadily up until point s in Figure 11b. To see why this is so, note that this segment of the total revenue product curve corresponds to the points on line segment RS (along which $y = 4$) in Figure 11a. There indifference curves are crossed at a constant rate as input x increases. But once we move to the left of point S in 11a (we cross ray OP_2), we leave the vertical segments of the indifference curves, and it now takes a larger increase in x to yield a given rise in total revenue. Finally, to the left of point H no expansion of the use of x can increase revenue any further, and so the corresponding segment of the total revenue product curve (the portion to the left of point h) becomes horizontal. The reader is left to examine for himself the construction of the average and marginal revenue product curves (Figures 11c and 11d). He should notice that the discontinuities in the marginal revenue product curve occur precisely at the input levels where one finds the kinks, s and h, in the total revenue curve. This is so, of course, because marginal revenue product at any input level is measured by the slope of the total revenue curve (cf. Chapter 3, Section 4).

In our diagrams we observe that the productivity curves of linear programming do exhibit diminishing returns and, in particular, diminishing marginal products. But the decreases characteristically occur in discontinuous jumps.

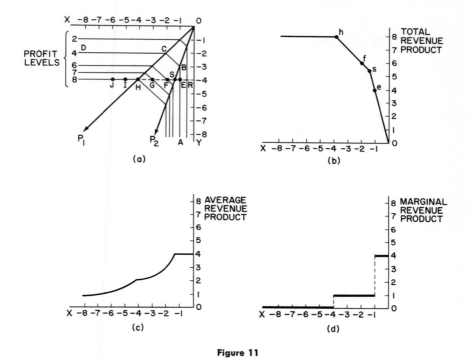

Figure 11

12. Conclusion

We have seen in this chapter that the points of view of marginal analysis and linear programming are not so different after all. The programming view of production is restrictive only in that it assumes that the production function is linear and homogeneous and that it deals with changes that are abrupt and discontinuous, so that we do not have the smooth indifference and marginal productivity curves of classical production analysis. In at least one respect the programming approach probes more deeply than the other because it enables us to see what lies behind the production function in terms of the optimal choice of process combinations for any set of input or output levels.

REFERENCES

Dorfman, Robert, "Mathematical or 'Linear' Programming: A Nonmathematical Exposition," *American Economic Review*, Vol. XLIII, December 1953.

————, *Application of Linear Programming to the Theory of the Firm*, University of California Press, Berkeley, 1951, esp. Chapters I and II.

Dorfman, Robert, Paul A. Samuelson, and Robert Solow, *Linear Programming and Economic Analysis*, McGraw-Hill Book Company, New York, 1958, Chapter 6.

Hicks, John R., "Linear Theory," *Economic Journal*, vol. 70, December 1960.

Wu, Yuan-li, and Ching-wen Kwang, "An Analytical and Graphical Comparison of Marginal Analysis and Mathematical Programming in the Theory of the Firm," in Kenneth E. Boulding and Allen W. Spivey (eds.), *Linear Programming and the Theory of the Firm*, The Macmillan Company, New York, 1960.

Comparative Statics
and Optimization:
Consumers and Firms

13

This chapter undertakes a systematic introduction to a set of analytic tools, the calculus methods of comparative statics. These powerful methods have yielded valuable results in a wide variety of subject areas including welfare economics, the theory of taxation, stabilization policy, and micro- and macroeconomics in general. They have proved particularly effective in providing *qualitative* conclusions indicating the direction (i.e., the sign) of the effects of a given change in policy or in underlying economic circumstances. The results have also been useful in quantitative analysis, that is, in the evaluation of the magnitudes of such effects. It is no exaggeration to say that some of the most widely noted theorems in economics are the products of comparative-statics analysis.

1. Comparative Statics: Parameters and Endogenous Variables

Consider a model used to describe the firm's production decisions, i.e., the quantities of its various outputs and inputs *given the prices* of all these items. In such a case, the input and output quantities can be referred to as the *endogenous variables*, that is, they are the variables whose values are determined *within* the system. On the other hand, the *price* of an input or an output, say the hourly wage rate, is in this case described as a *parameter*, that is, it is a magnitude which may be changed by outside forces but which, from the point of view of the behavior of a competitive firm, must be taken as fixed.

It should immediately be clear that one person's parameter is another's endogenous variable. To the consumer or the firm, the level of a tax on cigarettes is a parameter. To the legislator who may be interpreted to be seeking to determine a socially optimal value of that tax rate, the rate is an endogenous variable of his optimization calculation. Thus it is the nature of the problem being studied, as encompassed in the structure of the appropriate model, that determines whether some entity is to be considered a variable or a parameter for the purposes at hand.

Parameters may at first be confused with variables because, ordinarily, neither of them is given numerically. The symbol p_j, representing the price of commodity j, may seem as much a variable as y_j, denoting the output of that commodity. But for a study of competitive firms p_j is to be interpreted as a constant, albeit one whose magnitude may not be known. Moreover, that constant value may conceivably be replaced by another constant value in response to change in outside forces. A fiscal crisis can force a rise in the sales tax from 5 to 7 per cent. But from the point of view of business decisions the latter figure is as much a given as was the former. No change in the firm's output level, in advertising expenditure, or in the value of any other of its endogenous (decision) variables will affect that tax rate once it is determined by the legislature.

In seeking to select an optimal tax rate the legislature must consider the range of reasonable alternatives and must estimate or guess at their effects. For example, it may guess at the tax revenues that will accrue if the rate is set at 4 per cent or if, instead, the selected figure is 5 or 6 or 7 per cent. But that tax revenue figure will depend on the reaction of consumers and firms to the magnitude selected. If demands and production levels (the endogenous variables of the consumer's or firm's decision problems) are very little different under a high than under a low tax rate, a 7 per cent sales tax will bring in far more money than a 5 per cent tax, and the reverse will clearly be true if demands and outputs are highly responsive to that choice.

It is therefore important to know how the behavior of endogenous variables will differ with different parameter values. This is essentially what is meant by a problem in comparative statics. More formally, we have the definition

> *Comparative statics* is the comparison of the *equilibrium values* of the endogenous variables of an economic model corresponding to alternative values of the parameters selected for study.

Two features of this definition merit emphasis:

1. The parameter values investigated are always taken as alternatives, *not* as sequential changes. That is, the issue is what will happen if a 5 per

cent tax rate is chosen or if a 7 per cent rate is chosen *instead*; comparative statics does not examine what happens if a 5 per cent tax rate which prevails until next January is thereafter replaced by a 7 per cent tax rate. Behavior over time never enters a calculation in comparative statics.

2. Comparative statics concerns itself only with equilibrium values of the endogenous variables, i.e., it concerns itself only with the system after it has adjusted fully to the selected values of the parameters. This is just another side of the static character of the analysis.

2. Comparative Statics Without Optimization

Optimization is often an essential ingredient of a comparative-statics analysis, as we will see; but sometimes it is entirely absent. A simple example is the elementary analysis of the effect of an excise tax on the price and output of a competitive industry. Using the Marshallian supply-demand diagram (Figure 1), we recall that if SS' is the supply curve in

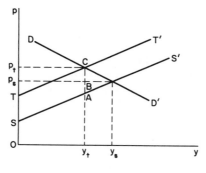

Figure 1

the absence of a tax, then with a tax rate equal to $ST = AC$ dollars per unit of output the supply curve will instead be TT', which lies uniformly above SS' by the amount of the unit tax. We see at once that y_t, the equilibrium output under the tax, will be less than y_s, the equilibrium without a tax, a result that is hardly surprising. Moreover, price will be higher under the tax $p_t - p_s = BC$ but the price difference may well be less than the tax $BC < AC$. In other words, pure competition and the slopes of the supply and demand curves may force suppliers to absorb part of the tax.

This, then, is a standard illustration of a comparative-statics analysis making no explicit use of any maximization or minimization process. This is a characteristic of the use of comparative statics in macroeconomics, for a typical issue in that field is the difference for the equilibrium values of national income, employment and inflation rates of alternative modes of behavior of the money supply, governmental expenditure, etc.

Before turning to the comparative-statics analysis that incorporates a maximization process, let us use our supply-demand example to re-emphasize for the last time a fundamental matter of interpretation. It is easy but incorrect to say that the analysis shows that the imposition of an excise tax will lead price to *rise* from its previous level, but by less than the amount of the tax. That is an intertemporal interpretation which is valid only if none of the other relationships happen to shift during the period to which such a statement applies. That is, it assumes implicitly that the production costs or demand patterns are not changed either by the tax rise itself or by other unrelated influences. But, in any event, comparative-statics analysis makes no such intertemporal assertions. Instead, its alternatives always represent substitute scenarios for an identical time interval: either a zero tax rate for the next year or a 5 per cent tax rate during the same period.

3. Comparative Statics and Optimization: Example I—Cournot

The comparative-statics analysis to which we turn now has a simple structure which can easily be lost sight of in the course of the calculation. It takes some values to the parameters, $t_1, \cdots, t_m$, as given, and it supposes that the values of the endogenous variables, $y_1^0, \cdots, y_n^0$, then emerge *from an optimization calculation* attributed to the decision-maker. One or more parameter values are then permitted to vary, usually by the small amount dt_i, and then one calculates the corresponding variations, dy_j^0, in the optimal values of the endogenous variables, i.e., the variables under the control of the decision-maker.

Probably the earliest and simplest examples of such a calculation are those that were provided by the French mathematician A. A. Cournot in his little masterwork of 1838.[1] The structure of the analysis is still used today in totally unchanged form.

Cournot's model, which we turn to now, is that of a profit-maximizing monopolist turning out a single product whose quantity is y and which he sells at price p. For simplicity, Cournot assumes the cost of providing the product to be zero (he describes it as a mineral water which flows costlessly from the monopolist's spring). Cournot then shows that if a tax rate of t francs per unit had been imposed on the product the monopolist

---

[1] A. A. Cournot, *Mathematical Principles of the Theory of Wealth*, N. T. Bacon, trans. (Irving Fisher, ed.), The Macmillan Company, New York, 1897.

would have found it profitable to sell a smaller amount than he would have in the absence of the tax.

The model which shows this is straightforward. Let

(1) $$y = f(p), \qquad f'(p) < 0$$

be the demand function for the mineral water. Then with costs assumed zero, the profit function is

(2) $$\pi = (p - t)y = pf(p) - tf(p).$$

Using standard simplified notation for the derivatives we write

$$\pi_p \text{ for } \partial\pi/\partial p \quad \text{and} \quad \pi_{pp} \text{ for } \partial^2\pi/\partial p^2, \quad \text{etc.}$$

Then the requirements for profit maximization are

(3) $\pi_p = f(p) + pf'(p) - tf'(p) = 0$ (first-order condition)

(4) $\pi_{pp} < 0$ (second-order condition).

So far we have carried out no more than the ordinary maximization process. Now, however, we ask what change in value of p is consistent with maintenance of the equilibrium condition (3) if for the value of the tax rate t there is substituted an alternative tax rate, $t + dt$. To determine this we permit t to vary by the amount dt in (3) and simultaneously permit the seller's price, p, to vary by the amount dp and see what combinations of the two are consistent with maintenance of the equilibrium requirement $\pi_p = 0$, that is, which values of dp and dt result in a *zero change* in π_p, i.e., in $d\pi_p = 0$.

To answer this question we must find $d\pi_p$, the total differential of (3) when t and p are both permitted to vary.[2] This gives us [since $\pi_{pt} = -f'(p)$ by (3)],

(5) $$d\pi_p = \pi_{pp}\, dp + \pi_{pt}\, dt = \pi_{pp}\, dp - f'(p)\, dt = 0.$$

[Here we could, of course, also have calculated an explicit expression for π_{pp} by partial differentiation of (3) with respect to p, but as we will see in a moment, that is unnecessary for our purposes.]

---

[2] The reader may find it helpful to review the discussion of the total differential in Section 7 of Chapter 4.

From (5) we can now solve for dp/dt, obtaining

(6) $$dp = [f'(p)/\pi_{pp}]\, dt \quad \text{or} \quad dp/dt = f'(p)/\pi_{pp}.$$

From the second-order conditions, (4), we see that the denominator, π_{pp}, is negative. From the assumption that the demand function (1) has a negative slope, we see that the numerator $f'(p)$ is also negative. Hence we conclude

(7) $$dp/dt = f'(p)/\pi_{pp} > 0,$$

and so, by (1),

(8) $$dy/dt = (dy/dp)(dp/dt) = f'(p)\, dp/dt < 0.$$

These are the comparative-statics results we were seeking. A higher tax rate, dt, will induce the profit-maximizing supplier to charge a higher product price and to provide a lower output.

4. Dissection of the Process: The Crucial Step of Total Differentiation

As a guide for some of the more complicated examples that follow, and in order to make clearer the logic of the analysis, we pause now to characterize and interpret each of the steps in the comparative-statics calculation.

The first few elements encompassing relationships (1)–(4) may be summarized in the following two obvious steps:

Step 1: Gather the information that we take as given, including premises such as that about the shape of the firm's demand curve (1) and the nature of the objective function. These preliminaries also include

Step 2: Carry out the optimization calculation, spelling out the *assumption* that the second-order conditions, such as (4), are satisfied. This premise, which plays a crucial role in this sort of comparative-statics analysis, must of course hold for the calculus optimization procedure to be legitimate.

We come next to the critical step which constitutes the core of the process and whose logic requires some explanation:

Step 3: Set equal to zero the total differential of *the first-order conditions* permitting, in the process, variation in the values of *all* of the endogenous variables and of the parameters whose influence is under examination.

There are several natural questions about this step: (a) Why is it the first-order condition (π_p in our example) and not the maximand (π) which is differentiated totally, and (b) what right have we to set the total differential equal to *zero*?

The answer to question (a) is that comparative statics deals with equilibrium relationships, which we determine with the aid of the first-order conditions such as $\pi_p = 0$, not the maximand, π. In any event, we do not have a usable relationship between π and the parameters. With one value of the parameter it will take some value π^* and with another value of the parameter we will instead have $\pi = \pi^{**}$, but we have no prior information about the comparative values of π^* and π^{**}. However, we do know the equilibrium values of π_p^* and π_p^{**}, the partial derivatives of the objective function under the two values of the parameter, for if with the one value of the parameter we are to attain equilibrium, then (3) tells us we must have

$$(9) \qquad\qquad \pi_p^* = 0,$$

and, similarly, if we attain an equilibrium under the substitute parameter value (as the comparative-statics analysis requires), we must also have

$$(10) \qquad\qquad \pi_p^{**} = 0.$$

This tells us at once why we differentiate the first-order expressions π_p and not the maximand, π, for we know *precisely* what values π_p must have with each of the different parameter values but we do not know that about π. Moreover, we can now immediately answer question (b), why we can set the differential of π_p equal to zero, for we have, by comparison of (9) and (10), for the two choices of parameter values

$$(11) \qquad\qquad \pi_p^* = \pi_p^{**} \quad \text{or} \quad d\pi_p = 0.$$

Looked at another way, the monopolist in the illustrative Cournot problem is faced with a *fait accompli*. Instead of the tax rate t he must pay the tax rate $t + dt$. To minimize the resulting damage he must change price by that quantity, dp, that restores the first-order conditions. Thus, if instead of the parameter value t, the tax rate is set at $t + dt$, then unless p is adjusted we may expect π_p to be affected. The best the monopolist can now do is to adopt a different price $p + dp$, which offsets any change in π_p and restores it to zero, as the first-order condition requires. That is precisely what is accomplished in the total differentiation equation (5), which is the crucial step in the comparative-statics process, because it gives us the desired relation between changes in parameter values, dt, and the corresponding changes in the equilibrium values of the endogenous variables such as dp and dy.

The remaining steps of the comparative-statics analysis are now easily described.

Step 4: Solve the total differential equations for the derivatives of the endogenous variables with respect to the parameter values (dp/dt in the Cournot example). Here it is useful to regard the total differential equation (5) as a single equation whose two variables are dp and dt. That is, we take as our variables for the purposes of this calculation not the price and tax rate p and t but the *changes* in their values. By the fundamental rule for total differentiation the variables dp, dt, etc., never enter in a more complicated form such as $(dp)^2$ or $\log dp$ or anything of that sort. The total differential equation will always be a *linear* relationship in the dp, dt and the other changes in endogenous variable and parameter values. This always makes it much easier to solve for the derivatives such as dp/dt than if nonlinear relationships were involved. We come finally to

Step 5: Evaluate the sign of the derivatives whose expression is obtained in the preceding step. Note, however, that it is *not* always possible to determine that sign, because in some cases the corresponding derivatives can in fact go either way. For example, if x is a consumer's purchase of some good and m is his income, we expect that $\partial x/\partial m$ will be negative for an inferior good and positive for a normal good. Consequently, we might well question any mathematical result which claimed to determine the sign of $\partial x/\partial m$ unambiguously. But in other cases, as in the Cournot model, an unambiguous sign will be arrived at. Here two types of information will normally be helpful: (a) the second-order conditions, such as $\pi_{pp} < 0$, and (b) premises about other economic relationships obtained from wider considerations; for example, we used in the Cournot discussion the premise that the firm's demand curve has a negative slope. It transpires that the second-order conditions *always* make an appearance in the expression for the derivatives obtained in Step 4 and, in particular, that they determine the sign of the denominator of that derivative just as they did that of π_{pp} in the solution expression (7) for the Cournot problem. This, too, is no mere accident but a necessary consequence of the logic of the problem, as will be seen later in this chapter.

In seeking some qualitative result one must never be hasty in accepting the conclusion that the behavior of the term in question is generally indeterminate. A sign may appear to be ambiguous at first, and yet some ingenuity may suddenly reveal its secret. Very frequently the first-order conditions will be helpful here, indicating relationships that prove crucial in the solution process.

5. Digression on Second-Order Conditions in Multivariable Models

Since the second-order conditions play so important a role in the comparative-statics analysis, we will have to discuss explicitly the form they take in models more complicated than the one we have examined so far. The generalized form of those second-order conditions will be reported in Section 7. For the moment we will only discuss why these conditions are not merely a straightforward extension of the requirements for the case $z = f(x)$. As soon as we deal with a model containing a multiplicity of variables we enter a new realm of complication if calculus methods are to be used exclusively.

To understand the source of the difficulty we start off by reviewing the simplest case of a maximand with one (independent) variable, i.e., where the objective is to maximize some function such as

$$z = f(x).$$

Here the second-order condition assures us that we are dealing with a graph such as that in Figure 2a rather than in 2b or 2c.

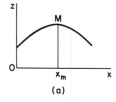
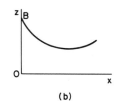
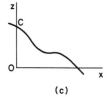

Figure 2

The graph in 2a, it will be recalled, can yield a unique interior maximum[3] because the first derivative is constantly declining (i.e., the second derivative is negative). This means that from the maximum point m it does not pay to go in either direction. Where, instead of our simple objective function $z = f(x)$, we are attempting to

$$\text{maximize } z = f(x_1, x_2)$$

---

[3] It will be recalled that an interior maximum is one that does not occur at a "corner" of the diagram, i.e., at a point where a constraint, such as a nonnegativity condition, prevents further movement of a variable. For example, if we require $x \geq 0$, then Figures 2b and 2c do have maxima at points B and C, respectively, but these are *corner maxima*, not *interior maxima*. Cf. Chapter 3, Section 10, above.

we hope, analogously, to have a graph such as that in Figure 3. Now in such a graph all the second (partial) derivatives must, indeed, still be negative. For example, by taking a cross section parallel to the x_1 axis of the hill in the previous diagram, we see that we obtain a curve RMV with the same shape as that in Figure 2a, that is, we will have $z_{11} = \partial^2 z/\partial x_1^2 < 0$. Hence, we still have as necessary conditions for our calculations the negativity of the second partial derivatives, i.e.,

(12) $$z_{11} < 0 \qquad z_{22} < 0.$$

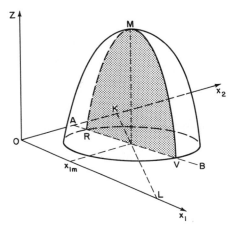

Figure 3

However, conditions (12) are not *sufficient* by themselves to do the job. That is, we can have cases where (12) is satisfied and yet there is no ordinary interior maximum. Such a case is illustrated in Figure 4 by surface $ARBCVD$, whose shape may be described as that of a sagging awning going diagonally above the floor of the diagram. As Figure 4 shows, z_{22} is negative because a cross section along HJ which is parallel to the x_2 axis yields an inverted U-shaped cross section HIJ, like the corresponding curves in Figures 2a and 3. Similarly, it is not difficult to see that in Figure 4 we also have $z_{11} < 0$ (cross section EFG). Thus, conditions (12) are both satisfied and yet surface $ARBCVD$ clearly has no interior maximum point M such as those in Figures 2a and 3.

It is not difficult to see what has gone wrong. $z_{11} = \partial^2 z/\partial x_1^2$ only tells us about cross sections taken in the east-west direction, i.e., cross sections parallel to the x_1 axis (like that above AB in Figure 3). Similarly, z_{22} gives us information just about the curvature of a cross section cutting through the relevant surface in the south-north direction (e.g., like that above HJ

in Figure 4). For the entire surface to have the proper curvature like that in Figure 3 any and every cross section of the graph of the maximand must have an inverted U shape. This must be true not *only* for cross sections taken parallel to the axes, such as those above AB in Figure 3 or above HJ in Figure 4, but also for any other cross section such as those above KL in Figures 3 and 4. Now it should be clear that the curvature of any such cross section goes in the right direction in Figure 3—it also has an inverted U shape. But the corresponding cross section above KL in Figure 4 is $RIFV$, which is an *uninverted* U; it is shaped like the curve in Figure 2b and is therefore not a well-behaved surface from the viewpoint of max-imization. Clearly, what is required is that the graph of the objective function (or of the Lagrangian expression in the case where the problem has constraints) be concave (downward) along every cross section,[4] as is

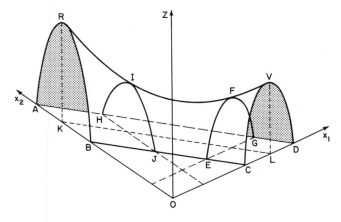

Figure 4

obviously true of the graph in Figure 3. Using the formal definition of concavity of a function that was given in Chapters 7 and 9, one can then proceed to draw many of the same conclusions as we obtain via the calculus methods. The means by which this is done are described in some detail in Section 10 of Chapter 14..Alternatively, we can formulate second-order conditions in terms of the effects upon the maximand not only of a change in x_1 itself, holding x_2 fixed (or vice versa), but also of simultaneous variation in the values of both variables, as indicated by the values of the cross-partial derivatives such as $z_{12} = \partial^2 z / \partial x_1 \partial x_2$ as well as the z_{11} and the z_{12}. This way of dealing with the matter will be described in Sections 6–8 of this chapter.

---

[4] Recall also that sometimes quasi-concavity will do. See Chapter 9, Section 19.

6. Example II: The Slutsky Theorem in a Two-Input Firm

As an intermediate step toward a description of the full comparative-statics analysis, let us turn to a classic example of this process: the derivation of the Slutsky theorem for a business firm, the statement that the profit-maximizing firm will always use a lower quantity of an input when a higher price of that input is substituted for a lower one.

To make the discussion easier we will take the firm to have only two inputs between which to divide its expenditures, which, as we will see in the following sections, permits a considerable simplification of the algebra.

The model requires our firm to minimize the expenditure it devotes to its inputs for any given output level, y^*, i.e., to

$$(13) \qquad\qquad \text{Min } E = p_1 x_1 + p_2 x_2$$

subject to its production-function constraint

$$(14) \quad f(x_1, x_2) = y^* \qquad \text{(for whatever level of } y^* \text{ happens to be selected),}$$

yielding the Lagrangian expression (Section 8 of Chapter 4)

$$(15) \qquad\qquad L = p_1 x_1 + p_2 x_2 + \lambda[y^* - f(x_1, x_2)].$$

This is a model with three endogenous variables, x_1, x_2, and the Lagrangian λ (whose optimal value, λ^0, has been shown in the Kuhn–Tucker analysis to give us $\lambda^0 = \partial E / \partial y^*$, i.e., the marginal cost of an increase in output). It also contains three parameters, p_1, p_2, and y^*. A comparative-statics analysis can then investigate the effects of a change in the value of any one or more of these parameters upon the values of each of the endogenous variables. Here we will be concerned with just one of these comparative-statics relationships, with $\partial x_1 / \partial p_1$.

To get this value, we start off, as usual, by differentiating (15) in turn with respect to the variables x_1, x_2, and λ to obtain the first-order conditions[5]

---

[5] The subsequent discussion can be simplified somewhat by using the first two equations in (16) to eliminate λ. This gives us, instead of the three equations in (16), the combined equation $p_1/p_2 = f_1/f_2$ plus the last of Equations (16). This step is avoided here for two reasons: first, because for expository purposes it is desirable to begin with the most standard procedures, and, second, because variables suppressed in the way just described may remain hidden in the model and may constitute a potential source of error.

$$(16) \quad \begin{cases} \partial L/\partial x_1 = p_1 - \lambda f_1 = 0 \\ \partial L/\partial x_2 = p_2 - \lambda f_2 = 0 \\ \partial L/\partial \lambda = y^* - f(x_1, x_2) = 0. \end{cases}$$

For the reasons discussed in the previous section, the second-order conditions of this problem with its multiplicity of variables is not a simple extension of the single-variable case. We would expect that in this minimization problem they require (writing L_{11} for $\partial^2 L/\partial x_1^2$, etc.)

$$(17) \qquad L_{11} = -\lambda f_{11} > 0, \qquad L_{22} = -\lambda f_{22} > 0$$

(though we note by direct differentiation that $L_{\lambda\lambda} = 0$ and is consequently not negative). Since from (16) $\lambda = p_1/f_1 > 0$ (where f_1 is the marginal product of input 1 and hence is presumably positive) conditions (17) amount to the plausible premise that inputs x_1 and x_2 each satisfy the "law" of diminishing marginal returns, i.e., that $f_{11} < 0$ and $f_{22} < 0$. However, for the reasons discussed in the preceding section, in such a multiple-variable case the conditions (17) are not adequate for our purposes. It can be shown (though it will not be proved here) that in the present case the second-order conditions require

$$(18) \qquad \lambda[f_{11}f_2^2 - f_1 f_2(f_{12} + f_{21}) + f_{22}f_1^2] < 0.$$

The general expression from which this inequality is derived will be given in Section 7. For the moment this expression merely serves to limit the degree of influence of the cross-partial terms, f_{12} and f_{21}. We note that if f_{12} and f_{21} happened both to be zero, then this condition would automatically be satisfied if indeed [6] $f_{11} < 0$ and $f_{22} < 0$.

Having gathered our premises and carried out our maximization calculations (steps 1 and 2), we are now ready for the critical step in which we differentiate totally our first-order conditions, permitting variation in each of our endogenous variables, x_1, x_2, and λ, and in the param-

---

[6] Moreover, if $f_{12} > 0$ and $f_{21} > 0$, condition (18) is automatically satisfied because then every term in the expression will be negative. Here $f_{12} > 0$ can be interpreted as a sort of complementarity between the two inputs—it means that increased use of one of the inputs increases the marginal product of the other. Thus, only in the case where $f_{12} < 0$, $f_{21} < 0$, and where these cross-partial derivatives are relatively large, i.e., the case of substantial substitutability (in the same sense in which "complementarity" was just implicitly defined), does satisfaction of condition (18) run into problems.

eter, p_1. Since our first-order conditions are composed of three equations we obtain, correspondingly, by this process, three total differential equations:

$$-\lambda f_{11}\, dx_1 - \lambda f_{12}\, dx_2 - f_1\, d\lambda + dp_1 = 0$$

$$-\lambda f_{21}\, dx_1 - \lambda f_{22}\, dx_2 - f_2\, d\lambda \qquad = 0$$

$$-f_1\, dx_1 - f_2\, dx_2 \qquad\qquad = 0,$$

where, since we are only permitting the parameter, p_1, to vary, $dp_2 = 0$ by assumption. For convenience, we bring the term involving the parameter change, dp_1, over to the right-hand side and then divide all three equations through by $-dp_1$ to obtain

(19)
$$\begin{cases} \lambda f_{11}\, dx_1/dp_1 + \lambda f_{12}\, dx_2/dp_1 + f_1\, d\lambda/dp_1 = 1 \\ \lambda f_{21}\, dx_1/dp_1 + \lambda f_{22}\, dx_2/dp_1 + f_2\, d\lambda/dp_1 = 0 \\ f_1\, dx_1/dp_1 + f_2\, dx_2/dp_1 \qquad\qquad = 0. \end{cases}$$

Taking dx_1/dp_1, dx_2/dp_2, and $d\lambda/dp_1$ as the unknowns we can now treat (19) as a set of three simultaneous linear equations in three unknowns and use the usual methods to solve for these unknowns.[7]

Our objective is to solve for dx_1/dp_1, which means that we wish to eliminate dx_2/dp_1 and $d\lambda/dp_1$ from (19). The straightforward way of eliminating the latter is to multiply through the first two equations, respectively, by f_2 and f_1 and then subtract the second equation from the first, to yield

(20) $\lambda(f_2 f_{11} - f_1 f_{21})\, dx_1/dp_1 + \lambda(f_2 f_{12} - f_1 f_{22})\, dx_2/dp_1 = f_2.$

Next, from the last equation in (19) we can eliminate dx_2/dp_1 by writing

$$dx_2/dp_1 = -(f_1/f_2)\, dx_1/dp_1,$$

which, when substituted into (20), gives us as the expression for dx_1/dp_1, which we are seeking,

$$\lambda[f_2 f_{11} - f_1 f_{21} - (f_2 f_{12} - f_1 f_{22})(f_1/f_2)]\, dx_1/dp_1 = f_2,$$

---

[7] The next few steps merely represent the tedious calculations needed to solve the simultaneous system for dx_1/dp_1, and the reader may prefer to go directly to the solution, Equation (21).

or, multiplying through by f_2 and dividing through by the expression that precedes $\partial x_1/dp_1$,

$$(21) \qquad \frac{dx_1}{dp_1} = \frac{f_2^2}{\lambda[f_2^2 f_{11} - f_1 f_2 (f_{12} + f_{21}) + f_1^2 f_{22}]}.$$

To interpret this result the reader will note first that the denominator in (21) is indeed the same as the expression in the second-order condition (18), a characteristic of comparative-statics arguments that had been pointed out earlier.

Moreover, from (18) we see at once that if the second-order conditions are satisfied, then the denominator of (21) is necessarily negative. It then follows at once that dx_1/dp_1 must be negative, which is what we wanted to prove. That is, we have proved that the competitive firm in equilibrium will indeed have a derived demand curve for inputs that is negatively sloping—they will use less of the input when its price is higher.

Question: Why is there no income effect in (21), the Slutsky equation for the firm?

The procedures illustrated in this section constitute the essence of the comparative-statics methods. The remaining sections of this chapter will extend them in just two ways. First, the second-order conditions will be given for the case where there are n variables and m constraints, and, second, we will employ Cramer's rule to help in the solution of the simultaneous equations constituted by the total differential equations of the analysis. The entire discussion will make fairly heavy use of determinants, and so the reader who is not acquainted with the elementary properties of determinants will either have to learn about them from any of the large variety of available sources,[8] or he will have to leave the chapter at this point.

7. Second-Order Conditions, Constrained n-Variable Problems: Bordered Hessians

We now report the second-order conditions for a constrained max-imization or minimization problem with a multiplicity of variables. Con-

---

[8] See, e.g., R. G. D. Allen, *Mathematical Analysis for Economists*, The Macmillan Company, London, 1938, Chapter 18.

sider the problem

$$(22) \quad \begin{cases} \text{Max (or Min) } \pi = f(x_1, x_2, x_3, x_4) \\ \text{subject to the constraints} \\ g(x_1, x_2, x_3, x_4) = 0 \\ h(x_1, x_2, x_3, x_4) = 0. \end{cases}$$

For explicitness, we deal with this case involving four variables and two constraints, but everything said about this case is extendable directly to cases involving n variables and m constraints for any positive integers, n and m, provided[9] $m < n$.

In that case, we have the Lagrangian

$$L = f(\,\cdot\,) - \alpha g(\,\cdot\,) - \beta h(\,\cdot\,),$$

where we use $f(\,\cdot\,)$ to denote $f(x_1, x_2, x_3, x_4)$, etc.

To state the second-order conditions, we need a number of definitions. Writing, as usual, L_{ij} for $\partial^2 L/\partial x_i\, \partial x_j$ and g_i for $\partial g/\partial x_i$, etc., we define the *bordered Hessian* determinant of the system (22) as

$$(23) \quad H = \begin{vmatrix} L_{11} & L_{12} & L_{13} & L_{14} & -g_1 & -h_1 \\ L_{21} & L_{22} & L_{23} & L_{24} & -g_2 & -h_2 \\ L_{31} & L_{32} & L_{33} & L_{34} & -g_3 & -h_3 \\ L_{41} & L_{42} & L_{43} & L_{44} & -g_4 & -h_4 \\ -g_1 & -g_2 & -g_3 & -g_4 & 0 & 0 \\ -h_1 & -h_2 & -h_3 & -h_4 & 0 & 0 \end{vmatrix}.$$

This determinant is composed of all of the second-partial and cross-partial derivatives of the Lagrangian, L, *bordered* by the last two rows and columns of the partial derivatives of the constraints.

We define next the first lower-order principal minors, H_{ii}, as the minors of H obtained by deleting the ith row and the ith column of H, i.e., as H_{11}, H_{22}, H_{33}, and H_{44}, where, for example,

$$H_{11} = \begin{vmatrix} L_{22} & L_{23} & L_{24} & -g_2 & -h_2 \\ L_{32} & L_{33} & L_{34} & -g_3 & -h_3 \\ L_{42} & L_{43} & L_{44} & -g_4 & -h_4 \\ -g_2 & -g_3 & -g_4 & 0 & 0 \\ -h_2 & -h_3 & -h_4 & 0 & 0 \end{vmatrix},$$

---

[9] If $m = n$, the system has as many constraints as unknowns, and, provided they are independent, these can determine the values of the variables, leaving nothing to be maximized. If $n < m$, we have more equations than unknowns, which may well not even have a consistent solution.

$$H_{22} = \begin{vmatrix} L_{11} & L_{13} & L_{14} & -g_1 & -h_1 \\ L_{31} & L_{33} & L_{34} & -g_3 & -h_3 \\ L_{41} & L_{43} & L_{44} & -g_4 & -h_4 \\ -g_1 & -g_3 & -g_4 & 0 & 0 \\ -h_1 & -h_3 & -h_4 & 0 & 0 \end{vmatrix}.$$

The reader may wish to write out the minors H_{33} and H_{44} for himself.

Similarly, we define the next lower-order principal minors H_{ijij} of the Hessian, H, as the minor obtained by deleting the ith and jth rows and the ith and jth columns of H. These fourth-order minors include H_{1212}, H_{1313}, H_{2323}, H_{2424}, and H_{3434}, where, for example,

$$H_{1212} = \begin{vmatrix} L_{33} & L_{34} & -g_3 & -h_3 \\ L_{43} & L_{44} & -g_4 & -h_4 \\ -g_3 & -g_4 & 0 & 0 \\ -h_3 & -h_4 & 0 & 0 \end{vmatrix}.$$

In the same way we can go on defining principal minors of the Hessian of successively lower orders.

We can now state the following two propositions for which we will attempt no proof [10]:

Proposition 1: The second-order conditions for a constrained *minimization* problem such as (22) required the bordered Hessian *and all of its principal minors* to be positive.

Proposition 2: The second-order conditions for *maximization* of a system such as (22) require that its bordered Hessian be negative if the number of its variables (other than Lagrange multipliers) is odd and that it be positive if the number of those variables is even. Moreover, if H is positive, its first-lower-order minors, H_{ii}, must all be negative, its next-lower-order minors, H_{ijij}, must all be positive, etc. Similarly, if H is negative, the H_{ii} must be positive, the H_{ijij} must all be negative, etc. In sum, *the H, H_{ii}, H_{ijij}, etc., must alternate in sign.*

In our example, since we have an even number of variables (the four x's), if we are maximizing we therefore require

$$H > 0$$

$$H_{11} < 0, \qquad H_{22} < 0, \qquad H_{33} < 0, \qquad H_{44} < 0$$

$$H_{1212} > 0, \qquad H_{1313} > 0, \qquad H_{1414} > 0, \qquad H_{2323} > 0, \text{ etc.}$$

---

[10] For a derivation, see, e.g., P. A. Samuelson, *Foundations of Economic Analysis*, Harvard University Press, Cambridge, Mass., 1948, Appendix A.

These conditions are used throughout the standard comparative-statics analyses. In particular, they make use of the requirement that in a minimization problem H and its principal minors must all have the same sign, while in a maximization problem they must alternate in sign.

PROBLEMS

1. Write out H_{2323} for H as given in (23).

2. Show that condition (18) of the previous section follows from Proposition 1 applied to the systems (13) and (14).

8. Illustration III: The Slutsky Theorem for the Consumer

We now derive the Slutsky theorem for the consumer who maximizes the utility he obtains from the consumption of n commodities, in quantities $x_1, \cdots, x_n$, subject to his budget constraint. We want to show that, after elimination of the income effect, $\partial x_1/\partial p_1 < 0$. The consumer seeks to

$$\text{Max } u = u(x_1, \cdots, x_n)$$

subject to

$$\sum p_i x_i = m,$$

whose Lagrangian is

$$(24) \qquad L = u(\,\cdot\,) + \lambda(m - \sum p_i x_i).$$

Differentiating in turn with respect to $x_1, \cdots, x_n, \lambda$ we obtain the first-order conditions

$$(25) \qquad \begin{cases} u_1 - \lambda p_1 = 0 \\ \cdots\cdots\cdots \\ u_r - \lambda p_n = 0 \\ -p_1 x_1 - \cdots - p_n x_n + m = 0. \end{cases}$$

This time we will vary two parameters, p_1 and m, in order to be able to determine dx_1/dm and dx_1/dp_1 so that by comparison of the two we can separate out the income and substitution effects in the latter.

Thus, differentiating totally each equation (25) we obtain

$$(26) \qquad \begin{cases} u_{11}\,dx_1 + u_{12}\,dx_2 + \cdots + u_{1n}\,dx_n - p_1\,d\lambda = \lambda\,dp_1 \\ u_{21}\,dx_1 + u_{22}\,dx_2 + \cdots + u_{2n}\,dx_n - p_2\,d\lambda = 0 \\ \cdots\cdots\cdots\cdots\cdots\cdots\cdots\cdots\cdots\cdots\cdots\cdots \\ u_{n1}\,dx_1 + u_{n2}\,dx_2 + \cdots + u_{nn}\,dx_n - p_n\,d\lambda = 0 \\ -p_1\,dx_1 - p_2\,dx_2 - \cdots - p_n\,dx_n \qquad\quad = x_1\,dp_1 - dm, \end{cases}$$

where for convenience we have brought over to the right-hand sides of these equations all terms involving dm and dp_1, the changes in the parameter values.

Next, to see the effect of a change in the consumer's budget alone on his purchases of x_1, let us separate out the role of dm and dp_1 by first taking $dm \neq 0$, $dp_1 = 0$. Presently, we will reverse these premises to examine the effect of a change in the price, p_1, on his purchases of x_1.

We may now use Cramer's[11] rule to solve the system of linear equations (26) in the variables dx_1, dx_2, $\cdots$, dx_n, $d\lambda$, obtaining from that rule

$$(27) \qquad dx_1 = \begin{vmatrix} 0 & u_{12} & \cdots & u_{1n} & -p_1 \\ 0 & u_{22} & \cdots & u_{2n} & -p_2 \\ \cdots & \cdots & \cdots & \cdots & \cdots \\ 0 & u_{n2} & \cdots & u_{nn} & -p_n \\ -dm & -p_2 & \cdots & -p_n & 0 \end{vmatrix} / H,$$

where the reader should verify that the denominator of (27), which by Cramer's rule is the determinant of (26), is indeed the Hessian, H, of our maximization problem.

---

[11] Cramer's rule gives us the solution in terms of determinants of a system of simultaneous linear equations. For example, suppose we are given the pair of equations $2x_1 + 3x_2 = 4$ and $5x_1 + 6x_2 = 7$. Then the determinant of the system is

$$D = \begin{vmatrix} 2 & 3 \\ 5 & 6 \end{vmatrix} = 2 \times 6 - 3 \times 5 = -3.$$

Cramer's rule states that provided $D \neq 0$ (as is true in our example) then

$$x_1 = \begin{vmatrix} 4 & 3 \\ 7 & 6 \end{vmatrix} / D = 3/-3 = -1 \quad \text{and} \quad x_2 = \begin{vmatrix} 2 & 4 \\ 5 & 7 \end{vmatrix} / D = 2.$$

More generally, in the system of simultaneous linear equations

$$a_{11}x_1 + \cdots + a_{1n}x_n = b_1$$
$$\cdots \cdots \cdots \cdots \cdots$$
$$a_{n1}x_1 + \cdots + a_{nn}x_n = b_n$$

We find the value of a variable x_i from the formula $x_i = A/D$, where D is the determinant of the system

$$\begin{vmatrix} a_{11} \cdots a_{1n} \\ \cdots \cdots \\ a_{n1} \cdots a_{nn} \end{vmatrix}$$

and A is another determinant obtained from D by replacing the ith column in D with the column of constants, $b_1, \cdots, b_n$.

Expanding the determinant of (27) in terms of the elements of its first column[12] we obtain

$$(28) \qquad dx_1 = -dm H_{n+1,1}/H \quad \text{or} \quad dx_1/dm = -H_{n+1,1}/H,$$

where $H_{n+1,1}$ is the cofactor (the signed minor) of the element in the $(n+1)$st row and the 1st column of H. We will see shortly that we know very little about the nature of the expressions in (28). However, it will help us a few paragraphs later to separate out the income effect.

First, however, we must return to the total differential equations (26) to determine the consequences of a price change. This time, therefore, we take $dp_1 \neq 0$, $dm = 0$. Again using Cramer's rule to solve for dx_1 we obtain this time, instead of (27),

$$(29) \qquad dx_1 = \begin{vmatrix} \lambda\, dp_1 & u_{12} & \cdots & u_{1n} & -p_1 \\ 0 & u_{22} & \cdots & u_{2n} & -p_2 \\ \cdots\cdots\cdots\cdots\cdots\cdots\cdots\cdots\cdots \\ 0 & u_{n2} & \cdots & u_{nn} & -p_n \\ x_1\, dp_1 & -p_2 & \cdots & -p_n & 0 \end{vmatrix} / H,$$

or expanding in terms of the first column and using (28),

$$(30) \quad dx_1/dp_1 = \lambda H_{11}/H + x_1 H_{n+1,1}/H = \lambda H_{11}/H - x_1\, dx_1/dm.$$

We will show next that $-x_1\, dx_1/dm$, the second term in (30), is the income effect of the change in price, i.e., that it is $(dx_1/dm)(\partial m/\partial p_1)$, so that the remaining term is the substitution effect. For this purpose first note that if p_1 changes (e.g., it rises), then the resulting fall in purchasing power (the "compensating variation" in income) will be $\partial m/\partial p_1 = -x_1$. If a person is purchasing, say, 7 shirts, and shirts rise in price by one dollar, then he will have lost 7 dollars in purchasing power, i.e., he will

---

[12] It will be recalled that when we expand a determinant such as

$$A = \begin{vmatrix} a_{11} & a_{12} & a_{13} \\ a_{21} & a_{22} & a_{23} \\ a_{31} & a_{32} & a_{33} \end{vmatrix}$$

in terms of its first column we obtain

$$a_{11} \begin{vmatrix} a_{22} & a_{23} \\ a_{32} & a_{33} \end{vmatrix} - a_{21} \begin{vmatrix} a_{12} & a_{13} \\ a_{32} & a_{33} \end{vmatrix} + a_{31} \begin{vmatrix} a_{12} & a_{13} \\ a_{22} & a_{23} \end{vmatrix} = \Sigma\, (-1)^{1+i} a_{i1} A_{i1},$$

where A_{i1} is the minor of the determinant A obtained by eliminating its ith row and first column. The same rule permits us to expand A in terms of any other column or in terms of any of its rows. The minor A_{ij} multiplied by $(-1)^{i+j}$ is called the cofactor of a_{ij}.

need 7 additional dollars to be able to purchase the same number of shirts as before. Similarly, if he is purchasing x_1 units of commodity 1 and the price of that commodity rises by a dollar, his loss on real income can be taken to be $-x_1 = \partial m/\partial p_1$. Substituting this result into the last term of (30) we obtain

$$(31) \qquad -x_1\,dx_1/dm = (dx_1/dm)(\partial m/\partial p_1).$$

This shows that (31) is indeed the income effect, i.e., it is the portion of the effect on x_1 of the rise in price that is transmitted via the effect of dp_1 on the purchasing power of m.

This means that the remaining term in (30) is the substitution effect whose sign it is our purpose to determine. We have by (25) $\lambda = u_1/p_1 > 0$ and by the second-order conditions (Proposition 2 of the preceding section) that H_{11} and H are of opposite signs. Hence we deduce, at last, that

$$(32) \qquad \text{the substitution-effect term} = \lambda H_{11}/H < 0.$$

This is the Slutsky theorem for the consumer, which we have sought to prove. It states that after elimination of the income effect (31) then $\partial x_1/\partial p_1$ as given by (32) will always be negative.

The role played by the income effect in our analysis should be noted. We really have no information about the cofactor, $H_{m+1,1}$, in (31), and so we can draw no general conclusions about the nature of the income effect. We can only say it may sometimes be negative (and call it "the inferior-goods" case) and sometimes positive (calling this the case of "normal" goods). But, fundamentally, the income term just serves as the unexplored component of (30), so that only after it is removed can we make useful statements about the remainder. The discovery that one *can* say a great deal about the remainder *after eliminating the income term* is a major contribution of Slutsky, Hicks, and Allen.

9. Illustration IV: The Linder Theorem

We end our display of comparative-statics problems with one which is simpler to follow than that of the preceding section and which to many will be much more interesting than the Slutsky theorem. After all, with all that effort, we have merely proved that under suitable restrictions the demand curve will have a negative slope, and one may easily wonder whether one might not have accepted that conclusion simply on intuitive grounds without all of the painstaking calculations which we have just gone through. Certainly, that result is not likely to be a major surprise to anyone.

A comparative-statics theorem which is, perhaps, rather more surprising has been provided by Staffan Burenstam-Linder in his fascinating book, *The Harried Leisure Class*.[13] He has challenged the conventional view that the great problem of the twentieth century will be excessive leisure with which man will be unable to cope. On the contrary, the substitution effect of rising hourly incomes always favors the purchase of goods whose consumption requires relatively little time (note that, once again, the ambiguity inherent in the income effect must first be removed before we can arrive at such an unqualified conclusion).

Specifically, the theorem we will prove asserts that, because the consumption of commodities requires time as well as money, the substitution effect of a rise in a person's real wages will always work to decrease the consumption of a commodity whose ratio of consumption time to price is relatively high.

In other words, as his rate of real earnings increases, the consumer will be driven to purchase commodities that, although more costly in money terms, conserve his increasingly scarce resource: time. To derive this result, we use a model that divides the economy into two sectors. We use the following notation:

x_1 = quantity purchased of the commodity under study,
x_2 = quantity of "all other goods" consumed,
x_3 = quantity of labor time spent earning income,
p_1, p_2 = prices of commodities 1 and 2, respectively,
w = wage rate,
t_1, t_2 = consumption time expended per unit of commodities 1 and 2, and
m = nonwage income (if any).

We will show that, neglecting income effects, $\partial x_1 / \partial w > 0$ if, and only if, $t_1/p_1 < t_2/p_2$ (that is, if commodity 1 has an unusually low ratio of consumption time to price). The consumer's objective is to maximize his utility:

$$u(x_1, x_2, x_3)$$

subject to his budget and time-availability constraints:

$$p_1 x_1 + p_2 x_2 = m + w x_3$$
$$t_1 x_1 + t_2 x_2 + x_3 = t.$$

---

[13] Staffan Burenstam-Linder, *The Harried Leisure Class*, Columbia University Press, New York, 1970, pp. 150–152.

We use the standard comparative-statics procedure to find our desired expression for $\partial x_1 / \partial w$. Our Lagrangian is

$$L = u(x_1, x_2, x_3) + \lambda(m + wx_3 - p_1 x_1 - p_2 x_2) + \mu(t - t_1 x_1 - t_2 x_2 - x_3),$$

with the first-order conditions

(33)
$$\begin{cases} u_1 - \lambda p_1 - \mu t_1 = 0 \\ u_2 - \lambda p_2 - \mu t_2 = 0 \\ u_3 + \lambda w - \mu = 0 \\ m + wx_3 - p_1 x_1 - p_2 x_2 = 0 \\ t - t_1 x_1 - t_2 x_2 - x_3 = 0. \end{cases}$$

Next, we set equal to zero the total differentials of our first-order conditions, which the reader may wish to write out as an exercise. Letting H represent the determinant of the system, we have, by Cramer's rule and expanding the numerator determinant in terms of its first row,

(34)
$$dx_1 = \begin{vmatrix} 0 & u_{12} & u_{13} & -p_1 & -t_1 \\ 0 & u_{22} & u_{23} & -p_2 & -t_2 \\ -\lambda\, dw & u_{32} & u_{33} & w & -1 \\ -x_3\, dw - dm & -p_2 & w & 0 & 0 \\ 0 & -t_2 & -1 & 0 & 0 \end{vmatrix} / H$$

$$= -\lambda\, dw H_{31}/H - (x_3\, dw + dm) H_{41}/H.$$

We can use precisely the same procedure as that in the previous section to show that the last term in (34) is now our income effect. This leaves us with the substitution effect

$$-\lambda H_{31}/H = -\lambda \begin{vmatrix} u_{12} & u_{13} & -p_1 & -t_1 \\ u_{22} & u_{23} & -p_2 & -t_2 \\ -p_2 & w & 0 & 0 \\ -t_2 & -1 & 0 & 0 \end{vmatrix} / H$$

which can be shown by expansion of this last determinant to equal

(35)
$$-\lambda(p_2 + wt_2)(p_1 t_2 - p_2 t_1)/H.$$

Now it can be argued that we must assume $\lambda > 0$. The argument, incidentally, illustrates clearly the use of first-order conditions in obtaining qualitative results in a comparative-statics analysis. Substituting from the third equation into the first equation of first-order conditions (33) we eliminate μ and obtain

$$u_1 - \lambda p_1 - u_3 t_1 - \lambda w t_1 = 0$$

or

$$\lambda = (u_1 - u_3 t_1)/(p_1 + w t_1) > 0$$

since presumably $u_1 > 0$, $u_3 < 0$ (marginal utility of commodity 1 is positive; marginal utility of labor, u_3, is negative).

Moreover, by the second-order conditions (Proposition 2) $H < 0$. Then since all the other terms in (35) are positive, we see that the substitution effect will be positive if, and only if, $p_1 t_2 - p_2 t_1 > 0$, i.e., $t_1/p_1 < t_2/p_2$ (that is, if the ratio of time-cost to price for commodity 1 is less than that of "all other goods"). This is our desired result.

The intuitive explanation of this result rests in what is, in effect, a rising cost of time. Because the amount of time available to an individual is fixed, it becomes increasingly scarce (and hence, expensive) relative to the expanding quantities of commodities that can be purchased with an ever-rising income (as well as the rising wages that can be earned in each hour). Those consumption activities that are time intensive then become correspondingly less attractive. To paraphrase Linder, as the individual's time becomes more valuable he is driven to seek to spend his money "more efficiently," that is, more quickly.[14]

REFERENCES

Silberberg, E., "A Revision of Comparative Statics Methodology," *Journal of Economic Theory*, vol. 7, No. 2, 1974 (mathematical treatment, but not too difficult).

---

[14] Our discussion has dealt only with the substitution effect. As usual, the income effect can work either way. Where leisure is not an inferior good, the income effect will make for a secular rise in its demand, offsetting the substitution effect, at least in part. However, casual observation suggests that precisely those individuals with the educational background and occupations associated with attendance at theatrical performances and the utilization of museums and libraries are the persons who have not demanded more free time as their incomes have risen—if anything, they have tended to grow increasingly busy at their "responsible" jobs.

Towards Observability:
Revealed Preference
and
Expenditure and Cost Functions

14

Ordinalism was only a first step away from an analysis based on introspective utility. Even indifference maps and subjective rankings are not observable directly, and they certainly do not lend themselves to statistical estimation. In recent years two new structures for consumer analysis that move us a long step toward direct observability have become available. The first of these, the revealed preference analysis, was designed almost entirely by Samuelson,[1] with the finishing touches to the analysis contributed by Houthakker.[2] Samuelson also made major contributions to the second of these innovative constructs, the use of expenditure functions as a substitute for utility analysis, whose full formalization must, however, be attributed to the earlier work of R. Roy.[3]

This chapter provides an introduction to both these approaches. The second of them, which is also described as the duality analysis of consumer behavior, has its analogous counterpart in the theory of production and the decision-making of the firm, where the central source is the work of Shephard.[4] Some of the most suggestive applications of duality theory

---

[1] P. A. Samuelson, *Foundations of Economic Analysis*, Harvard University Press, Cambridge, Mass., 1948, Chapter VI.

[2] H. S. Houthakker, "Revealed Preference and the Utility Function," *Economica*, Vol. XVII, May 1950.

[3] See R. Roy, *De L'Utilité: Contribution a la Théorie des Choix*, Paris, 1942.

[4] Ronald Shephard, *Cost and Profit Functions*, Princeton University Press, Princeton, N.J., 1953, 1970.

occur in production analysis, and so the discussion concludes with an examination of the application of duality analysis to production theory, which should also cast some light on our discussion of expenditure functions.

1. The Revealed Preference Model

The revealed preference analysis undertakes to reconstruct the theory of the consumer on the basis of concepts which, at least in principle, do not require the consumer to supply any information about himself. If his tastes do not change, observation of his market behavior can, conceptually, supply all the requisite data. For this purpose we need merely record what combinations of commodities he buys at different prices. Given enough such information, it is even theoretically possible to reconstruct the consumer's indifference map, as we shall see.

The entire revealed preference analysis is based on a rather simple idea. A consumer will decide to buy some particular set of items either because he likes them more than the other goods that are available to him or because they happen to be cheap. Suppose we observe that of two collections of commodities offered for sale the consumer chooses to buy A rather than B. We are, then, *not* entitled to conclude that he *prefers A to B*, because it is also possible that his decision just reflects the fact (if it is a fact) that A is the cheaper collection and he may even regret not buying B. But price information may be able to remove this uncertainty. If their price tags tell us that A is not cheaper than B, then there is only one plausible explanation of the consumer's choice—he bought A because he likes it better. More generally, we have the

Definition: If a consumer buys some collection of goods A, rather than the available collections B, C, D, etc., and it turns out that none of the latter is more expensive than A, we say that A has been *revealed preferred* to the others (or that the others have been revealed to be inferior to A).[5]

The complete set of combinations which are revealed inferior to A by one purchase can be found with the aid of the price line. In Figure 1a, let A represent the collection of commodities which is bought when the

---

[5] Let $p_a = (p_{1a}, p_{2a}, \cdots, p_{na})$ be the set of prices at which the individual buys collection $x_a = (x_{1a}, \cdots, x_{na})$ and spurns another collection $x_b = (x_{1b}, \cdots, x_{nb})$. Then x_a is said to be revealed preferred to x_b if it is at least as expensive as x_b at the prices p_a at which x_a is purchased. That is, x_a is revealed preferred to x_b if

$$\sum_{i=1}^{n} p_{ia}x_{ia} \geq \sum_{i=1}^{n} p_{ia}x_{ib},$$

where the right-hand sum represents the cost of collection x_b at the prices p_a at which in fact x_a was purchased.

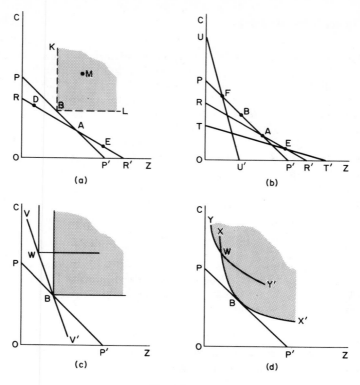

Figure 1

price line is PP'. By definition, any other point on PP', such as B, is just as expensive as A. Moreover, since every point, such as D, which is below and to the left of the price line, represents smaller amounts of both commodities than do some points on PP', it follows that such lower points are cheaper than A. Therefore, because the consumer bought A rather than any of these other collections that were no more expensive, it follows that every point on or below PP' is revealed inferior to A. Finally, since it should be clear that any point above PP' is more expensive than A, we see that none of these can be revealed inferior to A by the consumer's purchase of A.

We can now state the basic assumption of the theory, called the *weak assumption of revealed preference*. This asserts that[6]

---

[6] In terms of the notation of footnote 1, this premise asserts the following: Suppose at prices p_a some collection x_a would be purchased, while at some other set of prices, p_b, x_b would be bought. Then if

$$\sum p_{ia}x_{ia} \geq \sum p_{ia}x_{ib}$$

so that x_a is revealed preferred to x_b, then we can never have x_b revealed preferred to x_a. That is, at the prices p_b at which x_b is bought we must never have

$$\sum p_{ib}x_{ib} \geq \sum p_{ib}x_{ia}.$$

The consumer will never behave in a manner which is so inconsistent that some collection A will be revealed preferred to B and that B will simultaneously be revealed preferred to A.

Violation of this assumption must involve the consumer's buying A if it were the more expensive and then being induced by a relative *rise* in B's price *to above the price of A* to switch his allegiance to B! A Cadillac buyer who could be induced to switch to a Chevrolet by a rise in its price to $50,000 would violate the weak revealed preference assumption. We would not normally expect consumers to behave in this apparently peculiar manner. However, both snob appeal and the judging of quality by price can, clearly, be inconsistent with this weak revealed preference assumption.[7]

We shall also employ a second assumption:

Given any collection of goods, the consumer can be induced to buy it if its price is made sufficiently attractive, i.e., for any point in Figure 1a, there exists some price line involving positive prices and a positive income level which will lead the consumer to buy it.

The assumptions are all that is needed to derive any of the standard results of the theory of consumer behavior (with the exception of integrability, as noted in an earlier footnote).

As an illustration let us see how revealed preference theory can be used to prove the Slutsky theorem, which states that if the income effect is ignored, the demand curve must have a negative slope. Although a two-dimensional diagram is employed for expository purposes, every step of the argument carries over to a situation involving any number of commodities.

In Figure 1a let A represent the combination of commodities bought when the price line is PP'. We want to show, once again, that a fall in the price of commodity Z from PP' will increase (not decrease) purchases of Z

---

[7] The *strong* assumption of revealed preference is a sort of transitivity extension of the weak assumption. It asserts that if collection x_a is revealed preferred to x_b, if x_b is in turn revealed preferred to $x_c, \cdots$, and x_y is revealed preferred to x_z, then no set of prices will reveal x_z preferred to x_a. Houthakker showed that this premise is required to guarantee the existence of a utility function that is consistent with any given indifference map—the so-called problem of *integrability*. Given any ordinary indifference map in two dimensions it is always possible to construct many utility surfaces consistent with these preferences, but the same is not necessarily true in an n-variable case. However, it is true if the consumer's preferences satisfy the strong axiom of revealed preference. (The term *integrability* occurs here because indifference curves can be described by the differential equations, $du = 0$, where u is the consumer's utility, and integration of these equations, if it is possible, yields the equation of the corresponding utility surfaces.)

if we consider only the substitution effect. For this purpose, we insert the imaginary price line RR' which passes through point A, so that the consumer's real income remains constant in the sense that he can still just make his original purchase at the new prices, if he wishes to do so. RR' is flatter than PP' because Z has, by hypothesis, fallen in price. We want to prove that the new equilibrium point on RR' (if it is different from A) must be a point like E, which lies to the right of A (an increased demand for Z). To prove that this must be so, we show that any point on RR', such as D, which lies to the left of A, is ruled out by the weak revealed preference assumption. We know that, since D lies below PP', A is revealed to be preferred to D. But if D were chosen when the price line was RR', then since A is no more expensive than D at those prices (they lie on the same price line), D would be revealed preferred to A. Hence A would be revealed preferred to D and vice versa, which is precisely what the weak revealed preference assumption prohibits. Thus, no point on RR' which, like D, lies to the left of A can be chosen. The substitution effect of a fall in the price of Z will generally increase the demand for Z (or at least not decrease it), as was to be proved.

2. Revealed Preference and the Slutsky Theorem in n Variables

The nature of revealed preference analysis in n commodity problems is easily illustrated by an explicit derivation of the Slutsky theorem in n variables.

Suppose our consumer would purchase quantities $x_1, \cdots, x_n$ of these commodities at prices $p_1, \cdots, p_n$. However, if the price of good 1 were replaced by $p_1 + \Delta p_1$, all other prices held constant, *and the consumer's income were changed so as to leave him on the same indifference curve* (i.e., the income effect were removed), his purchases would change to some quantities $x_1 + \Delta x_1, \cdots, x_n + \Delta x_n$ and the increments $\Delta x_1, \cdots, \Delta x_n$ must represent the substitution effects of the price change, p_1. The Slutsky theorem asserts that the sign of Δx_1 will be the opposite of that of Δp_1, that is, if the commodity's price *rises*, the substitution effect is a *decrease* in purchase of that item and *vice versa*.

Now $x_1, \cdots, x_n$ and $x_1 + \Delta x_1, \cdots, x_n + \Delta x_n$ are indifferent because the income effect has been removed. Thus, the former cannot be revealed preferred to the other; at the prices $p_1, \cdots, p_n$ at which the former is purchased it cannot be as expensive or more expensive than the latter. That is,

$$p_1 x_1 + p_2 x_2 + \cdots + p_n x_n < p_1(x_1 + \Delta x_1) + p_2(x_2 + \Delta x_2)$$
$$+ \cdots + p_n(x_n + \Delta x_n).$$

Similarly, because they are indifferent, the second collection of goods $x_i + \Delta x_i$ cannot be revealed preferred to the first so that at the prices $(p_1 + \Delta p_1, p_2, \cdots, p_n)$ at which that collection is bought

$$(p_1 + \Delta p_1)x_1 + p_2 x_2 + \cdots + p_n x_n > (p_1 + \Delta p_1)(x_1 + \Delta x_1)$$
$$+ p_2(x_2 + \Delta x_2)$$
$$+ \cdots + p_n(x_n + \Delta x_n)$$

Subtracting the first of these inequalities from the second we obtain at once

$$\Delta p_1 x_1 > \Delta p_1 (x_1 + \Delta x_1)$$

or

$$0 > \Delta p_1 \, \Delta x_1,$$

which is our Slutsky theorem.

PROBLEM

1. Provide a different derivation of the Slutsky theorem from the revealed preference assumption using the alternative definition of removal of the income effect under which the consumer's money income is adjusted so that after the price change he can just purchase the initial collection of goods. That is,

$$(p_1 + \Delta p_1)x_1 + p_2 x_2 + \cdots + p_n x_n = (p_1 + \Delta p_1)(x_1 + \Delta x_1) + p_2(x_2 + \Delta x_2)$$
$$+ \cdots + p_n(x_n + \Delta x_n).$$

3. Revealed Preference and the Indifference Map

The revealed preference assumptions also permit us, in principle, to construct the consumer's indifference map on the basis of enough observations on his market behavior. Going back to Figure 1a, suppose this time that B is observed to be the combination which is chosen by the consumer when the price line is PP', and let us try to find the indifference curve through point B. We already know from our first observation that B is revealed preferred to every point on or below PP'. Moreover, it is easily shown that every point such as M, which lies in the region above and to the right of point B (the shaded region above KBL), is revealed preferred to B. It is, of course, highly plausible that M is preferred to B, for M contains more of one or both commodities than does B (it is above and to the right of B).[8]

---

[8] M is revealed preferred to B by the fact that it is always at least as expensive as B since it contains more of at least one commodity (and no less of either good). And

It follows that the remainder of the indifference curve through B must lie below area KBL and above price line PP', i.e., that it must lie somewhere in the unshaded region above line PP'. This proves at once that, at least near B, the indifference curve must have a negative slope (otherwise it would enter area KBL) and that it must be convex to the origin (it must be above PP' both to the right and to the left of B). Since this argument can be repeated for any other point in the diagram, we see how the revealed preference theory can be used to prove that all indifference curves must be of negative slope and convex to the origin throughout their length.

However, we still have quite a way to go before we find the precise shape of the indifference curve through B, since all we have seen so far is that it can lie anywhere in the unshaded region above line PP' (which has been called the *zone of ignorance*). But further observations of the consumer's behavior can, as will be shown now, permit us to extend the shaded regions by chipping away at the zone of ignorance, and thus to get closer and closer to finding the precise location of the indifference curve through B.

First let us see how we can extend the region OPP', which is revealed inferior to B. Consider any point other than B on PP', e.g., point A (Figure 1a), which has, therefore, been revealed inferior to B. By the second assumption of revealed preference theory, there is some price line, RR', which will lead the consumer to purchase A. We find RR' by watching the consumer and recording his income and the prices he pays when we see him buy A. Any point on or below RR' is now revealed inferior to A, and since A has, in turn, been revealed inferior to B, everything on or below RR' is revealed inferior to B.[9] Thus triangle $AP'R'$ is revealed inferior to B—it has been chopped off from the region of ignorance. We can repeat this procedure as many times as we wish. For example, we can take any other point, such as F, on PP' (Figure 1b), find its price line UU', and thereby show that triangle PFU is revealed inferior to B and thus remove this triangle from our zone of ignorance. Or we can take a point *on one of the added price lines*, such as point E on RR', and observe the price line TT' at which E is bought. Since every point on or below TT' is revealed to be inferior to E, and E is inferior to A, which is, in turn, inferior to B, all of these points are revealed inferior to B. Hence, triangle $R'ET'$ is now removed from the zone of ignorance, etc. In this way we can go on chopping away at the underbelly of the zone of ignorance indefinitely, getting closer and closer to the indifference curve through point B which we seek.

---

since, by the second assumption of revealed preference theory, some positive prices can induce the consumer to buy the more expensive collection, M, those prices must reveal that he prefers M to B.

[9] Note that this argument sneaks in an assumption of transitivity. If E is revealed inferior to A and A is revealed inferior to B, we assume that E is thereby revealed inferior to B.

Moreover, the upper portion of the zone of ignorance can also be hacked away bit by bit. Thus, in Figure 1c draw *any* new price line, VV', through B. We observe the consumer when prices and his income happen to correspond to budget line VV'. Let W be the point which is chosen with these prices and income. At these prices B is no more expensive than W, so that W (and, consequently, all of the region above and to the right of W) is revealed to be preferred to B. This procedure can be repeated with other price lines through point B, each of which yields a point like W that is revealed to be preferred to B. The locus of all such points, the curve XX' in Figure 1d, and all points above and to the right of XX' are, then, revealed preferred to B. XX' is called the *offer curve* through point B.[10] We can chop away still more of the zone of ignorance by choosing any point W on offer curve XX', observing what the consumer buys with various price lines through W, and so constructing the offer curve YY' through W. Since any point on or above YY' is revealed preferred to W, which is in turn preferred to B, these points are all shown to be preferred to B. Proceeding as long as we wish in this way, we can narrow down the region of possible location of the indifference curve through B (the zone of ignorance) as far as we like.

Unfortunately, the proof that the upper and lower chopping-away sequences converge, and so *exactly* narrow the zone of ignorance down to a single indifference curve, is rather difficult and involves more advanced theorems in differential equations.[11] However, the basic idea of the revealed preference approach to indifference curve construction should be clear from the foregoing discussion.

4. Revealed Preference and Index Numbers of Real Income

An index number formula for the measurement of real income undertakes to employ price and quantity information for each of two periods and to determine on the basis of these data alone whether real income has risen, fallen, or remained unchanged. One of the major difficulties in the construction of an index number formula lies in the problem of evaluating a real income change which involves many individuals, since it may be an improvement from the point of view of some people but an unfortunate development in the opinion of some others. But even though we will deal with only *one* person in order to evade this problem, we will see that the construction of an index number formula still runs into fundamental difficulties.

---

[10] That is because XX' shows the various commodity combinations, such as W, which the consumer will offer to buy at different relative prices (different price lines) any of which enable the consumer to buy combination B with no money left over.

[11] See H. S. Houthakker, *op. cit.*

Suppose that the consumer receives some collection of goods, B, in one period and some other collection, Q, in the next. In some ultimate psychological sense we can say that his real income will have risen if and only if Q lies above his indifference curve through B; his real income is unchanged if and only if B and Q are on the same indifference curve, and his real income will have fallen if point Q lies below the indifference curve which passes through point B. Thus, to accomplish its purpose the index number formula must somehow be able to indicate on the basis of two sets of price-quantity observations where the indifference curve through B lies in relation to point Q.

But we have just seen that such a small amount of price and quantity information must leave us with a considerable zone of ignorance as to the location of any indifference curve. Hence it is impossible to design any index number formula which *always* tells us whether real income has risen, fallen, or remained unchanged. In some cases, depending on the prices or quantities involved, it is possible to determine whether B or Q represents the larger income. For example, in Figure 1a if PP' represents the price situation when B is purchased and then if Q lies below PP', we know that B is revealed preferred to Q so that the change from B to Q represents a fall in real income. Similarly, if Q lies in region KBL, we know that real income must have risen. But if Q lies in the unshaded zone of ignorance, we may well lack information sufficient to determine what has happened to real income, and no formula can supply these missing data.

There are two cases in which we can be sure of what has happened to real income: If Q lies below B's price line, real income must have fallen, whereas if B lies below the price line when Q is purchased, so that Q is revealed preferred to B, then real income has risen. That is as far as the data will carry us—if neither of these situations happens to hold, no index number formula can determine what has really happened to real income.

Yet any one of the standard index number formulas is set up as a test of the direction of change of real income. The price and quantity data for points B and Q are inserted into the formula, and if the resulting index number turns out to be greater than 100, real income has allegedly risen; if it is equal to 100, it is supposed to be unchanged; and so on. It is natural to ask about the basis on which these judgments are made when the required indifference curve information is not available. The answer is that any index number formula implicitly sets up an imaginary and arbitrary indifference map and then treats it as though it were the consumer's true indifference map, using this arbitrary map to determine what has happened to his real income. Of course, if the individual's true indifference map differs from the artificial map implicit in the index number formula, the index number may well imply that real income has gone up when it has in fact decreased, and vice versa.

This can be illustrated by a brief analysis of that index number of real income which uses base-period prices as weights (the Laspeyres index). Let us, for simplicity, suppose there are only our two commodities, C and Z, and let p_{bc} and p_{bz} be their respective base-period prices. If the quantities held by the consumer in the base period were c_b and z_b and if c and z are his current possessions of the commodities, the expression for the Laspeyres index of current real income is

$$100 \frac{p_{bc}c + p_{bz}z}{p_{bc}c_b + p_{bz}z_b},$$

i.e., the value of current purchases c and z, at base-year prices $(p_{bc}c + p_{bz}z)$ divided by the actual base-year expenditure on the two commodities $(p_{bc}c_b + p_{bz}z_b)$, all multiplied by 100. Suppose, then, that we know the four base-year numbers p_{bc}, p_{bz}, c_b, and z_b and that we want to find which possible combinations of c and z will, according to this expression, leave our consumer's real income unchanged. Income will remain constant on this Laspeyres index calculation whenever we have

(1) $$100 \frac{p_{bc}c + p_{bz}z}{p_{bc}c_b + p_{bz}z_b} = 100,$$

where the reader should remember that the four base-year magnitudes p_{bc}, p_{bz}, c_b, and z_b are given, fixed numbers, not variables. Now divide both sides of the equation by 100 to cancel it out, and use m_b to designate the given (constant) total base-year expenditure on both commodities together, the denominator in (1). The indifference curve equation (1) then becomes

$$\frac{p_{bc}c + p_{bz}z}{m_b} = 1,$$

that is,

(2) $$p_{bc}c + p_{bz}z = m_b.$$

Equation (2) is just another version of the formula (1) for any combination of goods C and Z which the Laspeyres index considers indifferent with that of the base year (real income unchanged). It is the equation of a Laspeyres index indifference curve. But the reader will note that (2) is the equation of the price line with base-period prices p_{bc} and p_{bz} and base-period income (expenditure) m_b. In other words, the Laspeyres indifference curve is the base-period price line! Thus it is the very lowest edge (PP') of the zone of ignorance (Figure 1a)—any points below it are necessarily revealed inferior to the base-period point.

This result helps us to evaluate the Laspeyres index number, for we know that the true indifference curve through point B (which represents the combination of C and Z consumed during the base period) must lie above this price line PP' (Figure 2). We see that if the point representing current consumption is located below PP' (point Q) so that the Laspeyres index number says real income has fallen, this must actually be the case. But if the Laspeyres index number indicates that real income has risen, it may (point Q'') or may not (point Q') in fact have done so (for point Q'' also lies above the true indifference curve but point Q' lies *below* it). In sum, the Laspeyres indifference curve may charitably be considered the lowest possible curve in the zone of ignorance, and whenever it is wrong it must overvalue current real income. In other words, it is the most sanguine of all admissible indices of real income, since any index which is more biased in this direction (e.g., if it says Q is also better than B) must imply that the consumer's base-period indifference curve actually cuts below the base-period price line, into the region which is revealed inferior to B!

Although it is possible to conduct a similar analysis of the concealed implications of any other index number formula, such an investigation is usually somewhat more difficult than that of the Laspeyres case.

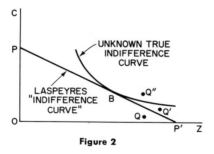

Figure 2

5. Duality and the Theory of the Producer and Consumer

We turn now to the second of the major reformulations of consumer analysis: duality or expenditure-function theory.

The last few years have witnessed a substantial flow of writings on this subject, which (like revealed preference theory) is designed in some sense to constitute a *re*formulation containing no more substantive materials than those contained (at least *implicitly*) in the older writings. But this new way of looking at matters does contribute important insights of its own and offers many *analytic* advantages both in tractability and in more immediate empirical application.

The newer analysis represents a dual approach to the more conventional analyses both literally and in spirit. It may be recalled from the discussion of Chapter 6 that when production decisions were interpreted as "the primal problem" the analysis was conducted in terms of activity (physical output) levels, whereas the dual problem instead emphasized money values. In an economic model in which physical quantities (e.g., consumer demands or outputs) can be taken to be determined by prices or prices by physical quantities one has a choice over which of these two types of variable to use in formulating the analysis. At least in principle, the business firm can choose how much it hopes to sell (and from this it can deduce a selling price), or it can instead decide how much it wants to charge for its product (and then estimate how much it will be able to sell at each price). In exactly the same way, the theorist can interchange the role he assigns in his analysis to the "real" and the pecuniary variables. This is precisely the changeover that occurs as one proceeds from the conventional formulation described in earlier chapters of the book to the dual analysis.

As we will see, one of the immediate fruits of this changeover is the replacement of relatively abstract concepts such as utility and production functions, which are not only difficult to deal with statistically but are even more difficult to explain to practitioners. Their place is taken by expenditure functions (indicating how a consumer's outlays vary with the amounts he purchases), by cost functions, and by profit functions, all of which are easily understood, conceptually, and all of which are expressed in terms of variables and parameters for which empirical data are more readily available.

It should be emphasized that the equivalence in principle between duality theory and the conventional analysis is no shortcoming of the former. On the contrary it is a substantial accomplishment to show that a relatively straightforward concept such as a consumer's expenditure function contains within it all the information obtainable from his (inaccessible) utility function and that under specified circumstances the properties of the utility relationship can be deduced from the expenditure function.

The dual approach then offers us at least three principal advantages:

1. It enables us to formulate many problems in a way that is "natural," i.e., translatable into intuitive ways of looking at the analyses.
2. It is often more readily adaptable to empirical estimation.
3. It facilitates the processes of theoretical deduction and proof.

In particular, as we will see, one important case of the last of these advantages lies in the field of comparative statics where it permits the elimination of many long and tedious calculations, substituting for them calculations which are basically simple, even though the unfamiliarity of their approach may make them seem somewhat more difficult than they actually are.

As often happens in a relatively new branch of analysis, the duality literature does not generally make easy reading for the uninitiated. Some of the materials are, indeed, inherently complicated, but there is also a great deal, encompassing some of the most fundamental parts of the analysis, that can be understood without too much trouble. These are of course the portions of the discussion upon which this chapter concentrates.

6. The Expenditure Function as a Substitute for Utility Analysis

The basic structure of the conventional theory of the consumer, it will be recalled, consists of a simple constrained maximization model. The consumer is assumed to want to select that combination of purchases that maximizes his utility subject to his budget constraint, i.e., he is taken to

$$\text{Max } u(x_1, \cdots, x_n)$$

subject to

$$\sum p_i x_i \leq m.$$

The dual of this problem, whose interpretation is obvious, describes the consumer as a minimizer of *expenditure*, $\sum p_i x_i$, for whatever level of utility he attains. He is taken to seek to

$$(3) \qquad\qquad \text{Min } E = \sum p_i x_i$$

subject to

$$(4) \qquad\qquad u(x_1, \cdots, x_n) \geq u^*,$$

where u^* is some given level of utility.

We may now define the *expenditure function*, $E(p_1, \cdots, p_n, u^*)$, as the minimum level of spending necessary to achieve the given level of utility u^* when prices are set at $p = p_1, \cdots, p_n$, i.e., it is the value of E obtained from the solution of problem (3), (4). More explicitly

$$(5) \qquad E(p, u^*) \equiv E(p_1, \cdots, p_n, u^*) = \sum p_i x_i^0,$$

where the x_i^0 are the optimal values of the x_i obtained from the solution to the dual problem (3), (4) and p represents the vector of parameter values, $p_1, \cdots, p_n$. The expenditure function, which is expressed entirely in terms of observable prices and outputs, involves none of the abstract and disputable issues that arise in an analysis basing itself on the utility function. Yet one remarkable feature of the theory is that a "well-behaved" expenditure function, i.e., one with certain desirable properties which will soon be spelled out, contains within it an *indirect* utility function which is also certain to be well behaved. That is, not only can one deduce the expenditure function from the utility function via (3), (4), but one can proceed in the reverse route, going from expenditures to utilities, and in each case, desirable properties of the function with which one begins the calculation imply analogous desirable properties for the function which has been deduced.

These and other significant properties of the expenditure function are contained in a number of theorems to which we turn next.

7. Three Properties of the Expenditure-Utility Relationships[12]

A utility function for our purposes may be considered to be well behaved if it possesses three basic properties:

1. There are some values of $x_1, \cdots, x_n$ for which the consumer is not sated[13] (the quantities with which our discussion deals will all be taken from the region of nonsatiation).
2. The utility function is strictly quasi-concave (Chapter 9, Section 7), meaning, in effect, that in the zone of nonsatiety its indifference curves are "convex to the origin."
3. The utility function is continuous in the variables $x_1, \cdots, x_n$.

These properties are not all required in order to arrive at all the propositions that follow, but they are sufficient for their derivation. To avoid complications we will therefore assume that they hold for any utility function from which we wish to deduce an expenditure function. For many purposes it is also convenient to assume a further property:

4. The utility function has first and second partial and cross-partial derivatives in all the variables $x_1, \cdots, x_n$, i.e., the derivatives $\partial u/\partial x_i$, $\partial^2 u/\partial x_i^2$, and $\partial^2 u/\partial x_i \, \partial x_j$ exist for all relevant commodities i, j.

---

[12] The materials in the remainder of this chapter are relatively advanced.

[13] It will be recalled, from Section 7 of Chapter 9, that nonsatiation means that the set of x values lies in a region such that consumers prefer larger quantities of any and all of the commodities in question and that, consequently, indifference curves for any pair of the n commodities must have negative slopes.

Obviously, if property 4 holds, then property 3 becomes redundant. We may note that the properties we have just discussed are essentially those assumed in conventional utility and indifference analysis as described in Chapter 9, and they permit us to deduce all the standard results of that analysis. That is why we may refer to a utility function that has these properties as being "well behaved." With these conditions satisfied the dual problem (3), (4) will possess a solution, i.e., the expenditure function then exists.

We now deduce immediately

Proposition 1: The expenditure function is a linearly homogeneous function of prices. That is, if all prices are increased k-fold, then the minimum expenditure necessary to attain the utility level u^* is also increased k-fold.

The proof of Proposition 1 is completely trivial. Suppose all prices are multiplied by k. Referring to (3) and (4) this will obviously not change the optimal consumption quantities, x_i^0, for whatever x's minimize $\sum p_i x_i$ must also minimize the value of the objective function after the price change, $\sum k p_i x_i = k \sum p_i x_i$ when both are subject to the same constraints since the price change merely multiplies the objective function by the constant, k. Thus, by (5) the new expenditure function becomes

$$(6) \qquad\qquad E(kp, u^*) = \sum k p_i x_i^0 = k E(p, u^*),$$

which is what we were to prove, i.e., that multiplication of each price by k also multiplies the expenditure function by k.

Proposition 2: The expenditure function is strictly monotonically increasing with utility level u^*. That is, higher utility levels can be attained by the consumer only if he increases his expenditure.

Proof: Because the consumer is not sated and prices are positive, if u^* is to be decreased slightly to $u^* - \Delta$, one way in which the consumer can certainly save money is by a small *proportionate* decrease in his consumption of all commodities sufficient to get him down to the lower utility level. Since he will be able to save at least this amount by the *cost-minimizing* level of expenditure, it follows that we must have $E(p, u^* - \Delta) < E(p, u^*)$.

We now come to a result which is far less obvious and only slightly more difficult to prove:

Proposition 3: If the utility function satisfies properties 1–4, then the expenditure function is concave in prices.

It will be recalled (Chapter 9, Section 16) that a concave function is defined as one which, intuitively speaking, is "concave downward." Mathematically,

Definition: the function $y = f(p_1, \ldots, p_n) = f(p)$ is concave if given the line segment connecting any two points on its graph, $p' = (p'_1, \ldots, p'_n)$ and $p'' = (p''_1, \ldots, p''_n)$, then for any $p^* = wp' + (1 - w)p''$ which is an interior point on the line segment connecting p' and p'' the "height" above p^* of the line segment connecting $f(p')$ and $f(p'')$, i.e., $wf(p') + (1 - w)f(p'')$, will be less than that of the corresponding point on the graph of the function, $f(p^*)$. That is, for any constant w such that $0 < w < 1$, $f(p)$ is concave if

$$(7) \qquad f(p^*) \equiv f[wp' + (1 - w)p''] \geq wf(p') + (1 - w)f(p'').$$

We now offer the proof of Proposition 3, leaving until afterward the discussion of its economic content.

Let $x' = (x'_1, \cdots, x'_n)$, $x'' = (x''_1, \cdots, x''_n)$, and $x^* = (x^*_1, \cdots, x^*_n)$ represent the optimal (least-cost) solutions under the three sets of prices p'_i, p''_i, and p^*_i, respectively, where $p^*_i = wp'_i + (1 - w)p''_i$; that is, the p^*_i are a weighted average of p'_i and p''_i, so that p^* is any point on the line segment connecting p' and p'' (see Section 15 of Chapter 9). By (4), x', x'', and x^* each yield at least the utility level u^*. Hence at prices p'_i the bundle $(x^*_1, \cdots, x^*_n)$ must be at least as expensive as $(x'_1, \cdots, x'_n)$, the least-cost purchase at these prices, i.e.,

$$(8) \qquad \sum p'_i x^*_i \geq \sum p'_i x'_i \equiv E(p', u^*).$$

Similarly, at prices p'' the bundle x^* must be at least as expensive as x'' so that

$$(9) \qquad \sum p''_i x^*_i \geq \sum p''_i x''_i \equiv E(p'', u^*).$$

Consequently, at the prices $p^* = wp' + (1 - w)p''$ for which the x^*_i are optimal,

$$
\begin{aligned}
(10) \quad E(p^*, u^*) &\equiv \sum p^*_i x^*_i \equiv \sum [wp'_i + (1 - w)p''_i]x^*_i \\
&= w \sum p'_i x^*_i + (1 - w) \sum p''_i x^*_i \\
&\geq wE(p', u^*) + (1 - w)E(p'', u^*) \qquad \text{[by (8) and (9)]}.
\end{aligned}
$$

But by (7) relationship (10) is precisely what we mean by the concavity of E.   Q.E.D.

Having completed our proof we turn next to the economic interpretation of the theorem. The discussion will also help to clarify the concept of concavity.

Taken literally, Proposition 3 asserts that if we consider two alternative sets of prices, then a (weighted) average of these prices will certainly not decrease (from the average cost under the initial sets of prices) the amount of money which a consumer must lay out to achieve a given level of utility, and, indeed, at the averaged prices the consumer may well have to spend more for the purpose. Thus the theorem says, in effect, that price averaging tends to make it more costly to maintain one's real income. But why should this be true? A simple example will show intuitively why it is so. Suppose that the only two items whose prices vary are two close substitutes, say, 1969 wines of two vineyards in Ste. Julien, call them *b* and *t*. Suppose in the first price set *b* sells for $4 per bottle and *t* sells at $8, while in the second set the prices are reversed. *In either case* the consumer can then obtain the 10 bottles needed to satisfy his craving for Bordeaux by purchasing 10 bottles of the less expensive wine at a total outlay of $40. If, however, the prices were simply averaged so that each wine sold at $6, obviously the cost of any 10 bottles would now be $60. In sum, the theorem indicates that nonuniformity in the price of substitute goods provides an opportunity for saving by purchasing the cheaper of the available substitutes and that averaging of prices, by making costs more uniform, eliminates such bargains.

8. Dual Properties of Utility and Expenditure Functions

We can now quickly summarize without proof[14] several key propositions about expenditure functions, before turning to another extremely important result whose proof will be outlined.

Proposition 4: If the utility function has properties 1–4, then the expenditure function is differentiable with respect to u^* and to commodity prices (assuming the prices in question are positive), and it is monotone nondecreasing with the prices, i.e., an increase in prices will never reduce the cost of attaining a given level of utility.

Next we have the *basic duality theorem*, which asserts that there exists a well-behaved utility function corresponding to every well-behaved expenditure function.

---

[14] For proofs, see e.g., Ronald Shephard, *op. cit.*, and Daniel McFadden, "Cost, Revenue and Profit Functions," in D. McFadden (ed.), *An Econometric Approach to Production Theory*, North-Holland Publishing Company, Amsterdam, forthcoming.

Proposition 5 (the Shephard-Uzawa duality theorem): If an expenditure function, E', has the properties specified in Propositions 1–4, i.e., it is linearly homogeneous, concave in prices, differentiable, and monotonically increasing with u^*, then there exists a utility function, $u'(x_1, \cdots, x_n)$, which has properties 1–4 and is such that if we deduce an expenditure function E'' from u' then E'' and E' will be identical.

Since the expenditure function is a continuous function of prices and "utility levels," $Y = E(p, u^*)$, one can, in principle, invert the relationship to solve for the value of u^* as a function of p and expenditure level, Y. A utility function derived in this way is called the *indirect utility function*. That such an inversion of the expenditure function to the indirect utility function is possible follows from Propositions 2 and 4, since if a function $y = f(x)$ is differentiable, it must be continuous, and if it is also monotonic, it must possess a well-defined inverse $x = f^{-1}(y)$. This is easy to envision graphically because on the graph of such a function every x must correspond to a unique y and vice versa since the curve can neither have gaps nor can it ever "bend back" to yield, say, two values of y for any x.

However, the importance of the fundamental duality Proposition 5 is not that it suggests a procedure for the determination of utility functions but that it permits us, for many purposes, to dispense with the utility function altogether. Proposition 5 tells us that the expenditure function, in effect, contains within it an implied utility function, and that to assure ourselves that this indirect utility function is well behaved we need never actually find that function explicitly. For if the expenditure function has the desirable properties of linear homogeneity, concavity, and differentiability, then we can be certain that the indirect utility function also possesses the properties usually desired of it.

9. The Compensated Demand Function. Shephard's Lemma.

We come now to one of the propositions that underlies many of the theoretical applications of the duality analysis. We will show that one can determine directly the demand relationship, which underlies so much of theoretical and empirical analysis, by simple differentiation of the expenditure function with respect to the price of the item whose demand is being studied. However, the resulting relationship is of the sort called a *compensated* demand function (see Chapter 9, Section 13). That is, it is a demand function from which the income effect has been removed so that it describes only the substitution effect. It does this by taking the consumer to have been compensated for the loss in his purchasing power that would otherwise occur when a price rises (or for the rise in his purchasing power resulting from a price fall). In other words, it tells us how a consumer's purchases will change when some price, p_i, is replaced by $p_i + \Delta p_i$ *and* the consumer is simultaneously provided enough additional income to keep his utility level (real income) unchanged. Thus, the derivative of the compensated demand curve, $\partial x_i / \partial p_i$, is precisely the substitution effect of a change in the price of good i upon the quantity of that good purchased.

We may now state

Proposition 6 (Shephard's lemma): The partial derivative of the expenditure function with respect to the price of commodity i (assuming its price is positive) is equal to x_i^0, the optimal demand for the ith good, i.e.,

$$(11) \qquad \frac{\partial E(p, u^*)}{\partial p_i} = x_i^0,$$

so that, since the value of u is held constant at u^*, (11) is the *compensated* demand for commodity i as a function of prices.

Proof:[15] By definition of the expenditure function

$$(12) \qquad \sum p_i x_i^0 - E(p, u^*) = 0.$$

Now consider any alternative set of prices, $p' = (p_1', \cdots, p_n')$, and the corresponding optimal set of consumption levels, $x' = (x_1', \cdots, x_n')$, yielding the utility u^*. Then since for the given utility level x' rather than x^0 is optimal (expenditure minimizing) under these alternative prices, p', we must have

$$(13) \qquad E(p', u^*) = \sum p_i' x_i' \leq \sum p_i' x_i^0$$

or

$$(14) \quad \sum p_i' x_i^0 - E(p', u^*) \geq 0, \qquad \text{for any set of positive prices } p'.$$

Comparing (14) and (12) we see that expression (14) reaches its lowest possible value for any positive prices when $p' = p$. Since the prices p represent a minimum, they must satisfy the first-order conditions for a minimum of (14) that the partial derivative of (14) with respect to any

---

[15] The reader may wonder why we do not get our result simply by differentiation of the expression $E(p, u^*) = \sum p_i x_i^0$ with respect to p_i. But two functions which have an equal value need not have equal derivatives! At their intersection point a supply and demand curve have equal coordinates, but we normally expect one to have a negative slope while the other's slope is usually taken to be positive.

positive price p_i must be equal to zero. That is, we must have

$$\frac{\partial[\sum p_i' x_i^0 - E(p', u^*)]}{\partial p_i'} = x_i^0 - \frac{\partial E(p', u^*)}{\partial p_i'} = 0 \qquad \text{at } p' = p,$$

which is precisely what (11) asserts.

One property of demand relationships now follows immediately from Proposition 1, which asserts that the expenditure function is linearly homogeneous. It will be recalled from Chapter 11, Section 10, that given a function homogeneous of degree r, its partial derivatives will each be homogeneous functions of degree $r - 1$. Consequently, from Propositions 1 and 6 we obtain

Proposition 7: The compensated demand relationship derived from a well-behaved expenditure function is homogeneous of degree zero. That is, a proportionate change in all prices will leave quantities demanded entirely unaffected.

10. The Slutsky Theorem and Other Results in Comparative Statics

The power of duality theory is perhaps most forcefully illustrated in its applications to comparative statics. It will be recalled that comparative statics examines the effects on the values of the endogenous variables of a model of a change in the value of one of its parameters. For example, it investigates the effects on the consumer's purchases of a change in his income or in the price of some commodity.

The expenditure function is well designed to deal with such issues because its formulation represents the role of prices much more directly than that in the conventional utility maximization model. We will see now that results which require tedious calculations in the conventional analysis almost fall into our laps from the expenditure function and the compensated demand relationship derived from it. For example, we have the standard Slutsky theorem:

Proposition 8: If the expenditure function is well behaved and has second-partial derivatives, then the substitution effect will be negative (or zero), i.e., holding utility constant an increase in the price of good i will lead to a reduction or at least no increase in the quantity of good i consumed.

Proof: Since by Proposition 3 the expenditure function is concave in prices, we must have

$$(15) \qquad \qquad \partial^2 E/\partial p_i^2 \le 0.$$

Now the substitution effect is given by $\partial x_i^0/\partial p_i$ (u^* constant). But by (11) and (15)

$$\frac{\partial x_i^0}{\partial p_i} = \frac{\partial^2 E}{\partial p_i^2} \leq 0 \qquad \text{(Q.E.D.)}.$$

This proof is so short and simple that the magnitude of its accomplishment may be recognized only by those who have gone through the tedious derivation of the conventional analysis with its many differentiations, its bordered Hessian determinants, and its Cramer's rule calculations. Here we see one of the major benefits offered by duality theory: It enables us to translate the painstaking arguments of the standard comparative statics into utterly simple terms. Once the building blocks of the duality theory are laid down, many further results begin to drop out with little additional effort, as we will illustrate now.[16]

Proposition 9: Every good i must have at least one substitute j, meaning that (neglecting income effect) if the price of j rises, people will switch demand to i. That is, for every good, i, there must be at least one good, j, for which $\partial x_i/\partial p_j \geq 0$ and for which, if the demand curve for i has a negative slope (so that $\partial x_i/\partial p_i < 0$), we have the *strict* inequality, $\partial x_i/\partial p_j > 0$.

Proof: Since $x_i = \partial E/\partial p_i$ is homogeneous of degree zero by Proposition 7, Euler's theorem (Chapter 11, Section 10) tells us

$$p_1\,\partial x_i/\partial p_1 + p_2\,\partial x_i/\partial p_2 + \cdots + p_n\,\partial x_i/\partial p_n = 0.$$

Thus, if the ith term, $p_i\,\partial x_i/\partial p_i$, is negative (nonpositive), at least one of the remaining terms must be positive (nonnegative).   Q.E.D.

Finally, we have the standard symmetry result

Proposition 10: $\partial x_i/\partial p_j = \partial x_j/\partial p_i$.

Proposition 10 follows directly from the assumption that the expenditure function has continuous second derivations so that $\partial x_i/\partial p_j = \partial^2 E/\partial p_i\,\partial p_j = \partial^2 E/\partial p_j\,\partial p_i = \partial x_j/\partial p_i$. This theorem asserts that the substitution effect of p_j on the demand for i must exactly equal the sub-

---

[16] We may note why the expenditure function approach is able to dispense with explicit use of the second-order conditions on which the conventional analysis relies so heavily. The answer, of course, lies in the strict quasi-concavity of the implicit utility function corresponding to a well-behaved expenditure function. Strict quasi-concavity assures satisfaction of the second-order conditions for maximization of the consumer's utility subject to a linear budget constraint.

stitution effect of p_i on the demand for j. In other words, if i is a net substitute for j, then j must be a net substitute for i to precisely the same degree, as measured by absolute price response.

This proposition shows the symmetry of the *net* substitution and *net* complementarity relationships, i.e., those that hold after removal of the income effect, as has been done in the compensated demand relationships with which we are dealing. That is, Proposition 10 shows that if good i is a net substitute for j meaning $\partial x_i / \partial p_j > 0$, then j must be a net substitute for i, and the same must hold for complementarity.

11. Cost, Revenue, and Profit Functions

The dual approach to consumer theory has been used with equal effectiveness in dealing with production decisions and the decisions of the firm more generally. Just as the expenditure function is used as a substitute for the utility function in consumer analysis, in the theory of the firm under perfect competition (where all input and output prices are parameters) the cost function, the revenue function, and the profit function have been used to replace the production function, each taking on a different role that is conventionally assumed by the production function. As we will see, their relationship to the production function is almost perfectly analogous to that between the expenditure and utility functions.

Specifically, the cost function relates to the firm's *input* decisions given its output levels and input prices. The revenue function, symmetrically, relates to the multiproduct firm's *output* decisions given the magnitudes of its inputs and the prices of its various products. Finally, the profit function relates to the combined decision: The choice of input and output quantities, given all input and output prices.

We may note that systematic duality theory as described in this chapter was first presented in terms of cost and production functions. While there had been earlier pieces dealing with duality in consumer theory more or less peripherally,[17] it was Ronald Shephard's pathbreaking work, *Cost and Production Functions* (1953), that first explored the subject thoroughly. Indeed, the fundamental theorem showing the relationship

---

[17] This includes writings by E. B. Antonelli (1886), A. A. Konus (1924), H. Hotelling (1932), J. R. Hicks (1946), P. A. Samuelson (1947), and, above all, R. Roy (1942, 1947) by whom the earlier work was carried to its furthest extent. For fuller discussion of the history of the theory, see W. E. Diewert, "Applications of Duality Theory," in M. Intrilligator (ed.), *Frontiers of Quantitative Economics*, Vol. 2, North-Holland Publishing Co., Amsterdam, 1971. For an excellent description of the subject matter overall, see D. McFadden, "Cost, Revenue and Profit Functions," *op. cit.*

between the cost function and the input-demand function is known as Shephard's lemma.[18]

First, as we did for utility functions, we must list some properties which one might expect to hold for a well-behaved production set (the set of possible input-output combinations):

1. *Outputs require inputs.* In any feasible input-output combination with some positive output there must be at least one nonzero input. In other words, if the input quantities are $r_1 = r_2 = \cdots = r_m = 0$, then the outputs must be $y_1 = \cdots = y_n = 0$ (with zero inputs nothing will be produced).

2. *Free disposal and feasibility of the origin.* The input-output combination corresponding to the origin of production space is included in the feasible production set, i.e., it is feasible to produce nothing using zero input quantities. This premise, which is not so innocuous as it sounds, implicitly contains a *free disposal* assumption, for if any undesired objects ("outputs") happen to be present, the feasibility of the origin requires that they can be removed without using any inputs to do so, because otherwise nonzero values of some of the inputs would be required to attain zero values of the outputs.

3. *Bounded production frontiers,* i.e., for any fixed set of input quantities $r_1^*, \cdots, r_n^*$, the production frontier is bounded (i.e., with those inputs there is some level y_i' of each output i that cannot be exceeded given the quantities of the other outputs).

4. *Closedness.* The feasible production set (as well as the production frontier for any fixed set of inputs and the production isoquant for any given bundle of outputs) is closed.[19]

5. *Convexity of the production set.* This means that physical returns are diminishing both in the sense that added inputs yield marginal products that diminish or remain constant and in the sense that marginal rates of substitution between inputs or between outputs either diminish or remain

---

[18] Recently, work in the area has multiplied, produced by newer writers such as D. McFadden, G. Hanoch, W. E. Diewert, S. N. Afriat, and H. Uzawa.

[19] A set is defined to be closed if, given any convergent, infinite sequence of points in the set, the limit point of that sequence is also contained in the set. Intuitively, a closed set is made up of an interior *plus* its boundary, while an open set includes the interior but *not* the boundary. Thus, the interior of a circle plus its circumference make up a closed set, while the set made up of the interior of the circle, but which does not contain its circumference, is open.

constant. That is, as the producer gives up more and more of a product y_1, the amount of product y_2 he can obtain instead from a given set of inputs does not increase at the margin, etc.

12. On Cost and Production Functions

A cost function $C(p, \ y^*)$ is defined as the solution of the cost minimization problem for the production of a given output bundle $y^* = (y_1^*, \cdots, y_n^*)$, i.e., it is the solution of

(16)
$$\begin{cases} \text{Min } \sum p_i r_i \\ \text{subject to} \\ g(y_1^*, \cdots, y_n^*, r_1, \cdots, r_m) \leq 0, \end{cases}$$

where $g(\cdot) \leq 0$ is the production function, and where p_i is the given price of input i. That is, if r_i^0 is the optimal value of input i in (16), then the cost function is

$$C(p, \ y^*) = \sum p_i r_i^0.$$

We will now state a number of propositions about the relationships between cost and production functions, each one the analogue of a proposition in the theory of expenditure functions. We offer no proofs because each proof follows the logic of the analogous proposition about expenditure functions.

Let us first offer the

Definition: The set T is called a *standard production possibility* set if it is not empty and if it is well behaved, meaning that it satisfies conditions 1–4 of the preceding section, i.e., the production frontier is bounded, the production set is closed, and zero inputs yield zero outputs.

If the production set is standard and convex, then a solution to the cost minimization problem (16) exists, and so the cost function has a non-negative finite value. Moreover, we have

Proposition 11: The cost function is a linearly homogeneous function in prices for producible output bundles and strictly positive input prices.

Proposition 12: The cost function is strictly monotonically increasing in outputs.

Proposition 13: The cost function is concave in input prices.

Proposition 14: The cost function is differentiable with respect to input prices and output quantities, and it is monotone nondecreasing in input prices.

Proposition 15 (Shephard): If the cost function, C', is *standard* in the sense that it satisfies Propositions 11–14, and if zero cost yields zero output and if cost is a continuous function of outputs, then there exists a standard production set T' such that if we deduce a cost function C'' from T' then C'' and C' will be identical.

The clear analogy between Propositions 11–15 for cost and production functions and Propositions 1–5 should illustrate their similarity. The reader can easily go through the remaining Propositions 6–10 for expenditure functions and formulate the cost function analogues for him- or herself.

13. Revenue and Profit Functions: Definitions

Since a similar array of propositions applies to revenue and profit functions, we will not even list any of them but confine ourselves to a formulation of their definitions, both of them obviously related to the production set.

The revenue function gives the revenue that can be obtained from the optimal combination of outputs for any fixed bundle of inputs. That is,

Definition: Given the output prices $p_1, \cdots, p_n$ for outputs $y_1, \cdots, y_n$, the *revenue function* for any fixed set of input quantities $r_1^*, \cdots, r_m^*$ is defined as

$$R(p, r^*) = \sum p_i y_i^0$$

for y_i^0 satisfying the revenue maximization requirement

(17) $\begin{cases} \text{Max } \sum p_i y_i \\ \text{subject to the production requirement} \\ g(y_1, \cdots, y_n, r_1^*, \cdots, r_m^*) \leq 0. \end{cases}$

Finally, the profit function is obtained from an implicit and simultaneous determination of inputs and outputs where we take z_i to represent either an output or an input quantity, with i being an output if $z_i > 0$ and an input if $z_i < 0$. Thus we have

Definition: Given the input-output prices $p_1, \cdots, p_w$ for output or input quantities $z_1, \cdots, z_w$, the profit function is defined as $\pi = \pi(p) = \sum p_i z_i^0$, where z_i^0 is the solution of the maximization problem

$$(18) \qquad \begin{cases} \text{Max } \sum p_i z_i \\ \text{subject to} \\ g(z_1, \cdots, z_w) \leq 0. \end{cases}$$

14. Illustration I: Deducing the Cost and Profit Functions from the Production Function

To give concreteness to the preceding discussion we now describe how one actually goes about finding the expenditure function from a given utility function, or the cost, revenue, or profit function, given the production function. We will illustrate the process by starting from a simplified though rather unrealistic production function

$$(19) \qquad\qquad y = aLK,$$

where y is output and K and L are the quantities of capital and labor inputs, respectively. The objective is to find the cost-minimizing values of K and L for some specified output level, y^*, substituting these optimal values into $P_L L + P_K K$ to obtain the corresponding value of the cost function with input prices P_L and P_K. Thus, substituting production function (19) into the cost minimization model (16) we obtain the Lagrangian

$$P_L L + P_K K + \lambda(y^* - aLK)$$

with first-order conditions

$$P_L = \lambda aK$$

$$P_K = \lambda aL$$

$$y^* = aLK.$$

Hence, eliminating λ, we get $P_L/P_K = K/L$, and substituting this into the last of the first-order conditions successively for K and L we obtain

$$y^* = aL^2 P_L/P_K \quad \text{or} \quad L = (y^* P_K/aP_L)^{1/2}$$

and, similarly,

$$K = (y^* P_L/aP_K)^{1/2}.$$

Consequently, the cost function is given by

$$C(P_K, P_L, y^*) = P_K K + P_L L = 2(y^* P_K P_L/a)^{1/2},$$

which involves the sharply decreasing marginal and average costs such as might be expected to follow from the extreme scale economies implicit in (19). From the analogue of Proposition 6 (Shephard's lemma) the implicit demand functions for labor and capital are obtained directly by differentiation of the cost function with respect to P_L and P_K to yield once again

$$L = (y^* P_K / a P_L)^{1/2} \quad \text{and} \quad K = (y^* P_L / a P_K)^{1/2}.$$

The same process can be used to derive the cost, revenue, and profit functions for other types of production functions, though the calculations are usually considerably more tedious. For example, the standard Cobb-Douglas production function

$$y = b L^a K^{(1-a)}$$

turns out, by exactly the same set of steps, to yield the cost function

$$C(P_L, P_K, y^*) = b^{-1}(1 - a)^{-(1-a)} a^{-a} y^* P_L^a P_K^{(1-a)}$$

with the implicit demand function for labor given by

$$\frac{\partial C(\cdot)}{\partial P_L} = ab^{-1}(1 - a)^{-(1-a)} a^{-a} y^* P_L^{(a-1)} P_K^{(1-a)}$$
$$= b^{-1}(1 - a)^{-(1-a)} a^{(1-a)} y^* P_L^{(a-1)} P_K^{(1-a)}$$
$$= L$$

and that for capital is obtained analogously from $\partial C(\cdot)/\partial P_K = K$.

By exactly the same process one obtains a revenue function for a given production function using the constrained maximum problem (17) instead of (16), which gave us the cost function. Finally, the profit function is deduced from (18) also using the procedure that has just been described.[20]

15. Illustration II: Useful Cost Functions Derived Independently of Production Functions

One of the most attractive features of the duality approach is that it permits us to postulate directly expenditure, cost, or profit functions in

---

[20] It should be noted that the Cobb-Douglas function does not have a profit function for, with constant returns to scale and constant input and output prices, profit per unit will be constant. Hence, if profit per unit is zero, the output level will be indeterminate and the total profit zero, no matter what the output level. If profit per unit is positive, then neither optimal output nor total profit will be finite.

convenient forms, without deriving them from any utility or production functions or even explicitly checking them against such associated functions. One need merely look at a specific cost or expenditure function to see that it satisfies several basic requirements such as linear homogeneity and concavity in prices, and we know by Propositions 5 and 15 that the associated production and utility functions will be well behaved. One can then design a cost or expenditure function that is convenient for whatever purposes are at hand and simply check the properties of the postulated relationship itself in order to infer from Proposition 5 or 15 that all is well with the associated production or utility functions.

A good illustration is provided by Diewert, who has devised what he calls a generalized Leontief cost function,[21] whose equation is

$$C(p, y^*) = h(y^*) \sum \sum b_{ij} p_i^{1/2} p_j^{1/2},$$

where p_i is the price of input i, y^* is the selected output level, and $h(y^*)$ is a function of y^* that is continuous, monotonically increasing, and such that $h(0) = 0$, with h tending toward infinity with y^*. It is also postulated that the parameter values satisfy $b_{ij} = b_{ji}$.

We note first that this cost function is linearly homogeneous in prices [multiplication of each p_i by the same constant, k, multiplies the entire function, C, exactly by $(k^{1/2})(k^{1/2}) = k$].

Second, the function obviously increases monotonically and continuously with y^* by the assumed properties of $h(y^*)$.

Third, provided the parameters, b_{ij}, satisfy a certain set of inequalities which there is no point in reproducing here, the function will be concave in prices.

In these circumstances the conditions for Proposition 15 are satisfied, and we are therefore sure without further investigation or without explicit specification of any production function that there exists a well-behaved production function (i.e., a standard production possibility set) that corresponds to Diewert's cost function.

Equally noteworthy is the linearity of the cost function in the parameters b_{ij}. This is important because if one is to use econometric methods to estimate the parameters of the cost function then the b_{ij}'s are the unknowns whose values must be estimated from the data. The linearity of the cost function in the b_{ij} means that one can make use of all the simplifications that become possible for econometric methods in a linear case.

To illustrate further the properties of this cost function we deal with the two-input case and set y at such a level that $h(y^*) = 1$. In that case the

---

[21] See W. E. Diewert, "An Application of the Shephard Duality Theorem: A Generalized Leontief Production Function," *Journal of Political Economy*, Vol. 79, May/June 1971, pp. 481–507.

cost function becomes (since $p_i^{1/2} p_i^{1/2} = p_i$, and we have assumed $b_{12} = b_{21}$),

$$C(p_1, p_2, y^*) = b_{11}p_1 + 2b_{12}p_1^{1/2}p_2^{1/2} + b_{22}p_2.$$

By Proposition 6 we now can obtain the demand functions for inputs 1 and 2 by differentiation of the cost function in turn with respect to the prices of these inputs. This yields the derived demand expression

(20)
$$\frac{\partial C}{\partial p_1} = x_1 = b_{11} + b_{12}(p_2/p_1)^{1/2}$$

$$\frac{\partial C}{\partial p_2} = x_2 = b_{22} + b_{12}(p_1/p_2)^{1/2}.$$

We can use these derived demand functions to obtain the iso-product curve showing the alternative input combinations (x_1, x_2) that can yield y^*, the given output quantity. If $p_1 > 0$, $p_2 > 0$, from the two equations (20) we obtain directly the equation of the iso-product locus relating x_2 to x_1:

$$(p_2/p_1)^{1/2} = \frac{x_1 - b_{11}}{b_{12}} = \frac{b_{12}}{x_2 - b_{22}}$$

or

(21)
$$(x_1 - b_{11})(x_2 - b_{22}) = b_{12}^2.$$

Writing $z_1 = (x_1 - b_{11})$ and $z_2 = (x_2 - b_{22})$ it becomes clear that the graph of Equation (21) is a rectangular hyperbola (curve II' in Figure 3).

The hyperbola is asymptotic to the z_1 and z_2 axes at which we have, respectively, $x_2 = b_{22}$ and $x_1 = b_{11}$. The graph can, consequently, be redrawn as in Figure 4 with x_1 and x_2 on the axes instead of the z_1 and z_2

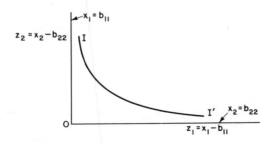

Figure 3

of Figure 3. In Figure 4 the unshaded portion of the diagram is identical to Figure 3, with point A in Figure 4 corresponding[22] to the origin of Figure 3.

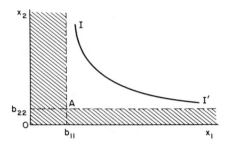

Figure 4

Note that the curvature of the iso-product curve II' depends on the magnitude of the b_{ij}, which consequently determine the elasticity of substitution between the two inputs (Chapter 11, Section 13), for we have by (21)

$$x_2 = b_{22} + b_{12}^2/(x_1 - b_{11}),$$

whose second derivative with respect to x_1 is

$$\frac{d^2 x_2}{dx_1^2} = 2\,\frac{b_{12}^2}{(x_1 - b_{11})^3}\,.$$

Thus, the curvature of the iso-product curve which determines the elasticity of substitution is itself determined by b_{12} and b_{11}.

In particular, if $b_{12} = 0$, then by (21) the II' curve will include only the point $x_1 = b_{11}$, $x_2 = b_{22}$ and all points with $x_1 > b_{11}$, $x_2 = b_{22}$ or any point with $x_1 = b_{11}$, $x_2 > b_{22}$ since redundant inputs do not reduce output. Consequently, the production indifference curve then takes the L-shaped form implicit in the Leontief input-output model,[23] as illustrated in Figure 5. This, of course, is why Diewert calls his relationship a generalized Leontief function.

---

[22] It is clear that if b_{11} or b_{22} (or both) are negative then II' will cross the x_2 or the x_1 axis (or both). In that case the corresponding input will be one which is dispensable, where x_i is said to be dispensable if it is possible to have a positive y even if $x_i = 0$.

[23] This is the case with zero elasticity of substitution (Chapter 11, Section 13) as we would expect for the fixed coefficients of the Leontief production relationships.

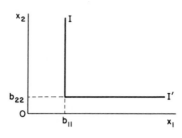

Figure 5

Thus, we see from this example how duality theory permits us to postulate cost (or expenditure) functions which are tractable statistically (as is illustrated by the linearity of the generalized Leontief cost function in the parameters, b_{ij}) and which offer us direct information on the properties of the underlying functions (such as the preceding expressions for the curvatures of the production indifference curves).

REFERENCES

Henderson, James M., and Richard E. Quandt, *Microeconomic Theory*, 2nd Edition, McGraw-Hill Book Company, New York, 1971, Chapter 2, Section 8. (On revealed preference.)

Lancaster, K. J., "A New Approach to Consumer Theory," *Journal of Political Economy*, Vol. 74, April 1966.

McFadden, Daniel, "Cost, Revenue and Profit Functions," in D. McFadden (ed.), "An Econometric Approach to Production Theory," North-Holland Publishing Company, Amsterdam (forthcoming). (On duality theory.)

McKenzie, Lionel, "Demand Theory Without a Utility Index," *Review of Economic Studies*, Vol. 24, June 1957 (advanced).

Samuelson, P. A., "Consumption Theorems in Terms of Overcompensation Rather than Indifference Comparisons," *Economica*, Vol. XX, February 1953. (On revealed preference.)

Shephard, Ronald, *Cost and Profit Functions*, Princeton University Press, Princeton, N.J., 1953, 1970. (Very difficult for a non specialist.)

FIRMS, GAMES,
AND
DECISIONS

three

The Firm
and Its Objectives

15

We have now discussed the data which the firm needs for its decision-making—the demand for its products and the cost of supplying them. But, even with this information, in order to determine what decisions are optimal it is still necessary to find out the businessman's aims. The decision which best serves one set of goals will not usually be appropriate for some other set of aims.

1. Alternative Objectives of the Firm

There is no simple method for determining the goals of the firm (or of its executives). One thing, however, is clear. Very often the last person to ask about any individual's motivation is the person himself (as the psychoanalysts have so clearly shown). In fact, it is common experience when interviewing executives to find that they will agree to every plausible goal about which they are asked. They say they want to maximize sales and also to maximize profits; that they wish, in the bargain, to minimize costs; and so on. Unfortunately, it is normally impossible to serve all of such a multiplicity of goals at once.

For example, suppose an advertising outlay of half a million dollars minimizes unit costs, an outlay of 1.2 million maximizes total profits, whereas an outlay of 1.8 million maximizes the firm's sales volume. We cannot have all three decisions at once. The firm must settle on one of the three objectives or some compromise among them.

Of course, the businessman is not the only one who suffers from the desire to pursue a number of incompatible objectives. It is all too easy to try to embrace at one time all of the attractive-sounding goals one can muster and difficult to reject any one of them. Even the most learned have suffered from this difficulty. It is precisely on these grounds that one great economist was led to remark that the much-discussed objective of the greatest good for the greatest number contains one "greatest" too many.

It is most frequently assumed in economic analysis that the firm is trying to maximize its total profits. However, there is no reason to believe that all businessmen pursue the same objectives. For example, a small firm which is run by its owner may seek to maximize the proprietor's free time subject to the constraint that his earnings exceed some minimum level, and, indeed, there have been cases of overworked businessmen who, on medical advice, have turned down profitable business opportunities.

It has also been suggested, on the basis of some observation, that firms often seek to maximize the money value of their sales (their total revenue) subject to a constraint that their profits do not fall short of some minimum level which is just on the borderline of acceptability. That is, so long as profits are at a satisfactory level, management will devote the bulk of its energy and resources to the expansion of sales. Such a goal may, perhaps, be explained by the businessman's desire to maintain his competitive position, which is partly dependent on the sheer size of his enterprise, or it may be a matter of the interests of management (as distinguished from shareholders), since management's salaries may be related more closely to the size of the firm's operations than to its profits, or it may simply be a matter of prestige.

In any event, though they may help him to formulate his own aims and sometimes be able to show him that more ambitious goals are possible and relevant, it is not the job of the operations researcher or the economist to tell the businessman what his goals should be. Management's aims must be taken to be whatever they are, and the job of the analyst is to find the conclusions which follow from these objectives—that is, to describe what businessmen do to achieve these goals, and perhaps to prescribe methods for pursuing them more efficiently.

The major point, both in economic analysis and in operations-research investigation of business problems, is that the nature of the firm's objectives cannot be assumed in advance. It is important to determine the nature of the firm's objectives before proceeding to the formal model-building and the computations based on it. As is obviously to be expected, many of the conclusions of the analysis will vary with the choice of objective function. However, as some of the later discussion in this chapter will show, a change in objectives can, sometimes surprisingly, leave some significant relationships invariant. Where this is true, it is very convenient to find it out in advance before embarking on the investigation of a specific problem. For if there are some problems for which the optimal decision will be the same, no matter which of a number of objectives the firm happens to adopt, it is legitimate to avoid altogether the difficult job of determining company goals before undertaking an analysis.

2. The Profit-Maximizing Firm

Let us first examine some of the conventional theory of the profit-maximizing firm. In the chapter on the differential calculus, the basic marginal condition for profit maximization was derived as an illustration. Let us now rederive this marginal-cost-equals-marginal-revenue condition with the aid of a verbal and a geometric argument.

The proposition is that no firm can be earning maximum profits unless its marginal cost and its marginal revenue are (at least approximately) equal, i.e., unless an additional unit of output will bring in as much money as it costs to produce, so that its marginal profitability is zero.[1]

It is easy to show why this must be so. Suppose a firm is producing 200,000 units of some item, x, and that at that output level, the marginal revenue from x production is $1.10 whereas its marginal cost is only 96 cents. Additional units of x will, therefore, each bring the firm some 14 cents = $1.10 − 0.96 more than they cost, and so the firm cannot be maximizing its profits by sticking to its 200,000 production level. Similarly, if the marginal cost of x exceeds its marginal revenue, the firm cannot be maximizing its profits, for it is neglecting to take advantage of its opportunity to save money—by reducing its output it would reduce its income, but it would reduce its costs by an even greater amount.

We can also derive the marginal-cost-equals-marginal-revenue proposition with the aid of Figure 1. At any output, OQ, total revenue is represented by the area $OQPR$ under the marginal revenue curve (see Rule 9 of Chapter 3). Similarly, total cost is represented by the area $OQKC$ immediately below the marginal cost curve. Total profit, which is the difference between total revenue and total cost is, therefore, represented by the difference between the two areas—that is, total profits are given by the lightly shaded area TKP minus the small, heavily shaded area, RTC. Now, it is clear that from point Q a move to the right will increase the size of the profit area TKP. In fact, only at output OQ_m will this area have reached its maximum size—profits will encompass the entire area $TKMP$. But at

---

[1] The word "approximately" is inserted because, in practice, a precise adjustment may be impossible to achieve. A 230,773rd car may bring in $2 more than it costs to produce but the production of a 230,774th auto may cost somewhat more than the revenue it yields, so that perhaps only at something like an (impossible) $230,773\frac{3}{4}$ automobile output level would marginal cost and revenue be equal.

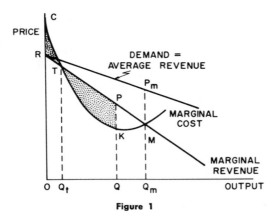

Figure 1

output OQ_m marginal cost equals marginal revenue—indeed, it is the crossing of the marginal cost and marginal revenue curves at that point which prevents further moves to the right (further output increases) from adding still more to the total profit area. Thus, we have once again established that at the point of maximum profits, marginal costs and marginal revenues must be equal.

Before leaving the discussion of this proposition, it is well to distinguish explicitly between it and its invalid converse. It is *not* generally true that any output level at which marginal cost and marginal revenue happen to be equal (i.e., where marginal profit is zero) will be a profit-maximizing level. There may be several levels of production at which marginal cost and marginal revenue are equal, and some of these output quantities may be far from advantageous for the firm. In Figure 1 this condition is satisfied at output OQ_t as well as at OQ_m. But at OQ_t the firm obtains only the net loss (negative profit) represented by heavily shaded area *RTC*. A move in either direction from point Q_t will help the firm either by reducing its costs more than it cuts its revenues (a move to the left) or by adding to its revenues more than to its costs. Output OQ_t is thus a point of *minimum* profits even though it meets the marginal profit maximization condition, "marginal revenue equals marginal cost."

This peculiar result is explained by recalling that the condition, "marginal profitability equals zero," implies only that neither a small increase nor a small decrease in quantity will add to profits. In other words, it means that we are at an output at which the total profit curve (not shown) is level—going neither uphill nor downhill. But while the top of a hill (the maximum profit output) is such a level spot, plateaus and valleys (minimum profit outputs) also have the same characteristic—they are level. That is, they are points of zero marginal profit, where marginal cost equals marginal revenue.[2]

We conclude that while at a profit-maximizing output marginal cost must equal marginal revenue, the converse is not correct—it is not true that at an output at which marginal cost equals marginal revenue the firm can be sure of maximizing its profits.

3. Application: Pricing and Cost Changes

The preceding theorem permits us to make a number of predictions about the behavior of the profit-maximizing firm and to set up some normative "operations research" rules for its operation. We can determine not only the optimal output, but also the profit-maximizing price with the aid of the demand curve for the product of the firm. For, given the optimal output, we can find out from the demand curve what price will permit the company to sell this quantity, and that is necessarily the optimal price. In Figure 1, where the optimal output is OQ_m, we see that the corresponding price is Q_mP_m, where point P_m is the point on the demand curve above Q_m (note that P_m is *not* the point of intersection of the marginal cost and the marginal revenue curves).

It was shown in the last section of Chapter 4 how our theorem can also enable us to predict the effect of a change in tax rates or some other change in cost on the firm's output and pricing. We need merely determine how this change shifts the marginal cost curve to find the new profit-maximizing price-output combination by finding the new point of intersection of the marginal cost and marginal revenue curves. Let us recall one particular result for use later in this chapter—the theorem about the effects of a change in fixed costs. It will be remembered that a change in fixed costs never has any effect on the firm's marginal cost curve (Chapter 3, Section 6) because marginal fixed cost is always zero (by definition, an additional unit of output adds nothing to *fixed* costs). Hence, if the profit-maximizing firm's rents, its total assessed taxes, or some other fixed cost increases, there will be no change in the output-price level at which its marginal cost equals its marginal revenue. In other words, the profit-maximizing firm will make no price or output changes in response to any increase or decrease in its fixed costs! This rather unexpected result is certainly not in accord

---

[2] Again, this problem arises because our marginal maximum condition must be supplemented by a second-order condition—that the second derivative of profits be negative, which means, in the present context, that the marginal revenue curve must cut the marginal cost curve from above (going from left to right). The reader should verify that this condition is satisfied at the profit-maximizing output OQ_m in Figure 1 but that it is violated at OQ_t. He should also give an economic interpretation of the condition. Compare Section 5 of Chapter 4.

with common business practice and requires some further comment, which will be supplied presently.

4. Extension: Multiple Products and Inputs

The firm's output decisions are normally more complicated, even in principle, than the preceding decisions suggest. Almost all companies produce a variety of products and these various commodities typically compete for the firm's investment funds and its productive capacity. At any given time there are limits to what the company can produce, and often, if it decides to increase its production of product x, this must be done at the expense of product y. In other words, such a company cannot simply expand the output of x to its optimum level without taking into account the effects of this decision on the output of y.

For a profit-maximizing decision which takes both commodities into account we have a marginal rule which is a special case of Rule 2 of Chapter 3:

> Any limited input (including investment funds) should be allocated between the two outputs x and y in such a way that the marginal profit yield of the input, i, in the production of x equals the marginal profit yield of the input in the production of y.

The reasoning behind this result is straightforward. If the condition is violated, the firm cannot be maximizing its profits, because the firm can add to its earnings simply by shifting some of i out of the product where it obtains the lower return and into the manufacture of the other.

Stated another way, this last theorem asserts that if the firm is maximizing its profits, a reduction in its output of x by an amount which is worth, say, $5, should release just exactly enough productive capacity, C, to permit the output of y to be increased $5 worth. For this means that the marginal return of the released capacity is exactly the same in the production of either x or y, which is what the previous version of this rule asserted.[3]

Still another version of this result is worth describing: Suppose the price of each product is fixed and independent of output levels. Then we require that the marginal cost of each output be proportionate to its price,

---

[3] The earlier rule states that the marginal *profitability* must be the same in both uses, whereas now we have the marginal *revenue* of the input the same in the production of either x or y. But if a unit of resources costs D dollars, the marginal profit of i in the production of x (MP_{ix}) equals its marginal revenue minus its cost, so that if marginal profitability is the same in both uses we have

$$MP_{ix} = MR_{ix} - D = MR_{iy} - D = MP_{iy}$$

so that we must also have $MR_{ix} = MR_{iy}$, and conversely.

i.e., that $MC_x/P_x = MC_y/P_y$, where P_x and MC_x are, respectively, the price and the marginal cost of x, etc.[4]

In this discussion we have considered only the output decisions of a profit-maximizing firm. Of course, the firm has other decisions to make. In particular, it must decide on the amounts of its inputs including its marketing inputs (advertising, sales force, etc.). There are similar rules for these decisions, as discussed in Chapter 11 and in Chapter 17, Section 6. The main result here is that profit maximization requires for any inputs i and j

$$MP_i/P_i = MP_j/P_j,$$

where MP_i represents the marginal profit contribution of input i and P_i is its price, etc.

Having discussed the consequences of profit maximization, let us see now what difference it makes if the firm adopts an alternative objective, one to which we have already alluded—the maximization of the value of its sales (total revenue) under the requirement that the firm's profits not fall short of some given minimum level.

5. Price-Output Determination: Sales Maximization

Sales maximization under a profit constraint does not mean an attempt to obtain the largest possible physical volume (which is hardly easy to define in the modern multiproduct firm). Rather, it refers to maximization of total revenue (dollar sales), which, to the businessman, is the obvious measure of the amount he has sold. Maximum sales in this sense need not require very large physical outputs. To take an extreme case, at a zero price physical volume may be high but dollar sales volume will be zero. There will normally be a well-determined output level which maximizes dollar sales. This level can ordinarily be fixed with the aid of the well-known rule that maximum revenue will be obtained only at an output at which the elasticity of demand is unity, i.e., at which *marginal revenue is zero*. This is the condition which replaces the "marginal cost equals marginal revenue" *profit*-maximizing rule.

---

[4] To see how this follows from the preceding version of our rule, suppose that $1 in inputs produces K dollars worth of x and K dollars worth of y. Then if one unit of x requires, say, $5 in inputs (marginal cost $5), one unit of x must be worth (approximately) $5K$ dollars. Similarly, if it costs $9 to produce a unit of y, that unit must be worth $9K$ dollars. Hence we must have

$$MC_x/P_x = 5/5K = 9/9K = MC_y/P_y.$$

All of these rules can also be derived with the aid of a Lagrange multiplier analysis, as shown in the last sections of Chapters 9 and 11. The reader can supply the proofs as an exercise.

But this rule does not take into account the profit constraint. That is, if at the revenue-maximizing output the firm does, in fact, earn enough or more than enough profits to keep its stockholders satisfied, then it will want to produce the sales-maximizing quantity. But if at this output profits are too low, the firm's output must be changed to a level which, though it fails to maximize sales, does meet the profit requirement.

We see, then, that two types of equilibrium appear to be possible: one in which the profit constraint does not provide an effective barrier to sales maximization, and one in which it does. This is illustrated in Figure 2, which shows the firm's total revenue, cost, and profit curves as indicated.

The profit- and sales-maximizing outputs are, respectively, OQ_p and OQ_s. Now if, for example, the minimum required profit level is OP_1, then the sales-maximizing output OQ_s will provide plenty of profit, and that is the amount it will pay the sales maximizer to produce. His selling price

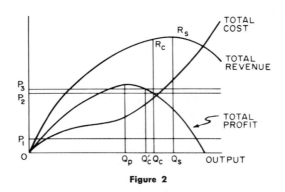

Figure 2

will then be set at Q_sR_s/OQ_s. But if the producer's required profit level is OP_2, output OQ_s, which yields insufficient profit, clearly will not do. Instead, his output will be reduced to level OQ_c, which is just compatible with his profit constraint.

It will be argued presently that in fact only equilibrium points in which the constraint is effective (OQ_c rather than OQ_s) can normally be expected to occur when other decisions of the firm are taken into account.

The profit-maximizing output, OQ_P, will usually be smaller than the one which yields either type of sales maximum, OQ_s or OQ_c. This can be proved with the aid of the standard rule that at the point of maximum profit marginal cost must equal marginal revenue, for marginal cost is normally a positive number (we can't usually produce more of a good for nothing). Hence *marginal revenue will also be positive when profits are at a maximum*, i.e., a further increase in output will increase total sales (revenue). Therefore, if at the point of maximum profit the firm earns more profit than the required minimum,[5] it will pay the sales-maximizer to lower his price and increase his physical output.

6. Advertising

The decision as to how far to carry advertising expenditure can also be influenced profoundly by the firm's choice of objectives—whether it chooses to maximize sales or profits. The relevant diagram for the advertising decisions is completely elementary. The horizontal axis in Figure 3 represents the magnitude of advertising expenditure and the vertical axis total sales

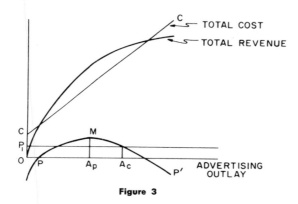

Figure 3

(revenue) and total profit. The drawing of the total revenue curve assumes, as most businessmen seem to do, that increased advertising expenditure can always increase physical volume, though after a point sharply diminishing returns may be expected to set in.[6] This means that total revenue must vary with advertising expenditure in precisely the same manner, for, unlike a price reduction, a *ceteris paribus* rise in advertising expenditure involves no change in the market value of the items sold. Hence, whereas an increase in physical volume produced by a price reduction may or may not increase dollar sales, depending on whether demand is elastic or inelastic, an increase in volume brought about by added advertising outlay must always be accompanied by a proportionate increase in total revenue.

---

[5] If it earns less than the required minimum at this output, there is obviously no output which will satisfy the profit constraint.

[6] Of course, this is not necessarily true—potential customers may perhaps be repelled by excessive advertising.

Incidentally, it should be noted that a more comprehensive analysis would take into account the interdependence between pricing and advertising decisions. This could be done with the aid of a three-dimensional diagram, with the axes representing price, advertising outlay, and revenue (and costs).

If all other costs are added to advertising cost, we get the line which depicts the firm's total (production, distribution, and selling) costs as a function of advertising outlay. Subtracting these total costs from the level of dollar sales at each level of advertising outlay, we obtain a total profits curve, PP'.

We see that the profit-maximizing expenditure is OA_p, at which PP' attains its maximum, M. If, on the other hand, the sales maximizer's minimum acceptable profit level is OP_1, the constrained sales-maximizing advertising budget level is OA_c. It is to be noted that there is no possibility of an unconstrained sales maximum which is analogous to output OQ_s in Figure 2. For, by assumption, unlike a price reduction, increased advertising always increases total revenue. As a result, it will always pay the sales maximizer to increase his advertising outlay until he is stopped by the profit constraint—until profits have been reduced to the minimum acceptable level. This means that sales maximizers will normally advertise no less than, and usually more than, do profit maximizers. For unless the maximum profit level A_pM is no greater than the required minimum OP_1, it will be possible to increase advertising somewhat beyond the profit-maximizing level OA_p without violating the profit constraint. Moreover, this increase will be desired since, by assumption, it will increase physical sales, and with them, dollar sales will rise proportionately.

The interrelationship between output and advertising decisions now permits us to see the reason for the earlier assertion that an unconstrained sales-maximizing output OQ_s (Figure 2) will ordinarily not occur. For if price is set at a level which yields such an output, profits will be above their minimum level and it will pay to increase sales by raising expenditure on advertising, service, or product specifications. This is an immediate implication of the theorem that there will ordinarily be no unconstrained sales-maximizing advertising level. Since its marginal revenue is always positive, advertising can always be used to increase sales up to a point where profits are driven to their minimum level.

7. Choice of Input and Output Combinations

The typical firm is a multiproduct enterprise (frequently the number of distinct items runs easily into the hundreds or even thousands) and, of course, it employs a large variety of inputs. This section examines briefly the effect of sales (rather than profit) maximization on the amounts and allocation of the firm's various inputs and outputs.

We obtain the following result, which may at first appear rather surprising: Given the level of expenditure, the sales-maximizing firm will produce the same quantity of each output, and market it in the same ways as does the profit-maximizer. Similarly, given the level of their total revenues, the two types of firm will optimally use the same inputs in identical quantities and will allocate them in exactly the same way. This result may be somewhat implausible because one is tempted to think of some products or some markets as higher-profit, lower-revenue producers than others and one would expect the profit-maximizing firm to concentrate more on the one variety and the sales-maximizing firm to specialize more in the other. But we shall see in a moment why this is not so.

It is easy to illustrate our result geometrically. In Figure 4 let x and y represent the quantities sold of two different products (or sales of one product in two different markets) or the quantities bought of two different inputs. The curves labeled R_1, R_2, etc., are iso-revenue curves, i.e., any such curve is the locus of all combinations of x and y yielding some fixed amount of revenue. Similarly, CC' represents all combinations of x and y which can be produced with a fixed outlay (total cost). The standard analysis tells us that the point of tangency, T, between CC' and one of the R curves, is the point of profit

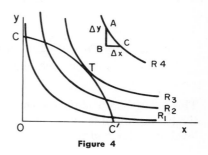

Figure 4

maximization. But it is also the point of revenue maximization because it lies on the highest revenue curve attainable with this outlay. This demonstrates our result.

A little reflection should now render the result quite plausible. The point is simply that, *given the level of costs*, since profit equals revenue minus costs, whatever maximizes profits must maximize revenues. Hence, differences between the profit and the sales-maximizer's output composition or resource allocation must be attributed not to a reallocation of a given level of costs (or revenues) but to the larger outputs (and hence total costs and revenues) which, we have seen, are to be expected to accompany sales maximization.[7]

Explained in this way, our theorem is completely trivial. But when the sales-maximizer's profit constraint is taken into account a more interesting but closely related conclusion can be drawn.

---

[7] We conclude that when the operations-researcher encounters the problem of allocating optimally some *fixed* quantity of a firm's resources, the values of all other decision variables being given, his answer will be exactly the same whether he is dealing with a sales- or a profit-maximizing firm. Such analytically derived equivalences can clearly permit significant economies in research. In this case, for example, it means that the operations-researcher may be able, when dealing with allocation problems, to avoid wasting effort in determining the order in which the company ranks sales and profit objectives.

We may view the difference between maximum attainable profits and the minimum profit level expected by the sales-maximizer as a fund of sacrificeable profits which is to be devoted to increasing revenues as much as possible. Since each output is produced beyond the point of maximum profits, *its marginal profit yield will be negative.* In other words, each time it increases the output of some product in order to increase its total revenue the firm must use up more of its fund of sacrificeable profits. This fund of sacrificeable profits must be allocated among the different outputs, markets, inputs, etc., in a way which maximizes total dollar sales. The usual reasoning indicates that this requires the marginal revenue yield of a dollar of profit sacrificed, e.g., by product x, to be the same as that obtained from a dollar of profit lost to any other product, y; i.e., we must have

$$\frac{\text{marginal revenue product of } x}{\text{marginal profit yield of } x} = \frac{\text{marginal revenue product of } y}{\text{marginal profit yield of } y}.$$

This relationship indicates that, even in the sales-maximizing firm, relatively unprofitable inputs and outputs are to be avoided, whatever the level of outlay and total revenue.

8. Pricing and Changes in Fixed Costs and Taxes

Students consistently find one of the most surprising conclusions of the theory of the firm to be the assertion that fixed costs do not matter to pricing and output decisions.[8] This piece of received doctrine is certainly at variance with business practice, where an increase in fixed costs is usually the occasion for serious consideration of a price increase. It is easy to show, however, that this is precisely the sort of response one would expect of the firm which seeks to maximize sales and treats its profits as a constraint rather than as an ultimate objective. For if, in equilibrium, the firm always earns only enough to satisfy its profit constraint, then a rise in overhead cost must mean that earnings fall below the acceptable minimum. Outputs and/or advertising expenditures must then be reduced in order to make up the required profits. The purpose of any such decrease in production is, of course, to permit an increase in selling price.

This is very easily restated in terms of Figure 5. An increase in overhead costs means, geometrically, a uniform downward shift in the total profit curve by the amount of the overhead expenses. Hence, if overheads rise by amount CD, output will fall from OQ_c to OQ'_c, for at OQ_c profits will now

---

[8] Cf. Chapter 4, Section 9.

be Q_cR, which is less than the minimum acceptable level OP_m. By contrast, the change in overhead costs will leave the profit-maximizing output unchanged at OQ'_p. For the added costs reduce the height of the "profit hill" uniformly, but they do not change the location of its peak. This result also has implications for tax policy. It has sometimes been held that there is nothing a company can do to shift any part of the corporation income tax on to the consumer or its employees. The profit-maximizing firm can gain nothing by raising its prices or changing its outputs in response to a change in corporation tax rates, provided that these rates are so structured that the higher the firm's earnings are before taxes the more it gets to keep after taxes. The argument is almost exactly the same as the fixed cost analysis.

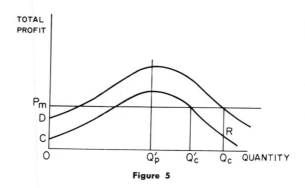

Figure 5

The corporation tax reduces the height of the total .profit curve, but it moves the peak of the curve neither to the right nor to the left.

But, once again, if the firm wishes to maximize sales subject to a profit requirement, rather than maximizing profits, this conclusion loses its validity. When taxes are raised, the firm will be motivated to increase its price (and, therefore, to reduce its output) in order to make up its lost profits. The explanation of the shiftability of this apparently unshiftable tax is simple—the sales-maximizing firm will, in effect, have a reserve of profits which it has not claimed (it has not maximized profit) but which it can fall back on when driven to do so by a rise in tax costs, though it can get back to its old profits only by some sacrifice in its sales.

This concludes the discussion of the implications of a sales maximization objective. In the present context the analysis is important primarily as an illustration of the effects of alternative objectives on the optimal decisions of the firm. It is designed to indicate the seriousness of the errors which can arise unless care is exercised in investigating the goals of a company before undertaking an analysis of its behavior and its policies.

9. Satisficing and Behavior Analysis

Professor Simon has offered yet another persuasive hypothesis about the objectives of firms. He has argued that in many cases management recognizes implicitly or explicitly the complexity of the calculations and the imperfections of the data which must be employed in any optimality calculation. As a result, firms frequently give up the attempt to maximize anything—profits or sales or anything else. Instead, they set up for themselves some minimal standards of achievement which they hope will assure the firm's viability and an acceptable level of profit. Firms which are satisfied to achieve such limited objectives are said to "satisfice" instead of maximizing. Starting from this hypothesis, a number of investigators led by Cyert and March have attempted to develop what they call a *behavioral* theory of the firm—one which seeks to show how firms really act, not just how they ought to act if their decisions were all optimal. Using computers to simulate observed decision processes of a number of companies, they have achieved remarkable success in employing some of these programs to predict company decisions. Though one may question whether they have provided a theory or an empirical approach and evidence for the construction of a theory, the significance of the entire analysis is undeniable. Certainly we can no longer operate comfortably on the assumption that profit maximization adequately explains all of the observed business behavior.

10. Profit and Sales Maximization: Sample Calculations

Example: Given the demand function $P = 20 - Q$ and the *total* cost function $C = Q^2 + 8Q + 2$.

(a) What output, Q_{II}, maximizes total profit and what are the corresponding values of price, P_{II}, profit, II_{II}, and total revenue (sales), R_{II}?

(b) What output, Q_r, maximizes sales and what are the corresponding values of price, P_r, profit, II_r, and total revenue, R_r?

(c) What output, Q_c, maximizes sales subject to the constraint $II \geq 8$, and what are the corresponding values of the other variables, P_c, II_c, and R_c?

Answer to a:

$$\text{total profit} = II = PQ - C = -Q^2 + 20Q - Q^2 - 8Q - 2$$

$$= -2Q^2 + 12Q - 2.$$

Therefore, to maximize profit, we require

$$\frac{dII}{dQ} = -4Q + 12 = 0 \quad \text{or} \quad Q_{II} = 3,$$

and so

$$P_{\text{II}} = 20 - Q_{\text{II}} = 17$$

$$\Pi_{\text{II}} = -2Q_{\text{II}}^2 + 12Q_{\text{II}} - 2 = -18 + 36 - 2 = 16$$

$$R_{\text{II}} = Q_{\text{II}}P_{\text{II}} = 3 \cdot 17 = 51.$$

Answer to b:

$$\text{total revenue} = R = PQ = -Q^2 + 20Q.$$

Therefore, to maximize sales, R, we require

$$\frac{dR}{dQ} = -2Q + 20 = 0 \quad \text{or} \quad Q_r = 10,$$

and direct substitution yields

$$P_r = 10, \qquad \Pi_r = -82, \qquad R_r = 100.$$

Answer to c:

Set $\Pi = 8$ so that

$$8 = -2Q^2 + 12Q - 2, \quad \text{i.e.,}$$

$$2Q^2 - 12Q + 10 = 0.$$

Solving for Q we obtain the two roots $Q = 1$ and $Q = 5$. Since (by direct substitution) the corresponding values of P and R are seen to be $P(1) = 19$, $R(1) = P(1)Q(1) = 19$, $P(5) = 15$, $R(5) = 75$, the constrained sales-maximizing value of Q is

$$Q_c = 5.$$

The corresponding values of the other variables are

$$P_r = 15, \qquad \Pi_r = 8, \quad \text{and} \quad R_r = 75.$$

PROBLEMS

In Problems 1 and 2, below, given the demand and total cost functions specified, determine the optimal output, Q, price, P, total profit, Π, and total revenue, R,

(a) under profit maximization,
(b) under unconstrained sales maximization,
(c) under sales maximization subject to the specified constraint.

1. $P = 12 - 0.4Q$, $C = 0.6Q^2 + 4Q + 5$, constraint $\Pi_c \geq 10$.
2. $P = 16 - Q + 24/Q$, $C = 43 + 4Q$, constraint $\Pi_c \geq 16$.
3. Let E be the price elasticity of demand and S be the price elasticity of sales, i.e.,

$$S = \frac{dPQ}{dP} \frac{P}{PQ}.$$

Prove that $S = 1 - E$. Show, therefore, that if demand is inelastic ($E < 1$), a fall in price will reduce total revenue (S), etc. (elasticity Theorem II, Section 4, Chapter 9).

4. Given marginal revenue $(MR) = \dfrac{dPQ}{dQ}$ prove that $MR = P\left(1 - \dfrac{1}{E}\right)$.

5. Use the two preceding results to show that

(a) If price elasticity of demand equals unity, then total revenue is not affected by the value of Q.

(b) If $P \neq 0$, then marginal revenue equals zero if and only if $E = 1$.

(c) The ratio between price and marginal revenue is constant if and only if E is a constant.

REFERENCES

Baumol, William J., *Business Behavior, Value and Growth*, Harcourt Brace Jovanovich, Inc., New York, revised ed., 1967, Chapters 6–8.

Cyert, R. M., and J. G. March, *A Behavioral Theory of the Firm*, Prentice-Hall, Inc., Englewood Cliffs, N.J., 1963.

Machlup, Fritz, "Marginal Analysis and Empirical Research," *American Economic Review*, Vol. XXXVI, September 1946. Reprinted (together with further comments by Lester and Machlup) in Richard V. Clemence (ed.), *Readings in Economic Analysis*, Vol. 2, Addison-Wesley Publishing Company, Cambridge, Mass., 1950.

Marris, Robin, *The Economic Theory of Managerial Capitalism*, Free Press, Glencoe, Ill., 1964.

Scherer, Frederic M., *Industrial Market Structure and Economic Performance*, Rand McNally & Company, Chicago, 1970.

Scitovsky, Tibor, "A Note on Profit Maximization and Its Implications," *Review of Economic Studies*, Vol. XI, 1943. Reprinted in American Economic Association, George J. Stigler and Kenneth E. Boulding (eds.), *Readings in Price Theory*, Richard D. Irwin, Inc., Homewood, Ill., 1952.

Simon, Herbert A., "Theories of Decision Making in Economics," *American Economic Review*, Vol. XLIX, June 1959.

————, *Models of Man*, John Wiley & Sons, Inc., New York, 1957, Chapter 14.

Williamson, Oliver E., *The Economics of Discretionary Behavior: Managerial Objectives in a Theory of the Firm*, Prentice-Hall, Inc., Englewood Cliffs, N.J., 1964.

Market Structure, Pricing, and Output

16

The determination of prices and output levels is very much affected by the competitive structure of the market. Here, "competitive structure" is a phrase which refers to the nature and extent of the monopolistic elements, if any, that are present in any particular market situation. There exists a large body of literature which discusses various types of competitive conditions running the range from perfect competition to pure monopoly, and which seeks to analyze their effects on prices and output. It is convenient to begin our discussion with a listing of some of the market categories which have been investigated.

1. Classification of Market Structures

The economist has classified industries or groups of firms into several categories, depending on the nature of competitive conditions. The following are fairly standard definitions:

1. *Pure competition*: An industry is said to be operating under conditions of pure competition when the following requirements are met:

(a) *Many firms.* There must be a large number of firms in the industry, each of which controls so small a proportion of total output that its addition to or removal from the market has little or no effect on the market price;

(b) *Homogeneity of products.* All firms must be known by buyers to produce identical products (cf. the definition of monopolistic competition below);

(c) *Freedom of entry and exit.* Any individual or company with the funds and inclination must be able to enter (start or buy a firm in) the industry without artificial hindrances being erected against him, and any owner of a firm in the industry who can find a buyer may freely sell his company;

(d) *Independent decision-making.* There must be no collusion.

2. *Pure monopoly:* A firm is classed as a pure monopolist if it is the sole producer of some commodity for which there are no close substitutes and if it faces no imminent threat of competitors.

3. *Monopolistic competition with product differentiation:* This is a market arrangement very similar to pure competition except for feature 1(b)—product standardization. Under product differentiation each firm produces goods which are different or which customers believe to be different from competitive products. The "product differences" may in fact not involve characteristics of the products themselves. More attractive wrapping, more convenient location, or special sales features such as better service or free gift coupons may be the basis for customer preferences and loyalties.

4. *Monopsony:* A buyer's monopoly.

5. *Discriminating monopoly:* A firm which charges different prices to different customers for the same commodity.

6. *Bilateral monopoly:* A single purchaser without competitors buying from a monopolist seller.

7. *Duopoly:* A two-firm industry. This is a special case of

8. *Oligopoly:* An industry with a small number of large firms producing the bulk of its output.

Pure monopolies have always been rare if they ever existed at all. Pure competition also is rare, although there exist a number of commodities which, for many purposes, provide a good approximation: Grains and the stock market are two outstanding examples.

Illustrations of the other market forms are readily found. For the defense industries the government is a monopsonistic buyer, and wage negotiation between unions and industry representatives sometimes closely resembles bilateral monopoly. Doctors are well-known price discriminators.

However, the bulk of our enterprises seems to fall into the two remaining classifications, monopolistic competition and oligopoly. Competing neighborhood retailers of all sorts are typically monopolistic competitors, each with his corps of more or less loyal customers and locational and personality differences which make his products and services at least somewhat distinct from those of his competitors. The lion's share of manufacturing is in the hands of oligopoly firms—steel, autos, tobacco—almost any present-day large industry, and it is in these industries that most privately sponsored operations-research work occurs.

Let us now discuss the price and output determination process in some of these market situations. The tools which have been described in earlier chapters will permit us to deal with these cases fairly briefly.

2. The Profit-Maximizing Competitive Firm

The bulk of the analytic literature on price-output determination has traditionally been devoted to the case of pure competition. The reason is at least partly that such a case is more readily amenable to analysis so that it is possible to develop a far richer theoretical structure for this situation than for other market forms.

First, let us examine some immediate consequences of the definition of pure competition. Under pure competition the demand curve of the firm is always horizontal (perfectly elastic). This follows from the first feature of the definition of pure competition—the relative insignificance of each firm so that no one of them can affect price noticeably. The single wheat farmer can do nothing about the day's price in Chicago. If he raises the price of his wheat above the going price, he will be unable to sell anything, whereas he can gain nothing by cutting his price below the market price for at the prevailing price he can sell any amount he can be expected to produce. For him, then, there is no price decision to be made—the price figure is simply handed to him.

In the short run the firm may, of course, end up making either profit or loss. But in the long run the free entry and exit feature of pure competition assures us that these profits or losses will disappear altogether! If the industry is profitable, new firms will be induced to enter it and compete with the already established concerns. The resulting increase in demand for inputs may bid up their prices and hence raise costs. Certainly the increased product supply can be expected to reduce its market price. Thus, profits will tend to be squeezed down toward zero or at least until no additional firms find it worth moving in.

Similarly, if there is initially a net loss to firms in the industry, the exit of concerns will raise profits and ultimately it will eliminate the loss.

Of course, this conclusion holds only if there are no autonomous changes in demands or costs during the period of adjustment. A foreign crop failure or the invention of more efficient equipment may suddenly restore high profits to wheat farming and so offset the influence of new entrants. Since, to some extent, such changes are always taking place, the adjustment toward zero profits will always be imperfect. However, the forces working in that direction will nevertheless be there.

Let us now examine in somewhat greater detail the nature of this competitive equilibrium toward which the market tends to adjust. Such a situation is depicted in Figures 1a and 1b. In these diagrams the horizontal line DD' is the firm's demand curve. The curve is horizontal because, as already stated, no change in the firm's output is a sufficiently significant contribution to total market supply to affect the price.

So long as there is no price discrimination, any firm's demand curve will also be its average revenue curve. The reason is that if all units of a

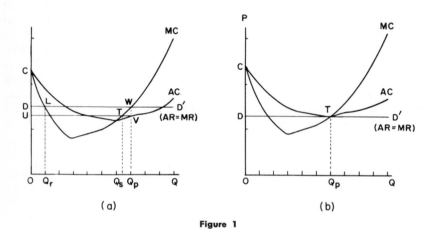

Figure 1

commodity are sold at the same price, the revenue brought in by an average unit must be its price. Hence DD' is also the average revenue curve. Also, we know that where an average curve is neither rising nor falling it will coincide with the corresponding marginal curve. Here, since the average revenue curve is horizontal throughout its length, it must everywhere coincide with the marginal revenue curve (Chapter 3, Section 5).

Figure 1a represents the situation of a competitive profit-maximizing firm in short-run equilibrium. Its profit-maximizing output is OQ_p, where its marginal cost curve, CMC, intersects the marginal revenue (demand) curve DD'.[1] At that point it is earning a profit, for on each unit it produces it obtains VW (= unit revenue minus unit cost). Thus its total profit (= unit profit multiplied by the number of units produced) is represented by area $UVWD$.

---

[1] Why is OQ_r not an equilibrium output in view of the fact that there, also, we have marginal cost = marginal revenue?

Figure 1b represents a long-run equilibrium situation. Here the average cost curve must be tangent to the demand curve, DD'. The reason is that if the unit costs were everywhere higher than price, every output would be unprofitable, and firms would leave the industry, thus shifting the curves toward tangency by raising DD' (price) and, possibly, lowering the cost curves as well. Similarly, if the average cost curve were to intersect the demand curve, there would be some outputs at which profits could be earned and an influx of new firms would soon shift the cost and revenue curves sufficiently to wipe out these profits. Only when there is tangency will the "no-profit, no-loss" position of long-run equilibrium be the best the firm can do, and no firms will be tempted to enter or leave the field if this is the typical situation of all firms in the area.

Since the demand curve is horizontal, the point of tangency, T, of the average cost curve with the demand curve must occur at an output at which the average cost curve is also horizontal, i.e., it will be at an output where unit costs are at a minimum. For that reason the marginal cost curve will also intersect the average cost curve at that point. In sum, at the point of equilibrium we have the impressive set of equalities, marginal cost equals marginal revenue equals average cost equals average revenue equals price (Figure 1b).

It is to be noted that in equilibrium every firm in the industry must have the same costs, for the product price will be the same for all such companies, and both marginal and average costs will equal price for all firms. This may appear to smack of the miraculous. Firms with dissimilar resources, production techniques, and operating procedures all end up with the same costs. But this is another work of the competitive mechanism. More efficient firms must have lower costs because some of their resources are better—items such as more convenient location, purer raw materials, or more skilled managers must account for the difference. But competition guarantees that if manager A can run a firm at $10,000 more cheaply per year than can B, then A's salary will tend to be bid up until it is $10,000 per annum higher than B's, for if A's firm pays him only $8,000 more, it will be in B's firm's interests to try to bid A away with an offer of $9,000 and it will pay A's firm to hold him with a $9,500 counteroffer, etc. (Of course, if A is the owner of the firm he will simply gather these wages of his special skills in the form of profit in the noneconomist's sense of the word.) In this way all cost savings will tend to be paid out to the more efficient inputs that make them possible. Hence, since we must include these bonus payments, the costs of the more efficient firms will tend to be driven toward equality with those of the less efficient.

One more point needs to be made here—the zero-profit rule may seem implausible at first glance. Why should anyone stay in business if it yields him no returns? But the term "profits" is used here in a rather strict sense.

A small businessman may earn a comfortable living. But if his earnings are no more than he could get by spending the same amount of time working for someone else plus the return he could get by investing his money elsewhere, the economist states that he is receiving just the wages for his labor and interest on his capital. Only if he receives any more than this sum is the excess counted as profit. It is surely true that many a small businessman has shown himself willing to work for even negative profits when the term is interpreted in this sense.

3. Equilibrium in the Competitive Industry

The standard and well-known analysis of pricing and output determination in the competitive *industry* (as contrasted with the single firm) involves the drawing of an industry supply curve and an industry demand curve with price and output determined by the intersection of the two curves.

The supply curve can be given an interpretation in terms of costs. In fact, in the long run it tends to approximate a curve of average costs for the industry. This, again, is a consequence of the free-entry-and-exit assumption and its zero-profit result. If the industry were to supply its commodity at a price which exceeded its average cost, some firms would necessarily be making a profit. We have seen how the entry of new firms could make short work of that profit.

One must examine the stability of this industry equilibrium in order to see whether this equilibrium point can be expected to be of direct relevance to any real market situations, i.e., whether there is any mechanism which pulls competitive prices and outputs into line with their equilibrium levels. It is not appropriate here to go into a full dynamic analysis of this stability question, but we will at least examine the outlines of the mechanism which can work in the direction of stability. Figure 2a shows the usual supply-demand diagram for the competitive industry. The equilibrium occurs at the point of intersection, E, of the two curves, and P_E and Q_E constitute the equilibrium industry price-quantity combination.

Suppose now that, for some reason, the market price falls below the equilibrium price, say to P_L. In this case the quantity demanded will exceed the quantity supplied by quantity $D_L - S_L$, and we may expect price to be pushed back up toward the equilibrium price. In the same way, a price like P_H, which is above the equilibrium level, will be pushed back down. In this situation, then, the equilibrium at least gives an appearance of stability which dynamic analysis can rationalize.

But it does not follow that the supply-demand equilibrium point will always be stable. On the contrary, it is easy to find a case where the machinery works in the wrong direction. Figure 2b depicts such a situation.

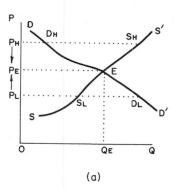

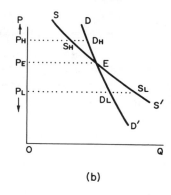

(a)   (b)

Figure 2

Here, when the price falls to P_L, below the equilibrium price, supply will exceed demand (by quantity $S_L - D_L$). Hence price will be driven down even further. Similarly, we have instability on the upward side. Doubtless such cases are rare in practice, but the illustration at least shows that we must be careful in assuming that our models are always well behaved.

The diagram can be used to study problems such as the effects of taxation on competitive pricing. A standard analysis seeks to determine what portion of a tax on manufactured goods will be paid by the producer and how much of it will be passed on to consumers in the form of higher prices. This is referred to as the problem of the *shifting* and *incidence* of taxation.

Figure 3 is another supply-demand diagram. The original supply curve is represented as RR'. Since, in the long run, this can be interpreted as an average cost curve, the addition of a fixed per-unit tax which raises businessmen's outpayments correspondingly results in a uniform upward shift of the cost curve to SS'. We see at once that, while the tax per unit is represented by length AB, the resulting increase in price will be only FB. In other words, part of the tax burden (FB) will be shifted from the manufacturer to the consumer. But the incidence of the remainder, AF, will be on the producer.

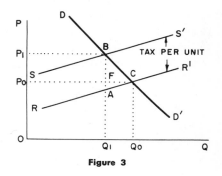

Figure 3

By experimenting with the shapes of the diagram, the reader can verify the following results:

1. The smaller the slope of the demand curve, the greater will be the proportion of the tax paid by the supplier.

2. The smaller the slope of the supply curve, the greater will be the proportion of the tax which is shifted to the consumer.

These rules have a ready intuitive justification. For example, a steep demand means that buyers are willing to continue to purchase pretty much the same quantity almost no matter what the price. It is natural to expect that such anxious purchasers will end up paying the bulk of the tax.

4. Supply Curves: Some Comments

A supply curve is, of course, defined as a graph which shows what quantities of a commodity will be offered for sale at different prices—i.e., it summarizes the seller's quantity reaction to various prices. We have just seen that the long-run supply curve for the industry will coincide with its average cost curve.

The competitive firm, too, will have a supply curve, and it will also be related to costs, but in a quite different manner. In fact, the profit-maximizing *firm's* supply curve will coincide with (a portion of) its *marginal* cost curve. This proposition can readily be demonstrated with the aid of Figure 1a. As we have seen, our firm will find it profitable to produce up to a point where price (marginal revenue) equals marginal cost. Thus, at price OD, the firm's supply will be OQ_p, and, similarly, at price OU it will supply quantity OQ_s. Both of these price-quantity supplied combinations are represented by points (W and T) on the marginal cost curve, CMC. Since a similar observation holds for any other price at which the firm is willing to produce, our result follows—the firm's supply curve is the same as its marginal cost curve.[2]

The supply curve is, strictly speaking, a concept which is usually relevant only for the case of pure (or perfect) competition, and it will therefore not be encountered in later sections of this chapter. The reason for this lies in its definition—the supply curve is designed to answer questions of the form, "How much will firm A supply if it encounters a price which is fixed at P dollars?" But such a question is most relevant to the behavior of firms that actually deal with prices over whose determination they exercise no influence. Only in two situations may we expect firms to encounter such preset prices—if there is a central authority who sets prices by fiat, and in conditions of pure competition where the price is set by an impersonal

---

[2] Strictly speaking, the supply curve includes only the rising segment of the firm's marginal cost curve. At price OD the firm will produce OQ_p and not OQ_r, as has already been noted in footnote 1, above. Therefore, a point such as L, on the descending portion of the marginal cost curve, will form no part of the supply curve. Moreover, even points on the ascending portion of the marginal cost curve must be excluded from the supply curve *if they lie below the average variable cost curve*. At any price which lies below average variable cost the firm is better off supplying nothing.

market mechanism outside the control of any buyer or seller. In most other circumstances the firm will be able to set its own price, so the information given by the supply curve will be inapplicable to the operations of such a company.

5. Pure Monopoly

In the case of pure monopoly the firm and the industry coincide by definition—the monopoly *is* the industry. The output of the monopolistic *firm* must therefore be compared with that of the *industry* under pure competition. This comparison can be made with the help of a diagram which combines the supply-demand analysis of the competitive in-dustry with the marginal ap-paratus of the theory of the firm. This is done in Figure 4.

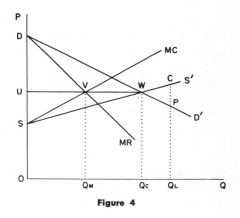

Figure 4

Here *DD'* and *SS'* are the competitive industry supply and demand curves. Suppose, now, that a monopolist takes over the competitive industry, and that in the process there occurs no change in the basic conditions of demand and cost (including rents). The demand curve now becomes the monopolist's average revenue curve. Moreover, as we have seen, the long-run supply curve tends to approximate the average cost curve.[3]

We can, therefore, construct the monopolist's marginal cost and mar-ginal revenue curves, *SMC* and *DMR*, from this information by the methods of Chapter 3, Section 5. The monopolist's profit optimum output will, then, be OQ_M, which is clearly smaller than the competitive output OQ_C. So long as the slope of the supply curve is positive, or, if it is nega-tive, so long as it is less steep than the demand curve, this will always be the case. For if the average cost curve cuts the average revenue curve from below, all outputs, such as OQ_L, above the competitive zero-profit point, OQ_C, will cause the firm to lose money, since average cost, Q_LC, will

---

[3] This assumes that the industry pays rent to suppliers of inputs because other industries compete for their use. If, in the competitive situation, some factor rents had been paid only because firms within the industry were bidding against one another for the inputs, then with monopolization these rent payments would disappear and the monopoly average cost curve would lie below the competitive supply curve.

there exceed price, $Q_L P$. Only to the left of the competitive equilibrium point will there be any profits.

This is the standard well-publicized result that the monopolist tends to restrict his output. But this result must be treated with caution for two reasons.

1. It is likely that cost and demand conditions will change when a monopoly takes over a competitive industry. By centralizing purchasing and, perhaps, having one man replace 100 independent buyers, by effecting economies of large scale through the combining of plants, inventories, etc., the monopolist may be able to reduce his costs. On the other hand, the larger monopolistic firm may require a more cumbersome, more costly administrative machinery. In addition, monopolistic advertising may increase the demand for the monopolist's products. It follows that the simple comparison of monopolistic and competitive outputs of Figure 4 cannot be relied on.

2. Even if the competitive industry does produce the larger output, it is by no means obvious that this is always desirable from the point of view of consumers or anyone else. In a period of full employment an increase in output in one industry takes away resources from elsewhere in the economy and forces a reduction in output and possibly a price rise there (the "guns vs. butter" problem). The basic point is that, under full employment, the determination of the outputs of the different industries is a matter of the *allocation* of resources. In popular discussions one tends to think that the larger the output of any industry, the better off is society, but it is easy to see that this can result in a misallocation of resources, just as, in the firm, a lopsided investment policy biased excessively toward one department may ease that department's operations but is hardly likely to be optimal from the point of view of the business as a whole.

6. Monopolistic Competition (Product Differentiation)

Chamberlin's analysis of monopolistic competition deals largely with the individual firm and does not refer directly to the industry. In fact, it may be almost impossible to define an industry in such a situation. Differentiation of product means that no two firms put out the same item. Some products may, perhaps, be easily recognized as the same sort of item, but as one gets to less and less perfect substitute products one industry will tend to shade off into another. Hence, rather than well-defined industries, one tends to get something more like a continuum of products, although this assertion probably overstates the situation in practice.

Under monopolistic competition the demand curve for the product of the firm may be expected to have a negative slope, even though the firm is as small as one operating under conditions of pure competition. For customers will have different degrees of loyalty to the firms from whom they make their purchases. A small reduction in one firm's price may only attract its competitors' most mercurial customers. But, as larger and larger price reductions are instituted, it may acquire more and more customers from its rivals by drawing on customers who are less anxious to switch.

The equilibrium of the firm involves the usual conditions—marginal cost equal to marginal revenue. Again, in the short run, the firms may or may not earn a profit. But under monopolistic competition one can also expect something like freedom of entry. Since firms are small, relatively

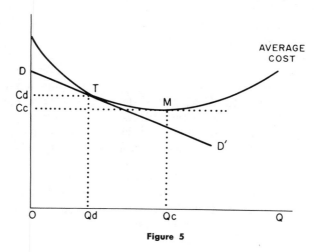

Figure 5

little capital is required to set up business and turn out a product not quite the same as but still very like those already on the market.

The result is that, as under pure competition, both profits and losses will tend to be eliminated in the long run. The average cost curve will be driven toward tangency with the demand curve, and we will end up with a situation like that depicted in Figure 5. The equilibrium point, T, will be the point of tangency between the average cost curve and the negatively sloping demand curve, DD'. For at any other output, unit costs will be larger than price and so such an output will involve a loss to the firm.[4]

---

[4] It follows that, since OQ_d is the maximum profit output, marginal cost must there equal marginal revenue. This also follows from the standard relationship

$$M = A + Q(dA/dQ),$$

where M and A represent marginal x and average x, respectively (see footnote 3 of Chapter 3). This result shows that if two average curves (in this case average *cost* and *revenue*) are tangent, so that $A_1 = A_2$, $Q_1 = Q_2$, and $dA_1/dQ_1 = dA_2/dQ_2$, we must have $M_1 = M_2$.

The average cost curve is ordinarily taken to have the "U" shape indicated in the diagram on the argument that both very small and very large outputs are difficult and expensive to produce. Even economies of large scale apply only up to a point, beyond which administrative costs and diminishing returns, because of the presence of scarce (bottleneck) inputs, are generally expected to raise the unit costs of production.

If this is so, the point of tangency T between the U-shaped average cost curve and the negatively sloping demand curve must be found somewhere to the left of the minimum average cost point, M. This is in direct contrast with the equilibrium of the competitive firm whose long-run position is M (cf. Figure 1b, above). Hence, the output of the firm under monopolistic competition must be smaller, and its unit cost and price higher than it would be under pure competition.

In this case it can be argued that there is, from the point of view of the economy as a whole, something to be said for the superiority of the competitive arrangement. What may be called for is some amalgamation of business firms. The diagram (Figure 5) shows that, by becoming larger, firms can reduce their unit costs from what they are at point T. That means that if a number of firms are eliminated, the total output may be kept the same (instead of 12 firms producing 500 units each we can, e.g., reduce the number of firms to 3, each producing 2,000 units, and so keep the total output at 6,000). But each of the firms will, as a result of its expansion, have lower average costs. It follows by elementary arithmetic that if the same output is produced at lower unit costs there must be a net over-all saving to the community (if unit costs are reduced from $8 to $6, the total cost to the firms producing the 6,000 total product, in our example, will be reduced from $48,000 to $36,000—a net gain to the community of $12,000 with no reduction in output!). This result has been called the *excess capacity theorem* of monopolistic competition.

Hence, only if the elimination of firms results in an important reduction in the variety of products available to the consumer, so that a real decrease in consumer choice opportunities occurs, is there any reason for society to "prefer" the product differentiation equilibrium point, T.

7. Monopsony

Under monopsony, a monopoly on the buyer's side, it is in the interest of the buyer to obtain his purchases (usually inputs) at as low a cost as possible, just as the monopolist seeks to obtain as large a return as possible. Thus the monopsonistic firm's output level will be chosen with an eye on the consequences for input prices of a change in its demand for inputs.

The optimizing buyer's demand curve is always a marginal curve. The business firm facing an input whose price is fixed will (Chapter 24, Section

2) purchase inputs up to the point where the input's marginal revenue product (the increase in revenue made possible by the purchase of an additional input unit) is equal to its price. The firm's input demand curve is, therefore, a curve of marginal revenue product, i.e., for every possible quantity of input purchase it indicates the value of its marginal revenue product. By exactly the same argument it can be shown that the optimizing consumer's demand curve must be a curve of marginal utility (with utility measured in money terms). That is, at any product quantity it shows the maximum money amount which the consumer would be willing to give up for an additional unit of the product.

From the point of view of the buyer, however, the *supply* curve of an input may be considered an average rather than a marginal curve. That is, it shows for every level of input purchase the price he will have to pay for each unit of this input—i.e., it gives the average cost to him of that input.

The profit-maximizing monopsonistic firm's equilibrium requires the usual marginal-cost-equals-marginal-revenue condition. This means that the monopsonist's input purchase must be at a level at which the marginal revenue product of the input is equal to its *marginal* cost to the firm. A similar argument would apply to monopsonistic purchasers of finished products (monopsonist–consumers).

Hence, the monopsonist's equilibrium point will be the intersection of the input's curve of marginal revenue product with the curve *marginal* to the supply curve of the input (the average input cost curve). If the input supply curve has a positive slope, the marginal input cost curve will lie above (to the left of) it, since when an average curve is rising the marginal curve will always lie above it. Therefore, the monopsonistic level of input purchases will tend to be smaller than those of a group of buyers for whom the input price is fixed. The reason is the same as that for the monopolist's output restriction. By restricting his purchases, the monopsonist forces down the price of what he buys, and that is to his advantage.

8. Remarks on Discriminating Monopoly

The basic condition which must be met before price discrimination, that is, the sale of different units of a product at different prices, can be practiced successfully is that the market for the seller's product be split off into separate sections and that it be difficult to transfer the seller's product from sector to sector. For example, the doctor can charge different prices to different patients because it is ordinarily impossible for a low-fee patient to resell his treatment to someone who pays more for the same services. An exporting firm can charge less abroad than the domestic price of his product because the costs of reimporting the product can be prohibitive or because of other obstacles to reimportation.

We may also note several other properties of the discriminating monopoly case:

1. If he sets his prices properly, the discriminating monopolist can always expect to earn at least as much as does an ordinary monopolist. For, in setting his prices independently in his different markets, he will always have the option of keeping the prices in several of his markets the same, if that is profitable. In other words, the discriminating monopolist can match every opportunity which is open to the ordinary monopolist and he has some others besides.

2. The basic rule of profit maximization in discriminating monopoly is that marginal revenue must be the same in all markets to which the firm sells. For if its marginal revenue is greater in market A than in B, it can increase its profits by decreasing the amount shipped to B and transferring it to A. Only when this transfer process raises the price in market B and lowers it in A to a point where marginal revenues in the two markets are equal will the firm have arrived at an optimal allocation of its goods between the two markets. The condition that marginal revenue must everywhere be the same thus determines the discriminator's shipments to all his markets, and his total output is determined by setting the marginal revenue equal to marginal cost.[5]

---

[5] The last section of this chapter describes the algebra of decision-making under price discrimination. Graphically the matter is handled by a horizontal summation of the marginal revenue curves for the company's submarkets. Thus in the diagram EF on the

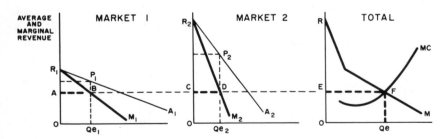

total marginal revenue curve RM equals $AB + CD$, the sum of the corresponding quantities on the marginal revenue curves of markets 1 and 2. The total quantity which will be supplied is OQe where the total marginal revenue, RM, equals the total marginal cost, MC (point F). This quantity is divided between the markets into amounts OQe_1 and OQe_2 at which the marginal revenues are equal in both markets as required for profit maximization. The prices in the two markets are given by the heights of points P_1 and P_2, the points on the *average* revenue (demand) curves corresponding to these quantities.

9. Bilateral Monopoly

In this analysis it is convenient to extend the concept of the indifference curve and, in the present context, to be able to interpret it either as a curve of constant utility (as in the usual theory of the consumer) or as a curve of constant profitability so that any two points on such a curve are equally profitable. We deal here with the case of two people who are exchanging two commodities. If one of the items exchanged is money, one of the bilateral monopolists (the money-payer) may be identified as the buyer and the other as the seller. Suppose that the buyer is an input-purchaser and that the seller is an input-supplier. We may draw an indifference map between money and X (the quantity of the input sold) for each

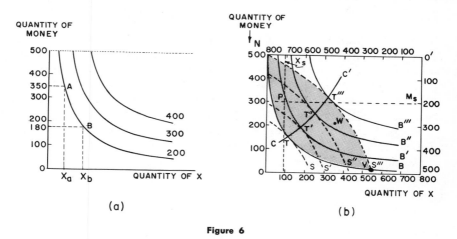

(a)   (b)

Figure 6

of these persons. In Figure 6a we have such an indifference map for the input-purchaser. Here it is assumed that the buyer starts off with $500 in money. In interpreting the indifference map it should be noted that we read *down* from this figure to determine the amount the buyer pays out. For example, at point A he ends up with X_a units of X and $350 of his original supply of money left. That means he must have spent the difference, $150, for the X_a units of A.

Each such indifference curve is a locus of money-input purchase combinations which are equally profitable. All points on the lower curve (such as B) yield $200 in profit. Those on the next curve yield $300, etc.

A similar diagram can be drawn to represent the circumstances of the supplier, only in his case it will be the quantity of X which is measured from his maximum supply capacity level downward, and any one of his profit indifference curves must be the locus of all combinations of quantity supplied and revenue which yield him a fixed level of profit (after deducting the cost of production of that quantity of output from his total revenue at that point).

The two indifference maps can now be combined in an ingenious rectangular diagram[6] (Figure 6b). One of the indifference maps is turned upside down and the ends of the axes joined. Thus the buyer's total money supply determines the length of the vertical axis, and the fixed input production capacity gives the length of the horizontal axis. Now, any point in the diagram may be interpreted as a trade. That is, it shows simultaneously where both of the bilateral monopolists will end up after an exchange. For example, point P represents a trade in which the buyer ends up with 100 units of input and 300 units of money, while the seller ends up with the remainder—\$200 (point M_s on the right-hand axis) and 700 units of X in the form of unused production capacity—point X_s on the top axis. (Note that the seller's holdings are read downward and to the left from the upper right-hand corner, O', which is the origin of his upside-down indifference map.) Any point thus automatically indicates the ending position of *both* buyer and seller. Because of the fixed total of \$500 in money, whatever does not remain in the hands of the buyer must go to the seller and the same applies to X (or, rather, capacity to supply X).

The solid indifference curves, B, are the buyer's indifference curves whereas the broken S curves are those of the seller.

Consider now the curve CC', which is the locus of all points of tangency (such as T) between the buyer's and seller's indifference curves. CC' is called the *contract curve*. It possesses two relevant features:

1. For every trade point off the contract curve, there exist trade points on the contract curve which are mutually advantageous to buyer and seller. For example, consider point V, which is off the contract curve. Since it is not a point of tangency, the seller's and buyer's indifference curves S''' and B which go through that point must intersect. Hence there will be a region between the two curves (shaded area) through which there passes higher profit indifference for both seller and buyer (e.g., indifference curve B' yields more profit to the buyer than does B, and S' is more profitable to the seller than S'''). We conclude that all points on the arc of the contract curve TT''' which lies in the shaded region will be preferred to point V by both buyer and seller.

2. Any move along the contract curve must be disadvantageous to *one* of the participants. Any move downward and to the left must be disad-

---

[6] This device, as well as the concept of the contract curve, described below, was invented by Edgeworth. See F. Y. Edgeworth, *Mathematical Psychics*, Kegan Paul, London, 1881, pp. 17ff. For a derivation of the equation of the contract curve see Chapter 21, footnote 11, below.

vantageous to the buyer (it gets him to a lower indifference curve), and any move in the opposite direction must adversely affect the seller, for an analogous reason.

It has therefore been argued that the actual trading point must end up somewhere along the contract curve, CC', for anywhere else it will be mutually advantageous to buyer and seller to renegotiate their deal, and only at a point on the contract curve will no such renegotiation be profitable to both.

The range of possible trading points can be narrowed down somewhat further. The point in the upper left-hand corner, N, represents the situation in which no exchange is made. The buyer holds on to his money and gets no X. Through this point there pass one of the buyer's and one of the seller's indifference curves (B and S'''). Neither buyer nor seller will be willing to accept any trade that leaves him on a lower profit indifference curve, for he can always refuse any such inferior proposition and stay at his "no-deal" point, N. This means that all possible trading points must lie in the region between the indifference curves through N, the shaded region in the diagram. For that reason, the only possible points on the contract curve are those on the arc TT'''.

Beyond this it is difficult to narrow down any further the possible locations of the final equilibrium point. Several suggestions have been offered— for example, the joint maximum point (the point which maximizes the sum of the profits of the buyer and seller together). However, it is difficult to see why one may expect that the bargainers should always be expected to end up at any one such point. For that reason, many economists have concluded that the bilateral monopoly problem is "indeterminate."

In fact, some have even suggested that the trade may well end up somewhere *off* the contract curve. If, for example, the trade happens to fall at point W, and the buyer feels that his bargaining position is so weak that a reopening of negotiation would move the trading point to somewhere along TT', he may prefer just to let sleeping dogs lie.

Similar indeterminacy problems will occur in the discussion of oligopoly which follows, and some degree of explanation will be offered in the course of the discussion.

10. Oligopolistic Interdependence

The oligopoly situation (including in this term the two-firm duopoly case) has one feature on which most of the economist's attention has been centered. This is the interdependence in the decision-making of the various firms, an interdependence which is recognized by all of them. In an industry which consists largely of a small number of sizable companies, if one of them opens a tremendous advertising campaign or designs a new model of his product which sweeps the market, he can be fairly sure that this will lead to countermoves on the part of his competitors. Every businessman in such a situation knows that at least some of his rivals' decisions depend on his own behavior, and he must take this fact into account in his own decision-making.

The reason for this interdependence in decision-making is, of course, that a major policy change on the part of one firm is likely to have obvious and immediate effects on the other companies which comprise the industry. As a result, the oligopolist has developed an armory of aggressive and defensive marketing weapons. For example, it is only under oligopoly that advertising comes fully into its own. Under pure competition no one has *any* motive to advertise because any producer can sell all of his product at the going price without incurring any advertising outlay. A monopolist will find some advertising to be profitable, perhaps when he is introducing a totally new commodity or where there exists a considerable body of potential consumers who have never tried his type of ware. But under oligopoly, advertising can become a life-and-death matter where a firm which fails to keep up with the advertising budget of its competitors may find its customers drifting off to rival products.

As a result, the oligopolistic businessman is sometimes rather surprised when the presence of competitive conditions in his industry is questioned. To him competition consists not in the quiescent stalemate of perfect competition where there is no battle because there is never anyone strong enough to disturb the peace. Rather, to him, true competition consists of the life of constant struggle, rival against rival, which one can only find under oligopoly (or, on a smaller scale, under conditions of monopolistic competition).

Oligopolistic interdependence has another consequence which is of more importance for the economic literature than for the operation of the economy. This feature of the situation has made the formulation of a systematic analysis of oligopoly very difficult. Under the circumstances a very wide variety of behavior patterns becomes possible. Rivals may decide to get together and cooperate in the pursuit of their objectives, at least so far as the law allows, or, at the other extreme, they may try to fight each other to the death. Even if they enter into an agreement[7] it may last or it may break down. And the agreements may follow a wide variety of patterns.

As a result, the literature of oligopoly theory is full of different models, many of which describe, at most, one particular arrangement—a price-

---

[7] In any event, oligopolistic collusion will always be somewhat limited by legal restrictions and, in fact, by definition, for where all firms in an industry take all of their decisions jointly, they are in essence amalgamated into a monopoly.

leadership agreement or some particular method of using freight charges as a means for apportioning out market territories.

An even more serious analytical difficulty arises directly out of management's need to take account of its competitors' reaction patterns. When a businessman wonders about his competitors' likely response to some move which he is considering, he must recognize that his competitor, too, is likely to take this interdependence phenomenon into account. The firms' attempts to outguess one another are then likely to lead to an interplay of anticipated strategies and counterstrategies which is tangled beyond hope of direct analysis, for in this way management is only led to advance along an infinite sequence of compounded hypotheses: "If I make move A, he may consider making countermove B, but he may realize that I might then respond by making move C, in which case . . . ," and so on *ad infinitum*.

There are several ways out of this state of confusion, which is as unsatisfactory to the economic analyst as it is to the businessman who is saddled with its problems. Each of these approaches has something to be said for it.

1. *Ignoring interdependence.* The firm may simply ignore the entire matter, on the assumption that its competitor will also do so. There is some reason to believe that this is, in fact, what many firms do in their more routine day-to-day decision-making. They ignore the interdependence of the returns to the various firms in the industry because, as a practical matter, these complex effects of minor policy changes are not worth the effort required to take them into account. Since interdependence disappears from decision-making with such an approach, the analysis of this case is simply the standard analysis of the theory of the firm which was discussed in the preceding chapter. However, in the analysis of a really major decision—when an automobile manufacturer considers introducing a radical new design or a cigarette manufacturer is about to embark on a major advertising campaign—the decision-maker knows he cannot afford to dodge the issue in this way, and the complex problems of interdependence must reenter the discussion.

2. *Predicting competitors' countermoves.* A second way of dealing with the problem is for a firm to attempt to anticipate the nature of competitive reactions on the basis of guesswork or past experience. For example, the decision-maker may know that his competitors have usually matched his price changes within a few days or he may simply guess that they are likely to do so. In such a case, it is possible to take this definite reaction pattern into account and decide on a strategy which is optimal in terms of this assumption. The remainder of this chapter describes models which employ this second approach to the analysis of the interdependence problem. One difficulty which arises here, as we shall see, is that if two competitors both

proceed on this sort of optimality calculation, each is likely to find that his prediction about the other was incorrect, *because the optimality calculation will lead him to act in a manner which was not predicted.*

3. *Preparing against optimal moves by competitors.* A third approach to the analysis of the interdependence problem in business decision-making is that of the theory of games. Here the businessman does not guess at his opponent's reaction pattern. Rather, he, in effect, calculates the optimal moves of the opposition—his rival's best possible strategies— and prepares his own defenses and countermeasures accordingly. Discussion of this third alternative has been postponed until Chapter 18.

11. Stability of Oligopoly Arrangements: Kinked Demand Curves[8]

Let us now examine several oligopoly models which have attracted considerable attention. First let us consider one which is *not* designed to deal with oligopolistic price and output determination. Rather, it seeks to explain why, once a price-quantity combination has been decided upon, it will not readily change.

The source of the problem is the fact that oligopolistic arrangements are notoriously undependable. For example, the history of price agreements contains case after case where "chiselers" seem to have found it advantageous to undercut the price which was agreed upon in order to grab off a larger share of the market. Yet, despite this phenomenon, prices in many oligopolistic industries appear to have exhibited a remarkable degree of stability, particularly in their resistance to change in the downward direction. The model which will now be described is one possible explanation of the "stickiness" of oligopoly prices.

Consider the effect on quantity demanded of a reduction in the price of a commodity. This is, as usual, shown by the demand curve for the product. Suppose, first, that the reduction in the price which is charged by our firm is matched by other competing concerns. In that case the company may expect to increase its sales slightly, but since it is not likely to get any customers away from its rivals in these circumstances, no large addition to its sales is to be anticipated. Its demand curve (*DD'* in Figure 7) will be relatively inelastic.

Now suppose, on the other hand, that our company is the only one to reduce its price. In that case a much larger increase in its demand is to be

---

[8] The analysis of this section is based on the work of Sweezy, Hall, and Hitch. See Paul M. Sweezy, "Demand Under Conditions of Oligopoly," *Journal of Political Economy*, Vol. XLVII, August 1939, reprinted in American Economic Association, *Readings in Price Theory*, George J. Stigler and Kenneth E. Boulding (eds.), Richard D. Irwin, Inc., Homewood, Ill., 1952, and R. L. Hall and C. J. Hitch, "Price Theory and Business Behavior," *Oxford Economic Papers*, No. 2, May 1939.

expected. Thus, where no one else follows its price moves, the firm is likely to have a relatively elastic demand curve like dd'.

Let point C represent the firm's current price-quantity combination. It has been argued that the large oligopolistic firm is likely to anticipate the following competitive reaction pattern to a price change:

1. *Price reductions:* If our company reduces its price, competitors will feel the drain on their customers quickly and so they will be forced to match this price cut. In other words, for downward price movements from point C, the relevant portion of the firm's demand curve will be segment CD' of the steeper demand curve DD'.

2. *Price increases:* If the company raises its price, it may expect that its happy competitors will welcome the new customers which they gain from

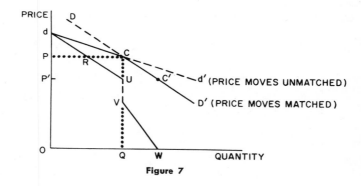

Figure 7

the price-raising firm as a result, and they will have no motivation to match the price rise. Hence, for price rises the relevant part of the demand curve will be elastic segment dC.

In sum, given this view of competitive reaction patterns the company's demand curve will be the composite curve dCD', characterized by a kink (a sharp corner) at the point C, which represents the current price-output combination.

It is now easy to see that a company with such a competitive response pattern will be extremely reluctant to change its price. For a fall in its price will yield no large increase in sales, while a price increase will result in a substantial cut in business, and neither of these is a very attractive prospect.

The reader should also be able to show with the aid of the geometric technique of Chapter 3, Section 5, that the marginal revenue curve in this case is broken line $dUVW$. If the marginal cost curve happens to pass anywhere through the gap VU in the marginal revenue curve, the profit-maximizing firm will have no motivation to leave the current price, P. Even if there is, for example, a sharp rise in costs, so long as the marginal cost curve does not rise above point U it will lead to no price change.

This analysis has been questioned on empirical grounds.[9] Certainly it seems clear that in an inflationary period oligopoly firms do often follow one another's price *rises*, contrary to what is assumed by this model. However, the analysis does show how the oligopolistic firm's view of competitive reaction patterns can affect the changeability of whatever price it happens to be charging.

12. Reaction Curves and Oligopolistic Pricing

Let us now see how the businessman may go about setting his price if he has some definite ideas about his competitors' reactions to his decisions. For diagrammatic simplicity the discussion is confined to the two-firm

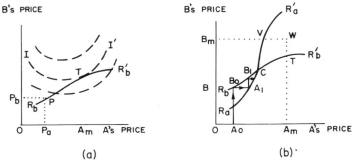

(a)　　　　　　　　　　　　　　　(b)

Figure 8

(duopoly) case. Figure 8a summarizes this anticipated reaction pattern. *Reaction curve* $R_b R_b'$ contains the relevant information about the price reaction of one firm, B, to the pricing decision of another firm, A. For example, point P on this curve indicates that if firm A sets price OP_a for its product, and if firm B reacts in accord with the information given by its reaction curve, the price of B's product will become OP_b.

If B does stick to this reaction pattern, A's optimal price decision can be represented quite simply. The broken curves in Figure 8a represent the indifference curves of A's objective function, that is, they are his iso-profit curves if A is a profit-maximizer. Then the highest indifference curve which

---

[9] See George J. Stigler, "The Kinky Oligopoly Demand Curve and Rigid Prices," *Journal of Political Economy*, Vol. LV, October 1947, reprinted in American Economic Association, *ibid.*; J. L. Simon, "A Further Test of the Kinky Oligopoly Demand Curve,"

A can attain (the highest indifference curve compatible with B's reaction pattern) is II', which is tangent to B's reaction curve at point T. To get to this point, A must set his price at OA_m and, accordingly, this must be his optimal price.

So far so good. But, unfortunately for the analysis, two can play at optimization. Figure 8b contains, in addition to B's reaction curve, R_aR_a', which indicates the manner in which B expects A to react to his prices. B, in turn, may now pick an optimum point, say V, on A's reaction curve, R_aR_a', and thus he will set his price at OB_m. But if both A and B choose these "optimal" prices, they will end up neither on point T nor on V. Rather, the resulting price combination will be represented by W, a point which lies on neither reaction curve.

The result will be that both players will be surprised at their earnings— they may either be pleasantly surprised (on higher indifference curves than they expected) or they may be disappointed. More important, they will both realize that the reaction curves have become falsehoods, for neither player is now reacting in accord with the dictates of his reaction curve. Once they realize this, they will know also that their optimality calculations have gone up in smoke. What was optimal for A so long as B stuck to his reaction curve need no longer be optimal once B strikes off on his own. Both firms must begin their calculations afresh, and we cannot say where they are likely to go from here.[10]

Thus we have not fully avoided the problems of interdependence in oligopoly price determination even if we have somehow found a reasonable method of constructing each oligopolist's reaction curve (and the number

---

American Economic Review, Vol. 59, December 1969; and W. J. Primeaux, Jr., and M. R. Bomball, "A Reexamination of the Kinky Oligopoly Demand Curve," *Journal of Political Economy*, Vol. 82, July, August 1974. These authors have collected data indicating that oligopoly prices are no stickier than those of monopoly firms and that price increases by one firm are as frequently followed as are price decreases contrary to what the model indicates.

[10] An alternative oligopoly model investigates what will happen if both firms stay on their reaction curves. It is easy to show that if the curves have the correct relative slopes the price combination must tend toward C, the point of intersection of A's and B's reaction curves, for if A sets price OA_0, B will move to point B_0, the corresponding point on his reaction curve (price OB), but then A will raise his price accordingly (he will move to point A_1 on his reaction curve), etc. Prices will then move along the path $A_0B_0A_1B_1\cdots$ toward intersection equilibrium price combination C. This is a generalization of the granddaddy of all oligopoly models, that of Cournot. See A. A. Cournot, *Researches into the Mathematical Principles of the Theory of Wealth* (1838), English translation, The Macmillan Company, New York, 1897. It is also possible to construct an Edgeworth contract curve from Figure 8b and Section 9, this chapter. This is, again, the locus of points of tangency of the participants' indifference curves, and it has properties similar to those of the contract curve of bilateral monopoly.

of models which have been proposed indicates that this matter is far from cut and dried).

This concludes our brief discussion of the theory of oligopoly and with it, our survey of the standard analysis of the various alternative market forms. A number of significant results have emerged from the analysis, but the need for a theory which is richer in empirical content seems quite apparent. Particularly, one is left with the feeling that the oligopoly analysis has involved a number of interesting observations and has provided us with a number of helpful analytical concepts, but some of its most critical questions remain unanswered.

13. *Monopoly, Duopoly, and Discrimination: Elementary Mathematical Analysis*

Example 1: The Calculus of Price Discrimination

Given two isolated markets supplied by a single monopolist, let the two corresponding demand functions be

$$P_1 = 12 - Q_1 \quad \text{and} \quad P_2 = 20 - 3Q_2.$$

Suppose the monopolist's total cost function is

$$C = 3 + 2(Q_1 + Q_2).$$

A. What will prices, sales, and marginal revenues be in the two markets under a regime of price discrimination, and what profit will the monopolist earn?

Answer: The total profit in the two markets together will be

$$\Pi = P_1Q_1 + P_2Q_2 - C = 12Q_1 - Q_1^2 + 20Q_2 - 3Q_2^2 - 2(Q_1 + Q_2) - 3$$

$$= 10Q_1 - Q_1^2 + 18Q_2 - 3Q_2^2 - 3.$$

Taking partial derivatives and equating them to zero we have

$$\frac{\partial \Pi}{\partial Q_1} = 10 - 2Q_1 = 0 \quad \text{or} \quad Q_1 = 5$$

$$\frac{\partial \Pi}{\partial Q_2} = 18 - 6Q_2 = 0 \quad \text{or} \quad Q_2 = 3.$$

Hence, substituting these values of Q_1 and Q_2 into the demand and profit functions,

$$\Pi = 49, \qquad P_1 = 7, \qquad P_2 = 11$$

and

$$\text{marginal revenue in market 1 } (MR_1) = \frac{\partial P_1Q_1}{\partial Q_1} = 12 - 2Q_1 = 2$$

while

$$MR_2 = \qquad 20 - 6Q_2 = 2.$$

B. Find the corresponding values if the monopolist cannot discriminate.

Answer: Profits must now be maximized subject to the constraint[11] $P_1 = P_2$, i.e.,

$$12 - Q_1 = 20 - 3Q_2.$$

Using the same profit function as before, we have the Lagrangian expression

$$\Pi_\lambda = 10Q_1 - Q_1^2 + 18Q_2 - 3Q_2^2 - 3 + \lambda(8 - 3Q_2 + Q_1)$$

so that we require

$$\frac{\partial \Pi_\lambda}{\partial Q_1} = 10 - 2Q_1 + \lambda = 0$$

$$\frac{\partial \Pi_\lambda}{\partial Q_2} = 18 - 6Q_2 - 3\lambda = 0$$

$$\frac{\partial \Pi_\lambda}{\partial \lambda} = 8 + Q_1 - 3Q_2 = 0,$$

whose solution is $\lambda = -2$, $Q_1 = 4$, $Q_2 = 4$. Substituting into the relevant expressions we obtain

$$\Pi = 45, \qquad P_1 = 8, \qquad P_2 = 8,$$

$$MR_1 \left(= \frac{\partial P_1 Q_1}{\partial Q_1} = 12 - 2Q_1 \right) = 4, \qquad MR_2 = -4.$$

Note that in the discrimination case marginal revenues were equal in both markets while, where prices were equal in both markets, marginal revenue in one of the markets was actually negative. It should also be observed that one price rose and the other fell under discrimination but that the monopolist's profits were higher in the discriminatory case.

Example 2: Cournot Equilibrium vs. Joint Maximization

Let there be two firms in an industry and let the profits of each be dependent

---

[11] It is also possible in simple cases to proceed just by adding the demand functions. We do this by first solving them for Q_1 and Q_2 in terms of P_1 and P_2 thus: $Q_1 = 12 - P_1$, $Q_2 = 20/3 - P_2/3$. Since $P_1 = P_2 = P$ we may then add these to obtain the total demand,

$$Q = Q_1 + Q_2 = \frac{56}{3} - \frac{4}{3}P \qquad \text{or} \qquad P = \frac{56}{4} - \frac{3}{4}Q.$$

on both its output and the output of its competitor, thus:

$$\Pi_1 = 24Q_1 - Q_1^2 - 2Q_2^2 - 8$$
$$\Pi_2 = 30Q_2 - 3Q_2^2 - 2Q_1 - 9.$$

A. What will be the magnitudes of outputs and profits if each firm, following the Cournot assumption, chooses its output to maximize its own profit on the assumption that the other firm will not react to this output decision?

Answer: In this case the firms will just set the partial derivatives of their own profits with respect to their own outputs equal to zero, thus:

$$\frac{\partial \Pi_1}{\partial Q_1} = 24 - 2Q_1 = 0 \quad \text{or} \quad Q_1 = 12$$

$$\frac{\partial \Pi_2}{\partial Q_2} = 30 - 6Q_2 = 0 \quad \text{or} \quad Q_2 = 5.$$

Hence, by substitution, $\Pi_1 = 86$, $\Pi_2 = 42$, $\Pi = \Pi_1 + \Pi_2 = 128$.

B. What will the firms' profits and outputs be if they set output levels by collusion so as to maximize their joint (total) profits?

Answer: Our objective function is now

$$\Pi = \Pi_1 + \Pi_2 = 22Q_1 - Q_1^2 + 30Q_2 - 5Q_2^2 - 17.$$

Setting

$$\frac{\partial \Pi}{\partial Q_1} = 0 \quad \text{and} \quad \frac{\partial \Pi}{\partial Q_2} = 0$$

and solving, the reader should be able to show that we have

$$Q_1 = 11, \qquad Q_2 = 3, \qquad \Pi_1 = 117, \qquad \Pi_2 = 32, \qquad \Pi = 149.$$

Note that while total profits have risen, the profits of the second firm have decreased under joint maximization, and a redistribution of profits may be required to secure its agreement to the arrangement.

PROBLEMS

1. Prove that if the demand and *average* cost functions of an industry are linear, the monopoly (maximum profit) output will be exactly half the competitive (zero-profit) output. Show this both algebraically and geometrically.
2. Given the following demand functions for two separated markets and the total cost function of the monopoly supplier, what will be the prices, outputs, and

---

The profit function can now be written

$$\Pi = PQ - C = \frac{56}{4} Q - \frac{3}{4} Q^2 - 2Q - 3 = 12Q - \frac{3}{4} Q^2 - 3,$$

whose maximum is $Q = 8$, $P = 8$, as before.

marginal revenues in the two markets, and the company's total profits, (i) under price discrimination; (ii) with prices equal in both markets?

(a) $P_1 = 17 - 2Q_1$ $P_2 = 25 - 3Q_2$ $C = 2 + Q_1 + Q_2$

(b) $P_1 = 2 - Q_1$ $P_2 = 9 - 6Q_2$ $C = Q_1 + Q_2$.

3. Prove that if the marginal cost of supplying two markets is equal, then, under price discrimination, the marginal revenues in both markets must be equal.

4. Given the following pairs of profit functions for two firms in an industry, find the profits and outputs (i) corresponding to a Cournot equilibrium; (ii) corresponding to maximization of joint profits

(a) $\Pi_1 = 8Q_1 - Q_1^2 - 2Q_2$ $\Pi_2 = 10Q_2 - Q_2^2 - 4Q_1$

(b) $\Pi_1 = 12Q_1 - 2Q_1^2 - Q_2$ $\Pi_2 = 6Q_2 - Q_2^2 - Q_1$.

REFERENCES

American Economic Association, George J. Stigler and Kenneth E. Boulding (eds.), *Readings in Price Theory*, Richard D. Irwin, Inc., Homewood, Ill., 1952, Articles 18–22.

Bailey, Elizabeth E., *Economic Theory of Regulatory Constraint*, D. C. Heath and Company, Lexington, Mass., 1973.

Baumol, William J., *Business Behavior, Value and Growth*, Harcourt, Brace, Jovanovich, Inc., New York, revised ed., 1967, Chapters 3–8.

Chamberlin, Edward H., *The Theory of Monopolistic Competition*, 7th edition, Harvard University Press, Cambridge, Mass., 1956.

Fellner, William, *Competition Among the Few*, Alfred A. Knopf, Inc., New York, 1949.

Machlup, Fritz, *The Economics of Sellers' Competition*, Thè Johns Hopkins Press, Baltimore, 1952.

Marshall, Alfred, *Principles of Economics*, 8th edition, Macmillan & Company, Ltd., London, 1922, Book V.

Robinson, Joan, *The Economics of Imperfect Competition*, Macmillan & Company, Ltd., London, 1933.

Scherer, Frederic M., *Industrial Market Structure and Economic Performance*, Rand McNally & Company, Chicago, 1970.

Shubik, Martin, *Strategy and Market Structure*, John Wiley & Sons, Inc., New York, 1959.

Telser, Lester G., *Competition, Collusion and Game Theory*, Aldine-Atherton, Chicago and New York, 1972.

Neumann-Morgenstern
Utility Theory

17

1. Utility, Risk, and Game Theory

We have already seen (Chapter 9) that the neoclassical economists constructed a cardinal utility theory as part of their analysis of consumer demand. This cardinal utility measure was designed to convey information about the psychological state of the consumer (or the businessman and the worker)—the magnitude of his desires, and the psychic gains and losses incurred by the alternative actions which are available to him.

We also saw that it is possible to dispense with this utility analysis in much of the theory of consumer behavior and in the analysis of economic decision-making in general. A large class of decision processes can be explained simply with the aid of information about the individual's preferences, with no attempt to assign magnitudes to them.

Game theorists have had no dispute with the resulting ordinalist (indifference curve) analysis, so far as it goes. However, in their work they have found it exceedingly useful to go beyond an ordinal utility measure wherever questions of risk arise.[1] The outcomes of the alternative choices available to the decision-maker are sometimes known only in probabilistic form, e.g., if he does A, he has one chance in three of ending up with $1,000 and two chances of three ending up with only $40. In such a case it is

---

[1] The role of this utility analysis in game theory will be indicated in the next two chapters in the discussion of the concept of "mixed strategies."

essential in game theory to do more than just examine the decision-maker's ranking of A as against his other similar alternatives, $B, C, \cdots$, etc.

In the course of their work on game theory, von Neumann and Morgenstern were therefore led to construct their much-discussed cardinal utility measure for the ranking of situations involving probabilities (risky situations). This nomenclature turns out to have been highly unfortunate. The resemblance between the Neumann–Morgenstern construct and the neoclassical utility measure ends largely with the use of the term "cardinal" to designate both analyses. Much misunderstanding and unnecessary controversy can be traced to this usage.

Let us now turn to a general discussion of the mathematician's use of the term "measurement" and its varieties to make clear what is meant by the term "cardinal utility" in the N–M (Neumann–Morgenstern) sense. Only then will it be possible to explain its relationship to the neoclassical analysis.

2. Classes of Measures and Their Strength

A measure, in its most general sense, is simply a device which is designed to convey information about the phenomena to which it refers. Normally the information is conveyed by means of numbers. This requires a linguistic convention which indicates the meaning of the number "105" when we say that the measure of some feature of an object is 105. For example, if this number represents length or temperature, its meaning has been well defined (once the system of measurement—say, Fahrenheit vs. centigrade—is specified).

It is sometimes desirable that such a number convey a great deal of information whereas in other circumstances very little needs to be communicated by a "measurement." As a result, one encounters measures which vary considerably in power to convey information. Let us examine three such classes of index, starting with the least powerful and describing them in order of increasing information content. It will then be shown that an ordinal utility index and the N–M utility index belong, respectively, to the second and third classes.

Class 1. Associative measures: The weakest type of index (one which conveys very little information) is one which serves only to *associate* items in two different collections. For example, persons in a newspaper group photograph are sometimes identified by placing a number next to each face and the same number beside the corresponding name in a list printed underneath. Here we set up the linguistic convention that any one man's name and face are given the same number. The numbers themselves do not matter and can be transformed in any way we like (we can exchange any number for another), provided no two faces bear the same number.

Class 2. Orderings or rankings: A ranking is a measure which assigns an ordering to a set of items—it tells us which of two items is higher on the scale. To take the standard illustration, in a hardness scale, harder minerals are given higher numbers.

Note that such a ranking measure also contains associative information—two rocks with the same ranking number must be equally hard. Thus a ranking index does carry more information than an associative index. The former does everything which is done by the latter and more besides.

Suppose we assign a set of numbers in such a ranking. We may note that the same information can be conveyed just as well by any other set of numbers provided that we still satisfy our linguistic convention. Of two rocks the one with the higher number in the initial numbering (the harder rock) must also bear the higher number in any new index which is assigned.[2] We describe this by saying that the index which measures, or rather describes, a ranking is *unique up to a monotone transformation.* Thus, while we still have quite a bit of choice in the assignment of numbers, we have considerably less option than in the case of an associative measure. That is because a ranking conveys far more information; thus the meaning of the numbers must be far more rigidly specified by the linguistic convention.

It is clear that an ordinal utility measure is a ranking, so that it falls into this second class of indices.

Class 3. Cardinal measures: Finally, we come to "cardinal measurement," which conveys still more information than did either of the other types of measure. It permits us, from what we know about two items in isolation, to *predict* something about them in combination. Consider the problem of finding two pieces of cloth in a shop which together are large enough to cover a table at home. We wish to *predict* which two pieces will do this *without having to take them home and try them* (and return them for exchange if they turn out to be too short). A measure of length can help us here. We know that a table 3 yards long can easily be covered by two cloths whose lengths are $1\frac{1}{2}$ yards and $2\frac{1}{4}$ yards.

It will be observed that a length index can be used to rank and to associate as well as for this sort of prediction. For example, we know just from the numbers and their standard interpretation that a 7-foot board is longer than a 3-foot board (ranking) and that all 3-foot boards are of equal length (association).

Because we want a cardinal measure to be capable of making the sort of prediction which has just been described, we have very little choice in

---

[2] Clearly other linguistic conventions might do—*softer* minerals might be given higher numbers.

the numbers which are to be used. We wish to convey the prediction that whenever two items, A and B, are combined, we obtain some item, C, as a result. For this purpose it is customary to represent the process of combining A and B by the *addition* of the index of A to the index of B. For example, if A is a 6-foot board (a board of length index 6) and B is an 8-foot board, we employ the linguistic *convention* that the length which is obtained by laying these two pieces of lumber end to end (item C) is $6 + 8 = 14$ feet long.[3] That is why some cardinal measures are called *additive*.

The convention that we make our prediction by adding leaves us very little option in choosing the numbers of any such measure. Indeed, we have no more than two numbers which are up to us (two degrees of freedom)[4] and the rest are then beyond our control—they are automatically dictated to us by our linguistic convention. For example, because we add lengths, we know that the length of two pieces of cloth must sum up to the number which we assign to the length they cover together. A cloth as long as a 3-foot piece and a 1-foot piece *must* be assigned the number "4 feet," and the three pieces together *must* be called "8 feet," etc.

The N–M utility index is cardinal in this very specific sense—it is intended to be used for making predictions. It is employed to predict which of two lottery tickets (or which of two other risky alternatives) a person will prefer. We are given this individual's ranking of the alternative prizes offered by the lottery tickets and the odds on each prize. From this we wish to be able to infer by numerical calculation, and *without actually asking the person*, which lottery ticket he will choose.

---

[3] Here again we might use other conventions. Any process which uniquely assigns a third number to any pair of numbers will do the trick. We might, for example, use logarithmic rulers with slide-rule scales and get used to multiplying lengths—10 inches and 5 inches = 50 inches But the point is that to convey information we must start off with some sort of language. We must first set up our linguistic conventions in any convenient way and then find the numbers which correctly convey the information in this language.

[4] Actually a length measure conveys even more information than this, and so we have only one choice in assigning numbers to lengths—we can only decide on a unit of length—whether we will measure in centimeters or inches. The point is that in a length measure we have a well-defined zero. Mathematically, zero is defined as a number which, when added to another, leaves the latter unchanged. A nonexistent piece of cloth (a piece of zero length) has an analogous (the mathematicians call it *isomorphic*) property. Hence, in measuring length we have only one degree of freedom, the choice of units of measurement, and a length measure is said to be *unique up to a proportionate transformation*. When measuring utility or temperature (without an absolute zero) we have two degrees of freedom—the choice of unit and the zero (freezing of water, or some other point, as in Fahrenheit measure), and hence these measures are said to be *unique only up to a linear transformation*.

In N–M utility measurement we want to assign to lottery-ticket *prizes* utility numbers which, when they are processed arithmetically in accord with the linguistic convention which is described in the following se tion, will assign a utility number to the *lottery ticket itself*. This lottery-ticket utility number should have the property that it ranks the lottery ticket correctly in relation to any other possible ticket. That is, lottery ticket *A* should be assigned a higher utility number than is given to *B* by this calculation if and only if the person prefers *A* to *B*. In sum, the N–M utility index is intended as a calculator of lottery-ticket preferences. (The term "lottery ticket" is of course meant to denote any alternative involving risk.)

Here again, once we pick such utility numbers for any two alternatives, we will see that we are left no choice on the numbers to be assigned to other alternatives. This, then, is the sense in which the N–M utility measure is cardinal—it is richer in that it conveys more information than does an ordinal utility ranking obtained, for example, by directly asking any individual to state all his preferences. In effect, the N–M index is an economy device which requires an interviewer only to ask the subject to state *some* of his preferences—his ranking of lottery-ticket *prizes*. With the aid of the N–M utility index (if it is applicable to this person) the interviewer can then *deduce* by himself the person's ranking of all other alternatives from the answers he has already received.

3. Construction of an N–M Index

If an individual exhibits some degree of consistency in his preferences, it is possible and convenient to construct an index which describes these preferences numerically. This "utility index" does so by assigning a higher "utility" number to some item, *a*, than to another item, *b*, if the individual happens to prefer *a* to *b*. However, for their purposes von Neumann and Morgenstern required a somewhat stronger index than this—one which would enable them to make the sort of deduction which has just been described. For this purpose it was necessary to make a few more assumptions about the consistency of the preferences of the individual in question. These assumptions are described in Section 5, below. First, however, let us examine the mechanics of their special utility index.

Consider a lottery ticket which offers two prizes: The first prize is a Cadillac and the booby prize is a pair of roller skates. Suppose the odds are one in one thousand of winning, that is, the probability of winning is 0.001 so that the probability of losing is 0.999. Suppose also that, somehow, we obtain some information about our individual's attitudes toward the two prizes, and that, by a method to be described presently, we express this psychological information by means of the statement that he values the Cadillac at 2,000 utils and the skates at 1 util. Then the N–M utility convention requires us to evaluate the lottery ticket at

$$0.001 \times 2,000 + 0.999 \times 1 = 2.999 \text{ utils.}$$

More generally, if a lottery offers two prizes, A with probability P and B with probability $1 - P$,[5] and if their respective utilities are $U(A)$ and $U(B)$, then the utility of the lottery ticket, L, is defined to be

$$(1) \qquad\qquad U(L) = PU(A) + (1 - P)U(B).$$

This simple calculation is all there is to the N–M evaluation of the utility of a lottery ticket, *once we know the person's evaluation of its prizes.* The crucial question is, then, how do we find the utility of these prizes?

In principle, this is accomplished by an extension of the preceding convention (1). For this purpose we design a special (artificial) lottery ticket which will serve as a standard of comparison. Consider two extreme prizes, E and D. These are chosen so that E is, in his opinion, as good as anything our individual is likely to end up with (mnemonic device: $E =$ eternal bliss) and D is as unpleasant as anything he may plausibly expect ($D =$ damnation).[6] Our standard lottery ticket, which we designate as $S(P)$, offers our individual E with probability P and D with probability $1 - P$, where the probability number P is not specified (it is left free to vary). Let us assign any two arbitrary utility numbers to E and D, say $U(E) = 100$ and $U(D) = 1$.[7]

Now consider any ordinary prize, A, and let us see how a utility number is assigned to A. For some values of P in the standard lottery ticket, $S(P)$, the individual will prefer $S(P)$ to A, and for other values of P the reverse will be true. For example, if $P = 1$ (certainty of eternal bliss), he will surely prefer $S(P)$ to A, and if $P = 0$ (certainty of damnation), he will prefer A to $S(P)$. It is therefore plausible that there will be some in-between value, P_a, at which our individual is indifferent between A and $S(P_a)$. Once we have found this in-between probability number, P_a (say $P_a = 0.3$), there is no difficulty in finding the utility of A. For A must

---

[5] If one or the other of A and B is certain to occur, their probabilities must, by definition, sum up to unity. Thus, if the probability of A is P, that of B *must* be $1 - P$.

[6] Actually it is not necessary to employ such extreme prizes—any two arbitrarily chosen prizes will do the trick. However, the E and D concepts make the logic of the construction easier to follow.

[7] This is where we use up our two degrees of freedom. There is, of course, one restriction on our choice of these numbers. By convention, we must have $U(E) > U(D)$ since E is preferred to D.

have the same utility number as $S(P_a)$ since they are indifferent. But the utility of this standard lottery ticket, $U[S(P_a)]$, is easily calculated with the aid of our N–M linguistic convention equation (1). We have

$$U[S(P_a)] = P_a U(E) + (1 - P_a) U(D) = 0.3 \times 100 + 0.7 \times 1$$

$$= 30.7 \text{ utils,}$$

i.e.,

$$U(A) = 30.7 \text{ utils.}$$

To summarize, in order to find a utility number which represents some individual's attitude toward any prize, X, we interview or observe the person to find out the probability P_x at which he is indifferent between the standard lottery ticket, $S(P_x)$, and X. We then evaluate the utility of X by using the standard N–M rule, Equation (1), to determine the utility of $S(P_x)$. That is all there is to it.

But where does the N–M prediction come in? Suppose we have two lottery tickets L_1 and L_2 and we wish to predict which of these our individual prefers. If ticket L_1 offers alternative prizes A and B, and L_2 carries with it prizes C and D, we find the utilities of each of these prizes in turn by the procedure which has just been described. From these figures, in turn, we can evaluate, by the N–M calculation [Equation (1)], the respective utilities, $U(L_1)$ and $U(L_2)$, of L_1 and L_2. We then have the prediction that the person will prefer the lottery ticket with the larger *calculated* utility number.

Observe what has happened here. In order to assign utilities to the (riskless) prizes, we did have to interview or observe the person in question. But once he has committed himself on these we need ask him no further questions in order to predict his ranking of any lottery tickets in which only these prizes are involved. We do not have to ask him how he feels about the odds involved in these tickets—this can be determined for him from our computation.

4. Expected Utility vs. Expected Payoff

One feature of the N–M utility convention (1) should be pointed out. According to this rule a lottery ticket is evaluated at the actuarial (expected) value of its *utilities*, not at the actuarial value of the prizes themselves, as one might more usually be tempted to do. This assertion, which may not be clear to the reader, is most easily explained by example. Consider a lottery ticket whose prizes, A and B, are amounts of money. Let these amounts and their respective utilities be the figures shown in the following table:

	A	B
Prize (dollars)	500	2
Utility of prize (utils)	40	2
Probability	P	$1 - P$

A standard actuarial evaluation of this lottery ticket is

$$500P + 2(1 - P),$$

so that, e.g., if $P = \frac{1}{2}$ (50–50 odds) this ticket's *actuarial value* will be

$$\tfrac{1}{2}500 + \tfrac{1}{2}2 = 251 \; dollars.$$

But in Neumann–Morgenstern utility analysis it is necessary to translate the prizes into utility terms before one can evaluate the ticket. In N–M analysis the ticket would then be valued at $40P + 2(1 - P)$ or

$$\tfrac{1}{2}40 + \tfrac{1}{2}2 = 21 \; utils.$$

There is something inherently attractive in the latter procedure. The rational individual may be taken to be interested not in the money value of a prize, but in just how much winning it will mean to him (its utility). For example, a prize of $10,000 is ten times as large as a $1,000 prize, but if he needs the $1,000 very badly the utility of $10,000 may, in some sense, not be quite ten times as high. In evaluating the lottery ticket he should surely take this into account.

In fact, diminishing (or increasing) marginal utility can easily affect the person's attitude toward a lottery ticket. Suppose that $0 is evaluated at 0 utils by some individual, that $50 gives him 60 utils, while a second $50 yields him only 40 more utils. We have the following utility table which thus clearly involves diminishing marginal utility:

Prize (dollars)	0	50	100
Utility (utils)	0	60	100

Now consider a lottery ticket which offers a 50–50 chance of zero or $100. Its actuarial value is, of course, $(\frac{1}{2})100 + (\frac{1}{2})0 = \$50$. But to an expected utility-maximizer it is worth only 50 *utils*, which according to the table is far less than the value of $50. That is, this person will be willing to pay much less than $50 (its actuarial value) for the lottery ticket. Actually, this makes good common sense. If the ticket costs him $50, he stands a fifty-fifty chance of either winning or losing $50. But, if to him the marginal utility of money is diminishing, an added $50 is worth less (40 utils) than the disutility of a $50 loss (60 utils). Hence, he should never accept the ticket in exchange for $50. This is an old observation which has been made a number of times by economists and mathematicians. It illustrates how results which are more plausible intuitively can be obtained from expected utility rather than from actuarial (dollar) calculations.

Another example from a totally different field may help to bring out the difference between utility and nonutility calculations. Suppose we are trying to evaluate two alternative bombing strategies. One of them offers a 1 in 10 chance of getting through and destroying 80 per cent of the enemy's productive capacity. The other, more conservative strategy offers eight out of ten chances of destroying 10 per cent of this productive capacity. On a straight actuarial evaluation the two strategies are equivalent (0.1 × 80 = 0.8 × 10). But in terms of a doubtless more relevant utility analysis, this is not necessarily so. For example, experience suggests that a 10 per cent loss in productive capacity is easily made up and will result in no real long-run difference in enemy military strength, so that it may be almost worthless. On the other hand, an 80 per cent loss is likely to weaken him very substantially and may be of crucial military value, and a utility analysis might therefore definitely recommend this latter strategy over the other. We see, then, that in decision-making it seems more appropriate to use a calculation based on the utilities of the alternative outcomes rather than on the magnitudes of the outcomes themselves. It seems much more appropriate to maximize expected utilities than expected prize values.[8]

---

[8] Some critics, notably Professor Allais, have argued that although these calculations should be based on utility, they should include all the facts about the utility calculation and not just the expected value. For example, fifty-fifty odds of 100 and 200 (utils) have the same expected utility (150) as do fifty-fifty odds of 125 and 175. However, it may be argued that since the former pair of utility payoffs is more widely spread out (dispersion = 200 − 100 = 100) than is the latter (175 − 125 = 50), the former lottery ticket subjects the player to greater risk, and that, therefore, he need not be indifferent between the two. Expected value does not tell the whole story!

However, it has been answered that the utility calculation already takes the dispersion of the prizes into account. That is, if one lottery ticket offers a greater risk than another, its utilities are calculated in such a way as to discount for this fact. The utility of the riskier lottery ticket has already been reduced to take the risk into account. Hence if we make a second adjustment for the risk involved in dispersion of *utilities*, we would be double-counting. Those who take this position say that this is why the psychological assumptions described in the next section can be shown (see the appendix) to *require* the person always to pick the lottery ticket with the highest expected utility, no matter what the dispersion of utility payoffs. Since Allais disputes the appropriateness of these assumptions, of course this argument carries no weight with him.

5. Psychological Premises Behind the Prediction

Let us return now to our main theme, the prediction which is obtained from a N–M utility calculation. We have seen how from a purely numerical manipulation we are able to make a forecast of human behavior—to predict which of two lottery tickets our individual will prefer.

Clearly such a prediction need not always turn out to be correct. Its validity must rest on some sort of psychological assumptions, for only people of some particular psychological constitution will behave in accord with the N–M predictions. Those who have worked with the index are fully aware of this, and various sets of psychological premises have been formulated for the analysis. Let us now examine briefly a set of five assumptions which suffice to produce an N–M psychology. The appendix to this chapter contains a proof which shows that someone for whom these five premises are valid must always do as the N–M calculation predicts.

Assumption 1: Transitivity: If our individual is indifferent between two prizes A and B, and he also happens to be indifferent between B and C, then he will be indifferent between A and C. As we have seen in Chapter 9, this assumption also plays a role in indifference map analysis, so that it is no more restrictive than the usual ordinal utility analysis.

Assumption 2: Continuity of preferences: This is, in effect, the plausible assumption (which has already been employed) that if our standard lottery ticket, $S(P)$, is preferred to some prize, A, when $P = 1$, and if on the other hand, A is preferred to $S(P)$ when $P = 0$, there exists some in-between value of P at which $S(P)$ and A are indifferent.

Assumption 3: Independence: If our player is indifferent between a Ford and a Chevrolet, he will be indifferent between two lottery tickets which are identical in all respects except that one of them offers a Ford as a prize while the other offers a Chevrolet instead. This assumption is also taken to hold for lottery tickets, e.g., if the person is indifferent between the Ford and a lottery ticket, R, which offers him a chance at a Rolls Royce, he must also be indifferent between two lottery tickets one of which offers a Ford and the other of which offers as a prize (the lottery ticket) R.

Assumption 4: Desire for high probability of success: Given two lottery tickets with identical prizes, our individual will prefer the lottery ticket with the higher probability of winning. This assumption is so persuasive that it hardly seems worth stating but it has been pointed out that there are exceptions even to this premise. Players of Russian Roulette and, sometimes, mountain-climbers seem to *prefer* to live dangerously! Finally we have

Assumption 5: Compound probabilities: If the person is offered a lottery ticket whose prizes are, in turn, other lottery tickets, his attitude toward this compound lottery ticket will be the same as though he had gone through all the probability calculations to find out what ultimate odds of winning and losing this compound ticket really offers him. (Luce and Raiffa cite Kuhn's example of very real compound lottery tickets, which is worth recalling here. All over Paris one sees wheels of chance whose prizes are, in turn, tickets in the French National Lottery.)

Some controversy has arisen out of the third and fifth premises. It is, of course, clear that few people will, or even can, go through the elaborate calculations envisaged in the last assumption, and no one has ever claimed otherwise. But the question which has been raised is whether they even *ought* to do so as a matter of self-interest. To illustrate the sort of objection which has been raised, let us consider one which has been advanced against the 3rd (so-called independence) assumption. Many, if not most people will offer considerably less than $500 for a lottery ticket, T, which gives them a fifty-fifty chance of $1,000 or zero. Let us say that to one person T is worth $200 (he is indifferent between T and $200). Why is it worth so little to him? The answer, this argument asserts, is that he wishes to avoid risk. Two hundred dollars is a sure thing whereas T is not, so that he is willing to forego the difference between the $500 actuarial value of T and the $200 in hard cash to avoid the gambling element involved in taking T.

But suppose we consider two lottery tickets L_1 and L_2 which differ only in that T is a prize in L_1 and $200 is the corresponding prize of L_2. Should he necessarily be indifferent between L_1 and L_2 as Assumption 3 requires? The answer, says this argument, is no, because the $200 is no longer a sure thing—it has become a prize in a lottery ticket. In this case since the person is gambling in any event, he may well prefer L_1, which offers T (actuarial value $500) as one of its prizes, to L_2, in which the corresponding prize is only $200. For the second choice—the $200 option—no longer keeps him safe from risk. In other words, this argument maintains that the relative value of T and $200 is *not independent* of the context in which they are offered. They will be indifferent in one case but not in the other.

It is not intended here to offer any judgment on the acceptability of the N–M psychological premises. Many economists consider them to be rather attractive assumptions but, as we have just seen, they have not gone unchallenged. The main thing to be recognized is that the validity of the N–M predictions must rest on this or some other set of psychological assumptions.

6. N-M vs. Neoclassical Cardinal Utility

There remains one more subject to be explored—what relationship, if any, does the N–M cardinal utility theory have to that of the neoclassical utility theorists? It is generally (though not universally) agreed that there is none—the two utility measures have nothing in common insofar as their cardinality is concerned.

It is *not* the purpose of the Neumann–Morgenstern utility index to set up any sort of measure of introspective pleasure intensity. Such a measure of "strength of feelings" is totally unnecessary in the theory of games for which the N–M utility theory was constructed. Rather, the utility measure was set up for purposes of calculation, or rather of prediction (in the subtler sense of the word), to permit the theorist to *determine in the absence of the player* which of several risky propositions the player will *prefer*, for the solution of a duopoly game must predict which strategy each player will choose (prefer), and the theory must therefore be able to predict how each player will *rank* risky strategic decisions.

Then where does the "cardinal utility measurement" enter this matter? The answer is that the word "cardinal" has been used, misleadingly, to mean two entirely different things. One denotation is the neoclassical, introspective, *absolute* marginal pleasure measurement. The other, game-theoretic, use of the word "cardinality" is entirely operational. The prediction as to which of the two lottery tickets will be chosen is most conveniently made with the aid of a numerical calculation. We are given the person's ranking of the prizes and intend to predict from these data which ticket he will choose. For this purpose N and M have constructed an index far more powerful than the ordinalists'.

But note that this is not cardinal utility in the old-fashioned sense. Not a word has been said about successive increments of some item yielding diminishing (or increasing) marginal joy. Indeed, to a strict neoclassicist the N–M index is a sheep in wolf's clothing—to him (but not to the mathematician) it is nothing but an ordinal measure, for while it can be used to predict, it can predict only *rankings* of lottery tickets!

It is true that once we have derived a numerical N–M utility index we can use it to compute numerical marginal utilities[9] and some of the other measures encountered in neoclassical utility theory, measures which dis-

---

[9] For example, if $U = f(M)$ is the N–M measure of the utility of money, M, to our individual, we can compute the marginal utility of money to him as $\Delta U / \Delta M$ or dU/dM.

appear in the ordinalist's analysis. But this kinship between the two cardinal theories is also illusory. It will be recalled that the ordinalist is perfectly happy to use a concept of marginal utility of X measured in terms of money (he calls it the marginal rate of substitution between X and money), or, for that matter, marginal utility of X measured in terms of any other commodity. He objects only to an introspective evaluation of marginal utility in absolute psychological units.

But the marginal utility which can be derived from a N–M measurement is just this sort of marginal rate of substitution. To evaluate the marginal utility of apples in money terms we would ask, "How much more money are you willing to pay for an additional apple?" In N–M theory we ask, instead, "How much of an increase in the probability, P, of winning E in our standard lottery ticket, $S(P)$, is worth the same as an additional apple?" The N–M marginal utility of X therefore ends up as no more than the marginal rate of substitution between X and the probability of winning the prespecified prize (E) of the standard lottery ticket. This is surely not cardinal measurement in the neoclassical sense.

APPENDIX: THE PSYCHOLOGICAL PREMISES AND THE INDEX

Let us now prove that the calculation of Section 3 of this chapter will predict correctly the lottery-ticket preferences of any person who satisfies the psychological assumptions of Section 5.

First, it is necessary to restate these assumptions in somewhat greater detail. For this purpose it is convenient to employ the following notation: For any alternatives A and B let AIB mean A is indifferent with B, and for any alternatives A and B and any (probability) number P where $0 \leq P \leq 1$, let $[P:A, B]$ represent a lottery ticket which offers the probability P of obtaining prize A, and $1 - P$ of obtaining prize B. Using this notation, our assumptions become:

Assumption 1: Transitivity: If for this person AIB and BIC, then AIC.

Assumption 2: Continuity of preference as a function of P: For any three outcomes, E, A and D, if E is preferred to A and A is preferred to D, there exists a (probability) number P_a such that $0 < P_a < 1$ and $AI[P_a:E, D]$.

Assumption 3: Independence: For any four prizes, A, B, C, and F, if AIB and CIF, then $[P:A, C]I[P:B, F]$ for any probability P.

This states that if two investments (lottery tickets) involve equal probabilities of attaining outcomes which are different but which are valued equally, then the two investments will be equally attractive.

Assumption 4: For any alternatives E and D, and any probability numbers r and r', if E is preferred to D, then $[r:E, D]$ is preferred to $[r':E, D]$, if and only if $r > r'$.

This states that, other things being equal, we will always prefer the investment opportunity with the greater probability of a favorable outcome.

Assumption 5: Compound probability arithmetic: For any alternatives E and D and any probability numbers P, P_a, and P_b,

$$[P:[P_a:E, D], [P_b:E, D]]I[r:E, D],$$

where r is a probability number given by $r = PP_a + (1 - P)P_b$.

This requires some explanation. The long bracketed expression to the left of the I represents a compound lottery ticket which offers the probability P of winning. If the ticket-holder wins, however, rather than a definite prize he obtains another lottery ticket $[P_a:E, D]$. If he loses, he is given, instead, the inferior lottery ticket $[P_b:E, D]$, with the same prizes but poorer odds. What is the probability of eventually coming out of all this with the grand prize, E? There is a probability P of winning the better lottery ticket which offers E with probability P_a, so the probability of getting E in this way is PP_a. However, if he loses the first draw, a loss which will occur with probability $1 - P$, the ticket-holder still has the probability P_b of getting E, so that there is a probability $(1 - P)P_b$ of his obtaining E in this way. The total probability of obtaining E is then $PP_a + (1 - P)P_b$, which we have called r.

We may now interpret this last assumption to say that the person's psychology is such that he will evaluate a compound lottery ticket in terms of the probabilities of winning the ultimate prizes.

Let us now choose the lottery ticket to be used as a standard against which other alternatives can be evaluated. It is still convenient (but not necessary) to assume that this ticket offers to the winner eternal bliss (E) and to the loser damnation (D), so that any alternative, A, which we bring to be evaluated against this standard ticket will presumably be no better than E and no worse than D.

By Assumption 2, for any such A, there will be a probability number $P_a(0 < P_a < 1)$ such that $AI[P_a:E, D]$. We can now prove the following:

Theorem 1: Possibility of predicting: Given any two lottery tickets $[P:A, B]$ and $[P':A', B']$ and a person whose preferences never violate Assumptions 1–5, if we obtain (say by his introspection) the four probability numbers P_a, $P_{a'}$, P_b, and $P_{b'}$ chosen so that

(2) $AI[P_a:E, D]$ and $BI[P_b:E, D]$, etc.,

then *from these numbers it is possible to predict which of the two lottery tickets will be preferred.*

Proof: We begin by evaluating our first lottery ticket in terms of E and D. This we can do by replacing A and B by their equivalents in terms of our standard lottery ticket, to obtain

$$[P\!:\!A,\,B]I[P\!:\![P_a\!:\!E,\,D],\,[P_b\!:\!E,\,D]] \qquad \text{(by Assumption 3)}$$

$$\therefore\;[P\!:\!A,\,B]I[r\!:\!E,\,D] \qquad \text{(Assumptions 1 and 5)},$$

where r is the probability number $PP_a + (1 - P)P_b$. Similarly, the second lottery ticket can be evaluated in terms of E and D as

$$[P'\!:\!A',\,B']I[r'\!:\!E,\,D] \qquad \text{where} \qquad r' = P'P_{a'} + (1 - P')P_{b'}.$$

Therefore, by Assumption 4, the individual must prefer $[P\!:\!A,\,B]$ to $[P'\!:\!A',\,B']$ if and only if

$$(3) \qquad r = PP_a + (1 - P)P_b > P'P_{a'} + (1 - P')P_{b'} = r',$$

and he will be indifferent between these tickets if and only if $r = r'$. But by hypothesis, P, P' are numbers given by the terms of the two lottery tickets, and P_a, P_b, $P_{a'}$, and $P_{b'}$ were found out by observing or questioning our individual. Then r and r' can be evaluated directly and the higher of these two numbers must, by Assumption 4, correspond to the preferred lottery ticket. (Q.E.D.)

Let us now see how the N–M index is constructed and prove that it can be used to predict correctly the choice of lottery ticket. As already indicated, we employ the following linguistic convention (definition) for evaluating the utility of a lottery ticket in terms of the utilities of its prizes:

$$(4) \qquad U[P\!:\!A,\,B] = PU(A) + (1 - P)U(B).$$

That is, if $P = \frac{3}{4}$ so that the odds of winning are 3 to 1, we evaluate the utility of the lottery ticket at three-fourths the utility of victory plus one-fourth the utility of defeat. But we note again that this is only a convention. To show that it is usable we must first restate, in terms of our present notation, how these utility numbers can be found, and then we must prove that they must always assign a higher utility number to the preferred lottery ticket.

To find the utility of any alternative, A, we first assign arbitrary "utility" numbers

$$(5) \qquad U(E) > U(D)$$

to eternal bliss (E) and damnation (D) in our standard lottery ticket.

Now we find $U(A)$ by recalling (2) and defining

(6) $U(A) = U[P_a:E, D]$, $U(B) = U[P_b:E, D]$, etc.,

so that by (4)

$$U(A) = P_a U(E) + (1 - P_a) U(D), \text{ etc.}$$

Hence by finding P_a in (2) the utility number $U(A)$ can be computed.

Finally, let us prove

Theorem 2: Validity of the prediction: These utility numbers rank lottery tickets correctly so that $U[P:A, B] > U[P':A', B']$ if and only if the former is the preferred lottery ticket, i.e., if and only if (3) holds.[10]

Proof: The utility of the first lottery ticket is

$$U[P:A, B] = PU(A) + (1 - P)U(B) \qquad \text{[by convention (4)]}$$

$$= PU[P_a:E, D] + (1 - P)U[P_b:E, D] \quad \text{[by (2) and (6)]}$$

$$= P\{P_a U(E) + (1 - P_a)U(D)\}$$

$$+ (1 - P)\{P_b U(E) + (1 - P_b)U(D)\} \qquad \text{[by (4)]},$$

which gives on multiplying out and rearranging terms

$$= \{PP_a + (1 - P)P_b\}U(E)$$

$$+ \{P(1 - P_a) + (1 - P)(1 - P_b)\}U(D)$$

$$= \{PP_a + (1 - P)P_b\}U(E)$$

$$+ \{1 - PP_a - (1 - P)P_b\}U(D)$$

(7) $$= rU(E) + (1 - r)U(D),$$

where r is defined as in (3), above. Similarly, the utility of the second lottery ticket is

(8) $$U[P':A', B'] = r'U(E) + (1 - r')U(D).$$

Thus comparing (7) and (8) we see that since by (5) $U(E) > U(D)$, the first lottery ticket will have the higher utility number if and only if $r > r'$. But we have just seen (3) that this condition also guarantees that that lottery ticket will be preferred. Thus we have proved that convention (4) will always assign a higher utility number to the preferred lottery ticket, as we require.

---

[10] The proof can easily be extended to the case of indifference.

REFERENCES

Alchian, Armen A., "The Meaning of Utility Measurement," *American Economic Review*, Vol. XLIII, March 1953.

Ellsberg, Daniel, "Classical and Current Notions of Measurable Utility," *Economic Journal*, Vol. LXIV, September 1954.

Friedman, Milton, and Leonard J. Savage, "The Utility Analysis of Choices Involving Risk," *Journal of Political Economy*, Vol. 56, August 1948, reprinted in American Economic Association, *Readings in Price Theory*, J. G. Stigler and K. E. Boulding (eds.), Richard D. Irwin, Inc., Homewood, Ill., 1952.

Luce, R. Duncan, and Howard Raiffa, *Games and Decisions*, John Wiley & Sons, Inc., New York, 1957, Chapter 2.

Strotz, Robert, "Cardinal Utility," *American Economic Review*, Vol. XLIII, May 1953.

More Difficult Readings

Allais, Maurice, *Fondements d'une théorie positive des choix comportant un risque et critique des postulats et axiomes de l'école américaine*, Imprimerie Nationale,

Arrow, Kenneth J., *Essays in the Theory of Risk Bearing*, Markham Publishing Company, Chicago, 1970, Chapter 2.

Borch, Karl, *The Economics of Uncertainty*, Princeton University Press, Princeton, N.J., 1968.

Herstein, I. N., and John W. Milnor, "An Axiomatic Approach to Measurable Utility," *Econometrica*, Vol. 21, April 1953.

Marschak, Jacob, "Rational Behavior, Uncertain Prospects and Measurable Utility," *Econometrica*, Vol. 18, April 1950.

Samuelson, Paul A., "Probability, Utility, and the Independence Axiom," *Econometrica*, Vol. 20, October 1952.

Von Neumann, John, and Oskar Morgenstern, *Theory of Games and Economic Behavior*, 2nd edition, Princeton University Press, Princeton, N.J., 1947, Chapter 1 and Appendix.

Game Theory *

18

1. Taking Account of Competitive Decisions

One of the most vexing and persistent problems of the businessman is that of outguessing his rival. If only he could calculate in advance what the competition was going to do, his planning would become far easier and more effective.

As we have seen in Chapter 16, this problem can be dealt with in a variety of ways. The simplest approach is applicable where experience with the behavior of a competitor makes it relatively easy to predict his strategies. Where such information is available, it is, in effect, possible to choose that decision which maximizes the firm's expected return after the effects of the rival's countermoves are taken into consideration. Procedures which resemble this are frequently encountered in business practice.

But it is often against the competitor's interests to permit this sort of a calculation. Management may therefore avoid too obvious a pattern in its decision-making in order to keep the opposition guessing. When it succeeds in this goal, no such simple prediction of competitive behavior will be possible. At best, one may be able to say something such as, "The

---

* There is a considerable literature on this subject. The classical source is, of course, John von Neumann and Oskar Morgenstern, *Theory of Games and Economic Behavior*, 2nd edition, Princeton University Press, Princeton, N. J., 1947. For a superb exposition and further references, see R. Duncan Luce and Howard Raiffa, *Games and Decisions*, John Wiley & Sons, Inc., New York, 1957.

odds are about two to one that he will match our price cut, but if he doesn't, there's a fifty-fifty chance that he will do nothing or try to underbid us," and even the validity of the estimate of these odds is apt to be questionable.

It is also possible to approach the analysis of competitive behavior by a more deductive route. Instead of asking, inductively, what we can infer from the competitor's past behavior, one seeks to determine a rival's most profitable counterstrategy to one's own "best" moves and to formulate the appropriate defensive measures. This is the approach which game theory has adopted.

2. The Zero-Sum, Two-Person Game

Consider a competitive struggle for share of the market by two firms (a duopoly). Here, every percentage point gained by one of the firms is necessarily lost by the other. This situation is called a *two-person, zero-sum game*. It is called *zero-sum* because, no matter what is done by either competitor, the total gain in market share to the two players is zero, so that the interests of the competitors are diametrically opposed. There is nothing to be gained by collusion. In our example, so long as their number remains unchanged, the share of the market which the two firms have between them is necessarily 100 per cent.[1] But the game is zero-sum only because of the nature of the company objectives. Decisions which are taken by the firms may very well increase or reduce both the absolute size of their market and the total profits of the two taken together. Increased advertising outlay and price-cutting may, for example, increase their combined sales volume and reduce their profits, and if the firms' objectives were maximization of either profit or sales rather than market share, the game would not be of the zero-sum variety.

Returning to the "battle for share of market" case, let us view the situation from the point of view of one of the firms, company A. Suppose that it has three strategy choices under consideration. A new package for its product is being investigated and the choice has been narrowed down to a red, yellow, or blue package, which we call strategies 1, 2, and 3, respectively. Suppose also, that its competitor is considering four alternative strategy moves involving, say, four different combinations of advertising media. Thus in an extreme, unrealistic case, these might involve

---

[1] Strictly speaking, this is a "constant-sum" rather than a zero-sum game because the sum of the two market shares is the fixed number 100 (per cent), not zero. However, there is no significant analytic difference between the constant-sum and the zero-sum games. This is because there is no change in strategic possibilities from a given game to another game in which some constant amount that cannot be changed by the players is added to the original payoffs.

exclusive use of television, radio, newspaper, or magazine advertising (e.g., strategy 4: put all advertising money into magazine ads).

Consider now any pair of strategies open to the two players (e.g., player A employs strategy 2, a yellow package, and B uses strategy 3, newspaper advertising). Such a pair of decisions will (other things being equal) determine A's market share. Say, it will result in a 9 per cent share of market for this firm. This figure is called A's *payoff*.

All the information of this variety can be summarized in a *payoff matrix* such as the following, which shows what A will receive as a result of each possible combination of strategy choice by himself and by his competitor:

B's strategy

		1	2	3	4
	1	50	90′	18*′	25
A's					
strategy	2	27	5*	9	95′
	3	64′	30	12*	20

Thus we see the number 9 recorded in the space which is at the junction of the second row and third column, indicating that if A chooses strategy 2 and B chooses strategy 3, A will receive a payoff of 9. Since in a constant-sum game one competitor gains only that part of the fixed total prize which the other fails to obtain, there is no need to record B's payoff separately. It is obvious that if A has 9 per cent of the market, then B's payoff from this strategy-counterstrategy combination must be 91 per cent.

We assume that both A and B are acquainted with all the information contained in this table. Using these data, each player must decide on a best strategy without knowing the countermove which will be made by his opponent.

3. Maximin and Minimax Strategies

The cautious approach to this problem is to assume the worst and act accordingly. Thus, in terms of the preceding payoff matrix, if firm A employs strategy 1, its management would, on this approach assume that firm B will employ its strategy 3, *thereby reducing A's payoff from strategy 1 to its minimum or security value*, 18, which is therefore marked with an asterisk. Similarly, the fatalistic view of A's strategy 2 is that B will employ its strategy 2 and so A will obtain a payoff of 5 per cent of the market, the lowest figure in the second row of the matrix, which records the possible payoffs of A's strategy 2. Finally, the corresponding security payoff level for A's strategy 3 is 12.

With this dyspeptic view, A can make the best of the situation by aiming at the highest of these minimal payoffs. That is, management will choose that one among its strategies for which the starred figure is highest. It will seek the *maximum* among these minimal payoffs. This decision rule is, for obvious reasons, called a *maximin* strategy.

Firm B can, of course, employ a similar strategy. Only for B to assume the worst means that A receives a very *large* payoff, so that B is, residually, left with very little. Thus if B plays its strategy 1, its worst possible (security) payoff level is 64, which is therefore marked with a prime. The worst possible payoff for each of B's other strategies (the highest figure in each column) is marked in the same way. The best of these (pessimistic) payoffs for B is, of course, the lowest of these figures, the 18 in column 3. Hence the best of these choices, which is called B's *minimax* (not maximin) strategy, is strategy 3.

4. Equilibrium (Saddle) Points

In the example which has been chosen, A's security payoff from its maximin strategy 1 is exactly the same as the amount which B expects A to receive when B employs a minimax strategy 3. That is, the starred entry in the first row coincides with the primed entry in column 3. In such a case the payoff matrix is said to possess an *equilibrium point*, 18 (which, for geometric reasons that will be described presently, is also called a *saddle point*). It is to be emphasized that this coincidence of maximin-minimax strategy payoffs does not always occur. What happens in cases where the payoff matrix possesses no equilibrium point will be discussed later.

The maximin or minimax strategies have a number of important properties, some of which hold only if the payoff matrix possesses an equilibrium point:

PROPERTY 1. *The protective power of maximin strategies:* By definition, a strategy of this variety offers both parties a measure of protection in that A's maximin strategy gives him the largest share of market which B can be prevented from reducing any further, and B's minimax strategy offers B the lowest share of market for A which A can be prevented from increasing any further. A has set up the highest absolutely defensible floor under his earnings. Thus, when A plays strategy 1, anything B does will either leave his market share at its maximin level, 18, or raise it above that figure. Similarly, B's use of his minimax strategy, 3, places the lowest possible ceiling over A's payoffs.

By contrast, suppose A had chosen strategy 2 instead of his maximin strategy 1. It is true that if B miscalculates and plays strategy 1 or 4 this offers A a greater market share than the maximin payoff, 18. But B then has available a better counterstrategy. He can choose strategy 2, which (with A using his strategy 2) will confine A to a 5 per cent share of market. In other words, by choosing a strategy other than his maximin strategy, A has left himself unprotected against a countermove by B which gives him, A, less than his maximum-security-level share. Thus the maximin or minimax strategy is designed to offer both sides maximum protection—it may well be described as the coward's (or if one prefers, the prudent man's) strategy.

PROPERTY 2. *The minimax-maximin combination and equilibrium:* Where the payoff matrix possesses an equilibrium point, a maximin strategy also has the attractive property of being a most advantageous strategy available to the one firm *if the other firm chooses a minimax strategy.* Indeed, this is why the coincident payoff matrix entry of the minimax-maximin strategy combination is called an *equilibrium point.* That is, if one of the two firms plays its minimax (maximin) strategy, the other is motivated to employ its maximin (minimax) strategy because that is how it can achieve its largest market share. Equilibrium points therefore possess an element of inner stability in that if one player adopts a strategy consistent with the attainment of such a point, the other player is also motivated to do so.

This property can be illustrated with the aid of our payoff matrix. If B plays its minimax strategy 3, the most which A can obtain is an 18 per cent share of the market, which he gets by playing his maximin strategy 1. The reason this is so is that since 18 is also B's minimax payoff, it must represent the largest figure in column 3 (the worst market share for B when he plays strategy 3). Similarly we see that if A employs his maximin strategy 1, the best B can do in response is to employ his maximin strategy 3, because any other strategy will give A more than 18 per cent of the market.

PROPERTY 3. *All equilibrium pairs are minimax-maximin strategies:* A pair of strategies a and b (where a is *any* one of the strategies open to firm A and b is one of those open to B) is defined as an *equilibrium pair* if, whenever firm A chooses a, B's most profitable countermove is b, and vice versa.

The previous property of minimax strategies, stated in this terminology, is that the minimax-maximin strategy combination constitutes an equilibrium pair. In addition, we may now assert that the converse of that proposition is also valid, i.e., that any equilibrium pairs of strategies are necessarily minimax-maximin strategies.[2]

PROPERTY 4. *Equality of payoffs of different equilibrium pairs:* A payoff table may possess more than one equilibrium pair of strategies. Suppose we call them (a, b) and (a', b'). However, since by the preceding property, both a and a' must be maximin strategies for A, they must yield the same security payoff to A. Similarly b and b' must yield the same security value to B. In other words, any of the *four* strategy combinations (a, b), (a', b'), (a, b'), and (a', b) must yield the same payoffs. Therefore if there are several equilibrium pairs of strategies and if one of the players picks any such strategy, then the other player can achieve the same degree of protection (minimum payoff) no matter which of these he chooses.

PROPERTY 5. *Maximin strategies may be poor countermoves to nonminimax strategies:* The minimax strategy also has an important unattractive feature. Suppose one of the firms is run by managers who are poorly informed or are not very clever, or who simply are willing to take risks, and who, for any of those reasons, do not employ a maximin strategy. Then, the maximin strategy is likely to be unprofitable to the other firm. For example, if B employs strategy 1, then it will be strategy 3 which yields A its highest market share (64 per cent) and A's maximin strategy, 1, will not do as well. In other words, the prudent maximin strategy is only guaranteed to be good when playing against another prudent man!

5. Geometry of Equilibrium Points: Saddle Points

A's payoff as a function of his and B's strategy choices can be represented in a three-dimensional diagram such as shown in Figure 1. In order to obtain a smooth diagram it has been necessary to assume that both A and B have entire (continuous) ranges of strategy choice open to them, involving decisions such as the prices to be charged for their projects or the amounts to be spent on advertising. Thus either player has an infinite number of choices open to him (one corresponding to each point on his strategy axis). This contrasts with situations involving only a finite num-

---

[2] For if b is B's most profitable move against a, this combination of strategies must yield to A his smallest possible return from a, i.e., his security-level evaluation of strategy a, call it $S(a)$. Now, consider any other one of A's strategies, and call it a'. The security value of a', that is, $S(a')$, is the minimum yield of a' so that the combination of strategies a' and b must yield a payoff, $c(a', b)$, which is at least as large as $S(a')$. Hence $c(a', b) \geq S(a')$. Moreover, since a is A's most profitable countermove to b, the combination (a, b) must pay A at least as much as does combination (a', b), i.e., we must have $S(a) \geq c(a', b)$. Comparing the two inequalities, we see that $S(a) \geq S(a')$, i.e., no other strategy, a', has a security value greater than that of a. Hence a must be A's maximin strategy. A similar argument shows that b must be B's minimax strategy.

ber of strategy possibilities (such as the three strategies assumed available
to A and four to B in the previous payoff matrix) to which most theorems
of game theory refer.

In this diagram A's market share is shown directly by the height of the
surface above any point on the floor of the diagram (representing a combination of strategy choices by A and B). B's market share can be inferred
just as easily, since whatever per cent of the market is not held by A must
be in B's hands. B's share of market surface is thus what is left of the
three-dimensional cube in the diagram after A's share of market surface
has been removed.

It will be noted that A's surface has been drawn to involve two very
special characteristics. It has the crest of a hill running roughly north to
south and the trough of a valley running roughly east to west. The valley
is the locus of security levels for A's strategies. For example, if he chooses

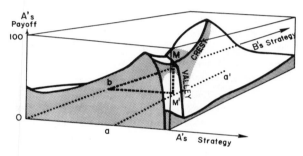

Figure 1

strategy a in the diagram, the worst payoff he can possibly receive is
$M'M$, the payoff at the point where line aa' (the line which represents
strategy a) falls under the trough or valley line of the payoff surface.
Similarly, the crest line is the locus of B's minimal payoffs (i.e., the
maximal payoffs to A for any of B's possible strategy choices).

The altitude of the point of intersection, M, between the trough and
the crest lines is A's payoff from the combination of A's maximin strategy
a and B's minimax strategy b. A's maximin strategy a is his maximin
strategy because that is where the trough line reaches its highest point,
i.e., where it crosses the crest of the hill. For similar reasons b is B's minimax strategy. Thus, M is an equilibrium point and M' represents the
equilibrium pair of strategies a, b.

Because the graph of the payoff surface has the shape of a somewhat
distorted saddle, a point such as M, which is the intersection of a hill
crest and a valley trough, is called a *saddle point* (see also Figure 1 of
Chapter 6).

6. Payoff Matrices Without Equilibrium Points

We have yet to deal with the case where A's share of market payoff matrix has no saddle point. An illustration is provided by the following payoff matrix for A:

	1	2
1	80′	20*
2	40*	100′

Here A has a maximin strategy, 2, because 40 is the maximum of the lowest numbers in the two rows. Similarly, B has a minimax strategy 1 which will guarantee that A obtains a market share no larger than 80 per cent. This is not a saddle point because the maximin strategy combination (2, 1) and the minimax combination (1, 1) do not coincide. The lowest point on the crest of the surface is at a different location from the highest point in the valley. Note that if the maximin-minimax combination of strategies is employed, A will obtain 40 per cent of the market so that B will be pleasantly surprised.

Even in this case, the maximin-minimax procedure will still be the coward's strategy. By definition, it provides maximum protection against one's competitor.

But now this strategy pair lacks the second attractive feature which it possessed in the saddle-point case. It is no longer an equilibrium pair. That is, *if B is certain to employ his minimax strategy 1, A is better off employing his non*maximin strategy 1, which will raise his market share from 40 to 80 per cent. It is also easy to see that B will want to change his strategy if A changes from his maximin to his nonmaximin strategy, and that A's best counterstrategy will depend, equally, on B's strategy choice. Thus, in the absence of a saddle point, the choice of strategies becomes a highly unstable affair.

This does not mean that maximin or minimax strategies are now necessarily undesirable. Especially when A and B are highly uncertain of one another's plans, they may still both prefer to play it safe and to stick to this decision no matter what the risky temptations.

7. Mixed Strategies

There is another interesting type of strategy alternative open to A and B. Its analysis will require the aid of the utility theory developed in Chapter 17. It turns out that if the number of possible pure strategies with which we began is finite, this alternative type of strategy has the effect of replacing A's share of market payoff matrix with another which has the following remarkable property: If the original share of market surface had a saddle point, the new surface will also have one at the same location. And even if the original share of market surface had no saddle point, the new one *always* will!

The way in which this additional set of strategic possibilities enters can be indicated in a somewhat roundabout manner. It was remarked at the beginning of the chapter that good business policy will often seek to prevent the competition from predicting one's own strategy. One way of doing this is to choose one's strategy randomly, e.g., to pick two fairly good strategies and choose between them by the toss of a coin or some other chance device such as a spinner. The combination of the two strategies and the probabilities assigned to the two strategies[3] is itself called a *mixed strategy*, as compared with the *pure strategy* which involves no such random elements.

Mixed strategies can easily be shown to have a very interesting property. They can often increase the security levels available to both competitors when the pure-strategy payoff matrix has no saddle point. This is easily demonstrated with the aid of the preceding payoff matrix.

Suppose that the payoffs in the table, instead of representing share of market, are measured in utility terms. We can then compute the (expected) N–M utility of a mixed strategy to compare its value with that of a pure strategy.

Consider the mixed strategy which offers A a 1-to-3 chance of having to employ strategies 1 and 2, respectively. If B employs his strategy 1, the expected value of the utility of the outcome to A will be $\frac{1}{4}80 + \frac{3}{4}40 = 50$. On the other hand, if B employs his other strategy, 2, the expected value of A's payoff is $\frac{1}{4}20 + \frac{3}{4}100 = 80$. Either of these outcomes exceeds the 40 guaranteed to A by his maximin pure strategy, and so, simply by turning his decision into a gamble, A has increased the level of protection which is available to him. In the same way, B can also increase the value of his minimum payoff by the use of mixed strategies.

There appears to be an element of sleight of hand in this procedure, and some writers have questioned the value of mixed strategies except as a means of confusing the competition. The businessman in question must always assume the worst in situations in which his competitor is not kept in the dark by the use of a random decision device, but he must accept a more temperate evaluation of his own prospective payoff when his own

---

[3] The odds can be set any way the player prefers to have them. For example, if the pointer in a spinner can fall on any number from 1 to 12, the odds are set at 2 to 1 in favor of strategy 1 by deciding to play strategy 1 if the pointer falls anywhere on 1 through 8 and to play strategy 2 otherwise. Since there is an infinite number of possible sets of odds, the number of mixed-strategy alternatives open to a player is infinite.

decision is made into a gamble. If the individual were to adopt as pessimistic a view of the outcome of a mixed strategy as he does for a pure strategy, he would act as though he were always sure of losing and a mixed strategy could not increase his degree of protection.[4]

Mixed strategies have proved advantageous to A by enabling him (*only in his anticipations*) to take his eggs out of one strategy basket. Actually, however, by using such a strategy he has opened himself to the worst of contingencies. If luck is against him, and B uses strategy 2 while against 3–1 odds he is led to employ 1, his payoff will be only 20, the lowest possible payoff in the table, which is well below the 40-util payoff to his maximin pure strategy. The mixed strategy has really provided him with no absolute protection in the ultimate outcomes, unlike his pure maximin strategy. But, in return, the mixed strategy has permitted him the luxury of anticipating far more desirable outcomes, e.g., the 100 payoff which the maximin pure-strategy approach would have required him to keep out of his calculations altogether.

8. Optimal Mixed Strategies and the Saddle-Point Theorem

The theorem that there must be a saddle point on the surface which represents the payoffs from a finite number of pure strategies and, in addition, all possible mixed strategies into which these can be combined, was first proved by J. von Neumann. It has been called the fundamental theorem of two-person, zero-sum game theory.

To discuss the derivation of this theorem the concept of the *optimal* mixed strategy must first be described. The odds attached to the different pure strategies which make up the mixed strategy need not be chosen arbitrarily. By changing the odds in our previous illustrative computation, it is easy to show that different mixed-strategy odds yield different maximum security levels for a player. He should therefore look for a set of probabilities for his own mixed strategy which will make his security level as large as possible.[5] This so-called optimal mixed strategy will set the

---

[4] Such a person, in fact, would not possess the second characteristic of the expected-utility maximizer as listed in Chapter 17. To him the value of a gamble will not vary with the magnitude of the probability of winning. A ten-to-one chance of making $50 or $5 would be worth exactly the same to him as a similar bet at fifty-fifty odds—both would be worth exactly $5. This again suggests that the extreme pessimism of a maximin strategy may not always be appropriate.

[5] This is the point where the Neumann-Morgenstern utility theory is required. We wish to find which of the infinite number of possible mixed strategies is preferred by the maximining player. But the utility axioms tell us that he will prefer the one for which the *expected* security (utility) value is highest. We therefore compute the general expression for this expected value in accord with the procedures of the utility theory, and are then in a position to use linear programming methods to find the odds which maximize this expected value, in the manner described below.

highest possible floor, L, under A's expected earnings. If A plays this mixed strategy, the best B can hope to do is keep A's *expected* earnings down to level L.

If we go back to the first payoff matrix in this chapter for an illustration, the probabilities which constitute this optimal mixed strategy can be found with the aid of the following linear program: Let q_1, q_2, and q_3 be the probabilities which player A will assign to the pure strategies one of which is to be chosen by his random device. Then he seeks those values of the q's which maximize L, the floor to his payoff. Since the q's are probabilities, their sum must equal unity and none of them may be negative. We also require (in order to be sure L is a floor) that no matter what his opponent does, A's expected payoff is at least L. The symbol q_1 represents the probability that A will be told by his random device to employ his pure strategy 1, so that, if his opponent plays his strategy 1, A will have the probability of q_1 of receiving the corresponding payoff, which we denote by $P_{11} = 50$ (our first payoff matrix). If his opponent plays strategy 1, he can also expect payoff $P_{12} = 27$ with probability q_2, etc.

Considering all these possibilities together, we see that if B plays his strategy 1, A's payoff must turn out to be one of the numbers 50, 27, or 64 ($= P_{13}$) and A's *expected* payoff will then be 50 multiplied by the probability, q_1, that he will end up with strategy 1 plus 27 multiplied by the odds on strategy 2, q_2, plus $64q_3$. A will seek q's which guarantee that this sum is no less than L. Similarly, if B were to play his strategy 2, A's expected payoff would be $90q_1 + 5q_2 + 30q_3$, and this, too, must be no less than L. Similar conditions must also take care of A's expected payoff if B should employ either strategy 3 or 4. Taking all of these constraints into account, we see that the determination of A's optimal mixed strategy constitutes the following linear programming problem:

Maximize L (the floor to A's payoff) subject to

$$50q_1 + 27q_2 + 64q_3 - L \geq 0$$

$$90q_1 + 5q_2 + 30q_3 - L \geq 0$$

These conditions state that A's expected earnings are never less than L, i.e., that L is truly a floor.

$$18q_1 + 9q_2 + 12q_3 - L \geq 0$$

$$25q_1 + 95q_2 + 20q_3 - L \geq 0$$

$$q_1 + q_2 + q_3 = 1$$

$$q_1 \geq 0, q_2 \geq 0, q_3 \geq 0$$

These conditions must be satisfied for the q's to be probabilities.

Since whatever B gains A must lose, B will be equally anxious to minimize A's expected payoff. His optimal mixed strategy will impose on

A's expected maximum payoff (the most A can get for himself) a ceiling, S, which is as low as possible. It is easy to check that the probabilities, v_1, v_2, v_3, and v_4, which accomplish this are found with the aid of the dual of the preceding program:

Minimize S subject to

$$50v_1 + 90v_2 + 18v_3 + 25v_4 - S \leq 0$$

$$27v_1 + 5v_2 + 9v_3 + 95v_4 - S \leq 0$$

$$64v_1 + 30v_2 + 12v_3 + 20v_4 - S \leq 0$$

$$v_1 + v_2 + v_3 + v_4 = 1$$

$$v_1 \geq 0, \qquad v_2 \geq 0, \qquad v_3 \geq 0, \qquad v_4 \geq 0.$$

We can now apply the two duality theorems of Chapter 6, Section 3, to this zero-sum, two-person game.[6] Theorem I tells us that if both players employ their optimal mixed strategies, then L, the highest floor which A can set under his payoff, will be equal to S, the lowest ceiling which B can place over A's earnings. This means that there will always exist a pair of *mixed* strategies which constitute an equilibrium pair in the sense that neither player can do any better for himself when the other employs his optimal mixed strategy. A can guarantee himself no more than $L = S$, and B cannot force him to take less. This is the fundamental theorem of the zero-sum, two-person game. This theorem paved the way for most further game-theory analysis. It may be added that von Neumann's original proof is much more complicated than that which was just outlined.[7]

Our duality Theorem II also has an interesting game-theoretic interpretation. Since both players know the payoff figures, player B can, of course, compute A's optimal mixed strategy and its expected yields just as well as can A. We would, therefore, expect B not to play any strategy which offers to A more than his minimum expected return, $L = S$. Duality Theorem II tells us that this is precisely how he will behave if his strategy is optimal. For suppose the probabilities of A's optimal mixed strategy are

---

[6] The duality theorems of Chapter 6 must be extended somewhat for the present purpose since our pair of dual programs contain not just inequality constraints but also the equations

$$q_1 + q_2 + q_3 = 1 \quad \text{and} \quad v_1 + v_2 + v_3 + v_4 = 1$$

(which, as they stand, contain no slack variables).

[7] Actually, for this argument to constitute the outline of a proof, it is necessary to show that the pair of dual programs in question possess optimal solutions.

such that strategy 1 turns out to be a poor one for player B; that is, if B plays strategy 1, A's expected earnings will be greater than the minimum, L, to which B can force them. This means that in the first constraint condition in A's linear program the expected value of A's payoff, $50q_1 + 27q_2 + 64q_3$, will actually be *greater than L*. Duality Theorem II then tells us that the optimal value of v_1, the corresponding variable in the dual problem, will be zero. But, it will be recalled, v_1 is the probability that when B spins his mixed-strategy spinner it will tell him to play pure strategy 1. In other words, duality Theorem II tells us that the linear programming calculation will assign such odds to B's mixed strategy that he takes no chance on his random device, leaving him stuck with undesirable strategy 1. More generally, we see, then, that duality Theorem II *always* assigns probability zero to an inferior pure strategy. An optimal mixed strategy will automatically ensure the player against any risk of employing a pure strategy which enables his opponent to do well.

The programming view of the two-person, constant-sum game yields one other significant observation. We would normally expect that in an optimal solution a number of slack variables will take zero values. The corresponding constraints must then become equalities, i.e., the corresponding expected yields are all exactly equal to L. The economic interpretation is that a player picks the odds in an optimal mixed strategy in a way which offers his opponent little real choice—the opponent can choose among a number of strategies, but, typically, *most of these offer him exactly the same payoff* (the rest offer him even less since they give the first player *more* than L).[8]

---

[8] Where the payoff matrix has exactly two rows and two columns and has no equilibrium point containing any pure strategy, it is clear that the equilibrium pair must consist of mixed strategies, i.e., all four numbers q_1, q_2, v_1, and v_2 must be positive. Hence, in a *basic* solution to such a problem all four slack variables must be zero. This states that the expected payoff to a player must be the same for both of his pure strategies if his opponent uses an optimal mixed strategy.

This observation yields an easy method for the determination of the optimal mixed strategies in such simple (two-row, two-column) games. For example, in the second payoff table of this chapter the expected payoff to B's strategy 1 is $80q_1 + 40q_2$, and that to B's strategy 2 is $20q_1 + 100q_2$, where $q_1 + q_2 = 1$, i.e., $q_2 = 1 - q_1$. If these expected payoffs are to be equal, we must have

$$80q_1 + 40q_2 = 20q_1 + 100q_2$$

or

$$80q_1 + 40(1 - q_1) = 20q_1 + 100(1 - q_1),$$

that is,

$$80q_1 + 40 - 40q_1 = 20q_1 + 100 - 100q_1 \quad \text{or} \quad 120q_1 = 60$$

so that $q_1 = \frac{1}{2}$ and the optimal mixed strategy for A involves $q_1 = \frac{1}{2}$, $q_2 = \frac{1}{2}$. The reader can check for himself that the optimal mixed strategy for B involves $v_1 = \frac{2}{3}$, $v_2 = \frac{1}{3}$.

9. Strategy; the Extensive and Normal Form of a Game

There is a matter of interpretation which it is well to take up before proceeding further. The term "strategy choice" has been employed in a way which makes it appear to denote a single move. However, as the concept is used in game theory it has been interpreted to mean a great deal more. The strategy really becomes an extensive book of rules indicating what the player intends to do, in every contingency, from the beginning of the game to the end. Thus the strategy commits the player to an entire sequence of moves which is contingent in a fully specified manner upon what is done by the other player.

This clearly artificial device serves to collapse the entire game into two strategy choices, one by each player. Once these choices have been made, the subsequent history of the game is completely determined. One can, in principle, figure out all the rest. Of course, only in the simplest of game situations can a player even be conceived of as thinking in terms of strategies in this extreme sense.

Some studies have been made of games considered move by move. Such an analysis is said to deal with games in their *extensive form*. However, the bulk of the literature discusses games in the collapsed form that uses the strategy concept, referred to as games in *normal form* (meaning that the games have been rewritten in accord with this convenient mathematical norm—not that games are normally played in this way!).

10. Two-Person, Nonconstant-Sum Games

So far the discussion has dealt only with constant-sum games, i.e., only with games in which the behavior of the players has no effect on their combined payoff. Real economic problems are usually of the nonconstant-sum variety. For example, collusion can normally increase the total profits of a pair of duopolists, and two countries can usually do better by getting together than by declaring war on one another. Unfortunately, the theory is in a far less satisfactory state outside the area of the two-person, constant-sum game.

In the literature, nonconstant-sum games are divided into two classes: *cooperative* and *noncooperative,* i.e., into games where collusion does and those where it does not occur.

In the cooperative case the game theorists have tended to argue that the players will be sufficiently rational to discover and make full use of all opportunities which can be mutually advantageous. That is, the players are taken to cooperate on any and every action which can increase the payoff of either player (provided it does not, at the same time, reduce the payoff of the other). In the terminology of Chapter 16, Section 9, this states, then, that they will always end up somewhere on the contract curve.

Of course, it is doubtful whether players are really so rational in practice. Moreover, the problems involved in arriving at an acceptable division of the "take" may well prevent the players from maximizing their total loot as this rationality assumption requires! It is noteworthy that most of the novelty in the cooperative-case analysis occurs in investigation of the division of the spoils between colluding players. Nash has supplied a criterion for a reasonable or "fair" division which has been the subject of considerable attention and some criticism. [9]

Noncooperative, nonconstant-sum games will also be discussed briefly. They possess a number of interesting features:

1. If such a game possesses several equilibrium pairs of strategies, they need not all yield the same payoff. Moreover, if (a, b) and (a', b') are equilibrium pairs, neither (a, b') nor (a', b) need be equilibrium pairs. Thus two properties of the zero-sum case no longer hold (cf. Section 4, above). This can greatly complicate the planning problems of both players since, if they do not aim for the same equilibrium pair, both may lose out.

2. In the noncooperative, nonconstant-sum case it will often pay a player to publicize his plans, in marked contrast with the rather obvious advantage of secrecy in the zero-sum case. Disclosure may be useful either as a threat or as a means for transmitting information which permits a degree of tacit collusion:

(a) *Threat information:* To a player who announces that he will drop a jar of nitroglycerine which will blow everyone up if he does not have his way, disclosure of this information is necessary for him to win his point. Curiously, a reputation for stupidity and stubbornness can be useful to the player who poses a threat because it will help convince the others that he really means it! Many mundane economic examples, such as strike threats, are easily cited. [10]

(b) *Information for quasi-collusion:* A company will often make certain that any price increases are well publicized in the hope or even the confident expectation that this move will soon be followed by other

---

[9] The Nash criterion states that if the *status quo* is (as a matter of convenience) evaluated at zero for both players, and if the players' payoffs are evaluated by the recipients at u_1 and u_2, then a fair division is one which maximizes the product of these utilities, $u_1 u_2$. Nash derives this rather surprising arbitration formula from a set of axioms which are set up as reasonable criteria for a fair division of the spoils. A Zeuthen-Harsanyi model, which assumes that the bargainer who makes a concession is always the one whose percentage utility loss is the smaller, has also been shown to lead to the Nash solution. See John C. Harsanyi, "Approaches to the Bargaining Problem," *Econometrica*, Vol. 24, April 1956.

[10] For a highly suggestive analysis of this and other related problems, see T. C. Schelling, *The Strategy of Conflict*, Harvard University Press, Cambridge, Mass., 1960.

firms in the industry, to their mutual advantage. Other examples will doubtless occur to the reader.

3. Another peculiarity of the nonzero-sum, noncooperative case is that both players will often be led by self-interest to take decisions which are mutually disadvantageous. This has been illustrated sharply by a game called the *prisoners' dilemma*, which is attributed to A. W. Tucker. Two prisoners are brought in and interrogated separately. Each knows they will both get off if neither prisoner "talks." However, they are both told that if one confesses and the other does not the one who fails to confess will receive a particularly heavy penalty. In this situation both players may well decide to protect themselves by confessing.

This point is of considerable economic importance. It shows why citizens may not contribute taxes voluntarily even though each wants the government to function—the citizen sees nothing to be gained by paying taxes unless there is some guarantee that others will contribute too, just as one prisoner will confess unless he has some assurance that his fellow prisoner will not do so. Similarly, many storekeepers will keep their shops open on Sunday although they all prefer a holiday, each fearing that if he does not do so he will lose customers to his competitors. This argument is involved in the logic behind conscription and rationing in wartime, governmental anti-inflationary measures, etc. All of these measures are designed, at least in part, to achieve the cooperation which alone can prevent the loss to each player from his trying to protect himself when he has no assurance that others will behave as required for their mutual interest.[11]

11. n-Person Games: Some Concepts

Of most widespread potential economic application is the theory of many-person games, for most industries contain more than two firms, most real international trade problems involve more than two countries, and so on. But *n-* (many-) person games have so far proved rather intractable to analysis. Writings on the subject and results have been much fewer than in the case of the two-person, zero-sum game. Certainly there is nothing in *n*-person theory resembling the well-rounded analysis of the two-person case.

Nevertheless, the literature is rich in suggestive ideas—definitions and concepts rather than theorems. Some but not all of these concepts are matters of common sense and common observation and it is only remarkable that they were given little attention in pre-game-theoretic economic theory.

---

[11] Indeed, I have suggested that this argument is central to the rationale of governmental control in a democratic society. See my *Welfare Economics and the Theory of the State*, G. Bell & Sons, Ltd., London, 2nd ed., 1965, esp. Chapters 7–9 and 12.

So far, in economic application, such suggestive concepts have been the most fruitful aspect of game theory—they have served to provide an illuminating way of looking at difficult problems rather than a source of cut-and-dried calculations. For these reasons the discussion of n-person games which follows is little more than a description of concepts and definitions, and it is organized accordingly. These will, however, enable the reader to form an impression of the present state of n-person theory.

In this theory, games are again divided into the cooperative and noncooperative varieties. Only one result will be reported for the noncooperative case. Nash has proved that *every* noncooperative game in which each player has only a limited number of strategy alternatives open to him has at least one (mixed- or pure-strategy) equilibrium point. In other words, there exists at least one combination of mixed or pure strategies $(a, b, c, \cdots, n)$ such that, if they are employed by players $(A, B, C, \cdots, N)$, respectively, it will be unprofitable for any one of these players to switch to any other strategy. Thus there exist strategy combinations which have this self-policing feature: If all players but one follow this pattern, the self-interest of the remaining player will also lead him to stick to the equilibrium pattern.

However, an n-person game may possess more than one equilibrium point, and there may then arise the difficulties which were mentioned in the two-person, nonconstant-sum case: Different equilibrium points may yield different payoffs to the players, and if some players aim for one equilibrium point and the remaining players aim for another, they may all end up at a nonequilibrium point! Hence, in the absence of coordination of their plans, if a game possesses a number of equilibrium points, the players may find it difficult to attain any one of them.

We now turn to a listing of the central concepts of the theory of n-person cooperative games:

1. *Coalitions.* In the two-person game there is no possibility of several players combining against the rest. Such collusive arrangements can obviously arise in a many-person game. In game theory this sort of combination of players is called a *coalition*.

Obviously there are many cases where a coalition can add to the "take" of its members by successfully exploiting the remaining players. However, there are some games in which coalitions offer no net advantage to their members (an economic example might involve the costs of administration eating up the profits of any coalition). A game of the relatively uninteresting variety in which there is no motivation for coalition formation is called an *inessential game,* as contrasted with *essential games* in which its members can benefit from the formation of a coalition.

2. *Side payments.* Sometimes, in order for a coalition to maximize its

returns, it may be necessary for a member to undergo some sacrifice. For example, a cartel may find it profitable to close the inefficient plant of one of its members rather than getting every member to reduce his scale of operations. In this case, in order to induce the short-changed individual to serve the interests of the coalition it is necessary to set up an equalization payment (bribe) for him. In game theory such a redivision of the spoils is called a *side payment*.

3. *Imputation*. Any assignment of payoffs to the players is called an *imputation* if it meets two acceptability requirements:

(a) Each player must receive at least as much as he can get for himself when all other players are arrayed against him. If this condition is not met, any player who receives the short end of the payoff allocation can refuse to go along with the coalition structure from which these payoffs result. Obviously, he can always hold out for at least the amount which he can obtain for himself without anyone's help.

(b) A second requirement for an imputation is that the total of all the payoffs to all of the players combined equals the maximum amount they can get by forming one grand universal coalition in which every member is included.[12] This second condition of group rationality is, in fact, widely violated in practice. When farmers fail to get together to restrict their total outputs, they end up with a total "take" which is lower than the maximum (monopoly) amount. The same is true when several countries adopt restrictive tariff policies and all of them end up poorer as a result. In other words, an imputation may be described as a set of payoffs which could be achieved by the players in a game if they were more rational than they are in reality.

4. *The core*. Some imputations may satisfy a condition of group rationality which is even stronger than (b) above. This more stringent condition requires that *any* set of individuals jointly earn from the proposed imputation at least as much as they can obtain by getting together and forming themselves into a coalition. Of course, people do not, in fact, think out every possible coalition they can conceivably form and what they may hope to earn by joining it, so that this condition is certainly not met in practice. The set of all possible imputations which meets this difficult

---

[12] This implies that any imputation must be Pareto optimal (cf. Chapter 21, Section 3, and Chapter 23, Section 5), for otherwise it would be possible to make a change which was advantageous to some of the players and disadvantageous to no one, i.e., the group would initially not have obtained the maximum "take" as rationality condition (b) requires. It also follows that a Neumann-Morgenstern *n*-person game solution (defined below) must be Pareto optimal.

requirement is called the *core* of a game. However, many games have no core, Indeed, it has been proved that any zero-sum game which has a core, i.e., for which such imputations exist, must be inessential!

5. *Characteristic function.* But how does one determine how much will be paid to each player in different circumstances? Given the coalitions which are formed, what payoffs will be received by the members of each coalition? Von Neumann and Morgenstern approached this question by describing lower limits to these amounts. Given any coalition C, the worst that can possibly happen, from its point of view, is that all other players will combine against it in one grand countercoalition. But if the total take of the two coalitions is *fixed* at its maximum possible value [group rationality requirement (b) of an imputation] this transforms the problem into a constant-sum, two-person (two-coalition) game. Since such a game can always be solved by the linear programming methods described in Section 8, above, we can calculate how much will be earned by our coalition C in these unfavorable circumstances.

In this way a minimum-earnings figure can be computed for every possible coalition. If payoffs are measured in utility terms, the relationship $R = v(S)$, which gives this minimum payoff, R, for every possible coalition S, is called the *characteristic function* of the game. The Neumann–Morgenstern analysis of the n-person game is based largely on the characteristic function. However, such an analysis is bound to leave out much relevant information about the game because it concentrates exclusively on the worst outcomes for each coalition.

The following plausible result is among the theorems on characteristic functions: If two coalitions combine, the value of the characteristic function for the combination will equal or exceed the sum of the values for the uncombined coalitions, i.e., the combined coalition will earn at least as much when the rest of the world is against it as the two subcoalitions can earn for themselves in similar circumstances.

6. *Domination.* An imputation, I, is said to dominate another imputation, J, if there exists at least one coalition C which can be sure (in terms of the characteristic function) of earning for its members an amount, $v(C)$, which is at least as large as that prescribed for them by imputation I and if, in addition, every member of C receives more from imputation I than from imputation J. In other words, J is dominated by I if a set of players who are in a position to prevent imputation J from supplanting I find it profitable to prevent J. It is, of course, possible for two imputations to dominate one another if coalition S prefers I to J and can prevent J, and if coalition T prefers J to I and is in a position to prevent I.

7. *Solution.* Von Neumann and Morgenstern define a solution of an n-person game as a *set* of imputations which has the following

characteristics:

(a) If I and J are any two of the imputations in a solution, then neither I dominates J nor J dominates I.

(b) If K is an imputation which is not included in the solution set, then there is at least one imputation, K^*, which dominates K and which is included in the solution. Thus, a solution consists of a set of imputations none of which dominates any other, and which can among them dominate any excluded imputation.

There are several difficulties involved in this concept. First of all, a solution usually includes a number—sometimes an infinite number—of possible imputations. That is, a solution only lists for us a number of possible outcomes to a game. Thus it does not usually tell us how the game will or should end up. It only confronts us with a list, and sometimes a very large list, of possible alternatives.

This situation is even worse than this suggests, because a game may, and often does, possess a number of alternative solutions (each with its multiplicity of imputations). It is clear, then, that the solution concept does not permit us to calculate any unique outcome for the general game.

Moreover, although it is known that the number of solutions in the three-person game is usually embarrassingly large, it is not known whether there are games which do not possess even a single solution even where the number of players is restricted to a number as low as five. Shapley has also shown that there are games for which the solutions constitute strange and unpredictable sets, that is, cases which make it very difficult to set up general rules about the nature of solution sets.[13]

Because the solution concept permits so much indeterminacy and is not fully satisfactory in other respects, a number of alternative concepts have been explored. Milnor has set up several sets of criteria which, he suggests, an imputation should meet in order to be considered reasonable. These criteria are designed primarily to get rid of some of the possible imputations on the ground that they are in some sense not "reasonable." Vickrey has proposed a concept which he calls a *strong solution*, consisting only of imputations and coalitions such that if anyone defects from one of the included coalitions he is apt to regret it because there exist alternative imputations which tempt his new partners to "double-cross" him in turn. Luce has constructed a theory which takes into account the fact that there are institutional constraints on the formation and breakup of coalitions.

---

[13] The solution concept has also been criticized for its reliance on the characteristic function. That is, in practice, one imputation, I, may in effect "dominate" another, J, even though the characteristic function indicates that no coalition C can prevent J profitably. For the characteristic function gives only the most conservative estimate of what C can hope to achieve, and in practice C may often be expected to do much better than that.

That is, it recognizes that social mores may well prevent the formation of certain types of coalition. This points up what is admittedly the main weakness of game theory in its present stage of development—the relative lack of specific sociological, psychological, and economic content in its premises. Until such material is supplied, it is unreasonable to expect the mathematics to yield the empirically applicable results which are not contained in its assumptions.

This concludes a rather disjointed discussion of concepts of n-person theory, which should nevertheless at least offer the reader a hint of its flavor.[14] At any rate this section should suggest both the strength and weaknesses of game theory from the points of view of the economist and the operations researcher—its weakness as a source of devices for the calculation of categorical answers to competitive problems, and its strength as a suggestive frame of reference within which the structure of these problems and the alternatives available to the decision-maker may be seen more clearly.

REFERENCES

Luce, R. Duncan, and Howard Raiffa, *Games and Decisions, Introduction and Critical Survey*, John Wiley & Sons, Inc., New York, 1957.

McDonald, John, *Strategy in Poker, Business and War*, W. W. Norton & Co., Inc., New York, 1950. (Very elementary.)

McKinsey, J. C. C., *Introduction to the Theory of Games*, McGraw-Hill Book Company, New York, 1952.

Rapoport, Anatol, *Two-Person Game Theory*, University of Michigan Press, Ann Arbor, Mich., 1966.

———, *N-Person Game Theory: Concepts and Applications*, University of Michigan Press, Ann Arbor, Mich., 1970.

Telser, Lester G., *Competition, Collusion and Game Theory*, Aldine-Atherton, Chicago, 1972.

Tucker, A. W., *Game Theory and Programming* (mimeographed), Oklahoma State University, Stillwater, 1955.

Von Neumann, John, and Oskar Morgenstern, *Theory of Games and Economic Behavior*, 2nd edition, Princeton University Press, Princeton, N.J., 1947.

Weintraub, E. Roy, *Conflict and Cooperation: Game Theory in Economic Analysis*, Macmillan and Company, Ltd., London, forthcoming.

Williams, J. D., *The Compleat Strategyst*, McGraw-Hill Book Company, New York, 1954.

---

[14] For further details the reader is again referred to Luce and Raiffa, *Games and Decisions*, Chapters 7–12.

Decision Theory*

19

1. The Subject Matter of Decision Theory

Contemporary theory follows Knight's distinction between risk and uncertainty.[1] Risk refers to situations in which the outcome is not certain, but where the probabilities of the alternative outcomes are known, or can at least be estimated. Uncertainty is present where the unknown outcomes cannot even be predicted in probabilistic terms, that is, it refers to contingencies against which one cannot protect oneself on ordinary insurance principles.

In game theory, choice problems which involve risk are analyzed with the aid of utility theory, as we have seen in the last two chapters. One makes that decision whose expected utility (the average utility of the alternative outcomes each weighted by its probability of occurring) is highest. Decision theory has been developed to deal with problems of choice or decision-making under uncertainty, where the probability figures required for the utility calculus are not available.

---

* As in the last chapter, the reader who wishes to learn more about the theory, or who desires further references, is advised to consult R. Duncan Luce and Howard Raiffa, *Games and Decisions*, John Wiley & Sons, Inc., New York, 1957, especially Chapter 13.

[1] F. H. Knight, *Risk, Uncertainty and Profit*, Houghton Mifflin Company, Boston, 1921. Reprinted by the London School of Economics, series of reprints of scarce tracts in Economics No. 16, 1933.

Quite a bit of the games apparatus has been carried over into decision theory. As will soon be shown, the payoff matrix, the strategy concept, and the minimax approach all make their appearance again. But there is one fundamental difference between the problems of game and decision theory which cannot be overemphasized. In game theory, at least in the zero-sum, two-person case, there is a major element of predictability in the behavior of the second player. He is out to do everything he can to oppose the first player. If he knows any way to reduce the first player's payoff, he can be counted upon to employ it. In decision theory the second player is not even, strictly speaking, an opponent. Often this second player is referred to as *nature* and the corresponding decision problems are called *games against nature*. But our player cannot count upon nature to oppose him. In fact he cannot count on nature to do anything in particular.

This chapter follows the bulk of the decision-theory literature by treating only the so-called *complete*-ignorance case, that is, the case where the player who is to make a decision has absolutely no clue as to what the other player is going to do. Once there is available any information about his rival's likely behavior, however fragmentary, the requirements of the complete-ignorance case are violated.

However, the standard complete-ignorance analysis supposes, at least implicitly, that the player has at his disposal a large amount of other types of information—more, in fact, than a relatively well-informed businessman is likely to have in practice. In assuming that he can describe his problem in terms of a payoff matrix, the player is taken to possess a list of the strategy alternatives which are open to himself as well as those which are available to his opponent. In addition, he is assumed to know the magnitudes of all of the elements in the payoff matrix. This means, for example, that if a businessman player adopts a particular inventory policy and the demand for his product turns out to follow some particular time pattern, say falling at first, subsequently rising sharply, and finally, leveling off (this time pattern is considered "nature's strategy choice"), then the businessman knows, or believes he knows, exactly what payoff he will receive as a result of this (and every other) pair of his and nature's strategy choices. This is the sort of information which is conveyed by the numbers in his payoff matrix.

The player must also be recognized to have at his disposal a very different kind of highly pertinent information, for he knows something about *himself*—his own financial position and his attitude toward taking chances. Together, these must determine to what extent he will desire and can afford to gamble. The validity of any rules for rational decision-making under uncertainty must, then, be contingent upon at least these two elements—the player's psychological makeup and his pecuniary circumstances.

2. Some Proposed Decision Rules

Since attitudes toward gambling and financial circumstances differ from person to person, it is clear that there can be no one universally valid rule which tells a player how to choose among the strategies that are open to him. The appropriate decision criterion must vary from person to person and from one situation to another.[2]

It is not surprising, therefore, that a considerable number of alternative decision rules have been proposed. At present, the bulk of the literature of decision theory relates to such decision-rule proposals. Let us now examine in turn the most frequently discussed of these decision criteria.

1. *The maximin criterion.* As in game theory, one of the most conservative of decision rules is the maximin criterion. For each possible strategy the player determines the worst that can possibly happen, and then picks the strategy which is "least worst," i.e., whose most unattractive contingency is least disastrous.

In the present context the maximin strategy is somewhat less attractive than it is in a games situation, where the player has an active opponent whose interests are in direct conflict with his own. In such circumstances there can be good reason for fearing the worst. But where one's opponent is nature, who, at least in calmer moments, cannot be considered a systematic and calculating opponent, the maximin approach is rather clearly a manifestation of pure cowardice. This is not meant to imply that cowardice is necessarily irrational. On the contrary, there is much to be said for the Falstaffian position on self-preservation. There are persons and situations where the maximin strategy is entirely appropriate, but it's well to recognize the criterion for what it is.

As an illustration, consider the following payoff matrix (which is carefully chosen to make the maximin criterion show up badly):

	C	D	E
A	100	2	1
B	99	98	0

If our player employs strategy A, his worst payoff is one (1) (which he receives if nature employs strategy E), whereas if he employs strategy B

---

[2] It must be made clear, however, that this relativistic view is my own, and it is not a standard feature of the writings on decision theory. But cf. the Hurwicz α criterion described below.

his lowest possible payoff is zero. Hence his maximin strategy is A, because it offers him the larger of the two minimal payoffs.

This table also illustrates an objection which has been raised against the maximin rule whose conservatism will now be shown, in some circumstances, to be somewhat specious. From the point of view of the rational conservative, there is much to be said in favor of strategy B, because its highest and lowest payoff (in case nature employs strategies C or E) are fairly close to those of A, whereas B's intermediate payoff, 98 (if nature's strategy is D), is much higher than A's intermediate payoff, 2. Hence B appears to offer an excellent hedge against the possibility that neither the best nor the worst possible outcome will be realized.

The source of the difficulty is that the maximin criterion disregards most of the information in the payoff matrix. It considers only the worst possibility in each row, and makes its recommendation with complete disregard for the values of the other elements. Hence it is always possible to find cases in which the nature of these other numbers in the payoff matrix casts doubt upon the wisdom of the maximin choice. As will be seen presently, a similar criticism applies to most, but not all, of the other decision criteria which have been proposed.

2. *The maximax criterion.* A second decision criterion, which does not seem to have been put forth seriously anywhere in the literature, is worth describing because it is at the very opposite end of the scale of venturesomeness from the maximin rule. The maximax criterion, which is a decision rule well suited to the temperament of a plunger, considers only the most glittering prize offered by any strategy and is blind to any other contingencies. It calls for the player always to choose that gamble whose first prize is highest, no matter what the dangers in the relative values of the other prizes and penalties.

In terms of our payoff matrix, it is clear that the maximax criterion advises the decision-maker to employ strategy A, whose highest payoff, 100, exceeds the 99 first prize of strategy B. Two observations are relevant: (a) This illustration shows that the extremely gambling-oriented maximax rule can sometimes recommend the same course of action as the maximin rule, the counsel of timidity—their advice will coincide when one strategy carries with it the best of both first and booby prizes; (b) like the maximin criterion, the maximax rule ignores all intermediate prizes and so may suggest to a player that he give up a very great advantage in the less glittering payoffs, for a negligible difference in the highest prize.

3. *The Hurwicz α criterion.* As a (reportedly somewhat tongue-in-cheek) compromise, Hurwicz has proposed that a weighted average of the minimum and maximum payoffs of each strategy be employed as a decision criterion. For example, if we weight the minimum payoff (security value)

of any strategy at $\alpha = \frac{3}{4}$, and the maximum payoff $\frac{1}{4}$, then the Hurwicz α criterion would evaluate strategy A in the payoff table at

$$1 \cdot \tfrac{3}{4} + 100 \cdot \tfrac{1}{4} = 25\tfrac{3}{4}$$

and strategy B at

$$0 \cdot \tfrac{3}{4} + 99 \cdot \tfrac{1}{4} = 24\tfrac{3}{4}.$$

Hence, it would again select strategy A. This is to be expected, since both the maximin and maximax criteria selected A, and the Hurwicz criterion is, in effect, a weighted average of the two in which the weights are designed to reflect the player's psychology. Like the other two, the Hurwicz criterion clearly ignores a strategy's less extreme payoffs in its computations.

4. *The Bayes (Laplace) criterion.* A criterion whose history is far older then the others that have been described is the Bayes, or equiprobability-of-the-unknown criterion. This states that if we have absolutely no information about the relative probabilities of nature's strategies A, B, and C, we must assign equal probabilities to them in our calculations and then adopt the strategy whose expected payoff is highest.

In our payoff table, this criterion evaluates A at

$$\tfrac{1}{3} \cdot 100 + \tfrac{1}{3} \cdot 2 + \tfrac{1}{3} \cdot 1 = 34\tfrac{1}{3}$$

while B is rated at

$$\tfrac{1}{3} \cdot 99 + \tfrac{1}{3} \cdot 98 + \tfrac{1}{3} \cdot 0 = 65\tfrac{2}{3}.$$

Unlike the others which have been examined, then, the Bayes criterion ranks B ahead of A. It does so because the Bayes rule is the only one of the criteria so far examined which takes all possible payoffs into account. For the first time the 2 payoff possibility of strategy A and the corresponding 98 payoff of strategy B have entered the calculations, and these have turned the tide in favor of B.

In this respect, then, the Bayes criterion is more appealing than the others.

However, the Bayes criterion does suffer from a serious limitation. The difficulty is that it is not clear in advance what unknown possibilities are to be considered equally probable. To illustrate this point, let us consider an economic situation which can lead to a payoff matrix like ours. Suppose our player is considering whether to sell ice cream (strategy A) or hot dogs (strategy B) at a baseball game. We may divide nature's strategies into the three possibilities, C: sunshine, D: cloudiness, and E: rain (or other forms of precipitation). In the complete absence of meteorological information we might consider C, D, and E to be equally probable and assign them each the probability $\frac{1}{3}$ as was just done.

Alternatively, however, we might have decided that the major contingencies to consider are rain vs. nonrain. Because we possess no relevant information, it can be argued just as persuasively as before that these two contingencies are equally likely and each should be assigned the probability $\frac{1}{2}$. We see, then, that by a simple act of reclassification, the *a priori* probability assigned to the rain contingency (nature's strategy E) has been raised from $\frac{1}{3}$ to $\frac{1}{2}$! In other words, unless we have some advance information on the number of categories into which the alternatives should be classified, the Bayes equiprobability-of-the-unknown approach can leave the relevant probability figure completely ambiguous. By breaking the alternatives down into enough different categories, we can assign any one strategy a probability as low as we like.

A variant on the Bayes procedure is to ask the decision-maker to assign subjective probabilities to nature's possible strategies. If for some intuitive reason he feels that C, D, and E may reasonably be assigned probabilities of $\frac{2}{10}$, $\frac{5}{10}$, and $\frac{3}{10}$, respectively, the expected value computation can be repeated using these figures instead of the $\frac{1}{3}$, $\frac{1}{3}$, and $\frac{1}{3}$ probabilities of an equiprobability-of-the-unknown calculation. With these figures, strategy A, for example, would be evaluated at

$$100 \cdot \tfrac{2}{10} + 2 \cdot \tfrac{5}{10} + 1 \cdot \tfrac{3}{10} = 21.3.$$

5. *The minimax regret criterion.* The last criterion to be discussed was proposed by Savage. His rule concentrates on the opportunity cost of an incorrect decision. The approach is to protect the player against excessive cost of mistakes. From the original payoff matrix, a second matrix showing the cost of mistakes (the regret) is calculated. For this purpose it is necessary that the elements of the original payoff matrix be expressed in utility terms. Suppose that this is true of the data in our illustrative matrix and that nature's strategy turns out to be D. If the player employs his strategy B, he obtains the maximum payoff against D (98 as against 2 utils) and so he has nothing to regret. The corresponding regret figure is, consequently, zero, which is entered in the regret matrix at the juncture of row B and column D as shown. But if our player had instead employed A

Regret Matrix

	C	D	E
A	0	96*	0
B	1*	0	1

against nature's D, he would have earned only 2 utils as compared with the maximum possible payoff of 98, so that his net loss, his degree of regret, is $98 - 2 = 96$. This is entered in the row A, column D space. The rest of the regret matrix is computed similarly from the original payoff matrix, as the reader should check for himself. To protect himself against excessive loss, the player may now apply a minimax rule to this matrix. In each row the maximum loss is starred, and that strategy is chosen whose row contains the smallest of the maximum regret elements. In this case, strategy B is recommended by a minimax regret rule, because the worst that can happen to the player who chooses B is a 1-util regret.

At first glance it may appear that this criterion, because it recommends strategy B rather than A, overcomes the problem that was raised in connection with the maximin, maximax, and Hurwicz criteria. It is true that the minimax regret criterion can take into account large disparities in intermediate payoffs. In our illustration, nature's strategy D, with its prohibitive 96-util regret figure, assumes a crucial role even though it offers neither the maximum nor the minimum payoff for any of our players' strategies (see the original payoff matrix). However, the minimax regret criterion runs into the same problem in a slightly different manner. Since it is a minimax criterion, it considers *only the largest regret figure* in any row, and ignores any other data. Hence low and intermediate regret numbers are disregarded. If one strategy, F, has a very slightly smaller highest regret figure than another strategy, G, the criterion will recommend F even if every other regret figure in G is much lower than the corresponding number in F.

The appropriateness of the measure of regret which is employed by the criterion has also been called into question. It is not clear from the Neumann–Morgenstern utility index that the difference between the utilities of two payoffs is a good measure of the player's regret when he receives the smaller of the two. Perhaps the regret measure can be considered a somewhat crude and arbitrary, though not a totally unreasonable measure of the player's loss in choosing the wrong criterion.

6. *Mixed strategies.* Rather than choosing a pure strategy directly, the decision-maker may prefer to let a random device—a coin or a spinner— make his choice for him. As in the game-theory case, such a decision is called a mixed strategy. As before, the player can, by using the utility calculus, compute the expected utility yield of any mixed strategy corresponding to any one of nature's strategies. For example, if the player employs that mixed strategy which involves 50–50 odds of choosing either strategy A or B, then if nature plays its strategy C, the expected payoff will be

$$\tfrac{1}{2} \text{ the } A \text{ payoff} + \tfrac{1}{2} \text{ the } B \text{ payoff} = \tfrac{1}{2}100 + \tfrac{1}{2}99 = 99.5.$$

Continuing the calculation, one obtains the following augmented payoff matrix:

	C	D	E
A	100	2	1
B	99	98	0
$[\frac{1}{2}:A, \frac{1}{2}:B]$	99.5	50	$\frac{1}{2}$

The last row indicates the alternative expected payoffs of the mixed strategy $[\frac{1}{2}:A, \frac{1}{2}:B]$ which represents a 50 per cent chance of either A or B.

By varying these odds, e.g., to three to one, etc., these expected payoffs of the mixed strategy are, of course, changed. It then becomes possible to calculate at which odds the *mixed* strategy will yield the largest maximin value, or, if we prefer, the odds which give the lowest minimax regret figure.[3] Such a set of odds is said to constitute an *optimal* mixed strategy. The decision-maker may then prefer to employ an optimal mixed strategy.

Some comment on the concept of the mixed strategy is called for at this point. It may seem rather irrational for the decision-maker to permit a coin to make up his mind for him, and few if any businessmen are prepared to adopt this as a standard decision-making procedure. However, the maximiner is a fundamentally timid man who fears that his opponent (whether it be nature or another player) will always outguess and outplay him. This is the logic behind his disregard of anything but the least favor-

---

[3] Mixed strategies are not helpful to the player who employs a maximax or a Bayes criterion. Since the expected utility figure is a weighted average of the pure strategies, it will give something intermediate between the highest and the lowest of the items being averaged. This process of averaging therefore tends to raise lowest figures (it increases the security level) of a pure strategy, and is therefore useful to the maximiner. However, because it is an average, the expected values will tend to fall short of the maximum figures, i.e., a mixed strategy will tend to reduce the expected return of a maximaxer.

The user of a Bayes criterion never benefits from a mixed strategy for a similar but somewhat more complex reason. On a Bayes criterion, both strategies A and B are themselves evaluated by means of a weighted average of their payoffs. Thus, as we have seen with our payoff matrix, strategy A is evaluated at $34\frac{1}{3}$ and B at $65\frac{2}{3}$. A mixed strategy will in turn be evaluated, on the Bayes criterion, at a weighted average of these two figures (their expected value). This average must be less than the $65\frac{2}{3}$ value of B, so that the pure strategy B will always be preferred to the mixture of A and B. Thus, a Bayes calculation always evaluates a mixed strategy at some figure intermediate between the highest and lowest values of the pure strategies, and so one of the pure strategies will always be preferred on this criterion.

able outcome for any pure-strategy choice. A mixed-strategy calculation, however, no longer disregards these more favorable payoffs—rather, it deals with their average or expected value. This can be rationalized by the argument that when the player's decisions are made by a coin or some other random device he can be sure that no one will outguess him and so those more favorable payoffs which he formerly left out of his calculations now become very real possibilities, and they must therefore appear in his mixed-strategy calculations. Thus, the higher security value of a mixed strategy must be treated as a subtle reflection of the fact that a mixed strategy can prevent the player's opponent from predicting his decision.

PROBLEM

In the following payoff matrix (constructed by John Milnor) show that strategy A will be chosen by a Bayes criterion, strategy B will be selected by the maximin criterion, C by the Hurwicz α (for $\alpha < \frac{1}{2}$), and D by a minimax regret criterion:

A	2	2	0	1
B	1	1	1	1
C	0	4	0	0
D	1	3	0	0

3. Geometric Interpretation of the Decision Rules

The decision rules which have been described undertake to rank the strategies that are available to a player in terms of the alternative payoffs which they offer him. This suggests that each criterion implicitly postulates some set of indifference curves for the player so that they can rank the strategies for him. As will be shown presently, that is precisely what they do.

First, it is necessary to describe the nature of the indifference map which is involved. To keep the diagram down to two dimensions we shall deal only with pure strategies each of which offers exactly two possible payoffs. That is, the general pure strategy in this set offers our player a payoff which will be designated by V if nature plays some strategy C and some other payoff, W, if it employs its *only* alternative strategy, D. Two such strategies are shown in the following payoff matrix, which will provide our illustrations throughout this section:

	C	D
A	6	3
B	2	8

Here pure strategy A has two possible payoffs, $V = 6$ and $W = 3$; for pure strategy B we have $V = 2$ and $W = 8$.

Given the payoffs, a point representing such a strategy can be plotted at once on a diagram which measures off the magnitude of payoff V on its horizontal axis and that of W on its vertical axis. Thus strategies A and

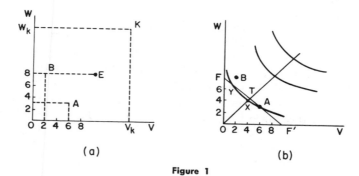

(a)   (b)

Figure 1

B are represented in this way in Figure 1a. Any point in the diagram clearly represents a pair of payoffs and, therefore, some (hypothetical) strategy, and, conversely, every possible strategy with a pair of alternative payoffs can be represented by such a point. If V and W are interpreted as *expected* payoffs, *such a point can also represent a mixed strategy* whose expected payoffs are the coordinates of the point. We may familiarize ourselves with the nature of the representation by noting the following:

1. If (and only if) one strategy, such as E, has possible payoffs *both* of which are greater than the corresponding payoffs of another strategy, A (we say then that E strongly dominates A), point E will lie above and to the right of A.

2. If and only if one strategy, E, has payoffs no smaller than those of another, B, and if just one of E's payoffs is higher than the corresponding payoff of B (E weakly dominates B), point E will lie either directly above or directly to the right of point B.

3. If some strategy point lies directly on the 45-degree line through the origin (point T in Figure 1b), the corresponding strategy will involve no uncertainty, since the two alternative payoffs will be equal. Thus, T has a payoff of 4 dollars if nature employs strategy C and (also) 4 dollars in the alternative event that nature plays D. At any point, such as A, which is not on the 45-degree line, the two possible payoffs V and W are unequal and we say that there is *dispersion* in the payoffs.

Suppose now that the player's preferences among these possible strategy points can be described by a set of indifference curves drawn through the diagram (Figure 1b). This is a rather strong premise since it means that the player must be able to rank every such possible strategy. However, that is precisely what is done by any one of the criteria which have been described. In any event, it does not seem much less plausible than the corresponding assumption behind the ordinary indifference map construction.

The only difference between this and the ordinary indifference map construction is that in the usual case the payoffs V and W represented on the axes are received by the player together (at point K he receives V_k *plus* W_k) whereas in our diagram the payoffs are alternatives (he receives either V_k or W_k but not both).

The shapes of the players' pure-strategy indifference curves will vary with their attitudes toward uncertainty. For example, we might expect that the indifference curves of a person who has an aversion to gambling will be convex to the origin like those in Figure 1b (or in the extreme case, like those of Figure 2a). To see why, we note that this shape (a diminishing marginal rate of substitution of W for V) means that successive equal increments in one of the payoffs will compensate the player only for ever-smaller reductions in the other payoff. He considers one increasingly glittering prize to be poor compensation for a continued proportionate deterioration in the alternative payoff.[4]

Similarly, the gambler who is anxious to give up the protection of a fairly good, second-best payoff in return for a more glittering first prize

---

[4] The connection between convexity to the origin and desire for a low dispersion in payoffs can be shown somewhat more rigorously as follows. For any probability numbers q and $1 - q$, the straight line $qV + (1 - q)W = K$ (FF' in Figure 1b) is the locus of combinations of payoffs, V and W, all of which yield the same expected payoff, K. If the player is averse to gambling, he would therefore presumably prefer point T on the 45-degree line, where the dispersion in the payoffs is zero, to either points A or Y on line FF' since all three points represent pairs of payoffs whose expected values are the same. Choose Y to be a point which is indifferent to A. If both points are indifferent also to some point on the 45-degree line, it must be a point which is inferior to T, i.e., Y and A must be indifferent to a point such as X nearer to the origin (i.e., of lower payoffs) than T. Thus the indifference curve YXA must be convex to the origin.

may be expected to have pure-strategy indifference curves which are concave to the origin.

It will now be shown that the maximin, the maximax, the Hurwicz, and the Bayes criteria each require that the decision-maker's pure-strategy indifference curves be of a very special shape which varies from criterion to criterion. For example, in the maximin ranking of a strategy, only the smaller of its payoffs is taken into account. This means (Figure 2a) that

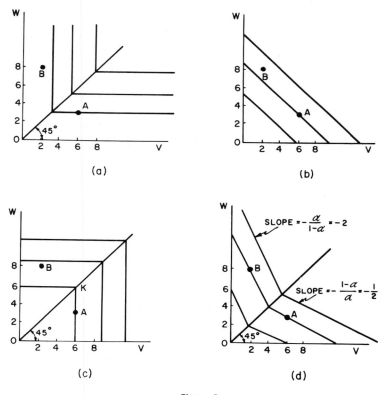

Figure 2

below the 45-degree line where payoff W (the ordinate of any point) is the smaller of the two coordinates, an indifference curve is any horizontal line W = constant, because the player will never be indifferent between two strategies for which the smaller payoffs, their W's, are not the same. For the same reason, above the 45-degree line the indifference curves must be the vertical lines V = constant. In other words, only for an individual whose pure-strategy indifference curves are like those in Figure 2a will it be appropriate to use the maximin criterion.

Similarly, since the Bayes criterion evaluates strategies at $\frac{1}{2}V + \frac{1}{2}W$, the equation of a Bayes indifference curve is $\frac{1}{2}V + \frac{1}{2}W = K$ (constant), i.e., $W = -V + 2K$. These curves are the parallel straight lines of slope -1 which are shown in Figure 2b. The use of other subjective probability numbers instead of fifty-fifty odds only changes the slope of these parallel straight lines. The reader can readily show that a maximax criterion (according to which the larger of the numbers V or W is constant along an indifference curve) and a Hurwicz α criterion (α multiplied by the smaller of the numbers V and W, plus $1 - \alpha$ multiplied by the larger of these two numbers $=$ a constant) require indifference maps of the kinds shown in Figures 2c and 2d, respectively.[5] The reader should note that strategy A is on the higher indifference curve in Figure 2a, that B is the preferred move in 2b and in 2c, and that in 2d they are indifferent.

Since there is no reason to believe that every person's indifference map will assume (the same) one or even any of the forms in these figures, it follows that no one of these criteria is a universal prescription for rationality. Strategies can be ranked, but only by the criterion which happens to be appropriate to the particular decision-maker in light of his psychological and financial circumstances as reflected in the shape of his indifference map.

4. Axiomatization

An alternative approach to the decision problem has employed what is called the *axiomatic method*. By setting up as axioms a number of requirements for an acceptable decision criterion, several authors have been able to come up with unique decision rules, e.g., several writers have shown that the Bayes criterion is the only one which satisfies the sets of axioms which they have proposed. Before we go into further detail, a few preliminary words on the axiomatic method are appropriate.

Axiomatization is one of the mathematician's very powerful and fruitful methods. In using it, the analyst sets out in explicit mathematical form the assumptions which he is willing to use in his investigation. He then employs rigorous mathematical techniques to deduce from these axioms as many of their implications as he can. Often the derived theorems

---

[5] The convexity to the origin of the indifference curves of the extremely conservative maximining player, and the concavity of the extreme gambling maximaxer's curves are in line with the interpretations of convexity and concavity given above.

The Savage minimax regret criterion cannot be represented in so simple a diagram since it involves direct comparison of all the elements in several strategies so that more than two dimensions are required for the indifference map even where each strategy has only two possible payoffs. However, if we deal with the regret matrix rather than the payoff matrix, the indifference map is again that shown in Figure 2a, since Savage applies a minimax (maximin) criterion to the regret data.

are extremely surprising and bear little *obvious* relationship to the axioms from which they are deduced. The axiomatic method, then, has two very attractive features. It forces the analyst to set his assumptions out explicitly, and it puts him in a position to deduce rigorously the implications both obvious and obscure of his *a priori* notions about the problem as expressed in these axioms.

However, it must be recognized that while mathematical statements are always explicit, they are often not transparent. The literature abounds with axioms whose meaning is in dispute or which turn out to mean something other than what their author intended. It is true that a mathematical axiom must have everything there—the author cannot simply hint at some of its features and keep reservations in back of his head in a fuzzy statement, as he is able to do in a literary discussion. But if the axiom requires a complex mathematical formulation (though simplicity, too, can sometimes be deceptive), the more subtle nuances of its meaning may be obvious neither to the analyst nor to his audience. There are a number of innocuous-sounding premises in the literature whose critical implications belie their apparent innocence. None of this is meant as a criticism of the axiomatic method. It amounts only to the trite injunction that powerful weapons should be used with very great caution.

The axiom systems which have been employed in the decision-theory literature are fairly complex and abstract, and there will be no attempt to describe any of them here. Implicitly, such a system must specify something about the needs and desires of the decision-maker if it is to be used to derive some specific decision rule.

The next section describes such a derivation. It is selected for its simplicity and it is unfortunate that it is not one of the standard axiomatic treatments of the literature of decision theory, all of which are too difficult for our expository purposes. Like a number of the standard analyses, this illustrative axiomatization will be shown to rule out all decision rules except the Bayes criterion. However, it does not follow that this is true of any axiom system. Indeed, Milnor has described a set of axioms corresponding to each of the decision rules which this chapter has described.

5. Neumann-Morgenstern Utility and the Bayes Criterion[6]

It will be shown in this section that a simple extension of the Neumann–Morgenstern utility assumptions rules out anything but the Bayes criterion. That is, a person whose psychology is as described by these axioms must, if he is consistent, employ a Bayes decision rule (with subjective *a priori* probabilities assigned by him to nature's strategies, if he prefers).

---

[6] This section is somewhat more difficult than the preceding portions of the chapter.

First it is necessary to discuss the applicability of the utility axioms to the decision problem. Consider a player who is trying to make up his mind between one of two equally priced refrigerators. The theory is willing to assign utility numbers to these objects and to assume that the player will choose that refrigerator whose utility is highest. But suppose, e.g., that refrigerator A is better adapted to storing tall objects and that B is designed primarily for heavy items. Since the consumer cannot be entirely certain in advance what he will be buying over the lifetime of the refrigerator, the choice between A and B must represent a strategy decision against an uncertain future. Similarly, the acquisition of any other durable item, such as a factory, can also be interpreted as a strategy choice.

Generalizing from this we may interpret two strategies A and B in a payoff matrix as two refrigerators, or two factories, or two tickets to a game with fixed prizes but unknown odds. The player may be certain of possessing ticket A and hence he may evaluate the utility of the ticket just as he does that of a refrigerator. Moreover, it is possible to assume that the player's ranking of these strategies satisfies the Neumann–Morgenstern utility axioms. Certainly, casual inspection of the axioms suggests that they are no less persuasive than usual when applied to refrigerators, to factories, or to any other tickets of admission to a game involving uncertainty rather than risk. Thus we adopt for our illustrative purposes

AXIOM 1. The player's ranking of strategies satisfies the Neumann–Morgenstern utility axioms.

In addition, it is necessary for our purposes to specify explicitly an essential feature of a game against nature—the fact that nature is not a calculating opponent so that the decision-maker has nothing to gain by camouflaging his strategy intention. Thus

AXIOM 2. The utility of a strategy is dependent only on the payoffs and probabilities which it involves. (In particular, its utility is not affected by an attempt to conceal from a competitor the fact that one has decided to play it.)

These two axioms together permit us to make a standard calculation

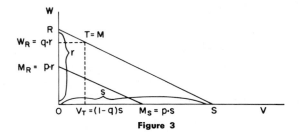

Figure 3

of the utility of a mixed strategy. For if M is the mixed strategy which chooses A with odds $\frac{3}{5}$ and B with odds $\frac{2}{5}$, we have, by the usual rules: the utility of $M = \frac{3}{5} \times$ utility of $A + \frac{2}{5} \times$ utility of B; or, in symbolic notation[7] (with generalized odds q and $1 - q$ instead of $\frac{3}{5}$ and $\frac{2}{5}$)

$$U(M) = qU(A) + (1 - q)U(B).$$

Finally we adopt

AXIOM 3. The decision-maker is indifferent between any two strategies whose payoffs or expected payoffs are identical.

The theorem about the Bayes rule can now be derived geometrically.

In Figure 3 consider two strategies R and S which are represented by points lying on the W and V axes, respectively, so that for the former strategy we have the payoffs $V_R = 0$ and $W_R = $ length $OR = r$ (some number), etc.; thus the payoff matrix is

$$
\begin{array}{c c c}
 & C & D \\
R & 0 & r \\
S & s & 0 \\
\end{array}
$$

Any strategy point T which lies on the straight line connecting R and S divides that line into some proportions which we designate $1 - q$ and q. Point T can be interpreted in either of two ways: It can be taken as a (hypothetical) pure strategy T, or as the mixed strategy M, which consists of R with probability q and S with probability $1 - q$, whose expected payoffs $V = qr$ and $W = (1 - q)s$ (see figure) are the same as those of T. We can now proceed with our proof in two parts, which shows that the indifference curves must be straight and parallel as a Bayes criterion requires (compare Figure 2b, above):

Part 1: Let S be chosen so that it is indifferent with R. Then the indifference curve connecting them is a straight line.

---

[7] Axiom 2 is required for this result. For if the opposition is likely to outguess and outplay the decision-maker unless he employs a mixed strategy, the evaluation of a mixed strategy given by the equation in the text is no longer valid because the values of $U(A)$ and $U(B)$ are changed by the very act of randomization. Strategy A will be much more valuable if there is a fair chance that the enemy will not make the right countermove so that randomization will increase $U(A)$ to, say, $U^*(A)$, and $U(B)$ to $U^*(B)$, and the utility of the mixed strategy becomes

$$U(M) = qU^*(A) + (1 - q)U^*(B) > qU(A) + (1 - q)U(B).$$

Proof: By hypothesis, since R and S are indifferent, we have $U(S) = U(R)$, i.e., the utility of S equals that of R. By the usual Neumann–Morgenstern formula, our mixed strategy, M, has the utility

$$U(M) = qU(R) + (1 - q)U(S) = qU(S) + (1 - q)U(S)$$
$$= (q + 1 - q)U(S) = U(S)$$
$$= U(R).$$

Thus the mixed strategy M is indifferent with both S and R. But by Axiom 3, pure strategy T is indifferent with M (since they have the same expected payoffs). Hence any pure strategy T on the line RS must be indifferent with both strategies R and S.

Part 2: All of the decision-maker's remaining indifference curves are parallel to RS.

Proof: Consider the pure strategy O both of whose payoffs are zero, and which is therefore presented by the origin of the diagram. Form the two mixed strategies, M_R and M_S, where M_R is defined as R with any fixed probability p and O with probability $1 - p$, and where mixed strategy M_S is S with probability p and O with probability $1 - p$. We have

$$U(M_R) = pU(R) + (1 - p)U(O)$$

and

$$U(M_S) = pU(S) + (1 - p)U(O).$$

Since S and R have been chosen to be indifferent, so that $U(R) = U(S)$, it follows at once that $U(M_R) = U(M_S)$, i.e., that the two mixed strategies are indifferent. Hence by the argument of part 1, the straight line $M_R M_S$ connecting the mixed strategy points is an indifference curve. But (Figure 3) M_S has coordinates $(ps, 0)$, and M_R has coordinates $(0, pr)$. Hence $M_R/M_S = pr/ps = r/s$, that is, the slopes of the two lines are equal, and the straight-line indifference curve $M_R M_S$ is therefore parallel to RS.

This proves our theorem because any parallel straight-line indifference curves satisfy the Bayes criterion. This has already been indicated in the discussion of Figure 2b.[8]

---

[8] More rigorously, any one of these lines has an equation of the form $W = -kV + c$, where k and c are any numbers and $k \geq 0$. Let r be a number defined by $r = k/(1 + k)$. Then we have $0 \leq r \leq 1$, so that r can be a probability number. Moreover, solving for k in terms of r we have $k = r/(1 - r)$. Substituting this expression for k into the equation of our line, we get

$$W = -[r/(1 - r)]V + c \quad \text{or} \quad rV + (1 - r)W = (1 - r)c = \text{a constant},$$

which is the equation of a Bayes indifference curve with probability r of payoff V and $1 - r$ of payoff W.

Thus we have proved the theorem that a simple extension of the Neumann–Morgenstern utility axioms requires the rational decision-maker to employ a Bayes criterion. It follows, incidentally, that there is some conflict between the maximin strategy and these utility axioms. The source of this difficulty is the extreme pessimism of the maximin strategy user which is not shared by a person to whom the utility axioms are applied. The former views the worst possible payoff of any strategy as the only possibility worth considering, whereas the utility calculator takes all payoffs into account. As already indicated, this difference in outlook can be rationalized by arguing that a mixed strategy protects the player from being outguessed by his opponent, a possibility which seems doubtful in games against nature, and which is therefore ruled out by Axiom 2 of this section.

6. Decision Theory and the Foundations of Statistics

Before concluding this chapter it is worth indicating briefly how the decision analysis has been used to reorient some of the literature on the foundations of statistics.

To illustrate the nature of this application, consider a simple problem of statistical quality control. A television tube manufacturer has a sample of tubes taken out of each day's production and tests every tube in the sample. Unless too many of the sample tubes are found to be defective, the entire day's production is just packed up and shipped without further examination. The statistical problem is how large a sample should be chosen for inspection and what proportion of defectives in the sample ought to be considered excessive, i.e., what is the proper border line between an acceptable and an unacceptable sample.

In conventional statistical analysis it is customary to make some probabilistic calculation indicating the degree of assurance provided by different sample sizes and rejection levels that the number of defectives in the total output batch will fall short of some specified number. Ultimately, the sample design decisions are made more or less arbitrarily, after a check that these decisions can be considered reasonable.

But the statistical problem is really one in which it is meaningful to look for an *optimal* decision. Too small a sample or too liberal a rejection level means that the percentage of defectives in the firm's shipments is likely to be high, and this can prove costly both in the cost of servicing under the manufacturer's guarantee, and in the loss of customer good will. On the other hand, as many firms have found to their sorrow, excessively rigid quality-control standards can be very expensive and can force the manufacturer to price his product out of the market. Clearly, some intermediate quality-control standards must be optimal, and an analytic approach to this problem of statistical design must seek such an optimum.

This problem is now readily translatable into standard decision-theoretic terms. Each relevant sample-size, rejection-level combination may be considered a strategy of the quality controller and, for each of these, the alternative possible payoffs to the firm may be entered in a payoff matrix. The rest of the analysis can then employ the methods of decision theory.

The same sort of comment applies to statistical problems more general than that of commercial quality control. The entire theory of testing of hypotheses is subject to the same considerations. The customary use of tests conducted at a 95 or a 99 per cent level of significance is essentially arbitrary and does not take into explicit account the costs and benefits (payoffs) of alternative significance levels.

These considerations have, as yet, had little influence on the methods of applied statistics. Rather, they have affected mostly the relatively abstract and philosophical discussions of the foundations of statistics. In part, this is because decision theory is still in a rudimentary state and can offer no firm and final answers to the questions of statistical design. Among the sources of the unsolved problems are the difficulties involved in obtaining data for the payoff matrix and the fact that the results of a decision-theoretic calculation depend on whether one chooses to employ a maximin, or a Bayes, or some other decision rule, and we have, as yet, no systematic procedure for making this choice. However, the discussion has served to call attention to the optimality problem—which is fundamental to most statistical problems—and to indicate some new and illuminating ways in which these problems can be viewed.

REFERENCES

Chernoff, Herman, and Lincoln E. Moses, *Elementary Decision Theory*, John Wiley & Sons, Inc., New York, 1959. (Statistical applications of decision theory.)

Luce, R. Duncan, and Howard Raiffa, *Games and Decisions, Introduction and Critical Survey*, John Wiley & Sons, Inc., New York, 1957, Chapter 13.

Milnor, John, "Games Against Nature," in R. M. Thrall, C. H. Coombs, R. L. Davis, eds., *Decision Processes*, John Wiley & Sons, Inc., New York, 1954.

Raiffa, Howard, *Decision Analysis*, Addison-Wesley, Reading, Mass., 1968.

GENERAL EQUILIBRIUM, WELFARE, AND DISTRIBUTION

four

General Equilibrium

and

the Theory of Money

1. Interdependence in the Economy: Substitutes and Complements

General equilibrium theory was developed to take account of a cardinal feature of the structure of our economy: the interdependence of its parts. A rise in the price of automobiles can reduce the demand for tires and increase the demand for bus transportation. A rise in wages may increase imports, reduce exports, and increase the use of labor-saving machinery. The set of examples can be expanded indefinitely.

Two types of interdependence relationship which have received considerable notice are substitutability and complementarity. *Substitute goods* are items which serve similar purposes, so that the buyer may choose from among the set of substitutes which serve his desires. Usually substitutes are imperfect so that the buyer will not be indifferent between them—they serve somewhat the same purpose, but do so imperfectly. Some examples of substitutes are raincoats and umbrellas, chicken and turkey, coal and fuel oil (which are also substitute inputs as well as substitute consumers' goods). *Complementary goods* are items which people (at least sometimes) wish to use jointly: cheese and wine, shirts and neckties, needles and thread. Note that labor and machinery may be either substitute or complementary inputs, depending on the context of the problem.

Substitute and complementary goods have been defined in terms of the effect of a change in the price of one of such a pair of goods on the demand for the other. If we omit the income effect, a reduction in the price of one of a pair of substitute items should decrease the demand for the other (a fall in the price of leather should reduce the demand for plastic furniture coverings) whereas the reverse holds for complementary goods (a reduction in the price of television sets may increase the demand for beer and aspirin).

It follows that many commodities whose relationship is only slight will be at least mild substitutes because they are competitors for the consumer's limited stock of purchasing power. A fall in the price of houses can reduce attendance at concerts because more houses may be bought and the new house owners may not be able to afford as many evenings out after meeting their monthly bank payments.

The upshot of the discussion is that a demand (or a supply) function for commodity x should not just include the price of x as its only price variable. In fact, to be on the safe side, it is customary in a general equilibrium demand function to include every price in the economy as a possibility, i.e., to say that the demand for any item is, at least potentially, dependent on the price of every other item in the economy.

2. Equations of General Equilibrium

Suppose an economy has 2,053 different commodities, including bonds, stocks, and factories as well as ordinary consumer's goods. Let us treat money as another one of these goods—item 2,054 in the list. In accord with the discussion of the last section, if hats are item no. 12, the demand for hats will be given by an expression

$$Q_{12} = D_{12}(P_1, P_2, \cdots, P_{2054}, A, M).$$

This states that the number of hats demanded depends on the price of every one of the 2,054 commodities, $P_1, P_2, \cdots, P_{2054}$. In addition, demand will depend on the wealth of the economy (presumably the wealthier the economy, the greater the demands for commodities). The wealth of the economy is summed up by the variables A (an index of its holdings of physical assets—buildings, farmland, factories, etc.) and M, the stock of cash in existence. It will be noted that there is no explicit income variable included in this discussion since consumers' income is presumably given by the prices of the commodities which they sell for a living—e.g., the price of labor time (the wage rate)—and these prices already appear in the demand function.

There is a similar *supply* function for item no. 12 (hats), which may be expressed as

$$S_{12}(P_1, P_2, \cdots, P_{2054}, A, M).$$

The economy is said to be in a state of *general equilibrium* if the supply of every commodity is equal to the demand for it. That is, for the 2,054 items in the economy, the following 2,054 equations must all be satisfied:

$$S_1(P_1, P_2, \cdots, P_{2054}, A, M) = D_1(P_1, P_2, \cdots, P_{2054}, A, M)$$

$$S_2(P_1, P_2, \cdots, P_{2054}, A, M) = D_2(P_1, P_2, \cdots, P_{2054}, A, M)$$

. . . .

$$S_{2054}(P_1, P_2, \cdots, P_{2054}, A, M) = D_{2054}(P_1, P_2, \cdots, P_{2054}, A, M).$$

If we are given the values of A and M, we have as many unknown prices as equations and the system can therefore, presumably, be solved for the equilibrium values of the prices, $P_1, P_2, \cdots, P_{2054}$. Substitution of these values into the demand (or supply) expressions will then indicate the quantities of the various commodities which will be exchanged. This, in essence, is the general equilibrium system and the method by which it determines the prices and quantities sold of the various commodities. It has been and can be, expanded and complicated in various ways, by including other variables explicitly, e.g., *exogenous* variables (variables whose values are determined by noneconomic phenomena) such as temperature, and *endogenous* variables such as advertising expenditure, both of which clearly affect demand. We can also go beyond the supply relationships to take explicit account of the behavior of firms and the availability of natural resources. But until some recent developments, which will be discussed in Chapter 23, the structure of general equilibrium analysis did not differ essentially from that just described.

3. The Redundant Equation: Walras' Law

There is one complication which arises even in this simple system. It requires discussion here because of the ideas to which it leads—and despite the fact that it turns out to be far less important than the earlier general equilibrium theorists believed. Of the 2,054 prices which have been included as variables, the last, the price of money, is a rather peculiar animal. By definition, the price of any item, say a hat, is the number of dollars it takes to purchase a unit of that good. But the unit of money is a dollar so that the number of dollars it takes to purchase a unit of money is exactly one (1). It is, therefore, inconceivable that the price of money should be anything but unity. In other words, P_{2054}, rather than being a variable, must be the number "1." We have thereby lost one of our 2,054 variables though we are still apparently left with 2,054 equations. Now, as will be shown in Chapter 23, Section 1, having the same number of equations and unknowns does not guarantee that the system can be solved, nor is the absence of equality in the number of equations and unknowns necessarily fatal to the solvability of a simultaneous equation system. Nevertheless, earlier general equilibrium theorists set great store by this equality, so they considered it important to prove that one of the 2,054 equations is redundant—that in reality we have only 2,053 significant equations to match the 2,053 unknowns.

For this purpose they discovered an important identity which has since come to be called *Walras' law.* Any person who demands a commodity is, by definition, prepared to supply, in exchange, an amount of money (or other commodities) of equal value. Similarly, anyone who supplies some amount of goods on the market demands in exchange its value equivalent in money or other commodities.

Every demand is thus matched by an equal supply (in dollar terms) of some other items and vice versa. It follows at once that the total money value of all items supplied must equal the total money value of all items demanded. In algebraic notation,

$$(1) \qquad \sum_{i=1}^{2054} P_i S_i \equiv \sum_{i=1}^{2054} P_i D_i,$$

where the three-pronged *identity* sign, $\equiv$, means that (at least in an ordinary economy) this relationship must hold no matter what—whether there is equilibrium, or disequilibrium, whether prices are high or low. This identity, which is little more than an accounting relationship (it is difficult to imagine an economy in which it does not hold), is Walras' law.

To show how Walras' law can be used to indicate that one of the general equilibrium equations is redundant, suppose that we find prices which satisfy all but one of the supply-demand equations, say every equation except the first. The sums of the money values of the supplies of all commodities (excluding the first) must equal the money values of their demands. Walras' law then tells us, by subtraction, that the supply and demand of the first item must then also necessarily be equal.[1] That is, if $P_1 S_1$ is unequal to $P_1 D_1$ but the values of all other supplies, $P_i S_i$, equal the corresponding demand values, the sums of all of these supplies together cannot possibly add up to the values of the demands as Walras' law requires. It follows that $P_1 S_1$ cannot possibly be unequal to $P_1 D_1$, i.e., if all other supplies and demands are equal, we must necessarily also have $S_1 =$

---

[1] *Proof:* Since $S_2 = D_2$, $S_3 = D_3, \cdots$, $S_{2054} = D_{2054}$, we have, multiplying by the corresponding prices, $P_2 S_2 = P_2 D_2$, $P_3 S_3 = P_3 D_3$, etc., and adding these equations together we obtain

$$\sum_{i=2}^{2054} P_i S_i = \sum_{i=2}^{2054} P_i D_i.$$

Subtracting this equation from the Walras' law identity we obtain our result,

$$P_1 S_1 = P_1 D_1 \qquad \text{or} \qquad S_1 = D_1.$$

D_1. Hence, if we find any prices which satisfy every supply-demand equation except the first, we need not bother testing them in the first equation, for we know, without trying them, that S_1 will equal D_1 at these prices. The first equation is then harmless and redundant—it adds no information which is not already given by the other equations, and causes no difficulties. We can drop the first equation and solve the others for the prices as if the omitted equation had never existed.

It is important to realize that the first supply-demand equation was picked for omission purely as a matter of expository convenience. Actually, *Walras' law permits us to drop any single equation of our choice.* Much confusion can be saved by realizing that no substantive issue is involved in the choice of the equation to be omitted, since whatever information it provides about any equilibrium prices and quantities will still be contained in the remaining equations.

4. Pitfalls in Determination of the Price Level [2]

Since the general equilibrium equations which have just been described presumably determine all prices in the economy in money terms, they also determine the level of prices—whether prices in general are high or low—inflated or deflated. If the matter is left here, no trouble need arise. However, for a long time the economic literature has contained fairly detailed and separate discussions of the theory of money and the price level. But what they wrote in these discussions often skated perilously close to contradictions with what had been said in the general equilibrium sections. It turns out that there are a number of well-concealed pitfalls in this area, in which some writers have, indeed, been caught.

In order for there to be a determinate price level, there must be one price level which is consistent with equilibrium, and all other price levels should produce disequilibrium and therefore be untenable. This is, for example, what is postulated by the quantity theory of money which states, in effect, that the higher the price level, the more cash people will demand in order to be able to carry on their day-to-day business. Hence, given the supply of money, if the price level is very high, the demand for cash will exceed the supply. People will hold on to money rather than other assets (reduce their demands for goods) and the price level will be forced down toward its equilibrium value. Similarly, with a fixed money supply, if

---

[2] The next few sections are based on work of Lange and more particularly on that of Patinkin. See Oskar Lange, "Say's Law: A Restatement and Criticism," in Oskar Lange, Francis McIntyre, and Theodore O. Yntema (eds.), *Studies in Mathematical Economics and Econometrics; In Memory of Henry Schultz,* Chicago University Press, Chicago, 1942; and Don Patinkin, *Money, Interest, and Prices,* Harper & Row, Publishers, Inc., 2nd ed., New York, 1965.

prices are below their equilibrium levels, the demand for money will be less than the supply; people will try to get rid of money by spending more, and prices will be forced to rise. This, then, is the classical mechanism of price-level determination. The central point merits repetition: In any theory of price-level determination there must be one price level which produces equilibrium, and the others must result in disequilibrium, for otherwise there will be nothing to select out the price level so that any monetary theory must be impossible.

But here is where the conflict between price-level analysis and the rest of general equilibrium theory can arise. It is the essence of general equilibrium theory that what happens in one sector affects what goes on elsewhere. In particular, as we shall soon see again, Walras' law provides a strong link between the monetary sector and the rest of the economy. Assumptions about the structure of the nonmonetary aspects (the so-called *real* sector) of the economy can therefore affect the mechanism which determines the price level. But a number of more or less plausible-sounding assumptions have been made about the real sector which, without its being realized by those who made them, served effectively to destroy any mechanism for the determination of the price level, for *these assumptions make it impossible for any change in the price level to produce equilibrium or disequilibrium.* That is, under these assumptions, if there is equilibrium with price level *A*, there will also be equilibrium, other things being equal, with any other price level, *B*, whereas if one price level produces disequilibrium, any other price level will produce disequilibrium! There is, thus, no such thing as a unique equilibrium level of prices. Any attempt to graft a price-level theory onto this kind of system must produce a contradiction since such a theory, as we have seen, must state that some price level produces equilibrium, and the others disequilibrium.

The assumptions about the real sector of the economy which have such unexpected and distressing effects on the monetary analysis are the pitfalls of the general equilibrium analysis which were mentioned at the beginning of this section. Let us examine these assumptions one by one and see how they lead to trouble.

1. *The homogeneity postulate.* It has sometimes been argued that the demands for and supplies of commodities are affected only by relative prices, and not by their magnitudes in money terms. It makes no difference to hat and shoe purchases, in this view, whether hats are $1 and shoes $3, or hats $5 and shoes $15. In both cases the *relative* price—the hat-shoe price ratio—is three to one. The argument is that if, suddenly, the government were to double the face value of all coins and pieces of paper money—if all dollar bills were to have the legend "two dollars" stamped over their faces—nothing in the economy need be affected except its accounting

records. Umbrellas would nominally cost twice as much, but the buyers' dollar incomes would be twice as high. Thus, the argument runs, if we increase all money prices but raise them strictly in proportion, no commodity's supply or demand will be affected.

This assumption has been called the *homogeneity postulate*, the terminology being drawn from the mathematical expression for a relationship in which a *proportionate* change in all of the variables (the prices) has no effect on the dependent variables (quantities supplied and demanded). Demand and supply relationships in which a proportionate change in prices leaves things unchanged are said to be *homogeneous of degree zero in prices alone*.

This homogeneity assumption is inconsistent with the determination of any price level. It will be recalled that, by Walras' law, if there is supply and demand equilibrium in every market except one, then the remaining market must also be in equilibrium. Hence, in particular, if demand equals supply in every market in the real sector of the economy (demand equals supply for every commodity except money), then the supply of and demand for money must also necessarily be equal. In this case we must have an equilibrium price level. Suppose, now, that the price level changes, with all prices varying in exactly the same proportion. If the supply and demand relationships are homogeneous, then none of them will be affected by this change in price *level*—the demand for neckties will remain equal to the supply of neckties, the demand for pianos will remain equal to their supply, etc. This change in price level, with no change in relative prices, cannot disturb the equilibrium in any market of the real sector, so that, by Walras' law, the supply of and demand for *money* must also remain equal. Thus, it is impossible for any change in price level alone (leaving relative prices unaffected) to produce disequilibrium in the money market. In sum, we see that the homogeneity postulate, because it precludes the price level from affecting the real sector, also prevents it from affecting the money market. If we accept that assumption, it is impossible to have any monetary theory or any determinate price level—any price level will do as well as any other because they will all be equally consistent with equilibrium.

2. *Dichotomy of pricing in the real and monetary sectors.* A second and closely related assumption, which leads to similar difficulties, is the premise that it is possible to divide price determination into two completely independent parts—the determination of the absolute price level occurring entirely in the monetary sector of the economy and the determination of relative prices only in the real sectors of the economy. That is, relative prices are determined by the supply-demand equations for commodities, and then the price level is determined separately by the money supply-demand equation.

If this two-part, or dichotomized, price determination premise implies that the price level has absolutely no effect on the real sector of the economy, it runs into the same trouble as the homogeneity postulate. If no change in price level can produce disequilibrium in any commodity market, by Walras' law, it cannot produce money-market disequilibrium either. Hence, this extreme form of the dichotomous price determination assumption also produces a contradiction with any monetary theory. If the price level does not affect the commodity markets, it cannot be determined in any market. However, we shall see later that there is another closely related, but entirely legitimate form of this dichotomy assumption.

3. *Say's identity.* A third and final assumption which can preclude the determination of a price level is one of the several (no longer fashionable) propositions which have at one time or another been labeled *Say's law.* This version of the proposition attributed to Say is the one which is found in most modern references. It asserts that people offer things for sale only because they want other goods and services in exchange. If they accept money for the goods they sell, they do not do so because they want the money for its own sake but because they desire to take the money *at once* and buy other goods with it. In this way, every supply of a good brings with it a demand for an equivalent amount of *goods.* Whether prices are high or low, rising or falling, the supply of all goods taken together must equal the demand for all goods taken together. This version of Say's law is compatible with an overproduction of hula hoops or some other particular commodities, if, for example, people's tastes have unexpectedly swung away from hula hoops. But the overproduction of these items must be matched by an undersupply of some other goods on which suppliers do want to spend their money. Thus, it is possible for producers to turn out the wrong goods but they can never turn out too many goods for the buying public. General overproduction of commodities is impossible.

This version of Say's law is a first cousin of Walras' law which states that supplies of goods and money together must equal demands for goods plus money. Say's law is the stronger assertion that people don't want money except to buy goods at once, so that the total supply of commodities alone (excluding money) is necessarily *identical* with the total demand for commodities alone. For this reason it has been proposed that this version of Say's proposition be called *Say's identity.*[3]

Since Say's identity requires that the goods markets, taken as a whole, must always be in equilibrium (total supply for all goods equals total demand), it follows by Walras' law that the remaining market, the money market, must also always be in equilibrium. It is impossible for any change in the price level (or any change in anything else, for that matter) ever to produce disequilibrium in the money market. As a result, Say's identity also precludes the determination of any price level by any relationship of monetary theory.

To summarize, we have now examined three assumptions which have at some time or another appeared in the economic literature—the homogeneity postulate, the dichotomization assumption, and the Say's identity assumption. We have seen that any one of these causes serious trouble for general equilibrium theory by making a monetary theory impossible. Only in a barter economy where money plays no role and there is no absolute price level can any of these assumptions be made without causing such difficulties.

5. The Real Balance Effect

In practice, a change in the price level can have very profound effects on demands for and supplies of commodities. Perhaps the most powerful influence of a price change is that which operates through the public's expectations. A rise in price level has, for example, been known to stampede buyers into purchasing goods in the fear that their prices will go up even further. Thus, a price change, by leading buyers or sellers to expect further price changes in the future, can induce them to speed up or to postpone purchases and sales of commodities.

Another influence of a change in price level is its effect on the purchasing power of a stock of cash. If a man has $1,000 in cash, and prices fall by half, the value (purchasing power) of his stock of cash will have doubled. More generally, it can be seen that a rise in prices will lower the real value of cash holdings (it will reduce the real wealth of the owners of the money) whereas a fall in prices will raise the real value (purchasing power) of cash holdings. A proportionate fall in all prices may leave real *incomes* unaffected (if wages and commodity prices both fall 50 per cent, the purchasing power of workers' incomes are unaffected). But we see that the fall in prices must increase the *real wealth* of people who hold cash.

---

[3] In algebraic terms Say's identity may be written, using the notation of Walras' law identity (1) in Section 3, as

$$\sum_{i=1}^{2053} P_i S_i \equiv \sum_{i=1}^{2053} P_i D_i.$$

This differs from the Walras' law identity only in one respect. The numbers above the $\sum$'s are 2,054 in the Walras' law case but they are 2,053 here. That is so because the supply of and demand for the 2,054th commodity, money, do not enter into Say's identity.

Let us now make the reasonable assumption that an increase in a person's wealth will lead him to increase his expenditures either on consumption or on investment goods, even if only by a small amount. Then the fall in price level must increase the public's demand for goods and services because, as we have just seen, it increases the real wealth of cash-holders. Thus, changes in the price level must also affect demands for and supplies of goods.

The effect of price-level changes on demands and supplies which operates through the resulting change in the purchasing power of cash has been discussed in the literature under a variety of names. In different places it has been called the *Pigou effect*,[4] the *real balance effect* (the effect which operates via the purchasing power of cash balances), and the *wealth-saving relationship* (the effect of the change in real wealth on saving and expenditure).

The real balance effect amounts to a direct denial of the homogeneity postulate and the dichotomization assumption which were described in the previous section, for through this effect, a change in price level (a proportionate change in all prices) does cause variation in demands for and supplies of goods (unless, of course, cash stocks were also to change in the same proportion). In this way, absolute prices play a role in the real sector of the economy and not just in the money market. The real balance effect is also incompatible with Say's identity for it implies, e.g., that a sufficiently large rise in the price level can lead to such a reduction in the purchasing power of cash-holders, so that the demand for goods will, taken as a whole, fall below the supply—there will be general overproduction—a phenomenon which, Say's identity asserts, is impossible.

The real balance effect is an essential piece of the machinery which works to produce equilibrium in the money market. Suppose, for example, that for some reason prices fall below their equilibrium level. This will increase the real wealth of cash holders, lead them to spend more money, and that in turn will drive prices back up toward equilibrium. Thus, the real balance effect is a part of the equilibrating mechanism of the money market. It is a force behind the working of the quantity theory or whatever analysis we wish to use to explain the determination of the equilibrium price level.

6. Comparative Statics: General Equilibrium Analysis

Suppose, however, we were to decide to ignore problems of disequilibrium and confine our attention only to general *equilibrium* problems. For example, if there is an influx of money into the economy, we may ask not

---

[4] After A. C. Pigou, to whom the idea was attributed.

about its impact effects, but rather, what it will have done to the economic situation after the economy has had a chance to adjust to the new money supply—after it has reached its new equilibrium. This approach is called the method of *comparative statics*. If an exogenous change occurs, we do not, as in dynamics, trace out the course of the resulting developments as time passes. Rather, we compare the initial equilibrium position only with the new equilibrium which might eventually result from this change. We compare only two static equilibrium situations.

In such a comparative-statics analysis, it turns out that the real balance effect may lose much of its importance so that in such cases a modified sort of homogeneity postulate and dichotomization assumption may become legitimate.

Suppose there is a doubling of the supply of money. Suppose, moreover, that after the smoke has had a chance to clear away, all prices will have doubled, and the demand for money will also have doubled. In this situation there is no change in relative prices, and the supply and demand for money are once again equal (at twice their original level). The purchasing power of stocks of money will have been reduced back to its original level (there are twice as many dollars but each dollar is worth only half as much as it was).

With all relative prices unchanged, and with the purchasing power of money stocks back where it began, there is no reason for any change in the demand for or the supply of any commodity. In sum, whereas a change in price level may have affected these supplies and demands, once prices have doubled any change in the real value of cash balances may well have disappeared, and the consequent effects on commodity demands and supplies will then also have disappeared. Hence, if we began from a position of equilibrium, a doubling of all prices as a result of a doubling of the money supply may well restore equilibrium again.

The change in money supply will thus have affected the absolute price level, but it will not have had any effect on the real sector of the economy. Equilibrium relative prices and commodity supplies and demands will all be back at their old levels.

We see that these assertions come very close to the homogeneity postulate (price-level changes do not affect demands for and supplies of goods) and the dichotomization assumption (events in the money market determine only the price level and have no effect on the real sector of the economy, which can be analyzed separately). However, these two assumptions are legitimate only in their modified form in which they refer just to equilibrium prices and equilibrium supply and demand levels. Only in such a comparative-statics context are these premises acceptable. It is important to recognize that the classical and neoclassical economists often used equilibrium concepts and comparative-statics techniques without specifying explicitly that they were doing so. When homogeneity and dichotomization assumptions are encountered in their writings, it is necessary to recognize, therefore, that they may well have been meant in an innocuous comparative-statics sense so that no error need have been committed at that point in their discussion.

This section has argued that only where questions of dynamics and disequilibrium are considered do the homogeneity and dichotomization assumptions *necessarily* run into trouble. However, the reader should realize that even *equilibrium* supplies and demands *may* be affected by price-level changes. If in the course of a price rise there is, for example, a redistribution of real wealth, as will often be the case, demands will shift in accord with the tastes of those whose purchasing power has been increased. All that the preceding argument has shown is that it is *possible* for equilibrium demands to be unaffected by a price rise so that there is no logical impossibility in the homogeneity postulate when applied to equilibrium supplies and demands. It has *not* been maintained, even in a comparative-statics analysis, that this postulate must always, of necessity, be valid.

7. Optimal Cash Balances

Before leaving our discussion of the theory of money, let us inquire a little more closely into the structure of the demand for money.

Keynes, in his *General Theory*, divides the demand for liquid funds into three categories: that which is desired for transactions purposes (the cash needed to meet foreseen payments like a firm's payments which are required by contract); that for precautionary purposes (cash needed to meet payments whose magnitude is not known in advance); and that to be used for purposes of speculation. Keynes implies that the demand for cash for transactions and precautionary purposes will be rather strongly responsive to changes in expenditure levels, but that these demands will be relatively interest inelastic.[5]

It is, of course, possible to accept this as an assumption or as an impression garnered from observation, but usually, on such a question, the theorist prefers to probe somewhat more deeply. Why should people and firms keep more cash when their expenditures rise? And if there is a reason for their balances to be increased in these circumstances, what determines the amount by which their money holdings should rise? Finally, we may well ask whether interest rates should not also influence *significantly* the magnitudes of these cash holdings. These are all questions of good management. Cash is kept not for its own sake but because it helps the consumer

---

[5] See J. M. Keynes, *The General Theory of Employment, Interest and Money*, Harcourt, Brace & World, Inc., New York, 1936, pp. 196–97.

and the businessman to carry on his activities. The questions to be asked, then, are whether there is some way in which an optimal cash balance can be computed and, if so, how this optimal cash balance figure will be affected by changes in incomes and interest rates. These are obviously important questions for business management, as well as for economic theory.[6]

A firm's cash balance can usually be interpreted as an inventory—an inventory of money which its holder stands ready to exchange against purchases of labor, raw materials, etc. It is really no different in principle from a shoe manufacturer's inventory of footwear which he stands ready to trade for the distributor's cash. The reason for comparing cash on hand with a commodity inventory is that we already possess a body of techniques for determining optimal inventory levels.[7] These techniques can be used to balance off the advantages of a sizable cash balance against its costs.

It is, of course, convenient to keep a sizable cash balance on hand because that can make it so much easier to meet required disbursements, particularly because it is not always possible to foresee in advance the precise magnitudes of required expenditures. But it is expensive to tie up large amounts of capital in the form of cash balances. For that money could otherwise be used profitably elsewhere in the firm, or it could be used to pay off debt and reduce the firm's interest burden, or the money could be invested profitably in securities. When tight money limits the funds which are in practice available to the businessman, he must recognize that every dollar he keeps in the form of cash on hand means one dollar less available for the purchase of labor, raw materials, etc.

To see precisely how the optimum cash inventory computation is handled, let us go directly to the calculation of the optimal level of that portion of a company's cash inventory which is used to meet payments whose magnitude is known in advance. Suppose the company receives $80,000 in cash on the first day of each month which it will pay out in regular daily installments over the next month. Rather than keep all of this cash idle, some of it can be invested in securities, say at a return of 5 per cent. But each time some cash is invested or withdrawn there is a fixed brokerage charge, say $25. The company may then consider the three alternatives shown in Table 1 for a four-week month.

Notice that as the frequency of withdrawals increases, the average investment goes up from 0 to $20,000 to $30,000; thus, the annual interest

---

[6] Much of the analysis which follows is based on my article, "The Transactions Demand for Cash: An Inventory Theoretic Approach," *Quarterly Journal of Economics*, Vol. LXVI, November 1952. See also James Tobin, "The Interest Elasticity of Transactions Demand for Cash," *Review of Economics and Statistics*, Vol. XXXVIII, August 1956.

[7] See the illustrative inventory analysis of Chapter 1 and the list of references at the end of that chapter.

earnings at 5 per cent rise from 0 to $1,000 to $1,500. But in method *A*
there are no brokerage charges. In method *B* there is one investment and
one withdrawal per month, or 24 broker transactions per year, which result

TABLE 1

	Week				Average Investment Holding
	1	2	3	4	
Possibility A: No investment (zero broker transactions per month)					
Investment purchases	0	0	0	0	
Investment holdings	0	0	0	0	0
Withdrawals	0	0	0	0	
Payments	$20,000	$20,000	$20,000	$20,000	
Possibility B: Two broker transactions per month					
Investment purchases	$40,000	0	0	0	
Investment holdings	$40,000	$40,000	0	0	$20,000
Withdrawals	$40,000*	0	$40,000	0	
Payments	$20,000	$20,000	$20,000	$20,000	
Possibility C: Four broker transactions per month					
Investment purchases	$60,000	0	0	0	
Investment holdings	$60,000	$40,000	$20,000	0	$30,000
Withdrawals	$20,000*	$20,000	$20,000	$20,000	
Payments	$20,000	$20,000	$20,000	$20,000	

* This amount is in fact never invested or withdrawn—it represents the amount
withheld from the initial investment.

(at $25 per transaction) in a total brokerage fee of $600. Method *C* requires
four investment and withdrawal transactions per month, or forty-eight
per year, which will cost just $1,200. Thus we have the results shown in
Table 2.

Clearly, method *B* is the more profitable way for the firm to manage its
cash.

More generally, it is possible to show how the optimum balance (inventory) of cash not held in short-term investments will increase when the
volume of transactions or the brokerage fee increases, and decrease when
the interest rate increases. The inventory analysis of Chapter 1 indicates
that these will not be proportionate variations. For example, the optimal
cash balance will increase only as the square root of the volume of transactions—i.e., there will be economies of large scale in the firm's optimal
cash balance.

TABLE 2

	Average Investment	Annual Interest Earning	Broker Trans- actions Per Year	Annual Broker Cost	Net Gain (Interest Minus Broker's Cost)
Method A	0	0	0	0	0
Method B	$20,000	$1,000	24	$ 600	$400
Method C	$30,000	$1,500	48	$1,200	$300

The reasons for this result can be suggested without the aid of mathematics. Most important, it must be noted that a given volume of payments can be met with different cash withdrawal levels. We observed that the $80,000 could be paid by keeping the entire $80,000 on hand, or by investing it and withdrawing $40,000 twice a month, etc. In other words, even when the firm's total payments are fixed, the average cash balance used to meet these payments can be varied. We can see why this amount will vary directly with the value of the brokerage fee and inversely with the interest rate. Clearly, if the brokerage fee goes up, it will pay to cut down the number of withdrawals, i.e., the optimal cash balance will rise. Similarly, if the level of the interest rate goes up, it will pay to make withdrawals as small and as late as possible, i.e., the optimal balance of idle, noninterest-earning cash will fall. In sum, if firms are efficient profit maximizers, Keynes was probably wrong in playing down the influence of the interest rate on the transactions demand for cash.

In addition, we now have a firmer foundation for his view that the demand for cash should increase with the volume of transactions. But why should they not increase proportionately (as Keynes suggests)? That is—why should the most economical cash holding increase relatively less than the volume of expenditures which this cash is used to finance? The answer is to be found in the nature of the cost of investment transactions. The minimum broker's fee is what makes it unprofitable to take cash out of investments in frequent small driblets, although doing so will keep cash invested until the last possible moment. But the larger the amounts involved, the smaller, relatively speaking, will be the brokerage costs. On a $1,000 bond purchase, minimum brokerage fees can be costly. On a million-dollar transaction they are negligible. Hence, the larger the total amounts involved, the less significant will be the brokerage costs, and the more frequent will be optimal withdrawals. For this reason optimal withdrawals and cash balances will rise when the volume of transactions per firm increases, but will rise less than in proportion with the volume of transactions payments.

For expository simplicity, this discussion has assumed that any reduction in cash holdings is used to purchase short-term securities. In practice, tight money means that frequently funds can more profitably be invested inside the firm. This does not alter the nature of the analysis in any fundamental way. The same methods can be employed to take this fact into account in determining the way in which the firm can use cash most effectively and most economically.

It is also interesting to note, without any attempt at explanation, that on not entirely implausible assumptions, somewhat similar results can be derived for the precautionary demand for cash, though the method of analysis is considerably different from that which has just been described.

Some final remarks are appropriate to tie in the discussion of this section with the rest of the chapter. We have seen throughout the general equilibrium discussion how large a role was played by the demand for cash balances. Now, with the aid of inventory analysis we have been able to make some deductions about the nature of that demand.

In particular, we can now say something about the relationship between changes in the price level and the demand for cash balances. Suppose prices rise by 37 per cent; will people end up demanding 37 per cent more money as is so often assumed in the general equilibrium discussions? Our inventory model tells us that (if the pattern of the cash-holders' purchases does not change)[8] they will—that optimal cash balances will increase in precisely the same proportion as the price level. If price level goes up by this percentage, the money value of the buyer's transactions will clearly also rise by 37 per cent, and this might lead us to suspect that the demand for cash will rise by only a smaller proportion. But a uniform rise in prices means that brokerage fees will also rise by 37 per cent so that larger cash balances will become desirable in order to avoid investments and withdrawals and the brokerage costs which they incur. The two effects together—that of the increased money value of transactions and that of the increased brokerage fee—can easily be shown to lead to a rise in the optimal demand for cash in precise proportion with a change in the price level.[9]

---

[8] This implies either that full equilibrium has been achieved or that the real balance effect can, for present purposes, be ignored.

[9] To prove this the reader need merely glance at the final expression for the optimal inventory in Section 6 of Chapter 1. This result states that

$$D = \sqrt{\frac{2a^*Q^*}{k^*}} \, .$$

In terms of the current discussion we can interpret D (or, rather, $D/2$) as the optimal average cash inventory, Q^* as the volume of transactions (payments to be met), k^* as

REFERENCES

Becker, Gary S., and William J. Baumol, "The Classical Monetary Theory: The Outcome of the Discussion," *Economica*, Vol. XIX, November 1952.

Gurley, J. G., and E. S. Shaw, *Money in a Theory of Finance*, The Brookings Institution, Washington, D.C., 1960.

Hicks, J. R., *Value and Capital*, 2nd edition, Oxford University Press, New York, 2nd edition, 1946, Chapters IV and XX.

Lange, Oskar, *Price Flexibility and Employment*, Cowles Commission Monograph No. 8, Principia Press, Bloomington, Ind., 1944.

Leijonhufvud, Axel, *On Keynesian Economics and the Economics of Keynes*, Oxford University Press, London, 1968.

Malinvaud, Edmond, *Lectures on Microeconomic Theory*, North-Holland Publishing Company, Amsterdam, 1972. (Somewhat advanced.)

Orr, Daniel, *Cash Management and the Demand for Money*, Praeger Publishers, New York, 1971.

Patinkin, Don, *Money Interest and Prices*, Harper & Row, Publishers, Inc., New York, 2nd edition, 1965.

Walras, Léon, *Elements of Pure Economics* (trans. and ed. by William Jaffé), Richard D. Irwin, Inc., Homewood, Ill., 1954.

---

the interest cost of carrying cash (the interest rate), and a^* as the brokerage fee (reorder cost). Then, if brokerage fee and the volume of transactions are each increased by a factor of W (each rises to W times its former level), the expression under the square root sign then rises by W^2 so that the optimal cash balance also goes up to exactly $\sqrt{W^2} = W$ times its initial level.

General Equilibrium
and Welfare Economics

21

Welfare economics is the branch of economic theory which has investigated the nature of the policy recommendations that the economist is entitled to make. Its literature has mostly discussed two types of subject: (1) the fundamental but quasi-philosophical problems involved in distinguishing a "legitimate" from an "illegitimate" recommendation and (2) the construction of a theoretical framework which can be applied to some actual policy problems. We shall be concerned primarily with the latter, leaving the first, more methodological problem until the end of the chapter.

1. Resource Allocation and General Equilibrium

Welfare economics has concerned itself mostly with policy issues which arise out of the allocation of resources—with the distribution of inputs among the various commodities and the distribution of commodities among the various consumers.

This is a general equilibrium problem because if resources are moved into one industry, they must presumably be taken out of another, and the interrelationships of the two industries constitute the heart of the matter. The problem of determining the optimal outputs of the various commodities produced in the economy arises only because the quantities of all resources are limited. In such circumstances, it is no answer to say that more of any commodity is a good thing. If we produce more guns, there will be less farm labor available to produce butter. It may be highly undesirable to increase the output of product a because the required concomitant decrease in product b is (on some criterion) more valuable. The optimal allocation of resources between the two items is a matter of the relative urgency of the demands for them and their relative costs of production. No product's optimal output level can therefore be determined in isolation but only in a comparison with other commodities with which it competes for society's limited resources. This is the basis for the conclusion that, at least in principle, resource allocation is necessarily a matter for general equilibrium analysis.

2. The Maximands: Consumers' and Producers' Surplus

Before getting to the specific criteria of optimality that have been derived by welfare economists, we must first ask what is meant by optimality of resource allocation—what it is that society can be taken to be maximizing. Here we are not concerned with the matter as a philosophical issue—that aspect of the subject will be touched on later in the chapter. Rather, the issue is operational. As elsewhere in microeconomics, optimization is taken to denote maximization of the value of some objective function. In the conventional theory of the consumer that maximand is the utility function. In the conventional theory of the firm it is the profit function. What can we use for the purpose in dealing with the welfare of the entire community?

Whatever their shortcomings, two approaches have so far proved most fruitful. One involves maximization of consumers' and producers' surpluses, and the other is the approach which can be described as Pareto optimality. These will be discussed in turn in this and the following section.

The notion of consumers' surplus always seems on a superficial view to involve a bit of flimflam. The idea is that every consumer gets out of each transaction something more than he pays for the item he purchases. This *must* be so because no one forces him to make a purchase.[1] If he were to end up with no net benefit, he would not bother to make that purchase. This is the secret of the mutual gains from trade which even Marx was at pains to emphasize.[2] In a voluntary trade both parties must end up with a net gain even though their total holdings after the trade must be exactly as much as they held between them before. The explanation of this bit of

---

[1] One may be tempted to argue that one is forced to buy food no matter what its cost. But that is equivalent to saying that since it preserves the lives of the members of our family it is priceless and certainly worth more to us than the price we pay for it *no matter how exorbitant we may consider that price.*

[2] See *Capital*, Volume I, Charles H. Kerr and Co., Chicago 1906, p. 175.

magic, of course, is that each has obtained from the other something *he* valued more in exchange for something he valued less—I traded some milk which I do not like for some cheese which I find delicious. Since we have the opposite tastes, we both obtained a surplus from the transaction.

Thus, the notion that each consumer obtains a surplus from each voluntary transaction involves no moral judgment about the desirability or fairness of the prices that are charged or the generosity (or rapacity) of the seller. It merely is an observation about the nature of voluntary participation in economic transactions.

Since in the last analysis all economic activity involves giving up something (money or physical inputs) in exchange for something else, it seems an appropriate objective to maximize the sum of the *net* gains, i.e., the surpluses obtained from consumption and production. The problem is, how does one measure these net gains? Consumers' surplus is the economist's answer to that question, one which often permits him to make actual numerical estimates in practice.

Jules Dupuit, who is credited with the invention of the concept,[3] proposed that one measure the net benefit in *monetary units* and that one use as the measure of consumers' surplus the area between the demand curve and the horizontal line indicating the price paid for the commodity. The reason is simply this: since consumer equilibrium requires the consumer to equate the price of a commodity with its marginal utility (measured in money),[4] the demand curve for commodity i becomes a curve of marginal utility of that good. In terms of Figure 1a, since quantity x_a will be bought at price p_a, the marginal utility of X at quantity x_a must be $x_aA = p_a$. The total utility of that quantity of X must therefore be the area under the curve between the origin and x_a, i.e., it must equal Ox_aAD, for it must be the sum of the marginal utility rectangles such as those marked B, C, and D, representing, respectively, the marginal utility of the first, second, and third units of X. The amount the consumer pays if he purchases x_a is price times quantity, i.e., the rectangle Ox_aAp_a. The consumers' surplus from this purchase is the difference between these two

---

[3] J. Dupuit, "On the Measurement of the Utility of Public Works" (1844), translation in K. J. Arrow and T. Scitovsky (eds.), *Readings in Welfare Economics* (American Economic Association), Vol. XII, Richard D. Irwin, Inc., Homewood, Ill., 1969.

[4] Strictly speaking, the equilibrium requirement is $p_i/p_m = mu_i/mu_m$, where p_i is the price of good i, p_m is the price of money, and mu_i/mu_m is the marginal rate of substitution of money for good i; that is, it tells us how much money the consumer is willing to give up for an additional unit of i. But since the price of money is unity (how many dollars exchange for a unit of U.S. currency?), we have $p_m = 1$, and the preceding equation becomes $p_i = mu_i/mu_m =$ marginal utility of i measured in money.

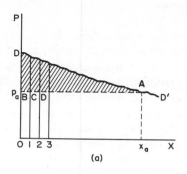

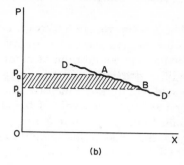

(a)

(b)

Figure 1

areas, i.e., the difference between the money value of the total utility of his purchase and the money he actually pays for it. It is therefore represented by[5] the roughly triangular area, $p_a A D$.

The preceding measure of consumers' surplus offers a great advantage in application. One can often at least approximate its magnitude empirically. Where a reliable econometric estimate of the demand curve is available one can measure its area, thereby obtaining a calculation of consumers' surplus.

Even if one does not know the *entire* demand curve, one can determine a great deal from a partial knowledge of its shape. For example (Figure 1b), by knowing only the segment of the demand curve that is shown, one can evaluate the gain to consumers of an innovation that permits price to fall from p_a to p_b. That gain will be indicated by the resulting expansion in the area representing consumers' surplus, which is represented by $p_b B A p_a$.

There are some theoretical objections to this procedure which are potentially significant but which, fortunately, seem likely to be unimportant in many cases. We have measured total utility and, hence, surplus in money terms. But at different points of the demand curve the consumer will be left with different amounts of money, and so the value (marginal utility) of money to him will have changed. We are back at the rubber-yardstick problem.[6]

---

[5] Similarly, producers' surplus is the difference between total revenue from his output, minus the area under his marginal cost curve. Under pure competition, the producers' surplus is captured by the landlord in the form of rent (see Chapter 24). That is how it is possible to have a producers' surplus and yet zero profit in competitive equilibrium.

[6] We can get rid of the problem in theory by keeping the consumer's real income constant so that its value to him does not change. In this case we have eliminated the income effect and our demand curve becomes a *compensated* demand curve (Chapter 9, Section 15). Consumers' surplus *can* be measured as the area under this compensated demand curve, but, unfortunately, we have no way of observing this compensated curve statistically.

The issue is brought out by an indifference diagram which also illustrates some alternative ways of measuring consumers' surplus. In Figure 2 the consumer is in equilibrium at point a, where his budget line pp' is tangent to indifference curve, I. If he were not permitted to buy the commodity, he would end up at point p (with Op dollars and zero units of good X) on lower indifference curve J. Obviously, a quantity of money sufficient to get him from lower curve J to higher curve I is a measure of consumers' surplus. But what is this amount? Is it quantity of money pc on the vertical axis? Or the length ba above x_a? Or the vertical distance between the two indifference curves at some intermediate location? These will not all be the same unless the indifference curves are parallel throughout. The point is that the amount of money that constitutes a given gain in utility to the consumer varies with the amount of money (and X) in his possession, and so there is no one correct *money* measure of the net benefit he gets from his purchase of X, and hence there is no one correct consumers' surplus figure. Only if the variation in the money measure is small, i.e., if the indifference curves are nearly parallel, can one calculate the consumers' surplus from a demand curve with any degree of confidence.[7]

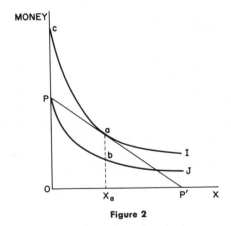

Figure 2

[7] Robert Willig of Bell Laboratories in his important work on the subject has designed operational criteria which permit the analyst to judge from observed data how large the error in a consumers' surplus can be in any particular case. Moreover, he concludes "... it is clear that in most applications the error of approximation will be very small. In fact, the error will often be overshadowed by the errors involved in estimating the demand curve." R. D. Willig, "Consumers Surplus Without Apology," *American Economic Review*, Vol. 65, 1976.

3. Pareto Optimality and Productive Efficiency

An alternative approach to the choice of social maximand which has proved very fruitful analytically is associated with the work of Vilfredo Pareto. Again leaving its underlying philosophy to a later section, we will discuss it here only as an operational concept. Taking the objective of society to be in some sense the maximization of the welfare of *all* of its members we run at once into an intractable problem. We simply cannot add up the utilities of different individuals, any more than we can add up its production of salami and its output of brandy. Even if we were to know how to measure absolute pleasure (utility) for each individual (which ordinalists deny), we certainly would not know how to compare 4 units of individual a's utility with 6 units of utility for b.

A similar problem obviously arises in the aggregation of consumers' surplus for different individuals. Even though consumers' surplus is measured in a unit that is ostensibly common, i.e., money, it is apparent that a dollar means different things to different individuals. We may not know how to *prove* that $10 is worth more to a poor man than it is to a wealthy vice president of the United States, but few of us would be prepared to deny it. Therefore we are hardly comfortable in arguing that a given proposal is socially desirable even though it reduces the poor person's consumer surplus by $8 because it increases the wealthy individual's surplus by $12, for is this really a net gain of $4? One can, of course, assign different weights to different individuals in the process of aggregating consumers' surplus, but how such weights should be chosen is not quite clear.

The welfare economist therefore retreats to a second line of argument which does not offer us the possibility of measurement that a consumers' surplus approach often provides, but it does often yield significant results nevertheless. This alternative approach asserts that, at the very least, a social optimum must not succumb to the error of the dog in the manger— that is, at the very least, a maximum must offer everything to any one individual that it can provide him *without harming anyone else*. More concretely, a very weak requirement for optimality is that selecting any one member of society arbitrarily (call him individual 1) his utility, u_1, should be made as large as possible while making sure that there is no loss in the utility $u_2, \cdots, u_m$ of any other one of the m persons in the community.

This approach, which is referred to as *Pareto optimality*, then treats social optimality as a problem in *constrained* maximization, with the utility of some one person maximized and each other person's utility function serving as a constraint. That is,

Definition: Pareto optimality: Letting x_{ij} be the quantity of commodity i consumed by individual j, and letting that person's utility function be $u_j = f^j(x_{1j}, \cdots, x_{nj})$, *Pareto optimality* requires that society maximize the utility of some arbitrarily selected individual, i.e., that it

$$\text{maximize } u_1 = f^1(x_{11}, \cdots, x_{n1})$$

subject to the requirement[8] that there be no loss in the utility of any other individual $2, \cdots, m$

$$u_2 = f^2(x_{12}, \cdots, x_{n2}) = k_2$$

$$\cdots\cdots\cdots\cdots\cdots\cdots$$

$$u_m = f^m(x_{1m}, \cdots, x_{nm}) = k_m.$$

In the next section we will see what sorts of results can be obtained from such a formulation. First we pause briefly to illustrate the flexibility of the approach by noting how it can be adapted to other problems. For example, since we can no more add up the outputs of different commodities than we can add the utility of different individuals, we adopt an analogous approach to productive efficiency:

Definition: Productive efficiency: Let $y_i = g^i(r_{1i}, \cdots, r_{wi})$ be the output of any commodity i using the quantity r_{ki} of input k, etc. Then efficiency requires (for commodity 1, any arbitrarily selected commodity) that we

$$\text{maximize } y_1 = g^1(r_{11}, \cdots, r_{w1})$$

subject to the requirement that there be no reduction in any other output

$$y_2 = g^2(r_{12}, \cdots, r_{w2}) = c_2$$

$$\cdots\cdots\cdots\cdots\cdots\cdots$$

$$y_n = g^n(r_{1n}, \cdots, r_{wn}) = c_n$$

---

[8] Actually it is appropriate to write the constraints as inequalities

$$u_j = f^j(x_{1j}, \cdots, x_{nj}) \geq k_j$$

since there obviously is no objection to a *beneficial* change in j's utility. This requires the use of Kuhn-Tucker methods rather than the standard Lagrangian techniques of the differential calculus, and so we use the equality forms of the constraints as an expository simplification.

and the constraints given by the available quantity of each input

$$r_{11} + \cdots + r_{1n} = r_1 \qquad \text{(total amount of input 1 in the economy)}$$
$$\cdots \cdots \cdots \cdots \cdots \cdots \cdots$$
$$r_{w1} + \cdots + r_{wn} = r_w \qquad \text{(total amount of input } w \text{ in the economy).}$$

It should be noted that to be Pareto optimal an allocation of resources must be efficient. For if it were not efficient, it would be possible to increase output 1 without a loss in any other output. Hence, if there is at least one individual in the economy who prefers more of item 1, it is possible to benefit that individual without harming anyone else by giving him the increased output of commodity 1. Thus, the initial situation cannot have been Pareto optimal.

In sum, efficiency is necessary for Pareto optimality since the absence of the former means that society has not taken advantage of every opportunity to benefit one person without harming others. However, the converse proposition is *not* valid. An allocation of resources may be efficient and yet not Pareto optimal. This is obviously so because society can turn out combinations of goods which are not ideally suited to the tastes of the individuals in the community and yet it can be efficient in the way it produces that nonoptimal combination. In a world of coffee drinkers it would not be Pareto optimal to produce lots of tea and no coffee, and yet that does not preclude efficiency in the production of tea!

Obviously, Pareto optimality analysis sidesteps the issue of income distribution. Economists tried various approaches, none of them fully satisfactory, to the problem of income distribution.[9] But the marginal optimality rules, which generally rest on a Paretian foundation, themselves have benefitted little from this discussion. They remain either silent or prejudiced in favor of the *status quo* on the issue of income distribution and are, therefore, necessarily incomplete or unsatisfactory even on matters for which distribution is not the primary issue. Ultimately, the Paretian approach can be considered the welfare economists' instrument *par excellence* for the circumvention of this issue.

4. Optimal Distribution of Products Among Consumers[10]

Given the amounts of the various goods which have been produced, how can these commodities best be divided up among the members of the

---

[9] For a review of the available analysis, see Amartya Sen, *On Economic Inequality*, Oxford University Press, Inc., New York, 1973.

[10] For an excellent alternative discussion of the materials of the next few sections see F. M. Bator, "The Simple Analytics of Welfare Maximization," *American Economic Review*, Vol. 47, March 1957.

consuming public? It would seem that this problem runs us right into insuperable problems involved in deciding who deserves what. But we can avoid this issue and yet arrive at

Proposition 1. Pareto optimal allocation of goods among consumers: For any two products X and Y and any two consumers 1 and 2, consumer 1's marginal rate of substitution of X for Y must be the same as that of consumer 2; that is, to both consumers the ratio of the marginal utilities of the two products must be the same.[11]

To show why this must be so, we note that if the condition were violated so that an additional unit of X were not worth the same number of units of Y to both consumers (unequal marginal rates of substitution), they could both benefit by a simple exchange. Suppose that to consumer 1

---

[11] *Proof:* Using the model of Pareto optimality described in Section 3, we see how far we can increase the utility, $u_1 = f^1(x_1, y_1)$, of, say, the first consumer without reducing the utility, $u_2 = f^2(x_2, y_2)$, of the other, using any arbitrary utility index consistent with the preferences of the two consumers. Here x_1 is the amount of X in the hands of the first consumer, y_2 is the amount of Y which the second consumer possesses, etc. Our task, then, is to

$$\text{maximize } u_1 = f^1(x_1, y_1)$$

subject to

$$f^2(x_2, y_2) = k_2^* \quad \text{(a constant)}, \quad \text{i.e., the second consumer must not be hurt, and}$$

$$\left.\begin{array}{l} x_1 + x_2 = X^* \\ y_1 + y_2 = Y^* \end{array}\right\} \quad \text{i.e., the total available amounts of } X \text{ and } Y \text{ are fixed.}$$

To find this maximum we form the Lagrangian expression (Chapter 4, Section 8)

$$u_\lambda = f^1(x_1, y_1) + \lambda_a[f^2(x_2, y_2) - k_2^*] + \lambda_b(x_1 + x_2 - X^*) + \lambda_c(y_1 + y_2 - Y^*).$$

Differentiating partially in turn with respect to x_1, x_2, y_1, and y_2 and setting each of the results equal to zero we obtain

$$\frac{\partial u_\lambda}{\partial x_1} = \frac{\partial f^1}{\partial x_1} + \lambda_b = 0, \qquad \frac{\partial u_\lambda}{\partial x_2} = \lambda_a \frac{\partial f^2}{\partial x_2} + \lambda_b = 0$$

$$\frac{\partial u_\lambda}{\partial y_1} = \frac{\partial f^1}{\partial y_1} + \lambda_c = 0, \qquad \frac{\partial u_\lambda}{\partial y_2} = \lambda_a \frac{\partial f^2}{\partial y_2} + \lambda_c = 0.$$

Now we know $\partial f^1/\partial x_1 = mu_{x1}$ (the marginal utility of X to individual 1, etc.), and solving the preceding equations for these marginal utilities we obtain

$$mu_{x1} = -\lambda_b; \qquad mu_{y1} = -\lambda_c; \qquad mu_{x2} = -\lambda_b/\lambda_a; \qquad mu_{y2} = -\lambda_c/\lambda_a.$$

Thus by straightforward division

$$\frac{mu_{x1}}{mu_{y1}} = \frac{mu_{x2}}{mu_{y2}} = \frac{\lambda_b}{\lambda_c},$$

which is Proposition 1.

an additional unit of X has the same utility as 1.7 additional units of Y, whereas to consumer 2 the marginal unit of X is worth 1.9 additional units of Y. If they trade, consumer 1 giving a unit of good X to 2 and receiving, say, 1.8 units of Y in exchange, each consumer must consider himself 0.1 units ahead. Each consumer receives a higher utility in exchange for a lower—a clear gain for both parties. This same sort of mutually profitable trade can for the same reasons always be arranged if the conditions of Proposition 1 are violated, so that the distribution of commodities cannot then be optimal because some opportunities to improve the situation remain unused.

The graph of the Pareto optimal solution to the problem of exchange turns out to be the contract curve in the Edgeworth box diagram (Figure 3a). It will be recalled from our discussion of this diagram in Chapter 16, Section 9, that the length of the horizontal axis of the diagram represents the total quantity of X in the hands of both individuals together and that the length of the vertical axis is the total quantity of Y. With the lower left-hand corner serving as the origin for individual 1 and the upper right-hand corner as that for individual 2, any point in the diagram represents a distribution of the total X and Y between the two persons. If some point, A, represents the initial pretrade distribution of the goods between the two individuals, a trade is represented by a move to another point in the diagram. Any move from A to a point such as E in the shaded region must represent an improvement to both parties since it puts each one on a higher indifference curve relative to his origin.

A Pareto optimal solution is represented by any point on the contract curve, CC', which is the locus of points of tangency, T, between indifference curves of the two persons. It is clear that these are the points that satisfy Proposition 1, since at any such point the slopes of 1's and 2's indifference

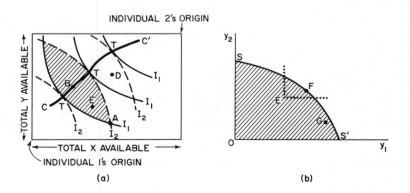

(a)   (b)

Figure 3

curves must be equal; i.e., their marginal rates of substitution between the two goods must be the same. We see at once why any point such as B on CC' must be Pareto optimal and why any point such as A off CC' is not. For we have seen that any move from A anywhere into the shaded area is mutually beneficial and hence A is not Pareto optimal (it does not provide the maximal benefits available to 1 without harming 2). On the other hand, *any* move from a point on the contract curve must put at least one person on a lower indifference curve. Thus B is Pareto optimal because it permits no change which benefits one party without harming the other.

We conclude

(a) That there is never just one Pareto optimal solution; indeed, there is generally an infinity of Pareto optima, each given by a different point in the diagram, i.e., each representing a different distribution of benefits between the two persons;

(b) We are not entitled to conclude that every Pareto optimal solution is better than every nonoptimal solution. For example, we cannot compare, with the aid of the Pareto optimality analysis alone, the Pareto optimal point B with the nonoptimal point D since while individual 2 prefers the former, individual 1 prefers the latter. So without an explicit interpersonal comparison we simply cannot judge the relative desirability of the two distributions represented by the two solutions.

Proposition 1 consequently tells us something about how commodities should be distributed among individuals *without saying anything about how income should be distributed among them*! It does this by telling the consumers that they should end up somewhere on the contract curve but dodging the important problem of their optimal location on the contract curve. The rule avoids talking about distribution by committing itself to little more than the apparently trivial assertion that if you have a bottle of whiskey (which you dislike) and I have a fifth of gin (which I detest), why—let's swap! However, the result should not be scorned. Many a sage has missed this apparently simple point and argued that whatever one of the traders gains he must have taken away from the other, so that there can be no net advantage from trade. Moreover, out of such apparently trivial statements are formed the axiom systems on which powerful theories are built and important insights gained. We shall see presently how the weak result of this section can be used as a basis for some conclusions about the design of a rationing system.

5. Optimal Use of Resouces in Producing Given Outputs

We come now by a completely analogous argument to a second marginal rule for social optimality:

Proposition 2. Productive efficiency in the allocation of several inputs: An efficient use of any two inputs i and j, in the production of outputs X and Y, requires that

$$mp_{ix}/mp_{jx} = mp_{iy}/mp_{jy};$$

i.e., it requires that the ratio of the marginal physical products of i and j in the production of X be the same as the corresponding ratio for commodity Y.

This is so because if equality does not hold, say if the first fraction is larger, i will be relatively more efficient in producing X than is j (i will have a *comparative* advantage in X production), and it will pay to shift some of input i into X production and out of Y production and to shift some of j the other way, from X to Y. The argument is precisely analogous with that involved in the preceding marginal rule. Suppose (as an illustration) we have the figures

$$mp_{ix} = 20, \quad mp_{jx} = 8, \quad mp_{iy} = 4, \quad \text{and} \quad mp_{jy} = 2$$

so that, as the reader can verify, the left-hand fraction in Proposition 2 is the larger of the two. Now move one unit of i out of Y production and into the manufacturing of X so that the output of Y decreases by four units. Next, move enough input j in the other direction *to keep the output of Y on the same level as it was originally*; i.e., move two units of j into Y production (where each unit produces two units of Y) so that the output of Y goes up by $2 \times 2 = 4$ units, back to its old level. The result is a net increase in the output of X (with the output of Y remaining unchanged), for X's output has first been raised $(\Delta i)(mp_{ix})$ units $= 1 \times 20 = 20$ units and then been decreased by $(\Delta j)(mp_{jx}) = 2 \times 8 = 16$ units, leaving a net gain of four units. The reader can try other illustrative figures and see that they always yield similar results.[12] Moreover, we can instead keep the output of commodity x unchanged and increase that of y or obtain smaller increases in both outputs.

The upshot is that if this last marginal equation is violated, a switching around of inputs can give us something for nothing—it can increase one or both outputs without any increase in input use! Hence, because there are such unused opportunities, the input cannot possibly be optimally em-

---

[12] The mathematical proof of this theorem is virtually the same as that in footnote 11. The relevant maximand and the constraints were described in the discussion of productive efficiency in Section 3. From these the reader can form the Lagrangian expression for this constrained maximization problem and complete the proof of Proposition 2 by direct analogy with footnote 11.

ployed when this last equation is violated. Where the marginal analysis is applicable, production is therefore said to be *inefficient* when this equation does not hold and *efficient* if the equation is satisfied (along with the second-order conditions).

The diagrammatic representation of the analysis can again be expressed in terms of the box diagram with the axes indicating the total input quantities available and the indifference curves interpreted as iso-product loci. The contract curve is, this time, the locus of efficient points. The matter can also be represented in terms of the production possibility locus (Figure 3b). Let the points in the shaded region represent every combination of outputs that can be produced with the available combination of inputs. Then every point such as *E* that is inside the region is *inefficient* since it is possible to move from it to a point such as *F* at which more of each output is available. The northeast boundary of the region, curve *SS'*, is the locus of *efficient* points. Again note that there is an infinity of efficient points and that one cannot say that every efficient point is preferable to every inefficient point. For example, we cannot rank *F* and *G* from the information at our disposal in this discussion.

6. Marginal Rule for Pareto Optimal Output Levels

We come now to what is perhaps the most important and most controversial of the marginal rules of welfare economics. This is the rule which tells us how much coffee and how much salami should be produced with society's scarce resources.

The allocation of a limited quantity of resources among alternative outputs is dealt with by the following optimality rule, which is closely related to the one we have just discussed:

Proposition 3. Optimal relative outputs: If resources are to be allocated optimally between any two outputs X and Y, then the marginal rate of substitution between X and Y for every individual $j = 1, 2, \cdots, m$ who consumes some of each good must be equal to the ratio of the marginal (social) costs of production of the two goods. That is, we must have

$$\frac{mu_x^1}{mu_y^1} = \frac{mu_x^2}{mu_y^2} = \cdots = \frac{mu_x^m}{mu_y^m} = \frac{mc_x}{mc_y}.$$

Here marginal cost of X, mc_x, can be interpreted to mean the value of the resources needed to produce an additional unit of X, etc. Note that the equality of the marginal rates of substitution mu_x^j/mu_y^j for all consumers, j, is the requirement of Pareto optimality in the distribution of society's outputs (Proposition 1).

The reasoning underlying Proposition 3 is so close to that behind the previous marginal rules that it need not be repeated. The reader should be able to show that if output levels are such that the equation is violated, total social utility can be increased by an increase in one output together with such a decrease in the other that there is no net change in total social costs (the use of society's resources). So once again, if this equation is violated, society has missed an opportunity to get something (utility) for nothing, and therefore output levels cannot be optimal.

7. An Optimal Price System

Let us temporarily ignore the distinction between *social* and *private* costs and benefits. Then we can state

Proposition 4: Suppose we institute a price system which has the following characteristics:

    1. All inputs and outputs have fixed prices which are the same for every buyer and seller and which no buyer or seller can change.

    2. All quantities supplied are demanded and hence sold, i.e., these are the equilibrium prices of the general equilibrium system.[13]

    3. Any firm can enter (or leave) the production of any commodity at these prices if it finds it profitable to do so.

Then, under these circumstances, if every consumer maximizes his utility and every firm maximizes its profits, *all of the preceding marginal optimality requirements will automatically be satisfied.*

This is a fundamental theorem of welfare economics. It is a refined version of the invisible hand proposition, and the reader would do well to convince himself how very remarkable it is.

Outline of proof that Proposition 1 must hold under such a price system: We know (Chapter 9, Section 5) that if prices are fixed, each consumer will, if he behaves optimally, buy any two commodities X and Y in such amounts that for him the marginal rate of substitution of X for Y is equal to the ratio of the prices of the two items. Since these prices are the same for all consumers by characteristic (1) of our price system,

---

[13] Here we have to ignore free goods and goods which are a drug on the market. Not all the water near a large lake will find buyers, and desert land in the middle of the Sahara is likely to go begging for customers. This skips over the problem of deciding which goods will be free, for that cannot be known in advance. Whether or not some item will be unwanted depends on how much money customers have left over from their other purchases. See Chapter 23, Section 5.

the marginal rates of substitution of X for Y must be the same for all consumers, as Proposition 1 requires. Note that this result follows with *any* fixed prices, no matter how arbitrarily or randomly they are selected.

Proposition 2 must be satisfied for exactly the same reason. As is shown in Chapter 11, if its input and output prices are fixed, it will pay a firm to hire any two inputs, i and k, in such proportions that the ratio of their prices equals the ratio of their marginal products. Proposition 2 follows at once, since for any two firms, one of which uses the two inputs to produce X and the other to produce Y, we must have $mp_{ix}/mp_{kx} = p_i/p_k = mp_{iy}/mp_{ky}$. Again, it is remarkable that this result holds with *any* arbitrarily chosen prices!

Proposition 3 is considerably more difficult to derive, and the argument will only be sketched in. In outline, the argument consists of showing that every industry will expand each of its outputs to a point where the ratio of their marginal costs is equal to the ratio of their prices. Moreover, all consumers will determine their purchases to a point where the marginal rates of substitution are equal to the products' price ratios. Marginal cost ratios and marginal rates of substitution will therefore all be equal to the same price ratio and, therefore, equal to each other, as Proposition 3 requires.

The pricing arrangement of Proposition 4 does its job because it provides the right signals to producers and consumers. For example, its relative prices are set equal to relative marginal costs (i.e., costs to society in terms of its resources). Thus, when the consumer divides up his budget in such a way as to get the most from his own money resources he also automatically makes the decisions that get the most out of society's resources. He will not be induced to consume a set of items that gives him no more pleasure than another but which requires twice as large a quantity of resources to produce. A similar argument shows that these prices provide the correct financial signals to producers.

However, the consumer side of the argument still suffers from a fundamental weakness arising out of the issue of income distribution. In effect, this procedure tells us to determine the allocation of resources on the basis of the marginal rates of substitution of the different consumers as indicated by their expenditures. This has been compared to an election in which some voters get to vote many times—where each dollar the consumer has to spend entitles him to another vote so that the wealthy can exercise an influence proportioned to the magnitude of their wealth. We decide that an optimal allocation of resources requires us to produce more marmalade for Ellen rather than more jam for Daniel if Ellen can afford to pay for it and Daniel cannot. Thus, in this interpretation of Proposition 3 we have not avoided committing ourselves on the question of a good distribution of wealth—rather we have, by default, decided to accept the *status quo*.

8. Pure Competition and Monopoly

Using Proposition 4, which states that the price system of the preceding section guarantees the satisfaction of the marginal optimality rules, we can at once deduce several of the best-known results of welfare economics.

First, there is

Proposition 5: Perfect or pure competition will tend to yield an optimal allocation of resources.

Under pure competitive equilibrium prices are fixed as far as any individual consumer or businessman is concerned; supplies and demands are all equal, and, in the long run, all firms which can produce any product profitably will enter that industry. Thus all three requirements of the price system of the preceding section will be met by a pure-competition equilibrium, which must therefore satisfy all of the marginal requirements for an optimal allocation of resources. Hence, there is a presumption that under pure competition the allocation of resources will be optimal.[14] This result and the material of the two previous sections constitute the elaborate superstructure which has been superimposed on the old commonsense notion that competition is a good thing because it prevents monopolistic exploitation of consumers and labor. However, one may well wonder whether the commonsense notion is still not more persuasive than its highly subtle and ingenious rationalization.

The nature of the theoretical argument is brought out intuitively by contrasting the world of pure competition with one in which there are a few monopolistic industries. Since the price of the product falls as output expands, a monopoly will produce an output which is smaller than that of an otherwise identical competitive industry (unless there are very extreme economies of large-scale production), as was shown in Section 5 of Chapter 16. This means that, given the total level of the employment, less resources will be used in the manufacture of monopolistically produced outputs and more of these resources will go into the remaining industries than would have been the case in an economy where pure competition was universal. Too little will be produced by the monopolies and too much by the com-

---

[14] Actually this is no more than a presumption, and there remain a number of flies in the competitive ointment. We know that any optimal allocation to which marginal analysis is applicable must satisfy these marginal rules, but the converse is not necessarily true—an allocation may satisfy these rules yet not be optimal. There are two specific and important sources of possible difficulty: The second-order conditions (see Chapter 4, Section 5) may not be satisfied, and social and private costs and benefits are unlikely to be equal throughout the economy. The second of these problems is discussed in Section 11 of this chapter. For an explicit and extremely lucid discussion of the relevance oi the second-order conditions, see J. de Graaf, *Theoretical Welfare Economics*, Cambridge University Press, New York, 1957, esp. pp. 22–26 and 66–70.

petitive industries. Resources will be overallocated to competitively produced commodities and monopolistic output restricted—to the social detriment.

However, the reader should observe that the argument breaks down in a world of monopolies where there are no industries operating under a regime of competition. Given the level of employment of resources, a misallocation can arise only if the demand for inputs of one set of industries (the monopolists) is low *in comparison with* that of the remaining industries. If each of a number of runners slows down, none of them need come in ahead of the others, and if each industry is weak in its bidding for resources, no lopsided allocation of these resources need result. We see, then, that some competition may conceivably be worse than none![15]

9. Centralized Planning Without Central Direction

The theorem about the optimality results which can be achieved with the aid of the pricing system of Section 8 has had yet another application—to the economies of socialism and central planning. A number of theorists have argued that government planning does not have to involve elaborate controls and instructions, such as factory-by-factory production targets.[16] The central authority need only compute a set of prices which satisfies the three conditions described in Section 8 and order factory managers to maximize their profits (profit maximization, too, could be made more or less automatic by basing managerial wages on the profits shown by the plants which they run). The result would then be automatic—a self-policing system for the achievement of an optimal allocation of resources. One would achieve the alleged economic benefits of central direction without the costly administrative burden and unpleasant bureaucratic interference which goes with detailed central supervision.

The "socialism by price guidance" proposal has come to be known by one of its characteristics, *marginal cost pricing*. Every firm would be forced to sell as much as it produced and to sell this output at a price equal to its marginal cost. This is the essence of the pricing arrangement.

The idea is attractive, but it encounters a number of important difficulties. Perhaps the most important is that the equilibrium which results will maximize private rather than social net benefits. If, for example, it is important for the nation, on some criterion, to sacrifice some current consumer welfare for long-run economic growth, the price system of Section 8 does not take these social goals into account. Other problems of differences

---

[15] This is an illustration of the theorem of the second best—Proposition 12, below.

[16] See, e.g., Lerner, *op. cit.*, and Oskar Lange and Fred M. Taylor, *On the Economic Theory of Socialism*, University of Minnesota Press, Minneapolis, 1938.

in social costs and returns will be discussed presently. The upshot is that the proposed pricing system may fail to accomplish one of the main purposes of central planning—the achievement of social goals which are not reflected in private returns.

Another somewhat more technical problem which plagues such a scheme for decentralized control arises if the firm's average costs decrease when the scale of its production increases (increasing returns).[17] If average costs are falling, by the standard rules of the average-marginal relationships (Chapter 3, Section 3), marginal cost must be less than average cost. Therefore, if the firm sells at a unit price equal to *marginal* cost, price must be less than average cost, i.e., unit costs will exceed unit returns so that the firm must lose money on each and every unit it sells! There is nothing the management of such a firm can do to make any profits, no matter how efficient its operations, if it sticks to a marginal cost price. Thus (even though it may sometimes be socially desirable to operate some industries which are unable to produce a profit) marginal cost pricing must, at the very least, lead to serious administrative difficulties in decreasing cost firms.

10. Breakeven Constraints and Optimal Deviations Between Prices and Marginal Costs

The discussion of the preceding section indicates that whatever its desirable properties, marginal cost pricing simply may not be possible for society. If, for example, the preponderance of economic activity were carried out by single-product firms with declining average cost curves, then most industries would either end up losing money or charging prices not equal to marginal costs. Even if every product were sold by firms at its marginal cost and the government were willing to subsidize firms by covering any resulting losses, the problem would not be solved, because the funds for the subsidies must be derived from taxes. Any tax on a commodity (including an income tax, which can be interpreted as a tax on hours worked) must itself introduce a deviation between the price of the product to the consumer and its marginal cost, for the price to the consumer is then equal to the producer's marginal cost *plus* the tax.

The issue, then, is what is the second-best set of prices, given the undeniable fact that production costs must be covered from somewhere? The answer was supplied in 1928 by Frank Ramsey, a Cambridge philosopher, who, unfortunately, died very young. The Ramsey theorem can be expressed in many forms. Two which are most widely recognized can be described as follows: Suppose we are given any two commodities 1 and

---

[17] This problem is closely related to the difficulties which arise when the second-order maximum conditions are not satisfied.

2 whose total cost is $c(y_1, y_2)$, with marginal costs mc_1 and mc_2 and marginal revenues mr_1 and mr_2. Suppose we must meet a budget requirement such as

$$p_1 y_1 + p_2 y_2 = c(y_1, y_2).$$

Then one form of the Ramsey theorem asserts that

Proposition 6a: The Pareto optimal prices p_1 and p_2 of two goods whose outputs are subject to a budget constraint must satisfy

$$p_i - mc_i = \lambda(mr_i - mc_i) \quad \text{or} \quad \frac{p_1 - mc_1}{p_2 - mc_2} = \frac{mr_1 - mc_1}{mr_2 - mc_2}.$$

That is, the optimal deviation between price and marginal cost will be proportionate to the deviation between the marginal revenue and marginal cost of that commodity. A second, and more widely known, form of the theorem asserts

Proposition 6b: If E_1 and E_2 are the elasticities of demand of two goods whose outputs are subject to a budget constraint and all cross elasticities of demand happen to be zero, then Pareto optimality of their pricing requires

$$\frac{p_i - mc_i}{p_i} = \frac{k}{E_i} \quad \text{or} \quad \frac{(p_1 - mc_1)/p_1}{(p_2 - mc_2)/p_2} = \frac{E_2}{E_1}.$$

This form of the theorem, which is known as the inverse elasticity formula, asserts that the optimal *percentage* deviation of the price of any item from its marginal cost $(p_i - mc_i)/p_i$ will vary inversely with the elasticity of demand for that item, E_i.

To understand the logic of this rule we must first consider what it is that is undesirable about a deviation of price and the corresponding marginal cost. Suppose two products A and B have equal prices but A has a marginal cost twice as great as B's. With their prices equal, in equilibrium the individual who buys some of each must obtain just as much marginal utility from a unit of the one as from the other. But in that case, the allocation of resources cannot be Pareto optimal, for since A costs twice as much in resources as B, a net gain can be achieved by shifting some quantity of resources from A to B, producing two units of A for every unit of B given up. Since the two goods have the same marginal benefit to consumers, obviously this change is a net advantage to them, and failure to carry it out is a violation of Pareto optimality. Every deviation of price from marginal cost introduces such a distortion in consumers' demands by leading them to purchase goods in accord with their relative *money* costs, which must then be different from their true *social* costs, i.e., their costs in terms of the resources used up in producing them.

However, where society faces a budget constraint, as we have seen, prices *must* deviate from marginal costs. For example, where marginal cost pricing would yield a deficit because of widespread increasing returns, prices may have to exceed marginal cost to prevent that deficit. But this can be carried out in a variety of ways with prices for different items exceeding their marginal costs by different percentages. The objective of Pareto optimality, now, is to find that set of deviations which meets the budgetary requirement while producing distortion in the allocation of resources no greater than the minimum necessary for the purpose.

To determine what relative prices produce this minimal distortion we must consider relative demand elasticities for society's different outputs. The statement that a product, i, has a highly elastic demand while product k does not means that the former is highly sensitive to a given percentage price change while the latter is not. It follows that if prices must be changed from marginal costs but in a way that produces relatively little distorting effect on demands, then the bulk of the price rise should fall on items whose demands are comparatively *in*elastic. The more inelastic the demand for a good, the less a given percentage change in price from its marginal cost will distort its use from the Pareto optimal level. Thus, to meet the budgetary requirement, prices of items with inelastic demands should deviate from marginal costs by a relatively large percentage, and the reverse should be true for items with elastic demands.

This result has played an important role in the recent literature of welfare theory, of taxation, and of the theory of regulation of public utility rates. In tax theory it is used in an obvious way to discuss optimal tax rates on different commodities given the size of the government's budget. In the theory of regulation it is used to determine Pareto optimal relative prices for the various products of a public utility which meet the budgetary requirement that the firm earn just enough to cover its costs (including a return on its capital) but without giving it any monopoly profit. It can be shown, incidentally, that the theorem automatically calls for prices that are exactly equal to marginal costs where such a pricing policy does just happen to cover total costs.

To outline the proof of the theorem, first recall that for any product, i, consumer equilibrium requires that the marginal utility (measured in money) of that commodity to each individual be equal to its price. Suppose now that we construct an artificial social utility function $u(y_1, \cdots, y_n)$ also measured in money which is designed to have the same property, i.e.,

$$\frac{\partial u}{\partial y_i} = p_i \qquad \text{for all commodities } (i = 1, \cdots, n).$$

We assume that society's objective is to maximize net surplus, which is the difference between this total money utility of its outputs and the (money) cost of the resources used in their production, $c(y_1, \cdots, y_n)$. Then the problem is to

$$\text{maximize } u(y_1, \cdots, y_n) - c(y_1, \cdots, y_n)$$

subject to the budget requirement which characterizes the problem:

$$p_1 y_1 + p_2 y_2 + \cdots + p_n y_n = c(y_1, \cdots, y_n).$$

This yields the Lagrangian function [writing $u(\cdot)$ for $u(y_1, \cdots, y_n)$, etc.]

$$u_\lambda = u(\cdot) - c(\cdot) + \lambda[p_1 y_1 + \cdots + p_n y_n - c(\cdot)].$$

The first-order maximum conditions then include

$$\frac{\partial u_\lambda}{\partial y_1} = \frac{\partial u}{\partial y_1} - \frac{\partial c}{\partial y_1} + \lambda\left(\frac{\partial \sum p_i y_i}{\partial y_1} - \frac{\partial c}{\partial y_1}\right) = 0$$

$$\cdots\cdots\cdots\cdots\cdots\cdots\cdots\cdots\cdots\cdots\cdots\cdots\cdots\cdots$$

$$\frac{\partial u_\lambda}{\partial y_n} = \frac{\partial u}{\partial y_n} - \frac{\partial c}{\partial y_n} + \lambda\left(\frac{\partial \sum p_i y_i}{\partial y_n} - \frac{\partial c}{\partial y_n}\right) = 0.$$

Thus, substituting (for any good k) the consumer's equilibrium condition (which was just reviewed) $p_k = \partial u/\partial y_k$ and noting that by definition $\partial c/\partial y_k = mc_k$ and $\partial \sum p_i y_i/\partial y_k = mr_k$ these equations become

$$p_1 - mc_1 = -\lambda(mr_1 - mc_1)$$

$$\cdots\cdots\cdots\cdots\cdots\cdots\cdots\cdots$$

$$p_n - mc_n = -\lambda(mr_n - mc_n),$$

which immediately gives us the first Ramsey theorem.[18]

---

[18] The second theorem is now also obtained directly by noting that when cross elasticities are zero, for example, $mr_1 = \partial (y_1 p_1 + \cdots + y_n p_n)/\partial y_1 = p_1 + y_1(\partial p_1/\partial y_1) = p_1 - (p_1/E_1)$, where $E_1 = -(p_1/y_1)\partial y_1/\partial p_1 =$ price elasticity of demand. Thus, substituting such expressions for mr_i in the last set of equations in the text they become

$$p_i - mc_i = -\lambda(p_i - mc_i - p_i/E_i)$$

or, collecting terms,

$$(1 + \lambda)(p_i - mc_i)/p_i = \lambda/E_i,$$

which yields our second Ramsey theorem when we write $k = \lambda/(1 + \lambda)$.

11. Beneficial and Detrimental Externalities of Production and Consumption

Much of the discussion of this chapter requires reevaluation when we take into account divergences between private and social costs and returns. The basic idea behind the argument that the competitive price system is optimal is roughly that the businessman (like other members of the economy) can make money only by producing and marketing useful products and services. Hence he benefits only by benefitting the community, and, conversely, by promoting his own interests he necessarily promotes those of the rest of the community as well. Unfortunately, there are many cases where this crucial premise breaks down—when members of the economy do things which benefit others in such a way that they can receive no payment in return, or where their actions are detrimental to others and involve no commensurate cost to themselves. In such cases of divergence between social and private returns, self-interest and social interest do not coincide. This statement must be interpreted carefully—it is not meant to contrast the welfare of individuals with some sort of abstract "social good." Rather, it says that when each person independently pursues his own interests he may end up less well off than he would under an optimal arrangement. Where social and private returns do not coincide, it is possible that all members of society will lose out if each of them does his best to promote his own aims.

Let us see, now, how such divergence between private and social returns are likely to arise and how they can lead to a misallocation of resources. Specifically, let us examine how they affect the theorems of the preceding sections. For this purpose it is convenient to deal, in turn, with four types of divergence between private and social returns: beneficial externalities of production, detrimental externalities of production, and beneficial and detrimental externalities of consumption. It should be noted that *most of these are, in the last analysis, market imperfections*—cases where the market offers no price for the provision of a service or a disservice.

1. *Beneficial externalities of production:* This category of divergence between private and social returns has received a great deal of attention in the literature. The concept was first formulated explicitly by the English economist, Alfred Marshall, at the end of the last century.

The case of economies of large-scale production in which a firm can produce each unit of output more cheaply when it expands can be referred to as a case of *internal* economies—the benefits of the firm's expansion are reaped internally, within the company. By contrast, the *external economies* case is one where an increase in the firm's production produces benefits part (often a substantial part) of which devolve on others.

This may arise in at least two ways: (a) By expanding its operations the firm may perform a direct service to others. The standard example is the training of a labor force. If one glass-blowing firm on the island of

Murano expands its operations, it may have to train more glass-blowers, who are potentially available for employment by its competitors, and those competitors will incur no training costs if they recruit any of those workers.

(b) A second sort of external economy arises when an expansion in the operation of one company makes it cheaper to supply services to all the firms in the industry. A rise in the production of Ford automobiles will result in an increase in steel production. If there are internal economies in steel manufacturing (ordinary economies of large-scale production), steel prices may subsequently fall, and so Ford's competitors also will obtain their raw materials more cheaply as a result of the increased output of Ford cars. In sum, economies which are external to the firm may arise when the expansion of one firm makes it cheaper for all firms in the industry to obtain their inputs.

Both of these types of external benefits of large-scale production clearly involve divergence between private and social returns. The firm's expansion makes it cheaper for other companies to operate, but under the prevailing price system there is no remuneration to the expanding firm for these benefits which it has conferred on others.

2. *Detrimental externalities of production:* An expansion of the scale of a company's operations can also have analogous disadvantageous effects such as pollution and other forms of damage to the environment as an incidental by-product of economic activity. If one company's increased output leads it to keep more trucks in operation, it will crowd the roads and, in particular, make it more expensive and time-consuming for other companies to ship goods by truck. Increased fishing by one group depletes the supply of fish and makes it harder for others to obtain their catch. Increased use of water or more drilling of oil wells can make it harder for others to get these resources. Increased farming of land which erodes the soil very often makes it more difficult for neighbors to produce and maintain the fertility of their territories. There is no need to add still further to these illustrations.[19]

3. *Beneficial and detrimental externalities of consumption:* An increase in consumption can also cause analogous advantages or disadvantages to others—advantages or disadvantages which are not reflected in the returns

---

[19] These are all examples of what are called *technological* externalities—increased output by one enterprise requires the use of larger physical inputs by other firms to produce any given result. A different type of externality which has no such significance for welfare economics is called a *pecuniary* externality. This occurs when one firm, by increasing its output, causes a rise in the price of its inputs. That makes it more expensive *in money terms* for other companies who use similar inputs. But it does not increase the social cost of their production because this production requires no larger input quantities or expenditure of time and effort than before. Increased use of leather by a shoe manufacturer may raise leather prices and hence the money costs of other shoe firms, but it need not make it any harder for them to make shoes.

of the person who produces them. As in the production case, these beneficial and detrimental externalities arise from interdependences which cannot readily be reflected in the pricing arrangements. A affects B's welfare not just by delivering some goods to him and receiving money in return.

For example, where the Smiths try to keep up with the Joneses, if Jones buys a new cream-colored Cadillac convertible, he makes life harder for Smith. Smith must now consume more than he did before in order to accomplish no more than just maintain his old level of satisfaction. Here is a detrimental externality of consumption. On the other hand, if I purchase more education for my children, I make them better citizens (or, at least, so educators would have us believe). This confers an advantage on others—it makes it possible for others to achieve a given level of satisfaction with a smaller expenditure of their own resources. In sum, any increase in consumption which makes the consumer a more efficient or inefficient producer, or any increase in consumption which affects the consumption patterns and desires of other buyers, will produce beneficial or detrimental externalities. If many women purchase more short skirts, they will make those with long hemlines feel increasingly dowdy and less able to resist the pressure to buy short skirts themselves; the fact that a book enters the best-seller lists may help promote its sales, etc.—in each case, any consumer's purchase has had an indirect but very real effect on his fellows.

Here, then, are some of the most significant classes of cases in which social and private returns diverge.[20] Some of the illustrations may not seem to represent cases of great social significance. But one must not conclude that externalities play no major role in the economy. Taken together, they assume very great significance. The fact that a large industrial firm finds it incomparably easier and more profitable to operate in an industrial community than in an underdeveloped area is in large part a result of external economies. The presence of other firms makes it far easier to run a plant— they bring with them a skilled labor force, financial institutions, organizations which can efficiently supply technical services and raw materials, and so on. Indeed, the scarcity of operating firms and the external economies which they provide has often been cited as a major problem of the backward areas—without such an initial group of firms and the external economies of their operations, it is very difficult to get enterprises started. Industry is needed to encourage further industrialization.

On the consumer side, the externalities are also very powerful. The

---

[20] Many other examples can easily be cited. The Piazza San Marco in Venice is the site of a case of an externally conferred benefit which, by overextension, incurs an external social cost. The cafes hire bands to serenade their customers. But, being outdoors, they cannot avoid providing music to the patrons of adjoining bistros. Unfortunately, however, with four or five of these going at once it becomes impossible to hear the music anywhere.

tastes and the demands of consumers are very heavily conditioned by the societies in which they live. Food, clothing, housing, and many other tastes differ from country to country and from region to region, at least partly because the consumption pattern of one consumer is highly dependent on those of other members of society. In sum, the externalities of consumption are by no means negligible.

It remains for us to see how these externalities affect the allocation of resources. The connection is easily suggested. If a firm or an individual makes a contribution to social welfare for which he receives no payment, he is likely to engage in this activity to a smaller extent than the interests of society require. If the production of some commodity confers external benefits, private enterprise may easily produce a less-than-optimal amount of this item. Company A, in deciding whether to expand its output, will not usually be led to do so by the fact that this will make things cheaper for companies B and C.

Similarly, where there are detrimental externalities of production or consumption, private enterprise will perhaps overallocate resources (produce an excessive amount) because part of the cost of the operation is external to the firm—it is borne by others. Notoriously rare is the firm which refrains from expanding its operations because it will increase the pollution of the atmosphere or because it leads to soil erosion or the depletion of a natural resource (such as fish in the sea) which it does not own.

To summarize,

Proposition 7: Externalities can lead to a misallocation of resources even in the world of perfect competition. Too little may be produced by industries in which external benefits prevail, while there may be more than an optimal output of commodities whose production involves detrimental externalities.

In principle, it is even possible that where there are detrimental externalities the presence of monopolies can lead to outputs smaller, and therefore more nearly optimal, than those which would result from competition.[21]

---

[21] Moreover, if any industry is taken over by a monopoly, external economies or diseconomies may sometimes disappear in the process. If the expansion of one firm saves money for another firm in the same industry, this external economy becomes internal when the two firms combine into one—all the benefits accrue to the same management. This also illustrates the danger of decentralized decision-making in a single company—the manager of one division will not always pay adequate attention to the effects of his decisions on other divisions in the company (the effects of his decisions which are external to his division). As a result, a set of decisions which are optimal for the branches of the company, taken by themselves, may be far from optimal for the company as a whole. Cf. Charles Hitch and Roland McKean, "Suboptimization in Operations Prob-

12. "Market Failure" and Public Goods

We have seen that the market mechanism will fail to produce ideal results as the result of at least three influences: monopolistic elements, economies of scale, and externalities. A fourth source of market failure closely associated with the phenomenon of externalities is also important. This is the category of public goods, for which we have the

Definition: A *pure public good* is one which can serve a small or a large number of persons at exactly the same total cost (the marginal cost of an additional user is zero). This characteristic is called *supply jointness* or *undepletability*. In addition, public goods are often taken to be characterized by the impossibility of *exclusion* of anyone from enjoying its benefits once the good has been provided.

Standard examples of public goods are television broadcasts which cost the same whether they have 50 or 5 million viewers and improvement of the quality of the atmosphere since reduced smoke emissions from factories cost the same whether 50 or 5 million nearby residents benefit from the cleaner air. Note that exclusion is virtually out of the question in the second case because you cannot stop anyone from breathing, at least not without committing a felony, while in the broadcasting case exclusion is technically possible—a scrambling device can prevent someone from receiving a broadcast without prior payment.

It is often difficult or impossible for private enterprise to supply a public good profitably, particularly where exclusion is not possible, since if no one can be prevented from using the good, no one can be forced to pay for it. Moreover, from the point of view of consumption decisions, the Pareto optimal price of a pure public good is zero once it has been produced,[22] for since it costs society nothing if another person uses the good, there is a net opportunity loss in inducing anyone to refrain from consuming it because of a price charged for the item. This does not mean that it is desirable socially to produce every public good but merely that once produced their use should be opened to as many people as want to take advantage of them even if the benefit they obtain is very small.

To decide whether a public good should be produced, we must *add together* the benefits to all the people who will consume it and see whether

---

lems," in Joseph F. McCloskey and Florence N. Trefethen (eds.), *Operations Research for Management*, The Johns Hopkins Press, Baltimore, 1954. See also Charles Hitch, "Economics and Military Operations Research," *Review of Economics and Statistics*, Vol. XL, August 1958.

[22] That is, it is zero unless there is a budget constraint to be met. Where such a constraint is present the Ramsey theorem of Section 10 applies.

they are at least equal to the cost. We can measure individual j's marginal benefits from public good X in terms of the money j is willing to give up for it, that is, in terms of j's marginal rate of substitution between X and money (commodity N), mu_x^j/mu_n^j. Then the sum of the marginal benefits to all m individuals in the community will be $mu_x^1/mu_n^1 + mu_x^2/mu_n^2 + \cdots + mu_x^m/mu_n^m$.

Proposition 8: At an optimal output of public good X its social marginal benefit must (for the usual reasons) be equal to its marginal cost, that is,

$$mu_x^1/mu_n^1 + \cdots + mu_x^m/mu_n^m = mc_x.$$

It is instructive to compare this condition for optimal output of a public good with the corresponding requirement for a private good given in Proposition 3.

In any event, it is clear that desirable public goods will often not be produced or at least not produced in adequate amounts if their supply is left to private enterprise. Typically, public goods from national defense to improvement of the environment require either governmental intervention or direct supply by the public sector.

13. Some Additional Results of Welfare Theory

By way of illustration of the results obtained with the aid of welfare theory, let us now summarize briefly three standard theorems of welfare economics. Each of them can be criticized in a number of respects, but each result, if taken with a grain of salt, yields some useful policy insights.

Proposition 9: In a world of pure competition a tariff must result in a misallocation of resources and in a reduction in net social welfare when all affected nations are considered together.

This result is almost a direct consequence of the results of Section 8. If the allocation of resources which results from competitive prices is optimal, any reallocation of resources which results from the imposition of a tariff and the consequent modification of prices must be presumed to reduce welfare in all countries as a group, though the tariff-levying country may conceivably gain at the expense of others. Specifically, a tariff reduces welfare by causing relative prices to be different for importers and exporters, thus violating the optimal price system requirements given in Section 7.

Before we go on to the next proposition the reader should be reminded that *points rationing* is a method of distributing limited supplies by providing each consumer with some fixed number of ration "points," say 250 points tokens, and requiring that he give up 5 points for every pound of beef he buys, one point with every pound of sugar, etc. In this way the consumer still retains a fair amount of discretion in the choice of his purchases even though his total consumption is restricted. By making its "point price" (the number of points given up with a purchase) sufficiently high, consumption of any item can clearly be cut down as far as is appropriate. We can now formulate

Proposition 10: Wherever it is necessary to restrict the use of a number of commodities, it is better to do so by means of a system of point rationing, in which each consumer is assigned an equal number of points to be used by him as he prefers, rather than the more usual method of assigning an equal amount of each good to each consumer.

Thus, if each consumer is, for example, assigned 1 pound of beef and 1 pound of lamb per week, in an ordinary rationing procedure, the result is necessarily disadvantageous both to consumers who prefer beef and to those who prefer lamb. If, on the other hand, each consumer is given 10 points and told that he must give up 5 points with every pound of meat he purchases, beef lovers will get their 2 pounds of beef and lamb eaters their 2 pounds of lamb.

Indeed, if points are really so effective in restricting consumption that money income is no longer a real limit of consumption, the ration points, rather than the money prices, will become the relevant prices in the purchases of these rationed commodities. Then each rationed consumer will purchase commodities in such proportions that the marginal rate of substitution of any one commodity for another will be equal to the ratio of their fixed point prices. Hence, under points rationing, these marginal rates of substitution must be the same for all consumers, as Proposition 1 requires, whereas the rule will almost certainly be violated under a more rigid rationing system.

Points rationing may only be undesirable for one of two reasons: (a) If some consumers are considered irresponsible—say, if they will spend points on gin rather than orange juice for their children (or vice versa, depending on the point of view)—it may then be preferable to issue a fixed orange juice (gin) ration which cannot be traded for anything else. (b) If money prices are permitted to rise so much that the poor cannot afford to use up all their ration points, fixed rations may be desired for morale purposes, to keep the wealthy from getting too large a share of the available produce in times of scarcity.

This theorem on rationing illustrates how the relatively innocuous Proposition 1, which requires equality of marginal rates of substitution for all consumers, can help lead to significant policy conclusions.

(*alleged*) *Proposition 11:* If the government decides to obtain some *fixed amount* of money by means of taxation, it is better to do so by income taxation rather than by excise (sales) taxation.

The central idea of the argument is that a taxpayer who has K dollars taken from him by means of an income tax can, *if he wishes*, always afford to purchase the combination of goods which is the most preferred of the combinations available to him if he had *exactly the same amount* taken from him by a sales tax on *some single commodity*. It follows at once that if the man pays the income tax he must be *at least* as well off as he would be after the sales-tax payment, for the income-tax payer has available the best of the options which would be open to him as a sales-tax payer (as well as some options which would then not be available).

Consider a consumer who has an income of $100 and buys 3 units of commodity X at $10 each (Table 1). If, say, a tax of $1 on each unit of X sold leads the buyer to reduce his purchase of X down to U units (his *preferred* purchase of X at this new price), a $1 excise tax on X will clearly yield the government U dollars in sales-tax money from this person (second line of the table).[23] Since the consumer now spends $11 (including $1 tax) on each of U units of X, he will be left with $100 - 11U$ dollars to spend on his other purchases.

TABLE 1

	Income	Income After Tax	Price of X	Units of X Bought	Income Left to Spend on Items Other than X
Before tax	100		10	3	70
Excise tax	100		11	U	$100 - 11U$
Income tax (possible)	100	$100 - U$	10	U	$100 - U - 10U$
Income tax (actual)	100	$100 - U$	10	?	?

Suppose, on the other hand, that the government were simply to collect an equal amount, U dollars, out of the income of the consumer instead of setting up a sales tax. The consumer could, if he wishes (third line of the table), still buy U units of X (now at $10 each) and be left with 100 minus the U dollars tax minus his $10U$ dollars outlay on X, again leaving him

---

[23] More generally, if with a sales tax the person would buy x units of X at a price of P dollars and the government wishes to collect K dollars, it must levy a tax K/x dollars on each unit of X sold, so the consumer ends up with $100 - px - K$ dollars.

$100 - 11U$ dollars in total to spend on other commodities. Thus, this hypothetical allocation of his money after payment of an income tax would, if he chose it, leave him exactly as well off as the sales tax, because in either case he ends up with exactly U units of X and $100 - 11U$ dollars to spend on other items. But, in fact, the income-tax-paying consumer may not wish to do exactly what he would have done in the presence of a sales tax. He will, very likely, spend the $100 - U$ he has left after income taxes in some way other than buying U units of X (fourth line of the table). If so, he presumably adopts this alternative because he prefers the situation in line 4 to that in line 3. But since line 3 is identical with line 2, the *best* of the alternatives available to him under a sales tax on commodity X, *he must prefer his state after payment of income tax* (line 4) *to his situation after payment of the sales tax.* Any other numbers or algebraic symbols can be substituted in the table and the reader can see they lead to the same results—the income tax generally hurts the consumer less than does the excise tax.

In intuitive terms, what is the logic of this result? It is simply that an excise tax distorts prices from their optimal levels and forces the consumer to reallocate his expenditures among commodities in a less desirable manner. An income tax reduces the consumer's over-all purchasing power but does not directly change relative prices and so does not force him to redirect his expenditures.

The validity of the argument has been questioned on a number of grounds. First of all, an income tax also motivates the individual to change his pattern of behavior. It distorts his income-earning plans rather than his consumption pattern. It can lead him to work either harder or less hard than he would have if no tax had been imposed on his earnings. This does not show up in Table 1, which assumes that the consumer's total income before taxes is fixed at $100. It is true, of course, that an excise tax *also* reduces the consumer's real income so that we may still argue that the sales tax distorts consumer behavior in two ways, whereas an income tax does so in only one. But it is easy to show the important

Proposition 12. The theorem of second best[24]: It is not necessarily worse for society if a large number of optimality conditions are violated than if only a few are violated.

We have seen, for example, that the presence of only one monopoly firm which violates the optimal-pricing conditions may be worse than having many firms that do so (Section 8) and that the monopolist's output

---

[24] See Richard Lipsey and Kevin Lancaster, "The General Theory of Second Best," *Review of Economic Studies*, Vol. 24, December 1956.

restriction which is a violation of the requirements of Pareto optimality may help to offset the violation of the optimality conditions resulting from detrimental externalities (Section 11). The second-best theorem is a somewhat unfortunate result from the point of view of policy applications of welfare theory for it tells us that piecemeal elimination of violations of the optimality conditions is not necessarily beneficial.

14. Criteria for Welfare Judgments

As mentioned earlier, a decade ago there was much discussion of the circumstances under which the economist is entitled to make any welfare pronouncements—when he can say that policy *A* will, in some sense, increase the welfare of the community as a whole. This problem lies at the foundations of welfare economics, for unless the economist knows how to distinguish between a policy change which is an improvement and one which makes things worse, he is in no position to make any recommendations at all.

It is my opinion, however, that the protracted discussion of this issue was neither very necessary nor very illuminating. I believe that there is a wide variety of policy recommendations which economists have long made and can continue to make with clear consciences. On many issues the desires of the community are rather obvious. For example, during the Great Depression it required little justification for the profession to adopt the reduction of unemployment as a prime objective. Similarly, in an impoverished country, an increase in per capita income can surely be assigned a high priority. Even where the situation is not so clear-cut, the economist has enough to say on policy matters by sticking to questions of the means appropriate for the achievement of given ends. For example, in a country in which the government is seeking to build up gold and dollar reserves, the economist is clearly the person who must consider whether a devaluation will make things better or worse in this respect.

In any event, I believe that the discussion of welfare criteria was relatively sterile and was largely foredoomed to failure. Any attempt to construct a rigorous and universally applicable criterion for distinguishing what policy change is an economic improvement must founder on the problem of interpersonal comparisons. Where a policy change affects some persons favorably and others adversely, as is usually the case, there is no *a priori* way of weighing the net result. Of course, we can and must make interpersonal comparisons—we judge, reasonably, that flood victims must occupy the government's attention and receive emergency assistance at the cost of other taxpayers. We decide that the building of a hospital will serve the general welfare even if it is inconvenient for a few homeowners who were located at its site, and so on. However, these judgments must be rough and ready and can only be handled case by case. No abstract and general formula can be invented which handles all such problems satisfactorily.

It is nevertheless worth examining several of the general criteria which were proposed for this purpose—criteria designed to test whether or not a proposed policy change is an improvement.

1. *The Pareto criterion.* We have already discussed this first criterion, originally formulated by the Italian Vilfredo Pareto about half a century ago, which states simply that

> Any change which harms no one and which makes some people better off (in their own estimation) must be considered to be an improvement.

This statement is certainly persuasive, and it is less empty than may at first appear. Some rather striking analytical results can be obtained with its help. For example, the argument of Section 13, that points rationing is ordinarily better than fixed ration quantities, relies on no more than the Pareto criterion. Points rationing may permit *every* consumer to benefit by adjusting his purchases in accord with his own tastes and desires, and no one need be harmed by it. For a similar reason, Proposition 1 of Section 4 can be considered to be founded upon the Pareto criterion.

Unfortunately, there are many policy proposals which cannot be judged with the aid of this criterion. The Pareto criterion does not apply to any proposal which will benefit some and harm others. In other words, the Pareto criterion works by sidestepping the crucial issue of interpersonal comparison and income distribution, that is, by dealing only with cases where no one is harmed so that the problem does not arise.

To compare it with the other criteria, it is convenient to translate the Pareto criterion into graphic terms. For simplicity, let us deal with a community in which there are only two persons, X and Y. In Figure 4a, let us represent the utility of individual X along the horizontal axis and that of Y along the vertical axis.[25]

The Pareto criterion then states that if we start off from a situation which is represented by a point like A, then a policy change is an improvement if it results in a move to any point like B, C, or D which lies to the right of A, or above A, or above and to the right of A, for at B, X is better off than at A with Y as well off as before, whereas the move to C benefits Y without harming X, and the move to D benefits both persons.

---

[25] For this purpose it does not matter how we measure this utility. The utility scales of the two individuals need not be comparable. All that is required for our purposes is that a movement toward the right in the graph, say from point A to B, always corresponds to some (unspecified) increase in X's welfare and that an upward movement represents an improvement in Y's well-being.

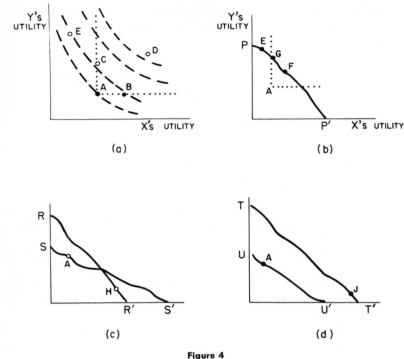

Figure 4

However, a move from A to E cannot be evaluated on the basis of the Pareto criterion, for this change increases Y's welfare but it does so at X's expense.

2. *The Kaldor criterion.* In order to permit the economist to pass judgment on a move such as that from A to E, Kaldor proposed the following criterion.[26] Suppose we ask individual Y how much he would pay (the maximum amount) rather than forego the move from A to E, and call this amount K_y. Similarly ask X how much he is willing to pay to prevent this change (call the amount K_x dollars). Then if K_y exceeds K_x, Kaldor argued that Y could compensate X for his loss in welfare and yet keep some part of the gain for himself. In other words, the change is a net gain, on balance, according to Kaldor, because, at least in money terms, the gain to Y outweighs the loss to X. Note that Kaldor does not require that X actually

---

[26] A very similar criterion was formulated by Hicks, and, later, Little drew on these to put forward a more guarded criterion of his own.

be compensated so that no one would end up with a loss. Such a change *with compensation* would be an improvement even under the Pareto criterion. Kaldor merely requires that the gainer be able, *potentially*, to make this compensation out of his gains. The Kaldor criterion then states that

> A change is an improvement if those who gain evaluate their gains at a higher figure than the value which the losers set upon their losses.

To translate this into graphic terms we must introduce a device called the utility possibility curve (PP' in Figure 4b). Suppose we start off at point F and consider what happens if X gives up some of his wealth and presents it to Y. This might result in the move to point G where X is worse off and Y better off than at F. Still another such redistribution of wealth might move us to E and so on. Thus, PP' is the locus of all combinations of X's and Y's utility levels which can be achieved by a redistribution of wealth between individuals X and Y and where this redistribution is accompanied by no other change.

Consider now the change from point A to E, which, we have seen, cannot be evaluated by means of the Pareto criterion because it involves a gain for Y but a loss for X. PP' is the utility possibility curve through point E. But there are points such as F and G which can be attained from E by a redistribution of wealth and which lie above and/or to the right of A. On the Kaldor criterion, then, the move from A to E is in this case an improvement because it is possible to redistribute wealth at E in such a way that no one loses as a result of the change. At G and certainly at F, X has been compensated for his loss. We conclude that, on the Kaldor criterion, any move from a point A to a point E is an improvement if and only if A lies underneath the utility possibility curve through point E.

3. *The Scitovsky double criterion.* Scitovsky soon pointed out that the Kaldor criterion suffers from a serious weakness. Suppose there is an economic change that not only affects the utility of each individual (the change from A to H in Figure 4c) but that simultaneously shifts the utility possibility locus. The issue is whether the entire change is a good thing. It is possible, on Kaldor's criterion, that a move from A to H will be considered an improvement but that, at the same time, the return from H back to A will be an improvement as well! This is shown in Figure 4c, where A lies below the utility possibility curve RR' through H, but at the same time H lies below SS', the utility possibility curve through A! It will be observed that this odd situation occurs as a result of the intersection of the two utility possibility curves in Figure 4c.

To avoid this embarrassing possibility, Scitovsky proposed a stricter test involving two parts:

(a) Use the Kaldor criterion to see if the move from the initial point to the new point is an improvement.

(b) Use the Kaldor criterion to make sure that the return move from the new point back to the initial point is not an improvement. On this criterion, *if and only if the move passes* both *parts of the double test* is the move an improvement, according to Scitovsky.

In my view, both the Kaldor and the Scitovsky tests operate on the basis of an implicit and unacceptable value judgment. By using a criterion involving potential money compensation, they set up a concealed interpersonal comparison on a money basis. If Y's gain is worth \$200 to him whereas X evaluates his loss at \$70, we are not entitled to jump to the conclusion that there is a net gain in the move from A to E in Figure 4a. If X is a poor man or a miser, \$70 may mean a great deal to him, whereas if Y is a rich man or a profligate, the \$200 may represent a trifle hardly worth his notice. Thus, unless X is actually compensated for his loss (in which case the Kaldor criterion is unnecessary—and the Pareto criterion can do the job) the change from A to E may represent a major loss to X and a trivial gain to Y even if it passes the Kaldor criterion with flying colors.

The Kaldor and Scitovsky criteria have thus ducked the basic problem —the interpersonal comparison required to evaluate a policy change which harms X but aids Y. They duck it by saying, implicitly, that the economist's recommendation should be based on X's and Y's relative willingness and ability to pay for what they want. They accept the *stàtus quo* distribution as a measure of the relative strength of feeling of the two individuals.

It is no answer to this criticism to say that these criteria are just designed to measure whether production, and hence potential welfare, are increased by a policy change—that these criteria disentangle the evaluation of a production change from that of the distribution change by which it is accompanied. Consider a change in production which increases gin output but reduces the output of whiskey. If X likes highballs but Y prefers martinis, the question whether this is an increase in *production* is inextricably tied in with the distribution of these beverages between X and Y.

Even if the utility possibility curves never intersect (Figure 4d), the same problem can arise. At point J, X is better off but Y is worse off than at A. Thus, even though the Kaldor and the Scitovsky criteria both tell us that J is better than A because J's utility possibility curve lies above A (but not vice versa), it is not at all clear that we are entitled to this conclusion.

4. *The Bergson criterion.* A final criterion to be described here is due to

Bergson. He suggests, reasonably, that the only way out of the problem is the formulation of a set of explicit value judgments which enable the analyst to evaluate the situation. These judgments as to what constitutes justice and virtue in distribution may be those of the economist himself, or those set up by the legislature, by some other governmental authority, or by some other unspecified person or group.

In effect, this amounts to the construction of an indifference map ranking different combinations of the utility which may accrue to the various members of society (the broken lines in Figure 4a). Such an indifference map is called the *social welfare function*, and it does permit the analyst to judge definitively whether or not a proposed policy change is an improvement. Thus, in Figure 4a, E must be considered better than A (the change from A to E is an improvement) because E lies on a higher indifference curve of that social welfare function.

Essentially, the Bergson criterion must be judged right, if not very helpful. To decide whether E is better than A, we must certainly employ some value judgments, and unless these judgments are explicit they must be treated with suspicion. Implicit value judgments only too often are at variance even with the intentions of those who make them, as would seem to be the case with the Kaldor and Scitovsky criteria.

But the Bergson criterion, though it provides us with a highly useful frame of reference, unfortunately does not come equipped with a kit and a set of instructions for collecting the welfare judgments which it requires. Thus, it still leaves us with the difficult part of the job unsolved. At any rate, it is not advisable to approach the problem as one noted economist is supposed to have done—by confronting the chief executive of a large underdeveloped country and saying to him, "Please describe your social welfare function to me."

15. A Theorem on Democratic Group Decisions

Several economists have recently devoted considerable attention to the relationship between individual and group decisions. That is, given information about the desires of the various persons who make up the group, the problem is that of setting up reasonable procedures for the reconciliation of those desires into a group decision. It will be noted that this problem has a family resemblance to that of the preceding section.

The discussion of this subject stems largely from the work of Kenneth J. Arrow.[27] His procedure is to list some plausible acceptability criteria

---

[27] See, particularly, his *Social Choice and Individual Values*, Cowles Commission Monograph No. 12, John Wiley & Sons, Inc., New York, 1951. See also Duncan Black and R. A. Newing, *Committee Decisions with Complementary Valuation*, Hodge, London, 1951, and the references to Black's work in Arrow, *op. cit.*

for social decisions and to examine their implications. He originally proposed the following four minimal conditions which social choices must meet in order to reflect individuals' preferences: (1) Social choices must be consistent (transitive) in the sense that if A will be decided in preference to B, and B in preference to C, then C will not be decided in preference to A; (2) the group decisions must not be dictated by anyone outside the community or by any one individual in the community; (3) social choices must not change in the opposite direction from the choices of the members of that society; that is, an alternative which would otherwise have been chosen by society must never be rejected just because some individuals come to regard it more favorably; and (4) a social decision as between two alternatives must not change so long as no individual in the community changes the order in which he ranks these alternatives in accord with his preferences. In other words, the social preference as between two alternatives, A and B, must depend *only* on people's opinions of *just these two alternatives*, A and B (and not on any other alternative which does not happen to be immediately relevant).

At first glance, these requirements for social choice may seem a rather appropriate set of conditions for democratic decision-making. However, Arrow has shown that the matter is not so simple. He has demonstrated that it is impossible to choose among all possible sets of alternatives without violating at least one of his four criteria. In other words, it would appear that social choice must be in a sense inconsistent or undemocratic! This negative result is the central theorem of Arrow's book.

Let us illustrate how such difficulties can arise. The obvious and most standard procedure for reaching group decisions is the ballot. But it has long been known that the voting-procedure runs afoul of Arrow's first requirement. That is, majority rule can lead to a pattern of social choices which is not transitive even though *every* voter has transitive preferences. This can be illustrated by an example. Three individuals, Smith, Jones, and Mznch, are to vote among three alternatives, A, B, and C, by writing a "3" next to the alternative they like most, a "2" beside the one they rank next highest, etc. Suppose, then, we get the following record of this balloting:

	A	B	C
Smith	3	2	1
Jones	1	3	2
Mznch	2	1	3

A glance at the table shows that both Smith and Mznch prefer A to B, that Smith and Jones both prefer B to C, and that Jones and Mznch prefer C to A. Hence, the majority prefers A to B and B to C, but it also prefers C to A! We see then that majority voting can easily lead to intransitive social choice patterns.

Later examination of the problem has suggested, however, that Arrow's requirements are more strict than they seem at first view and that inconsistent or "undemocratic" social choice-making is not really the only alternative.[28] The difficulty pointed out by Arrow's research can be ascribed, in part, to the fact that the fourth condition, above, is considerably more restrictive than first appears and is not merely the postulate of popular sovereignty that it seems. First, it implies that in deciding as between two alternatives the public's preferences as among still other alternatives be treated as irrelevant.[29] Suppose, for example, that half the

---

[28] See Clifford Hildreth, "Alternative Conditions for Social Orderings," *Econometrica*, Vol. XXI, January 1953; and Leo A. Goodman and Harry Markowitz, "Social Welfare Functions Based on Individual Rankings," *American Journal of Sociology*, Vol. LVIII, November 1952. For a more technical criticism of Arrow's argument, see Julian H. Blau, "The Existence of Social Welfare Functions," *Econometrica*, Vol. 25, April 1957.

[29] As an example of the intent of this assumption of "independence of irrelevant alternatives" consider the balloting described in the following two tables which violate the premise:

	A	B	C	D			A	C	D
Smith	4	3	2	1		Smith	3	2	1
Jones	4	3	2	1		Jones	3	2	1
Mznch	2	1	4	3		Mznch	1	3	2
Total point vote	10	7	8	5		Total point vote	7	7	4

In the left-hand table A wins by 10 points to 8 points for C. But if only irrelevant alternative B is dropped from consideration (the right-hand table), A and C become tied. In effect, the assumption states that the decision of a third party to put up a candidate who stands no chance of winning himself should not affect the outcome of the election as between the Democratic and Republican candidates.

However, it may be questioned whether it is really socially desirable to exclude such "irrelevant alternatives" from consideration. A weaker third party, such as the Liberal Party in Great Britain, derives much of whatever power it possesses from the possibility that its decision to run candidates may affect the outcome of an election. Elimination of this sort of influence may materially weaken the protection which the political system affords to the "irrelevant" minority groups. One may suspect that the popularity among mathematical economists of the axiom of "independence of irrelevant alternatives" stems as much from its spectacular consequences as from its attractiveness as a political tenet.

public prefers the erection of a bridge to the digging of a tunnel under a river at comparable cost, while the other half ranks the projects the other way. The fourth condition requires that the government's decision be uninfluenced by the fact that the tunnel advocates feel this to be the most important of the public works projects currently under discussion, while those who want the bridge really think that almost any other project is of greater significance.

In addition, Arrow's fourth condition requires that only *rankings* be considered. This means that no weight be given to the intensity of desires. For example, if 50 per cent of the public demands the tunnel with consider-able emotion because it feels that the bridge will deface the beauty of the area, while the other half of the public has a slight preference for the bridge because of its slightly lower cost, the difference in intensity of these preferences must, on this fourth condition, be disregarded.

Of course, we do not know how to measure intensity of feeling. Still there are cases where there would be consensus on this and where, in fact, a choice in accord with the Arrow condition would be unacceptable in principle to most of us. For example, in deciding whether to allocate labor to the production of some drug needed to treat a rare but dangerous disease or to the manufacture of Scrabble sets, we may recognize that, compassion aside, more people will want the Scrabble sets than the medicine. Yet on the crudest sort of interpersonal comparison of benefits, we may decide that the public as a whole will gain more from the production of the medicine because its potential users feel much more strongly about their preference than do the others.

However we may feel about the outcome of this discussion, it must be agreed that Arrow has again called our attention to the presence of pitfalls and treacherous problems in the analysis of group decision-making. More-over, although the reader is given no hint of their flavor here, Arrow has made a very important contribution in his choice of mathematical tools, for he has shown that the subject matter lends itself well to the methods of symbolic logic, and by means of this demonstration he has made what may well prove to be a significant addition to the economist's stock of useful analytic equipment.

16. Concluding Remarks

In this chapter we have seen that welfare economics has run the gamut from specific (though abstractly derived) policy conclusions on particular issues like rationing to broad, rather philosophical investigations into the proper foundations for the entire area of investigation. More recently, welfare economics seems to have gone off into a relatively new direction.

It has been used in operations-research type of analysis of specific problems of government[30] and as training material for operations researchers who can learn from the special concepts of welfare economics to avoid some frequently encountered analytic booby traps. For example, the idea of external economies and diseconomies has taught us to beware of policies which yield optimal results for each of the various divisions of a firm taken by themselves, because by not taking into account the effects of its decisions on the rest of the company, policy-making, division by division, may yield results which are far from optimal for the company as a whole. We see, then, that the emphasis in welfare economics has swung from its rather abstract subject matter in the 1940s toward the other extreme—to very applied work and concrete problems of day-to-day economic decision-making.

REFERENCES

Arrow, Kenneth J., *Social Choice and Individual Values*, Cowles Commission Monograph No. 12, John Wiley & Sons, Inc., New York, 1951.

Bator, F. M., "The Simple Analytics of Welfare Maximization," *American Economic Review*, Vol. 47, March 1957.

——, "The Anatomy of Market Failure," *Quarterly Journal of Economics*, Vol. 72, August 1958.

Baumol, William J., *Welfare Economics and the Theory of the State*, Longmans, Green & Co., Ltd., London, 1952.

—— and David F. Bradford, "Optimal Departures from Marginal Cost Pricing," *American Economic Review*, Vol. 60, June 1970. (The Ramsey theorem on optimal pricing under a budget constraint.)

—— and Wallace E. Oates, *The Theory of Environmental Policy*, Prentice-Hall, Inc., Englewood Cliffs, N.J., 1975.

Coase, R. H., "The Problem of Social Cost," *Journal of Law and Economics*, Vol. 1, October 1960.

Graaff, J. de V., *Theoretical Welfare Economics*, Cambridge University Press, New York, 1957.

Hicks, J. R., "The Foundations of Welfare Economics," *Economic Journal*, Vol. XLIX, December 1939.

Kahn, Robert F., "Some Notes on Ideal Output," *Economic Journal*, Vol. XLV, March 1935.

Kaldor, Nicholas, "A Note on Tariffs and the Terms of Trade," *Economica*, Vol. VII, November 1940.

---

[30] See, e.g., Roland McKean, *Efficiency in Government Through Systems Analysis*, John Wiley & Sons, Inc., New York, 1958: John V. Krutilla and Otto Eckstein, *Multiple Purpose River Development*, Johns Hopkins Press, Baltimore, 1958; and J. R. Nelson (ed.), *Marginal Cost Pricing in Practice* (the important French contribution), Prentice-Hall, Inc., Englewood Cliffs, N.J., 1964.

Lange, Oskar, and Fred M. Taylor, *On the Economic Theory of Socialism*, University of Minnesota Press, Minneapolis, 1938.

Lerner, Abba P., *The Economics of Control*, The Macmillan Company, New York, 1946.

Little, I. M. D., *A Critique of Welfare Economics*, 2nd edition, Oxford University Press, Inc., New York, 1957.

Mishan, Ezra, *Welfare Economics*, Random House, New York, 1964.

Pareto, Vilfredo, *Manuel d'Économie Politique*, 2nd edition, Girard, Paris, 1927, pp. 617–618.

Pigou, A. C., *The Economics of Welfare*, 4th edition, Macmillan & Co., Ltd., London, 1932.

Reder, Melvin, *Studies in the Theory of Welfare Economics*, Columbia University Press, New York, 1947.

Samuelson, Paul A., *Foundations of Economic Analysis*, Harvard University Press, Cambridge, Mass., 1947, Chapter VIII.

———, "The Pure Theory of Public Expenditure," *Review of Economics and Statistics*, Vol. 37, November 1954.

Scitovsky, Tibor, "A Note on Welfare Propositions in Economics," *Review of Economic Studies*, Vol. 9, November 1941.

Tribe, L. H., "Policy Science: Analysis or Ideology," *Philosophy and Public Affairs*, Vol. 2, Fall 1972. (On the limits of welfare economics.)

Willig, Robert D., "Consumers Surplus Without Apology," *American Economic Review*, Vol. 66, 1976.

Input-Output Analysis

22

1. The Economic Problem and the Assumptions

Input-output analysis, for which we are indebted to Professor Leontief, is the name given to the attempt to take account of *general equilibrium* phenomena in the *empirical* analysis of *production*. The three italicized elements in this statement are crucial and merit further discussion. Reversing their order, we observe, first, that the analysis deals almost exclusively with production. Demand theory plays no role in the hard core of input-output analysis.[1] The problem is essentially technological. The investigation seeks to determine what can be produced, and the quantity of each intermediate product which must be used up in the production process, given the quantities of available resources and the state of technology.

The second distinctive feature of input-output analysis is its devotion to empirical investigation. This is primarily what distinguishes it from the work of Walras and later general equilibrium theorists. A consequence of this no doubt long-overdue concern with the facts is that compromises have been forced on the investigator. Input-output employs a model which is

---

[1] This is strictly true only of the *open model* which is described here. In this model the final demand sector is, in effect, taken to be outside the production economy and final products are "exported" to the consumer inhabitants of this "foreign" demand sector. There is, however, *a closed model* in which labor is treated as a produced commodity and consumption as the raw materials used up in the production of labor. Here at least some rudimentary demand analysis must enter to show how the levels of consumption demands are related to the levels of labor outputs supplied.

more severely simplified and also more narrow in the sense that it seeks to encompass fewer phenomena than does the usual general equilibrium theory. Its narrowness lies in its exclusive emphasis of the production side of the economy. Its oversimplifications I shall discuss presently.

The third distinctive feature is its emphasis of general equilibrium[2] phenomena. Input-output seeks to take account of the interdependence of the production plans and activities of the many industries which constitute an economy. This interdependence arises out of the fact that each industry employs the outputs of other industries as its raw materials. Its output, in turn, is often used by other producers as a productive factor, sometimes by those very industries from which it obtained its ingredients. Steel is used to make railroad cars and railroad cars are, in turn, used to transport steel and the coal and pig iron which are used in its manufacture. Other examples should come to mind at once.

The basic problem, then, is to see what can be left over for final consumption (consumer, military, etc.) and how much of each output will be used up in the course of the productive activities which must be undertaken to obtain these net outputs. It should be clear that a successful attack upon these problems can result in an abundance of applications. It can be used in predicting future production requirements if usable demand estimates can somehow be obtained. Particularly, it can be used for economic planning including problems of economic development in "backward areas" and problems of military mobilization. A more modest purpose which it has already successfully begun to serve is the provision of a very illuminating detailed structure for national income accounting.

As we stated earlier, the intransigence of the empirical materials and the computational problems have forced on input-output analysis a number of simplifying assumptions even more extreme than those usually employed in our theoretical models. Particularly noteworthy are two assumptions, each of which has to some extent been relaxed in practice. One assumption, which will not be discussed, states that no two commodities are produced jointly. Each industry produces only one homogeneous output. But this restriction can be somewhat relaxed by interpreting this good as a composite commodity which is made up of several items produced in fixed proportions. Such a compound good can, for example, consist in packages of chewing gum and fertilizer in which there are always ten sticks of gum and one pound of fertilizer.

Perhaps more serious is a second assumption which states that in any

---

[2] The term "equilibrium" is misleading here. The outputs found by this method need not satisfy market equilibrium conditions. The analysis qualifies for the title "general equilibrium" in that it takes account of the interdependence of the various sectors of the economy. Perhaps we can say, more properly, that the model is characterized by the "general" without the equilibrium.

productive process all inputs are employed in rigidly fixed proportions and the use of these inputs expands in proportion with the level of output. This is a special case of an assumption of constant returns to scale (see Chapter 11, Section 5). But the fixed-proportions assumption is far more restrictive. Constant returns to scale is perfectly consistent with the substitution of one factor for another. A linear homogeneous production function (constant return to scale) permits both labor-intensive and capital-intensive processes. The firm whose production function exhibits constant returns can if it wishes have one hundred workers for every $1,000 invested in machinery, or it may use machines which require only ten workers per $1,000 machine investment. A linear homogeneous production function requires only that if the firm decides to triple the scale of either of these types of operation, the result will be a tripling of output. Not so the Leontief fixed-proportions premise, which requires that a manufacturing process which is labor intensive offer no option of a capital-intensive alternative.[3] If fifty-three men per $1,000 of investment are required at any level of operation, it is assumed that the same ratio will be required no matter how much the size of the firm expands or contracts. Whether this assumption is relatively innocuous or does considerable violence to the input-output results is still under dispute. But the premise is certainly never absolutely true, even in those cases where chemistry and engineering dictate fixed proportions between some ingredient and output.

2. The Mathematics

Basically, the input-output analysis consists in nothing more complicated than the solution of a set of N simultaneous linear equations in N variables. To illustrate this, let us consider a three-industry economy which produces coal, steel, and the service of railroad transportation. Each of these is measured in dollar terms. Each of these industries employs the products of the others in its manufacture, say in proportions shown by the following table:

User of Output

		Steel	Coal	R.R.
	Steel	0.2	0.2	0.1
Producer	Coal	0.4	0.1	0.3
of	R.R.	0.2	0.5	0.1
Input	Labor	0.2	0.2	0.5
	Total	1	1	1

---

[3] But cf. the Samuelson substitution theorem described in Section 4 of this chapter.

For example, the first column of the table states that every dollar's worth of steel uses in its manufacture 20 cents in steel, 40 cents in coal, 20 cents in railroad transportation, and 20 cents in labor.

Suppose, now, that somehow there have been set consumer output targets of $100 million in steel, $20 million in coal, and $40 million in railroad transportation. How much of each of these goods will have to be manufactured for both consumer and industrial use to meet the final output goals? Let S, C, and R represent the dollar value of this total output of steel, coal, and railroad transportation, respectively. Let us first examine the demands on the steel industry: In addition to the 100 demanded by final consumers, there will be the demand for its product for internal use which (the table tells us) amounts to $2/10$ of the total steel output or $0.2S$. Similarly, the railroad industry will require $1/10$ of a dollar of steel for every dollar of its service, so that the total railroading demand for steel will be $0.1R$, etc. Thus we have the equation

(total steel output) equals (amount used in steel mfg.)

$$S \qquad = \qquad 0.2S$$

plus (use in coal mfg.) plus (R.R. use) plus

$$+ \qquad 0.2C \qquad + \qquad 0.1R \qquad +$$

(amount left over for consumption)

$$100$$

or $\qquad S = 0.2S + 0.2C + 0.1R + 100.$

Similarly, we have the following two equations giving the amounts of coal and rail transportation available for final consumption:

$$C = 0.4S + 0.1C + 0.3R + 20$$

and $\qquad R = 0.2S + 0.5C + 0.1R + 40.$

These are three simultaneous linear equations in the three unknowns, S, C, and R. If we solve the equations for the values of these variables, we find what we started out to seek—the total outputs of the three commodities needed to meet the stated consumer targets. Only one more step is required. We note from the input-output table that $0.2 of labor time are consumed in the manufacture of $1 of steel, so that $0.2S$ dollars of labor will be needed to produce the required S dollars of steel production. Continuing in this way we see that $0.2S + 0.2C + 0.5R$ dollars worth of labor will be needed to produce the outputs of the three commodities required by our program. Taking the price of labor to be fixed, we see that this involves a specific requirement of labor man-hours. If this computed number does not exceed the available supply, all is well—the targets are feasible. Otherwise more modest targets must be substituted. That is the core of the theory of input-output.

We can see now why it is so convenient to work with fixed coefficients of production. With variable input proportions, single numbers will not suffice in the input-output table. Instead we would have to deduce, from the available statistics and engineering information, functional relationships between the level of output of each industry and the quantity of each input which would be required to produce it. The enormous statistical problems should be obvious enough. It is equally clear that the relevant equations would be complicated enormously. Even with the huge economy effected by the fixed-coefficients premise, the statistical and computational difficulties are tremendous. We can see that the first three rows of our table contain nine figures, the three inputs required by each of the three industries. Similarly, a four-industry model would require more than 16 figures, and so on. The number of required pieces of statistical information increases as the square of the number of industries considered, although in practice the work is reduced by the fact that many of the entries in the input-output table are zeros because some industry, A, does not use as an input any of the products of some other industry, B. It can also be shown that the number of computational steps involved in solving the equations increases as the cube of the number of industries. Thus, the labor involved in an input-output analysis rapidly becomes astronomical as the breakdown of industrial classifications becomes finer. A table has been constructed for a model involving some 450 industries, but most computation has involved considerably fewer industries. Certainly even 450 industries is too coarse a breakdown for most detailed planning purposes in an economy where the number of items produced can be considered to go well into the millions.

3. A Dynamized Input-Output Model

The Leontief model has appeared in a number of modified forms. One which is of considerable analytical interest is a dynamic model in which specific account is taken of the interrelationship of current and past outputs, and, in particular, of the building up of stocks of capital goods (factories, goods in process, machinery, etc.).[4] For purposes of this discussion we may consider that a current output can be used for any or all of the following three purposes: for current consumption; as an input in the production of some other output; and, finally, as an addition to the economy's stock of capital. The first two uses of an output have already made their

---

[4] See Wassily W. Leontief and others, *Studies in the Structure of the American Economy*, Oxford University Press, Inc., New York, 1953, Chapter 3. For a critical discussion, see Robert Dorfman, Paul A. Samuelson, and Robert M. Solow, *Linear Programming and Economic Analysis*, McGraw-Hill Book Company, New York, 1955, Chapters 11 and 12.

appearance in the static input model. It is the last possibility, capital investment, which is the novel feature that characterizes the dynamic model.

If the output in question is a building material or a piece of machinery, it is clear how it can be used to add to the stock of equipment, factories, and other productive facilities. But other outputs can also help to facilitate economic activities—production and marketing in the future. Inventories of raw materials and goods in process are obviously indispensable for smooth production, and effective marketing clearly requires stocks of finished goods. Hence the accumulation of outputs which are not used up when they are turned out can be essential for future production. This observation constitutes a tie-in between present and past (or between present and future), which is the crucial characteristic of any dynamic model.

The mathematical relationships which make up the dynamic system are a fairly straightforward extension of the ordinary input-output equations. The dynamic conditions are of two kinds:

1. Current output of each commodity must suffice to cover consumption demands plus interindustry demands plus demands for addition to inventory. Thus, the first equation of the preceding section would now read

$$S \geq 0.2S + 0.2C + 0.1R + 100 + (K_{st+1} - K_{st}).$$

Here K_{st} is the current (period t) accumulated capital stock of steel and K_{st+1} is therefore next year's steel stock. Assuming away wear and depreciation, the difference, $K_{st+1} - K_{st}$, is, therefore, the amount which is added to steel capital stocks out of current production. The reason for the use of inequality rather than an equation will be discussed presently.

2. The second type of relationship which constitutes the dynamic Leontief system requires that the capital stock be as large as is necessary to produce the planned output levels for the current period. For example, if each unit of steel output requires 4.2 units of steel capital goods (in the form of equipment, etc.), and if each unit of coal production requires 2.7 units of steel capital, and each unit of railroad transportation output requires 3.6 units of steel equipment, we need a capital stock sufficiently large for all three purposes, i.e., we must have

$$K_{st} \geq 4.2S + 2.7C + 3.6R.$$

These are the basic requirements of the dynamic input–output system. Together they can help us to plan not only for present production, but for future output as well. The model takes explicit account of what must be put aside today in order to be able to achieve our plans for tomorrow.

The presence of the inequality signs in the preceding relationships takes account of the possibility of overproduction and excess capacity. If, for example, in the last relationship we end up with K_{st} *greater than* the sum of the terms on the right-hand side, it must mean that the economy's steel equipment is not being fully used—there is excess capacity in this type of equipment. The reason such excess capacity can arise is that capital equipment is inherited from the past, and it can easily turn out that its composition does not fit in precisely with current output needs. It may involve too much steel and too little coal for our current production pattern. In an extreme case, excess steel capacity can become unavoidable because we simply do not have enough coal on hand to run the machines. But, in any event, we have the choice of producing various different combinations of final outputs *and investment goods*. Consider one such set of commodities, A, whose manufacture uses a great deal of steel and very little coal, whereas another, B, involves the opposite sort of input requirement. If it is decided to produce collection A, the economy may well end up with an excessive coal inventory, whereas if collection B is produced, there may be excess steel-equipment capacity. Even given the set of consumers' goods which the economy wishes to turn out, different production patterns will arise depending on the quantities of the various goods which it is decided to put into capital investment. It follows that the dynamic input-output system cannot just be solved to give us a unique set of output requirements for any set of final output goals. Production goals can be achieved by a variety of means, and somehow society must make up its mind among them, presumably on the basis of some sort of optimality computation. Planning for the long run cannot be reduced to a simple matter of the solution of a system of simultaneous equations as in the static input-output case.

4. Some Theorems of Input-Output Analysis

Before ending the discussion of input-output analysis it is appropriate to describe three noteworthy theorems on the subject and to indicate their function.

1. *The Samuelson substitution theorem:* It will be recalled from the first section of this chapter that a restrictive assumption of the input-output analysis is the premise that there are fixed technological coefficients—that it takes X man-hours, Y units of raw material of a given type, and so on, to produce each unit of an output, and that there is no possibility of any other input proportion. The firm has no choice of using or rejecting, e.g., labor-saving devices.

Professor Samuelson has proved that in some circumstances this restriction is not as serious as it appears.[5] He has shown that even where variation

---

[5] See Chapters VII, VIII, and IX (written, respectively, by Paul A. Samuelson, Tjalling C. Koopmans, and Kenneth J. Arrow) in Tjalling C. Koopmans (ed.), *Activity Analysis of Production and Allocation*, Cowles Commission Monograph 13, John Wiley & Sons, Inc., New York, 1951.

of input proportions is possible, *it will never be advantageous* provided that there are constant returns to scale, only one scarce input (labor, in the discussion of Section 2), and no joint products. In other words, the input-output proportions may be fixed as is assumed, but they will then be fixed by considerations of productive efficiency rather than immutable techno-logical requirements. For each commodity there will simply exist one *most efficient* capital-labor ratio (e.g., seventeen men per $1,000 of equipment), and no changes in the level of output of that commodity will affect this ratio.

There is really a simple logic behind this result. We saw in Section 10 of Chapter 11 that with fixed input prices and a linear homogeneous produc-tion function it will never pay to change input proportions no matter what the level of output. Suppose that there is only one scarce factor, labor, and nothing else preventing the indefinite expansion of national output. This means that the real cost to society of the manufacture of any output or any other input must be calculated in terms of the amount of labor required to produce it. The real price of input A will be, say, two man-hours per unit that of input B will be twelve man-hours. With constant returns to scale and unchanged input proportions these labor "prices" will not change. It follows that any output should always be produced in a manner which uses the same input proportions. The most efficient input proportions will in fact be those which make the smallest (direct and indirect) drains on the economy's scarce labor supply.

Unfortunately, if there is more than one resource in limited supply, this substitution theorem no longer holds, and so we are then back to our original problem. If the fixed input-output proportions assumption is to be accepted at all, it can only be as an approximation to the technological facts of the case.

2. *The Hawkins-Simon conditions:* Let us now turn to a second theorem of input-output analysis, one which is somewhat more abstract but of more general applicability than the one which was just discussed.

After collecting the data for an input-output table it is conceivable that the solution of the corresponding input-output equations will yield one or more negative numbers. This would imply that negative outputs of some commodities are required in order to achieve the final consumption targets! Clearly something has gone seriously wrong in such a case.

Hawkins and Simon have derived mathematical conditions which tell us the circumstances that will lead to such a pathological phenomenon and help us to understand it.[6] These conditions are useful as a check on input-output data to see whether a mistake has been made in collecting them.

---

[6] See D. Hawkins and H. A. Simon, "Some Conditions of Macroeconomic Stability," *Econometrica*, Vol. 17, July–October 1949.

More important, these conditions provide us with mathematical requirements which must be met by any acceptable input-output system, and the
conditions can therefore be used as a basis for further theoretical analysis.

In intuitive terms, what the Hawkins-Simon conditions show is that if,
say, our solution calls for a negative coal output, this must mean that more
than one ton of coal is used up (directly and indirectly) in the production of
every ton of coal output. If we have such an unfortunate productive situation, only a negative amount of coal will be left over for consumers' use,
and this deficit in consumer coal supplies will be smaller the smaller is the
economy's total production of coal. In such a topsy-turvy production
system, the only way to meet consumer targets is to produce negative coal
outputs— an obvious nonsense possibility.

In the dynamic Leontief model the situation is only slightly less serious.
If the Hawkins-Simon conditions are violated by the numbers in the input-
output table, it may be possible, for a time, to meet consumer demands out
of inventories. But, eventually, these inventories will be used up and it will
be impossible to build them up again because an attempt to produce more
will only hasten the drain on stocks since more of the items in question must
be used up by the production process than it is able to turn out.

The nature of the Hawkins-Simon conditions can perhaps be made
more specific with the aid of a graph. Consider a very simple two-industry
(steel-coal) input-output model in which neither the steel nor the coal
industry uses up any of its own product. Then we have the input–output
equations

(1) $$S = \quad aC + T_s$$
(2) $$C = bS \quad + T_c,$$

where S and C are steel and coal output, respectively, T_s and T_c are the
final net output targets for steel and coal, and a and b are constants. The
first equation, the demand curve for steel, may be represented by a straight
line (drawn as the flatter line) in Figure 1. Similarly, the second equation,
the demand for coal, may be solved for S in terms of C, and rewritten as

$$S = (1/b)C - (1/b)T_c.$$

This curve can then also be plotted in Figure 1 (the steeper line). The intersection point, B, gives us the solution to the input-output equations, the
required outputs of coal and steel thus being OC_b and OS_b, respectively.[7]

---

[7] Note the role of the limited labor supply in the input-output system. Its limited
availablity means that only input combinations represented by points on or below the
labor constraint line, LL', can be produced (shaded region). Points like P, which lie beyond this line, represent outputs which cannot be produced because the requisite labor is
not available. Fortunately, in the case shown, the solution point B is feasible. Note also
the similarity to the linear programming diagrams.

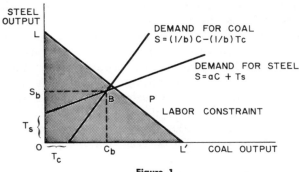

Figure 1

But suppose the two lines were parallel or that the steel demand curve were steeper than the coal demand curve. In that case, the two lines would not intersect in the positive quadrant. The input-output system would have no solution, and the Hawkins–Simon conditions must be violated. What are those conditions in this case? To prevent the problem of nonsolvability, the slope of the coal demand equation $(1/b)$ must exceed that of the steel demand equation (a) so that we must have $1/b > a$. That is the Hawkins–Simon condition for this simple model.

The economic implication of these conditions which was given above is now easily shown to apply in this case. Substitute the coal demand equation (2) into the steel demand equation (1) to eliminate the coal output variable, C, and obtain

$$S = a(bS + T_c) + T_s = abS + aT_c + T_s.$$

This last equation tells us that if steel output increases ΔS units, the amount of steel needed to produce the coal which is used to produce that additional steel will be $ab \, \Delta S$. But if the Hawkins-Simon conditions are violated so that $1/b \leq a$, we must have $ab \geq 1$, i.e., more than a ton of steel (ab units) will be used up in the course of producing an additional ton of steel!

3. *Series approximation to the solution:* A final theorem to be discussed here arises out of the need for computationally efficient methods of solution of the simultaneous equations of the static Leontief system. Since the work of numerical computation in the solution of a set of simultaneous equations grows so complex as the number of equations increases, it becomes highly desirable to find labor-saving methods. One method[8] which has received much attention involves an approximate solution which is analogous with the computation of the first few terms in the multiplier series $1 + c + c^2 +$

---

[8] See, e.g., Frederick V. Waugh, "Inversion of the Leontief Matrix by Power Series," *Econometrica*, Vol. 18, April 1950.

$c^3 + \cdots$ as an approximation to the value of the multiplier $1/(1 - c)$. As we know, in the multiplier case this will work if the marginal propensity to consume, c, is less than unity. In the Leontief computation we have a similar condition which states that this procedure will work if the sum of the first n elements in any column in an n-industry input-output table is less than unity. We may generally expect this to be the case for an operating industry in a profit economy because this total is the sum of the costs of all the inputs except the labor input going into the production of a dollar's worth of any commodity, and the costs of these inputs must usually be no greater than one (dollar), for otherwise it will not pay to produce the item.

Again, there is a simple piece of intuitive logic to the procedure. The purpose of the input-output computation is to answer questions such as "How much steel production is needed to satisfy consumer demands?" And the answer can be given in the form of the following infinite series:

	The economy will have to produce
	as much steel as consumers will use directly
plus	as much steel as is needed to produce other final consumer products
plus	as much steel as is needed to produce the inputs for these final consumer products
plus	as much steel as is needed to produce the inputs which are in turn used to manufacture those inputs which go into those final products
plus	as much steel as is needed for the inputs to make the inputs to make the inputs for the final products

and so on, *ad infinitum.* [9]

The idea in the series-approximation formula is to compute the total steel requirements involved in several such stages (say the first fifteen of

[9] This is readily illustrated with the aid of a trivial one-industry (steel) model, in which aS tons of steel are used up in producing one ton of steel. Here we have one input-output equation

$$S = aS + T,$$

where T is the final output steel target. This equation has the obvious solution

$$S(1 - a) = T \quad \text{or} \quad S = T/(1 - a).$$

But the same solution can be arrived at by the multiplier argument used above. To end up with T tons of steel we need to produce the T tons plus aT tons (to be used up in producing the T tons) plus $a(aT) = a^2T$ tons (to be used in producing the aT tons), etc. Thus we have the infinite geometric series

$$S = T + aT + a^2T + \cdots,$$

which has the well-known solution $S = T/(1 - a)$.

these rounds), and to take this subtotal, after some upward adjustment, as an estimate of total required steel production.

REFERENCES

Carter, Anne P., *Structural Change in the American Economy*, Harvard University Press, Cambridge, Mass., 1970.

Chenery, Hollis B., and Paul G. Clark, *Interindustry Economics*, John Wiley & Sons, Inc., New York, 1959.

Dorfman, Robert, Paul A. Samuelson, and Robert M. Solow, *Linear Programming and Economic Analysis*, McGraw-Hill Book Company, New York, 1958, Chapters 9–12. (Relatively difficult reading.)

Leontief, Wassily W., *Input-Output Economics*, Oxford University Press, New York, 1966.

———, and others, *Studies in the Structure of the American Economy*, Oxford University Press, Inc., New York, 1953.

Morgenstern, Oskar (ed.), *Economic Activity Analysis*, John Wiley & Sons, Inc., New York, 1954. (Contains both expository material and some rather difficult mathematical papers.)

Activity Analysis
and General Equilibrium

23

The term "activity analysis" may be taken to refer to the applications of linear programming methods to general equilibrium *theory*. The last few years have seen a new burst of effort devoted to this area, which, at least until the 1930's, had remained pretty much as it was left by Walras. The three outstanding developments relate to the solvability of the Walrasian equations, the development of general equilibrium growth models, and the application of general equilibrium theory to welfare economics. In all three cases the main advance has consisted in the development of powerful methods rather than in the discovery of surprising new theorems. For this reason much of the discussion which follows is devoted to the description of mathematical arguments and analytic techniques, and its economic content may on first reading leave one rather disappointed.

1. The Existence and Uniqueness Problems

Walras was much concerned with the solvability of his equation system. That is, he wanted to be sure that the system of equations he had set up sufficed to determine the values of his variables—the prices and quantities of the economy's outputs and inputs. Some writers approached this by counting the number of his equations and unknowns. They found he had the same number of equations as unknowns and assumed that the problem was solved.

Unfortunately, the matter is much more complicated. We usually expect a supply and a demand equation (curve) to determine a single equilibrium price-quantity combination, but this is certainly not true of either of the following pairs:

$$\text{Demand:} \quad Q = 1{,}000 - 5P \qquad Q = 1{,}000 - 5P$$

$$\text{Supply:} \quad Q = \phantom{1{,}}900 - 5P \qquad 2Q = 2{,}000 - 10P,$$

where P is price and Q is the quantity sold. The pair of equations on the left has no solution (no solution *exists*)—any price-quantity combination which satisfies the one cannot possibly satisfy the other because $Q + 5P$ cannot be both 1,000 and 900 at the same time. The trouble here is that the supply and demand curves are parallel straight lines and never intersect. In this case we say that the equations are *inconsistent* and the system is *overdetermined*.[1] By contrast, the other set of equations offers us an embarrassment of riches. It is compatible with an infinite number of price-quantity combinations. (The solution is not "unique.") In fact, since negative prices and quantities have not been excluded, every price can be an equilibrium price. In this case the difficulty is that the supply and demand curves coincide, so that at every point of this single-curve demand will equal supply. Here we say that the equations are *not independent* and the system is *underdetermined*.[2]

If there are scarce resources, the Walrasian system may get into trouble in yet another way—the solution to the equations simply may not be feasible because the available resources do not suffice to produce it. It may rightly be suspected that this is where programming enters in, for we are almost[3] back at the production-with-limited-capacity problem.

An *existence theorem* (a theorem which states that some equation or set of equations possesses at least one solution) does not tell us anything about the operation of the economy—rather, it tells us something about the operation of the Walrasian model. We know by observation that the market somehow determines unique prices and quantities. Thus the

---

[1] Just as it might be if we had three well-behaved equations in two unknowns.

[2] As would ordinarily be the case where a system consists in one equation in two unknowns.

[3] But not quite—because we have not found anything to maximize. It should be recalled that this capacity problem also occurred in the input-output analysis where the labor requirements of any output target had to be checked against the available labor supply. Incidentally, note that if resources are available in the wrong proportions it may be impossible to use them up completely, i.e., to satisfy the resource-use equations of the Walrasian system. For example, consider a world of only one output, a unit of whose production requires 2 hours of labor and 3 pounds of raw material. If the available amounts of labor and raw material are 400 hours and 300 pounds, respectively, the two equations $2Q = 400$ and $3Q = 300$ clearly cannot be solved. They must be replaced by inequalities which indicate that some labor or raw material will be left unused.

market's "solution" always exists. An existence analysis can serve only as a test for a general equilibrium model, in that if it turns out that the model possesses no solution we will perhaps want to reject it on the grounds that it may therefore be neither very helpful analytically nor very realistic.

An existence theorem is a rather esoteric idea. It assures us that a problem can be solved but it may tell us nothing about how to go about solving it. Nevertheless, it is more important—even to an economist—than it may at first appear to be. We know that a system which has passed the test of an existence theorem can contain no contradictory elements since, clearly, any contradictions within the system would make a solution impossible. This may even have some direct economic implications. For example, an existence theorem for a system which postulates both full employment and an "ideal" allocation of resources proves that these two desiderata are not incompatible goals. In other words, such a theorem can tell us whether we are pursuing aims which involve having our cake and eating it.

An existence theorem or a *uniqueness theorem* (a theorem which states that the system has no more than one solution) can have further economic relevance in another way. Often it will turn out that we can prove an existence theorem or a uniqueness theorem for a system only if it satisfies some special requirements. For example, we shall see later how such a restriction on the nature of consumer demand is used to prove uniqueness in a general equilibrium model. Now these requirements can be highly suggestive in indicating conditions which may be necessary for such an equilibrium to occur in the real world. This will become clearer in our discussion of the uniqueness problem below.

2. Solution of the Existence Problem

Existence theorems are closely tied in with the so-called fixed-point theorems. First, let us see what is meant by a "fixed point." Suppose we have some functional relationship $Y = f(X)$ which associates different values of Y with X. Then a fixed point is a specific value of X, say $X = X^*$ (some number), for which $Y^* = f(X^*) = X^*$, i.e., for which the value of Y is equal to the value of X. The reason such a value of X is called a fixed point can be made clear with the aid of the following illustrative table, which gives Y as a function of X:

X	1	2	5	6
Y	9	7	5	11

These data may be given the following geometric interpretation: We have four markers (e.g., paper clips) on a rule, one at each X figure, i.e., one at the 1-inch mark, one at the 2-inch mark, etc. The function gives us directions for moving these markers. It tells us to move the paper clip at the 1-inch mark to the 9-inch mark, the one at the 2-inch mark to the 7-inch mark, etc. Note, however, that the instructions tell us not to move the paper clip from the 5-inch mark. That is, $X = 5 = Y$ is a fixed point for this function. As another example, we note that $X = 1$ is a fixed point for the equation $Y = 3 - 2X$ because for $X = 1$, $Y = 3 - 2 = 1$.

But how are fixed-point theorems involved in existence proofs? The answer is that for a wide class of problems they are practically one and the same thing. Suppose, for example, we want to prove that there exists a root for the equation $f(X) - 5 = 0$. This is the same as finding a fixed point for the equation $Y = f(X) - 5 + X$. For if $X = X^*$ (where X^* is some number) is such a fixed point, we have $Y = X^*$ so that the equation becomes $X^* = f(X^*) - 5 + X^*$. Subtracting X^* from both sides, we see that $0 = f(X^*) - 5$; i.e., X^* must be a root of our original equation. More generally, we see that X^* is a root of the equation $0 = G(X)$ if and only if it is a fixed point for the related function $Y = G(X) + X$.

There is another way in which we can see the relation between a fixed-point theorem and an existence proof, this time for the solution of a pair of simultaneous equations. Suppose we are, for example, trying to find a solution to the standard supply-demand problem. A clumsy way to go about it is to draw the demand and supply curves one above the other as in Figure 1. We then pick some price, OP_d, on the Y axis of the demand diagram, see what quantity, OQ, buyers are willing to buy at this price, and then, by moving vertically to the supply curve, we find the price, OP_s, at which sellers are willing to supply that quantity. In this way we obtain a relationship which gives supply price as a function of demand price, $OP_s = f(OP_d)$. If it turns out for some particular demand price, OP_d^*, and its associated supply price, $OP_s^* = f(OP_d^*)$, that we have $OP_d^* = OP_s^*$, it is clear that price OP_s^* is a fixed point for this function. But it is also obvious that OP_s^* and OP_d^* are the equilibrium supply and demand prices. We see, then, that if the function which relates supply price to demand price has a fixed point there must exist a solution to the supply-demand equations. This, as we shall see presently, is in essence an outline of the McKenzie proof of the existence of equilibrium in the general equilibrium system.

The proofs for fixed-point theorems are generally very deep and complex. However, there is one very simple case which is usually used as an illustration. This simple theorem states that in *any* two-variable equation, $Y = f(X)$, if $f(X)$ is continuous (roughly, if there are no breaks in its graph—kinks, though, are permitted) and if Y is never negative and never

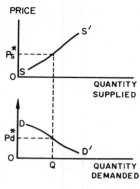

Figure 1

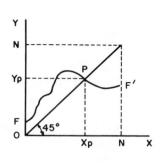

Figure 2

larger than some (any prespecified) number N, the function will possess a fixed point. This is shown in Figure 2, which plots the function $f(X)$ as FF' between $X = 0$ and $X = N$. The graph also contains a 45° line through the origin, and it is clear that any point such as P where FF' intersects the 45° line is a fixed point, for there we will have $Y = X$. There are two possibilities: If $Y = 0$ at $X = 0$, this is our fixed point. On the other hand, if $Y \neq 0$ at $X = 0$ so that FF' starts out above our 45° line, it can "try to avoid" the 45° line by staying above it. But since, by assumption, Y can never be greater than N, FF' will be kept from rising above the upper dotted line and the 45° line must catch up to it and corner it at $X = N$, if not sooner.

The first proof of the existence of a solution to the Walrasian system was published by A. Wald in 1933. His proof was exceedingly difficult. Like the authors of the more recent proofs, Wald had to impose further assumptions on the Walrasian model. Several of Wald's assumptions have been considered excessively restrictive and economically unjustified. Since then several alternative proofs have been offered involving much weaker and more plausible assumptions.

Without going into details we can now very briefly outline one of these proofs, that of Lionel McKenzie. His model contains two sets of inequalities and one set of demand equations. The first set of inequalities states that production takes place under constant returns to scale, and uses up no more than the physical resources which are available. The second set of inequalities states that since we are dealing with a case of perfect competition, profits will be zero.[4] All products sell at a price which is no higher

---

[4] It turns out, surprisingly, that these two sets of inequalities are the respective inequalities of the primal and dual programs in the linear programming production model of Chapter 6!

than the cost of production. (Processes which involve a cost greater than the price of the commodity will, of course, not be used.) The problem is, then, to show that there exists a set of factor prices, commodity prices, and outputs which are consistent with those resource limitations, profit limitations, and the market demand relationships.

We now proceed exactly as in the discussion of Figure 1, only here we must deal with many prices and quantities at once. Pick some arbitrary set of prices and find the quantities which the demand functions tell us consumers will buy at these prices. Suppose that these quantities are producible within the given resource limitations.[5] Then use our second set of inequalities to see what supply prices are just compatible with these output plans and the no-profits perfect-competition requirement. In this way we deduce a set of supply prices from any assumed set of demand prices exactly as we did in Figure 1. As in the discussion of that diagram, to show that an equilibrium price-quantity combination exists, it is necessary to prove that the assumed demand prices and the deduced supply prices can coincide. It is here that we must appeal to a fixed-point theorem. It can be shown that there is such a theorem which applies to our problem and proves that there is one set of demand prices which is the same as the set of supply prices deduced from it. At these prices and quantities, then, the demand conditions, the production conditions (resource limitations), and the profit conditions are all satisfied. This, in outline, is the McKenzie proof of the existence theorem for a general equilibrium model.

3. Solution of the Uniqueness Problem

Uniqueness is mathematically somewhat simpler to prove, though perhaps it is less plausible economically. There is really no good reason to believe that there will be no multiple intersections of supply and demand curves and hence a multiplicity of equilibrium points.

Further, the demand assumption which is used to prove uniqueness, although plausible enough for an individual consumer, is, at best, questionable when applied to the economy. This premise, which is employed in the uniqueness proof, turns out to be the basic assumption in Samuelson's revealed preference analysis, which we now review briefly (Chapter 14, Section 1).

Suppose that an individual buys a collection of commodities *A* rather

---

[5] It can be shown that at the prices which finally emerge the quantities demanded will indeed be feasible. Their production will require no more than the available resources.

than some other collection B which is also available on the market. Presumably he will have made this choice either because he likes A better than B or because A is cheaper than B. If, in fact, A is more expensive than B when the consumer buys A, then the second possibility is ruled out—our consumer must have bought A because he actually prefers it to B. We therefore say, when a consumer buys the more expensive of these two collections, that A has been *revealed* preferred to B. Suppose that a different set of prices could have led the consumer to change his mind and buy B. If his tastes do not change so that he still prefers A to B, he presumably will not buy B when it is more expensive than A. At least this will be the case if his tastes are consistent, for otherwise his buying of B rather than A when B is the more expensive collection reveals that he also prefers B to A! That is the basic revealed preference premise. In sum, it states that consumer tastes are consistent in the sense that if one set of prices reveals A to be preferred to B, then there exists no other set of prices which can reveal B to be preferred to A, i.e., which makes B more expensive than A and yet leads the consumer to buy B.

Now although this is a plausible requirement for consistent consumer behavior, it has much less intuitive appeal when applied to market demand. It may be perfectly consistent for the *community* to buy A rather than B when A is more expensive and yet buy B rather than A when prices change so that B is the more costly. This is because the price change redistributes real income among consumers whose expenditure patterns differ. Thus *different* consumer groups may foot the bulk of the bill in the two cases.[6] Despite these reservations, let us examine the line of reasoning which shows that the revealed preference premise for the market is violated if we have a multiplicity of equilibria. But, before the argument can be completed, one more preliminary theorem must be explained. This preliminary result will also be needed in the discussion of a later section.

At any *fixed level of input and output prices*, competitive outputs will tend to maximize total net profits; e.g., if there is any opportunity to increase profit by increasing some output at the expense of another, individual businessmen will make this switch until the opportunity disappears.[7] But it shall be argued now that this also means that *the value of the final products* (at these fixed prices) *will also be maximized*.

To make the argument clearer, consider a simplified production arrangement in which the economy's fixed resources are used only by the producers of raw materials who sell their entire product to the makers of

---

[6] For a fuller discussion see J. R. Hicks, *A Revision of Demand Theory*, Oxford University Press, London, 1956, pp. 54–58.

[7] What goes wrong with this argument in the presence of external economies or diseconomies? (See Chapter 21, Section 11.)

finished goods. The total profits in the economy are given by

The profits of
finished-goods = { 1. The value of finished products.
producers   { 2. Minus the cost of produced raw materials.

   plus

The profits of
raw-materials = { 3. The value of produced raw materials.
producers   { 4. Minus the cost of the economy's fixed resources.

But the cost to finished-goods producers of their raw materials is exactly the same as the value of the product (revenue) of the raw-materials producers. Hence, in adding items 1 through 4 on the right above, to obtain a figure for the total profit of the economy, items 2 and 3 must cancel out. We see, then, that the total profit earned in the economy will equal the value of the output of finished products minus the cost of the economy's fixed resources.

With a given set of positive prices for all products and resources, what can businessmen do to increase the economy's total profit? Since, by definition, the quantities of the various fixed resources are fixed, then with the prices of these items given, nothing which businessmen do will affect the cost of society's scarce resources. Hence, anything which can be done to add to the total value of final output will add an equal amount to total profits (equals the value of final output minus the cost of fixed resources). It follows that businessmen will have maximized the total profits of the economy if, and only if, they have maximized the total value of finished products. And, as we saw at the beginning of the discussion, with any given set of positive prices, the maximization of total profit may be expected in competitive equilibrium. Therefore, *competitive equilibrium will involve maximization of the total value of all finished commodities produced in the economy.*

We are now only one step from the end of the uniqueness argument. Suppose, on the contrary, that equilibrium is not unique—that there are two alternative equilibrium output combinations A and B, each with its own equilibrium prices. We have just seen that, at the prices which lead to the manufacture of A, the value of final outputs will be maximized, i.e., A will be at least as expensive as B. Similarly, at the prices at which B is produced, B will be at least as expensive as A. But if A and B are competitive equilibria, demand must match supply, that is, A must be demanded in the first situation (when it is most expensive) and B must be demanded in the second (when it is the most costly). A is then revealed preferred to B and vice versa. This clearly violates the revealed preference assumption for the market, so that if that assumption is to hold, there cannot be two equilibrium outputs, A and B. The equilibrium output must be unique.

4. The Von Neumann Model of an Expanding Economy

From existence and uniqueness theorems we turn now to the second of our activity-analysis topics: general equilibrium growth models. Two years before Wald published his existence proof, von Neumann delivered a paper which is perhaps the most virtuoso performance in the literature of mathematical economics. In this article von Neumann developed what is presumably the first general equilibrium analysis of economic growth. In this respect (though not in some of its other properties) the model is more complicated than the Walrasian system. Nevertheless, von Neumann developed an existence theorem for this model using a fixed-point theorem in a way which is somewhat similar to the later existence theorem for the Walrasian economy. Moreover, in the course of this argument there are clearly discernible features of both linear programming and game theory,[8] and, in particular, of the duality theory of linear programming.

The structure of the model itself can be outlined fairly briefly. Von Neumann describes an economy characterized by a linear homogeneous production function and in which all outputs serve only as raw materials for further production. Consumption can be interpreted as the process whereby finished goods are used as inputs in the production of labor. Thus consumption also becomes a purely technological phenomenon and ordinary demand relationships disappear from the model.[9]

The production function is described as a set of processes each of which turns some inputs into outputs, all in fixed proportions. To make sure his economy is completely integrated so that it is not decomposable into unconnected subsectors, von Neumann also assumes that each commodity is either an input or an output in every process, e.g., it is assumed that *every*

---

[8] As we saw in the chapter on game theory, every zero-sum, two-person game can be interpreted as a pair of dual linear programs (and the converse is also true), so it is really not so surprising that elements of *both* of these are involved in the von Neumann model.

[9] Actually, the absence of any demand functions removes a major difficulty in the proof of the existence theorem. In this respect the problem of the existence proof is considerably simpler than that for the Walrasian system.

process either produces size 7-B brown moccasin style shoes or uses them as a raw material![10]

Suppose now that this economy is expanding; the manufactured outputs of the production processes taken together exceed the outputs of the preceding period (which are the inputs for the current period's products). Moreover, assume with von Neumann that there are no limited supplies of land, labor, or other factors to put an end to this expansion. Von Neumann then asks whether there is a constant equilibrium rate of growth of the economy which will yield no profits, as required by perfect competition, and which satisfies the technological requirement that the process intensities during any period require no more than the available raw-material inputs (the outputs of the preceding period).

Equilibrium is defined as a constant proportionate rate of growth of all outputs, inputs, and process intensities which satisfies the profit and technological conditions just described. (Here a proportionate rate of growth, P, means that in every period each output is *at least* P per cent higher than it was in the previous period.)

Let α be the equilibrium rate of expansion of the slowest-growing item of the economy, i.e., the production of each item grows at a rate greater than or equal to α per cent per year. Let the money rate of interest be β dollars per annum. The no-profit condition then can be restated as follows: The money outlay on the inputs of any process plus the interest cost of that money for one period must be greater than or equal to the value of the outputs of that process. Similarly, the technological condition can be formulated as follows: The sum of the current inputs of any item in all processes (which is α per cent greater than the amount used in the preceding period) must be less than or equal to the output of that item in the preceding period. That is, the amount of coal used during the current period [equals $(1 + \alpha)$ multiplied by the amount of coal used last period] must not exceed the coal made available by last period's output. We see, then, how inequalities play a fundamental role in this model as they do throughout activity analysis.

Von Neumann then proves the following results:

1. There exists *one* such equilibrium rate of growth α (existence and uniqueness).

---

[10] This is not as ridiculous as it may sound—probably some steel worker wears out such shoes somewhere in American steel production. Moreover, there have been two recent articles which analyze the behavior of a von Neumann economy without the use of this assumption. See John G. Kemeny, Oskar Morgenstern, and Gerald Thompson, "A Generalization of the von Neumann Model of an Expanding Economy," *Econometrica*, Vol. 24, April 1956; and David Gale, "The Closed Linear Model of Production," in *Linear Inequalities and Related Systems*, H. W. Kuhn and A. W. Tucker (eds.), Annals of Mathematics Studies 38, Princeton University Press, Princeton, N.J., 1956.

2. This equilibrium rate of growth will equal the interest rate so that the rate of increase of output will just exactly suffice to cover the interest cost of investment in inputs. This is an intuitively obvious consequence of the no-profit condition. Thus, there will be a unique value for both α and β. However, it should be noted that a von Neumann model can be consistent with many equilibrium output-price combinations—in this respect, then, the solution is not unique.

3. There may be some processes whose employment involves a financial loss. These processes will not be used—i.e., all processes actually operated will yield exactly zero profits, as the theory of perfect competition has always taught us.

4. Some outputs may grow at a rate greater than α per cent per period. There will be a surplus of such an item over and above what is required as input in the next period for the equilibrium growth of the economy. Because there will be an excess supply of each such commodity, it will be a free good; that is, its marginal utility and hence its price will be zero.[11]

5. There will be no sustainable rate of growth greater than the equilibrium rate of growth α. For if there were available alternative processes capable of yielding a higher growth rate, α', then the α growth rate would not be consistent with equilibrium. Entrepreneurs would switch to these alternative processes because with interest at the old rate, β, they would make a profit. With the interest rate then raised to $\beta' = \alpha'$, to eliminate this profit the old nonmaximal growth-rate processes would only be operable at a loss.

The extreme abstraction involved in the von Neumann model hardly needs to be pointed out. Later work has removed some of the more unpalatable assumptions. The conclusions are of considerable interest in themselves. Nevertheless, primary interest in the model continues to reside in the analytic tools which were developed and exhibited with its aid.

5. Activity Analysis and Welfare Economics

Doubtless the best-known theorem of elementary welfare analysis asserts that a long-run, perfectly competitive equilibrium will yield an optimal allocation of resources. Not only is the theorem elementary and well known—as has already been shown in Chapter 21—it is also, strictly speaking, untrue, or rather, true only under some fairly restrictive assumptions.

In recent years there has been much work devoted to the development of an alternative activity-analysis proof of this theorem. It may well be

---

[11] Results 3 and 4 are directly related to the second duality theorem of linear programming which is described in Section 3 of Chapter 6.

asked why this has been thought to be necessary. For one thing, activity analysis has made no attempt to dispute the restricted validity of the result. In fact, no way has even been found to apply the methods of activity analysis to external economies and the related difficulties which are incompatible with the optimality of perfect competitive equilibrium. Rather, the new approach has been helpful in another way.

The standard welfare economics deals only with commodities which are actually bought in the market and not with those which are free goods or for which no customers can be found at a profitable price. For old-fashioned welfare theory leans heavily on the marginal conditions of equilibrium, e.g., the condition of equality of price ratios to the marginal rates of substitution. But these conditions need not hold for free or unsalable goods. In old-fashioned terms, if each consumer chooses not to buy a commodity, the marginal utility of that item may well be *less* than its price (note the inequality again). Moreover, the cost of production of such an unsalable good must be greater than its price. For free goods the ratio of prices is not even defined. It follows that the standard version of the theorem which we are discussing must be restated to read that (where the theorem is valid) a competitive economy will allocate resources optimally *among commodities which are salable without loss and which are not free*. But which commodities will these be? We cannot assume we know the answer in advance, for the answer is an economic question of costs of production and demand patterns. Moreover, though our intuition may tell us that this is so, we must prove rigorously that there can be no preferable allocation of resources to free or unsalable goods.[12]

Old-fashioned welfare theory, by taking marginal utility to equal price, may end up requiring negative consumption of an unwanted commodity since even with zero consumption its marginal utility may turn out to be less than its price. Similarly, it cannot preclude the economic absurdity of negative prices for "free goods." But since activity analysis can cope with inequalities, it can specify that (1) prices and quantities exchanged must all be greater than or equal to zero, (2) the average cost of production must be equal to price for all items which are produced, and greater than the price at which any item that no one considers worth producing can be sold, and (3) production must not exceed the levels made possible by the available resources of society. Subject to these and the limitations of competition, businessmen and consumers are then taken to do the best they can for themselves. Marginal equalities and inequalities do not even make an explicit appearance.

---

[12] Pigou long ago pointed out that the production of some items which it would be unprofitable to produce under pure competition can conceivably yield a net benefit to society. See *The Economics of Welfare*, 4th edition, Macmillan & Co., Ltd., London, 1938, pp. 283, 810–811. However, Pigou's case requires decreasing costs, and these cannot be handled by the activity-analysis approach as developed to date.

Before outlining the proof of the theorem, let us first recall two related concepts. A production arrangement is called *efficient* if any alternative productive arrangement which increases the output of some commodity must also involve a decrease in the output of some other commodity. The motivation of the definition is obvious. Any productive arrangement which is not efficient in this sense requires that the economy forego the opportunity to get something for nothing—the opportunity to increase the output of some item, X, without giving anything up in exchange. Related to efficiency is the concept of *Pareto optimality* (cf. Chapter 21, Section 31, for the reason for this nomenclature). A situation is said to be "Pareto optimal" when it is impossible to effect a change which benefits some individual without any deleterious effects on someone else. Efficiency is then a purely technological concept whereas Pareto optimality is the corresponding concept for individuals as consumers and in their other economic roles.

Let us now see how activity analysis can be used to prove that every competitive equilibrium is technologically efficient and that every efficient output combination is a competitive equilibrium, i.e., that for each efficient point there can be found a set of prices which would under perfect competition produce the efficient output combination in question. This part of the theorem amounts essentially to the standard result that a competitive output can occur at and only at any point on the *production possibility locus* (transformation surface), the graph which shows the various output combinations which society can produce with its available resources (curve TT' in Figure 3). For the production possibility locus is the locus of all efficient points. For example, we see that, with output OX_1 of X, the largest possible output of Y is OY_1 so that point C is efficient. But, on the other hand, a point like A which lies inside the transformation locus TT' represents an inefficient combination of output X and Y because it is possible to move to an efficient point like B which lies on TT' northeast of A, so that B involves greater outputs of both commodities. Note that although C is also efficient, as we have just seen, activity analysis as so far described has not settled whether it is or is not more desirable socially than is A.[13]

How do we know that a competitive output is technologically efficient? The answer is simple. With fixed prices, an inefficient output cannot in-

---

[13] We see, then, that there will usually be many efficient output combinations represented by the points that make up the transformation locus. The locus can be found with the aid of programming techniques. The trick is to choose any output of X, say OX_1, and find the *maximum* output of Y permitted by the resources left over from the production of that quantity of X. This is clearly a programming computation, and it will show that OY_1 is the maximum amount of Y then producible. In this way point C on the transformation curve will have been located, and, by starting with other values of X, other points on TT' can be found in the same way. For the details of the analogous derivation of the contract curve equation, see footnote 11 of Chapter 21.

volve a maximum money value of output. For we can increase the output of, say, X without decreasing that of any other commodity and end up with an output combination whose money value is obviously increased. Thus, with fixed prices, the money value of E in Figure 3 is clearly higher than that of A. But we have seen earlier (Section 3) that a competitive equilibrium necessarily involves a maximum value of output when valued at the equilibrium prices. Hence, no competitive equilibrium can be inefficient.

More difficult is the proof of the converse, which states that every

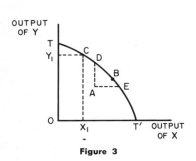

Figure 3

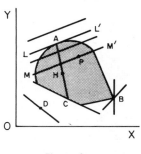

Figure 4

efficient output combination is a competitive output. However, the method of proof is interesting in and of itself. This employs an "intuitively obvious" mathematical theorem whose proof is, in fact, rather difficult. The theorem states that, given an (N-dimensional) convex geometric figure (convex set) and any point R on the boundary of or outside this figure, it is always possible to draw at least one line (N-dimensional hyperplane) through R in such a way that the convex figure lies entirely on one side of this line.[14] Thus, in Figure 4 the shaded region is convex. Through points A, B, and C on its boundary, and point D outside the figure, lines have been drawn which have the required property. Such a line through a boundary point like A, B, or C is called a *supporting line* (plane) of the convex set. Such a line can be taken to divide the plane into two half-planes (*half-spaces*) and in each case the shaded figure lies entirely within one of the half-spaces produced by the lines in the figure. Supporting lines represent a generalization of the concept of tangency to cover the case where the boundary curve has a kink (e.g., at point B—note that there are many supporting hyperplanes at such points).

---

[14] For the definition of a convex set, see Chapter 7, Section 4. The theorem does not hold for nonconvex regions as can be shown with the aid of Figure 5b in Chapter 7, where any line through point E must intersect the nonconvex shaded figure.

Consider now one of the supporting lines of the convex set, e.g., line LL' through point A in Figure 4. Since the convex set lies entirely on one side of such a line, then (if the line is not vertical) either no portion of the convex set will lie above this line or no part of the set will lie below this line. Suppose the convex set does not lie above the supporting line in question (as is the case with LL'). Then any point of the set (e.g., point P) must lie on or below LL', and any line parallel to LL' which goes through a point in the convex set (e.g., line MM' through point P) must either coincide with LL' or lie entirely below it. In other words, *such a supporting line must be the highest of all the lines which are parallel to it and which meet the convex set at any point.* We shall employ this result by interpreting the family of lines parallel to our supporting line as a set of price lines which, as usual, involve price ratios that are given by the (constant) slope of these lines. Then the italicized result may be translated to read as follows: If only output combinations which are represented by points within the convex region are attainable, the highest attainable price line goes through A, the point of tangency with the convex region. Of course, this final statement sounds at least vaguely familiar.

Now to get back to our theorem that every technologically efficient point is a competitive equilibrium. We note first that the set of points representing all the feasible outputs in a linear program must form a convex geometric figure.[15] Suppose now that some output is efficient. We have seen that the point which represents this output combination must lie on the upper boundary of the feasible region (compare curve TT' in Figure 3). Moreover, we know that through every such point there passes (at least) one supporting line. This line can be interpreted as a price line giving the value of the output through A, and its slope can be taken to represent the ratio of the prices of X and Y. In other words, for any efficient point there will always exist relative prices at which the efficient point maximizes the value of output.[16]

With these prices, moreover, businessmen under pure competition will (in the absence of external economies and diseconomies) be motivated to produce the technologically efficient output in question, for, as we have argued, it will pay them to maximize the value of output. Thus any such

---

[15] See footnote 1 of Chapter 7.

[16] The economic interpretation requires that the price line have a negative slope. But we can show that at an efficient point the slope of the price line must be negative, for we know that if all prices are positive, the slope of a price line will be negative. (Indeed this is why we want the price line to have a negative slope.) But suppose the contrary, that one of the "prices" deduced from the supporting price line is negative. We can then increase the value of output by decreasing the quantity of the commodity whose price is negative, which means that we can increase output value by leaving the efficient point, contrary to what has just been shown, i.e., that the value of the efficient output with this price line will be a maximum.

efficient output combination is a competitive output combination; at some set of prices competitive businessmen will produce it.

This, then, proves the theorem about the efficiency of competitive equilibrium. There is some similarity between this proof and the proof of the Pareto optimality theorem, which will not be described in detail. Clearly the latter theorem must take into consideration consumer demands, and this involves a number of complications. In effect, what we want to prove is that every competitive equilibrium involves tangency between the transformation locus and some sort of consumers' community indifference curve (an indifference curve which, in some sense, represents the tastes of all consumers taken together), and that any such point of tangency is a competitive equilibrium. For then society will have attained the highest state of welfare compatible with the available production possibilities. The tangency can be assured by the tangency of both the transformation curve and the community indifference curve with the same price line.

Here too we have a theorem on convex sets which comes to our assistance. The theorem states that if two convex sets meet only at boundary points, there will be at least one line such that one convex set lies in one of the half-spaces generated by the line and the other convex set lies in the line's other half-space.

Consider all output combinations above and to the right of some indifference curve, i.e., all the points which involve outputs that are preferred to or indifferent with the outputs at some point, R, on the indifference curve QQ' (Figure 5). Such a preferred point is defined in the Pareto sense as one that involves an output combination which can make some consumers better off than they were at R, without hurting anyone. It can be argued that the set of points preferred to or indifferent with R (shaded region in Figure 5) is convex. The set of feasible output points (the points in region OTT' which lie on or beneath the transformation curve, TT')

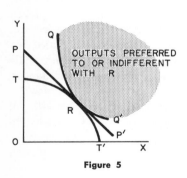

Figure 5

also constitutes a convex set, at least in cases involving constant returns (linear programming) or diminishing returns (see Chapter 7, Sections 4 and 5). There will then be a line, PP', which separates these two regions. If, in addition, point R lies on the transformation locus, PP' will be a supporting line for both sets and R will be a feasible efficient point which lies on the highest possible indifference curve.

6. Dual Prices and Decentralized Decision Making

Section 9 of Chapter 21 discussed a pricing scheme which was designed to achieve the results of central planning without detailed centralized direction. The idea is simply to establish such a set of prices that the individual plant or company manager is forced to make the "right" decisions in order to maximize his profits.

Some light can be thrown on the nature of this sort of arrangement with the aid of the analysis of the preceding section and the duality theorems of linear programming (Section 3 of Chapter 6). It will be recalled that one of the properties of the dual program is that the optimal values of its variables can be interpreted as accounting prices of the scarce resources in the primal production problem. Moreover, these accounting prices have the following properties:

1. The cost of the scarce resources used by the firm when evaluated at these accounting prices will be exactly equal to the firm's total profits.

2. If the firm is charged these dual prices whenever it uses its scarce resources, any output or process which should, optimally, not be employed by the firm will actually involve the firm in a loss—i.e., only negative profits can be earned on a commodity which the firm should, optimally, not be producing or on any process which the firm should, optimally, not be using.

Suppose, now, that the economy's production function is linear and homogeneous, and that the central authority were to look for a set of commodity prices and input prices which will lead individual businessmen to produce some efficient combination of outputs. As we saw in the previous section, for every such output combination, Q, there exists some set of prices, P, such that Q is the output combination of maximum value when evaluated at these prices, P. In other words, this output combination would be the solution of a mathematical programming problem: Maximize the value of output subject to the constraints imposed on the economy by its scarce resources. Moreover, since the production function is, by assumption, linear and homogeneous, this will be a *linear* programming problem. Such a problem will therefore have a dual whose solution will be a set of accounting prices, R, for society's scarce resources.

The planning authority now can proceed as follows: (1) Set prices P for all final products; (2) set accounting prices R for all scarce resources, meaning by this that whenever a plant or company manager uses any such resource he will be required to pay to the government the dual price of this item for every unit he uses.

In that case every business firm will find it unprofitable to produce any outputs or to use any processes which are not included in the optimal (efficient) output combination, Q, for by the standard properties of the dual prices every nonoptimal output or process will incur a loss.

Moreover, if every businessman expands his output to capacity (as he can do without loss since the dual prices just permit zero profits), the result will be the production of exactly the efficient output combination, Q. For as we have seen in Section 3, with fixed input and output prices, businessmen can only maximize their profits by maximizing the value of outputs, and the officially enforced prices P have been chosen so as to make Q the output whose value is a maximum. Thus by choosing output prices P and dual input prices R, businessmen will be forced by the pursuit of self-interest to make decisions which are socially optimal. No detailed central output directives will be required to achieve this optimal result.

7. Integer Programming and Welfare Economics

Most of the preceding results hold for cases involving linear or other convex relationships (constant or diminishing returns to scale) and where there are no problems of indivisibilities (a steam shovel is indivisible because we cannot produce one-half or one-fourth of a steam shovel). However, the presence of indivisibilities and increasing returns complicates the situation, and we shall see now that in these cases things do not work out so well.

These problems can be treated with the aid of integer programming analysis in which the answer is always required to contain no fractional parts. Its relevance to the indivisibilities case is clear since we desire an analysis which can avoid nonsense answers involving fractional parts of steamships, or drill presses. At least in principle, the increasing-returns case can also be reduced to an integer programming computation. Let us see, then, what follows for our welfare theorems from the integer programming analysis.

As in ordinary linear programming, it remains true in the integer programming case that every value-maximizing (competitive) output will also be efficient. This can be shown by exactly the same argument as that of Section 5. Unfortunately, the converse does not hold. There may be efficient outputs which are not competitive, i.e., for which there exist no prices at which this output combination maximizes the total value of output. This is easily proved by counterexample, as shown in Figure 6. Here the shaded triangle, OBC,

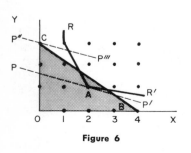

Figure 6

contains all of the feasible lattice points (the points representing all possible solutions with no fractional coordinates). Point A, with coordinates $(2, 1)$, lies in the interior of this triangle. But (because the feasible points are isolated) it is possible for such an interior point to be efficient. This is in fact the case with A, for there is no feasible lattice point which "dominates" A, i.e., no point which lies directly above it, directly to the right of it, or above it and to its right.

Now consider any straight (price) line, such as PP', through A. Any such line must lie below either lattice point B or lattice point C. This means that there must exist another parallel price line such as $P''P'''$ which lies above PP' and goes through one of these corners of triangle OBC. In other words, in the case shown in Figure 6, at the prices involved in the price (iso-output-value) lines shown, the value of output at point C exceeds that at A. And, similarly, at any other possible set of output prices the value of output at A will be smaller than that at B or that at C. This shows how, in the discrete programming case, there are likely to arise efficient outputs which are not competitive (value-maximizing) outputs and which therefore cannot be enforced by the standard type of decentralized control procedure of the economic literature, in which the central authority makes only simple price decisions.

It is to be noted, however, that it is possible to find families of nonlinear or piecewise linear price curves such as RR' for which the value of output is maximized at A. This has a simple interpretation. The prices which are set up are discriminatory and vary with the magnitude of output. Output combinations which are close to A are given relatively high prices, but as outputs move farther and farther from A prices are made increasingly unfavorable to the seller so that there are sharply diminishing returns to departures from A. In other words, an output, t_1, of any commodity at A is broken arbitrarily into a sum of suboutputs

$$t_{11} + t_{12} + \cdots + t_{1n} = t_1$$

and each of the suboutputs t_{1i} is assigned a different price, P_{1i}, as just described. Such an arrangement could, in principle, be enforced by government fiat. But it is difficult to see much advantage to a decentralized control procedure when it becomes so complicated, and in any event it would never result from the spontaneous operation of competitive market forces which preclude the existence of different prices for different units of a homogeneous product.

The so-called basic theorem of welfare economics runs into even more serious trouble in integer programming. It is in this situation not generally possible to attain a Pareto optimal point by means of a price system.

This is obviously so for the case of interior efficient points such as A in Figure 6, for let RR' now represent a community indifference curve so that A is now the optimal feasible point. There obviously exists no line which separates the remainder of the feasible lattice points from the region socially preferred to or indifferent with A (the region above RR'). This means that with any fixed price arrangement producers will find it more profitable to manufacture either output combination B or C than to turn out the social optimum combination, A.[17]

Let us summarize the results of this section:

1. Every competitive output combination is efficient and any such point can be attained by a system of fixed prices set by central authority, all other decisions being left to the individual firms in the economy. This is no different from the result for the ordinary linear programming case.

2. However, unlike the ordinary linear programming case, not every efficient output can be achieved by simple centralized pricing decisions or by competitive market pricing processes.

3. Moreover, it is possible in the integer programming case that there exists no hyperplane which separates the feasible lattice points from those which are preferred to or indifferent with the optimal lattice point. In other words, there may exist no set of prices which simultaneously makes the optimal point, Q, the most profitable among those which can be produced and the cheapest among those which consumers consider to be at least as good as Q. That is, at any set of prices either producers will try to make, or consumers will demand, some other output combination.

It should be observed, in conclusion, that these limitations on the price system in the integer programming case should not be entirely surprising. For, as has already been indicated, cases of increasing returns to scale can, at least in principle, be reduced to integer programming problems. And in such cases it has long been recognized that the price system runs into difficulties.

REFERENCES

Expository Material

Dorfman, Robert, Paul A. Samuelson, and Robert M. Solow, *Linear Programming and Economic Analysis*, McGraw-Hill Book Company, New York, 1958, Chapters 11–14.

---

[17] Moreover, it can be shown in the three-or-more variable case that even if the optimum point, Q, is a competitive efficient point (a point on the boundary of the convex hull of the feasible points), there may well exist no hyperplane which separates the feasible (producible) points from the lattice points which are preferred to or indifferent with Q.

Hicks, J. R., "Linear Theory," *Economic Journal,* Vol. 70, December 1960.

Koopmans, Tjalling C., *Three Essays on the State of Economic Science,* McGraw-Hill Book Company, New York, 1957, especially Essay I.

Source Materials

Arrow, Kenneth J., "An Extension of the Basic Theorems of Classical Welfare Economics," *Proceedings of the Second Berkeley Symposium on Mathematical Statistics and Probability,* University of California Press, Berkeley, 1951.

Arrow, Kenneth J., and Gerard Debreu, "Existence of an Equilibrium for a Competitive Economy," *Econometrica,* Vol. 22, July 1954.

Kemeny, John G., Oskar Morgenstern, and Gerald Thompson, "A Generalization of the Von Neumann Model of an Expanding Economy," *Econometrica,* Vol. 24, April 1956.

Koopmans, Tjalling C. (ed.), *Activity Analysis of Production and Allocation,* Cowles Commission Monograph 13, John Wiley & Sons, Inc., New York, 1951, Chapters II and III.

Koopmans, Tjalling C., *Three Essays on the State of Economic Science,* McGraw-Hill Book Company, New York, 1957, esp. Essay I.

Malinvaud, Edmond, *Lectures on Microeconomic Theory,* North-Holland/American Elsevier, Amsterdam and New York, 1972, Chapters 4, 5, 8, and 9. (Rather advanced.)

McKenzie, Lionel, "On the Existence of a General Equilibrium for a Competitive Market," *Econometrica,* Vol. 27, January 1959.

Quirk, James, and Rubin Saposnick, *Introduction to General Equilibrium Theory and Welfare Economics,* McGraw-Hill Book Company, New York, 1968.

Sen, A. K., *Collective Choice and Social Welfare,* Holden-Day, San Francisco, 1970.

Von Neumann, John, "A Model of General Economic Equilibrium," *Review of Economic Studies,* Vol. 13, 1945–1946.

Wald, Abraham, "Über die eindeutige positive Lösbarkeit der neuen Produktionsgleichungen," *Ergebnisse eines Mathematischen Kolloquiums,* Vol. 6, 1933–1934.

Theory of Distribution

The theory of distribution deals with the determination of the levels of payment to the various factors of production—the prices of the economy's inputs. Since general equilibrium analysis seeks to account for the determination of every price in the economy, it includes the pricing of inputs within its scope; that is, the analysis of distribution must ultimately be considered a segment of general equilibrium theory. Since a change in the level of wages, interest rates, or rents has significant ramifications throughout the economy, the general equilibrium aspects cannot easily be ignored.

In this chapter, there is no attempt at a systematic discussion of the three traditional input categories, land, labor, and capital. So simple a breakdown is somewhat out of fashion, since each of these categories includes within it so huge a variety of heterogeneous elements. It is often not helpful to treat coal, cloth, and a drill press as one homogeneous element—capital. Nevertheless, the categories still retain considerable convenience as shorthand analytic devices, and they will be used where they prove handy.

1. Controversies in the Theory of Distribution

Recently the theory of distribution has become the subject of a rather spirited debate between writers associated with Cambridge, Massachusetts, and Cambridge in the United Kingdom (including a group of Italian economists associated with the latter). Much of the argument has centered about fairly technical topics in the theory of capital and, accordingly, it will be considered later, in the chapter on Capital and Distribution. But the broad subject of the discussion can serve as a useful introduction to the materials of this chapter.

The basic issue is what one can reasonably expect from distribution theory. Three possibilities come to mind: (a) One can hope for a sophisticated analytical (micro) model which passes various tests of logical consistency and completeness and whose complexity reasonably reflects the complexities of the real world; (b) one can want a tractable macro model which rests on some well-chosen simplifications that exact only a small cost in distortion of reality but in return offer us a firm intuitive grasp of the main relationships and a reasonable basis for policy design; (c) one can aspire to a model which enables us to evaluate the fairness and morality of the distributive arrangements in our own or some other society.

We can immediately and most firmly dispose of the last possibility. Value judgments do not emerge from a behavioral model without first being put into it. We may all agree that more equality in income distribution is a good thing, but that is a view which does not emerge from our theory. Adam Smith and Ricardo could have espoused the same distribution model (though in fact they did not) but Smith in the spirit of the eighteenth century might have considered a call for more equality to be quixotic, while Ricardo, as an early liberal of the nineteenth century, might have taken it to be a goal which was obviously desirable but difficult to attain.

Few economists have argued that our theory tells us anything about *justice* in distribution, though there have been several exceptions. At the end of the nineteenth century J. B. Clark concluded from marginal productivity theory that "the different classes of men who combine their forces in industry have no grievances against each other," and that the distributive arrangements under pure competition ". . . treat men fairly" and are ". . . determined by a principle that humanity can approve and perpetuate" because it "gives to every agent of production the amount of wealth which that agent creates".[1] Similarly, some of the analytically weaker of the utopian socialists sought in the theory of distribution a basis for the condemnation of capitalism. But with these exceptions such

---

[1] John Bates Clark, *The Distribution of Wealth*, The Macmillan Company, New York, 1899, pp. v, 7–8.

a quest has elicited the universal derision of modern economists[2] and even that of Karl Marx.[3]

There is good reason to reject marginal productivity analysis as evidence of the virtue of the distributive arrangements. Even if Nature does contribute a marginal product that is equal to the rent of land, is there any inherent virtue in this sum going to the landlord acting as a representative of Mother Nature in absentia?

Let us consider next the macroeconomic models of distribution. Such models lump together large numbers of moderately diverse economic variables and relationships and treat the resulting aggregates as homogeneous economic elements. In this way, manageable models involving small numbers of variables and relationships are obtained. Some violence is always done to the facts in the process of aggregation. For example, the statement that the labor market is in equilibrium when the total effective demand for labor equals the total supply can conceal serious difficulties of oversupply in some industries and shortages in others. One must therefore seek fruitfulness rather than rigor in a macroeconomic model. A completely formalistic macro model is likely to be the worst of both worlds because it is apt to offer neither empirical insights nor an accurate analytic mechanism.

At least two such models are available and have been subjects of considerable discussion. The first is the classical theory of David Ricardo and the second is the model of Nicholas Kaldor, which can be taken as an example of the approach associated with Cambridge University.[4] Accordingly, this chapter will provide a review of these discussions and of some of the criticisms to which they have been subjected.

---

[2] Samuelson, for example, has felicitously described the imputation of virtue to payments based on marginal productivity as making ". . . idols of partial derivatives," *Foundations of Economic Analysis*, Harvard University Press, Cambridge, Mass., 1948, p. 225.

[3] See, e.g., *Das Kapital*, Vol. I, Chapter VI, Kerr edition. "The value of labour-power is determined, as in the case of every other commodity, by the labour-time necessary for the production, and consequently also the reproduction of this special article. . . . It is a very cheap sort of sentimentality which declares this method of determining the value of labour [in terms of the labor cost of production of subsistence], a method proscribed by the very nature of the case, to be a brutal method . . ." (Kerr ed., pp. 189, 192.)

[4] The reader may wonder why there is no discussion of a Marxian distribution model. However, it can be argued that Marx never formulated any such model and that he deliberately avoided doing so. He considered his analysis to be related primarily to production. (Thus, Volume I of *Das Kapital*, the only one of the three volumes completed by Marx, is entitled *The Process of Capitalist Production*.) Marx certainly held little brief for work that separates out distribution as a subject to be studied by itself. See,

Finally, there is *the* theoretical micro model of distribution, the marginal productivity analysis which is the basis of most theoretical writings on the subject. With all of its restrictive assumptions, most notably those of universal perfect competition and stationary equilibrium, no one claims that it is a very accurate representation of the facts. What is claimed is that it describes a consistent mechanism which bears at least some resemblance to the workings of our economic institutions and that embodied within its general equilibrium relationships there are the forces which determine the payments going to laborers, capitalists, landlords, etc. It used to be thought that these complex relationships in fact followed certain simple patterns at least roughly and that from these patterns one could safely formulate intuitive generalizations and draw conclusions relevant for policy. It has been the contention of the Cantab(Cambridge)-Italian school that no such generalizations are possible—that any simple conclusions drawn from the general equilibrium models will encounter so many exceptions of such significance that they become untenable. The right question, it would then seem, is not whether a marginal productivity analysis (with suitable modifications) is invalid or logically defective. Rather the issue is the degree to which it is useful.

2. On the Marginal Productivity Theory

The partial equilibrium elements of the marginal productivity theory are implicit in our discussions of the theory of the firm and the theory of production in earlier chapters. Under pure competition the profit-maximizing firm will hire any input up to the point where its wage equals the value of its marginal product, that is, to the marginal physical product of the input, multiplied by the money price of the product, for if the marginal value of the product exceeds the price of the input, the firm can, by definition, increase its profits by acquiring more units of the input since additional units bring in more to the firm than they cost. The reverse will be true if the price of the input exceeds the value of its marginal product.[5]

---

e.g., Karl Marx, *Grundrisse*, Martin Nicolaus (ed., trans.), Pelican Books, Harmondsworth, 1973, pp. 87. 94–98.

[5] Mathematically, in the single product firm, whose production function is $y = f(x_1, \cdots, x_n)$, where x_i is the quantity of its ith input, profit is given by

$$\pi = py - p_1 x_1 - \cdots - p_n x_n = pf(x_1, \cdots, x_n) - p_1 x_1 - \cdots - p_n x_n$$

where p is the price of a unit of output and p_i the price of a unit of input i. Hence, profit maximization requires

$$\partial \pi / \partial x_i = 0 \quad \text{or} \quad p \partial y / \partial x_i = p_i,$$

which is the result in the text.

The reader will recognize this as the usual argument behind any of the marginal conditions of equilibrium in any economic problem.

Where pure competition does not hold and product price varies with output (a negatively sloping demand curve for the products of the firm), the return to the input will be equated to its *marginal revenue product*, where marginal revenue product is equal to price times marginal physical product *minus* the loss in revenues to the firm that results from the fact that increased production forces it to reduce its price on everything it sells.[6]

If, for example, a firm has been producing 100,000 units of some product which sells at $5 per unit and an additional machine can produce an additional 32,000 units of output which, when dumped on the market, reduce the price to $4, the net effect is the following: It has added to the firm's revenues 32,000 units at $4 each, but this is partly offset by the $1 reduction in earnings on each of the remaining 100,000 units sold, making a net gain (marginal revenue product) of $128,000 − $100,000 = $28,000.

In terms of Figure 1 if DD' is the firm's demand curve, suppose an additional unit of input increases output from y_a to y_b (marginal physical product = $y_b − y_a$). Then the value of the marginal product is equal to price multiplied by $y_b − y_a$, i.e., to the heavily shaded area in the diagram. But this is not unadulterated gain to the firm which finds that simultaneously its product price falls by $p_a − p_b$, causing it a loss on its initial output represented by the lightly shaded area. The net revenue contributed by an additional unit of output, then, is the difference between the two areas, and that is the input's marginal revenue product. The firm will hire the input until its wage is equal to that marginal revenue product.[7]

The main point is that the marginal productivity analysis as it has been described up to this point has served to help us to determine the firm's *derived demand* for any given input. It shows how the quantity of the input demanded by the firm will vary with the input's price and makes it clear

---

[6] In terms of the discussion of the preceding footnote, we are no longer assuming that product price, p, is a constant but that it is a function of output, y. Consequently, by the chain rule of differentiation (Chapter 4, Section 2, Rule 8), the profit maximization requirement becomes

$$\partial \pi / \partial x_1 = 0 \quad \text{or} \quad p\partial y/\partial x_i + (ydp/dy)\partial y/\partial x_i = p_i,$$

thus adding the term $(ydp/dy)\partial y/\partial x_1$ to the requirement of the preceding footnote. The value of this term is normally negative since dp/dy is the reciprocal of the slope of the demand curve. ydp/dy is, then, the loss in total revenue resulting from the reduction in price that accompanies the rise in output.

[7] If the price of the input is affected by the quantity hired by the firm, this rule must again be amended in an obvious manner to state that in equilibrium the *marginal* cost of the input to the firm will equal its marginal product. But this and other such complications are peripheral to our interest here.

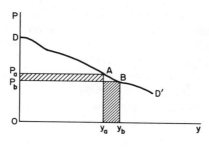

that, for a profit-maximizing firm, this demand relationship depends directly on the demand for the final product as well as the input's marginal contribution to output.

However, *so far it is not at all a model of input price determination.* It takes those prices somehow to have been determined outside the model and asks how much of each input will be hired in response. Thus, so far, it is an analysis of employment by the firm, rather than a model of wages and other input prices.

The determination of the input prices themselves requires one more step, but a crucial one. We now have obtained from the marginal productivity analysis a demand function for every input by every firm. We can take this information, along with the corresponding supply information for each input (whether purchased from another firm or a private individual like a worker selling his labor power), and embed it, along with the supply-demand information for every good in the economy, into a giant Walrasian model of general equilibrium. From this machinery we can assume that a set of equilibrium prices and quantities will emerge for every item in the economy, including wages for different types of labor, rents for different qualities of land, etc. *This* then is the marginal productivity model of price determination.

Unfortunately, no partial model will be able to do its job because if there is any place in the economy that interdependence of different activities manifests itself, it is in the market for inputs. A rise in wages in industry A soon enough affects labor costs in industry B. A rise in the price of fuels affects the relative demands for other inputs, depending on their comparative economy in fuel use.

Thus, we are left with the suspicion that the analysis, with all its assumptions, is fundamentally valid but perhaps not so illuminating as one might wish. To deal with this difficulty, economists in the neoclassical tradition have sought to aggregate large sectors of the marginal productivity model, permitting it to retain its general equilibrium character but cutting its scope down to two or three homogeneous inputs. In particular, models have been constructed containing only labor and capital, and qualitative conclusions have been derived from them. But this procedure, collapsing the vastly heterogeneous set of capital inputs into one artificial factor, has seemed particularly objectionable to the Cantab-Italo economists. This point will be discussed further in the chapter on capital and distribution, where more of the general equilibrium character of the marginal productivity theory will emerge.

3. Marginal Productivity, Cobb-Douglas Functions and the Constancy of Labor's Share

As illustrations of the workings of marginal productivity analysis, we offer brief discussions of two subjects that are of interest both as curiosa in the history of economic thought and as introductions to the role in distribution theory of the Cobb-Douglas production function and Euler's theorem on homogeneous functions.

There is a fair amount of empirical evidence that has been interpreted to assert that the share of wages in the national income of the United States has remained relatively constant for as long a period as is covered by our records.[8] There have been a number of attempts to explain this apparently remarkable fact. One proposed explanation of the relatively fixed proportion between wage payments and total national income is based on the hypothesis that the production function takes the special form of a Cobb-Douglas function (see Chapter 11, Section 11)

$$y = kL^a C^{(1-a)}$$

where k and a are positive constants (and $a < 1$). Here y represents *total national* output (income), L is the quantity of labor input, and C is the quantity of capital employed. It is easy to show, with the aid of some simple differential calculus, that if labor is paid a wage equal to its marginal product this production function will yield a share of wages relative to total output which is fixed and independent of the values of the variables, y, L, and C, as the empirical evidence seems to indicate. In fact, the ratio between total wage income and total output, y, must in these circumstances be exactly equal to a, the exponent of L in the Cobb-Douglas production function. A similar result must apply to the income of capital.

---

[8] For a sophisticated recent discussion, see Melvin W. Reder, "Alternative Theories of Labor's Share," *The Allocation of Economic Resources: Essays in Honor of Bernard Francis Haley*, by Moses Abramovitz and others, Stanford University Press, Stanford, Calif., 1959. See also Robert M. Solow, "A Skeptical Note on the Constancy of Relative Shares," *American Economic Review*, Vol. XLVIII, September 1958.

Proof: The marginal product of labor, $\partial y/\partial L$, is found by differentiation of the production function to be $akL^{(a-1)}C^{(1-a)}$. Since this is the wage per worker, total wage payments must equal this amount multiplied by the number of workers, L; i.e., the wage bill must be

$$LakL^{(a-1)}C^{(1-a)} = akL^aC^{(1-a)} = ay.$$

That is, total wages equal a times total output, as was to be proved.

Unfortunately, the argument fails in its central purpose. Its objective is to explain why the share of wages should have remained constant *despite vast technological change.* But it is just as difficult to see why with such technological change the exponent, a, in the production function should not have varied, which is the fundamental assumption of the preceding discussion. The argument, then, proposes to explain a constant wage share with the aid of a constant, a, for whose constancy it offers no explanation!

It is to be observed also that there is no *a priori* reason for accepting the validity of the Cobb-Douglas production function as an accurate depiction of the technology of the entire economy. It is merely an empirical hypothesis which has been proposed to explain an empirical observation.[9]

4. Euler's Theorem and the Adding-Up Controversy

Our second application of marginal productivity analysis has its roots in earlier discussions of distribution theory. When the marginal productivity theory first achieved acceptance just before the turn of the century, as we have already noted, some economists attempted to use it as a basis for showing that the distribution of income under free competitive capitalism must be morally just. In the course of the discussion there arose another question. Suppose every productive input is paid the value of its marginal product. Does this mean that the entire product will always thereby be handed out to those who worked on it, or may something be left over to fall into the clutches of an exploiter? Indeed, is there always enough on deposit in the production bank to pay out all of these marginal product claims or might there even be a deficit? It became important to the discussants to show that the sum of the marginal products *added up* to exactly the total output—that there was neither surplus nor deficit left at the end.

---

[9] See Robert M. Solow, "Technical Change and the Aggregate Production Function," *Review of Economics and Statistics*, Vol. XXXIX, August 1957, and Reder, *op. cit.* For evidence suggesting that an aggregate production function may not be of Cobb-Douglas form, see K. J. Arrow, H. B. Chenery, B. S. Minhas, and R. M. Solow, "Capital-Labor Substitution and Economic Efficiency," *Review of Economics and Statistics*, Vol. 33, August 1961, pp. 225–50.

Here the linearly homogeneous production function again came to the rescue. As was proved in Chapter 11, Section 10, there is a standard mathematical result, called *Euler's theorem*, which tells us that if a production function involves constant returns to scale, the sum of the marginal products will actually add up to the total product. That is, if each input i is paid $p_i = p \, \partial y / \partial x_i$, the value of its marginal product, we must have

$$py = \sum x_i p \, \partial y / \partial x_i = \sum p_i x_i.$$

Wicksteed's[10] injection of homogeneous linear production functions into the discussion opened a long controversy over the plausibility of the hypothesis that the production function will take this form in practice.[11]

As for the controversy itself, as Samuelson pointed out,[12] the discussion really seems to have missed the point. Whether there are any profits of exploitation left over for the capitalist to haul in is really a matter of market conditions. For example, as we have seen, in the long run under perfect competition prices of outputs and inputs will settle toward levels at which there is nothing left over for payment to the entrepreneur in excess of his managerial wages and interest on his capital, but under monopoly there will normally be profits in excess of this amount. The older Euler's theorem discussion abstracted entirely from the product and input markets in which competitive pressures, if anything, will rob the exploiter of the fruits of his exploitation.

But how does this conclusion square with Euler's theorem which says that marginal products add up to the total product when and *only* when the production function is linearly homogeneous?[13] The answer is implicit in a solution that was first proposed by Walras and then rediscovered by Hicks. They showed that, whether or not the production function is linearly homogeneous, in the vicinity of a competitive equilibrium point it must be *locally* linearly homogeneous, that is, all of its variable values *and*

---

[10] See Philip Wicksteed, *The Coordination of the Laws of Distribution*, Macmillan & Co., Ltd., London, 1894. Actually, it was A. W. Flux who, in his review of Wicksteed (*Economic Journal*, Vol. IV, 1894), explicitly injected Euler's theorem into the discussion.

[11] Edgeworth's much quoted comment merits repetition here: "There is a magnificence in this generalization which recalls the youth of philosophy. Justice is a perfect cube, said the ancient sage; and rational conduct is a homogeneous function, adds the modern savant." *Collected Papers Relating to Political Economy*, Macmillan & Co., Ltd., London, 1925, Vol. I, p. 31 (the remark was first published in 1904).

[12] *Foundations of Economic Analysis*, Harvard University Press, Cambridge, Mass., 1948, pp. 83–87.

[13] If the production function is homogeneous of some degree $r \neq 1$ (nonconstant returns to scale), Euler's theorem (Chapter 11, Section 10) tells us that $rpy = \sum x_i p \partial y / \partial x_i = \sum x_i p_i$ so that $\sum x_i p_i$, total payment to the firm's inputs, will *not* equal py, the value of its total output. One can prove a comparable result for a production function that is not homogeneous of any degree.

derivatives must be the same as those of a linearly homogeneous function. Thus, at that point all of the marginal products (the partial derivatives $\partial y / \partial x_i$) must coincide with those of a linearly homogeneous function, and so they too must satisfy the Euler's theorem condition.

To show why the production function must be locally linearly homogeneous in competitive equilibrium we note first that the simple function

$$(1) \qquad\qquad c = p_1 x_1 + p_2 x_2 + \cdots + p_n x_n$$

must be linearly homogeneous in the input quantities $x_1, \cdots, x_n$ since if each x_i is multiplied by k then c will obviously also be multiplied by k and that is just what we mean by linear homogeneity.

Now Equation (1) is simply the total cost to the firm of the collection of inputs $x_1, \cdots, x_n$, and its graph is a (hyper)plane through the origin, $c_a c_b c_c c_d$ in the two-input case represented in Figure 2. The oddly shaped surface (shaded area) in the diagram represents the production function (or rather the value of output) $py = pf(x_1, x_2)$. If the second-order conditions hold at the point of equilibrium, T, the two surfaces must be tangent there, since the zero-profit requirement assures us that at no combination of inputs and outputs will the value of outputs exceed the cost of the corresponding inputs, and at the equilibrium point the two will be equal. This gives us our result, for the tangency of the two surfaces at T means that there they will both have the same derivatives. In other words, $pf(x_1, x_2)$ must, indeed, be linearly homogeneous *locally* at T, as was to be shown. Euler's theorem must therefore apply, and the payment to each input of its marginal product must exhaust total product.

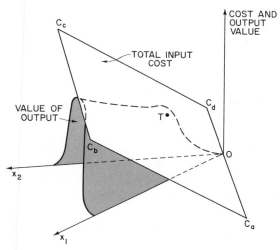

Figure 2

5. Alternative Distribution Theories, I: The Ricardian Model

Having discussed the structure and some applications of marginal distribution theory, we may note once again that in terms of logical consistency and formal completeness it has no equal. However, it has told us very little about the burning issues to which one might hope distribution theory will address itself, issues such as the magnitude of the income gap between the poor and the wealthy and its relationship to their role in the productive mechanism. For contrast, we therefore summarize briefly two macro models which are intended to come closer to dealing with such topics—Ricardo's analysis and the more recent Kaldor model.

Ricardo's distribution theory is still perhaps the one model which assigns distinctive roles to different economic classes, which deduces well-defined trends in their earnings, and which offers clear-cut policy implications. While few economists would concede that it constitutes a good description of a complex industrial economy, it has been held that its implications still retain some relevance at least for some less developed economies.

Ricardo's analysis rests on four central components: diminishing returns to labor utilizing a fixed quantity of land, the theory of rent, the tendency of universal competition to equalize returns to investment, and the Malthusian population principle. Though the roles of these four elements are interdependent, we must consider them individually.

The principle of diminishing returns has already been examined in the chapter on production. In sum, it asserts that as we increase the use of some inputs *holding the quantities of others constant*, the average and marginal yield of the expanding inputs must eventually fall. In classical theory this was applied to the increased use of labor (with growing population) and of capital (the product of capitalists' accumulation) on society's fixed supply of land, "the original and indestructible powers of the soil."[14] This can take the form of a decreasing yield either to investment of labor and capital on a given piece of land (their *intensive* yield) or to investment on successive and successively inferior pieces of soil (their *extensive* yield). In either case, the process of competition and the mobility of capital will in the long run tolerate no difference of return to different investments. The payment to landlords on higher-yielding units of investment will be bid up by competition to the point where all units provide the same net return to the investor. Thus the landlord will receive as rent the difference between the investor's return on his least productive investment (i.e., his return on the margin) and the higher return on all other units of invest-

---

[14] David Ricardo, *On the Principles of Political Economy and Taxation*, Sraffa ed., Vol. I, Cambridge University Press, New York, 1951, pp. 67, 71–72.

ment. If three units of output have, respectively, marginal costs of \$3, \$7, and \$9, then, as illustrated in Figure 5a, the first will earn a rent of \$6, the second a rent of \$2, so that all three will end up with a unit cost, including rent, of exactly \$9.[15]

This already describes the mechanism for the determination of one distributive share—that going to landlords. In the Ricardian model profits are determined residually as what is left over from production after payment of rent and wages. Consequently, we only have yet to discuss the wage determination process. For this we still lack one component of the analysis, the Malthusian population theory, which can be taken to assert, in oversimplified form, that whenever wages exceed some amount called "the subsistence level" people will marry earlier, and consequently reproduce more rapidly, thus eventually tending to increase the labor force to a point where diminishing returns and the competition of workers combine forces to drive wages back to the subsistence level.

All the pieces of the dynamic mechanism of the Ricardian distribution model are now in place, and its workings can be described very briefly. Capitalists, stimulated by high profits, are induced to save substantial portions of their earnings, which they invest as a means to earn still more profits. The increased investment demand brings with it a rise in demand for labor. That in turn raises wages and induces growth in population. In this process profits are eroded, and consequently investment is impeded by two forces—the rise in wage rates induced by the investment itself and diminishing returns, which are brought into play by increased population and expanded economic activity. The wage rise may only be temporary since the expanded population and its increased labor force ultimately depress wages once more. However, diminishing returns do not disappear by themselves. Unless there is technological progress on a scale sufficient to offset them, profits will suffer a persistent and cumulative erosion. This is the classical variant of the famous law of the falling of profit.

This process is illustrated in Figure 3, which shows the behavior of population, wages, rents, and output with the passage of time, on the assumption that there is a constant ratio between the size of the population and the size of the labor force. The curve OY shows how total output varies with the size of the labor force, with the curve leveling off toward the right as a result of diminishing returns to additional labor.

---

[15] For details of the argument see Section 10 of this chapter. It is ironic that this Ricardian rent theory was neither discovered by Ricardo nor claimed by him. Ricardo attributes the idea to Malthus but it can also be ascribed to Edward West, and perhaps to James Anderson some forty years earlier. See Sraffa's *Ricardo*, Vol. IV, pp. 3–8, and Joseph Schumpeter, *History of Economic Analysis*, Oxford University Press, Inc., New York, 1954, pp. 263–65.

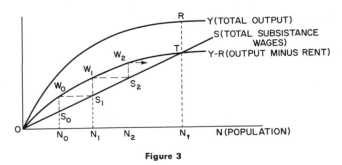

Figure 3

Total rent payments increase steadily with population growth and the resultant increase in land use. Therefore, curve $Y - R$, that is, total output minus rent, also levels off as we move toward the right, i.e., as population grows. $Y - R$ gives the portion of output available for division between wages and profits. Finally, the line OS shows how much output is required to pay every member of the population a *fixed* subsistence wage s. Since the expression for this curve is $S = sN$, where N is population size, this is a straight line through the origin.

In exaggerated form we may then take the dynamics of the classical distribution process to proceed somewhat as follows: Assume that population is initially N_0 and that the rate of accumulation is initially high so that the level of wages is bid up to a point where it absorbs most of non-rent output (point W_0), and is well above the subsistence level, $N_0 S_0$. This will encourage population to grow to N_1 at which the wage payment covers no more than subsistence, $N_1 S_1$. At this point profits will be high $(S_1 W_1)$, inducing increased accumulation and pushing total wages upward once more, this time toward W_1. The process repeats itself, moving roughly in the sequence of steps $W_0 S_1 W_1 S_2 W_2 \cdots$ toward point T, the point where output after rent is just equal to the requirements of subsistence. As population approaches N_t, the level corresponding to point T, the economy approaches its stationary state; at this, in the absence of new technology or other exogenous events, profits, accumulation, and population growth remain forever at zero, wage payments remain forever at subsistence, and rents remain at their maximum attainable level, TR.

Thus, in this process workers may gain little, and capitalists almost certainly lose out. The sequence of events also includes a diminishing propensity to accumulate as the rewards of accumulation decline, with the concomitant loss in the forces making for (at least temporary) wage increases. The landlords are the only ones who benefit from this dynamic process, gathering ever-increasing rents as the demand for their land grows with rising population, and inferior lands are brought into production, thus raising the rents on the better pieces of land. In this process, then, the interests of landlords are diametrically opposed to those of every other group. Workers and capitalists are not natural allies for they must compete for the remainder of the output of the economy, the portion not claimed by landlords. Yet workers and capitalists do have a common interest in the success of the accumulation process, as we will note again presently.

Two qualifications relating to the wage determination process are crucial for the policy implications of the Ricardian model: First, "subsistence" must not be taken to be some absolute bundle of consumption goods which constitutes the border line of starvation. On the contrary, the "subsistence" level depends on accepted standards of living:

> "It is not to be understood that the natural price of labour, estimated even in food and necessaries, is absolutely fixed and constant. It varies at different times in the same country, and very materially differs in different countries. It essentially depends on the habits and customs of the people . . . many of the conveniences now enjoyed in an English cottage, would have been thought luxuries at an earlier period of our history" (*Principles*, Sraffa ed., p. 97).

Second, when the demand for labor is sufficiently high, wages can be kept for indefinite periods of time above even this flexible "subsistence" level:

> "Notwithstanding the tendency of wages to conform to their natural rate, their market rate may, in an improving society, for an indefinite period, be constantly above it; for no sooner may the impulse, which an increased capital gives to a new demand for labour, be obeyed, than another increase of capital may produce the same effect . . ." (*Principles*, p. 95).

There is, then, no "iron law of wages."[16] It is important to understand that these two features of the wage determination process are no minor qualifications to his theory. Rather they are critical elements in its policy implications, for to Ricardo several conclusions followed immediately:

(a) The best way to contribute to the welfare of labor is to increase the standard of living, which serves as the acceptable minimum "subsistence level" below which the population will fail to reproduce itself. In

---

[16] The notion of an iron law is neither Ricardian nor Marxian. Indeed, Marx emphasized both points which have just been made. See, e.g., *Das Kapital*, Vol. I, p. 190, and Chapter XXV, Section 1. The notion of an iron law of wages is associated with Marx' nemesis, Ferdinand LaSalle. For Marx' scornful views on that subject, see his *Critique of the Gotha Program*, Section II.

other words, in the long run the most effective way to raise real wages is to decrease population growth, and a good way to achieve this is through a rise in the living standards considered necessary before embarking on the raising of a family;

(b) A second best procedure for raising workers' incomes is anything that encourages the continued accumulation of capital, which raises the demand for labor and hence bids up wages;

(c) Free trade is desirable because it reduces the cost of the "subsistence" of workers and decreases rents by reducing the demand for land within the country. Together these two influences augment the return to capital, stimulate accumulation, and raise wages;

(d) Payments to the poor must in the long run depress average real wages because they induce population to expand and thereby benefit no one but the landlord. They must hamper accumulation and decrease the marginal product of labor. Thus, though they appear to serve the interests of the poor, in the long run they work to their disadvantage.

Today the Ricardian model is generally considered a gross oversimplification. Population growth is not determined so mechanistically. The evidence on the proposition that payments to low-income groups stimulates their reproduction is hardly clear-cut, and it seems often to work the other way. Technological change permits real wages to rise even as population grows. Wage bargaining is a complex process affected by unionization and other institutions. Monopolistic elements and government agencies play more of a role than they are assigned in the classical analysis. Yet in spite of all this one comes away from the analysis with more than a little admiration for its comprehensiveness, its logical strength and its ability to deal with the workings of a complex set of phenomena with the aid of a simple and suggestive structure. Certainly Ricardo provided us with a macro model whose construction must be considered a major intellectual feat.

6. Alternative Distribution Theories, II: The Kaldor Model

The Cantab-Italo approach to distribution derives its roots both from Ricardian analysis and from Keynesian theory. A noteworthy example of its analysis is the Kaldor macroeconomic model,[17] whose primary aim is to analyze the share of wages in the total national product.

The basic premise of the model is that workers and capitalists save different proportions of their incomes. Consequently, given the level of (full employment) investment and total income there will be only one

---

[17] See Nicholas Kaldor, "Alternative Theories of Distribution," *Review of Economic Studies*, Vol. XXIII, No. 2, 1955–56.

proportion between workers' and capitalists' shares of that total income at which total saving will equal total investment, i.e., at which the total demand for output will equal its total supply.

The level of employment is, as usual in Keynesian analysis, taken to be a function of national output, Y. This level of employment, $f(Y)$, multiplied by the wage rate, W, is the total payment of wages, $W \cdot f(Y)$. The rest of output, $Y - W \cdot f(Y)$, is then the income which accrues to other classes of income earners.

Assume now that workers save a smaller proportion of their incomes than do other economic groups—say that workers save the proportion k of their incomes, whereas the corresponding figure for the rest of society is k^*, where, by assumption, $k < k^*$. Total desired saving will, therefore, be equal to that of the workers, $kWf(Y)$, plus that of the nonworkers, $k^*[Y - Wf(Y)]$. If I is a given level of investment, equilibrium is determined by the condition that desired saving be equal to the level of investment, i.e., that

$$(2) \qquad kWf(Y) + k^*[Y - Wf(Y)] = I,$$

where I, k, and k^* are assumed to be known constants. If for Y we substitute the full employment level of output, Y_f, this becomes a single equation with one unknown, W, which can be solved for the equilibrium level of wages, W_e.

The analysis suggests an interesting policy conclusion. Suppose that at some other wage rate equilibrium national income is below the full employment level and that the employment function, $f(Y)$, is independent of the level of wages. Then a rise in wage level will not depress the demand for labor. On the contrary, it will transfer income from a group of low spenders to a group of high spenders so that total effective demand and hence employment and the level of national income must all rise![18] The moral is,

---

[18] *Proof:* Since consumption equals income minus saving, a rise in wage level by amount ΔW will raise workers' expenditure to $(1 - k)(W + \Delta W)f(Y)$, and nonworkers' consumption expenditure will change to

$$(1 - k^*)[Y - (W + \Delta W)f(Y)]$$

so that total consumption demand will have changed from

$$(1 - k)Wf(Y) + (1 - k^*)[Y - Wf(Y)]$$

to

$$(1 - k)(W + \Delta W)f(Y) + (1 - k^*)[Y - (W + \Delta W)f(Y)].$$

By subtraction, we see that demand will have changed by $(k^* - k) \Delta Wf(Y)$, that is, effective demand must have risen, since $k < k^*$.

apparently, that during a period of depression a wage rise is likely to be a good thing and may produce at least part of the income necessary to pay for it. Boulding has called such a construct a "widow's cruse" model, after the legend of the widow who found that emptying her pitcher only filled it up again. Here the payment of higher wages out of national income helps to produce the wherewithal to pay them by increasing demand and therefore improving business receipts.

Another curious implication of the model is that in Kaldor's world capitalists can always increase their share of income by increasing their spending, i.e., by reducing their savings rate, k^*, to any point short of the level where it reaches that of the workers, k, for suppose total desired saving was previously equal to investment, so that after the decline in k^* desired saving is less than investment. If k^* is very close to k a given transfer of income from workers to capitalists will add very little to total saving, and so it will require a *large* transfer to the capitalists to produce the equilibrium in which desired saving matches investment.[19] Thus, capitalists will find that the more they spend the more they have, so that the capitalists then have access to a widow's cruse of their own.

The model has been the subject of considerable criticism. For one thing, it is never made clear why the economy in this model has an automatic tendency to approach the level of full employment. For another, the premise that employment depends only on output and not on wage level denies that higher wages will induce the adoption of labor-saving inventions. Tobin has suggested that the capitalists' widow's cruse is in fact a demonstration of the weakness of the theory. In a limiting case it permits them to capture all of GNP by spending enough of it for themselves!

It really is not easy to believe that this simple model encompasses all there is to the determination of labor's share or even most of the primary influences in this process. Yet it does offer some suggestive ideas, and it certainly represents a fascinating attempt to produce an analysis which lends itself more readily to interpretation in terms of policy than the general-equilibrium analysis with all of its complexities.

7. Backward-Rising Input Supply Curves: Labor and Saving

Having discussed some of the main theoretical approaches to the theory of distribution, we turn now to some special topics, most of them relating to particular categories of input.

---

[19] *Proof:* By (2), $(k - k^*)Wf(Y) + k^*Y = I$, so that total wage earnings equal $Wf(Y) = (I - k^*Y)/(k - k^*)$ and total profits, $\pi = Y - Wf(Y) = [Y(k - k^*) - I + k^*Y]/(k - k^*) = (kY - I)/(k - k^*)$. Since $k^* > k$ by assumption, this will be positive if $I > kY$. Then as k^* moves toward k so that the value of the denominator falls, total profits must rise.

In Section 2 we saw how the marginal productivity model provides us with derived demand functions for inputs. It is appropriate now to offer some remarks on the supply relationships. Because these are so dependent on particular institutional arrangements in the markets for the different inputs, no general pronouncements on this subject are possible, but a number of observations about particular types of input can be fruitful.

Most inputs are supplied by business firms. That is obviously the case with coal, iron, oil, lumber, and many other items. Given their demand, the analysis of the supplies of these items is therefore identical with that of the determination of any output level in the theory of the firm. The discussion of Chapters 11–16 applies here without change.

However, a number of important inputs are supplied by private individuals rather than by business firms. The worker who supplies labor time, the saver who supplies funds for investment, and even the small farmer may be considered to fall into this category. Each of these groups supplies items which they can also use for themselves. The worker can use in leisure pursuits the portion of his time which he does not sell, the investor can conserve the money which he does not lend out, and the farmer can use for himself at least some of the products which he does not sell. We say that each of these sellers has a *reservation demand* for his product—he wants to reserve some for himself.

The amounts of such inputs which will be supplied then depend both on the quantities which are produced and the amounts which the sellers choose to demand for themselves. The theory of demand of Chapter 9 therefore becomes highly relevant for the analysis of these input supplies.

What will happen to the supply of such an item when its price rises? Usually we expect that a rise in price will increase the supply of a good, but we shall see now that in the reservation-demand situation this will not always be true—a rise in price may well cause a reduction in supply.

To see how this works out, let us consider the supply of labor time provided by one worker. He has twenty-four hours to divide between work and leisure. His desired labor supply, then, is simply what is left over from the twenty-four hours after his reservation demand for leisure time. Suppose there is a rise in the hourly wage rate—the price of his labor time. This means that the price per unit (per hour) of leisure time has risen. The effect on his supply of labor time can then be determined residually by determining the effect of this price rise on his demand for leisure.

As in the ordinary theory of demand, we can divide the effect of the price rise on his demand for leisure into the substitution effect (the effect of the *relative* rise in the cost of leisure compared to that of his other purchases) and the income effect (the effect of the change in his real purchasing power which results from this rise in price). As in the ordinary theory of the consumer, the substitution effect of a rise in the price of leisure will make him want to purchase less. Other consumer goods will have become relatively cheaper, hence there will be more attractive ways to spend his money. Thus the substitution effect of a rise in wages will, indeed, tend to raise the labor supply since it will work to reduce the amount of time which he wishes to keep for himself.

But the income effect will work out quite differently from the way it does with an ordinary consumer product. First, the income effect is now virtually certain to be much stronger. The consumer usually spends only a small proportion of his income on any one product, so that a rise in its price alone will have very little effect on his real income. But a worker's income is largely or even entirely dependent on the sale of his labor time. Hence, a rise in hourly wages (the price of leisure) will have a substantial effect on his income and therefore, in turn, on his purchases. The income effect of a rise in the price of leisure will, therefore, be far more important than that of a rise in the price of shoes.

A second difference between the reservation-demand and the ordinary consumer-demand cases is that the income effects in the two situations will ordinarily be of opposite direction. A rise in the price of something he buys *reduces* the consumer's real purchasing power and therefore tends to reduce the demand for the item—it works in the same direction as the substitution effect. But a rise in the price of something he sells—such as labor power—makes the seller richer and permits him to afford more of the good things in life—leisure among them. Thus the income effect of a rise in wages—the price of leisure—is likely to be an increased demand for leisure. The (very likely substantial) income effect usually works in the reverse direction from the substitution effect. The net result may well be that a rise in the price of leisure increases its reservation demand; that is, a rise in wages may reduce the supply of labor. In this way we may have a negatively sloping (so-called backward-rising) supply curve of labor.

Of course, the individual worker does not usually have the option of reducing his working hours. If a factory is geared to a forty-hour week, it cannot very well suit the different preferences of individual employees by hiring some people for forty-seven hours and others for twenty-eight hours. But a negatively sloping supply curve of labor has nevertheless played a persistent role in the history of labor—via union demands for shorter hours, which accompanied rising hourly wages. The shorter work week has occurred with the consent—indeed, as a result of the demands—of an increasingly prosperous labor force.

For similar reasons, the possibility of negatively sloping supply curves arises also in the case of savings. It has often been assumed that a rise in interest rates—the price of savings which are loaned out—will lead people to save more. But a rise in interest rates also increases the income of the lender, and he may consequently prefer to increase the proportion of his income which he spends on himself. As in the case of wages, and for exactly the same reasons, the income effect of a rise in interest rates is likely to be substantial and in the opposite direction from the substitution effect—it will tend to make for reduced savings. The net result of the income and substitution effects is in this case in considerable doubt. Some have concluded that, for the community as a whole, the supply of savings which are available for lending is on balance relatively interest inelastic—a change in interest rate will make little difference to supply because the income and substitution effects will tend to cancel out. In individual cases, however, this will not always be so. Cassel and Keynes have described one extreme case in which the savings supply curve is likely to have a pronounced negative slope.[20] Suppose a man is saving money and lending it out at interest with the objective of having enough to buy a boat when he retires in five years. If the price of the boat does not change, the higher the rate of interest, the less he will have to put away in order to achieve his objective. A rise in interest rate will therefore clearly *decrease* his motivation for saving because it increases his income from his lendings.

8. Unions as Monopolies: Alternative Union Goals

It is a standard observation that unionization has made the analysis of wage determination a matter for the theory of monopoly rather than that of competition. Indeed, the wage-bargaining process is, in some discussions, taken to be a case of pure bilateral monopoly, with negotiation and the decision-making entirely in the hands of a set of union representatives on the one side and a monolithic industry (management) group on the other. The theory of bilateral monopoly with its superimposed sets of indifference curves (as described in Chapter 16, Section 9) has therefore sometimes been applied with little or no modification to the analysis of wage negotiation.

In any event, if labor is treated as a monopoly or a quasi-monopoly, the supply curve of labor becomes an inapplicable construct, for it will be recalled that under monopoly there is no overriding industry price which the firm is forced to accept and to which it adjusts its supply. It is therefore inappropriate for the analyst to look for the firm's supply response to various alternative given prices (the supply curve). Rather, the monopolist can set whatever price best suits his objectives by marketing an appropriate supply, and that is the only price which is applicable—there is no relevant range of supply prices to be recorded in a supply curve.

But what is this supply-price, labor-supply combination which best serves the unions' interest? Even the objectives of a firm are not self-evident, as we have seen (Chapter 15). Some firms may be interested in

---

[20] See J. M. Keynes, *The General Theory of Employment, Interest, and Money*, Harcourt Brace Jovanovich, Inc., New York, 1936, pp. 94 and 182.

maximizing their profits, others their market share; still others may pursue hybrid objectives, and all of these are usually only vaguely and only implicitly defined.

The plausible objectives of trade unions are perhaps even more diverse than those of business firms. Just to suggest the nature of some of the possibilities and to indicate some of their implications, let us consider the following three alternatives:

1. That the union wishes to keep all of its members employed;
2. That the union wishes to maximize the total income of its members;
3. That the union wishes to maximize hourly wages and keep at least a steady core group of its members employed.

Figure 4 shows some of the implications of these three objectives and demonstrates that they are likely to be incompatible.[21] Here DD' represents the industry demand curve for labor.[22] If the total membership of the union is OE_1, the union which seeks to get jobs for all of its members will have to settle for wage OW_1 per worker because any higher wage will cut the demand for labor to below OE_1. On the other hand, the union which wishes to maximize the total wage earnings of its members should demand wage OW_2, which corresponds to the point of unit elasticity, U, on the demand curve (for it will be remembered that where elasticity is greater than unity a fall in labor price will increase total industry expenditure on labor, whereas where elasticity is less than unity a rise in price will have the opposite effect). The total-wage-income-maximizing level of employment, OE_2, can also be identified by the condition that at OE_2 the marginal revenue curve, DE_2 (corresponding to the demand = average revenue curve DD'), must cut the horizontal axis, i.e., the additional wage payment resulting from an increase in employment must be zero.

Finally, if the union wishes to maximize wages for a small core group of its members, OE_3, the corresponding maximum wage per worker is OW_3. Thus, depending on which objective it adopts, the union will find different policies appropriate, and there will be no one decision which effectively pursues all three objectives simultaneously.

A union which maximizes the total wage receipts of its members (objective 2) must be prepared to accept the unemployment of what may

---

[21] The reader will recall the convention that inputs are measured as *negative* quantities. That is why the horizontal axis is taken to go to the left of the origin with higher negative values representing higher employment levels.

[22] The use of a demand curve implies that the industry is not a monopsonist—a single unified buyer of labor for whom there is no relevant input demand curve—for the same reason that the monopolist has no supply curve in the ordinary sense.

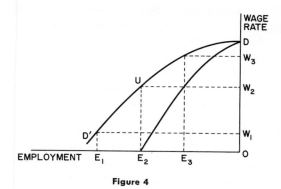

Figure 4

be a substantial number of its members (E_2E_1). Nevertheless, such a policy can make good economic sense. If the total wage "take" of the employed worker is somehow redivided among all of the union members (either by an unemployment assessment on the employed members or by long "vacations" which keep all members employed part-time), the income per worker (including those who are unemployed) will be higher than it would be if all union members were fully employed, for if the union membership is fixed at OE_1, then an increase in the *total* wage receipts, which are divided among this fixed number of men, must clearly raise the average wage level.

There is no need to expand this list of possible union objectives. It is clear that the matter is more complex than the discussion has indicated and involves considerations like the desire of the union leadership to stay in office, and the militancy of the membership. Enough has been said to indicate that no one *a priori* labor supply relationship is likely to be universally applicable.[23]

This completes our remarks on the supply of labor. Though they will not be discussed here, it must be emphasized that institutional considerations are also highly relevant for the analysis of the pricing of other inputs e.g., the rent of land and the interest on savings.

9. Inputs in Fixed Supply: Land

In standard analysis it is customary to treat some inputs as being absolutely fixed in supply. The economy is endowed with some set of natural resources, and there is nothing which can be done to change the amounts

---

[23] For a highly suggestive theoretical analysis of alternative union policy possibilities, see John Dunlop, *Wage Determination Under Trade Unions*, The Macmillan Company, New York, 1944.

of land, mineral deposits, and other such items. The supplies of these objects are therefore taken to be of zero elasticity—no rise in price can increase the available quantities.

In a geological sense this is perfectly correct, but from the economic point of view it is almost certainly false. What is important for our purpose is not the total territory of a country, but the amount which is in use; not the amount of oil under the ground, but the rate at which it flows into the pipe lines. But a sufficient rise in price can always be counted upon to increase the rate of flow of these items into the economy. More will be done to find new oil locations, and more speculative drilling will be undertaken. Mines which have been abandoned as uneconomic will be reopened, and less wasteful methods of mining will be developed and adopted. Poor land will be irrigated and fertilized. Only in the very short run, before there is time to do much about the level of production, will supplies of any inputs be fixed. And even then, it will be possible to do something. More of an input whose price has risen will be taken out of inventory and put into production; raw materials which become more expensive will be used more carefully to reduce waste—more thought will be given to cloth-cutting patterns, and gold dust recovery procedures will be tightened up by the goldsmiths; finally, other inputs, which are more abundant, will be used in larger amounts to help the firm economize on the employment of these scarce items—if there is a shortage of equipment, it can be worked on a three-shift basis, thus increasing the labor/capital ratio; if there is a shortage of one metal, another will be employed more frequently in its place.

In sum, as Professor Viner has pointed out, input supply functions are virtually never zero elastic from the economic point of view except, possibly, in the very short run.

Land, in particular, is customarily treated as an input whose quantity cannot be varied by human decision. That was the notion behind its description by Ricardo as the original and indestructible powers of the soil. But we know that landfill activities have extended the land area of many if not most major cities. New York and San Francisco have grown in that way, and the map of contemporary Boston bears surprisingly little resemblance to its eighteenth-century contours. Here, too, the available supply is affected by economic conditions—the value of real estate and the amount of wastes generated by the economy out of which the artificial land mass is often constructed. Nevertheless, in the discussion to which we now turn it is convenient for the exposition to treat land as an artificial limiting case—the input whose supply is absolutely fixed.

10. Economic Rent as Surplus. Heterogeneous Inputs and Increasing Costs

Though in the discussion of the Ricardian model the concept of rent referred, as it does in popular discourse, only to payments to landlords, today the concept is applied more broadly, to any type of input which earns a "surplus." By a surplus in this sense we mean any payment in excess of the amount necessary to have the input in question supplied. On our premise that the supply of land is fixed, any payment for the use of land obviously meets that criterion. Since land is there whether it receives any payment or not, the entire payment is a surplus *from the point of view of society as a whole*. Of course, it is no surplus from the viewpoint of any one industry or any one firm bidding for some land, for it must get that land away from others who also want to use it. It is precisely this competition among bidders for such an input which leads to the payment of a surplus or rent.[24]

As a most obvious generalization of the Ricardian model, these payments can occur in the bidding for inputs which differ in quality—not just lands differing in fertility, but equipment differing in state of repair and workers differing in "natural" skills. Consider two workers, c and d, both employed at similar jobs by different firms, and suppose that c is more productive than d, specifically, that the return on c's output per month is \$1,000 and that the corresponding figure for d is \$950. In the long run, competition among the firms will tend to make the monthly wages of c and d differ precisely by the difference in their *total* value output, \$50, for, suppose that c's wage is only \$20 higher than d's. It will then pay d's employer to offer to hire c (instead of d) at a wage increase of, say, \$10 per month, thereby increasing his (the employer's) receipts by \$50 and his wage payments by only \$20 + \$10 = \$30, which is clearly profitable. But when d's employer makes this bid to c, it will pay c's original firm to try to keep him rather than being stuck with the less efficient worker, d. This firm will therefore be forced to bid c's wage up even higher, and so on, until c is receiving exactly \$50 more than d—so that it will be equally remunerative to a firm to hire either of these inputs; c's wages will not be bid any higher than this, since if his monthly wage were, say, \$75 more than d's when his output is only \$50 larger, d's labor time will clearly be the better buy, and either c's wage will tend to fall or that of d will be bid up. In practice, of course, wage differences are never that closely matched to differences in productivity.

---

[24] The reader may well wonder how such surpluses can arise under pure competition in light of the Euler's theorem result of Section 4 of this chapter, which tells us that the total product is just used up by the marginal products paid to inputs. The answer is that in competitive equilibrium even rent surpluses are equal to the marginal products of the inputs that receive them. The landlord must, for example, be paid for each acre of land exactly the amount that would be yielded by an additional acre. A moment's thought assures us that this must be so because a competitive firm pays every one of its inputs, land included, exactly the value of its marginal product. Thus, it is clear that what from one point of view is a surplus, from another is just a marginal product. J. B. Clark may have been the first to point this out.

There are various obstacles which prevent firms from bidding against one another for their inputs and prevent inputs from moving from firm to firm, to where earnings are highest. Firms do not have complete information on the productivity of the inputs currently hired by other companies; there are *transfer costs* involved in moving an input from one firm to another, including the possible loss of seniority and pension rights for workers who move to a new firm, as well as transportation costs and family dislocation costs if a move requires a worker to change his home. Nevertheless, despite these reservations, the prices of inputs will often tend to reflect the differences in their total productivity. The rent on a more fertile piece of land will be considerably higher than that on a barren area. Land desirably located in the center of a large city rents for much more than land in a sparsely inhabited area. Skilled labor receives higher wages than unskilled labor. A new, efficient factory will sell for more than one which is obsolete.

However, such rent payments arise not only because of heterogeneity in input quality. Rent arises from any source of increasing marginal costs as output expands. Whether rising costs stem simply from an increasing disproportion of input quantities (more and more labor per acre of land), or because one must have recourse to increasingly inferior inputs, rent payments will arise alike and will follow an equivalent pattern, illustrated in Figure 5.

Figure 5a describes a case with discrete input units. There, if one unit is produced, the marginal cost is $3, but with the production of a second unit, marginal cost rises to $7. Since competition does not permit unequal returns on different units of output, the cost of the first will be bid up by the imposition of a $4 rent (heavily shaded area). If a third unit is added to output, marginal cost increases to $9, and so rent on the first unit rises to $6, and a $2 rent is now earned on the second unit. The rent is now shown by the entire shaded area.

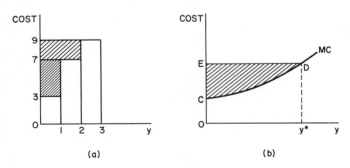

Figure 5

But note that this rent is a *transfer payment*, not a real cost in the sense of using up labor and raw materials. The production of a second and a third unit of output has not affected one iota the amount of labor and raw material needed to produce the first unit of output. The resources cost of the three units together is indicated by the sum of the areas of the three unshaded bars $= 3 + 7 + 9$. The shaded area (the rent), while it is a money cost to the firm that produces the output, represents no resources cost to society.

Figure 5b shows the same thing in the more familiar case where marginal cost is described by a continuous curve. Here the total resources cost of output y^* is, as usual, the area under the marginal cost curve, Oy^*DC. It is the sum of the marginal costs—the equivalent of the sum of the bars in Figure 5a. And for the same reason, shaded area CDE is the producers' rent or surplus which goes to the suppliers of the firm's productive resources. Area CDE is the same as the *producers' surplus*, which together with consumers' surplus is often taken as the appropriate maximand in the analysis of welfare economics (Chapter 21, Section 2).

One conclusion that follows is that total rent payment at any given level of output y is determined in a way that satisfies the condition

Average Cost of y *Including* Rent $=$ *Marginal* Cost of y *Excluding* Rent.

In terms of Figure 5a, when $y = 3$, marginal cost excluding rent, is $9. But then the cost including rent of the first unit of output is also $9 = $3 plus $6 rent and similarly, the cost of the second unit is also $9 = $7 + $2. Thus, since rent brings the cost of *every* unit up to the cost of the marginal unit, we have our result: average cost including rent $= (\$9 + \$9 + \$9)/3 = \$9 =$ marginal cost excluding rent. Obviously, the preceding argument does not depend on the particular figures chosen. If rent is set so that the cost of each and every unit of output (including rent) is equal to the resources (nonrent) cost of the marginal unit, then the average of all these (equal) figures must also equal that marginal cost.

This result has some significance for welfare theory. We saw in Chapter 16, Section 4, that the long-run supply curve of a competitive industry is the same as its curve of long-run average costs including rent. We see now that that curve is also the curve of long-run marginal cost excluding rent and this helps to explain the optimality of resource allocation under pure competition in the absence of externalities. For it shows, roughly, that where the demand and supply curves intersect, marginal social utility measured in money terms, as indicated by the height of the demand curve, will be equal to marginal resources cost, as given by the height of the supply curve. Thus, in competitive equilibrium marginal social utility of output will equal marginal resources cost, as optimality requires.

REFERENCES

American Economic Association, *Readings in the Theory of Income Distribution*, The Blakiston Company, New York, 1946.

Becker, Gary S., *Economic Theory*, Alfred Knopf Publishers, New York, 1971, Part Four.

Bronfenbrenner, Martin, *Income Distribution Theory*, Aldine, Chicago, 1971.

Douglas, Paul H., *The Theory of Wages*, The Macmillan Company, New York, 1934.

Dunlop, John, *Wage Determination Under Trade Unions*, The Macmillan Company, New York, 1944.

Haley, Bernard F., "Value and Distribution," in Howard S. Ellis (ed.), *A Survey of Contemporary Economics*, The Blakiston Company, New York, 1948.

Hicks, J. R., *The Theory of Wages*, The Macmillan Company, New York, 1932.

Johnson, Harry, *The Theory of Income Distribution*, Grey-Mills Publishing, Ltd., London, 1973.

Kaldor, Nicholas, "Alternative Theories of Distribution," *Review of Economic Studies*, Vol. XXIII, No. 2, 1955–56.

————, "Marginal Productivity and Macroeconomic Theories of Distribution," *Review of Economic Studies*, Vol. 33, 1966, pp. 309–19.

Pen, Jan, *Income Distribution: Facts, Theories, Policies*, Praeger Publishers, New York, 1971.

Robinson, Joan, "Capital Theory Up to Date," *Canadian Journal of Economics*, Vol. 3, 1970, pp. 309–17.

Tobin, James, "Towards a General Kaldorian Theory of Distribution," *Review of Economic Studies*, Vol. 27, February 1960, pp. 119–20.

Reder, Melvin W., "Alternative Theories of Labor's Share," *The Allocation of Economic Resources: Essays in Honor of Bernard Francis Haley*, by Moses Abramovitz and others, Stanford University Press, Stanford, Calif., 1959.

Capital

and

Investment Decisions

Capital budgeting refers to the investment decision-making procedures of business firms and other enterprises. The subject encompasses such topics as the selection of projects (which new factories, if any, should the company build), the timing of the investment, the determination of the amount to be invested within any given time period, and the arrangement of the financial means necessary for the completion of the projects. The calculations which are appropriate for these decisions for the most part derive directly from the theory of capital.

In keeping with the theoretical nature of the book, the materials of this chapter will not necessarily approximate capital budgeting procedures as they are currently encountered in practice. Rather, the chapter will deal, as far as possible, with methods which approximate optimality. However, there is an extremely important limitation which must be emphasized from the very beginning. Imperfect foresight into the future, risk, and uncertainty will for the most part be ignored, because economists have not devised really effective methods for taking them into account in the analysis. Later in the chapter something will be said about the matter, but the reader will readily recognize the limitations of that discussion. Unfortunately, capital budgeting is the one subject where we can least afford to abstract from limitations in our knowledge of the future, because, by its very nature, the investment decision can only be justified in terms of its prospective effects. Nevertheless, we must proceed, as does most of the literature, without the presence of this leading character in the drama.

The principles which will be described in this chapter are equally applicable to a wide variety of investment decisions, to net investment as well as to replacement, to scrapping and retirement. From the point of view of the analysis there is no structural difference in the decision which pertains to new investment and that which deals with replacement. When a company considers the purchase of a new machine, the fact that another one like it has served as a predecessor is, in a formal sense, a bit of irrelevant history.[1] The decisive question is whether the marginal profit contribution of the item justifies its acquisition, and if it does not, then the machine should go unpurchased whether or not it is a replacement item. Similarly, since scrapping or any other disinvestment decision (nonreplacement) can be treated as an act of negative investment, it is at least plausible that it should be based on the same principles and procedures as a decision to invest.

It is important to emphasize that, in an optimal investment decision, any *historical sunk costs*, such as the machine's employment of floor space, which would otherwise go unused, are *totally irrelevant*. For no current decision can change the past. Other examples of such irrelevant historical costs are the initial costs of provision of a railroad road bed, which should not affect the decision to purchase and run additional cars over the line, or the costs of a dam which have made a waterway navigable and which should not determine whether to operate another barge. In each case the added investment should be undertaken if and only if it more than pays *for itself*, whether or not it appears to bear its share of the outlays of the past.

To economists, the terms "capital" and "investment" do not refer to quantities of money or their use in purchasing stocks and bonds. Rather, we take them to denote "real" assets—factories, raw materials, machinery, inventories of finished and half-finished goods (goods in process), etc. *Capital*, in sum, is any previously produced input or asset of a business firm or any other producer.[2]

---

[1] Of course, if the firm previously possessed a similar machine, the company's labor force is more likely to be experienced in its operation, and this fact may contribute to the prospective profitability of a replacement. But this and other similar considerations must still enter an optimal investment calculation through their effects on *anticipated* profits.

[2] It may be noted that this is not how the term "capital" was used by Marx, who employed the term to represent both the physical assets without which the worker cannot put his labor power to use and the financial flows from these physical assets, both of which are the property of the capitalists. Physical capital, in whose construction the worker played a critical role, later confronts that same worker as "an alien object" without which he cannot function. Thus, capital to Marx is a social or institutional relationship, not a mere set of machines. It is only in the historical stage of capitalism that machines are transformed into capital by becoming simultaneously the instruments of control of the economic system and the private property of the capitalists.

Investment refers to the production or acquisition of any such real capital asset. Specifically, it is the time rate of increase of capital assets. If a firm has a capital of $17 million on January 1 and invests at the rate of $2 million per year, then its capital at the end of the year must be $19 million. Symbolically, if we designate investment and capital in year t respectively, by I_t and C_t, we must have[3]

$$I_t = C_t - C_{t-1}.$$

1. Discounting and Present Value: Valuation of Capital Assets

Before we can go on to the substance of capital theory we must examine the fundamental principles of its arithmetic, describing the procedure which must be employed to compare present and future receipts and outlays. It is characteristic of capital, as we have seen, that its construction and maintenance call for expenditures at different dates and that its yields are obtained at still other times.

Suppose, for example, that a $100 investment yields $20 at the end of the year and $25 at the end of two years, when the $100 is also returned to the investor. Would he have been better or worse off if he had, instead, received $22 each year? To answer such a question we must be able to compare the value of money (or other resources) at different dates. A dollar today, a dollar at the end of the year, and a dollar two years from now are all essentially different beasts.

The sooner we receive our money, the better off we are, for the sooner it can then be put to work earning more money for us. Let us see just how much more a quantity of money is worth if it is received sooner. Suppose that P dollars were invested for one year at a rate of interest i, compounded annually. Then at the end of the year it would yield iP dollars which, with the return of the principal, P, would give us $P + iP = P(1 + i)$ dollars. Let us call the initial sum P_0 (P dollars at our initial date, year 0) and write the equivalent sum at the end of one year as P_1 (meaning P_1 dollars receivable at the end of year 1). Then we must have the expression

$$P_1 = P_0(1 + i).$$

That is, P_0 dollars now must be worth the same as $P_1 = P_0(1 + i)$ dollars received at the end of the year. In other words,

$$P_0 = \frac{1}{1 + i} P_1 \equiv DP_1,$$

---

[3] Alternatively, we may use calculus notation to write $I = dC/dt$; investment is the rate of increase of capital over time.

where the symbol D, called the *discount factor*, is used to designate the fraction $1/(1 + i)$. DP_1 is called the *discounted present value* of P_1 dollars receivable one year from today. For example, if the rate of interest were 5 per cent so that $i = 0.05$, then we would have $D = 1/1.05$, and we would conclude that \$100 receivable at the end of the year is today worth only $(1/1.05)\$100 = \$95.24$ (approximately), because at a 5 per cent interest rate \$94.24 will grow to \$100 in one year.

What is the present value $P_0(2)$, of some amount, P_2 dollars, to be received two years in the future? If invested for one year, $P_0(2)$ will grow to $P_1^* = (1 + i)P_0(2)$. In a second year this amount will increase again to $(1 + i)P_1^* = (1 + i)(1 + i)P_0(2) = (1 + i)^2P_0(2)$. In other words, if $P_0(2)$ now is to be equal in value to P_2 receivable in two years, we must have $P_2 = (1 + i)^2P_0(2)$ or

$$P_0(2) = \left(\frac{1}{1 + i}\right)^2 P_2 \equiv D^2P_2.$$

Similarly, at compound interest, $P_0(n)$ dollars invested for n years will grow into $P_n = (1 + i)^nP_0(n)$. So the discounted present value of P_n dollars receivable in n years is readily seen [by division by $(1 + i)^n$] to be

$$P_0(n) = \left(\frac{1}{1 + i}\right)^n P_n \equiv D^nP_n.$$

This is the generalized formula of discounted present value which permits us to convert amounts payable or receivable at different dates into similar terms—they are all made comparable by being translated into their equivalent current value.

After this translation, amounts of money pertaining to different dates can be added or subtracted directly. If a firm spends \$90 today and receives \$105 a year from today, the net present value of the operation will be $105D - 90 = (1/1 + i)105 - 90$. At a 5 per cent rate of interest $(i = 0.05)$ this gives $(1/1.05)105 - 90 = 10$, that is, the net yield of the operation is \$10 in present value.

More generally, suppose that a firm expects to receive R_0 dollars currently, R_1 dollars in one year, R_2 dollars in two years, etc. The total *capitalized present value*, C, of this stream of expected receipts is given by

$$C = R_0 + DR_1 + D^2R_2 + \cdots + D^nR_n,$$

where, as before, D represents the discount factor $1/1 + i$.

An important special case arises if all these expected receipts (or payments) are equal, i.e., if we have $R_0 = R_1 = \cdots = R_n = R$. Then we have $C = R + DR + D^2R + \cdots + D^nR = R(1 + D + D^2 + \cdots + D^n)$. Now the terms of any geometric series such as $1 + D + D^2 + \cdots + D^n$ (call it S_n) can be totaled with the aid of the expression[4]

(1) $\qquad S_n = (1 + D + D^2 + D^3 + \cdots + D^n) = \dfrac{1 - D^{n+1}}{1 - D}$.

In the special situation where the stream of payments is expected to continue into the indefinite future, then, provided, as is normally the case, that $D < 1$, we obtain from (1)

$$S_\infty = (1 + D + D^2 + \cdots) = \frac{1}{1 - D}.$$

For since D is less than unity, D^2 is less than D, D^3 is smaller still, and, generally, D^n grows smaller and smaller as n grows larger and larger, and the term D^n in (1) tends to disappear; i.e., it approaches zero as n approaches infinity.[5]

2. Discount Rate and Opportunity Cost; Real vs. Nominal Rates

Before getting down to substantive conclusions it is appropriate to pause briefly to discuss the logic of the discounting process which has just been described. The discount factor $1/(1 + i)$ has been tied directly to the rate of return on investment. The discount rate is just a measure of what we lose by receiving our money later rather than now. It is the *opportunity cost* of not having those resources sooner. So long as there exists a perfect capital market, i.e., so long as a reputable businessman can borrow or lend as much money as he needs at the going rate of interest, the rate of interest is the required measure of the cost of postponing the receipt of money. For if he needs any money now, he can obtain it at once by borrowing and paying iP dollars per year for it, until the date when his postponed receipts finally arrive. Conversely, if he receives money now rather than later, he

---

[4] *Proof:* $S_n = 1 + D + D^2 + \cdots + D^n$, so that, multiplying and dividing by $1 - D$,

$$S_n = \frac{(1 + D + D^2 + \cdots + D^n)(1 - D)}{1 - D}$$

$$= \frac{(1 + D + D^2 + \cdots + D^n) - (D + D^2 + \cdots + D^{n+1})}{1 - D}$$

$$= \frac{1 - D^{n+1}}{1 - D}.$$

[5] For a discussion of the formula for continuous discounting, $P_0 = e^{-rt}P_t$, its rationale, and its advantages in differentiation, see the appendix to this chapter.

can always employ it to earn *iP* dollars per year by using it to pay off a portion of his debts or by lending it out at the current interest rate.

If the capital market is imperfect—if the businessman can only borrow limited amounts, or if the rate of interest on his loans rises as he borrows more, or if the rate of interest he can earn by lending his money is less than the amount it costs him to borrow—the connection between the interest and discount rates is not so simple. But, *in any event, the discount rate remains the opportunity cost of postponed receipts of money.* For example, if the businessman is limited in the funds he can borrow, he may be unable to build a new plant which is capable of returning say 9 per cent on investment. In that case, the relevant loss from postponement of receipts is not any of the market rates of interest but the 9 per cent profit foregone on the most lucrative of the investment opportunities from which he is precluded by not having his money now.[6]

In a period of changing price levels it is important to distinguish between *real* and *nominal* rates of interest. Suppose an investment of $1,000 brings in $100 but the price level is rising at an annual rate of six per cent. The nominal rate of interest is then ten per cent but in fact the investor is earning far less than that. For each year his $1,000 investment loses approximately 6 per cent or $60 in purchasing power. Thus, of his $100 nominal earnings, only $40 are a net return, with the remaining $60 just serving to make up for the loss in purchasing power of his capital as it is eaten up by inflation. In sum, we have the basic relationship

real rate of interest = nominal rate of interest − rate of inflation.

Failure to recognize this relationship can lead to serious misunderstandings. For example, a public used to 6 per cent rates of return on bonds at an earlier date is likely to consider a twelve per cent return to be exorbitant.

---

[6] For many purposes the interest concept itself must be extended to cover more than the direct pecuniary payment to lenders. Suppose a businessman has money tied up in inventory which he will sell in two years. Its interest cost, for our purposes, may be considered to consist of all the expenses which are incurred *simply as a result of the passage of time* during the period when the funds are kept in illiquid form in inventory holdings. In addition to payments to the bank on the money tied up in the inventory, there are several other types of cost of the relevant variety. Among these are taxes on inventory holdings; insurance costs; costs of warehousing such as inspection, rental, etc.; costs of spoilage and pilferage; obsolescence; and so on. The longer the funds are kept tied up in inventory, the longer these costs accumulate. In some timing decisions in practice—for example, in the decision as to how long to age brandy—tax rates on inventory holdings may play a more important role than do interest rates proper, particularly in the minds of the businessmen involved. Similarly, to the holder of stocks of military equipment or style goods such as women's clothing, the expected rate of obsolescence may be far more important than the interest rate proper.

However, if the rate of inflation has simultaneously risen from 1 per cent to 10 per cent per annum, we see that the real rate of interest, far from rising, has in fact fallen drastically from 5 to 2 per cent. The change is surely no bonanza for the investor!

We turn next to a fundamental issue: the criterion to be used in determining the profitability of a proposed investment project. Three of the criteria that are most frequently considered are the payout period, the internal rate of return (marginal efficiency of investment) and the discounted present value. These will be discussed and evaluated in the next three sections.

3. Payout Period

A criterion which is frequently employed to judge the profitability of an investment in practice is its payout (or payback) period. For example, if a factory costs $7 million to construct and is expected to yield $2 million per year, its payout period is taken to be three and one-half years. The payout period of a project, then, is defined as the number of years which is required to accumulate earnings sufficient to cover its costs. The payout period criterion ranks projects in terms of this figure, asserting that a project with a four-year payout period is generally to be preferred to a six-year payout investment and that two projects, each of which is expected to have a three-year payout period, are, without further information on anything but their prospective profit yields, to be viewed with indifference.

The payout-period criterion is a crude rule of thumb and it is rarely defended in the literature except as an easy and inexpensive device for dealing with risk—a role for the criterion which will be considered later in this chapter. It is described here because an explanation of its shortcomings is illuminating.

The basic weakness of the payout criterion lies in the limited period of time which it takes into account. A piece of equipment may well continue to operate for many years after it has covered its initial costs. Whether or not it will do so is highly relevant for determining the profitability of its purchase, but this element is nowhere taken into account by the payout calculation. To take an extreme example, consider two items with an equal cost and an equal payout period of seven years. Suppose the first of the candidate items is not likely to last much beyond these seven years, while the other may be expected to remain in use for a considerable amount of time thereafter. The latter is then clearly the better investment, but this it totally ignored by the payout criterion, which rates the two items equally.

Moreover, the payoff criterion completely ignores much of the time pattern of receipts. For example, an investment whose cost is 7 (hundred thousand dollars) will be paid off in three years by either of the following earnings streams: stream A which yields \$1 in the first year, \$1 in the second, and \$5 in the third, or stream B which offers \$5 in the first year and \$1 in each of the following two years. Yet it is clear that most firms will not be indifferent between the two propositions and, as a matter of fact, they will usually prefer stream B, which returns the investors' money much more promptly.

4. Marginal Efficiency of Investment

A second criterion, the internal rate of return or marginal efficiency of investment, carries behind it the prestige of some of the great names of economics. Keynes was among those who employed this measure of the profitability of an investment. Actually, this criterion does not work out too badly in most cases, but we shall see that, in principle, and sometimes in practice, it is subject to serious shortcomings.

The marginal efficiency of an investment project is defined as that rate of interest or return which would render the discounted present value of its expected future marginal yields exactly equal to the investment cost of the project. For example, consider a project whose anticipated yield is \$10 per year in perpetuity (beginning at the end of the year) and whose initial cost is \$100. If the rate of interest were 9 per cent [so that $i = 0.09$, and the rate of discount would be $1/(1 + i) = 1/1.09$], then the present value of this income stream would be $10(1/1.09) + 10/(1.09)^2 + \cdots = 10/i = \$111$ (approximately).[7] Clearly then, since 111 is greater than the \$100 value of the original investment, our trial interest rate, $i = 0.09$, is not equal to the marginal efficiency of investment. We need a higher discount rate, and hence a higher value of i to reduce the value of the income stream down to the 100 investment cost. If we try $i = 0.11$, we will find we have gone too far in the other direction, because the capitalized present value of the \$10 stream will now be equal to $10/1.11 + 10/(1.11)^2 + \cdots = 10/i = 91$ (approximately), which is less than the \$100 investment cost. If, finally, we try a 10 per cent interest rate ($i = 0.1$), we find that the present value of the income stream is exactly \$100, so that 10 per cent is the marginal efficiency of our investment. This measure is sometimes also called the project's *internal rate of return*, because it evaluates the internal profit-

---

[7] The general formula for the present value of K dollars in perpetuity, beginning at the *end* of the current period, is K/i. This is so because by footnote 4 of this chapter [and writing $D = 1/(1 + i)$], it is equal to

$$K(D + D^2 + \cdots) = KD(1 + D + D^2 + \cdots)$$
$$= KD[1/(1 - D)] = KD/(1 - D)$$
$$= \frac{K/1 + i}{1 - 1/(1 + i)} = \frac{K}{(1 + i) - 1} = K/i.$$

ability of a specific investment project, and it may have no relation to the company's cost of capital.

The marginal efficiency criterion tells management to undertake an investment so long as its marginal efficiency exceeds the rate of interest (or other costs) which the company incurs when it obtains more money. The argument is that if the company pays a 6 per cent rate of interest and can use these funds to purchase an item which will yield a stream of returns which can be evaluated at 10 per cent, then it will always pay the company to do so. And the argument is correct so far as it goes. The most important difficulty of the concept arises in circumstances not considered in the preceding discussion. Suppose that for some reason company management is limited in the number of investment projects which it can undertake. It must then assign priorities and settle upon the combination of projects which promises to be most profitable. Here marginal efficiency of investment runs into difficulties as a guide. To see how its problems arise we must compare it with the discounted present-value criterion.

5. Discounted Present Value vs. Marginal Efficiency

We have already seen earlier in this chapter how one calculates the discounted present value of the stream of returns expected to result from an investment project. The discounted present value criterion tells us simply that a project will be profitable if the discounted present value of its expected earnings is greater than its cost (including discounted future maintenance and operating costs). That is, it tells us to invest in a project if the discounted value of its revenues minus its costs is greater than zero.

To compare the behavior of the marginal efficiency concept with that of the discounted present value let us tabulate the results of the computation which we have just completed. This is done in Table 1. We see that since at a 9 per cent interest rate the present value of the illustrative investment is 111 (as we had already calculated), the net gain from our $100 investment is $111 − 100 = $11. A similar figure is shown for interest rates of 1 per cent, 2 per cent, etc.

We can now depict these results graphically in Figure 1, where we plot the net investment yields (their net discounted present value) against the various alternative interest rates. We see that the marginal efficiency of investment is the interest rate, E, at which our curve, VV', cuts the horizontal axis. For, by definition, the marginal efficiency of investment reduces the present value of the investment to the present value of its cost, so that its net yield must then be zero.

On the other hand, to determine the discounted present value we must know the appropriate rate of interest. Suppose the market interest rate, C,

TABLE 1. PRESENT VALUE OF $10 PER YEAR IN PERPETUITY
AT VARIOUS DISCOUNTING INTEREST RATES

Interest rate i	0.01	0.02	0.03	0.04	0.05	0.06	0.07	0.08	0.09	0.1	0.11
Discounted present value $V = 10/i$	1000	500	333	250	200	167	143	125	111	100	91
Net discounted present value $N = V - \$100$	900	400	233	150	100	67	43	25	11	0	−9

is 5 per cent ($i = 0.05$). Then, as point A indicates, the net discounted present value of the investment is $100.

The marginal efficiency of investment criterion tells the businessman to invest if the marginal efficiency of investment is greater than the interest rate (the marginal cost of capital), i.e., in the diagram if the intersection point E lies to the right of point C, the market interest rate. On the other hand, the discounted present-value criterion approves any investment whose net discounted present value, CA, is positive. We see, then, that in our illustrative case the two criteria are in agreement, and, in fact, we can normally expect them to be so. For, ordinarily, a rise in the discounting interest rate will reduce the present value of an investment, so that VV' will have a negative slope. Suppose in such a case that the net present value of the investment is positive (point A is above the horizontal axis at the current interest rate C). Then E, the point at which VV' crosses the horizontal axis, must clearly lie to the right of C, i.e., the marginal efficiency must also exceed the current interest rate.

But our net discounted present-value curve need not *always* have a negative slope, and that leads to the first (though, practically, perhaps not very important) shortcoming of the internal rate of return.[8] Suppose, for example, that a proposed investment project is expected to generate the following income stream in the five years of its anticipated life: first year −$100, second year $90, third year $110, fourth year −$60, fifth year −$60. We see that the project generates losses both at the beginning and

---

[8] This point and the one which follows were first called to the attention of economists by Lorie and Savage. See J. H. Lorie and L. J. Savage, "Three Problems in Capital Rationing," *Journal of Business*, Vol. XXVIII, October 1955, reproduced in Ezra Solomon (ed.), *The Management of Corporate Capital*, The Free Press of Glencoe, New York, 1959. In the following chapter we will see how this issue has recurred in pure capital theory in the debate over "reswitching of techniques."

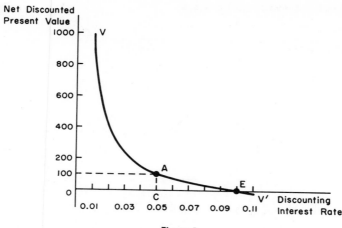

Figure 1

end of its life (the latter frequently occur in extractive industries, where the cost of closing a mine is high, or they may arise out of financial obligations incurred by the project over the span of its existence, obligations which are not covered by the investment's earnings in the fourth and fifth year because of the declining productivity of the item). Then VV' will take the form depicted by the solid portion of the curve in Figure 2 and will intersect the horizontal axis twice, once at R and once at S. The reason this will occur is that with a very low rate of interest, the negative returns in the fourth and fifth year will hardly be discounted at all, so that, together with the initial outlay, they can swamp the middle-period profits. For example, if the rate of interest were zero so that future returns were given exactly equal weight with current returns, our project would be evaluated at $-\$100 + 90 + 110 - 60 - 60 = -20$. However, with an intermediate rate of interest, the fourth- and fifth-year losses will fall in relative importance, and so the stream will assume a positive present value. Finally, if the interest rate is extremely high, nothing but the current year figure (the $100 initial loss) will retain any appreciable value after discounting, and so the stream will once again be ascribed a negative present value—hence the humped shape of the VV' curve in Figure 2.

Now in this diagram it is not clear whether point R or S is to be called the *marginal efficiency of investment*.[9] Moreover, the marginal-efficiency and

---

[9] It is also perfectly possible to encounter VV' curves which contain several more intersections with the horizontal axis, such as T and U, in the broken extension of our original VV' curve. The entire problem arises because to find the marginal efficiency of investment we seek to determine the discount rate, $D = 1/1 + i$, which satisfies $R_0 + DR_1 + D^2R_2 + \cdots + D^nR_n = 0$, where $R_0, R_1 \cdots, R_n$ is the stream of expected net returns from the project. Since this is an nth-degree equation, it may have as many as n distinct real roots, i.e., n different marginal efficiency figures.

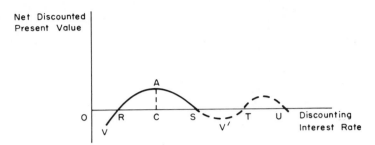

Figure 2

discounted-present-value criteria need no longer supply the same answer on the acceptability of a given investment project. If C is the current interest rate and R is taken to be the marginal efficiency of our investment, then the project should be rejected on the marginal efficiency criterion, because $R < C$. But at interest rate, C, the net discounted present value of the investment, CA, is positive, and so, on the present-value criterion, the project is profitable.

More serious, however, is the shortcoming of the marginal efficiency criterion which shows up when, for some reason, we are forced to choose between two mutually exclusive projects. Let their respective net discounted present-value curves be VV' and WW' in Figure 3, and let us refer to the corresponding projects as v and w. Then we can see at once that with the current interest rate at C, project w has the larger discounted present value $(CB > CA)$ but project v is characterized by the larger marginal efficiency of investment $(OS > OR)$!

Which, then, are we to choose? The answer is straightforward if the firm can borrow all the money it desires at C per cent so that it is some other consideration which has forced it to choose between v and w. For example, v and w may be alternative warehouse facilities and the company may need no more than one additional warehouse. In that case the present value is just what the title implies. It is the value which the rational firm must necessarily assign to a project, as was shown in Section 2. The project which has the largest discounted present value, by definition, makes the largest net contribution to the wealth of the firm. If some other criterion appears to tell us otherwise, that other criterion must somehow miss the point and we must ignore it.

The reason for the disparity of the two calculations is to be ascribed to their implicit treatment of two investment projects of different duration. Suppose one project brings in $100 and another brings in $105 one year later. How is the advantage of the earlier payment to be evaluated—at the rate of interest actually available on the market, as assumed by the discounted present value method, or is the hundred dollars to be assumed to earn the project's internal rate of return? That is, which of these two rates should be used in discounting the $105 to make it comparable with the $100? If the relevant project is in fact terminated when the $100 is received, that investment opportunity is now foreclosed and so only the *market* rate of interest is the relevant investment advantage offered by the earlier receipt of the $100. The answer given by the method of discounted present value is then the correct one.

Where there are limitations to the firm's borrowing ability, i.e., where its capital is rationed, and where that is the reason it is forced to choose between v and w, no such simple and categorical judgment can be offered, for in that case there is no well-defined current interest rate. The interest rate which the firm happens to pay on the money it borrows does not measure the true opportunity value of cash to the firm. If capital is really rationed, it means that management would like to borrow more at the current interest rate. Therefore the marginal value of further capital to the firm must exceed that interest rate. It is therefore no longer possible to make a direct identification of i, the rate of interest appropriate for the determination of discounted present value. We shall see in a later section the method of calculation which is appropriate for project selection where capital is rationed. It may only be indicated at this point that the problem is particularly intractable to methods of analysis like those which have just been described if capital is rationed to the firm in several of the periods when outlays will have to be made. For if the firm can only raise, say, $750,000 during the next year and no more than $1,250,000 during the year after, the marginal opportunity value of money in the two periods need not be the same. Even if the company needs the money more urgently during the former of these periods, it cannot arrange a transfer of funds from the second period to the first when borrowing is effectively rationed. It is as

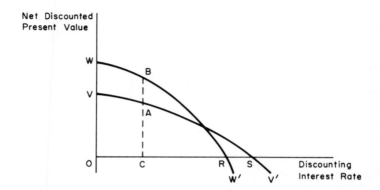

Figure 3

though an investment had two distinct prices, one involving payment in pounds and one in francs, and the purchaser were short of both types of currency and could not convert from one to the other. A very complex type of balancing between scarce dollars today and scarce dollars tomorrow is required in such a situation, and correspondingly more subtle calculations are required for an optimal selection of investment projects.[10]

6. Illustration: Use of the Discounted Present-Value Criterion

Case 1. A simple problem

Given investments A and B with expected payoffs as indicated in Table 2 below, which of these produces the higher present value, given a discounting rate of 6 per cent? With an interest rate of $i = 0.06$ the discount rate is $D = 1/1 + i = 1/1.06 = 0.94$ (approximately) so that we have

TABLE 2

| | Present | Year of Return | | |
		1st	2nd	3rd
Investment A	−1,000	500	700	500
Investment B	−600	400	800	0

$D^2 = 0.89$, $D^3 = 0.84$ (approximately). Therefore, the approximate discounted present value of investment A is

$$-1,000D^0 + 500D + 700D^2 + 500D^3$$
$$= -1,000 + 500(0.94) + 700(0.89) + 500(0.84) = \$513,$$

while that of investment B is

$$-600D^0 + 400D + 800D^2 = -600 + 400(0.94) + 800(0.89) = \$488.$$

Hence A is the more valuable investment in terms of net discounted present value.

---

[10] For other shortcomings in the discounted present-value analysis see J. Hirschleifer, "On the Theory of Optimal Investment Decision," *Journal of Political Economy*, Vol. LXVI, August 1958, reproduced in Solomon, *op. cit.*

Comparing this result with the payout period calculation, we see that investment A pays off $500 of its $1,000 cost after its first year, leaving the remaining $500 to be paid off during the second year when earnings accrue at the rate of $700 per year. Hence the payout period is one and five-sevenths years, approximately. Similarly, B requires approximately one and one-fourth years to recoup its investment cost. Thus, B has the shorter payout period and is the better investment on this crude criterion. But note that our payout calculation has taken no account of the fact that investment A is expected to earn $500 during its third year, while it is anticipated that B will yield nothing during that period.

Case 2. A more complex problem

To illustrate further the method of use of the discounted present-value criterion a typical problem from the literature of replacement theory (in operations research) will now be described in detail.[11]

Problem: *When to replace equipment with rising maintenance costs.* A firm pays $2,000 for its automobiles. Their operating and maintenance costs are about $500 per year for the first two years and then go up by approximately $300 per year. When should such cars be replaced?

First let us look at the problem in algebraic terms. The annual outlays during years 0, 1, 2 etc., of a given car's life, until it is replaced, are $C_0 = 2,000$ (the cost of the car), $C_1 = 500$, $C_2 = 500$, $C_3 = 800$, etc. If the car is replaced annually, we will have an outlay of $C_0 = \$2,000$ every year. If it is replaced every two years, we will have the outlay stream C_0, C_1, C_0, C_1, C_0, $\cdots$ whose elements repeat themselves every two years, and, in general, if it is replaced after t years, our stream of costs, S, becomes $C_0, C_1, C_2, \cdots$, $C_t, C_0, C_1, C_2, \cdots, C_t, C_0, \cdots$. To put these cost streams on a comparable basis, we translate them into an equivalent fixed annual payment, that is, an annual payment of a dollars whose discounted present value is the same as that of our stream, S. Since the elements in stream S repeat themselves every t years, we need only consider the present value of $C_0, C_1, \cdots, C_t$, and the present value of the a dollar payment for the same t years. With the discount rate, $1/(1 + i)$, represented by D, the present value of the a is given by [see Equation (1) of this chapter]

$$V = a + Da + \cdots + D^t a = a\,\frac{1 - D^{t+1}}{1 - D},$$

---

[11] This illustration is adapted from M. Sasieni, A. Yaspan, and L. Friedman, *Operations Research, Methods and Problems*, John Wiley & Sons, Inc., New York, 1959, p. 105 ff.

so that

$$a = \frac{1 - D}{1 - D^{t+1}} V.$$

Here, since V is the discounted present value of the outlays on the car for the t years before it is replaced, we have

$$V = C_0 + DC_1 + D^2C_2 + \cdots + D^t C_t.$$

Our object is to find the value of t which makes the fixed annual equivalent cost, a, as small as possible. Suppose, now, that the opportunity cost of having the receipt of money postponed for a year is such that a dollar one year in the future has a present value of only 90 cents, so that $D = 0.9$. That is, suppose that management estimates that it can invest its additional cash in such a way that by the end of the year each 90 cents will have, on the average, increased to $1.[12] We may then calculate a as a function of the length of life of an automobile in Table 3.

TABLE 3

Years (t)	C_t	D^t	V	$(1 - D)/(1 - D^{t+1})$	a
0	2,000	1	2,000	1	2,000
1	500	0.9	2,450	0.53	1,299
2	500	0.81	2,855	0.37	1,056
3	800	0.73	3,439	0.29	997
4	1,100	0.66	4,165	0.24	1,000
5	1,400	0.59	4,991	0.21	1,048
6	1,700	0.53	5,892	0.19	1,119

Clearly, the table indicates that a is at a minimum at about $t = 3$ or 4. That is, the cars should, optimally, be replaced at something between three- and four-year intervals.

Before leaving this example two extensions will be noted very briefly. First, observe that the scrap or trade-in value of the car when replacement takes place is easily included in the calculation. The amount received for the old car need only be considered a negative cost for that year and should be deducted from the value of C_t.

Second, exactly the same computation can be employed in deciding whether to switch to a more expensive vehicle which costs less to maintain. We need merely compare the minimum fixed annual equivalent cost for

---

[12] This is tantamount to having an interest rate, i, of approximately 11.1 per cent, for $D = 0.9 = 1/1 + i$, so that solving for i we obtain $i = 1/9 = 0.111 \cdots$.

our \$2,000 car, a, with the corresponding figure for the more expensive vehicle. The car which yields the lower a figure will clearly do the job most inexpensively in the long run.

The artificiality of the case which has been described should be apparent enough; however, it should adequately indicate the nature of replacement analysis.

PROBLEMS

1. Compute the discount rate if the interest rate is
   (a) 5 per cent
   (b) 7 per cent.
2. Suppose the interest rate is 5 per cent and that a certain investment is expected to yield \$500 at once, \$700 at the end of one year, \$200 at the end of the second year, and then be scrapped. Using the equation $a + aD + \cdots = a/1 - D$ calculate how many dollars paid out each year *in perpetuity* is equal in present value to the capitalized (i.e., discounted) present value of our investment. (Hint: Let a dollars per year be the amount paid in perpetuity. What is the capitalized value of this stream? What is the present value of the earnings of our investment? What is the value of a?)
3. Given three investment projects described in the following table:

Project	Current Payoff	1st Year Payoff	2nd Year Payoff
A	−300	600	0
B	−300	200	400
C	−300	300	$333\frac{1}{3}$

   (a) Assuming that the \$300 loss in the current year represents the cost of the project, calculate the payout period of each investment.
   (b) Calculate the marginal efficiency of each investment.
   (c) With the interest rate at 10 per cent, calculate the discounted present value of each project.
   (d) Which project is best on each criterion?

7. Indivisibility, Interdependence, and Capital Rationing Problems

Frequently, the investment decision is beset by a number of complications which require that its analysis employ tools which are rather more sophisticated. We shall see in this section that in order to satisfy the basic principles of optimality, the investment decision process must sometimes employ the methods of integer programming.[13]

Four such complications merit particular attention:

1. The first of these problems, which has already been mentioned, grows out of the funds limitations which sometimes circumscribe the investment decision. In the presence of capital rationing one is no longer concerned with the selection of an ideal set of investments whose acquisition might well require resources beyond those available to the firm. Rather, one must determine the best course which can be followed with the limited funds on hand.

2. A second problem arises because investment projects are, characteristically, indivisible, all-or-none propositions. If funds run short, it may be possible to scale down the plans for a proposed new building. But it is generally not possible to purchase 6.307 machines of a given variety. In practice, management is frequently offered several fairly definite alternative sets of specifications which can meet the requirements of a given job. It must then choose one among these alternatives, or it can reject them all, but frequently it cannot rescale or combine the options. This means that in deciding how many units of a given item a firm should acquire, fractional answers must be rejected as meaningless. And where an all-or-none decision is called for, the answer must be restricted to two possible values—0 or 1. Either one of the contemplated office buildings will be constructed, or the project will be abandoned altogether.

3. A third special characteristic of many investment decisions is that the available alternatives must be considered mutually exclusive. If management decides on project A, project B is thereby rejected automatically. Such a case arises, for example, where several alternative designs are proposed for a single warehouse or a single factory.

4. Our final source of analytical difficulty inherent in many investment decisions is encountered where one project should not be undertaken without another. The company should not purchase weaving machinery (project C) without a factory in which to house it (project D). Here project D may or may not be undertaken in the absence of C (the building might be used for other purposes), but C should not even be considered unless D will be adopted.

Let us examine these issues in turn, though we shall see at the end of the discussion how they can be handled together with the aid of a single calculation procedure. The approach required by the funds limitations which restrict management's freedom of action should be obvious to anyone

---

[13] This was first emphasized by H. Martin Weingartner, *Mathematical Programming and the Analysis of Capital Budgeting Problems*, Prentice-Hall, Inc., Englewood Cliffs, N.J., 1963.

who has studied linear programming or differential calculus.[14] The funds limitations simply must be treated as the constraints of the problem. To formulate our basic programming model, we shall require the following notation: Let

x_i represent the number of units of investment i which are undertaken (e.g., the number of trucks which are purchased by the firm);

N_i be the net discounted present value of the expected future returns on one unit of investment i;

m_{it} represent the amount of money required during period t to finance a unit of investment i;

M_i be the total amount of money available for investment during period t.

Then our objective function requires us to maximize the net discounted present value of all projects which are undertaken, i.e., maximize[15]

$$N = N_1 x_1 + \cdots + N_k x_k.$$

This is to be accomplished within the limited resources available to the firm as represented by the constraints corresponding to each of the pertinent time periods (from the present, $t = 0$, until some terminal date, $t = w$).

$$(2) \quad \begin{cases} m_{10} x_1 + m_{20} x_2 + \cdots + m_{k0} x_k \leq M_0 \\ m_{11} x_1 + m_{21} x_2 + \cdots + m_{k1} x_k \leq M_1 \\ \cdots\cdots\cdots\cdots\cdots\cdots\cdots\cdots\cdots \\ m_{1w} x_1 + m_{2w} x_2 + \cdots + m_{kw} x_k \leq M_w. \end{cases}$$

---

[14] The application of programming to this problem is due to Weingartner, *ibid.* For what may be the first such formulation employing differential calculus see Helen Makower and W. J. Baumol, "The Analogy Between Producer and Consumer Equilibrium Analysis," *Economica*, N.S. Vol. XVII, February 1950.

[15] Strictly speaking, the following construction oversimplifies matters considerably by assuming we know the interest rate with which to discount the returns from each project. For, since capital is rationed in our problem, the appropriate discount rate itself depends on the best use which can be made of the funds. In other words, the discount rate depends on the optimality calculation and vice versa. In principle, the solution of the problem requires a nonlinear programming analysis in which the dual prices are the marginal yields of money in the various periods, and, hence, the appropriate discount rates. In this problem the discounted present values, the N_i, themselves are functions of the dual prices, and hence are variable.

The following formulation also assumes that management is considering only a fixed number (k) of alternatives. These need not all be undertaken in the current period.

And, as usual, we also require

(3) $$x_1 \geq 0, \quad x_2 \geq 0, \quad \cdots, \quad x_k \geq 0.$$

Let us review the interpretation of each of these relationships. Our objective function multiplies N_i, the net present value per unit of project k, by x_i the number of units of i which is undertaken, to yield the total return from investment i. These returns for all potential projects are then added together to represent the total yield of any investment program which the company may adopt.

Our structural constraints (2) are constructed similarly. For example, the first of these deals with the capital requirements of the initial period, $t = 0$. It states that the sum of the moneys required in period zero for all investment projects which are undertaken, $\sum m_{i0}x_i$, must not exceed M_0, the quantity of money capital which will be available to the company during this period. Finally, our nonnegativity requirements (3) indicate that it is technologically impossible for the firm to construct a negative number of factories.[16]

These three sets of expressions represent our limited-funds investment problem in its entirety as a standard linear programming problem. It can then be solved by the standard linear programming techniques which have been described in Chapter 5, to yield an optimal investment program for the firm. If a problem which is encountered in practice involves significant nonlinearities, a nonlinear programming calculation can be substituted, in principle, though the very serious difficulties of data gathering and computation which such an analysis may incur cannot be overstressed.

Next we turn to the second difficult characteristic of the investment decision problem, the indivisibility of many investment projects. This means that our quantity variable x_i cannot meaningfully be permitted to take fractional values. If x_i represents the number of freight cars purchased, we can have $x_i = 1$, or 5, or any other integer value, but $x_i = 3.72$ is nonsense. In such circumstances we must therefore add to our previous re-

---

But the amount of a project to be undertaken in, say, period 5, must be represented by a variable x_i different from that (x_i) which corresponds to a similar project to be initiated in an earlier period. Of course, a project to be undertaken in period 5 is likely to require no investment funds in earlier periods, i.e., it may be characterized by the conditions $m_{j0} = m_{j1} = m_{j2} = m_{j3} = m_{j4} = 0.$

[16] A firm may, in fact, disinvest by selling some property. Such an activity can be handled by representing its amount by another variable x_v, where, since this symbol represents the amount sold, we may again require $x_v \geq 0$. For a method which deals with the possible dependence of the decision to sell on a prior decision to purchase see the discussion of interdependent investment decisions below.

quirement in our programming model

(4) x_i integer   (for all i corresponding to indivisible projects).

It will be recognized that this immediately transforms our construct into an *integer-programming* model. Highly promising integer programming techniques are already in existence, and these have frequently proved to be very effective and powerful.

The indivisibility of investment projects sometimes gives rise to a particular type of situation where the decision involved is whether or not to undertake a particular project. There is no question as to the number of these facilities—either the item will be constructed or it will not be. Thus the number of units of the item in question cannot exceed unity, i.e., the corresponding x_i can only take either the value 0 or 1. If $x_i = 1$, the project will be adopted; if $x_i = 0$, it will be rejected. This requirement can easily be incorporated into our model by means of the constraint

(5) $x_i \leq 1.$

For by (3) we must have $x_i \geq 0$, and by (4) x_i must take an integer value. There are then only two possibilities left, $x_i = 0$ or $x_i = 1$, just as we require. Our programming calculation then handles the all-or-none problem simply by the addition of constraint (5).

We come now to our last two special investment decision problems: mutually exclusive projects and the case of a project whose utility is conditional upon the adoption of some other investment. If a number of investments are mutually exclusive, a nonprogramming calculation becomes extremely difficult in the presence of funds limitations because of the combinatorial problems which arise. If investment B costs less than investment A, then should the company choose to invest in B this will release funds which can be invested in yet another project or in several other projects. Thus A is the better project only if its return is higher than that offered by the most lucrative available *combination* of projects (where project B is included in the combination). Such a complex decision problem can easily be handled by our programming model. If A and B are our mutually exclusive alternatives, we need merely substitute for constraint (5) the condition

(6) $x_a + x_b \leq 1,$

where x_a and x_b are the respective quantities of projects A and B undertaken. Since we already require $x_a \geq 0$, $x_b \geq 0$ and since both of these variables are restricted to integer values, we see that only three possibilities are permitted to us by condition (6):

$$\text{i. } x_a = 1, \qquad x_b = 0$$

$$\text{ii. } x_a = 0, \qquad x_b = 1$$

or

$$\text{iii. } x_a = 0, \qquad x_b = 0.$$

Our solution therefore permits us to undertake at most one of the two projects, which is exactly what is required in the case of a pair of mutually exclusive alternatives. Precisely the same sort of device (with the constraint this time being $x_a + x_b + x_c \leq 1$) will clearly work if only one of, say, three projects, A, B, and C, can be undertaken.

Finally, suppose some project C is not to be undertaken unless D is also adopted. We can arrange for our calculation to take this difficulty into account by requiring it to satisfy, instead of constraint (6), the condition

$$(7) \qquad\qquad x_c \leq x_d.$$

By (3), (4), and (5) x_d must either be 0 or 1. If x_d is 0 (project D rejected), then by (7) we must also have $x_c = 0$, so that C will then automatically be rejected also. If, on the other hand, $x_d = 1$, we may have either $x_c = 1$ or $x_c = 0$. Thus project C will certainly not be undertaken unless D is, but otherwise there is complete freedom of selection in the decisions on these two projects.

Let us summarize the results of this section. We have examined a number of problems which frequently beset investment decision calculations. While the difficulties to which these give rise have only been indicated very briefly and with no detail, the fact is that until recently no general method was known for finding an optimal solution to an investment decision involving any one of them. We have seen, however, how all of these circumstances can readily be incorporated into a programming model and how the corresponding programming calculation can be forced to yield an optimal solution which takes all of these requirements into account.

PROBLEM

Suppose five investment projects are under consideration and that they involve the following net present values and cost commitments:

Project	1	2	3	4	5
Net present value	70	20	60	30	10
Year 1 cost	20	7	15	8	2
Year 2 cost	10	8	20	5	3

Suppose that the company has 40 (million) to invest in the first year, and 30 in the second, and that projects 2 and 4 are mutually exclusive alternatives. Write out the programming formulation of this problem.

8. Risk and the Investment Decision

Up until this point the problems of risk and imperfect foresight have been ignored. But these are really crucial for the investment decision, which necessarily yields the bulk of its fruits in the future, sometimes in the very distant future. This section therefore reviews briefly some of the approaches which have been proposed for dealing with the consequences of our imperfect ability to predict events which have not yet occurred. We shall start with the most heuristic and operational methods of procedure and then we will outline some of the more subtle and abstract methods which have been devised.

a. *The finite-horizon method.* In practice, a number of decision procedures (which will be recognized as first cousins of the payback criterion) have just laid down a terminal date beyond which any prospective developments are simply left out of consideration. For example, in deciding whether to construct a dam or to undertake some other waterway development project, the Federal government has frequently adopted a fifty-year horizon, treating all facilities as though they were certain to disappear without a trace exactly one-half century after their erection. The logic of the procedure is the view that any forecast for a period longer than fifty years is so unreliable that it is best not undertaken at all.

But the economist cannot accept this resolution of the problem except, possibly, as a crude device which saves decision-making costs. After all, the view that a dam will vanish like the one-horse shay, precisely on its fiftieth anniversary, is itself a prediction, and a highly implausible one at that. A routine decision which implicitly treats this conventional flight of fancy as though it were fact can lead to some rather peculiar and indefensible conclusions. Suppose we are to decide between two canal locks which cost roughly the same and are equally serviceable in their early years. One of them, however, will probably last little more than fifty years, whereas the other is likely to remain serviceable indefinitely. The fifty-year horizon precludes us from deciding in favor of the latter even though it is so clearly preferable. Many public investment decisions do have considerable long-term effects which cannot be ignored in this way. Particularly the conservation effects of a project may become really important only in the fairly distant future, when in their absence, soil depletion, serious flooding, and a number of other untoward consequences might well assume significant, if not catastrophic, proportions. A finite and arbitrary horizon, then, is not really a defensible method for dealing with imperfect foresight. It takes no account of our limited ability to predict events in the more immediate future (which is sometimes as distant as twenty-five years from the present) and forces us to ignore totally what little we can forecast about the more distant future with some degree of confidence.

b. *Discounting for risk.* A procedure for dealing with risk which is far more attractive than the finite-horizon method is the use of a risk discount factor. This procedure consists in an addition to the rate of interest figure employed in the discounting calculation. For example, suppose the actual rate of interest is 6 per cent; the rate used in discounting might then be increased by what we can call a *risk factor* of, say, 1 per cent, to a total of 7 per cent for a mildly risky prospect, and we might add a risk factor of 3 per cent to get a 9 per cent total where a much more speculative investment is in question. Such a risk discount, δ, always reduces the value of the discount rate, for the discount rate becomes, under its influence, $D = 1/1 + i + \delta < 1/1 + i$. In other words, the higher the risk, the more we lower our evaluation of a given expected return because (if that return is expected n periods in the future) we multiply it by a smaller fraction, D^n (the nth power of the discount rate, D), where, of course, both D and D^n always lie between zero and unity.[17]

Since in the discounting process more distant returns are multiplied by higher powers of the discount factor, this procedure automatically assigns a higher weight to the risk factor in more remote future periods, unless (as is always possible) we use different risk factors for different dates. However, the risk factor will still take some account of the risk involved in more proximate returns and will never completely drop out of the calculation for expected returns for any future date, however remote. Thus, since the

---

[17] For if the interest rate and risk discount are positive, we have $D = 1/1 + i + \delta < 1$, and if the interest rate and risk discount are finite, we must, by the same equation, have $D > 0$. And with any such value of D we must have $0 < D^n < 1$ for any $0 < n < \infty$.

discount rate, D, lies between zero and unity, any power of D will also lie in the same interval. Thus, since, say, the second year return R_2 is multiplied by $D^2 = (1/1 + i + \delta)^2$ in discounting, its present value, $D^2 R_2$, will be somewhat reduced because of the presence of the risk factor, δ. But a nonzero return expected even in the 154th year, $R_{154} > 0$, will have a positive present value, $D^{154} R_{154}$, because $D^{154} > 0$. Thus we see that the risk-discounted method has some rather desirable properties and is relatively easy to handle. Its basic difficulty is that it comes with no explicit instructions which permit us to calculate the appropriate value of δ, the discount factor, and it must usually be estimated on the basis of some sort of judgment or intuition. Since, in any event, it must take into account the degree of the investor's risk aversion, i.e., the extent to which he is repelled by risk, the evaluation of δ must perhaps necessarily remain subjective in most cases. Moreover, the choice of a unique risk-discount factor to be used to discount all future revenues also assumes implicitly that the riskiness of investment is never affected by the passage of time, a premise which is certainly not always true.

c. *The probability theory approach.* A third procedure for the investigation of risky investment prospects bases itself on standard probability theory. The approach points out that no single expected-return figure can adequately represent the full range of possible alternative outcomes of a risky undertaking. Rather, a large number of alternative payoffs must be considered for each pertinent future date, and each such possibility must be accompanied by an associated probability. If the return at date t is represented by R_t and if only a finite set of values of R_t is considered possible, we must deal with a probability function $P = f(R_t)$ which asserts that, for example, there is a 5 per cent probability that the return in year t will exceed \$100,000, that the probability is 8 per cent that the return will fall between \$90,000 and \$100,000, etc.

The risk-discount method clearly takes no account of this full range of possibilities and their associated probabilities. It can therefore be argued with justice that the risk-discount approach ignores elements which are important in an effective calculation of an optimal investment policy.

Unfortunately, for most applications the discussion of the probabilistic approach has not proceeded much beyond criticism of the risk discount. If the full probability function were ever known (which is rarely, if ever, the case for any investment project), standard actuarial methods of evaluation could be used.

But even these procedures are fully defensible only if many similar investments are to be undertaken. An insurance company can confidently employ actuarial calculations because, with a large number of policyholders, the cases which turn out badly are virtually certain to be counterbalanced by the cases which turn out unexpectedly well. But in an investment decision which will never be repeated, the justification for actuarial calculations is somewhat more shaky. It follows that (with the probabilities typically unknown) such a method is often neither practical nor fully defensible.

However, there do exist some relatively standardized assets which have been in use sufficiently long to make possible at least crude estimates of some of the characteristics of the payoff-probability distribution. An important application is Markowitz' powerful analytic procedure which utilizes such an approach for the selection of portfolios of securities— combinations of stocks, bonds, and other financial instruments which constitute a significant portion of the total investment of certain types of company.

The Markowitz approach utilizes two focal measures: an index of expected earnings and an index of risk. Given any one security, one can estimate its anticipated average future earnings by extrapolation of past experience and the use of judgment based on knowledge of the issuer and of the circumstances of the market as a whole. On the same basis, one can calculate a rough figure for the standard deviation of these earnings which serves as the basis for the construction of a measure of risk. Using programming methods, Markowitz then calculates for any given level of expected earnings what portfolio (i.e., which combination of securities) minimizes the index of risk. For example, Figure 4 indicates that at an earnings level E the optimal portfolio will incur risk R. By calculating more such points we obtain AA', which we may call the *risk-earnings possibility curve*, i.e., the curve which tells us for each attainable level of earnings the smallest risk which can be incurred.

Now the entire curve consists, in some sense, of optimal combinations among which one cannot choose *a priori*. One investor may prefer lower risk even if it reduces his expected earnings, and so he may desire a rela-

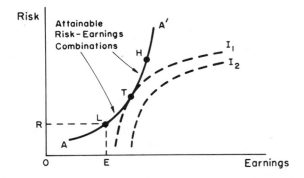

Figure 4

tively low risk point like L. Another investor who is more inclined to gamble may prefer a high expected earnings, high risk combination such as H.

For any prospective purchaser of such a combination of assets it is possible, in principle, to draw in a risk-earnings indifference map such as the I curves in the figure. These curves, it will be noted, are inverted in shape as compared with the standard indifference curves of the theory of consumer demand. This is because, other things being equal, we usually prefer lower levels of risk, i.e., we usually prefer points which are lower in the diagram. The curves have a positive slope because as risk increases, we require a higher level of earnings to keep us indifferent. If the diagram is turned upside down so that, as usual, higher points correspond to preferred combinations, we see that the indifference curves look quite normal.[18] For the investor shown, the optimal combination is, as usual, T, the point of tangency between the possibility curve and an indifference curve, because that gets him to his preferred earnings-risk combination, i.e., it tells him the portfolio which most effectively satisfies his goals.

In practice, the Markowitz calculation can take data pertaining to relatively large numbers of securities and select the "efficient" portfolio combinations from among them (i.e., combinations which are optimal in the sense that they correspond to points on the possibility curve AA'). However, the choice of the investor's preferred portfolio from among these efficient combinations is still left to the judgment of the individual investor and his attitudes on risk.[19]

---

[18] The reader will recognize that the slope of the indifference curve is the investor's marginal rate of substitution between risk and earnings. The flatter the curve, the less the added risk he is willing to undertake for a given increase in earning, i.e., the less of a gambler he is.

[19] One interesting result of the Markowitz analysis is that it will usually lead to the choice of a diversified portfolio of investments rather than one *best* (highest present value) investment. By not putting all of our nest eggs into one investment we are, in effect, hedging against the possibility that one of the projects will turn out very badly. Since the Markowitz calculation explicitly takes into account the effects of diversification on risk, it normally will recommend against concentration of funds on one or a very few types of investment. Recently Sharpe, Lintner, and Mossin have virtually simultaneously used the portfolio analysis as a basis for a powerful model of capital asset pricing. Assuming that all investors can borrow and lend as much as they want at a fixed rate of interest and that, given expected earnings, they seek to minimize the risk of their portfolio, the model leads to the curious conclusion that each investor will want to hold some stock of *every* firm in the economy and that any one security will constitute the same percentage of each investor's portfolio! See W. F. Sharpe, "Capital Asset Prices: A Theory of Market Equilibrium under Conditions of Risk," *Journal of Finance*, Vol. 19, September 1964, pp. 425–42; John Lintner, "The Valuation of Risk Assets and the Selection of Risky Investments in Stock Portfolios and Capital Budgets," *Review of Economics and Statistics*, Vol. 47, February 1965, pp. 13–37; and Jan Mossin, "Equilibrium in a Capital Asset Market," *Econometrica*, Vol. 34, October 1966, pp. 768–83.

d. *Sensitivity analysis and risk.* Still another method for taking risk into account in investment decisions employs what may be called *sensitivity analysis.* Here one decides which variables in the calculation are most crucial and most uncertain, and he tests how sensitive the calculated present-value figure is to likely changes in the value of this strategic variable. For example, suppose that a company is considering investing in a new product and that its plans are based largely on its hope of capturing 12 per cent of the market for this type of product within the next year. From this and its other information it can estimate in the usual manner (1) the expected present value of the investment if its expectations are fulfilled, (2) the effect of alternative possible market share figures on the calculated present value of that investment (all other things remaining equal), and, in particular, (3) the market share figure at which the net present value of the investment is zero, i.e., the *break-even* market share.

Suppose it turns out that this break-even market share is 8 per cent, so that unless it attains this market share within a year the investment will yield an absolute loss. This offers the firm some indication of the risk involved in the investment and enables management to associate with this project a subjective risk figure. In the same way, management can obtain such a risk index and a measure of expected yield (or present value) for each prospective investment. One can then proceed to construct a curve of attainable risk—earnings combinations as in Figure 4—and to select an optimal project or combination of projects as in the Markowitz procedure. Of course, a sensitivity analysis is more subjective and less powerful analytically than the Markowitz method. However, sensitivity analysis can be used in cases where the probabilistic information required by Markowitz is simply unavailable, and the relatively crude sensitivity calculation can be performed rather quickly and inexpensively.

e. *The use of decision theory and Neumann-Morgenstern utility.* The most recent, and perhaps the most sophisticated, methods which have been suggested for coping with risk and uncertainty are the Neumann-Morgenstern utility index and the criteria of decision theory. Since neither of these is, at least for the present, available in a form which permits its direct employment in concrete investment decisions and since both types of analysis are described in detail in other chapters in this book, there is no point in rediscussing the concepts here. However, the reader may well considerably increase his understanding of the entire problem by referring back to those chapters at this point.

We conclude, then, that among the variety of methods for dealing with risk which have been described, only three—the finite-horizon, the risk-discount, and the sensitivity-analysis approaches—are readily usable in practice. All three of them suffer from serious shortcomings, but economic analysis suggests that the latter two, the risk-discount and the sensitivity approaches, are far preferable to the former. Indeed, experience suggests that in many concrete applications they are reasonable and relatively trustworthy methods. In addition, the Markowitz approach can be extremely helpful, but it can be utilized only where reasonable estimates of the pertinent probabilities can somehow be obtained.

PROBLEMS

1. Suppose the risk discount, r, is 4 per cent. Recalculate the discounted present values of investments A and B in Table 2 of Section 6, assuming that the rate of interest, i, remains at 6 per cent.
2. Explain why though the risk discount is used for both projects, it has made B the better investment, whereas the calculation which ignored risk indicated that A was the more lucrative project.

9. Financing Investments: Alternative Methods

As is well known, there are several alternative methods whereby a firm can obtain the funds with which to finance an investment project. This section will list some of the more important of these financing techniques and will offer some relevant comments. In the next section, some of the considerations pertinent to an optimal financing program will be examined.

a. *Plowback.* By far the greatest portion of corporate investment in the United States is financed out of funds which are acquired internally. That is, rather than paying company earnings out to stockholders, they are plowed back into the firm. It avoids the heavy transactions costs which must be incurred in borrowing funds or in issuing new securities. It incurs less uncertainty for management, which can be sure of any funds it holds back, while it may not be completely confident of the results of an attempt to market new stocks or bonds. Finally, many stockholders seem to prefer this method of financing because it tends to transform income into capital gains by increasing the value of the company's stocks rather than providing dividend payments. This can offer a substantial tax advantage, particularly to shareholders in the upper income brackets.

b. *Issuing New Shares of Common Stock.* A second method whereby a company can obtain cash is through the sale of new common stock. Except from the point of view of any powerful stockholders who exercise real control over company policy, a share of stock can be considered to represent another form of loan to the company. True, it is more risky than a bond, but the shareholder receives from it dividends and capital gains if he is fortunate, and he can attempt to get his money back (terminate his loan) by selling the stock to another potential lender. The usual point of view that the stockholder is part owner of the company and that the bondholder is not is therefore a somewhat oversimplified view of the real distinction between the two.

c. *Sale of Bonds.* Management may borrow money directly by selling to the public some variety of bond, e.g., a mortgage bond, which supposedly pledges some piece of company property as security for the loan, or a debenture bond, which represents a general pledge of part of the value of the firm. The use of bond financing offers a distinct tax advantage since interest payments to bond holders are legally considered to be costs and are therefore not subject to the corporate income tax, whereas dividends, the corresponding payment for money obtained by the sale of stock, are considered to constitute income for the company and are therefore taxable.

To stockholders the sale of bonds is sometimes considered to be an advantage because it provides what is called *leverage*. Bonds are normally less risky than the stocks of the same firm because interest on its bonds represents a prior claim on company earnings which must be paid before any dividends are provided. Moreover, by holding a bond until maturity (the termination date of the loan which it represents) the bond holder can be sure of receiving the face value of the bond, provided the company remains solvent. The traditional view of the matter, then, is that their comparative safety makes bonds a relatively inexpensive way for the company to obtain money, i.e., the interest cost on a bond may be expected to be lower than it would be if the bond, as it were, absorbed its share of the company's risks, that is, interest cost normally is lower than the yield on a stock which is necessary to induce someone to purchase it. Hence, the higher the proportion of the external funds financing an investment project which is obtained by the sale of bonds, the greater the share of the returns from that investment available to current shareholders. If the return on an investment is 9 per cent, the interest on a bond is 5 per cent, and that on money obtained otherwise is 7 per cent, then the net yield to current stockholders of the investment will be 4 per cent if it is financed entirely by bonds. But if it is financed half by bonds and half otherwise, so that the average payment for money is 6 per cent, the net return on the investment will be only 3 per cent.

However, there is a catch to this. In effect, bond holders absorb less than their share of the company risk by passing it along to the stockholder. The more bonds there are outstanding, the greater the danger to shareholders and the company. If it has sold only so many bonds that its annual interest commitment is $100,000, then net annual earnings (before interest payment) of $250,000 will suffice to keep the company out of trouble and will leave $150,000 for plowback or dividends. However, if so many bonds are outstanding that the contracted annual interest payment amounts to

$400,000, a $250,000 level of earnings can lead to very serious results, and if continued long enough will result in insolvency. In other words, the leverage provided by the sale of additional bonds represents both an increase in the expected earnings of the stockholder and an increase in his risk.[20] It also means that the price of the company's stocks is likely to fluctuate more widely. Since his share of company earnings is a residue after the fixed-interest obligation, he does not have to share the company's unexpected prosperity with the bond holder. But, on the other hand, he gets no help from the bond holder in absorbing company losses. The stocks of the highly levered company, i.e., of the company with a high proportion of bonded indebtedness, are therefore likely to rise sharply when the market expects the firm to prosper and to fall drastically when adversity is foreseen.

From this it follows that a conservative managerial group (and a conservative stockholder) will typically dislike large amounts of bond financing because it magnifies the speculativeness of the company and its shares. We will discuss presently whether this reaction is entirely justified.

---

[20] To illustrate how increased bondholding is likely to increase the variance and likely range of stockholder earnings consider Table 4.

TABLE 4

1. Total earnings	100	200	300	400	500	600
2. Earnings per share at 100 shares	1	2	3	4	5	6
3. Earnings after interest ($200)	−100	0	100	200	300	400
4. Net earnings per share at 50 shares	−2	0	2	4	6	8

Here we have a company which is considering issuing either 100 (thousand) shares of stock, or 50 shares and 50 bonds. If it does the latter, it will incur a fixed interest obligation of 200 (thousand). The first row of the table simply lists some alternative possible earnings levels, ranging from 100 to 600. Row 2 indicates the corresponding earnings of any one of the 100 shares if no bonds were issued. Row 3 subtracts the fixed $200 interest debt from each possible earnings figure, and, finally, row 4 (= 1/50 times row 3) lists the earning to each of the 50 shares which would be outstanding under the stock-bond financing arrangement. Note that the lowest level of earnings per share has dropped from +1 in the pure stock case to −2 in the bond-stock case, while the highest earnings level has risen from 6 to 8! There are two reasons for this phenomenon. The fixed interest obligation reduces net stockholder earnings and produces losses at lower earnings levels. On the other hand, the reduced number of shares increases earnings *per share* once total earnings go beyond some minimal level.

Note also how leverage magnifies both gains and losses in earnings. In our example, when total earnings (line 1 in the table) rise by 100 per cent from 300 to 600, the levered earnings per share (line 4) rise 300 per cent, from 2 to 8. But if total earnings *decrease* 25 per cent from 400 to 300, earnings per share fall by 50 per cent, from 4 to 2.

d. *Convertible securities, direct loans, etc.* There are other instruments for financing which need not be discussed in detail. Firms may borrow directly from banks or insurance companies or Federal agencies. They may also issue hybrid securities, such as convertible bonds. A convertible bond is a bond which the holder can, subject to certain restrictions, trade in for company shares at a prespecified rate of exchange. A convertible is often safer than either a stock or a bond because the holder can, when he sells it, dispose of it either as a bond or as a corresponding number of stocks, whichever happens to have the higher market value at that time. Convertibles are issued by companies that wish to provide a somewhat safer type of security or that believe that the true value of its stock is not yet realized by the market. When the price of the company's stock rises sufficiently, the holders of convertibles will all find it profitable to transform them into stocks, and this will then automatically eliminate any bonded company indebtedness which the securities originally represented. Convertibles are also particularly salable because they are highly valued by some institutional purchasers whose rules of operation prohibit them from buying common stocks directly and who can therefore acquire them only through the purchase and conversion of this type of issue.

10. On Optimal Financial Policy

It would appear, then, that in financing its investment, management has a very considerable range of real options and that careful calculation is required for an optimal decision between the issue of bonds or common stock or between dividend payment and plowback (earnings retention). However, in a series of recent articles[21] Professors Modigliani and Miller have shown that these alternatives are not as different as they seem and that, in the absence of special tax problems, transactions costs, and market imperfection, there is little, if anything, to choose.

a. *Effects of leverage: stocks vs. bonds.* First of all let us examine the effects of added leverage on the shareholder, i.e., let us see how his interests are affected by the choice between the emission of more stocks and additional bonds. Modigliani and Miller show that in a market with no imperfections, taxes, or transactions costs the shareholder can arrange for himself any degree of leverage he desires. That is, if the company's leverage

---

[21] See Franco Modigliani and M. H. Miller, "The Cost of Capital, Corporation Finance and the Theory of Investment," *American Economic Review*, Vol. XLVIII June 1958, reproduced in Solomon, *op. cit.*, and M. H. Miller and Franco Modigliani, "Dividend Policy, Growth and the Valuation of Shares," *Journal of Business*, Vol. XXXIV, October 1961.

is too high for his taste, he can take steps to reduce the leverage which pertains to his own shares, or, if he wishes, he can increase the leverage associated with his holdings. What management does in this respect is thus of little or no interest to him, and the company's leverage decision consequently has no effect on the marketability of its securities.

To understand the argument we must see how one can decrease leverage. Though the answer is not complex, it is rather tricky and its comprehension may require the reader's concentration. One can reduce leverage to any desired degree simply by purchasing bonds and selling a number of stocks of equal value, thus reducing the risk of one's holdings. One trades a problematical income for a contractually fixed income, and the higher the proportion of the latter, the lower the leverage represented by one's holdings. Suppose the company has three times as many stocks as bonds outstanding. The individual investor who holds stocks and bonds in a three to one ratio has completely "unlevered" his holdings, i.e., his risks and returns are exactly the same as if the company had issued no bonds and he had purchased only stocks with the funds he had invested. For if any investor owns K per cent of the company's financial instruments, he will be entitled to exactly K per cent of its earnings, no matter what form those instruments and earnings may take.

Thus, we see that in the circumstances envisaged, any shareholder can arrange for "homemade leverage" sufficient to undo a managerial decision on leverage. By buying bonds he can reduce leverage and by the sale of bonds he can increase it. If he holds no bonds, so that he has none to sell, he can borrow money and achieve the same effect, for borrowing amounts to the same thing as selling bonds, since a bond is a loan, i.e., a "negative debt." Hence the welfare of the stockholder, in pursuit of whose interest the corporation is presumably run, is in this perfect market world totally unaffected by the choice between the issue of new stocks and new bonds.

Let us now introduce a "degree of risk" index which we can measure for any particular firm. It follows from the preceding discussion that in these ideal circumstances all firms with equal risk must yield the same earnings return on their total capital (stocks plus bonds), no matter what their leverage. For if one company's securities were underpriced in the sense that they earn a higher return per dollar of investment than the securities of another company, it would pay each investor to switch his funds from the too high-return company and then use homemade leverage to arrange for the degree of leverage he prefers. This would raise the price of the undervalued securities and lower the price of the other company's securities until they offered the same rate of return. Thus, in algebraic terms, if S is the total value of a company's stocks, B is the value of its bonds, E is company earnings (before deduction of interest), and r is the rate of return, we must have

(8)
$$\frac{E}{S+B} = r \text{ (constant)}$$

for all companies which are equally risky in some measurable sense.

We may deduce that the earnings per dollar of market value of shares increases linearly with the degree of leverage, i.e., with the proportion of the company's bond capital.[22] In other words, a graph with earnings-per-unit share value on the vertical axis and number of bonds on the horizontal axis will always be a straight line in these circumstances. That is, the higher proportion of its new investment which the company finances by means of bonds, the higher the return to each shareholder. Moreover, since the relationship is linear, it means that the marginal earnings yield per stockholder of an additional bond will be absolutely constant; there will be no diminishing returns to stockholders resulting from increments to the company's issuance of bonds.

Of course, as we have already noted, this is by no means pure gravy. As we have seen, the higher the amount of bonds, the greater the stockholder's leverage risk. This is why stockholders do not seek unlimited increases in leverage. As a matter of fact, that is precisely the explanation of our linear relationship. It tells us, in effect, that *in equilibrium, a linear increase in earnings per share will just suffice to compensate the stockholder for the risks which accompany enhanced leverage.* This price-earnings pattern is the means, according to Modigliani and Miller, by which market forces prevent the stockholder from either gaining or losing from an increase in leverage.

b. *Dividend payment vs. income retention.* Moreover, Modigliani and Miller have shown that in such circumstances, the shareholders' interests are unaffected by the decision between plowback and the issue of new shares in the current period as the means to finance a given investment project. This argument also is fairly subtle. We assume that none of the company's future plans and, in particular, investment decisions will in any way be affected by the decision in question. Now the value, V, of *all* company shares outstanding at the end of the period is determined by the ex-

---

[22] For if the interest rate per bond is i, so that the total earnings of the bond holders is iB, the amount left for stockholders will be $E - iB$, and the earnings per dollar of share value will be $(E - iB)/S$. Then, since by (8) $E = rS + rB$, the earnings per dollar of stock will be

$$\frac{E - iB}{S} = \frac{rS + rB - iB}{S} = r + (r - i)B/S,$$

which, so long as $r > i$, clearly increases linearly with the value of B.

pected value of future capital gains and future dividends which are by assumption given. V may therefore be treated as a constant, unaffected by the current decision between use of plowback and new stock financing to pay for the fixed level of investment. Suppose, therefore, that instead of financing all of the project out of current earnings, management pays the current shareholders D dollars in dividends which would otherwise have gone into the investment. To make up the deficit, the company must sell D dollars worth of additional securities to new stockholders. Let us see how the initial stockholders come out of all this. The value of *all* the company's shares at the end of the period is V dollars, as we have seen. But D dollars worth of these shares now belong to others. Hence our original stockholders' shares are now reduced in value to $V - D$ dollars. However, in addition they have received D dollars in cash. Therefore the net value of their assets is $(V - D) + D = V$! That is, the entire procedure has produced absolutely no change in the well-being of the original stockholders!

It would appear, then, that management has absolutely no grounds for choosing among methods of financing. In this crazy world, flipping a coin or consultation with an astrologer will produce an optimal decision since plowback or added stocks or added bonds are all equally happy decisions from the viewpoint of the current stockholder.[23] None of this seems to accord with common sense or the judgment of those experienced in these matters. We shall now see what has apparently gone wrong with the argument and why, despite its apparent conflict with the realities, the Modigliani-Miller analysis is so instructive.

c. *Effects of transactions costs, taxes, and market imperfections.* It has been emphasized from the beginning of this discussion that the absence of transactions costs, taxes, and market imperfections is assumed. Now we are entirely unused to a world without these characteristics and are surprised by its properties, as we would be by the physicist's theoretical construct of a world without friction, when a ball, once thrown into space, might continue in flight forever. Why do some stockholders prefer earnings to be retained? Because they thereby escape three costs: (1) the heavier income tax on dividends which they would have to pay instead of the lower tax on capital gains, (2) the transactions cost they would incur if they decided to reinvest their accumulated dividends through the purchase of more stocks—if dividends are retained they are automatically reinvested by the company, with no brokerage charges falling on the stockholder, and (3) the company avoids the transactions outlay required to raise funds to

---

[23] From the foregoing it follows that the cost of capital is, from the point of view of the stockholder, independent of the means whereby the funds are obtained. This conclusion, of course, is strictly true only in our highly simplified, frictionless world.

replace the dividends as a means for financing its investment program. These transactions costs, including the costs of compliance with government regulations, can be very substantial and represent a real drain on company earnings.

We can also understand in these terms why some other stockholders prefer the company to pay out dividends rather than retain earnings. Some investors who are uncertain about a company's future may wish to limit the amount of money they invest in it—that is, they want to keep their investment at a fixed level rather than have it grow automatically over a period of time. In that case, it may be less expensive for a small investor whose tax rate is relatively low to receive a substantial dividend than to undertake the transactions costs incurred by selling stocks as earnings are plowed back into the company.

In addition, some small investors prefer high dividends because they live on these regular payments. If there were no transactions costs, such a person could, as the value of his shares rose because of plowback, sell a corresponding small number of shares or fractions of shares. He would thereby receive his regular income without any consequent decline in the capital value of his holdings. But such a procedure brings with it brutal transactions costs. The smaller the number of shares involved in a given sale, the larger the brokerage cost per share, and when the number of stocks involved is very small, this charge becomes prohibitive. The regular monthly or quarterly sale of a few shares as a means for keeping up a steady income flow is just totally impractical.

We conclude that decisions on payout versus borrowing versus the issue of new stocks can matter to the company and to stockholders. They matter in the short run because a temporary high evaluation (overevaluation) of the company by the stock or bond markets may render outside capital particularly inexpensive as a means to finance investments by sale of stocks and (to some lesser degree) bonds. Moreover, dividend policy may have at least temporary effects on the value of company stocks. If, as is frequently alleged to be the case, many investors believe that the market considers high-dividend shares to be a better buy than other stocks which are comparable in all other respects, then the price of high-dividend stocks may be driven up accordingly. For even if the purchaser of such a share does not think it is worth more than a share in a high-plowback company, he will have to take into account the possibility that potential purchasers will take this view when he decides to sell the stock in the future.

Decisions on financing also matter in the long run because of transactions costs, taxes, and uncertainties, as we have already seen. As a result of all this, the decision on the form of financing remains an important one for management.

11. The Cost of Capital

We come, finally, to an important but ambiguous concept, the so-called cost of capital. This is the rate of yield against which prospective investment projects should be compared. That is, any investment which yields a rate of return greater than the "cost of capital" will be beneficial to stockholders, while any project whose return is less than the cost of capital will reduce the return to stockholders.

Strictly speaking, the cost of capital must be defined as the opportunity cost of money. It is the rate of return on the best alternative investment opportunity. So long as a project earns no less than would be returned by the best alternative use of the funds, stockholders come out ahead.

Where then are the complications? Let us consider them one at a time. We begin by assuming that there are no risks in the firm's operations.

1. *Interest rates and cost of capital in a perfect capital market.* Suppose that the firm can borrow or lend all it wants at a fixed interest rate; that rate is then the cost of capital. For any investment project which yields a return higher than the interest rate will already have been undertaken, financed by borrowing if necessary. Hence the highest earnings that can be obtained from *additional* funds are those which would be acquired by lending them out at the going interest rate.

2. *Variable cost of funds.* Sometimes the cost of obtaining money increases with the amount that is acquired. In that case it is the *marginal* cost of borrowing which constitutes the cost of borrowing, for to maximize return, the marginal yield of the investment must be equated to the marginal cost of borrowing.

3. *Pure capital rationing.* If the firm can neither obtain money from the outside nor dispose of funds elsewhere, then the cost of capital becomes the marginal return of money in the most profitable internal use available. If the investment decision problem is formulated with the aid of linear programming, as was done earlier in the chapter, then duality theory can help us, in principle, to determine the cost of capital. If M_t is the amount of money in period t and D_t is the optimal value of the corresponding dual variable, then duality theory tells us that D_t is the (highest attainable) marginal yield of money in period t, and so it must represent the cost of capital in that period.[24]

---

[24] Unfortunately, the calculation of the dual values in this problem is somewhat complicated. These values depend on the discounted present values of the various alternative projects (the coefficients of the objective function), but, simultaneously, the discount rates depend on the dual values.

4. *Cost of capital in a Modigliani-Miller model.* We introduced a risk index earlier into a Modigliani-Miller model and concluded that all equally risky firms in the construct must produce the same rate of earnings per dollar of money investment in accord with Equation (8). It is easy to show that in this model the cost of capital is r, the rate of return on investment for firms of the given degree of risk. This is so even if investment is financed by the sale of bonds (borrowing) at some interest rate i which is lower than r.[25] This result gives rise to the following paradox. Suppose our firm normally earns 8 per cent and is given a chance to borrow funds at 3 per cent which it can invest in the company at a return of 7 per cent. Management would then be making a serious mistake to undertake this apparently profitable transaction! For though it would increase the stockholders' earnings, it would not do so by an amount sufficient to offset the risk cost of the increased leverage produced by the new bonds, and hence stockholders would lose out on balance. This result follows rigorously and inescapably from the Modigliani-Miller premises. It should be said, in conclusion, that Modigliani and Miller feel their model and all its conclusions are widely applicable in the real world as reasonable approximations to the facts, though this evaluation is not universally accepted.

In this section, then, we have examined the important concept of the cost of capital. It is at the heart of the investment decision problem, for without this measure we can neither discount correctly nor decide on the proper amount of investment and the optimal selection of investment projects. We have seen that only in the simplest of circumstances is this measure given by the rate of interest, as was assumed in much of the discussion earlier in this chapter. Where (as it is in reality) the market for funds is more complex than the perfect capital market of pure competition theory

---

[25] For consider an investment costing I dollars which yields a rate of return, k, per dollar of investment. By (8), then, the initial value of the firm, $V_0 = S_0 + B_0$, is given by

$$V_0 = E_0/r.$$

But after the investment the new value, V_1, becomes

$$V_1 = E_1/r = (E_0 + kI)/r = V_0 + kI/r,$$

so that the company's common stock will now be worth

$$S_1 = V_1 - B_1 = V_1 - (B_0 + I) = V_0 + kI/r - B_0 - I.$$

But since $S_0 = V_0 - B_0$, this becomes

$$S_1 = S_0 + kI/r - I.$$

Hence the stockholders lose money if and only if $k < r$, and they make money if and only if $k > r$, i.e., if and only if the rate of return on the new investment, k, exceeds r, the rate of return for firms of this risk class. *This is so no matter what the bond rate of interest, i!*

and is affected by taxes and transactions costs, more subtle measures of the cost of capital are required. We have discussed the appropriate concept in a number of interesting cases which typify a wide variety of circumstances, but it should be obvious that there remain even messier conditions in which still other cost-of-capital constructs are likely to be appropriate.

12. Concluding Comment

This chapter has described some of the analytic tools which have been used to examine the company's investment decision and the means for its financing. It appears to follow from the discussion of our last sections that the decision on the nature of the physical investment project and its timing is likely to be more important for the company's welfare than is the selection of the pattern of financing, though, in practice, the latter may well influence the former. In any event, the development of powerful tools appropriate for the analysis of investment projects has gone much further than the design of methods for dealing with financing problems. We have seen the many types of problem which arise in the determination of investment plans and have gone over in considerable detail methods which can be used for their investigation. In the case of financial decisions, we have only been able to specify some of the alternatives and to provide some perspective on the significance of the choice among them.

APPENDIX: CONTINUOUS COMPOUNDING AND DISCOUNTING

The differential calculus is a very useful technique for the capital theorist. However, the discounting formulae of Section 4 do not lend themselves readily to differentiation. For example, to find the optimal duration of an investment, t, we might want to differentiate with respect to t an expression such as

$$C = R_0 + DR_1 + D^2R_2 + \cdots + D^tR_t.$$

There are two difficulties. First, the derivative dD^t/dt of a term such as D^t is given by a fairly messy and inconvenient formula. Second, and more serious, is the fact that in annual compounding t cannot be changed continuously. Rather, it must be varied in one-year jumps. And in going from t to $t + 1$ (the next higher value of t), our sum changes from

$$R_0 + DR_1 + D^2R_2 + \cdots + D^tR_t$$

to

$$R_0 + DR_1 + D^2R_2 + \cdots + D^tR_t + D^{t+1}R_{t+1}.$$

That is, the term $D^{t+1}R_{t+1}$ is suddenly added to the series. Such abrupt jumps make differentiation impossible.

To overcome these difficulties t must be permitted to vary continuously. This can be done in the following manner. If we were to reduce our period for compounding from a year to half a year, t could be varied from t to $t + \frac{1}{2}$ instead of having to go all the way to $t + 1$. Then our expression for gross earnings after t years, instead of being given by $P(1 + i)^t$, becomes

$$P(1 + i/2)^{2t}.$$

Similarly, with quarterly compounding, t can be changed by still smaller amounts, and the compound interest expression becomes

$$P(1 + i/4)^{4t}, \quad \text{etc.}$$

The direction in which we are heading should now be obvious. The object is to conceive of an unceasing compounding process which goes on at every moment so that, instead of moving in jumps, t can be varied continuously. We define the number [26] e as the limit of the expression $(1 + 1/n)^n$ as n approaches infinity—i.e., it is the yield on a dollar $(P = 1)$ invested for one year $(t = 1)$ at a 100 per cent rate of interest, if interest is compounded continuously. Thus, P dollars invested for t years at this rate of interest will yield with continuous compounding an amount

$$(1) \qquad\qquad\qquad A = Pe^t.$$

Finally, if the continuous interest rate is to be r rather than 100 per cent, the expression becomes[27]

$$A = Pe^{rt}.$$

It is now a simple matter to define discounted present value in terms of continuous compounding at an r per cent interest rate, for suppose P_t dollars are to be received t years in the future. In t years, P_0 dollars will grow into $P_0 e^{rt}$. Then if P_0 is the correct present value of P_t, we must have $P_t = P_0 e^{rt}$, i.e.,

$$(2) \qquad\qquad\qquad P_0 = (1/e^{rt})P_t = e^{-rt}P_t.$$

---

[26] It can be proved that e is approximately equal to 2.718.

[27] For the (instantaneous) interest rate is given by (1) as

$$\frac{dA/dt}{A} = rPe^{rt}/Pe^{rt} = r.$$

This basic expression has the advantage of an extremely simple differentiation formula:

$$dP_0/dt = -re^{-rt}P_t.$$

Illustration: The standard elementary examples of the point-input, point-output cases are the growing of wine and lumber. Letting the tree grow older means that we obtain more lumber from it, and, up to a point, as wines age they grow more valuable. What is the optimal age at which to consume such an item?

We have the marginal condition (attributed to W. S. Jevons) which states that, optimally, wine (or lumber) should be permitted to age until the point where diminishing returns reduce the *percentage* marginal yield of aging down to the level of the (per cent) rate of interest. To show this, let the value, V, of the total product be a function of the amount invested, I, and the length of time, t, for which the investment runs. This function may be written $V = f(I, t)$.

The anticipated profit, Π, of the businessman at the date he makes the investment is the present value of V, less the cost of his investment, I. Since the value, V, which he receives for his product only accrues to him at a point t periods in the future, it must be discounted at the appropriate interest rate, r, to obtain its present value, which, by the usual formula [Equation (2), above], is given by Ve^{-rt}.

Thus, the anticipated profit from the transaction is

$$\Pi = Ve^{-rt} - I = f(I, t)e^{-rt} - I.$$

Given the amount of the initial investment, I, we maximize Π by setting the partial derivative with respect to t equal to zero to obtain

$$\frac{\partial \Pi}{\partial t} = 0 = \frac{\partial f}{\partial t} e^{-rt} - rfe^{-rt},$$

or, dividing through by e^{-rt} and rearranging terms,

$$\frac{(\partial f/\partial t)}{f} = r,$$

which is the result we are seeking. It states that the relative yield of an increase in t, $(\partial f/\partial t)/f$, must in equilibrium be equal to the continuously compounded interest rate.

REFERENCES

Bowman, Edward H., and Robert B. Fetter, *Analysis for Production Management*, rev. edition, Richard D. Irwin, Inc., Homewood, Ill., 1961, Chapter 12.

Churchman, C. West, Russell L. Ackoff, and E. Leonard Arnoff, *Introduction to Operations Research*, John Wiley & Sons, Inc., New York, 1951, Chapter 17.

Grant, E. L., *Principles of Engineering Economy*, 3rd edition, The Ronald Press Company, New York, 1950.

Lutz, Friedrich, and Vera Lutz, *The Theory of Investment of the Firm*, Princeton University Press, Princeton, N.J., 1951.

Mossin, Jan, *Theory of Financial Markets*, Prentice-Hall, Inc., Englewood Cliffs, N.J., 1973.

Sasieni, Maurice, Arthur Yaspan, and Lawrence Friedman, *Operations Research, Methods and Problems*, John Wiley & Sons, Inc., New York, 1959, Chapter 5.

Smith, Vernon L., *Investment and Production*, Harvard University Press, Cambridge, Mass., 1961.

Solomon, Ezra, *The Management of Corporate Capital*, The Free Press of Glencoe, Inc., New York, 1959.

Terborgh, George, *Dynamic Equipment Policy*, McGraw-Hill Book Company, New York, 1949.

Capital
and
Distribution Theory

26

Besides seeking to explain investment decisions, capital theory also includes a second central topic: the determination of the rate of interest —the return to saving and investment. This, in turn, is taken to explain two phenomena of critical interest to society. First, it determines the share of national income going to capitalists rather than to workers. Second, it apportions output between present and future generations, with the level of savings (foregone consumption) today constituting the quantity of resources available for investments that permit larger outputs tomorrow.

This chapter will first examine more carefully the meaning of "Capital" and the measurement of its quantity. Next, it will show how the marginal productivity theory determines the rate of interest in its general equilibrium model and how this, in turn, regulates saving and investment behavior. Then we will examine some standard neoclassical models to show how the interest rate can affect the capital-output ratio, the productivity of labor, and other characteristics of the productive technology. Finally, we will review the grounds on which the Anglo-Italian school associated with Cambridge University has attacked the generality of these conclusions. Until recently, it was thought that low interest rates necessarily provide a powerful stimulus for economic abundance, always leading to the adoption of techniques using large quantities of capital relative to labor, and hence always increasing the productivity and incomes of the workers. This view of the matter has become a central issue in the discussion between the two Cambridges. While examining the substance of the debate we will also see how capital theory conducts its analysis.

The discussion will ignore risk and uncertainty, for we will have enough material to cover without dealing with the resulting complications.

1. Time as a Requisite of Production Processes

Early in the history of the labor theory of value it became clear that commodity prices cannot be explained simply by the amounts of physical labor needed to produce them. If one item, A, takes ten hours of labor to produce and is instantly ready for use, while another, B, also employs ten hours of labor but then requires some time before it is usable (e.g., the period required for lumber to dry after the trees are cut down), then item B will usually sell at a higher price than A's. For a businessman who is to be induced to invest in the manufacture of product B knows that he must not only lay out the wages needed to produce it—he must also be prepared to see his cash tied up for some considerable period.

From this observation two things are clear: first, that the mere passage of time can be a crucial requisite of production—indeed, that time can, in a sense, be considered an input very much on a par with labor and raw materials; second, like any other input, time has its price which is usually measured by the rate of interest.

Physical capital is defined to consist of all inputs used in the production process which are themselves products of the economy. Thus, it includes plant, machinery, inventories of raw materials, partially finished goods, and even inventories of finished commodities which must be kept on hand to make it possible to fill orders as they come in.

Any good whose manufacture makes use of capital must involve the passage of time in its production. For a capital asset is defined as a means of production which was itself produced *before* being put to its current use. Work on today's newspaper must already have been underway when metal was being mined for the production of the linotype machines, when the trees for making the paper were being planted, and so on.

Capital can be considered *the* input whose use inherently involves the passage of time. Any other input whose work requires time must by definition utilize capital in the form of goods in process. If a farmer produces a cheese which must be left to age before it can be sold, the product of his labor, in its unfinished state, becomes capital, a produced means of production. Moreover, the longer the cheese is left to ripen, the greater will be the capital cost of the project.

All of this means that the amount of capital employed in a production process cannot be measured by a single number, say, by its pecuniary value. One must also specify *time* measures along with such values. If the production of a unit of item C employs a \$20,000 machine for ten minutes, while a unit of D needs eighty minutes on this same \$20,000 machine, it is clear that, other things being equal, D employs more capital in its manufacture than does C. The measurement of capital is therefore likely to involve at least two variables—quantity and time—and in general *even two will not be enough*. In principle, the analysis of a productive activity requires specification of all its inputs and outputs *along with their dates*.

This also suggests that there are two basic ways in which the use of capital can be increased—we can either use more of the same type of capital (this is called *capital widening*) or we can switch to processes which involve longer investment periods (*capital deepening*). For example, we can widen our use of capital by employing 100 shovels (and 100 men) instead of 20, or, alternatively, we can substitute power-digging equipment for the shovels (and for some of the men), and since a steam shovel presumably takes more time to produce and to use up than do spades, this is an act of capital deepening. Such process, with relatively high capital-output and capital-labor ratios, is said to be relatively *capital intensive* or simply *capitalistic*. Unfortunately, as we will see, matters are not always so simple, and it will not always be possible to tell which of two production processes is the more capital intensive.

2. Heterogeneity and Homogeneity of Capital: Putty vs. Clay

In some analyses capital is treated·as a disembodied malleable substance. It is then treated as though it were homogeneous, movable at will from one sector of the economy into another, and usable in any of them as part of its productive process. This versatile substance has been referred to in recent discussions as "jelly" or "putty." At the opposite end of the spectrum is the interpretation of capital as a collection of vastly differing concrete objects: machines, factory buildings, unfinished products (working capital), and inventories of finished goods. There are also compromise "putty-clay" models in which capital starts out malleable but is then formed into specific objects and permitted to harden into shapes which can no longer be modified.

Both viewpoints have some truth to them. Obviously, capital does always take the specific forms of the clay models. Yet in the long run it has considerable mobility. If a new type of equipment or a new industry shows itself more profitable than an old one, then the older capital will not be replaced as it wears out. Instead, the depreciation funds will be "dissaved" in this process, and the real resources that they represent will, sooner or later, be reinvested in the new equipment or the new activity.

We can be mislead either by an analysis which abstracts completely from the specificity of capital assets or by one which concentrates on those differences and loses sight of the capability of resources to move to more profitable uses, the fundamental equilibrating mechanism of the competitive process common to classical, neoclassical, and Marxian analyses. The heterogeneity of capital goods means that a macroanalysis of production and distribution in terms of a few aggregative inputs such as labor and capital may be dangerous, though the seriousness of that danger is still a matter of lively debate. It is this problem that has forced much of recent neoclassical analysis to the use of full general equilibrium models treating each producers' good as a separate commodity, each with its own supply-demand relationships but which can generally only be "solved" and analyzed simultaneously.

In the absence of uncertainty, as assumed in this chapter, the putty-like property that capital acquires in the long run means that, under pure competition with freedom of exit and entry, all assets must yield precisely the same net return, for no one will ever invest in an asset that yields less than the maximum return available. It will be convenient to refer to that common rate of net return as the rate of interest, i.

3. On Measures of Quantity of Capital: Preliminary

Before turning to some of the results that have emerged from recent discussions on capital theory, we consider several attempts to define a numerical measure for the heterogeneous collection of inputs employed at different dates which together constitute the capital of a firm or an economy.

From the beginnings of neoclassical theory there have been attempts to define the quantity of capital. For example, Böhm-Bawerk, starting from the view that capital is essentially time, defined what he called the "average period of production" involved in a particular production process. He measured this as a weighted average of the time intervals between the utilization of the different inputs and the emergence of the final output. The weights can be the physical quantities of the inputs if they are homogeneous and so can be added together (e.g., if they all consist of a certain number of man-hours of labor of given skill), or these weights can be the values of those inputs. For example, if manufacture of a product ties up $100 for two years plus $50 for 1 year, the average period of production is (2 years $\times$ $100 + 1 year $\times$ $50)/($100 + $50) = $\frac{5}{3}$ years.

There are all sorts of objections to this measure, not the least of which is that a given input (e.g., a durable machine) can be used to produce a variety of outputs and we simply do not know what portion of that machine's cost to attribute to each product. More important, this measure of Böhm-Bawerk makes the error of forgetting the necessity of *discounting* if outlays at different dates are to be compared and added together. As we saw in the last chapter, it is not legitimate to evaluate the tying up of $100 for two successive years as twice $100, i.e., as equivalent to $200 tied up for only one year.

A second approach utilized by the general equilibrium analysis gives up the attempt to measure aggregative capital and simply treats its components separately, item by item, with drill presses not compared directly with switchboards, but each being treated as a separate intermediate product whose quantity is measurable directly and is determined by the general equilibrium process.

However, for some purposes this is an unsatisfactory solution. Just as it is often convenient to have a single index number to represent the more or less independent movements of a large multiplicity of prices, it can be useful to have a single measure of the complex of heterogeneous items comprising the capital stock of a firm, an industry, or even an entire economy. We have long ago given up the unrewarding search for an ideal index number since *no* single number can tell us correctly how all items in a large collection of prices are behaving. Similarly, any measure of capital is bound to give rise to anomalies. Yet it can be argued with some persuasiveness that the only thing worse than the use of such an aggregative measure is complete unwillingness ever to adopt one; for, without it, macroeconomic or econometric analysis of problems involving capital may be difficult or even impossible.

4. Capital Measurement: Dated Inputs and the Stationary State

A widely used approach to capital measurement (one which we will use later) goes back to Wicksell at the turn of the century. It has been called the *dated labor* or *dated input approach*. It is a measure of competitive equilibrium *value* of the capital stock, rather than, in any sense, of its physical quantity. It is therefore dependent on the pricing (market valuation) process and, as we will see, upon its choice of interest rate. Some anomalies may therefore result if prices or interest rates change, because we may be forced to say that the quantity of capital has changed even though the stock of physical capital has not varied at all.

To illustrate the approach, suppose a particular process requires four years to complete and each unit of output requires a sequence of outlays, x_1 dollars in its first year, x_2 in its second year, x_3 in the third year, and x_4 in the fourth and final year of the production process. Assuming prices are not changing, how much cost, in total, can we say the finished product incurs? The answer is that this cost, which is also *the value of the product* in competitive equilibrium, is equal to the money value of each of these outlays plus the interest on the amounts the producer has invested in them.

The competitive equilibrium cost of a product will be equal to the sum of the values of the inputs needed to produce it plus the accumulated interest on each such outlay:

(1) $$c = x_1(1 + i)^3 + x_2(1 + i)^2 + x_3(1 + i) + x_4.$$

Because x_1 is expended three years before the product is finished, by the end of the process it has had an opportunity cost of three years' compound interest, so that its accumulated value must now be $x_1(1 + i)^3$. A similar argument yields the remaining terms of the expression (1), which represents the labor and interest cost (value) of a unit of the finished product.

However, if this production process is not a one-shot affair, the value of the firm's total capital must include considerably more than that of its finished product inventory. In addition to the value of the finished product (1), it must include a considerable investment in goods "in the pipeline," some of which will emerge from the production process the following year, some the year after that, etc. The value of the firm's investment in these unfinished items must be added to value of the firm's inventory of finished products to determine its total capital.

We can illustrate this calculation by use of a construct, *the stationary state*, which is often employed in capital theory. Suppose the firm wishes to keep *a steady flow* of y units of output per year, each of which takes four years to complete. Then, at the end of each production year the company must have y units of goods that are completed (i.e., they were begun four years earlier), y units that are three-quarters complete (i.e., that were begun three years earlier), y units that are half complete, and y units that are just one-quarter finished.

To determine the total amount of capital all these finished and unfinished items represent we must find the cost (competitive equilibrium value) of each of them. For this we must know the outlays of labor (and their dates) per unit of output for the various goods in process and for the finished items. These data are given in Table 1a. It shows, for example, (last line), that goods $\frac{1}{4}$ finished have so far had expended upon them only their first set of inputs, whose cost is x_1. Similarly (second line from the bottom) items $\frac{1}{2}$ finished have so far received two doses of inputs, x_1 one year ago and x_2 in the current year. Table 1b includes the interest cost incurred by having these resources tied up by the expenditures specified in Table 1a. Naturally, the farther back the expenditures go, the larger the accumulated interest that represents their opportunity cost, so that outlays that occurred two years ago must be multiplied by $(1 + i)^2$, etc.

TABLE 1A. DATED INPUTS FOR FINISHED AND UNFINISHED GOODS

Batch of Goods	Date of Outlay	3 Years Ago	2 Years Ago	1 Year Ago	Now
Finished		x_1	x_2	x_3	x_4
$\frac{3}{4}$ Finished		0	x_1	x_2	x_3
$\frac{1}{2}$ Finished		0	0	x_1	x_2
$\frac{1}{4}$ Finished		0	0	0	x_1

TABLE 1B. DATED INPUTS AND ACCUMULATED INTEREST:
FINISHED AND UNFINISHED GOODS

Batch of Goods	Date of Outlay	3 Years Ago	2 Years Ago	1 Year Ago	Now
Finished		$x_1(1+i)^3$	$x_2(1+i)^2$	$x_3(1+i)$	x_4
$\frac{3}{4}$ Finished		0	$x_1(1+i)^2$	$x_2(1+i)$	x_3
$\frac{1}{2}$ Finished		0	0	$x_1(1+i)$	x_2
$\frac{1}{4}$ Finished		0	0	0	x_1

Now, *the sum of all of the terms in Table 1b is the total value of the firm's capital* per unit of output—the amount it must keep tied up in its production process year after year if it is to have a *stationary* annual output of one unit.

In summary, in a stationary state, with a process involving outlays of x_1, x_2, x_3, and x_4 in the first, second, third, and fourth year of work on a product, the total value of the firm's capital will be yK, where y is its output and K is its capital per unit of output and is given by the sum of the values of the inputs that have gone into its inventory plus the accumulated compound interest on each such outlay. Adding together all the items in Table 1b we see that this quantity of capital per unit of output is given by

$$(2) \qquad K = x_1(1+i)^3 + (x_1 + x_2)(1+i)^2 \\ + (x_1 + x_2 + x_3)(1+i) + (x_1 + x_2 + x_3 + x_4).$$

Obviously, the value of the firm's capital per unit of output, as given by (2), will be greater than the value of a unit of its finished product, as shown in (1), since the capital includes goods in process as well as finished product inventory.

From this calculation we can determine the firm's capital-output ratio simply by dividing (2) by (1).

We can also calculate the value of the firm's *annual* expenditure on inputs (labor) from either the last column of Table 1a or that of Table 1b, for we know that in (each) current year the firm spends x_4 on each unit of goods which it is finishing, x_3 on each unit of goods which will be $\frac{3}{4}$ finished, etc., so that, per unit of output, its total expenditure on inputs in (each) current year will be

$$(3) \qquad\qquad E = x_1 + x_2 + x_3 + x_4.$$

Since we are dealing with a stationary state in which expenditures are replicated precisely every year, the amount given by (3) must represent the firm's annual expenditure on inputs. In a simple model in which the only inputs are labor and capital one can then calculate a labor-output ratio by dividing (3) by (1) or a labor-capital ratio by dividing (3) by (2).

We observe, finally, that all these ratios are dependent on the value of i, the rate of interest, as is seen at once from the formula for value of output (1) and from that for the value of the firm's capital (2). This means that even if there is absolutely no change in a particular productive process, the quantity of the firm's capital, as we have defined it, will change if there is a change in the interest rate and so will its capital-output and its labor-output ratios. Thus, a given collection of buildings, machines, and goods in process whose physical makeup does not vary one iota will become a different quantity of capital (as evaluated by the dated input method) from what it was before a change in the interest rate. In other words, if there is a change in income distribution which modifies the rate of return to capital, then the *valuation* of the stock of capital will also (naturally) be affected. This illustrates a point that was mentioned earlier. The dated input method yields a measure of competitive equilibrium *value* of the capital stock and so does not correspond perfectly with any physical concept of capital.

It has also been suggested that this interrelationship between valuation of capital and rate of interest brings with it an unfortunate problem of circularity, for the quantity of capital plays a role in the process of determining the interest rate, but the interest rate, as we have seen, in turn affects the valuation of the quantity of capital. However, this in itself need not be a serious difficulty. It is a characteristic of all systems which require simultaneous solution and in which the value of every variable can affect that of every other.

5. Determination of Interest Rate in the General Equilibrium Model

Having discussed the measurement of capital we turn next to a more substantive issue, the determination of the interest rate. Today's neoclassical analysis determines the interest rate as just one element in the array of prices that emerge from the competitive general equilibrium. There is a simple but clever device which permits the analysis of an intertemporal equilibrium over a finite number of periods to be translated into that of a single-period case. In the latter, we have $y_1, \cdots, y_n$ representing the outputs of the n commodities produced by the economy. Corresponding to *each* such variable y_k in the single-period model, in multiperiod analysis we utilize h variables $y_{k1}, y_{k2}, \cdots, y_{kh}$, thus considering only some finite number[1] of periods, h, where h is called *the horizon*.

---

[1] While the choice of *any* finite value for h is arbitrary, it need not be a serious problem. In principle we can take the year h to lie billions of years in the future—beyond the likely span of human life.

For example, if commodity k is shoes, y_{k1} is the output of shoes in period 1, y_{k2} is the output of shoes in the second period, etc. For purposes of this analysis we treat y_{k1} and y_{k2} as the outputs of *two distinct commodities* not necessarily having more relation to one another than y_{kt} and y_{jt}, say the outputs of shoes and slippers (or shoes and bananas) in the same period, t. To each such variable there corresponds its own pair of supply-demand relationships and its own price. Thus the system involves the $n \times h$ output variables

$$(4) \qquad (y_{11}, \cdots, y_{1h}, y_{21}, \cdots, y_{2h}, \cdots, y_{n1}, \cdots, y_{nh})$$

and the $n \times h$ prices

$$(5) \qquad (p_{11}, \cdots, p_{1h}, p_{21}, \cdots, p_{2h}, \cdots, p_{n1}, \cdots, p_{nh}).$$

To treat the determination of the values of these variables as a problem for simultaneous solution, that is, to render them directly comparable, *these prices must all be expressed in terms of discounted present value.* Having done so, one can, in principle, solve the general equilibrium problem defined by the set of supply, demand, and production relationships in exactly the same way as one solves the problem with n output and n price variables for a single period.

Let us see now how that solution and its discounted prices also give us the equilibrium interest rate. As in the preceding chapter, let $D = 1/(1 + i)$ be the discount factor so that the present value of u dollars receivable one period in the future is $p = Du$.

Let k be a particular resource (commodity) and let its *undiscounted* future price in period $t + 1$ be written u_{kt+1}. We now take k to be the good in terms of which all intertemporal calculations are made; i.e., we use it as our standard of intertemporal price measurement, thus *defining* its price to remain constant[2]; i.e., for this good, its undiscounted future price, u_{kt+1}, is *defined* to be the same as its present price, p_{kt}. Therefore, the discounted value of that good's future price

$$(6) \qquad p_{kt+1} \equiv Du_{kt+1},$$

must satisfy

$$(7) \qquad p_{kt+1} \equiv Dp_{kt} = p_{kt}/(1 + i).$$

If one has determined p_{kt} and p_{kt+1} in the general equilibrium analysis, we can solve the preceding equation for the implied interest rate, i, obtaining

---

[2] For example, k can be money, whose unit price in every period is defined as unity.

(8) $$i = (p_{kt}/p_{kt+1}) - 1.$$

Thus the interest rate is always implicit in the general equilibrium calculation of prices. Consequently, if one accepts the analysis of price determination in a static *general equilibrium model*, one must automatically accept the neoclassical model of interest determination. One can argue that both of them neglect important real-world phenomena such as imperfect competition and institutional constraints, but that is a criticism applicable to most of microeconomics and not to neoclassical capital theory alone.

6. The Interest Rate and Producers' Demand for Investment

Since the interest analysis is, ultimately, a supply-demand model, we can learn more about it by examining more closely the capital supply and demand relationships, i.e., the relationship between the determination of desired investment and the desired saving which can be taken to supply the resources for that investment. We begin with the demand side—the demand of producers for net investment (additions to the stock of capital).

In neoclassical theory every act of investment is treated as a trade-off between present and future consumption. Labor and raw material which could have served consumption today are instead used to produce machinery or other capital goods which can increase the flow of consumers' goods tomorrow.

The equilibrium conditions for the firm's allocation of resources between any two periods are, naturally, the same as those for any other resource allocation decision by a multiproduct firm (for it will be remembered that shoes today and shoes tomorrow are interpretable simply as two *distinct* products of the same firm). An equilibrium in which positive quantities of two goods are turned out requires that the marginal rate of transformation of the two items be equal to (the inverse ratio of) their relative prices (see Chapter 11, Section 11). That is, for any two outputs j and k, if, by transferring a small quantity of resources from product j to product k, we give up $-dy_j$ of the former and obtain an additional dy_k of the latter, profit maximization requires that

$$-dy_k/dy_j \equiv p_j/p_k.$$

Similarly, in planning for the allocation of resources between shoe production in current period, t, and that in the next period, $t + 1$, we require (again using u_{jt+1} to represent the *undiscounted* price for commodity j in period $t + 1$)

$$-\frac{dy_{jt+1}}{dy_{jt}} = \frac{p_{jt}}{p_{jt+1}} \equiv \frac{p_{jt}}{Du_{jt+1}},$$

since otherwise it would be profitable to reallocate resources. If the first term were larger than the second, for example, it would pay the firm to expand future shoe production at the expense of that of the earlier period. The preceding equation can obviously be rewritten directly as

$$(9) \qquad - \frac{u_{jt+1} \, dy_{jt+1}}{p_{jt} \, dy_{jt}} = \frac{1}{D} = 1 + i.$$

Equation (9) is the basic equilibrium condition for intertemporal resource allocations by the firm. It tells that in equilibrium the transfer of a dollar of investment from current production (where it can earn $dp_{jt}y_{jt}$) to future output where it earns $u_{jt+1} \, dy_{jt+1}$, must bring a net gain exactly equal to $1 + i$, the amount that the dollar could have earned by being lent out at the rate of interest i. That is, at the margin the investment one period later must replace its original cost and *in addition* bring in a percentage return equal to i, the rate of interest, for otherwise it will pay to borrow and invest some smaller or larger amount. Thus, we have

Proposition 1: In equilibrium the marginal net yield of additions to each firm's capital must be equal to the rate of interest.

This is the basic condition in the neoclassical model that determines the demand for resources for investment—the decisions of firms on the amounts of the resources they wish to use for investment.

This can be represented in a diagram whose usefulness will become clearer presently. In Figure 1a we represent the undiscounted values of a single-product firm's outputs in the present period, t, and the following period, $t + 1$. The curve TT' is the transformation or production possibility locus expressed in monetary units. A point on that locus represents an efficient output combination in the sense that from any point such as A it is impossible to increase output in period $t + 1$ without some sacrifice of output in t. At a point such as A the producer is, in effect, investing ST' units of potential output now (that is how much he "abstains" from turning out now) and getting in return output valued at U dollars in the next period. Thus, as the producer moves leftward along the curve he is deciding to produce less and invest more now, in return for a larger output in the future. We now introduce a family of lines, corresponding to the iso-profit lines of the single-period theory of the firm. Each such line represents a constant sum of present values of current and future outputs. It is easy to show[3] that under perfect competition with prices constant for the firm,

---

[3] *Proof:* The present value of whatever output combination the firm selects is

$$(10) \qquad p_t y_t + p_{t+1} y_{t+1} \quad \text{or} \quad p_t y_t + D u_{t+1} y_{t+1},$$

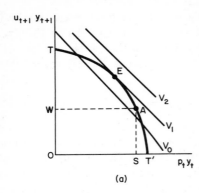
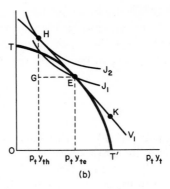

(a)   (b)

Figure 1

these are all straight lines with slope $-(1 + i)$, for a given future quantity of money, q_{t+1}, will have the same present value as the current amount of q_t if it is exactly $(1 + i)$ times as large as the former.

In Figure 1a we have several such lines, v_0, v_1, and v_2. The highest of these lines that is available to the producer, i.e., the one which is most profitable, is attained at the point of tangency, E, between the production possibility locus TT' and the line v_1. There the slopes of the two loci are clearly equal, and so we must have the slope of the transformation locus, $du_{t+1}y_{t+1}/dp_t y_t$, equal to the slope of the iso-profit line, $-(1 + i)$. But with prices fixed (under pure competition) that is the same as condition (9), the basic equilibrium condition for intertemporal resource allocation by the firm.

7. Interest Rate and the Supply of Saving: Lending and Borrowing

Saving is taken to be the source of the resources needed to produce capital. It represents new materials and labor which could have been used

---

where, as before, u_{t+1} is the undiscounted price of the product in $t + 1$. Setting the expression in (10) equal to any constant we obtain the equation of an iso-present-value locus

$$p_t y_t + D u_{t+1} y_{t+1} = k$$

that is,

$$u_{t+1} y_{t+1} = -p_t y_t/D + k/D$$

or, since $D = 1/(1 + i)$,

(11) $$u_{t+1} y_{t+1} = -(1 + i)p_t y_t + (1 + i)k.$$

This is clearly the equation of a straight line in our graph, with $u_{t+1} y_{t+1}$ represented on the vertical axis and $p_t y_t$ on the horizontal axis, and the slope of this iso-present-value locus is $-(1 + i)$.

for current consumption but which, instead, are held back (saved) in order to make possible the production of larger outputs in the future. Thus savings are the supply side of the supply and demand for new capital.

The consumers' intertemporal equilibrium relationships which determine the supply of savings are also no different from those in a single period model. Equilibrium can be taken to require tangency between the consumer's indifference curve for any pair of products and the corresponding price line. Thus the marginal rate of substitution between any such pair of products (the ratio of their marginal utilities) must be equal to their *discounted* price ratio. Letting x_{t+1} represent the amount of a given product consumed in period $t + 1$ and x_t the corresponding variable for period t, $-dx_{t+1}/dx_t$, the absolute value of the slope of indifference curve between x_t and x_{t+1} must therefore equal $p_t/p_{t+1} = p_t/Du_{t+1}$ so that

(12)
$$-\frac{u_{t+1}}{p_t}\frac{dx_{t+1}}{dx_t} = \frac{1}{D} = 1 + i,$$

where $dx_{t+1}/dx_t = mu_{x_t}/mu_{x_{t+1}}$ is the slope of the pertinent indifference curve. That is,

Proposition 2: Equilibrium of the consumer (saver) requires that his marginal rate of substitution between consumption in one period and consumption a single period later equal $1 + i$.

Condition (12) is the equilibrium requirement for the consumer's apportionment of his resources between present and future. Intuitively, this is so because every dollar's *reduction* in his current consumption represents saving which he can lend out at the current i per cent interest rate and therefore it permits him to consume an additional $1 + i$ dollars in goods in the following period. Condition (12) tells us that in equilibrium the i dollar interest return he obtains in this process must at the margin just compensate him for his subjective loss resulting from the postponement of consumption to the future (the substitution of dx_{t+1} for dx_t), or else it will pay him to change his present consumption (saving) level.

We can learn something more by combining the equilibrium diagram for the consumer with that for the producer.[4] Figure 1b reproduces from Figure 1a the transformation locus TT' and the iso-profit line v_1, which is

---

[4] This diagram is derived from the work of Hirshleifer and Fisher. See Jack Hirshleifer, "On the Theory of Optimal Investment Decision," *Journal of Political Economy*, Vol. 66, August 1965, pp. 329–352.

tangent to TT' at E. We left the producer in equilibrium at point E at which his equilibrium requirement (9) is satisfied and the present value of his earnings are maximized. But the producer is also a consumer—he must take his earnings and also divide them between consumption and saving. Will he necessarily be satisfied at point E in his role as consumer?

The answer is that in general he will not. The diagram contains two of his indifference curves, J_1 and J_2, between his present and future consumption. Equilibrium for him in his role as consumer requires that his indifference curve be tangent to his budget (price) line v_1. Here v_1 is his budget line (10) since its slope is $-(1 + i)$ and since it goes through point E where he is left by his productive activity. Now there is no reason to expect his indifference curve, J_1, through E to happen to be tangent to v_1 at that point, as consumer equilibrium would require. Indeed, as it is drawn the two are not tangent there.

Rather, his consumer equilibrium point, the point of tangency between one of his indifference curves and v_1, may well occur at some other point, point H in Figure 1b. That is, as drawn it is only at point H that tangency condition (12) for his equilibrium as a consumer is satisfied, while tangency condition (9) for his equilibrium as a producer holds only at E.

This is not an irreconcilable contradiction. Rather it means that the producer-consumer must be taken to move to his final equilibrium in two steps. As producer he first goes to E, which maximizes his purchasing power as a consumer [it puts him on the highest iso-profit line the technological possibilities (TT') permit him to attain]. Then he takes this purchasing power and divides it between present and future as best suits his tastes, moving to point H, the highest indifference curve he can attain with this highest of attainable iso-profit lines. How does he get from E to H? By lending or borrowing on the basis of his earnings at E, at the given interest rate, i. If his consumer equilibrium point happens to fall to the left of E, he will be a lender. That is, he will consume less than his current output at E, and the value of the decreased consumption $p_t y_{te} - p_t y_{th}$ is then lent out at interest rate i, enabling him to increase his consumption in the next period by GH, which equals $1 + i$ times the amount he has lent out. This follows from the fact that the absolute slope of v_1 is $1 + i$, so that $\Delta u_{t+1} y_{t+1}/\Delta p_t y_t = 1 + i$ or $\Delta u_{t+1} y_{t+1} = (1 + i) \Delta p_t y_t$.

Similarly, if his consumer equilibrium point on price line v_1 happens to fall somewhere to the right of E, say at K, it means that he will borrow to get from E to K and will consequently not be able to consume as much in the following period as he would have at E.

Thus, we have seen in this and the preceding section how the interest rate affects the behavior of producers and consumers, investors and savers. These relationships constitute component parts of the general equilibrium model which, as we saw earlier, can be taken to determine the interest rate which determines the savings-investment behavior we have just investigated.

8. Digression on Monetary Interest Theory

The reader may have been given the impression that the neoclassical theory operates in a totally different world from more recent approaches to interest analysis, for our discussion has been framed largely in terms of "real" magnitudes—the supply of saving (defined to consist of goods produced but not immediately consumed) and the demand for resources for investment (connoting the construction of machines and the accumulation of physical inventory, etc.). Where in all this is there room for concepts such as Keynesian liquidity preference, with its heavy emphasis on the role of money in the determination of interest rates?

Actually, classical and neoclassical theorists were well aware that interest is, in a way, a monetary phenomenon and that the rate of interest is affected by monetary occurrences. Indeed, their conception of the process involved was not entirely foreign to current views on the subject. However, in their opinion, monetary influences on interest rates were essentially transitory.

Let us outline their model briefly, roughly following the position of Alfred Marshall on the subject. For this purpose let us examine what happens if, starting from a position of full employment and general equilibrium, there is a sudden increase in the money supply, all other things remaining equal. Marshall readily concedes that this will cause a reduction in interest rates because there will now be more cash than people will wish to hold at the initial high interest rate, and so there will be a rise in the supply of loans (including the willingness to purchase bonds as one important form of lending).

However, the new lower interest rate will make it profitable to employ more roundabout processes. More money will be borrowed for investment, and more labor and raw materials will be demanded for the purpose. The result will be a bidding up of wages and prices.

But this very increase in price level must serve effectively to decrease the money supply. For example, a doubling of prices will cut the purchasing power of a given stock of money in half. We say that in this way rising prices serve to reduce the *real money supply*.

Thus the initial increase in money supply sets into motion a train of events by means of which it, at least partly, eliminates itself. How far will this process go on? The answer is that it will continue until the real money supply and, hence, the rate of interest have been returned to their original levels. So long as the real money supply is above its initial level, the rate of interest will remain depressed below the level which equates supply and demand for capital-producing resources. But this means that more resources are demanded by investors than are supplied by savers—there must be an excess demand for labor and raw materials to be used in the manufacture of capital goods. For this reason, the inflationary process must continue on until the cause of the disturbance, the increased money supply, has eliminated itself completely. Thus, the neoclassical theory is perfectly consistent with a short-run monetary analysis of interest rates. It maintains, however, that in the long run the influence of monetary events must eliminate itself and that interest rates must always return to the levels determined by the two relevant "real" phenomena, the supply of savings as governed by time preference and the demand for savings as determined by the marginal productivity of more roundabout processes, i.e., the marginal productivity of investment.

We observe that the full employment assumption implicitly plays a very important role in this neoclassical argument, for if there were extensive supplies of unemployed resources, an excess demand for these resources would very likely lead to more employment rather than to higher prices. In this way, the Marshallian model is apt to break down in a depressed economy.

9. Diminishing Returns and the Neoclassical Savings-Investment Parable

We now have at our disposal a formal model of the determination of the interest rate and the supply-demand relationships which it encompasses. We come now to the crucial question—what, if anything, does this model tell us about patterns of economic behavior? In this section we will describe some such results that do hold at least in certain cases. Until recently it was thought that they were valid generally. But as we will see, it is now agreed that they do not hold universally. The remaining issue is whether, in fact, they apply very widely or whether they represent only a very special sort of case.

Sections 9 and 10 gave us marginal (first-order) conditions (9) and (12) for equilibrium of saving and investment in a neoclassical world. As usual, to assure us that we are at a true maximum when these requirements are fulfilled, we need second-order conditions (corresponding to the requirement in a one-variable model that the second derivative of the maximand be negative). And, as usual, these conditions involve requirements about the concavity of the consumers' (intertemporal) utility functions, convexity of the (intertemporal) production relationships, etc. As in most of this volume, we will not review these second-order requirements in detail. Rather, the issue we turn to now is something these second-order conditions were until very recently, *thought* to imply but which has been shown to be a non sequitur in the Cambridge (England)-Cambridge (Massachusetts) discussion referred to in the chapter on distribution.

Implicit in the old-neoclassical analysis is a story involving increasing disutility of postponed consumption and diminishing returns to investment. Larger quantities of savings are assumed to involve a greater marginal disutility because the individual in question is thereby required to postpone the current consumption of items of increasing importance to him. When he is saving just a little, a small addition to saving only requires him to postpone the consumption of frivolities which matter very little to him. On the other hand, when he is saving a great deal his current consumption will already have been stripped down to a bare minimum of necessities, and the marginal cost of further saving will therefore be very high. The moral of this portion of the story thus appears to be that if an economy wants its members to save it must be prepared to pay the price in term of a higher interest rate. A high interest rate is the necessary reward to savers, one that is required to get them to save as much as is desirable for the social welfare.

The remainder of the tale relates to the allegedly diminishing returns to investment. Here it is held that if there is an autonomous increase in saving, with the highest net return, as more and more resources become available, they will have to be used in increasingly inferior investment opportunities. When only small quantities of resources are available they will be invested in activities which yield, say, 20 per cent or more, but if more resources are provided for investment, since the activities yielding 20 per cent will have been used up, society will have to be satisfied with others that yield perhaps only 15 per cent, and so on. Looked at the other way, this says that if there is no change in technology or any of the other production conditions, producers can only be induced to invest additional resources by offering them at a lower price (a lower interest rate). The demand curve for resources must be negatively sloping, and, other things being equal, a higher interest rate will always be associated with a lower quantity of investment.

These two key parts of the neoclassical story—the rising relative marginal disutility of saving and the diminishing marginal yield to investment—may actually be true, but what the recent Cambridge-Cambridge discussion has shown is that their truth or falsity can only be settled empirically. As we will see presently, they do not follow from the usual theoretical premises. This issue is of some importance because if the assumptions are false we can no longer take ourselves to be living in a world comfortable for analysis in which increased interest rates are required as a reward to savers to elicit from them more resources for society's investments, nor can we assume that declining interest rates will always lead producers to invest more and thus to provide more for the future at the expense of the present.

We will say little more about the role of savings in the neoclassical analysis and give only a short summary of the criticisms that have been levelled at it. Then we will turn to a far more detailed review of the other side of the neoclassical capital theory—its rich investment models.

10. Institutional and Sociological Determinants of Saving

The savings side of the Cambridge attack upon the neoclassical tale can be summed up briefly. The Anglo-Italian group has argued that in reality a rise in the rate of interest will *not* produce a significant increase in saving. Partly this is so because the income effect and the substitution effect of a rise in interest rates may plausibly be taken to work in opposite directions, as was shown in the chapter on income distribution. The substitution effect of increased interest does work to elicit more saving. But higher interest rates also increase savers' real incomes and enable them to satisfy their accumulation objectives (say, the desire to accumulate enough to buy a house or a car) at a lower rate of saving than they would have otherwise. The net result may well be that a change in interest rate produces a negligible effect on the amount saved up by society.

If not the interest rate, what then does determine the level of saving? In the Cambridge, United Kingdom, view it is largely decided by several institutional influences:

(a) The decisions by business management determining the amounts of their profits that they will plough back into their firms— the substantial amounts of savings of stockholders' resources carried out by firms themselves.

(b) The division of national income between workers and capitalists. Since capitalists are taken, as part of their historical function, to be accumulators par excellence, they are assumed to have a higher marginal and average propensity to save than workers. Thus with a given level of national income, the larger the share of it going to capitalists, the more society will end up saving. This is the foundation of the Kaldor model of income distribution described in the chapter on distribution.

Now there is no doubt some truth to both these assertions. For example, we do know that a very substantial share of the saving that takes place in the United States takes the form of plowback by the firm, which thereby holds back profits from the hands of the company's stockholders and appears to decide for them how much of this flow of company earnings should be reinvested. However, this relationship need not be just what it seems at first. Even with firms making plowback decisions, stockholders are not altogether powerless to control their total saving. Suppose a stockholder wanted to save $125 in a given year but finds that the firm in which he holds shares has retained $50 of his earnings that year. By saving only $75 instead of $125 as he had originally planned, he can still keep his total savings to the level he originally desired. The critical question is whether stockholders really do or do not make such offsetting adjustments. If they do, the level of saving will still be determined by such individuals *and their response to financial inducements such as the interest rates.* If they make no such adjustment, an important link in the neoclassical chain connecting saving and interest rates will have been broken. However, whether or not savers as a group make such an adjustment simply cannot be determined by *a priori* surmise. It is a matter for empirical investigation, and the issue is still far from being settled.[5]

11. On Some Simple Technologies and Neoclassical Investment Models

The other side of the Cambridge, United Kingdom, attack—its objections to the neoclassical story on choice of investment technique—is considerably more complex. In order to understand these objections, we must first examine in greater detail the relevant portions of the earlier neoclassical discussions, notably in the work of the Austrian economist, Eugen von Bohm Bawerk (1851–1914). We will deal with cases in which the Cambridge problems do not arise. In the next section, by comparison with these straightforward situations, we will see clearly how, in other situations, difficulties can arise.[6]

We will see how, in the neoclassical models, reduced interest rates *always* bring with them production processes that are more capital intensive and which (in the long run) yield higher outputs per member of the labor force. Thus, *reduced interest rates become a prime instrument of increased productivity and rising living standards.* They increase the income of the labor force by giving it more capital equipment to increase its productivity. However, we will find in the following section that things need not always follow this straightforward pattern.

---

[5] There is some preliminary evidence that household savers do adjust their savings to offset business and governmental saving decisions. See Paul A. David and John L. Scadding, "Private Savings: Ultrarationality, Aggregation and 'Denison's Law'," *Journal of Political Economy,* Vol. 82, March, April 1974, pp. 225–50.

[6] The discussion in this and the following sections relies heavily on the masterful exposition of the issues in Paul A. Samuelson, "A Summing Up," *Quarterly Journal of Economics,* Vol. 80, November 1966, pp. 568–83.

We deal with a type of production technology that is a modification of what has been described as the "point-input, point-output case." Labor is expended at one or several dates during the production of a commodity and then at some specific date the product is considered finished. In this model increasing capital intensiveness always takes the form of a longer (more time-consuming) process which permits labor to be saved. As an example we consider three processes for the production of a given quantity of firewood. In process I, one plants some fast-growing bushes and uses them one year later, with much labor needed to gather the required amount of wood. In process II, one plants two years before using the wood, expending an intermediate amount of labor in watering and weeding one year before the wood is used. In process III, the wood is permitted to grow for three years with small amounts of labor devoted to its care during each of the years of its growth. The processes have been ordered so that each one is more *capital intensive*, or *roundabout* than its predecessor—each involves an earlier expenditure of preliminary labor than the one before it. The earlier outlays of labor are undertaken because they decrease the amount of labor needed to produce the desired output by an amount sufficient to compensate for the earlier outlay of work. Thus, with increased round-aboutness there will be a reduction in the total expenditure of labor *per unit of output*. Table 2 gives some illustrative labor-input requirement figures showing this relationship for output of firewood in year $t + 3$ via each of our three processes:

TABLE 2

| | | Outlays of Labor | | | |
| | | Year | | | |
Process	Capital Intensity	t	$t + 1$	$t + 2$	Total
I	low	0	0	12	12
II	intermediate	0	4	4	8
III	high	2	2	2	6

We see that process I involves the outlay of 12 hours of labor in year $t + 2$, the year before the wood is used, process II uses 4 man-hours in each of the two years before the firewood is obtained, etc. As we go from process I to II to III the technology becomes successively more "round-about" or capital intensive, with the total labor expended per unit of output declining, as shown by the successively decreasing numbers in the last column of the table.

Which of the three processes in our example it will in fact pay to use (assuming that at least one of them yields a positive net benefit) depends on the discounted present values of the costs of the three processes and that, in turn, depends on the interest rate, i. Using c_j to represent the cost of process j and D once more as the discount factor $D = 1/(1 + i)$, those three discounted cost figures per unit of output are:

$$c_I = 0 + 0D + 12D^2 = 12D^2$$

$$c_{II} = 0 + 4D + 4D^2 = 4D + 4D^2$$

$$c_{III} = 2 + 2D + 2D^2.$$

We will see now that as the rate of interest rises [the value of $D = 1/(1 + i)$ falls] less roundabout techniques will become cheaper. At low interest rates the most capital intensive technique, III, will be cheapest. When i is sufficiently high, intermediate technique II will become less costly than III. Finally, when i is very high, the least roundabout technique I will become superior.

To take two extreme examples, if the interest rate were zero so that $D = 1/(1 + 0) = 1$ we have $c_I = 12$, $c_{II} = 8$, and $c_{III} = 6$, and the very capital-intensive process III is clearly the most economical way to get things done.[7] On the other hand, suppose the rate of interest were as high as 100 per cent per month ($i = 1$), where this unrealistic figure is used for simplicity of calculation. Then $D = 1/1 + 1 = \frac{1}{2}$ and $D^2 = \frac{1}{4}$ so that we obtain $c_I = \frac{12}{4} = 3$, $c_{II} = \frac{4}{2} + \frac{4}{4} = 3$, and $c_{III} = 2 + \frac{2}{2} + \frac{2}{4} = 3.5$. Thus, at this interest rate, processes I and II are equally expensive, while this time process III has become more expensive than either of the others. A repetition of the calculation for the still-higher interest rate $i = 2$ will readily show that now $c_I < c_{II} < c_{III}$.

The reason for the observed relationship between the magnitude of the interest rate and the roundaboutness of the least costly technique is not difficult to see—heavy discounting (a high interest rate) always favors processes whose outlays occur later because they permit postponement of the dates at which one ties up resources whose opportunity cost is the high i per cent per period.

Figure 2a shows how the present values of c_I and c_{II} behave as i increases, with the cost of the least capital-intensive technique, c_I, starting off much higher than c_{II} at $i = 0$ but dropping far more sharply than the latter so that it catches up at the crossover point[8] A. Figure 2b also in-

---

[7] This is the case in which there is no discounting so that an hour of future labor is precisely equivalent to an hour of current labor. Then it will then always pay to select the process with the lowest total labor outlay, whatever its timing.

[8] We find this crossover point by solving for D or i the equation $c_I = c_{II}$, that is,

cludes the curve depicting c_{III} as a function of i. Since the equation of that curve is $c_{III} = 2/(1 + i)^2 + 2/(1 + i) + 2$ we see that it starts off at $c_{III} = 6$ when $i = 0$ and asymptotically approaches $c_{III} = 2$ as i approaches infinity.

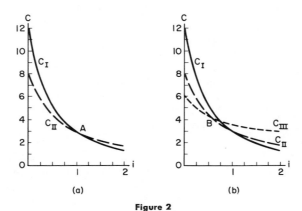

Figure 2

Several conclusions can be drawn about this sort of simple case (often referred to as the neoclassical parable)—the case in which increased roundaboutness consists of a spreading of the time interval over which labor is expended, along with a reduction in total labor outlay:

PARABLE PROPERTY 1. (As Figure 2 has shown) increased interest rates will always lead to the adoption of less roundabout processes.[9]

This in turn implies

$$12D^2 = 4D + 4D^2 \quad \text{or} \quad \frac{12}{(1 + i)^2} = \frac{4}{1 + i} + \frac{4}{(1 + i)^2},$$

which gives, multiplying through by $(1 + i)^2$,

$$12 = 4(1 + i) + 4 \quad \text{or} \quad 12 = 8 + 4i,$$

so $i = 1$ is our crossover point. Similarly, for the crossover point between, say c_{II} and c_{III} (point B in Figure 2b), we solve for i the equation $c_{II} = c_{III}$ or $2 + 2/(1 + i) + 2/(1 + i)^2 = 4/(1 + i) + 4/(1 + i)^2$ or $2(1 + i)^2 + 2(1 + i) + 2 = 4(1 + i) + 4$. This yields the quadratic equation in i, $2i^2 + 2i - 2 = 0$, whose only positive root is approximately $i = 0.6$.

[9] To show that this is always true in these neoclassical models, we can express the cost of the more roundabout of two processes (process r) as

$$c_r = \sum_{t=0}^{h} a_t/(1 + i)^t = a_0 + a_1/(1 + i) + \cdots + a_n/(1 + i)^h$$

PARABLE PROPERTY 2. There must be diminishing marginal returns to the increased use of capital involved in more roundabout processes. For, by Proposition 1, in equilibrium the interest rate will equal the marginal yield of capital. Thus, we see that increased roundaboutness (added investment) will always be associated with a lower interest rate and, hence, a lower marginal investment yield. In terms of Figure 3a, the slope of the curve of marginal product of capital must be negative if a reduced interest rate is always to increase the equilibrium use of capital.

PARABLE PROPERTY 3. Output per worker, y/k, will always *ultimately* fall as interest rates rise so that less roundabout methods are adopted, and less current consumption is sacrificed for future output. This follows directly from the premise that a decrease in roundaboutness involves a rise in the labor-output ratio, L/y. Thus, since with higher interest rates production becomes less roundabout, L/y will rise and hence y/L, output per person, will fall. In our example, as rising interest rates lead to a switch from most roundabout process III to process II and then to process I, output per labor-hour will decline from $\frac{1}{6}$ to $\frac{1}{8}$ to $\frac{1}{12}$ of a ton of firewood. This is so, since by Table 2, the labor required per unit of output is 6, 8, and 12 hours respectively for processes III, II, and I.[10]

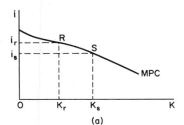 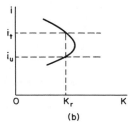

(a)   (b)

Figure 3

and that of a less roundabout process, s, yielding its output at the same time, as

$$c_s = \sum_{t=k}^{h} b_t/(1+i)^t = b_k/(1+i)^k + \cdots + b_h/(1+i)^h.$$

Here a_t is the tth period investment of labor in process r and b_t is that in process s and where $\sum a_t < \sum b_t$. It should be clear that at $i = 0$, $c_r = \sum a_t$ and $c_s = \sum b_t$, so that then c_r will then always be less than c_s. Therefore, at a zero interest rate the more roundabout process will be the cheaper. But as the interest rises, c_r will increase relative to c_s. Indeed, from the formulas it is obvious that as i approaches infinity, c_s will approach zero, while c_r will approach a_0, so that at a rate of interest sufficiently high, the less roundabout process *must* become less expensive in present value.

[10] After our discussion of the illegitimacy of adding together sums for different time periods, the reader may be uncomfortable about our adding of the labor spent in

PARABLE PROPERTY 4. In the neoclassical models output grows less and less capital intensive as the interest rate rises. For it can be shown that in any one given process, as the rate of interest rises, the ratio of the value of the total capital to the value of total output will fall.[11] The capital-output ratio will also fall when, as a consequence of a rise in interest rate, one switches to less roundabout processes. Thus any particular rise in interest rates will decrease the capital-output ratio whether or not it leads to a change in the process utilized.

12. Reswitching of Techniques and Contradiction of the Parables

We turn now to an illustrative pair of techniques in which, as we will see, the apparently normal behavior of the preceding cases breaks down and the four parable properties are no longer valid. That is, lower interest rates need not lead to more roundaboutness, a higher capital-output ratio, or increased output per man, and the marginal product of capital need not always decline. The examples we will now discuss involve the phenomenon of reswitching, which has been one of the foci of the debate between Cambridge (U.K.) and Cambridge (Mass.). It must, however, be noted that reswitching is not the only case in which such pathological

different periods to calculate the total labor used in process III, for example, at 6 man hours per unit of output. But this can be interpreted in terms of the stationary state model of Section 4 to yield the same result. Consider three fields each planted with what will someday be a ton of firewood, but in one of them the trees are just one year old, in one they are two years old, and in one they are three years old. If each year the field with the three-year-old trees is harvested and replanted, the process becomes continuous, yielding one ton of firewood each year. Moreover, it requires an outlay each year of 2 man-hours of labor in each of the three fields. Thus 6 hours of labor will be spent *each year* and output will be one ton each year, giving us an annual output–labor ratio of $\frac{1}{6}$ ton per man-hour with no problem about adding up inputs utilized at different dates.

[11] This can be verified by utilizing the measure of capital defined in Section 4. Equations (1) and (2), respectively, give the values of output and of capital in a process that lasts four years (the expressions can be generalized to an h-year process in an obvious way). The capital-output ratio, then, is obtained by dividing (2) by (1), yielding

$$\frac{\text{Capital}}{\text{Output}} = \frac{x_1(1+i)^3 + (x_1+x_2)(1+i)^2 + (x_1+x_2+x_3)(1+i) + (x_1+x_2+x_3+x_4)}{x_1(1+i)^3 + x_2(1+i)^2 + x_3(1+i) + x_4}$$

$$= \frac{x_1(1+i)^3 + x_2(1+i)^2 + x_3(1+i) + x_4}{x_1(1+i)^3 + x_2(1+i)^2 + x_3(1+i) + x_4}$$

$$+ \frac{x_1(1+i)^2 + (x_1+x_2)(1+i) + (x_1+x_2+x_3)}{x_1(1+i)^3 + x_2(1+i)^2 + x_3(1+i) + x_4},$$

where the next-to-last fraction is equal to unity, and the last fraction clearly approaches zero as i approaches infinity. Thus we confirm that for a single process of the sort described, the capital-output ratio will indeed decline when the rate of interest rises.

behavior can occur. There now seems to be a fair amount of agreement among the participants in the debate as to the immediate implications of reswitching and related behavior. Where the debate continues and opinions continue to be diametrically opposed is about the likelihood of their occurrence in practice and the seriousness of their implications for the neoclassical model.

Reswitching refers to a case in which there are two (or more) techniques, call them A and B such that A is cheaper when the interest rate is very high, B becomes less expensive at an intermediate interest rate, but when the interest rate is very low, A again becomes the cheaper way of producing their product. Thus, as interest rate decreases the optimal technique switches from A to B and then *re*switches back from B to A. Let us see how this can occur. Suppose method A involves the planting of firewood two years before it will be used, with no further work done on it before its utilization time, while method B involves its planting three years before utilization and requires a second expenditure of effort in tending the trees the year before they are used. Table 3 gives illustrative figures for the input requirements of the two processes.[12]

TABLE 3. OUTLAYS OF LABOR PER UNIT OF OUTPUT:
RESWITCHING CASE

Process	3 Years Before Harvest	2 Years Before Harvest	1 Year Before Harvest	Total
A	0	7	0	7
B	2	0	6	8

It will be noted that there is no way we can say *a priori* that one of these processes is the more "roundabout," i.e., more time-consuming than the other. Process B expends labor both earlier and later than A, so there is no direct way of rating them in terms of their relative use of time.

We can see why A will be favored both by a high and by a low interest rate. A very low interest rate favors A because it expends less labor than B in total so that when there is zero discounting the total cost of A will be 7 while that of B will be 8. Somewhat heavier discounting will, however, reduce most heavily the 6-labor-hour expenditure of B because it occurs two years after the beginning of the process and so is discounted at the rate $D^2 = (1/1 + i)^2$ while the 7-hour expenditure of process A is discounted only at the rate $D = 1/1 + i$. Thus at some intermediate level of interest rates (to be specified presently), B will become less costly than A.

---

[12] The figures are taken from Samuelson, *op. cit.*

But, finally, when the rate of interest goes high enough, *both* the second-year expenditure of process A and the third-year expenditure of process B will be reduced to negligible present values. Only the first-year expenditure of B, which is totally undiscounted, will continue to be substantial so that B will again be the more expensive process.

To take the extreme case, as i approaches infinity the present value of *any* postponed expenditure approaches zero since $D = 1/(1 + i)$ then approaches zero. The present value of the cost of process B will then approximate just the undiscounted 2 labor hours of the first year of that process, while the cost of A will approximate zero since its outlays are *all* discounted.

We can verify all this using the cost formulas for the two processes,

$$c_a = 0 + D \cdot 7 + 0 = 7/(1 + i)$$
$$c_b = 2 + 0 + D^2 \cdot 6 = 2 + 6/(1 + i)^2.$$

Substituting in successively the values $i = 0$, $i = 0.25$, $i = 0.5$, etc., we obtain the present values of the costs of the projects, shown in Table 4,

TABLE 4. COSTS OF PROJECTS A AND B AT SELECTED INTEREST RATES

i	0	0.25	0.5	0.75	1.0	1.25	$\cdots$	∞
C_a	7	5.6	4.67	4	3.5	3.1	$\cdots$	0
C_b	8	5.84	4.67	3.96	3.5	3.19	$\cdots$	2

which confirm the cost behavior that has been described. For $0 \le i \le 0.5$, c_a is less than c_b. For $0.5 < i < 1.0$, B is the less expensive technique, while for $1.0 < i$, A is once again the more economical. Furthermore, we see that the crossover points occur precisely at $i = 0.5$ and $i = 1.0$ at each of which[13] $c_a = c_b$.

---

[13] Clearly, reswitching requires that there be more than one crossover point. We will see now that this can occur because the relevant equation is of second degree and so it can yield two solutions for i; i.e., it can have two positive roots. To obtain the crossover points we proceed as we did in the neoclassical case, solving the equation $c_a = c_b$ or $7D = 2 + 6D^2$. We can obtain D directly from this quadratic equation, or we can substitute $D = 1/(1 + i)$ to get $7/(1 + i) = 2 + 6/(1 + i)^2$ or $2(1 + i)^2 - 7(1 + i) + 6 = 0$ or $2i^2 - 3i + 1 = 0$, which, by the usual formula for the solution of a quadratic equation, has the *two* positive roots $i = 0.5$ and $i = 1.0$, and hence there are two crossover points, as reswitching requires.

This result is generalized in the Appendix to this chapter. As discussed in Section 5 of the following chapter, the multiple roots of the crossover formula and its reswitching

Thus, we see that, at least in principle, it is possible for some technique to be superior both when the interest rate is very high and when it is very low, though not at intermediate interest rates. But this case, as we will see now, violates each of the four properties of the neoclassical parable described in the preceding section:

Violation of Parable Property 1. Obviously, where reswitching occurs, decreased interest rates do not always replace one technique successively by another, each of which is more roundabout than its predecessor. This no longer is true, first because reswitchable techniques, as we have seen, cannot be classed unambiguously as more or less roundabout! More important, if interest rates fall sufficiently, reswitching will bring back techniques which had also been favored at high interest rates. There is no longer a unique ranking of techniques as there was in the neoclassical models in terms of the order in which they are favored by successive reduction in interest rates.

Violation of Parable Property 2. In the neoclassical tale, there must be diminishing returns to increased capital use. That is precisely why decreasing interest rates will always favor the adoption of more capital-intensive ("roundabout") processes. That is, as shown in Figure 3a, the marginal product of capital (MPC) must fall monotonically (holding the quantity of labor constant), if a fall in interest rate (from i_r to i_s) is always to induce an increase in use of capital (from K_r to K_s). But the reswitching case has shown us that a sufficient reduction in interest rates can get society back to exactly the same technique which it would have used at a high interest rate and hence exactly the same use of capital. That is, the MPC curve must involve exactly the same quantity of capital[14] at interest rate i_t and i_u (Figure 3b) so that it may be "backward bending" as shown in the figure, or it may be C-shaped, or of some more complex shape but it cannot be steadily downward sloping as in Figure 3a. *That is, the reswitching case contradicts the claim that marginal returns to capital must always diminish.*

Violation of Parable Property 3. In the neoclassical case it was claimed that a rise in interest rate would always *ultimately* cause a fall in output per worker because it would reduce the utilization of capital. While a rise

---

implications are phenomena which have been recognized for some time for the investment plans of a single firm. However, the recent debate seems to have been the first time they were considered for an entire economy.

[14] Here we mean the same *physical* quantity of capital. The market price of the capital must change as the interest rate changes and varies the value of D at which one discounts the outlays that create the capital.

in interest rate will allegedly permit a temporary increase in consumption in the short run because it involves less investment for the future, less output per worker must be the ultimate consequence. However, the re-switching case again shows that this need not be true, because, with both a high and a low interest rate, society will use the same technique *with the same* present and future consumption and output levels. In fact, it is not difficult to show that as interest rates rise and society consequently goes from technique *A* to *B* and then from *B* back again to *A* that at some point the rise in interest rate can actually produce a decrease in current consumption and an increase in future output per worker—the very opposite of what had usually been assumed.[15]

Violation of Parable Property 4. Similarly, the reswitching case violates the conclusion that had previously been drawn from the neoclassical cases to the effect that a rising interest rate will always decrease the capital-output ratio. Roughly speaking,[16] it shows that at both a high and a low interest rate we may have the same process yielding the same output with the same amount of capital.

These, then, at least illustrate the main conclusions that have emerged from the reswitching discussion. As already indicated, all parties to the debate seem to agree about the validity of these results. Where the discussion rages hot and heavy is on the likelihood of the occurrence of the re-switching phenomenon in practice and the seriousness of its damage to the neoclassical position.

With respect to the first of these issues the Anglo-Italian group maintains that their discussion has shown the neoclassical model to represent "an entirely isolated case,"[17] while the partisans of M.I.T. have suggested that, for an economy as a whole, switching may be extremely rare and perhaps even nonexistent because "the conditions under which it can be ruled out are very weak."[18] Moreover, the Anglo-Italians suggest that "the implications of the phenomenon of reswitching of techniques for marginal capital theory appear to be more serious the deeper one goes in

---

[15] See Samuelson, *op. cit.*, p. 579.

[16] The argument is not quite right since the money value of both capital and output and, therefore, the capital-output ratio will be affected by the change in the value of *D* resulting from the variation in *i*.

[17] L. L. Pasinetti, "Switches in Technique and the 'Rate of Return' in Capital Theory," *Economic Journal*, Vol. 79, 1969, pp. 508–31.

[18] J. E. Stiglitz, "The Cambridge-Cambridge Controversy in the Theory of Capital: A View From New Haven," *Journal of Political Economy*, Vol. 82, July–August 1974, p. 897. The reference to New Haven should not be taken to be a claim to impartiality. Professor Stiglitz, who has, in any event, since moved elsewhere, makes no bones about his adherence to the M.I.T. views of the matter and expresses them with great lucidity.

uncovering them" (Pasinetti, *op. cit.*, p. 529), while the M.I.T. view is that "... reswitching has no implications for the validity of neoclassical distribution theory" (Stiglitz, *op. cit.*, p. 897).

13. Current Neoclassical Theory: The Factor Price Frontier and Labor's Share

The current neoclassical position on distribution theory can roughly be summed up in four assertions:

a. That the analysis of the distribution of income must ultimately be based on a full model of general equilibrium and its price determination process, as was discussed in Section 5 of this chapter.

b. That while there are dangers in the use of models based on aggregative production functions, with a single variable representing aggregate capital, such aggregation is quite unnecessary for a full general equilibrium analysis. Moreover, it is believed "... that, under most circumstances and for most problems, the errors introduced as a consequence of aggregation of the kind involved in standard macro analysis are not too important" (Stiglitz, *op. cit.*, p. 899). Thus, it is reasonable to build macro models for theoretical analysis or econometric estimation using a single figure for the aggregate quantity of capital which is as defensible as any other index number construct.

c. Though the reswitching phenomenon "causes headaches for those nostalgic for the old time parables of neoclassical writing, we must remind ourselves that scholars are not born to live an easy existence" (Samuelson, *op. cit.*, p. 583). In other words, it is not so easy as had previously been imagined to draw general qualitative conclusions from the neoclassical distribution theory, though the structure of that theory remains unaffected.

d. The theory does have an instrument of analysis from which one can draw a few general implications about the share of wages and capital in the national income, presumably the main issue to which distribution theory addresses itself. This analytic instrument is the *factor price frontier*.

The factor price frontier shows all the combinations of real wage rates and real interest rates made possible by any given technique or combination of techniques. In Figure 4a AA' is such a curve for some single process. It shows, for example, that if this process were the only one employed and the rate of interest were zero, then the competitive wage rate would be w^*, but it indicates also that as the rate of interest rises the real wage rate will decrease steadily from that maximum figure. Such a factor price frontier is deduced from the zero-profit conditions of competitive equilib-

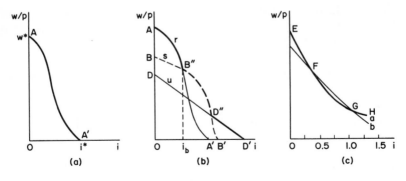

Figure 4

rium, which are critical components of the price determination process and which indicate, at each level of interest rate, for each technique, the maximum amount that a competitive firm can afford to pay its workers without incurring a loss.

Figure 4b shows what happens to the factor price frontier when, as is true in reality, there are a number of production techniques available. Here we see superimposed the factor price frontiers for three techniques r, s, and u. Technique r has the factor price frontier AA' of Figure 4a. But the frontier of technique s crosses AA' at point B''. To the right of that point (i.e., at interest rates higher than i_b) by using technique s firms can afford to pay wages higher than those indicated by AA'. Competition by firms for the available labor will therefore force them to adopt technique s and pay the higher wage. Thus for the pertinent range of interest rates the social factor price frontier will be $B''D''$. Similarly, to the right of D'', competition will force the adoption of technique u, and there the frontier will be $D''D'$. In sum, the social frontier will be $AB''D''D'$, the upper segments of the frontiers for the individual productive techniques.

Figure 4c shows us the same relationships for the reswitching case of the preceding section. Here we see that for $0.5 < i < 1.0$ technique b permits higher wages to be paid, and it will therefore be used. However, for interest rates below or above this range technique a will be utilized, just as our previous discussion showed. Here, then, the social factor price frontier will again be composed of the upper segments of the frontiers for the individual techniques; in this case it will be $EFGH$.

From the frontier it is possible to deduce for any level of the interest rate not only the real wage rate, w, but also the share of wages in total output, wL/y, where L is the size of the labor force and y is the value of total output. By subtraction, one also obtains, residually, the share of earnings of other types of income as $(y - wL)/y$.

One of the main conclusions drawn about the factor price frontier is its negative slope—the notion that lower interest returns to capital in a competitive economy will result in higher wage rates. Indeed, Samuelson concludes ". . . the neoclassical parable remains valid as far as the factor-price frontier trade-off between real wage and profit rate is concerned. But that is all that remains valid regardless of reswitching."[19]

14. Some Last Comments on the Debate

For an uninvolved observer[20] it is easy to come away seeing consider-able merits in both positions, more than the partisans in some of their more acrimonious pronouncements are willing to concede. First, it seems to me that with all its imperfections, and all the caveats with which one must circumscribe its conclusions, the general equilibrium model of neoclassical form is still the only complete analytical game in town. The alternative distribution models that have so far been proposed, while sometimes highly suggestive, are nevertheless rather *ad hoc*, are incomplete, and suffer from the same sorts of problems of aggregation as any neoclassical macro models.

Yet the debate seems to have revealed more clearly two serious de-ficiencies of the neoclassical model—first, it has shown the very limited conclusions we can derive from it that relate to policy and other forms of application. No longer can we be certain that the interest rate bears a simple and reliable relationship to the capital-output ratio, to the produc-tivity of labor and, hence, to workers' living standards. Second, it has reemphasized the absence of historical, institutional, or sociological content in the theory. Surely, these considerations do have a good deal to say about the process of distribution. The economic position of the worker in Western Europe and the United States is very much different from what it was before World War I, and in ways about which neoclassical theory by itself can tell us very little. There is an even more fundamental difference between the position of a workman in the late middle ages and his place in the economy after the Industrial Revolution. A theory of distribution which ignores such fundamental relationships is, indeed, a performance of Hamlet in which the prince of Denmark does not appear.

---

[19] *Op. cit.*, p. 575. It should be noted that Nuti has argued that even this conclusion can have its exceptions—that the factor price frontier can have positively sloping segments. See D. M. Nuti, "Capitalism, Socialism and Steady Growth," *Economic Journal*, Vol. 80, 1970, pp. 32–54.

[20] Since this section represents a personal view of the matter I should hasten to add that I have (or at least until now have had) friends on both sides of the discussion. I have written this section fully aware of the folly of trying to pass judgment on a debate that has not yet run its course.

But to make progress in the directions that are suggested here it is not necessary to throw away what has already been achieved. It seems to me that there is little to be gained by launching further attacks on the general equilibrium model. It does work, it does have valuable uses, and we have no substitutes for it. Rather, the urgent task is to extend the analysis or to produce supplementary or even alternative analyses which do give us insights into such issues as distribution and poverty, distribution and income inequality, and distribution and historical developments.

REFERENCES

von Böhm-Bawerk, Eugen, *The Positive Theory of Capital*, Wagner'schen Verlag, Innsbruck, 1889. English translation, Libertarian Press, South Holland, Ill., 1959.

Fisher, Irving, *The Theory of Interest*, The Macmillan Company, New York, 1930.

Harcourt, G. C., and N. F. Laing, *Capital and Growth*, Penguin Modern Economics Readings, Penguin Books, Ltd., Harmondsworth, 1971. (A good selection of readings on the Cambridge-Cambridge controversy containing many of the articles cited in this chapter.)

Hayek, Friedrich A., *The Pure Theory of Capital*, Macmillan & Co., Ltd., London, 1941.

Hirshleifer, Jack, "On the Theory of Optimal Investment Decision," *Journal of Political Economy*, Vol. 66, August 1958.

Lutz, Friedrich, and Vera Lutz, *The Theory of Investment of the Firm*, Princeton University Press, Princeton, N.J., 1951.

Smith, Vernon L., *Investment and Production*, Harvard University Press, Cambridge, Mass., 1961.

Solow, Robert M., *Capital Theory and the Rate of Return*, North-Holland Publishing Company, Amsterdam, 1963.

Wicksell, Knut, *Lectures on Political Economy*, Vol. I, Routledge & Kegan Paul, Ltd., London, 1934, pp. 144–195, 207–218, 258–299.

APPENDIX: COMMENTS ON THE MATHEMATICS OF RESWITCHING

Comment a. Degree of crossover equation and number of reswitches. The crossover-point equation $c_a = c_b$ in the example of Table 3 in the text is of second degree in the variable D (and therefore can have at most two positive roots) because some costs are incurred *two* periods in the future, and to these we apply the discount factor D^2. If, for example, c_a had also involved the expenditure of, say, 5 man-hours, three periods in the future, we would have $c_a = 7D + 5D^3$, and the crossover equation $c_a = c_b$ would be of third degree with the possibility of *re*-reswitching (three positive roots). That is, there might now be three discount rates at which a pair of techniques is equally costly. More generally, where at least one candidate technique involves expenditures n periods in the future, the crossover equation will be of nth degree with the possibility of as many as n positive solutions for D, and, at least in principle, of n switches of techniques.

Comment b. Why no reswitching in the higher degree equations of the neoclassical parable? Even in the neoclassical illustrations of Section 11 we had quadratic crossover equations such as $c_{II} = c_{III}$, i.e., $4D + 4D^2 = 2 + 2D + 2D^2$ and here, too, longer processes will introduce equations of higher degree. Why do these not involve two or more roots and hence, the possibility of reswitching? The answer is that such equations happen to have only one *positive* root (for example, the equation $c_{II} = c_{III}$ can be rewritten, by collecting terms, as $D^2 + D = 1$ whose solutions are $-0.5 \pm \sqrt{1.25}$). There is a mathematical theorem about the signs of the coefficients of an equation of the nth degree (Descartes's rule of signs) which tells us that if such an equation is the form $a_n D^n + a_{n-1} D^{n-1} + \cdots + a_k D^k = a_{k-1} D^{k-1} + \cdots + a_1 D + a_0$ *with all the constants a_i positive*, then it will always have exactly one positive root. This result is almost obvious because at $D = 0$ the left-hand side (*LHS*) of the preceding equation is zero and therefore less than a_0, the value of the *RHS* when $D = 0$. But because the *LHS* has the higher powers of D it will eventually catch up with the *RHS* at some sufficiently large value of D, call it D^*, and then remain greater than the *RHS* for all $D > D^*$. Thus, D^* is the *only* positive root of D. We show next that our neoclassical examples always satisfy Descartes's rule. For these models involve choices among techniques whose costs are of the form

$$c_w = w_0 + w_1 D + \cdots + w_n D^n \quad \text{and} \quad c_v = v_k D^k + v_{k+1} D^{k+1} + \cdots + v_n D^n$$

where $w_j < v_j$ for each $j \geq k$ and the former is clearly the more roundabout process. The crossover equation $c_w = c_v$ is then of the form

$$v_n D^n + v_{n-1} D^{n-1} + \cdots + v_k D^k = w_n D^n + w_{n-1} D^{n-1} + \cdots + w_1 D + w_0$$

or

$$(v_n - w_n) D^n + (v_{n-1} - w_{n-1}) D^{n-1} + \cdots + (v_k - w_k) D^k = w_{k-1} D^{k-1} + \cdots + w_1 D + w_0,$$

which is precisely the sort of equation that we know from Descartes's rule of signs to have only one positive root since every $v_j > w_j$ so that every coefficient is positive.

Answers to Problems

Chapter II, Section 6

1. (a) $y = \sum\limits_{i=1}^{4} a_i x_i$ (b) $y = \sum\limits_{i=0}^{2} a_i x^i$.

2. (a) $a_0 x^3 + a_1 x^2 + a_2 x + a_3$ (b) $1^2 + 2^2 + 3^2 = 14$.

Chapter IV, Section 2

1. $dy/dx = 77x^6 - 32x$.
2. $dy/dx = -48x^{11} - 8\sin 4x$.
3. $dy/dx = -42x^{-7}$.
4. $dy/dx = 3e^{3x}\sin x + e^{3x}\cos x$.
5. $dy/dx = (3e^{3x}\sin x - e^{3x}\cos x)/(\sin x)^2$.
6. $dy/dx = (3e^{3x}\log x - e^{3x}/x)/(\log x)^2$.
7. $dy/dx = 60x^3\cos 5x^4$.
8. $dy/dx = -32x^{-3}e^{2x^{-2}}$.

Chapter IV, Section 5

1. (a) $60x^3$ (b) $-2/x^2$.
2. Maximum at $x = 9$ (b) Minimum at $x = 0$.

Chapter IV, Section 6

1. $Q = 2$, $A = 3$.

2. $x = -4$, $z = 3$.

Chapter IV, Section 7

(a) $dy = 4x_1x_2^3\,dx_1 + 6x_1^2x_2^2\,dx_2$

(b) $dy = 4x_1\,dx_1 + 12x_2^2\,dx_2$

(c) $dy = (\partial f/\partial x_1)\,dx_1 + (2x_2 + \partial f/\partial x_2)\,dx_2$.

Chapter IV, Section 8

1. (a) $w = 5$, $x = 7$, $\lambda = -50$.   (b) $Q = 0.5$, $A = 1$, $\lambda = -6.5$.

2. $y_\lambda = \log x^3 w + \lambda_1(\cos x \cos w - 0.3) + \lambda_2(x/w^5 + e^w - 10)$.

Chapter IV, Section 9

2. The consumer maximizes $U(Q) - PQ$. Setting the first derivative equal to zero we have $dU/dQ - P = 0$ or $P = dU/dQ$.

3. From $PQ = K$ we have $Q = K/P$ and so $dQ/dP = -K/P^2$. Substitute these values of Q and dP/dQ into the elasticity expression and the result follows at once.

4. Using the rule for differentiation of a product,

$$\text{marginal cost} = \frac{dC}{dQ} = \frac{dcQ}{dQ} = Q\,\frac{dc}{dQ} + c\,\frac{dQ}{dQ} = Q\,\frac{dc}{dQ} + c.$$

But when c attains its minimum, $dc/dQ = 0$.

5. (a) 25   (b) no   (c) two: $Q_1 = 5$, $Q_2 = 20$

(d) second derivative of profit: $+0.9$ at $Q = 5$ and -0.9 at $Q = 20$.

Chapter V, Section 10

1. $R = 27$, $x = 0$, $y = 3$, $z = 1$, all slacks zero.

2. $R = 17\frac{2}{3}$, $x = 3\frac{1}{6}$, $y = \frac{5}{3}$, $s_3 = 1\frac{1}{6}$, $s_1 = s_2 = 0$ where s_1 is the slack variable of the first constraint, etc.

3. $R = 26$, $x = 2$, $y = 3$, $s_2 = 1$, $s_1 = s_3 = 0$.

4. $R = 5\frac{1}{3}$, $x = 1\frac{1}{3}$, $s_1 = 3\frac{2}{3}$, $s_2 = y = 0$.

Chapter VI, Section 1

$$\text{Minimize } \alpha = 5V_1 + 7V_2 + 3V_3$$

subject to

$$4V_1 + 3V_2 + 1V_3 \geq 6$$

$$1V_1 + 2V_2 + 1V_3 \geq 2$$

$$V_1 \geq 0, \qquad V_2 = 0, \qquad V_3 \geq 0.$$

Chapter VI, Section 5

1. $\alpha = 7{,}500, V_a = L_1 = 0, V_b = \frac{5}{6}, L_2 = -\frac{1}{3}$
3. (a) $\Pi = 300, U_2 = Q_1 = U_1 = 0, Q_2 = 9, U_3 = 7;$
3. (b) $\alpha = 300, L_2 = V_3 = 0, V_2 = 2, L_1 = 4, V_1 = 1$
3. (e) $\Pi = \alpha = 300$
3. (f) $Q_1 L_1 = (0)(4) = 0, Q_2 L_2 = (9)(0) = 0, U_1 V_1 = (0)(1) = 0,$ etc.
4. Because $U_1 V_1 \neq 0.$

Chapter VIII, Section 4

1. $L(Q, V) = 7Q_1^2 - 2Q_1Q_2 + Q_2^3 + V_1(400 - Q_1 - Q_2) + V_2(Q_1Q_2 - 200),$
$\partial L/\partial Q_1 = 14Q_1 - 2Q_2 - V_1 + V_2Q_2 \leq 0, \partial L/\partial Q_2 = -2Q_1 + 3Q_2^2 - V_1 + V_2Q_1 \leq 0, Q_1 \, \partial L/\partial Q_1 = Q_1(14Q_1 - 2Q_2 - V_1 + V_2Q_2) = 0, Q_2 \, \partial L/\partial Q_2 = Q_2(-2Q_1 + 3Q_2^2 - V_1 + V_2Q_1) = 0, \partial L/\partial V_1 = 400 - Q_1 - Q_2 \geq 0, \partial L/\partial V_2 = Q_1Q_2 - 200 \geq 0, V_1 \, \partial L/\partial V_1 = V_1(400 - Q_1 - Q_2) = 0, V_2 \, \partial L/\partial V_2 = V_2(Q_1Q_2 - 200) = 0.$

2. $L(Q, V) = 7Q_1^2 - 2Q_1Q_2 + Q_2^3 + V_1(Q_1 + Q_2 - 400) + V_2(200 - Q_1Q_2),$
$\partial L/\partial Q_1 = 14Q_1 - 2Q_2 + V_1 - V_2Q_2 \geq 0, \partial L/\partial Q_2 = -2Q_1 + 3Q_2^2 + V_1 - V_2Q_1 \geq 0, \partial L/\partial V_1 = Q_1 + Q_2 - 400 \leq 0,$ etc.

3. $L(Q, V) = 6Q_1Q_2^2 + V_1(50 - 2Q_1^2 - Q_2) + V_2(Q_1 - 10), \partial L/\partial Q_1 = 6Q_2^2 - 4Q_1V_1 + V_2 \geq 0, \partial L/\partial Q_2 = 12Q_1Q_2 - V_1 \geq 0, Q_1 \, \partial L/\partial Q_1 = 0, Q_2 \, \partial L/\partial Q_2 = 0, \partial L/\partial V_1 = 50 - 2Q_1^2 - Q_2 \leq 0, \partial L/\partial V_2 = Q_1 - 10 \leq 0, V_1 \, \partial L/\partial V_1 = 0, V_2 \, \partial L/\partial V_2 = 0.$

Chapter IX, Section 20

1. $x_a p_a = \$10.$
2. $x_a p_a = \$123.$
3. $x_a = (99p_a + 16)/(p_a^2 + 48).$

Chapter XI, Section 16

1. (a) $K = M/9$ $L = 4M/9$ $\lambda = 6M^{-\frac{1}{2}}$.
1. (b) $K = 4P^2$ $L = 16P^2$ $\lambda = -P$, $Q = 72P$.
2. (a) $K = (5M + 2)/16$, $L = (3M - 2)/8$, $\lambda = (-7M + 34)/8$.
2. (b) $K = (23P - 5)/14P$, $L = (11P - 3)/7P$, $\lambda = -P$,
$$y = (74P^2 - 4)/7P^2$$

Chapter XII, Section 5

1. (a) 500 square feet   (b) 2,000 square feet.
2. Any point on OP_3 involves ten hours of vat time per hour of labor time.
3. Your line should go through the point representing 7,000 vat hours and 300 labor-hours. OP_4 lies above ray OP_3 except at the origin.

Chapter XII, Section 7

1. 1,500 units of output via process 1 requires 600 labor hours and 3,000 vat-gallon hours. Five-hundred units of output via process 3 requires 175 hours of labor time and 1,750 gallon-hours of vat time. These add up to the coordinates of point G.
2. The coordinates of E_4 are 300 labor hours and 7,000 vat-gallon hours. The corresponding coordinates of F_4 are 600 and 14,000.
5. Both segments have slopes of -10.

Chapter XII, Section 9

$$Q_1 = 1,364, \qquad Q_2 = 0, \qquad Q_4 = 182, \qquad \text{profit} = \$1,427$$

Chapter XII, Section 10

At point 0 there are unused amounts of both inputs, so both slack variables are nonzero. At point S' only process P' is used (so $Q' > 0$) and some X is unused so its slack variable is nonzero. At point B we have no unused inputs but $Q > 0$ and $Q' > 0$, etc.

Chapter XV, Section 10

1. (a) $Q_\Pi = 4$, $P_\Pi = 10.4$, $\Pi_\Pi = 11$, $R_\Pi = 41.6$
   (b) $Q_r = 15$, $P_r = 6$, $\Pi_r = -110$, $R_r = 90$
   (c) $Q_c = 5$, $P_c = 10$, $\Pi_c = 10$, $R_c = 50$.

2. (a) $Q_\Pi = 6,$ $P_\Pi = 14,$ $\Pi_\Pi = 17,$ $R_\Pi = 84$
   (b) $Q_r = 8,$ $P_r = 11,$ $\Pi_r = 13,$ $R_r = 88$
   (c) $Q_c = 7,$ $P_c = 12\frac{3}{7},$ $\Pi_c = 16,$ $R_c = 87.$

3. $S = \dfrac{dPQ}{dP}\dfrac{P}{PQ} = \left(Q + P\dfrac{dQ}{dP}\right)\dfrac{1}{Q} = 1 + \dfrac{P}{Q}\dfrac{dQ}{dP} = 1 - E.$

4. $MR = \dfrac{dPQ}{dQ} = P + \dfrac{dP}{dQ}Q = P\left(1 + \dfrac{dP}{dQ}\dfrac{Q}{P}\right) = P\left(1 - \dfrac{1}{E}\right).$

Chapter XVI, Section 13

1. Let $P = a - bQ$, average cost $= c + kQ$, so that $C = cQ + kQ^2$. Then $\Pi = PQ - C = (a - c)Q - (b + k)Q^2$. Thus $\Pi = 0$ when $Q = 0$ or when

$$Q = \frac{a - c}{b + k}.$$

Also, setting $d\Pi/dQ = 0$ we get for profit maximization,

$$Q = \frac{a - c}{2(b + k)}.$$

2. (a) discrimination: $Q_1 = 4, Q_2 = 4, P_1 = 9, P_2 = 13, MR_1 = 1,$
                $MR_2 = 1, \Pi = 78.$
   nondiscrimination: $Q_1 = 3.2, Q_2 = 4.8, P_1 = P_2 = 10.6, MR_1 = 4.2,$
                $MR_2 = -3.8, \Pi = 74.8.$
   (b) discrimination: $Q_1 = 0.5, Q_2 = 0.67, P_1 = 1.5, P_2 = 5.0, MR_1 = 1,$
                $MR_2 = 1, \Pi = 2\frac{11}{12}.$
   nondiscrimination: $Q_1 = 0, Q_2 = 1\frac{1}{6}, P_1 = P_2 = 2, MR_1 = 2,$
                $MR_2 = -5, \Pi = 1.5.$

3. To maximize $\Pi = P_1Q_1 + P_2Q_2 - C(Q_1, Q_2)$ we require

$$MR_1 = \frac{\partial P_1Q_1}{\partial Q_1} = \frac{\partial C}{\partial Q_1}, \qquad MR_2 = \frac{\partial P_2Q_2}{\partial Q_2} = \frac{\partial C}{\partial Q_2}.$$

Hence, if $\partial C/\partial Q_1 = \partial C/\partial Q_2, MR_1 = MR_2.$

4. (a) Cournot: $Q_1 = 4, Q_2 = 5, \Pi_1 = 6, \Pi_2 = 9, \Pi = 15.$
   Joint maximum: $Q_1 = 2, Q_2 = 4, \Pi_1 = 4, \Pi_2 = 16, \Pi = 20.$
   (b) Cournot: $Q_1 = 3, Q_2 = 3, \Pi_1 = 15, \Pi_2 = 6, \Pi = 21.$
   Joint maximum: $Q_1 = 2\frac{3}{4}, Q_2 = 2\frac{1}{2}, \Pi_1 = 15\frac{3}{8}, \Pi_2 = 6, \Pi = 21\frac{3}{8}.$

Chapter XXV, Section 6

1. (a) $1/1.05 = 0.952$ approximate
1. (b) 0.935 approximate
2. $D = 0.95$ approximate, so present value $= 500 + 700D + 200, D^2 = 500 + 700(0.95) + 200(0.91) = 1347 = a/(1 - D) = a/(0.05)$, or $a = 67$, approximate.

3.

	Project A	Project B	Project C
Payout period	$\frac{1}{2}$ year	$1\frac{1}{4}$ year	1 year
Marginal efficiency	100%	$53\frac{1}{2}$%	$66\frac{2}{3}$%
Discounted present value	$246	$214	$250

Chapter XXV, Section 7

$$\text{Max } 70x_1 + 20x_2 + 60x_3 + 30x_4 + 10x_5$$

subject to

$$20x_1 + 7x_2 + 15x_3 + 8x_4 + 2x_5 \leq 40$$

$$10x_1 + 8x_2 + 20x_3 + 5x_4 + 3x_5 \leq 30$$

$$x_1 \leq 1, \, x_3 \leq 1, \, x_5 \leq 1$$

$$x_2 + x_4 \leq 1$$

$$x_1 \geq 0, \qquad x_2 \geq 0, \qquad x_3 \geq 0, \qquad x_4 \geq 0, \qquad x_5 \geq 0,$$

$$\text{all } x_i \text{ integer.}$$

Chapter XXV, Section 8

Present value of A = $416 (approximate)
Present value of B = $428 (approximate)

Index